THE CHURCH
IN THE
SEVENTEENTH CENTURY

Henri Daniel-Rops: *History of the Church of Christ:*

THE CHURCH IN THE SEVENTEENTH CENTURY

by

H. DANIEL-ROPS

TRANSLATED BY

J. J. BUCKINGHAM

LONDON: J. M. DENT & SONS LTD
NEW YORK: E. P. DUTTON & CO. INC.

H. Daniel-Rops: *L'Église des Temps
Classiques: Le Grand Siècle des Âmes*,
published in France by Librairie Arthème
Fayard, 1963

TRANSLATOR'S NOTE

This is a translation of *Le Grand Siècle des Âmes*, the first part of *L'Église des Temps Classiques*, which latter forms the fifth volume of M. Daniel-Rops' *Histoire de l' Église du Christ*.

CONTENTS

*

CONTENTS

MAP

CHAPTER I

A BUILDER OF THE MODERN CHURCH: ST VINCENT DE PAUL

1. THE RECTOR OF A DILAPIDATED PARISH

THAT year—the year of Our Lord, 1617—the holy time of Lent began as usual, with complete indifference and contempt. Châtillon, a medium-sized market town right in the middle of the Dombes, was neither more nor less Christian than hundreds of other French towns and villages; which meant that there was very little Christianity about it. The common people—peasants, fishermen, cattle dealers—cared little for anything beyond earning a living, in the hard way, from a lifeless soil straddled with a thousand pools and shrouded in fog during eight months of the year. The upper classes had become Huguenots; not that they practised Calvinism on that account. The neglected church was used for public meetings; the belfry, nicknamed 'the kingdom', had become a resort for drunken revels; the rectory was falling into ruins. For forty years the practice of religion had depended on the chance visits of the titular clergy who came to pocket the five hundred pounds which the living provided. There were at least six priests in the town, either curates or chaplains, whose morals were worse than lax and whose zeal was less than lukewarm; their sole liturgical occupation was the celebrating of a few Masses for the souls of dead persons long forgotten. No longer did the church bells ring to call the people to Mass or to Vespers. But that year they did ring.

A new parish priest had arrived. He came from Paris, they said—by the road leading from Pont-de-Veyle. Public opinion gave it as certain that he had been something in the nature of a chaplain or a tutor in the noble and powerful Gondi family, which was known as far away as the country round the Chalaronne. It was believed that he had resigned a wealthy living to come and officiate at Châtillon. Suspiciously everyone wondered why. But they liked the fellow. He was of medium height, robust and still young—not yet forty. He had a plain face, lengthened by the type of goatee beard which King Henri IV had made fashionable. He had an enormous nose, and his eyes were small and lively beneath the prominent brow ridges. A roguish smile played ceaselessly about his mouth. His pleasant face inspired confidence. When he spoke he emphasized his words with quick, imitative gestures and an animated voice with an accent foreign to those parts. Right

I

from the start he won sympathy, so easily, in fact, that Jean Beynier, a wealthy follower of Calvin, offered him a lodging at his home while the rectory was being made habitable—an offer which the new parish priest accepted without fuss.

It was immediately obvious to everyone that this priest was different from the others. He was up before dawn, he prayed for a good half an hour, tidied up his room and went to the church to say Mass—all of which was quite unusual. They saw him working with his own hands —cleaning, repairing and repainting the house of God, to which he earnestly summoned the faithful. The first to come were taken by surprise, and went off to tell others what they themselves had witnessed; that divine worship was conducted as they had never seen it done before, that his sermons were not boring, and that the ancient hymns warmed the soul when everybody joined in the singing. In a few weeks the Catholics of Châtillon had once more learned the way to their church. The 'unbeneficed' priests who loitered about the town, and whom the new rector had invited to come and live at the presbytery as brothers in community, had almost all accepted and were pleased with the arrangement.

This man was certainly amazing. The humblest peasants loved him —the harvesters of millet, to whom he lent a hand on the dried-up ponds, and the fishermen whom he helped when the ponds were full.[1] Even the rich respected him—the heretics too, and the violent, when they came in contact with his influence. One of these was honest Jean Beynier, his Huguenot host, who renounced his heresy. Another was the less accommodating Sire de Rougemont, an opportunist and adventurer for ever mixed up in brawls and squabbles. The rector stopped him on the road one day, and spoke to him so tenderly of God and his soul that the wicked man sprang from his horse and, there and then, snapped his formidable sword in half. Better still, no sooner did the new rector approach that shrewish magpie, Mlle de La Chassagne, a miserly, selfish, arrogant woman, than he led her back to the church and persuaded her to be mild and gentle towards the lowly. That was a real conversion!

Then came the greatest event of all. One Sunday, just as the rector was ascending the pulpit, someone came and whispered to him. One could see by his face that he was moved. He began his sermon: a sermon quite unlike any he had preached before. He related what he had just learned. A short distance from the town, in a house lost in the middle of the marsh, a family was suffering distress. All were ill at the same time, and were incapable of helping each other. Their poverty was pitiful. These unhappy souls had not a pound of bread left and no

[1] The marshes of the Dombes were regularly drained and then refilled; the dry periods were given over to tillage, while the wet years produced fish.

more fat or oil. They could not be left to die like that; the whole parish was responsible for its sons and daughters. He brought tears to many eyes; and when, after Vespers, the rector himself went to visit these forsaken people, he found fifty or more of his parishioners returning from the house of this unfortunate family with empty baskets on their arms.

The entire market-town had united in this charitable gesture, and felt better as a result of what they had done. That same evening this fine rector assembled around him the good people who had responded to his appeal, and suggested that they might organize permanent help for the destitute. The first congregation of the Ladies of Charity was thus formed, manifestly inspired by Providence. The rector drew them up a precise rule of life based on practical works; the document may still be seen in the church at Châtillon.

He was not to remain long at Châtillon—scarcely five months—but he left his mark. From this stagnant marsh of indifference, sordid vice and heresy, he had built a social brotherhood, a parish. As for himself, he learned much from his flock in the Dombes. He learned above all that the simplest methods, those nearest to hand, were the most efficacious in the fight against the corruption of Christian society—the theme of so many sermons—provided the heart was full of that charity of Christ which is so infectious. This young rector was called Vincent de Paul; his parishioners had at once called him 'Monsieur Vincent'.

2. THE SPIDER'S WEB

He was born [1] a long way from Châtillon, in a part of France even poorer than the Dombes, on the borders of the Landes and wealthy Chalosse; but on the bad side, among the sands and the marshy wastelands. In his native village of Pouy, three leagues from Dax—or d'Acqs, as it was then called—there were only fifty houses. They were built of clay with thatched roofs, and human beings and livestock often dwelt there together. There were four boys and two girls in the family, so his father had many mouths to feed; but he was able to give them only millet gruel and buckwheat cakes, and meat less than ten times a year. A hard school indeed, of which Vincent would retain the

[1] The date of his birth is not quite certain. According to the evidence he gave at the process of beatification of St Francis de Sales, he was born 'about' 1580. Abelly, his biographer, makes it 1576—perhaps merely with the pious intention of showing that Vincent was not as young when he was ordained as one might have believed. Coste, who bases his evidence on thirteen indisputable documents, places the date around 1581. His family name 'de Paul' obviously did not indicate a noble origin; it came from a distant forbear, so obscure that he was known neither by his trade nor even by a picturesque nickname: he was simply called by his baptismal name. The name Vincent was very common in the district. It came from a Spanish saint who brought the Gospel to south-west Gaul, and died a martyr under Diocletian.

lessons. In after days, when he became a familiar figure at court, and saw servants dancing attendance upon the rich, he would say: 'My mother never had a servant; she did all the serving herself. She was the wife of a poor peasant, and I am the son of a poor peasant.' He meant those words as a tender homage to his mother.

A poor peasant he was indeed. That is what he remained in spirit throughout his whole life; he insisted upon it so forcibly that one might have suspected a sort of discreet ostentation. Perhaps it was to safeguard his humility, or to show that his own humble origin gave him the right to stand up in defence of human misery. Perhaps it was a blend of both. He knew from experience that the spiritual itself was carnal, and that, to give the people back their soul, one had to give them first the wherewithal to live. He had learned that much in the days when he was growing up in his smoky cottage and in the communal *ériaou*, where, at the age of six, he had driven pigs to the acorns. He was not likely to forget it.

It seems that Vincent was a lively boy and of remarkable intelligence, for he had attracted the attention of M. de Comet, a person of some standing at Dax, whose duties as parish magistrate brought him to Pouy. At the request of a barrister at the presidial court, the Franciscans welcomed him to their college. To escape shabby, domestic surroundings Vincent, like many others of his day, was going to enter the Church. Whether he had any vocation at all at that time no one really knew, despite the touching stories told about him later on. In this simple French society at the beginning of the great century, social gaps were easily bridged through ecclesiastical channels, notwithstanding the frippery of doublets and lace ruffles. Young Vincent's father realized that only too well. And so, at fifteen, the youngster received the tonsure and Minor Orders.

If the boy was to become anything more than a country vicar he would have to proceed with his studies. His kind patron, Comet, saw to that. The boy's father made a grand gesture too: so that his son might attend the university he sold a pair of oxen—a great sacrifice. For four years Vincent remained in Toulouse, receiving a good classical education and then proceeding to theology. The life he led was certainly not as reprehensible as, later on through humility, he declared it to have been; though he might not have been very pious. Was there any hint of future sanctity in this little tutor to the children of noble families, this 'soup merchant' who, in order to gain a living, kept a boarding-house? It looked rather as though he were destined, like many another priest of that time, to be more interested in business matters, more concerned about benefices, than his ministry. In keeping with the deplorable customs of the age—customs which he was to fight tooth and nail—he passed through the various stages to the priesthood with alarming haste. In the year 1600 Vincent was ordained priest by a blind old man, François de Bourdeilles, Bishop of Périgueux, during a visit he paid to the bishop's palace. Vincent was then scarcely twenty years of age.

The time which he spent, to use his own words, 'in the spider's web'—the web of the world whose threads enmesh us all—dragged on for a good ten years and probably longer. Yet Providence did not fail to inflict such trials upon him as are commonly known to bring about conversions. In 1605 he went to Marseilles [1] to recover a debt which some rogue was not anxious to settle. On the return journey, having taken ship to Narbonne, he had the misfortune to see the vessel attacked by Turkish pirates in three brigantines. He was captured and taken to Tunis, where he was sold in the slave market of the town, wearing only a pair of breeches and a linen smock. That was a severe trial, but not perhaps so bad as he might have feared, for the masters who bought him proved to be quite humane. His first master was an alchemist who was searching for the philosopher's stone. Then came a farmer, Guillaume Gautier, who rented land from the Bey; he happened to be a former monk from the Franciscan monastery at Nici in Savoy (now known as Annecy). Vincent's charming manner caused him to be treated as a friend by the renegade and his three wives; so much so that the slave, bearing in mind that he was a priest, brought his master back to the faith of his baptism, and persuaded him to return to France so that he might be absolved there in due form. This afforded Vincent the opportunity to escape.

They disembarked at the end of June 1607 at Aigues-Mortes. Vincent and his companions hastened to Avignon, where the Papal Vice-Legate received them 'with tears in his eyes and a sob in his throat', happy to be able to edify the Catholic faithful with the touching spectacle of a solemn renunciation. What is more, this great

---

[1] Here we are following the traditional account given in two letters written by St Vincent de Paul himself, and dated 24th July 1607 and 28th February 1608. Some historians, however, have maintained that the saint invented the whole story of his captivity in Tunis in order to conceal from M. de Comet, his patron, other adventures possibly less commendable. The two letters in question remained in the archives of the Comet family until 1658. It seems certain that until that year no one close to the saint had heard of this picturesque chapter in his life. Could Vincent's captivity have been a tall story? It is a fact that, when one of his friends told him that these two youthful letters had been found, he immediately asked for them so as to destroy them. But the answer to those historians who have supported the argument in favour of 'Vincent's lie' is that there was no reason to doubt the truth of his letters since he never stated that they were untrue; in his life and actions there are definite traces of the influence which his stay in Tunis had on him; further, if he had wished to suppress the letters, it was because of the reference to alchemy—a subject on which the Inquisition was extremely touchy. See Granchamp, 'La prétendue captivité de Saint Vincent de Paul à Tunis', in the work *La France en Tunisie au XVIIe siècle*; Father Guichard, *Saint Vincent de Paul esclave à Tunis*, Paris, 1937; and P. Debongnie, 'Vincent de Paul a-t-il menti?' (*Revue d'Histoire Ecclésiastique Française*, XXXIV, Louvain, 1938).

dignitary of the Church was a passionate devotee of alchemy and the quest for the philosopher's stone, of which this one-time slave of the Tunisian doctor might know the secret. The Vice-Legate suggested to Vincent that he might like to accompany him to Rome, and the young priest accepted with joy. This was a happy period in his life. *Vixit in Urbe Aeterna*, as Montesquieu, another Gascon, was to repeat later. Introduced to the best people by M. Montorio, Vincent knew how to observe and keep silent—two valuable assets at the Roman court. He turned on his charm, and eventually came to the notice of the Pope (Paul V) and the French ambassador, Savary de Brêve. He succeeded so well that, when he left the Eternal City in 1609, rumour had it that he had been charged with a confidential mission.

What kind of a mission could it have been? No one knows exactly, or even if it existed. It did not concern the divorce of Henri IV and his queen Margot, which had already taken place several years earlier. Did it concern the nomination to the bishopric of Metz of the Duc de Verneuil, natural son of the king, which the Sovereign Pontiff wished to prevent? In any case Vincent met Henri IV, and was certainly well received by him—the Gascon by 'le Béarnais'; and perhaps it was to reward his silence that the king appointed him chaplain to his former wife. It was a good post and one which did not occupy much of his time. To distribute alms in the queen's name, to take his turn at celebrating Mass in her presence (for there were several chaplains), to be present at receptions given by the ex-queen—these things were hardly enough to fill his day. However, Vincent de Paul took advantage of his leisure to graduate in canon law at the Sorbonne. From a spiritual point of view did he gain much in this world of letters and elegant people—the rather mixed crowd which this one-time beauty, now grown wiser, liked to assemble about her? At best, by frequenting the *Fate bene fratelli* hospital, situated opposite Margot's mansion, he had apprenticed himself to a vocation which was later to become so magnificently his very own. Early in 1610 he was given the living of the Cistercian Abbey of Saint-Léonard-de-Chaumes, in the diocese of Saintes, which secured him against want. The career of which his gallant peasant father had dreamed was beginning to unfold before him.

But was it merely that he should live the life of a worldly abbé, a collector of livings, a shrewd and diplomatic priestling, that God desired him to have such a wealth of experience at thirty years of age? Was that why it had been given him to know one after another a peasant's life with its want, a student's life with its problems, a life of slavery with its sufferings, the life at Rome with its snares, court life and its delusions, and finally the life of the literary circle and its tricks? Was nothing to come of it all but a commonplace destiny which offered mediocre advantages? Round about 1610 he was, as he said himself, still on the surface of things, a man of limited horizons. But God had long since destined him for the great adventure of souls and had lain in wait for him.

3. THE REPLY TO THE CALL

What then had happened? We do not know exactly. Vincent de Paul was never much given to unbosoming himself, and on the major events of his spiritual life he has not said anything anywhere. It is, however, certain that from about 1610 he had changed interiorly, and soon afterwards exteriorly as well. Did he experience a 'night of fire' of the kind Blaise Pascal was to experience forty years later? This 'invasion by holiness', of which one of his biographers speaks, might have been a sudden ground-swell or a slow and thorough penetration. Contingent causes may have attended God's victory. There were, for instance, the many lawsuits in which he was obliged to engage with a Protestant magistrate of La Rochelle in order to secure the income from his abbey. There was also the more or less spicy relish of snobbery, of the man of letters, of pretty speeches, which the court of Queen Margot had to offer, whether he liked it or not. Despite these trials, these pieces of trickery, these little intrigues, no one doubted that he always remained an upright man, of rugged faith, and perfectly straightforward; it probably needed but little to make him reply to the interior call of Christ.

One man certainly helped him to become amenable to the Whisper: the saintly Bérulle, father of the French school of spirituality, the man whose austere figure dominated Catholicism in France at that time, and whose thought was destined to make a profound mark on the whole spiritual life of the century.[1] Pierre de Bérulle, born in 1575, was not much older than Vincent de Paul, but the little Gascon peasant was immediately filled with admiration for this aristocrat by birth and culture, the indefatigable herald of God's cause, the man who was to revive Carmel and establish the Oratory of France.

There is no doubt that Vincent had never before met anyone who had real experience of life in God; Bérulle certainly possessed such experience, and that was enough for Vincent. On bended knee he placed himself entirely in Bérulle's hands. The future cardinal therefore became his spiritual director, his confessor and, what is more, his living model. The worldly chaplain to Queen Margot had discerned all the problems which troubled Bérulle, such as the need of new leaven in the dough of Christian observance—the expressed desire of the

---

[1] On the subject of Bérulle see the preceding volume, *The Catholic Reformation*, pp. 363-8, and Chapter II of the present work, section 2, 'A Great Spiritual Fountain'.

Council of Trent, but one which was so slow to reach fulfilment. With all his being Vincent made these problems his own. It is believed, though the truth of the story is not certain, that Vincent made a retreat during the year 1611 with Pierre de Bérulle and Adrien Bourdoise, that energetic man who later gathered around him a number of pious priests at Saint-Nicholas-du-Chardonnet. The object of the retreat was to meditate upon these profound problems and to find answers to them.

This period of meditation was soon followed by action which betokened an interior development. Scarcely a year and a half after taking over the living of Saint-Léonard, Vincent surrendered an enormous sum of money—fifteen thousand livres, equivalent to at least five or six million francs—to the brothers for the care of their sick. The money had been left to him. It was the first indication of his obedience to his master's precept of renunciation. He not only gave his possessions to the poor, but his heart and his soul as well. He was to be seen more and more in the hospital wards and the slum areas of the town. He became keenly alive to every kind of misfortune, whether of the soul or of the body. There was, for instance, the case of the priest (a doctor at the Sorbonne) who suffered the tortures of temptation and doubt; by the transfer of merits, Vincent offered himself to God for this priest.[1]

Then there was the touching experience at Clichy, where Vincent eventually discovered his vocation. Bérulle wanted to take M. Bourgoing, the curé of Saint-Médard, a holy priest and a sound administrator, from Clichy to help him in the Oratory, which was about to come into being. To replace him Bérulle thought of his disciple de Paul, with the result that Bourgoing gave his parish over to him. Vincent never thought of disputing Bérulle's requests. Without surrendering his royal chaplaincy, he took over this parish, which stretched to the north walls of Paris, embracing not only Clichy, but the Garenne plain and a part of what are now the VIIIth, IXth, XVIIth and XVIIIth wards of Paris. Six hundred souls were given into his care. These market gardeners, poor country people, must have reminded him of those whom he had known as a child. They were hard-working, thrifty and possessed of a deep faith despite all appearances. And what a grand thing it was to be a parish priest! With all the enthusiasm of his youth he gave himself body and soul to his parochial

[1] The episode has a bearing on those mysterious aspects of the highest mystical and psychological experience. For the doctor of the Sorbonne was healed of his temptations, while Vincent himself was assailed for a long time, and in a frightful manner, by the very demon he had conquered in another. By all accounts this doctor was Nicolas Coeffetau, a Dominican and the future Bishop of Marseilles, whom the Abbé Urbain described as one of the creators of French prose. (Compare the article by Father Guichard in *Revue d'Histoire Ecclésiastique Française*, 1938, p. 134.)

duties, discovering its greatness and its bondage—an experience which served him later when he was instructing priests. For a year he preached, taught the Catechism, heard confessions, learned to sing with his flock, laying the foundations of a school and moving heaven and earth to rebuild his church: a model parish priest, and perfectly happy to remain one. One day when the Bishop of Paris [1] made his canonical visit to Clichy-la-Garenne, he received a rather unusual report from the lips of his curé: 'I am sure that neither you nor the Holy Father can possibly be as happy as I am!'

But God disposes of those whom he has reserved for Himself, and leads them by ways that they themselves do not understand. Vincent was sad when his spiritual director, Bérulle, asked him to give up his parishioners at Clichy and become a tutor in the powerful house of Philippe-Emmanuel de Gondi. Was he to return to the world again, to a life of ease and ostentation? He had since developed a taste for other dishes. Yet the Gondi atmosphere had nothing in common with that of Queen Margot. The Gondis were a family of Italian bankers who had come to France with the Médicis; they were fantastically rich, and all of them made careers in the higher administrative posts or in the Church. But the one in whose house Vincent came to live was the Général des Galères; that is to say, an admiral and head of the department of naval construction. He was an upright and pious man, and sufficiently engrossed in spiritual matters to become an Oratorian after his wife's death. His wife, Françoise de Silly, was a devout woman whose virtue and intellect were both praised at court. Vincent de Paul's real work in the family was the upbringing and education of the three Gondi boys. The eldest one eventually became Duc de Gondi; the second intended to become a Knight of Malta. Later Vincent took charge of the youngest; a thin, dark-complexioned boy who was one day to become the famous and much discussed Cardinal de Retz. But the young priest's position in the family soon developed into something more than that of a paid teacher. Mme de Gondi made him her confessor, and the Général des Galères himself was so much under the spell of Vincent's personality that the latter was once able to prevent him from fighting a duel—quite a praiseworthy feat in those days.

The period spent with the Gondis put the finishing touches to Vincent's training. Françoise de Gondi, like a number of women of the day—Mme Acarie, for instance—was haunted by the troubles which beset the Church, and she was anxious to remedy the evils which she

---

[1] In this chapter the terms Bishop of Paris and Archbishop of Paris are both used. That is because the bishopric of Paris, up to that time suffragan to Sens, was elevated to an archbishopric during the lifetime of Vincent, in 1622. The holder was called 'Monsieur l'évêque' or 'Monsieur de Paris'. It was the only term used until the end of the seventeenth century when, as the mischievous Saint-Simon says, they began to call each other 'Monseigneur' in order to get the title accepted.

saw around her. She soon sized up her sons' little tutor, recognizing him to be a man of God, and she determined to launch him into the great work which was so necessary. The pitiful state of the French countryside, too often a prey to influences which turned it away from Christianity, and the spiritual destitution of a large part of the clergy— all this she had seen on her own estates. She therefore made Vincent the companion of her journeys, so that he might observe the state of affairs for himself on the spot.

There were priests who no longer remembered the words of absolution, parishes that had been deserted for years, people of goodwill who were in danger of losing their souls. One day at Gannes, near Folleville, in the diocese of Amiens, Vincent was called to the bedside of a dying man whose conscience was torturing him. 'Madame,' the poor man said later to Mme de Gondi, 'I should have been damned had I not made a general confession to Monsieur Vincent.' There was plenty to upset one who believed in God. A few days later—it was early in 1617—at the request of Mme de Gondi, Vincent preached so earnestly and so eloquently from the pulpit in the village church that nearly all the villagers came to make a general confession; there were so many of them that it was even necessary to call the Jesuits from Amiens to the rescue. Thanks to him, that neglected vine, the father of the family, was brought back into cultivation, and he discovered from this experience the great pastoral reality to which he was to devote his life —the Mission.

Why did he suddenly break away from this great work of which he had caught a glimpse, from this life in which he could serve Christ so well? Once more the reason is wrapped in mystery, the mystery of a soul in so many respects hidden. It has been surmised that the extreme scruples of Mme de Gondi and her tumultuous spiritual conflicts might have wearied her confessor. But, if we go a little deeper, we might suppose that his exacting conscience reproached him: had he the right to enjoy this comfort and security, this luxury even, while so many of his afflicted brethren were given over to the direst perils? All through the saint's life it is possible to discern a sort of interior tug-of-war between his earnest desire to live in poverty among the poor and the compulsion he felt to live among the rich and powerful, to try to persuade them to incline towards the lowly and the outcast. The temptation to retire into obscurity is one which the most noble souls experience. If only he could escape from the Gondi mansion and its fashionable people, and take over some insignificant little parish, far away, and there serve God in silence. . . . Châtillon-des-Dombes needed a priest, a real priest; the Oratory at Lyons asked Bérulle for one. No one understood better than Bérulle the sentiments of his penitent, and he let Vincent go.

4. In the School of St Francis de Sales

Châtillon was not the ultimate refuge of Vincent de Paul's dreams; it was just a stopping-place on the road along which God was leading him. He soon began to receive letters, to which at first he did not reply; but it became more difficult for him to ignore them. M. de Gondi wrote begging him to return; Mme de Gondi went so far as to threaten to 'lay upon him before God the burden of all the good she would fail to achieve through lack of aid'. The Bishop of Paris intervened, and then Bérulle himself. Finally, M. Bence, superior of the Oratory at Lyons, made the curé of Châtillon realize that to remain buried in the marshes of the Dombes was not the destiny mapped out for him by God. Vincent obeyed and set out, as grieved at leaving his parishioners as they were to lose him.

Once again he was back in the world of fashion with his fine home and his pleasant relationships. Or so it seemed at first. The prospect of dazzling promotion awaited him in Paris: an appointment as chaplain to the de Gondi estates, to which was linked the office of Chaplain-General of the royal galleys. But during the few months he had been in Châtillon he had become aware of the tragedy of Christian souls threatened with apostasy; he had learned how easy it was to bring them back to God, if only one loved them just a little. From now on he would use the considerable influence he exercised to promote the cause of Christ, which is that of charity and justice. Since he had charge of the souls of the peasants on the Gondi estates, he would put into practice among them the methods which had been so successful at Folleville; he would give the French country mission its shape and its resources. Since he also had charge of the souls of the convicts in the galleys, he, a one-time slave in Tunis, would go himself and visit those condemned to penal servitude; he would shout from the house-tops the horror and injustice of their condition. And since Providence demanded that his poor cassock should rub against so much velvet and satin, he would remind the rich of the 'eminent dignity of the poor within the Church', as one of his young followers would one day declare. In his school he would teach them the gospel lesson of poor Lazarus.

So when Vincent de Paul returned to the Gondis, with whom he was to remain for nearly eight years, he found himself at the very centre of a movement which was at that time leading French Catholicism, in its most enlightened aspects, towards the reform desired by the Council of Trent. He took his place—modestly, for he never became in the least vain—in that enthusiastic circle of splendid souls who had been striving for fifteen years to give the Church a new look. Bérulle,

M. du Val—a master at the Sorbonne—the saintly Capuchin, Benoît de Canfeld, Father Cotton, those admirable men who, the following year, were to found the Company of the Blessed Sacrament, Mme Acarie, the Marquise de Meignelay, the Marquise de Bréauté—all had been labouring to strengthen the bases of faith, and for submission to the demands which faith makes. And it was in this atmosphere of Catholic reform that Vincent met, in 1618, the man in whom all these endeavours seemed to unite and be fufilled, the man who was to help Vincent to take the decisive step—St Francis de Sales.

Francis de Sales, Bishop of Geneva, was at that time in the prime of his life, in the full splendour of his achievement and the plenitude of spiritual perfection. He had a rather ungainly appearance; he looked more like a man from the mountainous country of Savoy than a member of the court, but his eyes shone in his bearded face, and his lips smiled with a tender mischievousness. This great mystic radiated human warmth, and no one could resist his firm gentleness and his calm wisdom. Vincent, like everyone else, had read the *Introduction to the Devout Life* which had been fashionable for the past ten years. During Francis' process of beatification Vincent spoke of the impression the book had made upon him; he had seemed to hear Christ Himself speaking, with the loving kindness that is discernible in the Gospels. Vincent had many talks with the bishop during the six months he spent in Paris.[1] He listened to him discussing matters of faith, the education of women, his missions, the direction of souls, politics, the duties of those in high places and many other things. He heard him speak too of the Order of the Visitation—Mother Jeanne de Chantal sometimes took part in these conversations. The bishop said he would like to see a society of women dedicated to charity in the world, rather than congregations of enclosed nuns—a suggestion which Vincent was to remember.[2] But above all, what the chaplain to the Gondis discovered most from his relationship with Francis de Sales was holiness itself, to which Bérulle had first pointed the way, a holiness to which his new master made him immediately susceptible by his example. Humility, serenity, self-control, joy in God—these were the virtues which Vincent was to practise in their fullness, and which the author of the *Devout Life* brought to maturity during those years in which Vincent enjoyed his enlightened direction. And we

---

[1] Francis de Sales was in Paris to negotiate the marriage of Christine de France, sister of the king, to the Prince of Piedmont, heir to Savoy.

[2] When Francis de Sales was dying, he entrusted to Vincent de Paul what was most dear to him—the Order of the Visitation. As Superior of the Visitation in Paris, Monsieur Vincent exercised his responsibility with care, but without seeking to exert a too rigid influence over the nuns, so that they continued with their teaching and their contemplative life. He was Mother de Chantal's spiritual director, and she looked for spiritual consolation from him rather than counsel.

know from what Vincent himself has told us that, on the death of his great friend in 1622, he suddenly got an impression of profound peace which put an end for ever to any violence of disposition that still lingered in him, that occasional irascibility, explosiveness even, which he had sometimes experienced; it was as though the saint's virtues had in a mysterious way been poured back into him.

The long trek towards God was nearing its end. Vincent's goal was in sight. He was nearly ready to undertake the many-sided work to which he would give his whole being. He was about to cut himself free from whatever moorings remained. He gave up his livings one after another. But there still remained the last bond to break: the secret sentimental link that united him to his family in the Landes. His heart sank when he thought of them and the home of his childhood—his mother, the humble housewife, and his brothers hard at work. He burned with a longing to snatch them from their poverty and the mud of their existence. Now that he was on familiar terms with the powerful, he was in a position to make their fortunes. What an agonizing temptation! But it is written in the Gospel that to follow Christ one must leave father and mother. . . . Once, however, he did return to Pouy. He visited again the scenes of his childhood; he went once more barefooted over the road to the *ériaou* to which, as a little swineherd, he had so often travelled with his pigs. He ate his last meal with his family, and then, in tears, he left them, never to return.

5. MONSIEUR VINCENT

The long trek and the phase of preparation may have seemed unending, but now it was nearly over. At forty-five years of age Vincent de Paul had not yet achieved any of the great foundations which he knew to be necessary. But did not Our Lord wait thirty years before taking His Word to the world? During those years of groping the fiery little Gascon acquired something very important, more important than immature successes: he learned that 'the works of God are not done when we want them to be done, but when it pleases Him', and that 'we must not jump ahead of Providence'. The virtue of holy patience was one that he was to practise to the full.

So at forty-five he had become entirely himself. He was no longer the young Gascon in a cassock whom we met at Rome and in the drawing-rooms of Queen Margot, nor even the young parish priest of Clichy whose vehement enthusiasm astonished his bishop. Something in him had sobered down, without in the slightest diminishing his bold fervour. His face had become lined. His brow bore the wrinkles of strain and anxiety. The time was soon to come when his back would be bent, and he would drag his legs along. In the end he would resemble that figure which film and portrait have made popular—a simple, bearded man, with a long, pointed nose and a short neck sunk into his shoulders. His head is completely covered by his black skull-cap, but his high forehead reveals his gifts of intellect; there is a sparkle in his piercing eyes; but in the smile of that large mouth his very soul shines through—the wisdom and charity of the saint.

This uncouth-looking priest who arrived at the court in his big boots, his frayed girdle, his cassock worn and turning green—where did he get that air of authority which flowed so spontaneously from him? 'There are neither holes nor stains, madame,' he replied proudly to the queen, when she teased him about his appearance. Here was the most notable, the most significant man in the whole history of French Catholicism, and perhaps even in the whole Church. What was his personality going to make of him during the thirty-five years of his active life? What strikes the historian above all is his readiness of mind. He was intelligent in the highest degree, although this might not be true in the sense in which the intellectuals use the word. He never sought to shine in dialectical argument, or in the play of ideas. But his little black eyes probed with a single glance the very depths of people; he could weigh up a situation in a flash. He was far-seeing, and therein lay his genius. He could put his finger on all the problems of his day, and even those which one could hardly predict; and he found logical solutions to them. Yet he was anything but a dreamer, a manufacturer of systems. He was, on the contrary, precise and realistic; his feet stood firmly on the ground. All empty dreams, or anything resembling mawkishness, horrified him. 'Horse and donkey love,' was the expression he used to describe any sentiment which lacked restraint. One saying of his describes his whole attitude, both practical and spiritual, and marks him as the contemporary of Descartes, a man of the classical age: 'God asks nothing of us which is contrary to reason.'

That is not the portrait of a doctrinarian or a starchy moralizer. This sound and sober-minded man did nothing in a flurry. 'He who hurries', he said, 'moves backwards in the things which concern God.' His calm soothed all men, and especially all women, who approached him; but it had the breath of joy and cheerfulness. A playful wisdom brought racy repartee to his lips and a ready Gascon wit. He told a son of St Francis, an eager candidate for a bishopric, that it would be a great pity to deprive his Order of a fellow as distinguished as he was; all the other could do was to enjoy the compliment. This watchful irony was never cruel. Vincent was anything but a controversialist. When engaged in the most lively debates he would always remain restrained and charitable towards those whose arguments he condemned. His extraordinary kindness was his most striking characteristic.

He loved men: to do so was an essential part of his nature. He loved them despite their smallness and their miseries—deficiences which he knew better than anyone; indeed he loved them because of these things. His first biographer, Abelly—'the soft Abelly,' as Boileau called him with an irony that was hardly just—relates that Vincent 'could not bear the mention of human distress without his face becoming immediately clouded over with sorrow and compassion'. His was a ceaseless charity blended with tact, a quality which this virtue sometimes lacks. He respected human dignity, even in the most poverty-stricken, because he recognized in the poor a resemblance to the divine. In this there was a Franciscan side to his character. In a century when Father Malebranche thought he was striking a machine when he beat his dog, the kindness of Vincent towards animals was soul-stirring. He communicated this sovereign charity constantly, by his words, his actions and his silence. That was the source of the radiating sweetness that proceeded from him. A lady under his spiritual direction said this of him: 'Could we not say, like the disciples on the road to Emmaus, that our hearts experienced the fire of the love of God while Monsieur Vincent spoke to us?'

The love of God: there is no need to look elsewhere for Monsieur Vincent's secret. This mainspring of his every action was embedded in his vigorous faith and his precise doctrine. If he loved men it was because he had irrevocably taken the first two commandments of the Gospel seriously, the two which Christ declared to be one: 'Thou shalt love the Lord thy God with thy whole heart, and with all thy soul, and with thy whole mind. . . . Thou shalt love thy neighbour as thyself.' In short, his overwhelming excellence depended entirely on the intensity of his spiritual life.

It is a fact which must be stressed, if only to remedy an injustice. There has existed an exaggerated tendency to set him apart from that glorious band of great spiritual men. First, because this saint of charity was very active, and because he was uncommunicative about what went on within himself, sincerely believing that it was all of no interest to anybody; then, because his humility drove him to demean himself with a persistence and a conviction which asserted themselves; finally, because some of his adversaries, especially those of Port-Royal, were anxious to relegate him to the ranks of the illiterate. In the film *Monsieur Vincent*, which has popularized his image in our day, he is made to look too much like a proprietor of some well-known brand of soup. We shall never grow tired of quoting the words of Bremond: 'It was not charity which made him a saint, but his saintliness which made him really charitable.' Admittedly St Vincent de Paul did not throw any new light upon religious theory; he did not, like his master Bérulle, set in motion a new school of doctrine. He did not even publish anything during his lifetime.[1] He scorned the idea of any deliberately systematic arrangement of his spiritual views; he left to his commentators the care of assembling the component parts. Yet there exist an admirable truthfulness and continuity in his spirituality; and who, among the great spiritual minds with which this period teems, was to leave so profound an impression upon the age?

His spirituality was essentially one of balance and moderation. He would have said of it what he did say of virtue: 'It is always based on the happy medium.' Even in matters of charity he condemned excessive zeal, just as he did the lack of it. His doctrine was a half-way house between the tenets of his two masters; or, better still, he united them: the ardent mysticism of Bérulle and the devout humanitarianism of St Francis de Sales—without forgetting the very precise influences of St Ignatius of Loyola. He had more confidence in man than Bérulle had, but even so his method was more rugged than that outlined in the *Introduction to the Devout Life*. His opposition to the Jansenist errors was obvious, but all the same he did not yield to the temptation of laxity. Here again, as in so many other matters, he spoke out. He prepared the Church to become *ours* in the present-day sense of the word. His successor in the following century was St Alphonsus of Liguori.

Finally, for him everything adds up to a fundamental principle, one which governs the metaphysic of the saints, and which St Paul stated in unsurpassable words: we must 'live in Christ'. If Monsieur Vincent rose at four in the morning and began his day with the use of the discipline—unto blood—and if he demanded of his body efforts and labour beyond measure, it was because he had Christ before his eyes: the man of sorrows, through whom all the sorrows of the world take on their true significance. To live the Cross, to live the Passion of Christ; that is to live also His infinite love of men. Bérulle initiated Monsieur Vincent into the contemplation of the incarnate Word, in every aspect of His sorrowful existence; St Francis de Sales taught him that humanity has but one model. Besides, Vincent adhered to Christ, according to the expression of the time, with all his soul—to Christ, 'this perfect model, this counsellor'.

That is why he remained so untroubled and so buoyant in the midst of life's difficulties; he had given over to God completely the task of guiding him. 'To will nothing but what God wills'; to know that 'He uses us if we give ourselves to Him'; 'to empty ourselves of ourselves, and allow God to act in us'; he was never to do anything but that, and it was the source of his success.

---

[1] His doctrine is to be found in his *Conférences et entretiens, Exercices spirituels*, which he gave to the Lazarists (the Congregation of the Mission), to the Sisters of Charity, and also in his vast correspondence (14 vols., published by Coste, between 1920 and 1925).

Hence the purpose of all his action was to obey God, to respond to God's beckoning; for Vincent was essentially a man who did things for God. In his eyes the Christian's task was to build the kingdom of the Father, *hic et nunc*; to bring more justice and love into the world. He was quite unlike those mystics, even the great ones, who are happy to live in solitude and meditation, not really scorning earthly things, but aspiring to charity through mortification and prayer only, on the principle of the transfer of merits and the Communion of Saints; as far as Vincent was concerned, he could not conceive of any impulse towards Christ which was not also an impulse towards his fellows. Here then is the decisive quality which puts the finishing touch to the saint's portrait: charity, poured out in works, is reunited at its pinnacle with pure contemplation. 'It is mysticism', says Bremond, 'which has given us our greatest men of action.'

6. THE GREAT FOUNDATIONS: THE MISSIONS

The hour of accomplishment had struck for Monsieur Vincent. He knew what Our Lord expected of him. Having returned to the Gondis, he was now able to exercise a great deal more influence, and he was going to use it to embark upon his multifarious enterprises, the fulfilment of which would carry him to every level of endeavour—an achievement at once social, moral, theological, pastoral, and even political; of astounding variety and scope, but the only kind of work which would enable him to display successfully his qualities of leadership, coupled with a veritable genius for organization.

We must note this final trait in Vincent's character as we watch the shaping in his competent hands of the great foundations which he bequeathed to the Church. Saintly founders often have these gifts: St Benedict, St Dominic and St Ignatius come to mind. Vincent was made in their mould. Amenable to circumstances, adapting himself to the environment in which he worked, always getting the best out of men and opportunities, he was precise, far-seeing and prudent; he knew that no man receives more help from God than the man who helps himself. Whatever he was responsible for, whether it was a big or a little thing, he dealt with in a strictly methodical manner. He laid down rules, both for himself and others, to provide for every contingency. He would not allow himself, and he forbade others, to take unnecessary risks or to embark upon badly prepared enterprises in which pious magnanimity so often comes to grief. Like a true leader he had a capacity both for visualizing things as a whole and for managing details. The further he went the more responsibilities fell upon his shoulders; but they did not bend them. Every task he undertook led to another. The Council of Conscience was linked with the reformation of the clergy; assistance for the devastated provinces led to the organizing of seminaries; political negotiations were followed by the struggle against Jansenism. He coped with everything and was never overwhelmed.

From his humble room at Saint-Lazare he inspired, governed and controlled a world. How many letters did he write? Above all, how many did he dictate to his secretary, the worthy Brother Ducournau? Probably from thirty to fifty thousand; no one knows for certain. The 'Coste' edition contains only three thousand. One of them is dated 'From the town, during the night'; but many, many others were scribbled hastily at odd times during a journey. His letters always made delicious reading, and even when they were stern they remained fragrant with charity. He replied to every report and to every request that was made to him. He entered into details; with one he discussed the cutting of the hay, with another the butchers' strike; but he also knew how to issue the kind of instructions which form the basis of a doctrine and call for action. An extraordinarily lucid brain was required to be able to handle so many different activities at once, activities so complex that the historian can only hope to give a superficial view of them by drawing artificial distinctions between things which, in Monsieur Vincent's case, took place in the gushing simultaneity of life.

His first achievement was basically the one around which everything else turned—the Mission. The idea took root spontaneously when Mme de Gondi enabled him to put his finger on the spiritual misery of the French countryside. In a heart that clings to Christ the very spectacle of an utterly forsaken people creates the urgent demand for an apostolate. Besides, the idea was already in the wind, as the saying goes. Other generous souls had undertaken to knead the heavy dough, to work into it the new leaven. Twenty-five years earlier Father Auger had stirred Bordeaux and the south-west. At the very moment when Vincent was about to enter the arena, Father Véron was scouring the country around Caen, and the amazing Michel le Nobletz was stirring the whole of Brittany. In Corsica a saintly Barnabite, Alexander Sauli, had been working valiantly for twenty years. What Vincent de Paul had begun at Folleville he was to continue elsewhere—at Paillart and Sèrevilliers, two other villages in Picardy, then at Villepreux, Joigny, Montmirail, and as far as Mâcon in Burgundy. The Church in France had not a lot of faith in these parish missions, the forerunners of our present-day missions. 'People used to laugh at me,' Monsieur Vincent admitted; 'they used to point their finger at me in the streets.' But he was not the man to give up an enterprise which seemed to him so obviously desired by God.

Before long he came to the conclusion that the results would be permanent only if the missions were arranged according to a plan; in other words, they should be organized institutions. This demanded the existence of teams of priests whose lives would be wholly devoted to the Mission. He became convinced that in order to achieve this end it was necessary to create a special society. So great was his humility that he hesitated to think of himself as the man for this foundation. But Providence made him see that he was, and he had no alternative but to obey. In the circumstances Providence made use of that splendid woman Mme de Gondi. She was rather inclined towards extremes, but she certainly had the charity of Christ in her soul and the interest of the Church at heart. She was so impressed by Vincent's sermon of January 1617 that she sacrificed little pleasures, reduced her expenses on clothes and put aside fifteen thousand francs—a considerable sum in those days—to establish permanent missions, which were to be given in rotation in all the villages on her estates. She approached the Jesuits, who declined the offer. The Oratorians did the same. These societies were not much concerned with the countryside. The good lady was therefore drawn towards the idea of setting up a new society. She nursed the project for seven years and spoke to her husband about it. He approved, increased the original endowment by thirty thousand francs and encouraged her in her intention to discuss the matter with her beloved chaplain.

The project made rapid progress. There was at that time in Paris, around the Montagne Sainte-Geneviève, a fair number of 'colleges' for students; they were more like boarding-houses than houses of study. The college known as the 'Bons Enfants', situated near the Porte Saint-Victor—where the Rue Monge now stands—was almost empty and in a bad state of repair. The Archbishop of Paris, Jean-François de Gondi, brother of the Général des Galères, put the premises at Vincent's disposal, and made him principal. That was in March 1624. The following year, on 17th April 1625, the contract setting up the foundation was duly signed in the presence of a notary, and the Gondis paid over the forty-five thousand francs, Vincent having already been granted the ownership of the college by the archbishop. Two months later the pious Mme de Gondi yielded her soul to God, for whom she had worked so hard.

It had been provided that the Congregation of Priests of the Missions would include six 'ecclesiastical persons', unencumbered by any benefices and free from all responsibilities; that they should undertake, under the control of the bishop, to go into the countryside to preach to the people 'who are almost abandoned, while the towns have a large number of doctors and religious to attend to their spiritual needs'. Three priests joined Vincent—three men of goodwill. One was André Portail, who served the future saint devotedly through every trial. The second was François du Coudray who, to give himself up to the poor who worked in the fields, sacrificed everything he loved most—his intellectual studies, his library, and even his Hebrew, at which he excelled. The third man was Jean de la Salle, whose dominating personality had already left its mark in various quarters. A splendid team! 'We went about preaching and giving missions from village to village,' Vincent said later. 'I had only one subject for my sermons, and I dealt with it in a thousand ways; it was the fear of God. That was our work, and God did what He had foreseen from all eternity: He blessed our labours. And some good priests, seeing this, joined up with us.'

The little congregation began to grow, although some people resented it. The priests of Paris, for instance, took the matter to the 'Parlement'; and the judgment it gave savoured of running with the hare and hunting with the hounds. The Parlement registered the royal patents under which the Mission was founded, which was a tactful way of dealing with the envious. It was necessary, therefore, to go to Rome to try to obtain from the Pope recognition of the new society as a congregation under pontifical approbation. It took nearly eight years of effort: the Congregation of Propaganda rejected the first application, and then the second. The problem was: since these priests did not wish to become a religious community, but aspired all the same to carry out a work similar to that for which the mendicant Orders formerly stood, what would they really be? Stranger still, it seemed that Vincent's friend, M. de Bérulle, far from helping his disciple in his undertaking, threw some altogether ecclesiastical spanners into the works. There is an occasional pettiness even among the greatest![1] It needed all the diplomatic skill of M. du Coudray to win the day. On 12th January 1633 Pope Urban VIII sanctioned the work of the Mission by the Bull *Salvatori Nostro*.

A few months later a new and serious obstacle was cleared. A monastic property was offered to Monsieur Vincent and his priests. And what a property! No less than the area now occupied by the former Saint-Lazare prison, the Nord Station (Gare du Nord), the Church of St Vincent de Paul and the Lariboisière Hospital—nearly a hundred acres in the heart of Paris! The last prior informed Vincent that he was making him a gift of it, and Vincent's first reaction was to decline it. 'We are poor priests,' he muttered; 'we live a life of simplicity. Our sole ambition is to serve the poor in the fields.' And he added: 'We are just born: we are scarcely a handful yet.' That was

---

[1] This explains why, when talking one day of the houses which were doing good work in Paris besides Saint-Sulpice and Saint-Nicolas-du-Chardonnet, Monsieur Vincent merely remarked: 'Let us leave the Oratory alone; don't let us talk about it.'

true, of course, but he knew in the depths of his faith that his work was destined to grow, just as the mustard seed grows. His friend and adviser, M. du Val, persuaded him to accept the property. The old priory, in which lepers were once cared for, was transformed into a vast dispensary of charity, an ever-open refuge for all human afflictions; and it became the mother-house of the new undertaking. It was an event of capital importance, destined to give the movement new possibilities and a new impetus. First Paris, then France, eventually Europe and the whole world would henceforth associate Monsieur Vincent with Saint-Lazare. The Congregation of the Priests of the Mission was to be called by the name which has made them famous— the Lazarists.

Priests of the Mission: the term is none the less quite precise; it describes them well. At the beginning they were secular priests; they lived among the country clergy, bound only by a promise of permanence, and by another, pledging them to the service of the poor, to which their founder attached the greatest importance. These were private promises which prevented them from being canonically members of a religious Order.[1] Monsieur Vincent never ceased to point out to his priests their purpose thus: 'To strive towards personal perfection by doing our best to practise the virtues which our Sovereign Master deigned to teach us by word and example; to preach the Gospel to the poor, especially to the poor of the countryside.' In that formula the personal spirituality of Monsieur Vincent is complete: to live in Christ in order to take Christ to others; nothing more than that, and nothing less. 'If only we knew', he said again, 'how to inspire souls with the spirit of the Gospel, we should be great missioners.' The 'if' is too modest a word; who could possibly be described as great missioners if not Monsieur Vincent and his sons?

Who were these men? They came from all classes of society—from the middle class and the nobility, but also from the poorer people. Whatever their origin, they all made themselves people among the people, poor with the poor, rubbing shoulders with the destitute without embarrassment or distaste. Above all, following the example of their leader, they invited the most humble to their tables. They were not famous men, and they did not seek to be; they were simple folk who knew how to speak to the common people, to laugh and joke with them; for their kind of charity was a light-hearted virtue. 'We are sent by their lordships the bishops,' one of them said, 'and we go along simply and naturally, preaching to the poor as Our Lord did.' They would arrive at a small market-town, a straggling village, or

---

[1] The final Constitution approved by Clement X in 1670 laid down the four vows which are still those of the Lazarists: the solemn vows of Poverty, Chastity and Obedience, and the special vow of Service to the Poor.

perhaps a large town, and spend a fortnight or a month there, preaching and talking anywhere, but in the churches mostly, or wherever it was necessary. And, of course, they never received payment: they never asked anyone for anything. 'We are just as much under an obligation to give missions for nothing as the Capuchin friars are to live on alms,' Vincent replied to Mme de Longueville who offered to pay for a mission. They had no other purpose beyond being carriers of the Word of God, and drawing the people to General Confession and to Holy Communion. And they were completely successful.

There was one point on which Vincent was very strict, and of which he never ceased to remind his sons: to make oneself understood when speaking of Christ one has to be simple. Simplicity was certainly not always the outstanding virtue of preachers. In those days sermons were too often an opportunity for a pompous showing off, and a display of cheap learning which, under the pretext of being symbolical, resulted in the most comical comparisons. Monsieur Vincent never tired of referring sarcastically to what he called 'monumental periods', 'cathedral' eloquence, those 'pieces of embroidery', and 'well-dressed sermons'. 'Enough of all these *Bibus* and *coeli coelorum*,' he would boom good-naturedly. 'These peacock-strutting speeches are a sacrilege; yes, a sacrilege!' What he called his Little Method consisted in speaking with all one's heart, without mincing matters, without bombast: that was the way to reach the heart. When he learned that one of his missioners still continued to make use of explosive eloquence, he wrote to him kindly, but with a sly dig: 'I have been told that you make too great an effort when speaking to the people, and that it is weakening your health. In the name of heaven, monsieur, be careful of your health, and moderate your speech and your feelings.'

We have seen the result of all this, and many in our day have had occasion to remember his words. The missions were, and always will be, an excellent method of moving souls. When Bossuet wrote to Pope Clement XI to request the canonization of Vincent de Paul, he stressed the decisive influence which the mission at Metz had had on his own spiritual development. The humble and the lowly, whom the missioners addressed primarily, were just as moved. The mission became an event: at Laon, for example, it was decided to suspend the market so that everyone might go and hear the missioners. One of the priests sent to Poitiers, who had at first encountered difficulties, wrote joyfully: 'These souls seemed as hard as stone, but they have become filled with a holy fire.' Mende, Arles, Angoulême, Cahors, Sens, Annecy, Châlons, Tréguier, Guingamp, Morlaix—all one after another begged the 'Messieurs' of Saint-Lazare to come back. But there were plenty of obstacles to overcome. At Sedan they had to contend with a large number of Protestants, a fact which created complications;

at Saint-Méen some envious Benedictines tried to prevent the Lazarists from settling down to work; at Saintes they had to deal with the devil himself. It was said that every night there was loud and terrifying banging in the cellar!

From Saint-Lazare Monsieur Vincent followed closely the development of his work, receiving reports not only from the superiors of houses which the Mission founded in large towns, but from missioners at work everywhere. It was a really Golden Legend that his sons created; expressions of gratitude reached him from all over France. He shed tears of joy when, one day, he received from Étienne Blatiron, one of his priests who was giving a mission in Corsica, the astonishing account of two mortal enemies giving each other a brotherly kiss of peace in public at the end of a sermon; yet there had existed between them a deadly family feud.

Then there were the two Saint-Germain missions which proved that Monsieur Vincent was not interested only in country yokels. First the court mission of 1638, while the king was in residence at the castle of Saint-Germain-en-Laye. It was the king himself who asked for the preachers, and Monsieur Vincent gladly sent them. He selected them from among those who attended his 'Tuesday Conferences', and instructed them to tell a few home truths to the beautiful and frivolous ladies in their low-necked dresses, the duelling nobles and the adventurers. The missioners carried out his instructions fearlessly. The mission that followed there three years later was given in a rather less fragrant atmosphere—the suburb of Saint-Germain in Paris, which the worthy Abelly described as 'a sink of iniquity'. There the disciples of Monsieur Vincent so stirred the souls of their audiences that M. Olier, the parish priest of Saint-Sulpice, was left flabbergasted. In days to come he would remember the lesson of that mission.

Right to the end of Monsieur Vincent's days the Mission remained his chief consideration, and he gave it his constant care. Since the death of Mme de Gondi another great lady had made herself the guardian of the young congregation; she was the Duchesse d'Aiguillon, a woman of high intellect and a soul which thirsted after that which was good. Thanks to her the congregation gained much, and many obstacles were smoothed out. There was no one, not even the suspicious Cardinal de Richelieu, who did not approve the work of Monsieur Vincent, or who refused to help him. Richelieu saw to it that a mission was established in the very market-town whose name he bore, and he left it a considerable legacy when he died. Old, worn out and crippled, Vincent never hesitated to go in person when necessary and visit the various mission foundations, riding in the carriage which the Ladies of Charity had given him, and which he called 'my infamy'. By the time he died, in 1660, Saint-Lazare had provided 840 missions; the congregation, distributed in 25 houses, numbered 131 priests, 44 clerics and 52 coadjutors. These may be impressive figures, but they show how heavy was the burden for every Lazarist. 'Three can do more than ten when Our Lord lends a hand,' said the smiling Monsieur Vincent. Thanks most of all to him and to his sons the movement of Catholic reformation in France was no longer an enterprise for scholars and intellectuals. The fair land of France was rediscovering its Christian roots, and, to the extent to which she has retained them, she owes much to the Lazarists.

7. 'IT IS ON ITS PRIESTS THAT CHRISTIANITY MUST DEPEND'

There was still another, a third, aim which Monsieur Vincent had entrusted to his sons. It was, of course, necessary to be holy oneself, and to take the Word to the people; but it was also essential 'to help clergymen to acquire the virtues necessary to their state'. This third purpose was indeed but the consequence of the first two: in order to preach the Gospel to the people, one had to do so to the pastors who, often enough, were equally in need of it.

The decrees of the Council of Trent had evidently not sufficed to halt at one stroke the decadence of the clergy. Much effort was needed if the Church were to climb back up the slope down which it had been sliding for more than two centuries. Too many priests, especially in country districts, were living on a level with the people, a people whose moral standard, after so many years of political, religious and social upheaval, was not very high. Strictly speaking, most of these priests did not lead bad lives, but their morals were not at all priest-like. Many of them were lazy—'Laziness is the vice of the clergy,' declared Monsieur Vincent; they were apathetic where parochial work was concerned. Because of lack of training, they were extremely ignorant. Vincent could remember a parish priest whom he met during his early missions on the Gondi estates, who did not even know the words of absolution. Absenteeism was common.[1]

This decline of the clergy racked the truly priestly soul of Monsieur Vincent. He had some terrible things to say about the state of affairs as he knew it. 'The priests, living as most of them do today, are the greatest enemies of the Church of God.' And again: 'The depravity of the priestly state is the principal cause of the Church's downfall.' These were severe criticisms; but to his generous nature they were just the expression of an urgent need. 'What the priests are, so are the people.' 'If a good priest can achieve a lot of good, think what harm a bad one can do. . . .' And he would add those words which give us

[1] See Chapter II, p. 67, on the condition of the clergy.

the feeling that we are already listening to the saintly Curé d'Ars: 'There is nothing as great as a good priest.'

And so he tackled eagerly the task of reforming the clergy. 'My dear brothers,' he said, addressing his Lazarists, 'the training of good priests is a most difficult undertaking, but it is the most exalted, and of the greatest importance for the salvation of souls.' Indeed it was a difficult task. One had to put an end to so many well-established practices, to insist upon a high moral standard in future priests, compel them to undertake special training, prevent people from assuming Holy Orders on the recommendation of some person in authority or for the sake of social position, or with a very meagre stock of theological knowledge. The whole edifice had to be rebuilt from the foundations. Monsieur Vincent was not the only one to carry in his heart the anguish of this enormous problem. The Council of Trent half a century earlier had studied it thoroughly and had laid down wise principles; it now remained to put them into practice. Bérulle with his Oratory and Bourdoise with his community of priests were both working at it, each in his own way. A little later there would be M. Olier and St John Eudes, Holzhauser in Germany and others. In this vast undertaking Vincent de Paul did not stand alone, but he assumed the leading role.

The first of his accomplishments was literally inspired by Providence. Throughout his life he often welcomed a suggestion, an idea or a scheme, as coming from God, and then, in humility, concentrated all his zeal and organizing genius into its fulfilment. It was in July 1628 that the Bishop of Beauvais, Augustin Potier de Gesvres, was riding in his carriage along a road in his diocese, accompanied by a few priests; Monsieur Vincent was one of them. The bishop seemed to be dozing. All at once he opened his eyes, and said: 'At last I think I see an easy and satisfactory way of preparing candidates for Holy Orders. I shall have them stay with me for a few days: they will carry out pious exercises, and be instructed in their duties and their functions.'

Monsieur Vincent started up, delighted. 'That thought comes from God, my Lord,' he said. 'I can think of nothing more suitable to put the clergy of your diocese on the right road.'

'It would be advisable to start as soon as possible,' replied the bishop. 'Get out a programme, and prepare a list of suitable subjects for discussion. About two to three weeks before the September ordinations, come back to Beauvais, so that we may get everything arranged for the retreat.'

Thus was born the *Exercises for Ordination Candidates*. During the following Ember Week Monsieur Vincent went to Beauvais to preach the first retreat. Within three years the formula was perfected, procedure was laid down and a little handbook prepared by Monsieur

Vincent in collaboration with other pious people. It was called *Homilies for Ordination Candidates* and was both a precise guide to spiritual perfection and a theological summary. Its success was remarkable. The archbishop wanted the Exercises carried out in his diocese; and he asked Monsieur Vincent to start classes at the Collège des Bons Enfants. Then, when Saint-Lazare was offered to the young Congregation of the Mission, the archbishop insisted that the Exercises be given regularly to all his future priests. The institution spread rapidly. It was adopted by other dioceses, such as Troyes and Noyon—then Savoy, and even Rome. To Catholics of the twentieth century the project might seem to have been very hastily improvised. Could anything really serious be achieved in three weeks? Yet it certainly bore fruit. Among the candidates who took the Exercises were Jean-Jacques Olier, the Abbé de Rancé and Bossuet, and both spoke highly of them; especially Bossuet who, after being a student, taught there several times.

However, Monsieur Vincent, more than anyone else, was aware of the shortcomings of his achievement. This retreat was certainly a beginning, but something more was needed. For five years he waited for Providence to tell him what he should do. The way was shown to him through some of the very priests who had followed the *Exercises for Ordination Candidates* at Saint-Lazare. Having gained a better understanding of the grandeur and responsibilities of the priestly office, they asked Monsieur Vincent to assemble them at Saint-Lazare 'to discuss with them the virtues and functions proper to their ministry'. The saint agreed to their request, and on 24th June 1633 he began his Tuesday Conferences. He kept these up, almost without interruption, until his death. They became famous and very popular. 'There was scarcely any ecclesiastic of note who was not anxious to join them,' said the illustrious teacher Lancelot, who was just as engrossed in problems of clerical reform as he was in Greek roots. A group of carefully selected priests was formed at Saint-Lazare; a profound faith and a warm-hearted emulation inspired them all. 'Every one of these gentlemen of the Conference', said Vincent, 'is exemplary, and there is nothing to be compared with the fruits of their labours.' It was from among those who attended the conferences that he chose his missioners to catechize the court at Saint-Germain. Bossuet, who worked hard there, has given this splendid testimony of the man who was the very soul of the conferences: 'He was like that minister to whom St Peter refers as speaking of God in a manner so elevated that God Himself seemed to speak by his mouth.' Bishops like Godeau could be seen at these conferences; de Grasse, and the Abbé de Coulanges, whom Mme de Rabutin-Chantal called 'le Bien Bon', and M. Olier, who was planning the foundation of Saint-Sulpice; and Abelly, the future biographer of Monsieur Vincent. All were to vie with one another in proclaiming their debt to this man of God.[1]

All this was splendid, but was it enough? Not yet. The very success of the Exercises and the Tuesdays induced Monsieur Vincent to start a third venture. The Council of Trent, in its XXIIIrd session, had asked bishops to set up seminaries in their dioceses for the training of their future priests,[2] but even seventy years after the closure of the Council the precise formula on which it was to be based had not yet been found. All the reformers were thinking about it, especially Bérulle and Bourdoise. So far the results had been poor. The Fathers of the Oratory had been trying unsuccessfully for twenty-two years to do something. M. Bourdoise, at Saint-Nicolas du Chardonnet, had, in thirty years, merely succeeded in founding a community of priests for the training of the young: a useful work indeed, but with limited possibilities. All the bishops with whose training Monsieur Vincent had been more or less directly concerned begged him to establish real seminaries. The saint still hesitated. Was that what God wanted of him? His sons had a vocation, to go and preach to the good people in the country districts, and there were not enough of them to enable him to branch out into such a vast undertaking as the establishment of seminaries. If only Heaven would give him a sign! Once more Providence did give him the sign he wanted; and it was through the medium of Cardinal de Richelieu himself who, during a memorable interview, invited Monsieur Vincent to resolve the problem which he had so much at heart.

Accordingly the Collège des Bons Enfants [3] became a seminary, situated less than 120 yards from the one controlled by M. Bourdoise. This action by Monsieur Vincent resulted in there really being two seminaries: *le Grand*, or the big one, which provided at the Bons Enfants twelve future priests, and *le Petit*, or the small one, situated in Saint-Charles, which was an annexe of Saint-Lazare and where children did their studies without necessarily intending to proceed to Holy Orders. Thus the separation of ordinary students from seminarists, which the French Episcopate had desired for seventeen years, was now realized. This took place early in 1642, during the period when M. Olier was founding the seminary of Vaugirard. A definite formula for the seminary had at last been outlined.

This does not mean that these early seminaries resembled our own of today. Students for the priesthood were received for six months to

---

[1] It should be added that Monsieur Vincent also started at Saint-Lazare the closed retreats which both priests and laity could attend if they wished. He entertained them without any charge.

[2] See *The Catholic Reformation*, p. 101.

[3] The expression *bons enfants* meant in those days *enfants de riches*, that is, 'children of the wealthy'.

two years, according to the locality, for the purpose of giving them spiritual and pastoral training rather than a sound theological education. Monsieur Vincent laid great emphasis on this training—and the somewhat Draconian regulations that he laid down were intended to instil this into his students. He was suspicious, he used to say, of the excessive 'scholasticism, which can be heard in Navarre or at the Sorbonne'. '*Scientia inflat,*' he would repeat. His desire to be practical never prevented him from wishing his seminarists to have a good basic education and to have their heads well screwed on. These seminaries produced a Vincentian type of student, and the outcome was immediately successful. The Lazarists linked this kind of work with that of the Mission by sending their young people to assist at the missions, and they opened seminaries in every town where bishops asked them to do so: at Cahors in 1643, at Saintes in 1644, at Le Mans in 1645, at Agen and Tréguier in 1648, and at Montauban in 1652. When their founder was dying, he was able to say of himself with truth that he had worked hard in the training of good priests, in trying to make them worthy of their priesthood.

8. 'CARITAS CHRISTI URGET NOS'

Missions, seminaries, mass conversions, the reform of the clergy—all were splendid achievements most certainly. And yet, to a tireless man like Monsieur Vincent, it was so very little. The love of God and of one's neighbour is a consuming passion: the man who yields to it has no time for rest. With misfortune appealing to him on all sides, Vincent responded to every entreaty; he even managed to get ahead of affliction before it manifested itself. One after another charitable works sprang from his hands—new institutions here, a regrouping there; and always the sole purpose was to make life on earth less painful to the lowly, less unjust and cruel. Before him social barriers fell away; money ceased to be the prisoner of the self-seeking. In an age of savage darkness, he caused the great light of kindness to radiate. He laid the foundations of what we today call Social Science; he did it in a straightforward and simple way, without worrying about theories. The watchword he gave to his Sisters was indeed the keynote of his own life: 'The charity of Christ crucified weighs upon us.'

So this is the picture which posterity, grateful for once, was to keep of this man of God. Vincent de Paul, 'the apostle of Charity'—that is how he is described in books; Vincent sheltering little waifs and strays under the folds of his enormous cloak—children whom he picked up at the corners of the streets; Vincent running to take the place of a galley slave who collapses at the oars beneath the blows of a galley sergeant; Vincent nursing the sick who lay huddled together in the hospitals, tending them without repugnance, without fear of possible contagion; Vincent made 'quartermaster' of the devastated regions, organizing a form of Catholic relief which was destined to inspire future similar efforts, and rescuing whole provinces from hunger. . . .

Such were the impressions of the saint which the people of France were to cherish in their minds and hearts—impressions upon which no Frenchman can dwell without emotion. Vincent was the most human of all the saints.

And yet, when one considers the accomplishments of Monsieur Vincent in the sphere of charity, it is important to remember the literally appalling conditions in which he achieved them, and which made his work so absolutely necessary. France was in an anaemic condition at the beginning of the seventeenth century; she was worn out as a result of the religious wars. Under the wise administration of Henry IV the great vitality which she possessed at that period enabled her wounds to heal quickly. The uncertain years of Louis XIII's minority did not entirely check this recovery; the only problems and misfortunes to be faced were those brought about by nature, without having to bear with those resulting from human folly. But the situation took a tragic turn from the moment when Richelieu, perceiving the downfall of his Swedish ally, Gustavus Adolphus, attempted to safeguard the balance of power in Europe and caused France to pass from a war of intrigue to open war against Austria and Spain. Invaded in the east, where the heroic Saint-Jean-de-Losne faced the attacks of the imperial forces, and in the north, where the Croats under Piccolomini stormed Corbie, the kingdom was threatened with extinction. While the most wealthy of the Parisians piled into their carriages and took to flight, Spanish skirmishers appeared in Pontoise. Champagne, Burgundy, Picardy and the Lorraine (which was French only in language and sentiment) gasped beneath the enemy's blows. It is important to bear in mind these calamities which lasted long after the year 1686, the 'year of Corbie', as it was called, had become just a nasty dream. Hordes of ruffians crossed the provinces in every direction, burning, pillaging and perpetrating even worse crimes. 'Every one of my soldiers', said the Duc de Lorraine, 'has a devil in his body, and at the sight of plunder the one devil becomes four!' Followed by their servants and womenfolk, some two or three hundred thousand men lived off the land of France for years, and one can imagine the state in which they left it by the time they were driven out and victory had been won.

It seems almost too hard to believe what the documents record of the misery of those calamitous years. The Lazarists admitted that they were frightened at what they saw: skeletons covered with sores, naked children wandering in search of roots, mothers who were said to have

shared the flesh of their children. 'The land is no longered ploughed!'
wailed a witness—the direst cry of indignation that can come from a
French peasant. To the misfortunes of war were added the horrors
of epidemics which usually accompany war. The plague renewed its
attacks nearly every year; smallpox was almost as deadly; so was a
scalp disease which took its toll. As a crowning misfortune, the climate
during those years made things worse: there were dreadful winters and
catastrophic floods. And then, when peace was signed at last and
everyone hoped for some respite, there were new troubles ahead. It
was not enough to have the Protestant war in the region of Montauban
and La Rochelle, the nobles plotting against the great cardinal, the
peasant risings in Périgord and the rebellion of the barefoot raga-
muffins in Normandy. Next, in Paris, the 'Messieurs du Parlement',
joined shortly by the princes and the dukes, carried on a revolt called
the Fronde against the Italian Cardinal Mazarin; and again the capital
became a prey to fear and famine. They were dreadful times.

The miracle of Monsieur Vincent was that he managed to cope with
all the misfortune brought about by events and the lack of understanding on the part of men, and that he succeeded in drawing forth
from this selfish, shallow and ruthless society treasures of charity to
help him in his tremendous task. For the strange radiance which proceeded from him attracted to the work he undertook hundreds, and
even thousands, of acts of self-sacrifice. His commanding sweetness
of manner compelled sacrifice. 'A queen has no need of jewellery!' was
his gentle thrust at Anne of Austria, who hesitated about giving up her
diamonds. Enthusiasm in self-denial and rivalry in generosity—these
were the virtues he could draw from souls, because his own overflowed
with them.

First there were the Ladies of Charity. As we have seen, they were
established spontaneously, in other words providentially, at Châtillon-
des-Dombes; they were a heaven-sent inspiration which was immediately put into concrete form with detailed rules. When Monsieur
Vincent returned to Paris to the house of Mme de Gondi, it was a
simple matter for him to gather together a few society women and
entrust them with works of charity like the one begun at Châtillon.
What he asked of them was to go and visit 'their Lordships the poor',
to take them food and clothing, to assist them materially and morally.
'If Our Lord had been asked, "What did you come to do on earth?"
He would have replied: "To help the poor." "Anything else?" "The
poor!" He would have repeated. "And what then?" "The poor! It is to
help them that I am here."' It was an extraordinary thing that so many
good people were able to understand that kind of talk. Was it perhaps,
as some have suggested, that charity was 'fashionable' at that time? It

may have been so; God uses everything for His purpose. But they were not all worldly-minded women. There was the rich lady Présidente Goussault, Superior of the Compagnie des Dames, who, with her nurses, was so gay in her charity; the splendid Mlle Polaillon, with her long nose and bright eyes, whom Monsieur Vincent playfully called Mlle Poulaillon, because her name was something like the French word for 'hen'. She would often be seen going bravely around the most disreputable parts of the town. Then there was the enchanting Mme de Villeneuve who, with her Daughters of the Cross, was so fond of teaching the little girls of the poor; and then Mme de Miramion, a delightful widow of sixteen who, turning her back on the court, took up work in the hospitals. Many were the ladies with famous French names to be seen around the beds in the Hôtel Dieu and Salpêtrière hospitals—Mme de Maupeou, the Princesse de Montmorency, the Duchesse de Nemours, Mme de Beauharnais, Mme de Hautefort, and even princesses of the blood, like Louise-Marie de Gonzague, the future Queen of Poland, and Anne of Austria herself, the Queen of France. From Paris the Compagnie des Dames radiated across the whole of France, to Beauvais, Senlis, Joigny, Meaux and Châlons. Good works were being done everywhere.

One of these Ladies of Charity stands out from the others: Louise de Marillac (1591–1660), the devout young widow of a middle-class lawyer; she discovered in charitable works the answer to her doubts and tribulations. She was a woman of powerful, lucid and well-ordered intellect. Her childhood and adolescence had not been too happy and, at twenty-two years of age, she agreed grudgingly to marry M. Antoine Le Gras, a forty-year-old secretary in the service of Marie dei Médici; when Louise was thirty-four her husband died. Having turned her back for so long on the pleasures of a world which had shown her such poor welcome, Mlle Le Gras too,[1] without realizing it, waited for a call from God. It was given to her. On the anniversary of her husband's death she had a Mass said, and the priest who said the Mass was Vincent de Paul. He had the charming idea of choosing the liturgy of the Nuptial Mass. Louise de Marillac was touched, and gave the care of her soul to the founder of the *Charités*. He immediately associated her with his budding enterprises. Four years later, having had time to study his penitent and become acquainted with her gifts of judgment and organization, he gave her the task of inspecting, and if necessary reforming, the existing charities, and even the setting up of others. She worked hard at Montmirail, Villepreux, Beauvais and other places.

Was it she or Vincent who first got the idea of a new foundation? Louise de Marillac remained so humble all her life that she is not always

---

[1] It was the custom at that time to confine the term 'Madame' to ladies of rank; while 'Mademoiselle' was used for the middle class.

given proper credit. Does not the popular term Sisters of St Vincent de Paul embody that voluntary circumspection of one who was also a foundress? But in any case Monsieur Vincent's merit lay in his acceptance of the idea and ensuring its realization. It was easy to establish that the *Charités* had to put up with two evils which are not unknown, by all accounts, to Catholic institutions of the present day: quite often the ladies did not pull together, each group wanting to be entirely responsible for its own activities, a thing which, as Monsieur Vincent told them, resulted in a 'hotchpotch'. Then again, after that grand enthusiasm which accompanies all beginnings, the good ladies, especially in the towns, became preoccupied with worldly matters, and no longer always found the time to prepare food for the poor, to take it to them and care for them. And so the idea of giving them assistants was considered; the result was 'The Confraternity of Charity for the poor sick of parishes', which became known as the Daughters of Charity.

There were difficulties at the beginning. To set these ladies up professionally in works of charity Monsieur Vincent had restricted himself to selecting during his missions young ladies of humble birth, who had no wish to marry, and sending them to parishes where *Charités* already existed. Recruited at random, and with very little preparation, these assistants were sometimes disappointing. It was absolutely essential to ensure better selection, and to insist on sound training in readiness for the task ahead of them. Mlle Le Gras took over this responsibility. On 29th November 1633, in a humble lodging in the Saint-Victor district, near Saint-Nicolas-du-Chardonnet, she mustered four simple peasant girls who had determined to become servants of the poor. It was there that the congregation of the Daughters of Charity was born. Vocations came to her so quickly that it was necessary three years later to move to the larger premises at La Chapelle, then the Rue du Faubourg-Saint-Denis, opposite Saint-Lazare.

That was the beginning of one of the institutions which have brought great honour to the Church; an institution which, while giving testimony to the charity of Christ, prevents us in our dark hours from despairing of humanity. One recalls the words of Napoleon one evening in the Tuileries, when a group of philosophers were extolling the benefits of philanthropy in the century of enlightenment. 'That's all very fine, gentlemen,' the emperor interrupted, 'but give me a Grey Sister!' [1] In the most depressing streets of large towns, and in the most

---

[1] The term 'Grey Sisters' may sound surprising to us who are accustomed to the blue habits and white cornets of the Sisters. For a long time the colour of their gowns was grey, hence their name. As for the cornet, it did not exist in the early days. The Sisters wore a toque, or bonnet, of white material, completely covering the head and hiding the hair. It was the customary dress of women living on the outskirts of Paris. The cornet was an extra, which poor women of delicate complexion wore to protect their faces in bad weather.

poverty-stricken country places, their habit (the normal peasant dress in Monsieur Vincent's day, as seen in Le Nain's painting 'The Peasants' Supper') and their white bonnet were living symbols of what the human heart, lifted up by the love of Christ, can give of the most sublime; and, when a Frenchman comes across these symbols in some foreign land at the other end of the world, he is unable to suppress a deep emotion, blended with tenderness and admiration.

Strictly speaking, the Sisters of Charity were not, and are not today, 'religious'; in the seventeenth century no one could imagine a *religieuse* to be anywhere but enclosed in a convent. It is true that St Francis de Sales had conceived the idea of forming a group of dedicated women who would live in the world, but work for Christ and the Church. He did not succeed, however, as the Sisters of the Order of the Visitation—the *Visitandines*—eventually became enclosed. But Vincent did succeed—though not without difficulty. On the first occasion that M. Blaise Méliand, Attorney-General to the king, received Mlle Le Gras to hear her request to have the articles of association registered by Parliament, he exclaimed with amazement: 'But that is impossible! You form part of the laity; all communities of women are regulars!' It was not for nothing that Vincent was a Gascon: he rewrote the articles so that there could be no possible confusion, and all obstacles were smoothed out. In 1646 the Archbishop of Paris approved the Rule; very cleverly Louise de Marillac arranged for the new institution to remain under the direction of her spiritual father, Monsieur Vincent, though he, through humility, did not wish it. In 1657 the king sanctioned the foundation by letters patent; and in 1668 —eight years after the death of the two founders—it was given pontifical approval.

Is it possible to measure the truly social revolution that is embodied in the foundation of the congregation of the Sisters of Charity? After all, works of charity up to then had been mainly the function of clerics, religious and wealthy ladies. Now one could see associated with it, and even taking the lead, women of the people, 'these good country girls' for whom Vincent had so much praise; girls whose names were perfumed with the soil of France—Madeleine Raporteblé, Marie Vigneron, Jeanne Gresier, Mathurine Guérin, Julie Hore Loret, Toussainte David and Françoise Fanchon. It was the virtues of these simple, pure, frugal, tough women, that Vincent wanted to see practised throughout the entire little band. To those who expressed a desire to enter this service of the poor he offered the example of *Marguerite Naseau*, the shepherdess from Suresnes, who had learned her alphabet alone—the 'Cross of God', as they called it in those days. She would sometimes ask a passer-by to help her with her reading, and then, armed with her small stock of knowledge, would go from village to village teaching the poorest children. When Vincent came across her, during a mission he was preaching at Villepreux, she put herself at his disposal—'the first Sister of Charity', he said of her, 'whom everybody loved.'

He made use of his daughters everywhere. There was not a single one of his undertakings with which the Grey Sisters were not associated in some way. In the parishes they used to visit the poor in their houses; [1] and they would teach little girls. But soon they were sent into the hospitals, which they lit up with their smiles. When Monsieur Vincent undertook to help prisoners and convicts the Grey Sisters again came to his assistance in this ghastly work. And when the queen, Anne of Austria, asked him for help with the sick and wounded soldiers, once more it was the Sisters of Charity who came to the rescue. Four of them—the first hospital nurses—were sent, and two died of contagious disease. Such was the work of these very unusual religious, who were not really nuns at all. 'Visit the poor instead of praying,' Monsieur Vincent told them. 'In this way you are leaving God for God.' The 'little band' soon grew; it was on the way to becoming the congregation of forty thousand women it is today. By 1660, when Vincent de Paul was about to die and to be followed almost immediately by Louise de Marillac, the Sisters had a hundred houses, of which thirty alone were situated in the capital; and everywhere people were asking for the Grey Sisters.

Such were the women, the bands of fellow workers whom he managed to raise up in large numbers to help him to achieve his aims. As to the achievements themselves, they were so numerous and varied that they defy any attempt to catalogue them. Each one gave rise to the next; one complemented the other in a remarkably smooth system.

Ladies of Charity and Sisters of Charity: but what about the men? Although, on the surface, Vincent seemed to have more confidence in women with their great spirit of devotion, he did not neglect to appeal to men. In 1619 he had set up his first Confraternity of Charity for men, the forerunner of the Society of St Vincent de Paul, which Ozanam was to organize two centuries later. He was most certainly one of the instigators of the Company of the Blessed Sacrament,[2] from which Catholic Action was to spring long afterwards. In many parts of France the members of the company helped Vincent's work to take root.

---

[1] In some places they were called 'the Soup Sisters'.

[2] Concerning the Company of the Blessed Sacrament, see p. 98. To explain the magnitude and the success of the undertakings of Monsieur Vincent, it has been claimed that he might have been the instrument and mouthpiece of the company, viewed as a vast attempt to sway men's minds; in other words, that he was a kind of tool of the *Cabale des Dévots*. No fact or document has ever been traced which gives serious grounds for accepting this slanderous supposition.

One day in 1634 Mme Goussault visited Monsieur Vincent to discuss the *Hôtel Dieu* hospital and the distressing condition of its sick. The hospital was too small, and the wards were overcrowded. The Augustinian nuns who tended the sick under authority of the Chapter of Notre Dame were unable to cope with everything; in any case, since they were an enclosed order, they were not in a position to find outside backing and help. At first Monsieur Vincent declined to assist: he had no wish to 'take a sickle into other people's harvest'. The lady president was adamant; she insisted that she wanted to take her Ladies of Charity to the Hôtel Dieu. Monsieur Vincent gave in; since it was the will of Christ, he would send his ladies to visit those sick and to take them 'jellies, soups and jam', besides books and games for their amusement; and they would work for the salvation of their souls. It became an amazing rivalry in goodness. The ladies of the congregation took over the care of the nine hundred sick. The Grey Sisters were installed near the hospital and worked in collaboration with society women like a really happy family. It was a heavy burden for the young congregation of Mlle Le Gras; but there was never any shortage of volunteers.

Then came another burden, heavier still—the care of abandoned children. This was certainly the most famous of Monsieur Vincent's undertakings, and the most touching. Conditions were lamentable. In those savage and gloomy days many mothers abandoned their children through poverty and despair. In Paris alone thousands were picked up every year on the steps of churches. What was to become of them? A government institution known as 'La Couche' was certainly responsible for collecting them, but it was a grim and shady organization. The children were placed with cruel foster-mothers who were supposed to feed them for a few pence a year; but many of the children died of hunger and neglect. And, worse still, some were sold for eight or ten sous and fell into the hands of professional beggars, who broke their arms and legs in order to excite pity and extract alms. It is recorded that not one of those abandoned children survived in fifty years. In 1638 Louise de Marillac took over the care of these tender victims. There was no question of trying to improve La Couche. The work of the 'Foundlings' was at first carried on as a relief, but eventually replaced La Couche. It was an expensive business. On several occasions Monsieur Vincent had to call together the committees of the 'Ladies'; he drew tears from them as he described the tragedy of these little creatures who, if money failed, would sink back into their former dreadful condition. But the work was destined to endure: first at the Château de Bicêtre, then in the suburb Saint-Denis; and finally in the Foundling Hospital which Louis XIV had built. The fact that from 1638 to 1660 forty thousand children were

saved indicates the importance of the undertaking, and how necessary
it was.

Another of the evils of Paris and other large towns was the beggars.
The rapid increase in mendicancy resulted from prevalent conditions.
Crippled ex-soldiers, bankrupt artisans and abandoned old people—
their name was legion. Deriving strength from their vast numbers, they
became insolent. Anyone who stopped to speak to a friend in the
street, or to pray in a church, was sure to be embarrassed by the
unwelcome and persistent voices of beggars demanding, even insisting
upon, alms, and becoming insulting if they were refused. Every now
and then the government took measures against them through the
police; but these measures proved quite useless. Monsieur Vincent
grappled with this problem too. By good fortune an anonymous
benefactor sent him a hundred thousand livres in 1653; he hastened to
found an almshouse for the most wretched of the beggars—the old
ones. With forty beds as a beginning, the Nom de Jésus Almshouse
was established, with the Grey Sisters, naturally, to take care of it. A
little thing in itself, but what an example! People vied with one another
to help: the Duchesse d'Aiguillon offered fifty thousand livres. The
officials in control of the 'Bureau of the Poor' at last began to take
notice of what was happening in the hospitals and almshouses, and
consigned the *Petites Maisons* in the Rue de Sèvres to the Sisters of
Charity: it had been rather a sorry-looking home for syphilitics and
people suffering from scurvy. Of course the Sisters flocked to it.
Before long Anne of Austria gave Monsieur Vincent La Salpêtrière,
an enclosure to the south of Paris where saltpetre was manufactured.
By 1657 the General Almshouse was completed and was capable of
housing two hundred destitute persons.

Was there any human distress at all to which Monsieur Vincent and
his associates did not turn? The little children were innocent, the sick
were to be pitied, most of the beggars were not to be blamed for their
plight; but what of the guilty—the convicts, the prisoners, the galley
slaves? Are they shut out from the charity of Christ? Monsieur Vincent
did not think so. To him—and it took humanity centuries to realize
it—the convicts, the prisoners and the galley slaves were also men.
It was his friends of the Company of the Blessed Sacrament who
made him acquainted with the facts concerning the dreadful condition
of those in captivity. 'They were rotting alive', wrote Le Voyer
d'Argenson after a visit to the Saint-Roche prison. There was no
discrimination: bandits, thieves, unfortunate people who had run into
debt, the harum-scarum sons of well-to-do families—all were imprisoned together. Monsieur Vincent went himself to see them. They
were soothed and consoled by his calmness of manner: one fellow, more
like an animal than a man, wept as he listened to Vincent. Then the

apostle would visit those in high places, protesting indignantly, 'demanding that these unhappy people might be treated a little better', that at least they be given spiritual comforts. He won his case; and, what is more, he opened a house of correction at Saint-Lazare for juvenile delinquents, in which he was two hundred years ahead of his time.

But that was not all. There were others even worse off than these inmates of prisons—poor wretches, some of whom had not committed great crimes, but whom royal justice had commanded to be sent to man the oars of the galleys. The king's galleys were beautiful; there were no ships to be compared with them—'their movement, as they skimmed the sea, was gay, smooth, sudden and rapid'—with their two triangular sails and their sixty-four oars, so rhythmically balanced. But men pulled on those oars—two hundred and fifty-six per ship; chained to their seats, and their shoulders always bared to receive lashes from the galley sergeants when their pull seemed too feeble. The lot of these wretches was horrible, and many noble souls were on their account moved to pity; among them the Oratorian, Jean-Baptiste Gault, Bishop of Marseilles, and the Chevalier Gaspard de Simiane. And no one knew better than Monsieur Vincent what it was to be a galley slave: he was so very near becoming one in Tunis!

From 1619, when Philippe Emmanuel de Gondi made him Chaplain-general of the Royal Galleys, he had taken an interest in the lives of the convicts. He visited them, protested to the authorities against the cruel harshness of the conditions under which they lived; and it is said that on one occasion he took the place of one of the convicts at the oars. When a chained gang left Marseilles, Monsieur Vincent would visit the poor fellows and talk kindly to them and send his Sisters of Charity. One of the galley slaves, Barbe Angiboust, eventually became famous for his consistent gentleness and infinite patience. Monsieur Vincent also sent his missioners to preach to them in the ports where the galleys called; the result were almost unbelievable, and the conversions amazing. Through his inexhaustible charity the saint managed to obtain from the French authorities a permanent ship's chaplaincy and an infirmary.

Where was this charity to stop? Not even in the face of the Turks. In Barbary—which Monsieur Vincent also knew better than anyone— there were Christian slaves who had been carried off by the Corsairs. He decided that someone ought to go and see them, and bring them spiritual consolation. The Moslem government refused permission: they wanted only priest slaves. The Gascon found a way of getting round the difficulty. Missionaries were appointed consuls by the king. Jean Le Vacher was one of them; he was both consul and Apostolic Vicar at Carthage, and he went so far as to open chapels in Barbary eventually suffering martyrdom at Algiers by being fastened to the mouth of a cannon.[1] 'I should envy you your happiness', Monsieur Vincent wrote to him, 'if it were right for me to do so.'

9. A ROYAL PENITENT'S MINISTER WITHOUT PORTFOLIO

Results like these are not merely evidence of the gifts and the holiness of a man: they also explain the high esteem in which he was held. As time went on and his undertakings grew in number, Monsieur Vincent, despite his humility, began to occupy a more prominent position in France. Richelieu realized his value, without perhaps fully understanding him. He gave Vincent his support, but not without some misgiving and mental reservation; for the founder of the Mission had no intention of breaking off his friendship with the Marillacs, one of whom—the Marshal—had been beheaded by the cardinal's orders. Nor did he break with his one-time pupil, the young and disturbing Jean-François-Paul de Gondi, the future Cardinal de Retz, that 'resolute spirit whom no one could love or hate by halves', as Bossuet said, and who boasted openly of having taken part in two plots against the powerful minister.[2]

But the king, Louis XIII, loved and admired Vincent unreservedly. That enigmatical man, fenced in by his shyness, was incapable of giving expression to the wealth of tender and lofty sentiments within him; but on the rare occasions on which he saw Monsieur Vincent he found him extremely attentive, understanding, responsive and discerning. In the saint's presence there was never that uneasy silence, when the speaker is lost for words, not knowing whether silence is the result of vexation, embarrassment or despondency. Although the king was very much attached to his confessor, Father Dinet, he loved to discuss his soul with Monsieur Vincent. And when he felt the approach of death, he desired to have him at his bedside. What little has been preserved of those conversations during the six weeks from early April to 14th May 1643 is sublime: Vincent comforted that soul beset with qualms despite its profound faith; he lavished an almost fatherly affection on the sick king, who, when he was near to death, asked the saint to tell him the details of his work and plans, and murmured: 'Ah, Monsieur Vincent, if I get better I want all the bishops to spend three years with you!'

When the king died little Louis XIV was a baby of five, and the

[1] See *The Church in the Eighteenth Century*, Chapter II.
[2] There are numerous works on Cardinal de Retz (the famous author of the *Memoirs*) dealing with the relations between him and Vincent de Paul; the two most recent are by P. G. Lorris (Paris, 1956) and F. Albert-Buisson (Paris, 1954)—not forgetting the work of Battifol.

child's mother, Anne of Austria, therefore found herself burdened with the responsibility of the Regency, which seemed likely to be long and probably encompassed with great difficulties. She too was a person of great faith, the devout and exacting faith of a Spaniard, which she inherited from Philip II; but it was a faith leavened with true charity—a quality somewhat lacking in the religion of her grandfather. Up to that time her life had been complicated, and often disturbed. At fifteen she married a king of the same age, and was for a long time almost deserted for the falcon and petty money grubbers; she listened, perhaps too readily, to dangerous friends. But Anne was also an open-handed woman: dressed in the black skirt worn by the common people, she used to visit the sick at La Charité and the Hôtel Dieu, or waited on them with her own hands at the Val-de-Grâce which she had founded out of her small savings. She is described by Mme de Motteville as a woman of extraordinary beauty, who could find a word of compassion for everyone; 'her lovely eyes tinged with green' shed tears of pity before the overwhelming spectacle of so much misery which she could never entirely relieve. That side of the queen was the work of Monsieur Vincent, who made her the first of his Ladies of Charity.

As soon as she became a widow she appealed to Monsieur Vincent for spiritual guidance, turning down both the Jesuits and the Capuchin friars who craved the honour of directing the royal conscience. After some hesitation he agreed, on condition that he might carry out his task with due strictness, and the queen consented. This spiritual direction was not to be an easy-going business; his penitent, an attractive woman of forty, was not without her temptations, and had perhaps too great a liking for parties and the theatre. It is to the credit of both saint and penitent that absolute harmony existed between them and they had confidence in each other. Not only was Monsieur Vincent the queen's confessor, but she confided in him in other matters; and he made no bones about discussing her *petites affaires*, which he regarded as *grandes affaires* when they concerned the Church and France. He thus became a force, a well-known personage whose influence was recognized; a kind of minister without portfolio, charged with what we might call today Public Assistance and social problems. 'Monsieur Vincent is the channel through which everything reaches Her Majesty's ear,' wrote a young Italian diplomat at the Nuncio's residence in the time of Louis XIII. The question was whether that state of affairs would continue during the Regency. For the Italian diplomat's name was Mazarin.

What sort of relationship existed between Monsieur Vincent and the second cardinal? Some have said that they were on very bad terms; but others that Vincent encouraged the queen's love for the handsome

Jules, and that he even gave his blessing to their secret marriage.[1] But that is only half the truth. There were so many points of difference between the two men that it is inconceivable that they should have seen eye to eye. A humble saint, generous and straight as a die, whose whole life was ordered on a spiritual plane, could never have been understood by a wily politician, greedy for money and honours, whose every act was subordinated to temporal interests—either his own or those of the state he managed. The disagreement between them went on growing until it almost reached boiling-point. But although Anne of Austria admitted her 'tender love for the mind' of the cardinal, she never for a moment agreed to give up for his sake the 'common fellow' in the threadbare cassock of whom Mazarin made fun.

Since Monsieur Vincent exercised a considerable semi-official influence from about 1643, he had but one purpose: to use it to broaden the scope of his charity, and to ensure the triumph of Christ and His Church. What has sometimes been called his political activity was an extension of the increasing part he played in French society. 'Simply and naturally' as ever, he put increased opportunity for action at the service of ideas which he had very much at heart.

It was thus that his sons were able to multiply the missions and found numerous seminaries in the provinces, that the Tuesday Conferences attracted a larger number of 'customers', that his charitable enterprises, his almshouses and hospitals received help which assured their establishment on a firm footing. One fact must be emphasized: having become a sort of Public Assistance agent, Monsieur Vincent never for a moment allowed the Charity of Christ to be confused with any method of state control; to him, love for man was not a thing to be portioned out administratively. The poor, even the abject, could not, as he saw it, be reduced to mere numbers in a list of classified cases; they remained people, and had to be treated with infinite delicacy. When, for instance, he set up his homes known as Petits Ménages (literally, small households), he did so to avoid separating elderly couples into different homes, and thus he allowed them to live out their lives in a two-roomed flat. And when, in 1656, the government, in an attempt to put an end to begging, decided to open in Paris the Hôpital Général, where sick beggars were obliged to report for admission, while the healthy ones were to be put into a workhouse or driven from the capital, Monsieur Vincent refused to back this juridical method of

---

[1] The facts have never been clear. Mazarin was a cardinal à *brevet*, that is to say, he was not a priest, and was therefore free to marry. But there is nothing certain to show that the secret marriage did in fact take place, and even less to suggest that St Vincent de Paul played a part in it. Again, even if it were true, we must realize that it would have been his duty as confessor to prefer marriage to a more or less conjugal relationship giving rise to scandal.

doing good, and he refused to allow the Lazarists to take charge of the new institution. It was an attitude rich in significance.

He was not, however, unaware of his powers as a 'Minister of charity without portfolio', and he did not make light of them. That became clear when he took over the work of relief in the provinces ravaged by war. The organization which Monsieur Vincent set up was a model of its kind. It brings to mind our own Catholic organizations for the relief of the poor. First, money had to be found; and that was undertaken by the generous band of the Ladies of Charity. Then relief teams were allotted their localities. For example, in Lorraine, bleeding and gasping from the ravages of war, seven centres were set up—run, of course, by the Lazarists and the Grey Sisters. Missioners were rushed from Paris; among them Mathieu Regnard (rightly nicknamed Renard—the Fox), who was given the task of conveying considerable sums of money. Many a time he managed to preserve it from the rogues he met on the way, through adventures and artfulness worthy of the most picaresque novel. Then, as the horrors of war resulted in a huge exodus of refugees, Monsieur Vincent, with the help of Gaston de Renty, a pious layman, organized reception centres in Paris to assist the refugees; they were so well treated that the Parisians were just a little jealous, and jokingly said that Monsieur Vincent had become a naturalized Lorrainer. Champagne and Picardy, where conditions were equally distressing, were the next objects of his solicitude. It is clear from the reports which Charles Maynart de Bernières wrote concerning the undertaking that the same procedure was applied there. There is ample evidence—and very moving it is—to show what Monsieur Vincent's relief work meant to the French provinces. In 1653 the municipal magistrates of Rethel wrote to him: 'For two years Champagne—and especially this town of Rethel—has existed entirely on your charity.' And every French history book should quote that amazing letter in which the Lieutenant-General of Saint-Quentin told the saint that, without him, the people of the district would have perished of hunger; and he went on to implore Vincent 'to continue to preserve the lives of so many who are at death's door, *and to be once more the father of our country*'. The words in italics tell the whole story.

Works of charity were not, however, the only things to which Anne of Austria's spiritual director devoted himself. There was another work just as necessary if Christ's charity was to be served: the defence of the truth of His message. To this end Monsieur Vincent got himself mixed up in all sorts of important matters—in anything and everything, in fact, which involved the faith and the Church. And in every case he acted with that determined gentleness, that blend of severity and mercy, for which he was always known.

Nothing could be more significant than his attitude in the great
conflict which arose at that time in the bosom of the Church concerning Jansenism.[1] Monsieur Vincent was only just beginning his work
when that little undercurrent of heresy, of which the Bishop of Ypres
was the source, first came to light and gradually developed into a
raging torrent. At first he showed no hostility whatever towards it.
And after all, were those personalities who started it really Jansenists
in the true sense of the word—Mother Angélique, Mother Agnès and
Monsieur de Saint-Cyran? Were they not rather just one small group
in the vast band which at that time was fighting so bravely for the
honour of God? Their spiritual standpoint had won the sympathy of
Monsieur Vincent. What is more, Saint-Cyran had been a friend of his;
in their impecunious days they had even shared a common purse.
None the less, when that austere theologian began to spread his theories
about Frequent Communion, Monsieur Vincent did not hesitate to
take a vigorous stand against them, because he held that they tended
to keep the faithful away from Holy Communion. The result was a
break in a friendship which had lasted fifteen years. But when Saint-
Cyran was arrested by order of Richelieu, and Monsieur Vincent was
summoned to give evidence, no one could drag from him a single
word which might compromise his old friend.

So much for charity. But when, about the beginning of 1650, it was
obvious that Jansenism constituted a serious danger, that it was tending
to become a heresy, then the queen's confessor used all his authority to
have it condemned. Nothing could be more remote from his direct
and active faith, his submissive Christianity, his generous enthusiasm,
than these strange doctrines weighted with torturing obscurity and the
leaven of rebellion. The condemnation of Jansenism by Pope Innocent
X in 1653 was partly the result of his efforts: he was concerned with the
drawing up of the 'Five Propositions' culled from the work of Jansen,
which were referred to Rome for a decision; and he went to a lot
of trouble to obtain the signatures of as many bishops as possible in
favour of severe measures. *Amicus Plato, sed major amica veritas.*

Was he concerned with the Protestant issue? To some extent he
was, but in a very humane and magnanimous way. In the days of the
great cardinal the question of Protestantism was especially a political
one, when the king had to take La Rochelle to prevent the setting up
of a state within the state. Monsieur Vincent, quite unlike those fanatics
who would have taken advantage of the opportunity to rub out 'the
religion', had nothing but words of kindness and understanding for its
adherents. He never forgot honest Jean Beynier who had so generously
opened his door to him at Châtillon-des-Dombes. It was not through
the medium of controversial books that he approached the Protestants

but as man to man with an open heart. There exists a letter from him to Gallais, one of his Lazarist priests, who was directing a mission at Sedan and happened to be faced with a number of Protestants. That letter is evidence of his high-minded principles and his admirable impartiality. In the words of Canisius, Monsieur Vincent literally regarded his 'separated brethren' as brothers. It is unnecessary to emphasize that this attitude was far and away ahead of his time. The revocation of the Edict of Nantes would have been unthinkable in the days when Monsieur Vincent stood beside the rulers of France.

That was what the saint understood by serving the Catholic cause and that of the Church. But there was another way, and another sphere in which he worked. For some time there had existed in government circles a congregation of ecclesiastical affairs, known as the Council of Conscience. Its business covered everything that concerned the Church, and especially the nomination of bishops. Anne of Austria appointed Mazarin to the Council, together with the Chancellor, Séguier, Charton, the Penitentiary of Paris, Potier de Gesvres, the virtuous Bishop of Beauvais, Cospéau, Bishop of Lisieux, and other persons of distinction as occasion demanded. Monsieur Vincent was, despite his protestations, nominated Secretary of the Council, and his duties were to investigate cases and take minutes of the proceedings. He thus found himself in the very heart of thorny problems which required decision. No one was more aware of their importance than he, nor of the dangers to the Church resulting from the bad old ways. He strove with all his strength to oppose those scandalous nominations, so firmly established by custom, under which children, society people and persons totally unsuitable were put in charge of dioceses. It was a hard battle. He had only just been nominated secretary when a rumour got around that he was in disgrace because of his express refusal to allow a living to be granted to the son of the Duc de la Rochefoucauld on the grounds that he was too young. That day he won his point, but on other occasions he was compelled to submit; customs were too firmly established, and Cardinal Mazarin was not the one to allow any interference in his schemes. Nevertheless Monsieur Vincent remained on the Council of Conscience for nine years and he made a deep impression upon it. Bishops who had attended Saint-Lazare, and others who came under his influence, went back to their dioceses with the intention of grafting on to them sound systems of reform. To others as well Monsieur Vincent sent directions, and even warnings, when things were not going right. The Council was wise enough to take steps to fix a minimum age for granting benefices: future bishops had to serve one year as priests; a check was put on the use of bishops' coadjutors, so as to remove fraud and nepotism. One can well imagine what out-cries and what fury these measures occasioned. Mazarin, who became more and more hostile towards this spoil-sport, got out of the difficulty by hardly ever summoning the so-called Council of Conscience after 1652, and shortly afterwards managed to get rid of its secretary with his too exacting conscience. It is true that by then he had another and greater reason for disliking Monsieur Vincent.

Monsieur Vincent was certainly never tempted to get mixed up with temporal affairs, like so many churchmen, or to join his old pupil de Retz in working against Mazarin. But the troubles of the Fronde broke out soon after the treaties of Westphalia, signed in 1648, had put an end to the war with the Empire. Once more the cruelty of the soldiery was let loose on the provinces. 'Worse than that of the Turks,' said Mother Angélique Arnaud. Paris soon rebelled against the government, and learned what it meant to go hungry. Monsieur Vincent was not content to provide widespread help for the refugees, to remedy the shame of the poor and relieve every kind of misery; he made himself the messenger, the herald of peace. On the first occasion, in January 1649, he hastened to Saint-Germain, despite terrible floods which had turned the Seine into a lake, and threw himself at the queen's feet to beg her pardon for the people of Paris. The peace of Rethel (March 1649) was the result. Three years later, when the Fronde was at its height and Condé had allied himself with the Spaniards in an attempt to get rid of Mazarin, Monsieur Vincent took another step—an extraordinary one: he, a simple priest, had the impudence to write to the first minister advising him to disappear from the scene, at least for a while, to allow tempers to die down. In the long run the cardinal took his advice, but harboured resentment against him who had given it. It mattered little to Monsieur Vincent; it was enough for him to have been a good servant of peace according to the dictates of his priestly conscience.

10. The Radiance of the Saint

It is not easy to imagine the significance of Monsieur Vincent's radiance during the last ten to fifteen years of his life. In France he was present everywhere through the works he had created, through the people he had chosen and set to work. The bishops whom he had trained at Saint-Lazare, or who had profited by his teaching, reflected his reforming principles in their dioceses. There were, for instance, Juste Guérin at Annecy, Pavillon at Alès, Solminihac at Cahors, Jacques Raoul followed by Dassompierre at Saintes, Sébastien Zamet at Langres, Antoine Godeau at Grasse, Lescot at Chartres, Perrochel in Boulogne, Brandon in Périgueux—a splendid pleiad; and there were others. Lazarist seminaries began to turn out young priests who were better trained and models of virtue. And other great reformers of the clergy, e.g. M. Olier and St John Eudes, experienced the direct influence of the saint; men who were to leave their mark on the succeeding age were called to God and trained for their task by the recluse of Saint-Lazare, including Jacques Bénigne Bossuet, the most famous of them all, to whom Vincent in 1659 entrusted the task of preaching to the Sisters of Providence. The Lazarists and the Sisters of Charity were scattered everywhere. A new breath of Christianity permeated middle-class society, and it sprang from the Ladies of Charity. And the poor came to know him who longed to make their condition less miserable. The humble priest with the cheap girdle stood like a lighthouse shining across France.

His radiance even overflowed the frontiers of the country. He saw those works which he had envisaged as personal efforts, and which had become national almost without his wishing it, now become international. The Mission had scarcely been set up when, in 1631, it was established in Rome; it was a flimsy affair at first, as was natural; but it was run by first-class men: du Coudray, one of the first four Lazarists, Berthe, the organizing brain, the enterprising Joly and the cultured Dehorgny. The first thing these sons of Monsieur Vincent introduced was the *Exercises for Ordination Candidates*, and then the missions in town and country. It did seem rather paradoxical that it had to be France, where the decrees of the Council of Trent were ignored by the state (since they had never been officially 'received'), who should send her sons to Rome to bear such splendid testimony to the ideal of Catholic reform. At Sabini and Viterbo, Subiaco and Mondovi, as well as Chiavari, Sestri, Raconiggi and many other places, the Lazarists gave missions in their usual way; the missions of Genoa and Turin proved an enormous success, thanks to Fathers Blatiron and Martin who were in charge of them. The ultimate triumph came when Alexander VII instructed young candidates for the priesthood to make a retreat with the missioners from France. Did Monsieur Vincent relish the piquancy of the situation? 'It has pleased our Holy Father', he noted, 'to send candidates for the priesthood to the poor wretches of the French Mission.' He must have realized what a great triumph that was.

Other countries also made calls on the untiring zeal of the Lazarists and the Grey Sisters; but when this happened the glory which came to him was a tragic glory, for their blood was spilt. Yet we know from Tertullian that blood has always been the seed of Christianity. First there was Poland. It was a great country in those days; Warsaw shone as a capital in an era when Berlin was still a mere village. French influence was considerable, which explains why a delegation arrived to ask the French king for a princess for their sovereign, Ladislas IV. That princess was Marie de Gonzague, daughter of the Duc de Nevers et de Mantoue and Catherine de Lorraine, who was French in her elegance, in her mind and in her education. When she became Queen of Poland she remembered that she had once been a Lady of Charity and had played an important part in works of charity, and she asked Monsieur Vincent to send her Mission priests, Sisters of Charity and Sisters of the Visitation. The man chosen as leader of the expedition, M. Lambert, was a person so outstanding that the founder regarded him as his future successor—'his eye and his right hand'. The early efforts were brilliant: missions, schools, charities, every Vincentian undertaking took root in Poland. But soon tragedy burst upon them. First there was the plague, bringing out the heroism of which these men and women were capable through Christ's charity; but the plague killed M. Lambert and several Sisters. Then came war, partly civil and partly foreign; it hurled the Muscovites, who answered the call of the insurgent Ukrainian Cossacks, and the Swedes against unhappy Poland. In Warsaw, which was captured in 1655, ruffianly bands, fighting in the name of Protestantism, hounded priests and Catholic institutions and attacked the churches; the Fathers of the Mission held on, remaining at their posts with their parishioners. Their leader, M. Ozenne, and every one of his Grey Sisters perished. Monsieur Vincent's heart bled when he heard these tidings, but his sorrow was not unmixed with pride.

In 'Hibernia', as Ireland was called, and in Scotland, the Orkneys and the Hebrides, the Mission also endeavoured to develop. The old country of St Columba welcomed the Lazarists with open arms; but when revolution broke out in England, and the era of Cromwell brought in its train that sanguinary repression in the Emerald Isle with which the name of the Puritan dictator has become linked, the missioners had to flee; not however, without leaving, as the seed of future harvests, the spirit of the Mission, which has borne so much fruit through the work of the Irish Lazarists in our time.

Monsieur Vincent was in no way disheartened by these setbacks. It was not for personal satisfaction, for the sake of petty applause, that a Christian had to obey the Word, and go forth and teach nations. Monsieur Vincent thought also of far-off lands across the seas. He thought of them for a reason which we, who belong to a century which proclaims the death of God, can understand; but it seems so extraordinary that a seventeenth-century saint could have formulated it. He admitted on several occasions that he asked himself whether France (today we should say the West) might not one day be absolutely de-christianized, and whether it was not therefore fitting, in anticipation of this happening, to sow the seed of faith in lands where it might germinate. He showed no haste, however, in establishing Lazarist missions in Africa; the French peasants still remained his first care. When the Congregation of Propaganda, newly formed in Rome, asked for missionaries for the Far East, Monsieur Vincent did not enter the lists, but he encouraged Monsieur Pallu, a staunch member of his Tuesday Conferences, to accept the challenge and to found what was to become the Society of Foreign Missions. Meanwhile, when the Société des Indes, which held the monopoly of commerce with Madagascar, asked him for priests to serve in the colony, and secured the good offices of Bagni, the Papal Nuncio, Monsieur Vincent regarded that as a sign from heaven, and complied with the request.

Another page of glory, stained with blood, was thus added to the history of the Congregation of the Mission, and it emphasized the significance of Vincent's methods. M. de Flacourt, the governor of the island, was all for using the mailed fist: humane treatment seemed to him to be out of place when dealing with creatures whom he regarded as scarcely human. Those whom Monsieur Vincent earmarked in 1648 for the Madagascar mission were the young and brilliant Father Nacquart and the humble, warm-hearted Father Gondrée. Both were true Lazarists; they loved these people whom Christ had committed to their care. They learned Malagasy, and lived with those under instruction. What anxieties and troubles that distant mission cost Monsieur Vincent! There was more to it than mere financial problems, long hours by candlelight working on his accounts to pay for the journey and the maintenance of the missionaries. The two fathers, worn out by the climate and excessive work, soon had to ask Monsieur Vincent for help. Before he was able to organize assistance Gondrée died, followed soon afterwards by Nacquart, and the little church which stands at Fort-Dauphin today is a touching memento of their short stay. Two more priests were sent, Fathers Bourdaise and Mounier; they too fell victims to their zeal and of that fascinating but terrible country. Others embarked at once to take their places in the hard fight—Fathers Herbron and Boussordec—and Monsieur Vincent exclaimed: 'I believe there is not one in the whole congregation who lacks the courage to go and take the places of those who have died!' The fact that Lazarist missions are to be found all over the world today, especially in Madagascar, is due to the tenacity and hopeful courage of Monsieur Vincent.

11. In Manus Tuas, Domine

Meanwhile the years went by. They bent and broke the peasant body of Monsieur Vincent; they chiselled deep lines in his face; they made his nose look longer and his bushy eyebrows more prominent. He resembled exactly the portrait which that conscientious artist Simon François painted of him at Saint-Lazare shortly before the saint's death. That painting has since been lost, but it was used by Van Schuppen and Edelinck in their engravings of the saint which have since become popular. He was weary, tired and in pain. He had constant and painful headaches, a daily recurrence of fever [1] and shortness of breath. At times his sufferings were intense, and he complained gently, murmuring: 'My Lord, my dear Lord . . . ' His legs would give way under him, and he had to be helped to walk; at times he even had to be carried, and he would say mischievously: 'Now I am like a great lord—the equal of bishops. . . .' He reached the age of eighty years.

His mind remained unimpaired in his weakened body; so did his will and his judgment. He never set foot in the court from the day Mazarin drove him from the Council of Conscience, but he continued to see the queen, and he gave her a lot of advice without exactly acting as her spiritual director. Above all he assumed full responsibility for the management of his great charitable organizations. He remained Superior of Saint-Lazare, and allowed no one else to guide the community; he also remained Superior of the Sisters of Charity, forcing himself, though obviously at the end of his strength, to visit them on foot, his stick in his hand (he had not far to go), and to lavish on them spiritual and practical advice. Right to the end he wanted to take to them all the message he had for them—the Ladies of Charity, the priests attending the Tuesday Conferences, the nuns of the Visitation. He used to say to everyone: 'Let us give ourselves to God, and may He give us the grace to remain strong. Let us stand fast for the love of God.'

On 3rd July 1660 he had the Grey Sisters brought to him so that he might praise their foundress, his dear Mlle Le Gras who had just died. On 24th July he presided at the election of the new superior. But he knew that God, in taking away the best of his fellow workers, was beckoning to him too. A gathering broke out in one of his eyes, which caused him cruel suffering. He remained calm and clear-headed and, according to those who witnessed his lingering end, as gay as ever. Around him the house of Saint-Lazare went on with its work for Christ, for the Church, for 'their Lordships the poor'. From everywhere letters flowed in, expressions of affection, good wishes, suggested remedies. The Pope himself sent him a message. A poor Negro sent herbs to soothe and refresh him. He died very peacefully on 27th September 1660—most certainly in the hands of Our Lord.

It was easy then to see in what consisted the glory of this humble man. A whole nation filed past the narrow bed on which lay the poor, spent body; Saint-Germain-l'Auxerrois was packed with the congregation gathered to hear Henri de Maupas, Bishop of Puy, speak in

---

[1] Was this perhaps malaria brought back from Tunis? If so, it is another argument in support of his having been a slave in Tunis.

praise of him. People argued over his relics; the Pope, kings and
sanctuaries clamoured for them, sharing out his very ribs, his knee-
caps, and even his heart. The Church knew that this man, who had
been so wonderfully faithful to her all his life, was destined for heaven
even while he lived. He was beatified in 1729; eight years later, in 1737,
Pope Clement XII raised him to the altar.

History sees in him one of the most outstanding men of his time,
so much so that there is not a textbook, however non-clerical it may
claim to be, which does not mention his name. He was the originator
of the social sense in an age which saw the final collapse of the solidarity of the city, the free town and the fief, which in the Middle Ages
had succoured the wretched—and this at a moment when wars and
internal strife made mutual aid and relief more than ever indispensable.
It was he then who found a way of linking all classes together in a
common effort to ease the misery of men, of rousing so much personal
generosity as to change the face of France. What is so often overlooked
is that everything noble and beneficent that has happened in the social
life of France in the last three centuries has its origin in him. We had
to wait for an atheist age for the social sense to change its spirit and
expression; for official organizations striving to take control of
charitable works, thus draining away what Monsieur Vincent knew so
well how to put into it—consummate humanity, true charity.

Such was the foundation of Monsieur Vincent's glory, so fundamentally non-clerical; and that is why Voltaire paid tribute to him in
these words: 'My favourite saint is Vincent de Paul.' But the Church
owes him more and can honour him for many other reasons. It is a
well-established law, and verifiable in fact, that the edification of the
Body of Christ occurs first in the secret depths of saintly souls, and
through their sovereign efficacy. Only the saints can discern the ways
which God maps out for His mystical Spouse, because they alone have
fully understood the evangelic mandate, and have fully grasped the
message which Our Lord addressed to their age. More than anyone
else, Monsieur Vincent laid the foundations of that modern Church
which was seeking to be born. His friend and master, St Francis de
Sales, was the living epitome of the aspirations and tendencies of an
age that closed with his own death, the age of Catholic Reformation.
St Vincent de Paul, on the other hand, laid the foundations of the
future—a more lively Christianity, kneaded by the new leaven; a
worthy priesthood, conscious of the majesty of its ministry and
utterly dedicated; a Church determined to be fraternal, open to all and
gentle to the lowly; a human religion in which Christ speaks to the
heart. All that, which we long for with all our being, we find in
Monsieur Vincent, in his words and in his actions. He lights up our
age, just as he enlightened his own.

It goes without saying that he was not alone in performing such a task. Beside him rises up an almost countless number of holy people who pursued the same ends and moved in the same direction, but on their own plane and within defined spheres. Such were Bérulle, Olier, Condren, St John Eudes and many others. But Monsieur Vincent was the only one to work in every field at once and to succeed in all. He is, in the works of Grousset, 'the figure-head on the ship'. There is no one who so perfectly sums up and completes within himself the fruitful age in which our Church was born—that great century of saints which ended at the moment of his death.

CHAPTER II

AN AGE OF SPIRITUAL GRANDEUR

1. The Youth of the Church in the Seventeenth Century

HAS it been sufficiently appreciated that the first sixty years of the seventeenth century stand out as a period of strength within the Church, an epoch of rare beauty and fruitfulness, certainly as rich as the greatest moments in the history of medieval Christianity? Has it been really appreciated that this was an era of youthful bloom and dazzling revival?

There stood Monsieur Vincent, dominating the age with his worn silhouette, his keen gaze bubbling over with kindness. Around him in their dozens rise those who, as history agrees, mirrored his achievements, tilling the same soil, ploughing other furrows, yet all gathering the same harvest of souls—men whose lives were perfectly ordered in God, and whose works had no other end than that of advancing His kingdom. There have been few centuries in the life of the Church which can muster so many great souls.

At the moment when, on 4th December 1563, in a little Alpine town which had suddenly become famous, the fathers who represented the entire Church, Catholic, Apostolic and Roman, announced the end of their labours, a twofold problem was set. The directions of the Council of Trent had to be introduced into the marrow and the blood of Christians, to be given the force of law by decrees; above all, souls had to become penetrated with the new spirit which had been unmistakably asserting itself throughout the assembly's discussions. Over the previous forty years it had become generally recognized that the task was not a simple one. Despite innumerable efforts—St Charles Borromeo had given the impetus to almost all of them—despite the intervention, whether cautious or downright dramatic, of missioners, pamphleteers, orators—of saints even; despite the work of religious Orders old and young, it was clear to all that, on the threshold of a new century, there still remained much to be done, and that those who really wished to serve God had much hard work on their hands.

What nation was likely to come forward and take over tasks which demanded such long and exacting labour? Christian Italy, which had provided such a strong force of men in the cause of Catholic reform, was passing through a period of pause. Germany had not yet emerged

51

from those severe clashes in which Catholics and Protestants were no longer fighting only for their beliefs; for thirty years the country had been exhausted by a dreadful war which left it little strength for religious effort. In England the Papist Church was too busy fighting heresy and schism to carry on anything but a chaotic struggle. And Spain, whose sumptuous and indolent kings were hardly interested in defending their faith except as a means of consolidating their power, no longer had Ignatius, or Teresa, or John of the Cross: it had only theologians. One country alone was capable of shouldering those tasks —the country which had been so charmingly described in the Middle Ages as 'the oven in which the bread of Christianity was baked'. That country was France. Her spiritual eclipse was over, and in the first years of the seventeenth century she resumed her vocation as 'the Church's eldest daughter', which her kings never ceased to proclaim her, even in her worst moments.

However, France was not yet out of trouble. Scarcely was she delivered from the ghastly discords in which her sons massacred each other, and set once more upon her feet by that wise king Henri IV, when she had to embark on a foreign war to safeguard her rights, perhaps her very existence. And when that was over she had another spate of revolution and civil war on her own soil. Despite these trying circumstances, however, it was France who grasped the torch of Christianity. Politically speaking she was moving towards ascendancy; but she had not yet attained it. Nor did she really lead in literature, notwithstanding the growth during this period of the '1660 school', in the midst of that seething creative fever which resulted in the classic period of art. But she had already produced Descartes and Pascal, and spiritually she was in the forefront. France beamed a light across the Christian world.

Paradoxically, however, France was also the land of conspirators, and of unscrupulous and ambitious men; it was the France of duels and love stories; a country in which heroines in lace collars fired cannon from the Bastille, and got up to all sorts of other pranks; where the Cardinal de Retz played the role of a refined cynic; where Paris crawled with beggars, and illegitimate children were abandoned in their hundreds at street corners. And yet another paradox: France was also the kingdom which failed to recognize as law the decrees of the Council of Trent. The Assemblée du Clergé approved and promulgated them in 1615 in a more or less personal manner only, without the consent of the state and contrary to the wishes of Parliament, which refused to register them.

Notwithstanding all this, it was France that was destined to lead the Catholic Reformation for over half a century. Her faithful were no better than those of other Churches; it contained just as many abuses and scandals as existed elsewhere. However, in the midst of it all there was a renewal of faith; basic principles found new methods of application; charity asserted itself in countless works. And what an atmosphere of holiness! That was the essential requirement. What gave rise to this amazing surge of revival had nothing to do with ministerial or royal commands—although Louis XIII and Richelieu were won over to these purposes; there were no parliamentary decrees, nor even resolutions voted in the Assemblée du Clergé. In this spiritual springtide the sap which welled forth everywhere rose from that good earth on which generations of good Christians had lived for centuries. Teams of men and women were already there, goaded by a purely interior urgency; men and women who longed with all their being to bear witness and to radiate the Word. Why were they so numerous in this place and in this age? But why did Renaissance Italy number so many great artists? There are no answers to these questions. The historian can surmise the work of Providence in the facts before him, but the purposes of Providence remain hidden. The historian sees only that this first upward movement of the seventeenth century makes it indeed the century of saints; and France was the home of saints.[1]

2. A Great Spiritual Fountain

The one fact which dominated all others during those fruitful years was an outpouring of spirituality. It was stupendous. It took Father Henri Bremond no less than eleven large and crowded volumes in his *Histoire littéraire du sentiment religieux* to paint what he regarded as but an incomplete picture of that spirituality. If the purpose assigned to men in the practice of Christianity—the salvation of their souls and the advancement of the Kingdom of God—has always been the same, the ways and means recommended have changed in the course of centuries; and this ceaseless renewal of its doctrines, this profusion of subtle shades of distinction, constitutes one of the most thrilling aspects of the history of the Church. There is perhaps no period which can muster so many great spiritual men, so many mystics—none which has so marvellously adorned the unique theme of essential unity. 'Well do I know the source which gushes forth and gleams . . . ' sang St John of the Cross. It is a source, an ejaculatory fountain whose teeming waters irrigate the whole body of the Church.

During the period immediately preceding the spring had gushed forth in Spain. Two great streams had flowed from it: one was the spirituality of Ignatius, and the other, more mystic, the waters of

[1] Twenty-seven French men and women of this period have been either canonized or beatified. How many others may have deserved to be raised to the altar!

C

Carmel. Both had flowed far beyond the country of their origin; in France especially they had contributed towards that 'mystic invasion' at which Bremond marvelled. Besides, was it not on the blessed hill of the Parisian martyrs that Ignatius of Loyola gathered together the first soldiers of the future Society of Jesus, on a brilliant morning in 1537— the Feast of the Assumption? And was it not the setting up in Paris of the Carmelites brought from Spain by Pierre de Bérulle that decided the international triumph of the reform of St Teresa of Avila? [1] Both of these streams remained a powerful influence throughout the seventeenth century. The Jesuit system became widespread: a vast number of those who made retreats practised the *Spiritual Exercises* of St Ignatius. Many members of the Society became great mystics, such as Father Louis Lallemand; [2] and the fundamental principle formulated by St Ignatius was to be found in the sentiments expressed by Bérulle: 'It is necessary first to look to God and not to oneself; to conduct a search not for oneself, but for the pure sight of God.' The same applied to Carmelite mysticism. The works of St Teresa, the founder, translated into French by M. Gaultier in 1621, met with an immense success; there were commentaries on the life and message of her followers, Madeleine de Saint-Joseph and Catherine de Jésus. The Carmelite Jean de Saint-Samson (1571–1636), one of the great mystics of the day, deserved to be called the French John of the Cross. Carmelite influences were to be found even in the sentiments of St Francis de Sales, M. Olier and St Vincent de Paul.

But the 'mystic invasion' did not take place in France without long-standing opinions being more or less modified. A method based on reconciling the whole being with a contemplated ideal, rather than on developing a consciousness of interior states and promptings, began to replace the Ignatian method of training the will. At the same time, that mighty take-off by which St Teresa and St John of the Cross sought to sweep the soul in a single bound towards God was attempted with more restraint in French spirituality: the tendency was to keep the feet on the ground. It was significant that Bérulle, the most mystic of the French spirituals of the time, expressed his admiration for the young Descartes and asked him to place an equitable philosophy at the

---

[1] See *The Catholic Reformation*, p. 372.

[2] The Jesuit Father Louis Lallemand (1588–1635) was master of novices at Rouen, and subsequently instructed aspirants to the Society who were in their third year. He was a great mystic; his *La Doctrine spirituelle* won the enthusiasm of Bremond. He is not to be confused with the many other priests called Lallemant, Lalemant or Lallemand who, from the seventeenth century onwards also belonged to the Society of Jesus: Charles Lallemand (1587–1607) and Jerome (1593–1610) two brothers who became missionaries in Canada; Jacques Lallemand (1660–1748), who spent his life fighting Jansenism; St Gabriel Lalemant was martyred in Canada. There was even a Father Lallemand who wrote a comedy entitled *The Monks*. The name was very common at that time and its spelling varied considerably.

disposal of religion. All this underlined the national character, its sense of proportion and its understanding of man.

It is difficult to get one's bearings in the sublime medley of spiritual men during those sixty years. Even in following the broad avenues which Henri Bremond uncovered in these thickly wooded forests, it is not easy to find one's way among those spiritual states, those surges, those graces, those subtle doctrines. Great souls and their spiritual works are so numerous that the most outstanding expert, despairing of listing them all, had to entitle one of his chapters 'Turba magna'. However, two main streams of thought are conspicuous: that of Devout Humanism and that of the French School; and to these streams the leaders in the divine quest are all more or less linked. All of them have in common the conviction that, since God is not an idea but three Persons, what is supremely important is to confirm the soul in its relations with those Persons, with whom it must be induced to unite. It is merely the ways and the means that differ.

Devout Humanism [1] was essentially the doctrine of St Francis de Sales,[2] the great Savoyard bishop, so French in every way, and especially from the point of view of his matchless literary style. He died in 1622. The starting-point of his thought was simply man himself: 'I am so much a man that I can be nothing else.' Like Terence, he regarded nothing human as being foreign to him; but with Shakespeare he thought humanity beautiful because it had been sanctified. He wanted this creature of blood and clay which is man to lift up his head to the light. The union of the soul with God was to be achieved by daily effort, by 'spinning the thread of little virtues'. This doctrine embraced the whole man, whom it dedicated as a votive offering to God. In the seventeenth century the words 'devote', 'devout' and 'devotion' still retained their full and original meaning, which time has weakened. To be *devoted* to God was man's way of expressing what Providence desired, and to that end a whole system of prevenient graces conducted the soul. It was a doctrine of hope and consolation.

Salesianism is therefore found to lie within the broad outline of Christian humanism. In some respect it was the heir of Erasmus and Picco della Mirandola, and later of the Jesuits Maldonat, Molina and Bellarmine; or again of Tolet, and of all those who had sought to promote a conception of life in which the advantages contributed by the Renaissance, such as discoveries and its culture, might be reconciled with Catholic teaching and morals. But while the early Christian Humanism was more speculative and aristocratic, Devout Humanism was addressed to everybody, and made it possible for all to lead an

---

[1] The term *Humanisme dévot* was first used by the Abbé Bremond, and has become common.

[2] On the subject of St Francis de Sales see *The Catholic Reformation*, p. 378 et seq.

interior life. Such is the genius of the *Introduction to the Devout Life*. Henceforward spirituality was not to be the prerogative of the cloister. 'It is a mistake, a heresy' to think so, the saint tells us. It can have place within a company of soldiers, in the workshop of the craftsman, in the domestic life of the married. St Francis de Sales is the 'teacher of teachers' of the modern spiritual life.

But, at the same time, there was nothing commonplace in this spirituality. It was to be wholly sustained by a great upsurge of love: 'All is love, in love and of love in Holy Church!' This is repeated in the *Treatise on the Love of God* (1607–16): love is the goal that we must reach and the means by which we reach it. Let no one say then that this sage was not a mystic! Whatever caution he might display in taking flight, how is it possible to doubt, when reading the last chapter of his *Treatise*, that he aimed at the 'farthermost point of the soul' and that he reached it? 'By dint of taking pleasure in God, becoming conformable with God, and transforming our will into that of His Divine Majesty'—is that not the very principle of all mystical experience?

This doctrine, of a breadth hitherto unknown, exercised a considerable influence. The extraordinary success of the *Introduction* swelled the number of the devout. Father Cotton, the king's confessor, and above all Father Richéome (1544–1625), supported during the lifetime of St Francis ideas similar to his; *La Peinture spirituelle ou l'art d'admirer, aimer et louer Dieu* is akin to the *Introduction*. The Bishop of Belley, Jean Pierre Camus (1583–1652), whose 186 volumes were unable to exhaust his apostolic zeal and vigour, circulated among the public his *Spirit of St Francis de Sales* (1631). The convents of his daughters, the *Visitandines*, made known his *Lettres spirituelles*. Father Binet, a Jesuit (*d.* 1639), the author of the two works *Les Attraits tout puissants de Dieu* and *Grand chef-d'œuvre de Dieu*, was such a consummate disciple of the great bishop that St Jeanne de Chantal asserts she 'never heard of a mind more conformable in prudent piety with that of St Francis de Sales'. Among the Franciscans, Father Boma, author of *Chrétien de tous les temps* (1655), is clearly of the same spiritual mould; so also is the anonymous poet who, under the rough habit of the Capuchin friar and the pen-name of Yves de Paris (1590–1679), spread the Salesian doctrine of humanity sanctified by grace. Where could one not find traces of these sentiments? Marie de l'Incarnation, that excellent Ursuline nun, and the Dominican Father de Chardon echoed them, so did St Vincent de Paul who, as we have seen, was the ardent disciple of the Bishop of Annecy, and M. Olier, and even Bérulle himself. 'Because nature is of God we shall avoid destroying it. . . . Man is indeed a great miracle; he is the most perfect and most wonderful blend in nature; it seemed as though God wished to make in him an epitome of all His works.' Are not these Bérullian sayings the echo of Salesian sentiments? Countless are the bonds which link Devout Humanism with the mysticism of the French School, although their emphasis is not always the same.

We have to thank Henri Bremond for shedding a ray of light on the long-forgotten French School. He more than anyone else demonstrated its originality and its riches. It was a school of the interior life, of eminent spirituality based on dogma, and especially on the Incarnation. During the whole of the seventeenth century, and up to the time of the Regency, it left a profound impression on the French mind, and even outside France. There is no doubt that its teachers contributed more than any others to the laying of the foundations of that modern Catholic spirituality which is still practised today.

The School had four masters during the period with which we are concerned. First there was the great and estimable Bérulle, the man who, while still very young,[1] introduced Carmel to France, who acted as a guide in the saintly parlour of Mme Acarie, who proposed to the Church an ideal of the priesthood which must certainly be regarded as unsurpassable, and founded the Oratory—'Indeed a truly eminent and estimable man,' as Bossuet described him, 'of such dignity that I would go as far as to say that not even the purple robe of the cardinal added anything to it.' There is no doubt that it was he who really founded the French School—'the doctor of so many doctors, the teacher of so many saints,' whom the Church has not yet seen fit to canonize, but to whose virtues so many splendid souls bear witness. 'Unctuous, ponderous, naïve, clumsy even in his niceties'—yes, and too often boring throughout the eighteen hundred columns which his work fills in the Migne edition; but sublime too in his best moments, always hungry and thirsty for the Word of God. 'When his genius flashes, he transcends everything,' rightly commented Bremond. His *Élévations à Jésus sur ses principaux états et mystères*, his treatise *Sur l'État et la grandeur de Jésus* (1623), and his exquisite *Vie de Jésus*, which unfortunately he did not complete, must be reckoned among the best works in spiritual literature. When he died in 1629, the characteristic features of the French School had been established.

His followers extended them. First, Charles de Condren (1588–1641), who succeeded him as superior of the Oratory, and whose personality seems to have exercised an extraordinary influence, although this is not altogether apparent from his books. Of him St Jeanne de Chantal said that he was 'born to teach angels'. Bremond calls him 'the incomparable'. On the practical plane his work was a continuation of that of Bérulle. His book, *L'Idée du Sacerdoce et du sacrifice de Jésus-Christ* (which did not appear until 1677) was a contribution towards the training of priests; but on the spiritual plane his

[1] See also *The Catholic Reformation*, p. 372.

Considération sur les Mystères de Jésus-Christ went even further than the opinions of his master in the direction of absolute theocentrism and self-abnegation. Jean-Jacques Olier (1608–57) also followed Bérulle in both spheres: in the practical sense his foundation of Saint-Sulpice was intended to bring to perfection the priestly ideal conceived by Bérulle; from a spiritual point of view he gave a new emphasis to the ideas of the great cardinal, a kind of consternation before the state of man as a sinner. His most outstanding merit was to make the dignity of doctrine more readily accessible to all the faithful generally; he stripped it of its technical formulae, even of its excessive sublimity; and in his balanced and lucid language he strove effectually to disseminate it. His *Journée chrétienne* (1655) and *Introduction à la vie et aux vertus chrétiennes* (1657) will be widely read for a long time to come. As for St John Eudes (1601–80) who, as we shall see,[1] flung himself unrestrainedly into the fray, he was for half a century a missioner, a tireless builder of seminaries and the founder of a community. He too taught a similar doctrine: 'Jesus, be everything on earth, as you are in heaven.' The purpose behind *La Vie et le royaume de Jésus* (1637) and *Le Mémorial de la vie ecclésiastique* was to comment on and develop that principle; but to the adoring and prostrate theocentrism of Bérulle, Condren and Olier, he added an impetuous and almost familiar movement of love, not much unlike that which swept away St Francis de Sales, and which was to lead to the cult of the Heart of Mary and the Sacred Heart of Jesus.[2]

These four men were all related in thought, and they may be spoken of as a school, although there existed perceptible differences between them. On the whole, the paths they offered to Christians were more rugged than those suggested by M. d'Annecy with his kindly smile. They certainly did not imply, as some Protestants and Jansenists did, the wholesale condemnation of human nature; it has been seen that Bérulle sought to respect, not destroy it. But they also knew that man, whose greatness they did not fail to recognize, was steeped in weakness and misery—'the glory and the outcast of the universe,' said Pascal, who was a follower of Bérulle. Cardinal Bérulle stated the fundamental definition in these incomparable words: '*Qu'est-ce que l'homme? Un néant capable de Dieu*' ('What is man? A mere nothing, capable of reaching God.') All the masters of the French School developed this apophthegm according to their individual genius. Nothingness—that is man's condition; to rise from it Bérulle advised him to adore, so that he might lift himself up towards God. Condren says man must get the measure of his weakness, the abyss from which God drew him by creation. Olier counselled him to become conscious of his sinful state

---

[1] See p. 73 et seq.

[2] See Chapter V, section 3 on devotion to the Sacred Heart.

and to plead for mercy; John Eudes, to put his trust in love. But all were alike in thinking that the first step was 'to recognize one's nothingness before God'. From that everything else would flow.

Before the nothingness that is man stands God. And the Bérullians cannot find adequate words to exalt Him and to acknowledge the enormous distance which separates us from Him. But He is a God who knows man, who has loved man and who has created him; He 'looked upon this miserable nothingness and set about forming our being'. The first and only duty of man then is to give back to God what He has given to us, in recognizing Him as man's only Master, 'the true centre of the world'. This absolute and final theocentrism means, therefore, that everything is to be related to the one and triune God.

This theocentrism could be discouraging. If God is so far away, how can we hope to reach Him? But the French School did not lead to despair. This nothingness that is man is capable of reaching to God— that must not be forgotten. And between man and God there is a mediator—Christ, God made man. It was towards Him that all the masters of the School turned their eyes; their spirituality was as Christocentric as it was theocentric. Father Bourgoing, one of Bérulle's successors, said of him: 'He was sent, like another John the Baptist, to point out Jesus.' The mystery of the Incarnation inflamed them all. Through Him humanity was consecrated, sanctified and redeemed; it was the divine exaltation of a genuine humanism. Through Christ we adore the Father, Bérulle emphasizes. Through Christ in the Blessed Sacrament we offer the Father the only meritorious sacrifice, adds Condren. Hence there is but one way to bridge the abyss which separates man in his nothingness from the divine infinity: 'to clothe himself with Our Lord; to annihilate within himself all interests other than those of God, according to the example of Christ Himself'. To Him alone must we *adhere*: that was the word the French School wished to propagate, and that doctrine was traditional. Does it differ from the words of St Paul, who declared: 'And I live, yet not I; but Christ liveth in me'? It was the same doctrine, expressed with incomparable vigour and completeness.

Bérullism radiated everywhere. Year after year books appeared which came back to the same theme: the *Méditations* of Father Bourgoing, the *Esprit de l'Eminentissime Cardinal Bérulle*, the *Œuvres complètes* of the master and many others. Father Amelote, Condren's biographer, Father Gibieuf, Father Métezeau, Father Hugues Carré, François de Saint-Pré and Jean-Baptiste Noulleau, who experienced severe trials in his spiritual life—all were disciples of Bérulle. There were plenty of others, apart from the Oratorians. At Evreux, the great archdeacon Henri-Marie Boudon rejoiced in the most bitter humiliations during eight long years, for they recalled to him the dereliction of Christ on the Cross. Chrysostôme de Saint-Lô, a penitent of the Third Order of St Francis, the Capuchin friar Alexandre de la Ciotat, Hercule Audiffret, Superior General of the Doctrinarians, and many others based their lives on the same ideal. Pascal came very near it : he read Bérulle so deeply that a great many of his sentiments seem to have been borrowed from him. And the glory of the French Church in the period that followed was to be Bossuet, the most unmistakable of all Bérullians.

Such were the two major streams which flowed from the fountain of living water, but they were not the only ones. Many others were recognizable; more or less original in thought, but often blending Bérullism and Salesianism, occasionally perfected by contributions from Italy, Spain and the Netherlands. We have seen St Vincent de Paul furnishing the example of a spirituality in which were combined in a living synthesis the influence of the Bishop of Geneva and that of the great cardinal. He, more than anyone else, wished 'to empty himself of himself', and 'unite his will so completely to the Will of God that it might become one with His'; but, at the same time, whence did he derive his large-hearted confidence in man, if not from the author of the *Introduction*? If there was such a thing as a Lazarist spirituality, it sprang from that felicitous agreement.

Dominican spirituality was revived, and it gave us that masterpiece by Louis Chardon (1595–1651), *La Croix de Jésus*, a treatise on mystical theology, throughout which the solid bases of Thomism are noticeable; but what aspiring sentiments are contained in its best pages! There are admirable pages dealing with the state of abandonment in which the soul may find itself, believing itself rejected and desolate, and, on account of this very abandonment, feel itself loved. St Teresa had already written that 'the more Jesus loves, the heavier are the crosses we have to bear'. Chardon thought the same; few spiritual writers have shown so profoundly that man's greatest good fortune is to be able to carry the Cross.

Marie de l'Incarnation (1599–1672) was an Ursuline nun, the namesake of another Marie, a Carmelite who had been known in the world as *La Belle Acarie*. Marie de l'Incarnation was the daughter of a humble merchant of Tours. She entered a convent when she became a widow, and soon set out for Canada 'to plant the Cross and the French Fleurs-de-Lis in full view of the English'. What a great mystic this champion was! Her accounts of the 'states of prayer' recall to mind the great Carmelite Teresa of Avila and, at times, St Bernard. Again the influence of St Francis de Sales, combined with that of her native soil, made her unerring and prudent. God heaped His favours upon her, but she analyses her experiences with an acuteness of perception worthy of a compatriot of Descartes. Her little book, *Révolte des passions dans une âme avancée*, is a marvel of psychology.

All the Orders and Communities participated more or less in this vast impulse. The great Father Joseph (1577–1638), the Capuchin friar Joseph du Tremblay, a much misunderstood man known as 'His Grey Eminence', was the author of an *Introduction à la vie spirituelle* and *Perfection séraphique*, two books which proved him to be a disciple of Benoît de Canfeld; though faithful to Franciscan spirituality, he also drew very near to Salesianism. Among the Carmelites there was Jean de Saint-Samson, a blind mystic and an admirable figure. For him the essential thing was 'aspiration', a kind of elevation, a raising up, which must spring from nature but reach beyond it, to fasten on to God alone, interiorly possessed. At Ghent, and later at Malines, Marie Petit, a native of Hazebrouck, and known as Maria a Sancta Teresia (1623–77), lived an astonishing life of union with Our Lady, and wrote about it from her solitude in moving words. Still more surprising, the Society of Jesus, a school of moral training and spiritual discipline, entered upon the road to lofty mysticism with Father Louis Lallemand (1588–1635) and his followers, French emulators of the Spanish Father Baltazar Alvarez, whose life had been written by Father du Pont; they were the Fathers Rigoleuc, Grasset, Nouet, Guilloré, Maunoir, and that strange and fascinating Father Surin (1600–63), who spent his life in a constant struggle between God and the adversary. These Jesuit mystics were so numerous that the Abbé Bremond set them apart as a separate school. One might list a great many more, and even outside the ranks of the clergy, for the laity were also swept along in the current. Indeed one of the greatest literary successes was the *Chrétien intérieur*, by Jean de Bernières-Louvigny (1602–59), a true man of his century; he was a Chief Treasurer with the bent of an apostle, who, with his friend Gaston de Renty, seemed to foreshadow the Christian layman of our own day. One might go on indefinitely describing the many hues in this vast tableau built up from works whose purpose was God.

That does not mean to say that everything has to be accepted unreservedly. As in all periods of active and fruitful spirituality there were excesses and deviations. Does not Devout Humanism, when carried to the extreme, run the risk of involving the mind in a profane contemplation of nature, under the pretext that the world is the work of God? Could not the desire to dedicate one's whole life lead to a familiarity hardly compatible with true religion? This sort of thing could make a mockery of the Commandments of God. A craze for mysticism was not without its dangers. Some went too far, forgetting that this was a delicate matter. Is there not, in the doctrine of Pure Love, which is the end of Teresian mysticism (though handled

* C

differently by St Francis de Sales and St John Eudes), the danger of an extreme facility if it is not properly understood? To say *God alone*, as the excellent Boudon does, and to cease to be interested in anything else, can lead to an all too easy rejection of asceticism, even of all moral or charitable purpose. The germ of *Quietism*,[1] which the Church was to condemn, may be discerned in some of the writings of the great century of saints, and the reaction against its excesses was to provoke the case of the mystics and their downfall. In the opposite sense, does not an excessive insistence on the consideration of man's nothingness and his misery also lead to an unduly pessimistic conception of Christianity? The tendency has always existed since the Church began. The mystics were to be opposed by the psychologists and the ascetics, who were impressed above all by the ravages made in our souls by sin; at the end of the century they were to attract a large body of opinion when Bourdaloue became their mouthpiece. But even before then the ascetic tendency among the great spiritual leaders of M. de Saint-Cyran's day inclined towards Jansenism, and Catholicism was rent by it.

Such was the human counterpart of this splendid page of spiritual history. But another danger could be detected: a division between the religious life and life itself. By dint of inviting pious souls to raise themselves towards God, might one not give them the notion of an entirely personal salvation? Might they not forget that, if the Christian's duty was indeed to save himself, this duty was inseparable from that of promoting the Kingdom of God? It seems extraordinary to have to say that some convinced and fervent Christians found it quite natural to obtain for their sons ecclesiastical titles and offices which they did not by any means deserve. Thus did M. de Gondi, the father of Cardinal de Retz; yet M. de Gondi became an Oratorian! There was no doubt about the dangers of this practice; and it explains why, despite the immense effort of all those great spiritual men, the christianization of society did not proceed more quickly. The fault lay with men, not with the saints.

For the saints—God's witnesses in their day—did not by any means separate faith from life. Indeed this was one of their most significant characteristics, and one which must be stressed. All these great spiritual men were men of action and women of action, for Marie de l'Incarnation was of the same mould. Did Bérulle remain lost in his prayers? He created and he strove; he founded his Oratory; he even played a part in politics. And what was Monsieur Vincent's life if not a daily battle in which action itself was prayer because it was charity? Maunoir, Lallemand, John Eudes, Rigoleuc, François Régis and many others were engaged to the full—missioners in France and outside it, the

[1] See Chapter VI, p. 367.

creators or the inspiration of great undertakings, leaders of teams striving to make the world Christian once more. It was not their fault if here and there the crust of the arid earth refused to allow itself to be penetrated. It was already wonderful that the water of the great spiritual fountain had flowed so far and had penetrated so deeply at so many points.

3. ECCLESIA IN EPISCOPO

This living water of the spirit could be seen flowing in every direction, revitalizing institutions and souls in every section of the Church. Students of Bérulle, of St Francis de Sales, of Father de Condren and St Vincent de Paul were to be found at every level. Their spirituality, relaying and developing the spirit of the Council of Trent, made its influence felt in all that constituted the Reformation, in the true sense of that word.

First, on the highest plane: the life of grace in the Catholic Church is essentially a hierarchical life. It was necessary therefore that the heads of the Hierarchy be the dispensers of the life of grace. *Ecclesia in Episcopo*, the famous expression of St Cyprian, was always held to be true. 'The bishop is in the Church, and the Church is in the bishop.' Let the episcopal body be transformed and the whole Christian people will be transformed.

This was perfectly understood. An episcopal theology was worked out; its numerous elements were to be found in the work of M. Olier and in the *Treatise on Holy Orders* by Antoine Godeau, Bishop of Grasse and Vence. Louis Abelly, Bishop of Rodez, summarized them in his *Episcopalis sollicitudinis Enchiridion*, 'the true guide of bishops'. This theology had long since been expounded by Barthélemy des Martyrs, the energetic Primate of Braga, in Portugal, and one of the leading lights at the Council of Trent, though not much notice was taken of it at the time. Henceforth it came to life and was put into operation.

A great obstacle, however, stood in the way. The Council of Trent, an assembly of bishops which laid down the duties of bishops, did not dare, or was not able, to resolve the preliminary problem of their own nomination; that is to say, the problem relating to the intervention of the temporal power in the choice of bishops. What a great rumpus there was when, during the XXVth session, the Fathers attempted to approach the question![1] The ambassadors of France and Spain, for once in agreement, tried to ride the high horse; even some of the bishops, among them the Ordinary of Prague, did their best to brush aside all serious discussion of the subject. In the end they confined

[1] See *The Catholic Reformation*, p. 81.

themselves to giving princes some very Platonic advice, and the same old practices continued with disastrous results.

In a great many countries bishops were nominated by the public authority, either legally or factually. In France the evil was firmly established by agreement under the Concordat of 1516. The king appointed the candidates; the Pope invested them canonically.

The episcopate therefore became a career dependent upon the State, and could moreover be merged with a different kind of administrative career: G. du Vair was Bishop of Lisieux and governor of Provence; Cardinal de la Valette was an army general; and François de Sourdis was both an admiral and Archbishop of Bordeaux. Some bishops bore noble titles: duke, count, prince or 'seigneur'. Since episcopal titles (sometimes augmented through their titles of nobility) carried with them material interests, the ambitions of their holders were not necessarily apostolic. A family which held an archbishopric would do everything to retain it: it was a part of its heritage and useful to younger sons. Thus Armand de Richelieu had to become a priest. There were real episcopal families whose members succeeded to their sees. The best-known was that of the Gondis, in Paris, of which the third archbishop, the future Cardinal de Retz, admitted that he was 'perhaps the most un-ecclesiastical person in the whole world'. All the great names of France were to be found at the head of dioceses, as well as those of families in the legal profession, such as the Matignons and the Séguiers. Why should not Richelieu nominate his beloved brother Alphonse to the See of Lyons? And what could one expect from titled bishops who were interested only in the revenues from their dioceses, and left the care of souls to some Vicar-General? Philippe Cospéau, Bishop of Aire, expressed indignation that bishops could be appointed 'while in their nurses' arms, or while still being bossed about at college'. And Monsieur Vincent complained distressfully: 'I tremble lest this detestable traffic in bishoprics bring the curse of God upon this country.'

However, notwithstanding such unfavourable conditions, very definite progress had been made, even as far back as the days of good King Henri IV. He did, of course, succumb to the evil custom when he reserved the bishopric of Metz for his natural son, Henri de Verneuil, who was five years of age. But on the whole his selections were good, and 'apart from a few bishops, like a Bourbon at Rouen, or a Lorrainer at Rheims, who thought their great names dispensed them from virtues great and small', the bishops selected by that lusty man were very edifying. His son, who was hard to please, kept a sharp eye on nominations. The episcopate in the time of Louis XIII was fairly good. Richelieu himself, though he had an unfortunate tendency to use for political or warlike ends men who should have been absolutely dedicated to the service of God, at least endeavoured to secure moral safeguards when he chose a bishop. Father Joseph prompted him along this path. In the same way later on, with Mazarin strongly inclined to jockey with bishoprics as he was with everything else, the influence of Anne of Austria and, through her, that of Monsieur Vincent—so long as he remained a member of the Council of Conscience—made itself felt in an endeavour to avoid the worst choices, and sometimes even to decide on excellent ones.

Thus we witness a complete and impressive restoration of the episcopate. Certainly there could not fail to be mistakes, and quite a number of them. There were worldly bishops, and there would be still more until the Revolution; men who were much too keen on their fine horses, like M. de Poiverel at Alet, or too enamoured of hunting, like M. de Montrouge at Saint-Flour, M. J. d'Estaing at Clermont [1] —and others even worse, whom there is no need to name. But it is certain that their number decreased, that their presence gave scandal, and that feeling against these bad pastors was so strong that Rome was able to oppose successfully nominations that were too high-handed. By 1660 good bishops were in the majority.

It would be impossible to name them all.[2] Some have been raised to the altar, and many others could have been; there are several who have been canonized unofficially, if one may dare use the expression. Although differing very much from each other as to character, methods, and even as to their particular form of spirituality, they were certainly all equally attached to a work which was essentially pastoral. Their influence was to be felt in the four corners of France, and all the more profoundly because most of them remained in the same see for a very long time—twenty, thirty, and even forty years.

To begin with there were those whom one might call the Borromeans, belonging to the spiritual family of the illustrious Archbishop of Milan.[3] The saint's writings, and the methods which he developed, exercised a great influence. And is not that extraordinary saint, Francis de Sales—an obvious imitator of St Charles in his episcopal activities— a saint at once so human and so spiritual, a leader of souls and a leader of the people?[4] When his turn came, he influenced others by his example and his teaching. Blessed Alain de Solminihac, Bishop of Cahors, who came later on, was also Borromean. He was made bishop against his will, by order of the king. For eighteen years, from 1636

---

[1] 'As he was blind, he saluted the ladies in a manner more than fatherly,' said a contemporary, 'feeling their faces with his hands to tell the canons round about him who they were . . . ' It must be said, however, that he worked for the reform of his diocese. His nephew, Louis d'Estaing, who succeeded him, was a good bishop and a reformer.

[2] See the excellent work by Father Broutin mentioned in the bibliographical notes.

[3] Concerning St Charles Borromeo see *The Catholic Reformation*, p. 110 et seq.

[4] Concerning St Francis de Sales see *The Catholic Reformation*, p. 378 et seq.

to 1654, he lived an up-hill-and-down-dale life in his poor diocese, giving an example of an extremely humble and canonical life with his priests. He strove to found a seminary; he trained his clergy at conferences over which he himself presided, and with sublime calmness he held his own in spite of the opposition of the second-rate. He has rightly been called 'France's St Charles Borromeo'.

Then there were those who had been trained by M. de Bérulle and his Oratory: Barthélemy de Donnadieu, Bishop of Comminges, a disciple of M. de Condren, an austere and enlightened soul. He took over his see from a pugnacious prelate who was more interested in politics and alchemy than in theology and pastoral work; and in eleven years (1626–37) he made his diocese one of the most zealous in the whole of France. Many miracles were wrought at the tomb of 'Monsieur Barthélemy'. There was also Jean-Baptiste Gault, Bishop of Marseilles, an Oratorian who spent no more than a year at the great port, but long enough to show his flock that a bishop could live poor among the poor, daring to take Christ into the low quarters of the town, into the convict prisons and the galleys; in that short time he showed that he knew how to die among his people, literally worn out by his work. And again there was Étienne de Vilazel from Toulouse, who stayed at Saint-Brieuc for forty years (1637–77), because he refused to leave the church to which God had married him. He said good-naturedly: 'Do we become bishops to destroy the work of the Cross or to build it up?'

Following narrower paths were also those on whom incipient Jansenism left its mark, but who were none the less excellent bishops, devoted to their flocks, expecting their priests to give an example of virtue, because they demanded much from themselves. At Alet, from 1657 to 1677, Nicolas Pavillon was another of St Vincent de Paul's friends; at Châlons-sur-Marne from 1646 to 1680, the son of a lady under the spiritual guidance of St Francis de Sales and second cousin to M. Olier, Félix Vialart de Herse, used to read a few pages from Charles Borromeo every day so as to become more imbued with his methods. But there were also men who to all appearances had chosen the broad and comfortable paths, men who had been attracted to a bishopric for political or family motives, but whom their sacred office had in some way transformed. These proved to be excellent leaders in their dioceses, bound to their pastoral work and often of exemplary conduct. Surprisingly enough, Armand de Richelieu was one of them. He was the perfect bishop in that wretched diocese of Luçon where, before him, no bishop had resided for sixty years. Another was François de Sourdis, Cardinal Archbishop of Bordeaux from 1600 to 1628; perhaps a little too violent occasionally, but an active prelate who brought his plans to maturity, founding missions and seminaries, and of whom Tallemant de Réaux rightly said that he 'governed his diocese exceedingly well, and was a sound man'. Another was Sébastien Zamet, Bishop of Langres from 1615 to 1654, the prototype of those prelates appointed by royal favour. Henri IV jokingly referred to his father, an immensely rich Italian banker, as 'my dear monied cousin'. Sébastien found his diocese in great confusion. He put it in order with remarkable courage, and at the same time gave himself body and soul to his poor flock, who were being crushed under the miseries of war. Antoine Godeau was yet another; at first a minion of Richelieu, it was while in charge of the dioceses of Grasse and Vence that he discovered fully the vocation of a bishop, and wrote profoundly on the subject.

One might easily add to the list of these bishops: Béthune at Puy, Fenouillet at Montpellier, du Louët at Quimper, Dinet at Mâcon, Raconis at Lavaur and so many others, apart from all those who moved in the world of Monsieur Vincent. All, or nearly all, employed the same methods: the forming of diocesan synods to study problems and find solutions to them, the appointing of non-resident vicars at the head of diocesan districts for the closer supervision of parishes, the multiplications of missions, and above all the creation of organizations and institutions for the purpose of restoring what M. Bérulle called 'the priestly state'. It would be impossible to overestimate the value of this work of restoring the episcopate.[1]

4. THE PRIESTLY STATE

The priesthood, 'the first order of the Church, essential and absolutely necessary to her', the order 'specifically instituted by the Son of God' (the words are again from Bérulle) was in a state of crisis; or rather, the condition of degradation in which it existed when the Protestant revolution began had not surrendered to the admirable injunctions of the Council of Trent. We may recall that this was a great source of pain to Monsieur Vincent; but also to all those who were solicitous for the things of God. A great priest of Châlons wrote: 'How many poor souls perish in our districts through the fault of their priests?' And St John Eudes said: 'Those who should work for the salvation of souls make it their profession to lose them.' Pathetic admissions, among hundreds. Was the austere Abbé de Saint-Cyran right when he declared: 'Among ten thousand priests, there is not one'?

[1] Strangely enough, the influence of these great bishops could be found even in civil matters. In the diocese of Coutances there was a large increase in the use of the names *Léonor* and *Charles-François*, because of the Bishops Léonor de Matignon and Charles-François Lomenie de Brienne.

Obviously he exaggerated. There were good priests—excellent priests; and undoubtedly many more good ones than bad ones, though one spoke less of the former than of the latter. But it must be admitted that the profusion of evidence of the vices of the clergy was disquieting. Catholics of the twentieth century, accustomed to the zeal and respectability of their priests, find it difficult to understand these things. They hesitate to believe that there could be many priests who had to be reminded by their bishops (like the worthy Vialart de Herse) that it was respectable to keep their cassocks buttoned up, that they had to put on liturgical attire when they celebrated Mass, that they should not drink in cabarets, or dance with girls, or allow persons of questionable character to stay at the presbytery. But more numerous than these obvious causes of scandal were certainly the priests who were interested in everything but their priesthood and their apostolate; they lived with their families after ordination, unoccupied; they frequented the court and the town, hoping for a good benefice—apart from all those in Minor Orders, subdeacons and other wandering monks who were to be found everywhere. Even among the clergy attached to parishes those who completely neglected their parishioners were innumerable. In the diocese of Langres 457 curés were non-residents, and only 138 lived in their parishes. A bishop in the Pyrenees said rather acidly that he thought it would be easier to tame a bear from his mountains than to persuade one of his priests to remain in residence. And as for those who were neither absent nor debauched, of what use were they? It seems that their ignorance was staggering. When young Adrien Bourdoise said he thought he would like to become a priest, some good man advised him in that case to work, because, he said, 'it is a splendid thing for a priest to know how to read and write'. Obviously there was no question of such clerics knowing any Latin. If they were capable of mumbling a minimum of liturgy it was as much as one could expect! It was one of these priests whom Monsieur Vincent met near Folleville who did not know the words of the Absolution; and in Provence Romillon came upon one who recited an *Ave Maria* on every occasion, because that was the only prayer he knew. Godeau thought he had put his finger on the basic reason for all these shortcomings when he said: 'The origin of this evil lies in the lack of vocation; from that, as from a poisoned spring, flow ignorance, scandal and the immorality of pastors whose bad example corrupts the people.' Unquestionably; but were there not also some very material causes? Why should the humbler substitutes, the priests in charge with their meagre *portion congrue*,[1] put so much

---

[1] *Portion congrue* really means a 'bare minimum', a sufficiency. The 'curés' were protected by the principle of *portion congrue*, but the 'vicaires', who were appointed by the 'curés', were not so protected.

zeal into ministering to parishes whose revenues were pocketed by the incumbents? [1]

It was precisely faults such as these that many people were resisting, and not without success. The Council of Trent had laid down principles for the reclamation of the clergy; it lavished excellent but insufficient advice. While it had given a new impetus to the extra-hierarchical clergy in establishing the formula for clerks regular, it had not determined the practical conditions under which discipline, learning and virtue might be reinstated. It was one thing to proclaim a sacerdotal ideal—as many authors did, e.g. François de la Rochefoucauld in his *Ecclesiastical State*; it was quite another to construct the institutional framework within which this ideal might assert itself. Indeed the two tasks were inseparable, as the leaders of the Church were well aware.

This aspect of ecclesiastical history is only now beginning to be studied. The Abbé Bremond concentrated on religious sentiment; pastoral work as such has only recently been considered. And the more one studies the great century of saints from this point of view, the more one becomes aware of the creative vitality, the inventiveness of which the French Catholics gave evidence. Therein lies a phenomenon quite comparable with that which we have witnessed during the last twenty years; amidst the seething variety of formulae there was a continual search for solutions to the major problems which presented themselves. The aim was to remake the clergy, so that the faithful might follow. How could it be achieved? Attempts, gropings and inevitable failures were followed by a little progress. Many labourers devoted themselves to this great task.

Some of them are famous. Foremost among them we again find Bérulle; [2] he was not only a master of the French spiritual school, whose influence was to make itself felt in the whole training of the clergy, but he was also a planner. Drawing inspiration from the example of St Philip Neri, he created in France the *Oratory* (1611–13), a 'Congregation of Priests of Jesus Christ', whose primary vocation was to work towards the restoration of the ideal of the priesthood, having, as Bossuet said, 'no other mind but the mind of the

[1] How could such a clergy control its flock? The pitiable state of the churches reflected this incompetence on the part of the priests. In many places ceremonies were performed without dignity—a fact which must be appreciated if one is to understand the insistence of the Company of the Blessed Sacrament and of St John Eudes on the veneration of the Sacrament of the Altar. Here low-necked women could be seen leaning against the altar during the Sacrifice of the Mass; there beggars stretched out their hands, even into the sanctuary; children brought to Mass played marbles or 'bilboquet'; it sometimes happened that the barking of dogs drowned the preacher's voice. To the priests all that was quite natural. Alain de Solminihac, during a tour of inspection in his diocese, came across a priest who did his cooking in the church!

[2] On the subject of Bérulle and Bourdoise as reformers of the clergy, see *The Catholic Reformation*, p. 365.

Church herself, no other rules but her canons'. Next, Adrien Bourdoise, a strange man, gruff and unswerving, ardent and rather unmethodical, who saw in the system of communities of priests a solution to every problem; in a space of thirty years he founded about twenty such groups in various dioceses, and his name is connected with the success, limited but definite, of the Paris Community of Saint-Nicolas-du-Chardonnet (set up between 1612 and 1638). Then, it goes without saying, there was St Vincent de Paul who, as we have seen, through his Retreats for Ordination Candidates and his Tuesday Conferences, strove to raise the moral and spiritual level of priests, while his seminaries effectively prepared young men for the duties of the priesthood.

All these are well-known names, but many others less familiar were pioneers. Few remember Jean-Baptiste Romillon and the little groups of 'Philippins' from Provence, who, from about 1600 to 1603, were a sort of link between the French Oratory and that of St Philip Neri. Few now give a thought to Bernard Bardon de Brun, the 'Bourdoise of Limoges', a mysterious personage who probably received the stigmata, and whose work hardly spread beyond his own province, but whose priests of Saint-Martial constituted a novel type of congregation of priests. Forgotten likewise are Charles Démia of Lyons, St Jean de la Cropte de Chanterac, the apostle of Périgueux, Christophe d'Autier de Sisgaud, Bishop of Bethlehem, who, with his eleven priests of the Blessed Sacrament, brought so powerful an influence to bear upon the clergy of Valence, Thiers and Clermont; and Jean de Fonteneil, a native of Bordeaux, who was a student under St Vincent de Paul. Well nigh endless is the list of those societies of priests which increased and multiplied at that time. They were unusual communities in which not everything perhaps was perfect, but which certainly achieved a great deal of good. The laity themselves put their shoulders to the wheel: one of them was the amazing Jacques Crétenet, a native of Franche-Comté, who settled at Lyons. A surgeon by profession, he became skilled in prayer, established a community of priest missioners and sent his teams of 'Josephites' throughout the territory watered by the Rhône and the Saône. He had to bear some heavy crosses, and even some knocks from his own spiritual children. After the death of his wife he was ordained priest and died a saintly death.

In striving for the reform of the clergy, all these apostles used more or less the same methods. The primary idea was to make the priests better than they were. They were to pass through fairly long stages of training, during which they would be imbued with sound principles. Monsieur Vincent's Retreats for Ordination Candidates were the model. Better still, among those who were more grounded in spiritual things, selections were made in advance, so that a collective effort might be made towards general betterment. This innovation included study circles in the manner of the Vincentian Tuesday Conferences, as well as certain diocesan synods. These initial efforts were approved by bishops who were anxious for reform: by Jean-Baptiste Gault at Marseilles, by Félix Vialart de Herse at Châlons, by François de la Fayette at Limoges and by others who presided personally at priests' conferences and took part in the retreats of their clergy. Undoubtedly none of them achieved results equal to the earlier triumphs of St Charles Borromeo; but many of them sowed seed that took root.

The positive issue quickly became manifest to all: it was not enough to take already ordained priests and instil into them virtues and principles more or less successfully; it would be more expedient to prepare young men for their priestly duties. The Council of Trent had expressly said so in the course of its XXIIIrd session. Chapter XXVIII contained a precise plan for the establishment of seminaries: 'If the young are not well brought up, they allow themselves to be drawn easily towards worldly pleasures.' Therefore colleges must be established where the children of both rich and poor would be received from the age of twelve and divided into classes; and from amongst them the bishop 'will allocate a certain number to the service of the churches'; the others would continue their studies with the object of becoming good Christian laymen. The idea had been put into effect in several places: in Milan under St Charles Borromeo, and at Rheims on the initiative of the Cardinal of Lorraine in 1567. The results had not fulfilled expectations. The institution of seminaries, of which Cardinal Pallavicini had said that it alone was a justification of the whole Council of Trent, and which appears to us today to be indispensable, was painfully slow in its fulfilment. This was probably because the Council of Trent had not prescribed practical conditions, especially financial, under which dioceses would establish their seminaries; perhaps because it had not imposed upon future priests the obligation of having to pass through a seminary. Moreover it had been laid down that a boy should be twelve years of age to be admitted to a seminary; candidates for the priesthood were accepted at this tender age, so that ordinary scholars were mixed up with true seminarists, and the institution thus became unbalanced.

Whatever the cause may have been, the failure at the beginning of the seventeenth century seems to have been quite evident. The seminary at Rheims, founded by Cardinal de Lorraine, became a choir school; at Rouen the seminary provided two priests in six years! More serious still, the Oratory, which had been founded by Bérulle for this purpose, was not a success; at Lyons, Mâcon, Langres, and Saint-Magloire near Paris, the Oratorian seminaries stagnated; and soon the flower of the priesthood who thronged around M. de Condren devoted themselves rather to missions, colleges and parishes.

The idea was not, however, abandoned. Work went forward, though with uncertain steps. There was some doubt as to whether candidates for ordination in religious houses and what were known as parochial seminaries should receive an essentially practical training according to the advice of M. Bourdoise, or whether they should be assigned to district seminaries. Cardinal Richelieu took an interest in the matter. In 1636 he laid the foundations of the Académie pour Mil Gentilshommes for the training of young noblemen—four hundred for the Orders and six hundred for the leading professions. In 1625 Charles Godefroy, a simple priest of Creteville (now called Quettreville, near Coutances), had written a dissertation entitled *Le Collège des Saints Exercices*, in which he indicated precisely how a seminary should be instituted, and he sent his paper to the French Assemblée du Clergé which met in that year. The Assemblée was impressed by this document, and though its pioneer died before he was able to embark upon anything really effective, his ideas gained ground. St John Eudes was to remember them later, and the Assemblée advised bishops to create two seminaries: one for young laymen, and the other for future priests.

Between March 1641 and October 1644 a scheme was evolved, and three splendid men of God set to work: St Vincent de Paul, M. Olier and St John Eudes. Lazarist, Sulpician and Eudist seminaries were the fruits of their labour, while the Oratory, of which Father Bourgoing had been elected General in 1641, returned to its original vocation, aware of the urgent need for true training establishments. Cardinal Richelieu lent the whole weight of his authority to this movement; he offered the castle of Rueil to M. Olier, sent a thousand *écus* to Monsieur Vincent, three thousand to M. Bourgoing and instructed the Duchesse d'Aiguillon to assist John Eudes. Everything was in full swing.

A majority of bishops was equally sympathetic; but a few held back, hesitating to confide the training of their priests to communities which would not be under their control. But those who sincerely wished for ecclesiastical reform entered wholeheartedly into the scheme. It is not possible to name them all. They realized that this was an indispensable work, and that, as Grammont, founder of the seminary at Besançon, said, it was not enough to have buildings and an income to maintain them; what was necessary above all was a spirit of holiness—which is of the very essence of reform. About the year 1669 things were very far from being perfect. Old priests and religious were still being allowed to mingle with candidates for ordination, and they all came at their own discretion. Though a number of seminaries did wonderfully, others still lagged behind; the spiritual climb was so laborious that in some dioceses a new start had to be made. A double result was achieved, however: the clergy became more scholarly and more worthy of its calling; and it co-operated with the bishops far more readily than hitherto.

It is with a feeling of admiration that one thinks of so many excellent priests, whose lives were so far removed from the spirit of their immediate predecessors. Their names are recorded in obscure chronicles, those holy French priests of the seventeenth century, whom Joseph Grandet has praised so beautifully.[1] Among them were Claude Bernard, known as 'the poor priest', who founded the Seminary of the Thirty-three, and was outstanding in the struggle to spread charity; Cotolendi, parish priest of Sainte-Marie-Madeleine at Aix from 1654 to 1659, then Vicar Apostolic in the Far East; Bénigne Joly, who edified the people of Dijon for over fifty years (1640–94); Bardon de Brun; Enguerrand Le Chevalier. All these would be paragons of their kind, were it not that Monsieur Vincent, the priest *par excellence*, towered above them all.

5. The Saint of the Seminaries of Normandy: St John Eudes

Among those who inspired the great movement which was to renovate the clergy of France, three figures stand out—three men whose activities were to prove decisive. We have seen the first, St Vincent de Paul, setting up one after another his retreats for ordinands, his sacerdotal conferences and his seminary; then Jean-Jacques Olier, who devised the ultimate scheme which was to be adopted in the future. Less familiar, however, to French Catholics—though his native town of Caen honours his name with a plaque at the corner of one of its streets, and his congregation has spread throughout the world—is that great saint of Normandy, John Eudes, who in so many ways resembles the Gascon saint.

It was while conducting missions in the district around Caen, during 1632 and the following years, that John Eudes became convinced that the major problem of his day was the improvement of the clergy, and that, in order to achieve this, it was imperative to establish seminaries. Like Monsieur Vincent he began with the sorrowful conviction that the French towns and countryside themselves were in sore need of reconversion. 'What are so many doctors and learned men doing in Paris', he asked in holy anger, 'while souls are perishing in their thousands?' As a young priest he was not content merely to bury himself in his books and studies, nor even in the schools, where his congregation, the Oratory, was doing well. He plunged into action 'to raise up the dead', as he said. Assembling a small band of priests, he gave them a short retreat and then spent eleven or twelve weeks

[1] Joseph Grandet's work was written about 1690 and published in an abridged form much later by Letourneau: *Histoire des Saints prêtres français au XVIIe siècle* (Paris, 1897).

rousing the parishes in the manner described during the process of his canonization. What is more, he succeeded.

He succeeded because he knew how to speak to his Norman audience. To begin with, he was one of them; born at Ri near Argentan in 1601, he came from a family that owned vineyards. His younger brother, François de Mézeray, became a member of the French Academy, and made the family name famous. John grew up among the people of Normandy and, like many another boy in the province, was educated by the Jesuits at Caen. When he became a priest his work during the plague showed clearly the splendour of charity. Then this man, whose robust appearance concealed many physical ailments, became a remarkable orator whose eloquence in the pulpit could alternate between the thrilling and the ardent, the terrifying and the poignantly tender. He exercised an amazing control over the crowds, who forgave him his ruggedness and redundancies. The people of Normandy came in their tens of thousands to hear him, and he converted them.

Converted, yes; but for how long? John Eudes soon found out. 'These poor people have excellent dispositions,' he grumbled, 'but what can we expect under the leadership of pastors such as we see all around us? Is it not inevitable that, forgetting the great truths which moved them during the mission, they fall back into their former errors?' So priests were necessary: good priests who would continue the work of the mission and perpetuate its influence. This was precisely what Monsieur Vincent was saying about the same time.

John Eudes set to work at once. In 1641, at the height of the mission at Remilly-sur-Lozon near Coutances, he called together the priests of the district to talks bearing upon the spiritual and pastoral life. They came in large numbers and went away pleased and undoubtedly better. But would it not be preferable to establish a real seminary? Many encouraged him to do so: Philippe de Cospéau, Bishop of Lisieux, Jacques d'Angennes, Bishop of Bayeux, M. de Renty, M. Jean de Bernières-Louvigny and Dom Tarisse, the Benedictine—the Jesuits too, and above all Marie des Vallées, the 'Saint of Coutances', that enigmatical visionary who assured him that she knew by divine inspiration that Providence expected this effort on his part.

John Eudes then spoke of his plans to his superiors, but met with a rebuff. The Oratory at that time was still not very successful with its early seminaries and preferred to steer its members towards missions and teaching. Besides, Father Bourgoing regarded Father Eudes as more qualified to preach missions than to administer seminaries, and he refused to authorize this undertaking. This refusal constituted a spiritual crisis for John Eudes; he was deeply attached to his community, his colleagues, and to the memory of twenty years as an

Oratorian. But, *Deo sic disponente*, as the decree of canonization expresses it, he remained firm; he refused to abandon his idea and left the congregation. He broke with them sorrowfully, as Father Eymard was to leave the Marists, as Father de Foucauld was to forsake the Trappist Order, and Father Anizan the Brothers of St Vincent de Paul; to be of more service to souls, he left to undertake a new task.

Two men encouraged him: Richelieu, who summoned him to a long talk and granted him the letters patent necessary for a foundation; and St Vincent de Paul who, in that autumn of 1642, had just opened his seminary, and lavished advice upon him. The following year John Eudes set to work, on 25th March 1643, after returning from a pilgrimage to the shrine of Notre Dame de la Délivrance at Caen. With five companions he opened his house, his seminary, without any official support, and founded the Society of Jesus and Mary [1] for the dual purpose of missionary work and the education of priests.

That was what the Eudist seminaries were destined to be. They were much more like novitiates than schools of theology, and aimed at combining preparation for the priesthood with the apostolate of the masses. It was a blend of theory and practice similar to what Monsieur Vincent was trying to do at Saint-Lazare and very similar to what Authier de Sisgaud was achieving with his priests of the Blessed Sacrament. This no longer represented the elementary formula of the houses established immediately after the Council of Trent; it very closely resembled that of Saint-Sulpice.

In any case the Eudist system undoubtedly supplied a need, for it succeeded—though not without setbacks. To begin with, four requests within less than eighteen months were received from Rome for similar foundations, and the brake had to be applied. The Oratory was not achieving much in this direction. As regards Normandy itself, the canons, parish priests and middle-class people were opposed to seminaries. Intrigues were hatched against the apostle, at least one of which succeeded—to such a point that his chapel at Caen lay for a while under interdict. There was even talk of imprisoning him. Jansenism was at this time in full vigour, and many of those whom he believed to be his friends, even among the Oratorians, were secretly working against the mystic herald of a doctrine which attested to the world the goodness of God, a goodness so great, so infinite, that only the holy Mother of Christ and the Heart of Christ Himself were capable of making men understand it.

John Eudes resisted every assault. He continued to journey from one Norman parish to another, exhorting the people from the pulpit. His

---

[1] At first it was called the Company of Jesus and Mary. The change in the name suggests the personal spirituality of the founder as the apostle of devotion to the Sacred Heart.

seminary at Caen prospered; the Assembly of French Clergy sent him a letter of congratulation. One after another the provincial bishops invited him to found seminaries in their cathedral cities—at Coutances in 1650, at Lisieux in 1653, at Rouen in 1658 and at Evreux in 1667. Even Brittany appealed to him in 1670. His books, perhaps rather too many of them, extended his influence, and implemented his doctrine. Meanwhile his Sisters of the Congregation of Our Lady of Charity, the forerunner of the Institute of Our Lady of Charity of the Good Shepherd, strove to reclaim fallen women. When he died in 1680 he had become a kind of patriarch; he was often called on for advice, and hundreds of good priests issued from the Eudist houses. It is surprising that he was not canonized by the Church until 1925.[1]

6. JEAN-JACQUES OLIER AND THE GENTLEMEN OF SAINT-SULPICE

The fact that Jean-Jacques Olier has not yet been canonized is the Church's secret. History, however, may declare that among the architects of clerical reform produced by the seventeenth century he stands out as the most thorough and the most effective. But it is not merely from this point of view that we can regard him as unappreciated. His image, in the eyes of an unenlightened posterity, appears rather hazy and faded. Even those who are better informed accord him a respect tainted with boredom. His sons, the Gentlemen of Saint-Sulpice, are renowned for their reserve, their determined self-effacement and their wholly interior piety. Was their founder cast in the same mould? In a sense he was; but he was not merely that. He led an astonishing life, with some highly coloured episodes, some unexpected crises and recoveries. And what a fascinating personality lay hidden beneath that mask of serenity which in the end became constant as a result of great effort!

Let us look at this little, softly spoken priest, laughing and joking with his companions at the Saint-Germain fair, where no priest ventured to show his cloth. At twenty years of age [2] he took life very much as it came. All at once a woman stood before him. Her name was Marie Rousseau, the wife of one of the twenty-five licensed wine merchants in Paris, and rather like Molière's Toinette or Martin. A pious uneasiness disturbed her soul. 'You make me feel so unhappy',

---

[1] No doubt on account of his connection with the strange Marie des Vallées, and also because of his many pamphlets, sent to Rome by the Jansenists whose implacable enemy he was.

[2] Jean-Jacques Olier was born in Paris on 20th September 1608; the incident referred to took place at the beginning of 1629. Marie Rousseau's wineshop was situated in the Rue des Canettes.

she said to him; 'I am praying for your conversion.' This eager and frivolous lad accepted the censure in silence; the strange appeal disturbed him. That was his first conversion. The next took place eleven years later, at Loretto, where he had gone more out of curiosity than from true piety. It was there that a prayer to Our Lady cured him of a painful optical disease. This second conversion set him on the road to perfection. And God was persistent; few souls have been so manifestly drawn. Jean-Jacques Olier found himself living in a world of mystery: what was his distress and confusion when confronted by a nun whom he recognized as someone he had seen on several occasions in a dream, and whom he knew to be praying for him! She was the Dominican Agnès de Langeac. The supernatural then became reality; here was plain evidence of the communion of saints. From now on he was *in via*.

But he had not reached the goal. It needed years more of torment and gradual progress. Jean-Jacques Olier was thirty-one years of age; he was not to be a little priest chasing after benefices, as he might well have been. With Monsieur Vincent, whom he met and heard preach, he discovered the meaning of the priesthood, which he had received without much enthusiasm. He discovered too the sovereign greatness of the poor whom he gathered round him. He flung himself into the generous labour of the mission. With M. de Bérulle he learned that true life meant life in Christ; but he had not yet made his decision. A dreadful spiritual crisis overwhelmed him, a terrible conflict in which the two men we all have within us confronted one another. He thought it would kill him, and he seemed to sink to the bottom of some great abyss. His friend and master, M. de Condren, almost despaired of him. Yet he gave proof of what was to come by refusing the bishopric which Cardinal de Richelieu pressed him to accept. Then suddenly he had peace—a silent acquiescence given so secretly that no details exist of this aspect of his life. But henceforward Jean-Jacques Olier knew that he was on the right path, and he advanced along it. What an adventure! Not even Augustine in his *Confessions* records anything greater.

It remained to ascertain the precise goal towards which God was leading him. For a little while longer he hesitated. Should he continue as a missioner in the towns and countryside of France? In Auvergne and at Chartres, despite obstacles, he had not fared badly. Or should he go off to Tonking with Father de Rhodes, or to Canada, where the Jesuits were so hard pressed? These were invitations to adventure, and he swept them aside. He also met M. Bourdoise and saw his work at close quarters; once again he came upon Monsieur Vincent, whose priests had just founded a seminary at Annecy; and his friend John Eudes was turning over similar projects in his mind. He made his decision. On 29th September 1641 Jean-Jacques Olier left Paris by the

Porte Saint-Germain, accompanied by François de Caulet and Jean du Perrier. Marie L'Huillier, formerly Mme de Villeneuve, who had installed her Sisters of the Cross in the small village of Val-Saint-Girard (now Vaugirard), about a league beyond the city walls, had shown him yet another sign from heaven, and he responded—at last!

From now on, as always happens in the great lives that God guides, plans materialized in quick succession, each one begetting another. At first, Jean-Jacques Olier thought of establishing a seminary, but he certainly did not decide right away to form a society charged with the special task of training the masters, the directors and the seminary professors. That development came of its own accord, as a kind of necessary sequence of events. The house at Vaugirard was set up; in a small way at first, but on a larger scale when a generous layman offered him a spacious building. Marie L'Huillier, like a true Martha, looked after the kitchen. The parish priest absented himself, deliberately of course, and left his flock to the three new priests. A few young people joined them: Gabriel de Quetplus, Louis de Gondrin, Antoine Ragnier de Pousse, M. de Bassancourt and M. de Chassagne, a professor of theology who insisted on the need for studies. This was the beginning of a seminary, but had they found a system? Would something be done comparable with what M. Bourdoise was trying to do at Saint-Nicolas-du-Chardonnet? When—probably in March 1642—the little band at Vaugirard was constituted as a society for the training of priests, here again it was a purpose rather than a plan.

The decisive stage was eventually reached. The parish priest of Saint-Sulpice despaired of achieving anything with his parishioners and wished to retire. The appointment was offered to Jean-Jacques Olier. It was not the kind of promotion suitable to a beneficiary already well provided for, and Mme Olier, his mother, was furious. But he remembered the work which Monsieur Vincent and his colleagues had done among this pack of heretics and wasters, and he accepted the post. With a few of his companions—four teachers and eight seminarists—he installed himself in the priest's house. The name by which the new community was to be known was conferred by the parishioners themselves; they called them the Priests of the Clergy, and this became their official title; they were to be known in history as the Priests of Saint-Sulpice.

The enterprise made rapid strides. M. Bourdoise's idea of training future priests in a sacerdotal community seemed to offer too limited a scope. That of mixed establishments, half college and half seminary, had proved unsatisfactory. At about the same time Monsieur Vincent was learning the lesson of practical experience, and opened his house for clerical training as distinct from his little seminary. A step or two away from the Church of Saint-Sulpice, in the Rue Guisarde,

Jean-Jacques Olier managed to buy a house which, though somewhat dilapidated, was good enough for the reception of a few boarders. That was at the beginning of the year 1642; and thus the first seminary of Saint-Sulpice was born.

How did it become in a short time so very different from others—the Lazarist seminaries, for instance? M. Olier has told us in his various writings. The seminary aimed at being 'a school of religion for those especially who will have the care of souls'. A school of religion—the phrase tells us everything, and characterizes what one might well call the style of Saint-Sulpice. As a student of Bérulle and M. de Condren, Jean-Jacques Olier was truly representative of the spirituality of the French school. He was therefore convinced that 'in the Church the priest is like a living Christ'; let him really be that, and all the rest will be added unto him. It was not therefore a question of blending practice with theory, and sending young priests to give missions around the countryside and into the suburbs before being fully trained. M. Olier himself was a very great missioner, but he realized that before going into battle the combatant must prepare himself; so he concentrated his main effort on the interior dispositions. There was to be nothing ostentatious, none of that 'dazzling learning' referred to by Fénelon. The training was to last five years—a very thorough training in moral and dogmatic theology, to prepare the soul of the priest to cope with all the problems of his ministry; and that included some training in pulpit oratory—an indispensable requirement. Above all, it was to be a 'school of holiness'. Such were the concepts under which the priests of France—and countless others in other countries of the world—were to be trained up to the present day.

From this idea sprang another. How did Jean-Jacques Olier discover it? It was all very well to train future priests, but the pupil, in every branch of learning, is no better than his teacher. If we want good seminarists, we must have good teachers. M. Olier therefore decided to detach from his group, and from others which he would form, the best and the most qualified, who would receive special preparation in a real 'interior seminary'; they were to be the masters of the seminaries. This then was the origin of those excellent instructors of the clergy who, even to our day, were to be known as Sulpicians.

The twofold work increased. By 1650 the little house had clearly become inadequate, and another more spacious was built on the same site—a property which occupied the present Place Saint-Sulpice, and which disappeared under the Empire. 'The frail and modest Society of Priests of the Clergy of France' grew under men's very eyes. To the first twelve companions were added seventy-two colleagues: twelve and seventy-two; these are biblical numbers. How were these men to respond to the requests from bishops who wanted Sulpicians to found seminaries in their dioceses? Before 1700 there were seminaries at Angers, Autun, Bourges, Clermont, Limoges, Lyons and Le Puy.

The immense task proved a heavy burden, which is the sting in all success. In 1652 M. Olier had to relinquish his beloved parish of Saint-Sulpice; that wretched place of which he had made a living church, so sturdy that the old edifice had to be replaced by a larger one, of which Anne of Austria laid the foundation-stone. He also left his thirty schools of charity, which he founded in the neighbourhood, and devoted himself henceforth to the sole business of supervising the training of seminarists and masters at Saint-Sulpice. It was on their behalf that he accepted a vast estate at Issy, situated on gently rising ground, where the mills turned at Les Moulineaux. There his work could grow; and here even today stands the great seminary of Paris, where thousands of priests, in the silence of solitude and along the *Allée de Lorette*, have breathed the perfume of that wonderful spirit of prayer which was inherent in the French School.

But M. Olier was worn out with ceaseless work. At forty-eight years of age he was tired and sick; it might be said that he had reached the end of his strength, were it not that his strength of soul remained unimpaired. He saw his work stretching beyond France: his sons, the Sulpicians, were preparing to establish a foundation at Montreal, to sow his spirit among the future clergy of French Canada, when cerebral haemorrhage struck him down. But he could now disappear from the scene (1657); the tree had such good roots that it was bound to thrive.

In 1649 Marie Rousseau made an entry in her diary which suggests that she was animated with a spirit of prophecy: 'The hour will come when, dying on his cross of labour, he will live only in the life of Jesus risen; and in the place to which he retires he will find interior peace; the consummation of his soul with God will be accomplished through the Blessed Sacrament.' Perhaps that was a fairly good description of the spirit of Saint-Sulpice; for these words referred to the little over-dressed priest whom she had met at the Saint-Germain Fair, for whose conversion she had prayed, and whom God had made the master of French seminaries.

7. UNDER THE LORD'S SCEPTRE

The regular clergy certainly did not lag behind the secular. In the past every movement of reform had been initiated by the religious Orders, who had carried the whole Church along with them: Cluniacs, Cistercians, Franciscans and Dominicans. It was they who showed Christians the road at a time when the Council of Trent was still laboriously seeking a way: Ignatius, the crippled Basque, with his

Jesuits; the tender Philip Neri with his Oratory; a little later the sublime Teresa, who gave new life to Carmel; and, well before that time, the humble Matteo de Bascio with his Capuchin friars.

The spring of living water had not dried up. Admittedly it had not yet been able to cleanse those Augean stables which certain sections of the so-called regular life had been for so long. Too many monasteries and convents knew scarcely any rule but that of Liberty Hall. The picture has been painted a hundred times, and there is no need to go over it again. The evidence of two writers will suffice. 'It was', says Father Faure, the reformer of Saint-Vincent-de-Senlis, 'a place where hardly a sign of religion and holiness remained; where games, festivities and dissolute songs constituted the normal relaxation of the religious.' And the Jesuit Polla said of the nuns of La Déserte, at Lyons: 'There remained no practice which suggested a community life, nor any vestige of enclosure. The habit which these ladies wore did not distinguish them from those who lived in the world; the only kind of observance they kept consisted in going into church when they felt like it and singing what pleased them. There was no knowing whether they were nuns or not.' It was not merely in works of fiction that enclosed nuns kept assignations in their convents or that monks went on the loose. Commendatory abbots, and abbesses of ten or fifteen years of age, made great fun of the spiritual life of the monks and nuns whom they were supposed to rule. The misfortunes of war, foreign and civil, added to these disorders. The amazing thing was that they were not more numerous, and that there should have been so many exceptions.

As a matter of fact the reaction against these abuses, so earnestly begun in the previous century, intensified and spread. The extraordinary growth of new foundations is especially noteworthy; they could be counted in their hundreds. In the diocese of Coutances alone six were established in twelve years. 'For twenty or thirty years so many and such a variety of Orders were introduced, that the number exceeded those that had been established during the previous thousand years. Whole streets were almost entirely occupied by new religious houses.' What the 'Parlement' of Rouen said in 1631 was equally true of France as a whole. The great century of saints was a century of monasteries and convents.

In these religious houses a vast and often heroic effort was made to ensure that the rule of God was better observed. Alongside the nuns in silk petticoats, rochets and flounced skirts, who took enclosure so easily and vied with each other in the display of jewellery, if not of lovers, must be placed the countless twenty-year-old abbesses, mostly of noble birth, who in so many houses burned with zeal for reform; who gathered around them all those who were tormented with a secret loathing for that sinful life; who talked counselled, persuaded, commanded even (were they not the daughters of soldiers?) and compelled almost everywhere, despite strong resistance, a return to obedience and to long neglected vows.

There was not a single Order of women which did not in some measure experience this reaction.[1] The Benedictine convents had a whole host of splendid abbesses who did wonderful work: at Montmartre, Marie de Beauvillier, who fitted her daughters for a life of perfection by means of St Ignatius's *Spiritual Exercises*; at Val-de-Grâce, Marguerite d'Arbouze, whose loving gentleness dispersed the furies that assailed her; at the Lyons convent of La Déserte, of which we have seen the deplorable condition, Marguerite de Quibly, as firm as she was good, put everything in order without fuss; elsewhere there were Jacqueline de Blémur, Madeleine de Chaugy, Françoise de Foix and Laurence de Budos. New female branches of the Benedictine Order sprang up: the Calvaire, founded in 1617 by Mother Antoinette d'Orléans, with the strong support of Father Joseph du Tremblay; the Benedictine nuns of the Blessed Sacrament whom Catherine de Bar, Mother Mechtilde, dedicated to the adoration of Our Lord in the Tabernacle (1653). Among the Carmelites there were successors of those good Spanish nuns who, with the help of Pierre de Bérulle, rekindled the flame. They turned their convent in Paris into a great spiritual centre which would one day receive Louise de la Vallière, a tender victim of the Passion, thirsting for mortification more than she had ever done for the flattery of courts. Their convent at Pontoise, where Mme Acarie ended her days, was hardly less famous, and in any case no less admirable. Among the Cistercians there was Louyse de Ballon (1591–1668), a little nun of sixteen, consumed by the fire of Christ, who turned her convent of St Catherine, in Savoy, into a model which many another imitated. Among the Dominicans, Charlotte d'Effiat, sister of the unfortunate Cinq-Mars, brought back her community to the rule of St Dominic from which it had drifted far. Many were the shining figures who illuminated this page of history; any attempt to list them in a roll of honour would involve unjust omissions. But Jacqueline Arnauld, 'Mother Angélique', must be mentioned. Thanks to her, Port-Royal, before it began to follow devious paths, was for countless souls a lighthouse, at which the 'Solitaires' assembled, and on which Pascal gazed with emotion.

The men were not behindhand, either in zeal or in courage. Eminent figures helped on the work of reform. One of these was Cardinal

---

[1] And, of course, there were some which obviously had no need of reorganization. Such was the *Visitation*, the great foundation (1610) of St Francis de Sales and St Jeanne de Chantal. After the death of the founders the community continued to be an example of virtues. Abandoning external activity, it persevered in that atmosphere of prayer upon which it had been grounded.

Richelieu, commendatory abbot of several monasteries; in order to advance the cause he set up a council composed of a Carthusian, a Cistercian of the Feuillant branch, a Benedictine, a Jesuit, a Franciscan of the Friars Minor and a Dominican. The Pope himself, Gregory XV, made the saintly Cardinal François de la Rochefoucauld, Bishop of Clermont and later of Senlis, his deputy. But in any case the movement towards reform did not wait for such guidance. It began at Pont-à-Mousson in Lorraine at the dawn of the century, when Canon Pierre Fourier joined forces with the Premonstratensian Servais de Laruelle and the Benedictine Didier de la Cour; the three friends resolved that each would lead his own Order back to its rule. They kept their word: in the first twenty years of the century the effort they made was powerful enough to prolong and widen its effects.

The movement was like a combined offensive. At St Vincent-at-Senlis, whose deplorable condition we have described, Father Charles Faure went into action; he dismissed those of his Canons of St Augustine who had obviously retained nothing of the saint whose name they bore but the questionable example of his youth. He succeeded so well that when François de la Rochefoucauld was appointed Abbot of Sainte-Geneviève he sent for a few religious from Senlis, set over them his own refractory monks and turned his house into a sanctuary on that Parisian mount, where the Library of Sainte-Geneviève and the neighbouring church (the lay Panthéon of the future) preserve the memory of his Order. Meanwhile Pierre Fourier, a forerunner of the Curé d'Ars, fulfilled his duties as parish priest of Mattaincourt in Lorraine, and at the same time acted in the capacity of 'visitor' of the Augustinians whom he reorganized, though not without difficulty. Far away, at Chancelade in Périgord, Alain de Solminihac, the future Bishop of Rodez, was doing likewise. In 1634 the fusion of these combined offensives ended in victory: the French Congregation of Canons Regular was created.

Servais de Laruelle on his part worked hard among the white-robed Canons Regular who followed—or failed to follow—the rule of St Norbert. The congregation observed the ancient and austere rule of Prémontré; it gained ground in Lorraine, Normandy, and in Paris, where the Carrefour de la Croix Rouge would keep alive the memory of the monastery which it established there. Around 1660 forty of its houses were reformed; even the Common Observance modified its statutes under the influence of Drosios, abbot of Pare.

The Benedictines also set to with a will, and it must be admitted that their need for reform was great. Of the monks of Saint-Denis Henri IV once joked: 'Our souls will spend a long time in purgatory if we wait for these people to pull us out.' As for the intellectual glory which had belonged to their Order, the 'Black Monks' no longer bothered about such things. The reform began at the abbey of Saint-Vanne in Lorraine, under Dom Didier de la Cour, and was soon followed by Dom Claude François at Moyenmoutier. The Vannist monks began to teach; their example was followed at Saint-Pierre de Jumièges; and in Paris Dom Laurent Bénard, prior of the Collège de Cluny, asked for their services. A new Benedictine congregation was created, and approved by the Pope in 1621; it took the name of St Maur, a disciple of St Benedict, and enforced a rigid reorganization under the direction of Dom Grégoire Tarisse. Saint-Germain-des-Prés in Paris became the headquarters of the new régime. In 1628 the Benedictines of Brittany joined the movement, and in 1630, those of the congregation of Chezal-Benoit. There was one distressing exception: the venerable abbey of Cluny hung back; mainly because it was in the hands of the commendatory Louis de Lorraine, Cardinal de Guise (by Royal Warrant), who was married to Charlotte des Essarts, former mistress of Henry IV; secondly, because its resistance was aggravated by the somewhat ruthless attempts to bring about reform. Richelieu certainly tried to bring about its participation by force; but after his death Rome allowed herself to be persuaded to end the effort, a fact which could only be prejudicial to Cluny; for Saint-Maur was to go on expanding, recovering eventually the great tradition of the Black Monks of former times—their learning, their real thirst for the works of the spirit, and their abundance of wisdom. Mabillon was one of their most distinguished members, and Dom Laurent Bénard bequeathed to them this splendid maxim: 'It is impossible for a truly learned man not to be also a great-hearted man.'

The White Benedictines, the sons of St Bernard, were in a very similar position. About 1575, at the monastery of Les Feuillants, in Languedoc, Jean de la Barrière introduced a reform. It was much too strict. Abstinence from wine, meat, bed and warmth was all well and good—but to use human skulls as cups, as some of them did! That kind of fanaticism fascinated the onlookers, including Henri III, who wanted to have a few Feuillants at the Louvre Palace. But the White Monks were somewhat discredited for the part they had played in the League, and bickering developed amongst them. Cardinal de la Rochefoucauld intervened, and in 1624 Clairvaux became the centre of a Congregation of the Strict Observance under Dom Largentier. Would Cîteaux join them? The monastery was occupied by lukewarm religious, and an amusing incident is recorded. These simpletons elected Richelieu himself as their Abbot-General, only to find that they had given themselves a king. They thought he was too far away and too busy to interfere; but the terrible cardinal took his role seriously, and imposed the reform of the strict observance, which by 1661 included about sixty monasteries.

In the other camp, that of the 'mitigated', there was still much to be done. But already a young and worldly commendatory abbot, who seemed ill-prepared for this momentous undertaking, had received from God the impulse which set him upon a new way of life. In the spring of 1657 the Duchesse de Montbazon died, and her lover meditated bitterly on human destiny. He was a godson of Richelieu, and his name was Armand Jean de Rancé.

The movement was thus general. It included all the mendicant Orders. First there were the Carmelites—Great Carmelites who were robed in white, and the Little Carmelites who went discalced and wore a rough brown habit. Louis Jacot, Chérubin de Saint-Joseph and Maur de l'Enfant-Jésus were outstanding among them. The Dominicans closed their Thomist ranks to fight Jansenism and Protestantism. All branches of the Franciscan Order were prominent in the work of reform, especially the Recollects, whose houses numbered more than two hundred by the end of the seventeenth century. The Capuchins were even more enthusiastic. Their one-time glorious habit had been somewhat compromised in the days of the Fronde; but it regained all its prestige when Father Benoît de Canfeld disembarked from England to speak so sweetly of God in the Hôtel Acarie, when Father Ange de Joyeuse, a former Marshal of France, became a much valued preacher and a very popular saint, and when Father Joseph du Tremblay—the Grey Eminence—a strong and noble soul, preached sermon after sermon and mission after mission.

One could go on indefinitely producing evidence of this prodigious revitalization among the regulars. The more recent institutes, founded in the preceding century with the specific object of working for reform, remained vigorous. The Jesuits who had been expelled from France after Chatel's attempt on the life of Henri III, won back in 1603 the legal right to exist, of which they were never officially deprived, and Father Cotton, the Society's hostage with the king, became his principal adviser. It was said that Henri IV had 'cotton in his ears'. The number of Jesuit colleges increased; Descartes regarded that of La Flèche as the most famous educational establishment in Europe. The Society numbered sixteen thousand members, spread over ten provinces, of which five were in France; and it was constantly growing. It was a real power in the land, as was clear from the wrath of its enemies. The Oratory was less numerous, but prospered none the less. The Theatines, the Barnabites and the Camillians also grew in great numbers. But that did not hinder the growth of quite new institutions such as the Lazarists, the Eudists, the Sulpicians and others. It was a remarkable sign of the times.

D

8. The Corn Springs Up: (i) The Missions

If the religious Orders were mending their ways and increasing everywhere, if the clergy were striving to become better, was it not in order that the mass of Christians might be more thoroughly imbued with the teaching of the Gospel? The anguish of souls threatened with destruction threw into the apostolate St Vincent de Paul, St John Eudes, Jean-Jacques Olier and many others—religious, priests and bishops. The saints were conscious of a dramatic situation: here was a world in which religion seemed doomed. 'Can faith be sincere if it does nothing?' They did something.

'France, the land of the Mission' is a term which has become popular in our time; it is just as true when applied to the early seventeenth century, and not only in regard to France. Society, from top to bottom, had to be rechristianized. It is true that customs, traditions, even the practice of religion, still survived—and certainly much more so than in the paganized masses of our day—but moral and spiritual life was in a sorry state of degradation. Violence, whether among duellists in doublets or ravaging bandits on the highways, together with debauchery, whether in the court or in the villages, was widespread in the land. Poisoning was not the monopoly of Mme de Brinvilliers. Sorcerers and witches prospered in the countryside; black magic was practised in the towns.

It was clear that more active measures were necessary if the Gospel grain was to be resown. First came the missions. The idea was born quite spontaneously on the morrow of the Council of Trent, in that return to first principles which marked the era of revival. It was imperative to do what Our Lord had commanded, what indeed the Apostles and the early Christians had done so well—to go and speak of Christ to the masses. This work was undertaken by St Philip Neri at Rome, by St Charles Borromeo at Milan and by St Peter Canisius in Germany. And with what success! The idea began to spread. The very word 'mission' was popularized by Monsieur Vincent. Catholic France made it her principal concern. And here again a comparison with modern times is inevitable: the Church in France elected to be 'in a state of mission'.

The method was simple; past experience had already determined it in outline. From the end of the sixteenth century priests and religious who wished to conduct missions applied first to the bishop, unless he himself had already inspired them. A deanery was assigned to them and they would visit all the parishes within it one after another, remaining two or three weeks in each, preaching, catechizing, reminding the people of the great truths of their faith, moving hearts and souls, and finally hearing confessions. When this work was over the bishop himself often came to the main town of the deanery to administer the Sacrament of Confirmation to those who had not yet received it, and to preside at the General Communion of the faithful. This would then be repeated in another deanery, or perhaps, if the number of available missioners allowed, several missions would be conducted at the same time. A certain amount of opposition was occasionally met with, some of it very unpleasant. There were times, for example, when the local clergy were afraid that these importunate visitors had an eye on their livings. But in a great number of cases the bulk of the faithful was sympathetic and welcomed the missioners. Vast areas were thus covered—whole provinces in fact. There were even what might be called today specialized missions, addressed to a particular section of the community, e.g. the galley slaves, soldiers under arms, or the royal court itself, all of whom needed missions as much as everybody else. The labour involved was prodigious, but the excellence of the work done was amazing.

All the great Catholic personages of the period, or almost all, were missioners in one way or another. Monsieur Vincent made the idea, the name and the method so popular that he seems almost to have monopolized its endeavours and its success; and it is true that he and his sons, the Priests of the Mission—for such was the real name of the Lazarists —worked wonders, and brought back life to many areas. John Eudes in his native Normandy was no less successful. And it must not be forgotten that M. Olier himself was a splendid missioner long before he founded Saint-Sulpice or dreamed of training seminary teachers. We are told that he roused such enthusiasm in Auvergne that whole villages went without food and drink from dawn to dusk in order to hear him preach and make their confessions to him.

Many bishops, too, played a part in this amazing rivalry. Not one whose mind was bent on ecclesiastical reform neglected this method of working. There were some who even lent a hand by going personally into the parishes to preach and hear confessions; Jean-Baptiste Gault, Alain de Solminihac and Authier de Sisgaud were among them. Many, like Danès at Toulon, Eléonor d'Estampes at Rheims and Sedan, Dominique Séguier at Meaux, established permanent missions in their dioceses. Others, following the example of St Charles Borromeo, set up communities of diocesan missioners. One such was founded by Jean de la Cropte de Chanterac at Périgueux; another was the Hall of Our Lord Jesus Christ, established by Planat at Clermont; and a third that of Raymond Bonal at Rouergue. Some of these local congregations overflowed the diocesan boundaries, e.g. the Missionary Priests of the Blessed Sacrament, founded by Bishop Authier de Sisgaud at Aix-en-Provence in 1632.

The impulse came from all quarters, even from very high places. In 1638 Richelieu himself contemplated a systematic plan for the re-evangelizing of France. Every year a large number of missions were to be preached in various districts, according to a prearranged scheme; the Jesuits alone were to undertake fifty a year. Louis XIII gave large sums of money to finance the missions, and Anne of Austria followed his example. The Company of the Blessed Sacrament was behind many of these enterprises, though secretly, as was its way. Even Mazarin earned some small indulgence from Heaven by assisting the missions!

Who exactly were the missioners themselves? First and foremost Lazarists, Eudists and all who were canonically dedicated to such work. But there are very many others who must not be forgotten. Secular priests buckled to: Michel le Nobletz was one, J.-B. Gault was another before his elevation to the episcopate. The Oratorians who chose this form of apostolate as well as that of teaching, met with wonderful success; Father Condren himself conducted missions, and so did Father Senault, the future panegyrist of Louis XIII. Picardy will long treasure the memory of Father Amelote and twenty-five other sons of Bérulle who worked so hard round about 1639. But the model, the prince, of the Oratorian missions was Father Lejeune (1592–1672), who for forty years stirred vast audiences from Rome to Metz, from Toulouse to Orange, in words that were at once passionate and simple, though occasionally, it must be admitted, somewhat trivial. Blindness struck him when he was still quite young. The Jesuits counted among their number two famous personalities: St François Régis and Father Maunoir, men so great that one is inclined to overlook the rest; but Father de Lingendes and Father de la Colombière should certainly not be passed over. As for the Capuchins, the more one studies this period of revival, the more considerable becomes their role. In Dauphiné the memory of Father Marcellin survives to this day; at Montmélian in Savoy, and in the district of Chablais, Father Chérubin did magnificent work; while at Gap people still speak of the ten Fathers who were preaching a mission when a plague broke out, and who devoted themselves so whole-heartedly to their flock that seven of them perished in the epidemic. Capuchins were also at work in Languedoc and the Cévennes, which was Protestant territory. Nor must we forget that Father Joseph made frequent and prolonged visits to western France not only for the purpose of winning back La Rochelle from the people of the so-called reformed religion, but also (and with even greater determination) to attack the Protestants by word and example. He was outstandingly successful.

Astonishing personalities were plentiful in this varied throng of evangelists. We may omit the saintly Lorrainer, Pierre Fourier, since Lorraine was not yet French. But there was Pierre de Kériolet, a missioner who had once been a public sinner; many were the villages of Brittany through which he carried the dust of his rags and the vehement ring of his sermons. There was Barthélemy Amilia, Vicar-General of Pamiers, who preached in dialect and whose hymns are still sung. Finally there was Andéol de Lodève who, in Dauphiné, Bresse, Velay and Vivarais, never failed to move his audience to tears, so touchingly did he speak to them of the misery of sinful souls and of the grief it caused Our Lord.

But of all the personages who deserve our notice, three are pre-eminent. In Brittany there was Michel le Nobletz (1577–1652)—Dom Michel, as he was called. He was one of the originators of the Mission, without doubt the most prominent predecessor of Monsieur Vincent; a simple priest who laboured in his beloved Brittany for forty years, speaking Breton to his listeners, making them sing hymns in their own language, not only in the church, but in the open air and along the roads. He conceived the idea of showing them the great truths of religion in the form of painted panels, strongly symbolical. There are some on the Our Father, on the principal scenes of the Gospel, on Christ's parables, on Our Lady—and even some terrifying panels on the seven deadly sins. He set up an organization of Lady Catechists, which met with such success in its teaching that the work long out-lived him.

The best and the most important of his disciples was Father Maunoir (1615–83), a young Jesuit, his true spiritual son. He succeeded in gathering around him three hundred co-operators, splendid material, of whom Father Rigoleuc, a leading authority on French mysticism, was one. With the assistance of these, and of two saintly women named Amice Picard and Catherine Daniélou, he took over from his master and laboured throughout Brittany. The method he preferred was the Procession of the Passion, which wrung the souls of the people. A priest took the part of Christ, and the whole story of Our Lord was demonstrated to the crowds; carried out by living people, up to and above all including the scenes of Maundy Thursday and Good Friday. When at the end the crowd gathered around the Blessed Sacrament, they listened to the sermon, and tears gushed forth, with cries and protestations of repentance. Closed retreats, organized in the main by Father Huby, sustained this fervour in the most ardent souls. Catholic Brittany owes an enormous debt to le Nobletz and to Father Maunoir.

The third was preaching far away, in the Cévennes and Vivarais—another Jesuit, a tender and sublime figure: St François Régis (1597–1640). While quite young he decided to live only for the poor, 'the most neglected part of the flock of Christ'. For all he was worth he wandered barefooted over that rugged country through wind and snow, or under the relentless August sun, from cottage to cottage, to the most remote and isolated spots in the high mountains, eating little more than the apples which his mother thrust into his pocket and giving to everybody the shining alms of his smile. At Viviers he was set upon; at the bishop's palace he was attacked by some nobles who took him to be a revolutionary—already! He then went to Puy where the bishop, Just de Serres, officially entrusted him with the mission in his diocese. His sermons drew crowds; there were often four or five thousand listening to him preach, and among them many Huguenots. His eloquence, at once so warm and striking, was his best medium, combined with the confessional where, as the curé of Ars was to do later, he remained shut up hour after hour. He was hardly forty-three when he died, completely worn out by his continual self-sacrifice. He took to the grave the secrets of the souls he had brought back to grace; in the last four months of his life alone they numbered ten thousand.

And what was the final result of these labours? Unqualified success, though it is always possible that contemporary writers may have exaggerated the figures. They declare, for instance, that St John Eudes on several occasions converted twenty or thirty thousand Normans on a single occasion; that Monsieur Vincent time and again drew entire villages to the confessional. The Capuchins, too, claim to have had eighteen thousand missioners; and Father Maunoir states in his diary that 'fifty thousand souls learned the Christian doctrine, and five thousand public sinners returned to God in a year'. Perhaps all this should not be taken too literally; but it is certain that this immense labour bore fruit, that the grain of Christianity sprouted afresh, and that there had been a change, as much in religious practice as in morals. Sociological studies carried out in our day have demonstrated that the areas which are still Christian in twentieth-century France are precisely those in which the missioners worked hardest three hundred years ago, and that the areas into which they did not penetrate, or hardly at all, are those unfortunately notorious areas which Canon Boulard has marked in red on his famous map indicating the frontiers of religious practice in present-day France. No homage more definite than that could be paid to the missions of the seventeenth century and to the admirable men who led them so effectively.[1]

9. THE CORN SPRINGS UP: (ii) CHARITY

This springtime of souls in the first half of the seventeenth century witnessed a renewal of faith. But what is faith without works? It is a

[1] The importance accorded to the Mission by seventeenth-century Catholics explains to some extent why they were less interested in the foundation of seminaries; they regarded the seminaries as supplementary to the missions. At Coutances the street leading to the old seminary is still called Rue de la Mission.

dead faith, as St James clearly says in his Epistle (ii. 26). The intense spiritual life of the time was accompanied quite naturally by countless works of charity; or, better still, since there is a real bond between charity and faith, both psychologically and theologically, the mighty current of generosity which flowed through society at that time tended to ennoble souls and to make the whole spiritual life more fervent. Monsieur Vincent confessed that he felt much more joy in the good that he saw done by others than in the good he was able to do himself. Those were the reactions not merely of a humble heart, but of a truly apostolic soul. The corn sprouted also in the form of charity.

Monsieur Vincent! His image forces itself upon the memory at the very moment we utter the word *Charity*. He was charity personified; its witness, its indefatigable instigator. Nothing that he did can be understood outside the vista of that most fundamental of the virtues. His Lazarists were just as much the agents of charity as they were missioners; his generous Ladies of Charity, his Sisters and his friends —they all served the cause of charity, whose name they carried so proudly.[1] As we look at the lives of these saintly figures we recall the words of Lacordaire: 'A Sister of Charity is a perfect demonstration of Christianity.' In that field Monsieur Vincent was not alone, though he may have been the first and the most distinguished. Many others demonstrated this charity in a different way. It must even be admitted that it is hard to steer a course amid the charitable ventures of that period; they are too numerous to list.

Humanity was passing through a time of suffering. Wars, both foreign and civil, had for so long brought their toll of calamities, famine and epidemics. Distress was widespread; and not only in the devastated provinces which touched Monsieur Vincent's heart, but in the large towns as well, where the poor dwelt in the misery of the slums and the sick in their tumbledown hospitals. Nor were all beggars malingerers. The task was formidable indeed, calling as it did for a simultaneous attack from every quarter upon the fortress of misery.

As for hospitals and asylums, the Council of Trent had earnestly drawn attention to the ancient traditions, and insisted upon bishops exercising 'a paternal care for the poor and all other unfortunate people'. The governors of hospitals and refuges were obliged to carry out the duties of their trust. Kings and princes too had similar obligations, and they responded to them. In 1606 Henri IV created the Chamber of Christian Charity, presided over by the Chief Almoner. Under his instructions all hospitals, Hôtels Dieu and other 'places of pity' were subject to inspection and administrative control. The

[1] See Chapter I.

foundation-stone of the Saint-Louis Hospital was laid, and the first military hospitals came into being. Under Louis XIII the number of medical establishments and poorhouses grew apace—La Pitié in 1612, the Convalescent Hospital in 1621; the hospice of Our Lady of Mercy, or the 'Cent Filles', which Chancellor Séguier established for orphan girls; in 1634 a hospice for the incurables—today called the Laënnec—financed by Marguerite Rouillé and Cardinal de la Rochefoucauld. Under Anne of Austria the hospice of the Holy Name of Jesus was instituted in 1657 by Monsieur Vincent; then the House of Foundlings and the General Institution were set up at the Salpêtrière to cater for cases of sickness, misery and mendicancy. Most of the large towns, in France at any rate, took up the movement, and created Hôpitaux de la Charité—Lyons in 1614, Rheims in 1632, Langres in 1638, Aix and Marseilles in 1640 and Dijon in 1643. Almost everywhere the Church took the initiative—often through the bishops—and the religious Orders both of men and of women assumed the responsibility of running them.

Some became famous. Since the publication of the Brief of Pope Paul V in 1617, the Brothers of St John of God added to their three traditional religious vows that of caring for the sick. Their founder, the heroic little Portuguese John Ciudad, taught them and proclaimed unceasingly that to devote oneself to others is to do good to oneself. *Fate bene Fratelli* was the name by which they were known. In France they had no less than twenty-four hospitals, of which the one in Paris was called La Charité—recently destroyed and so inadequately replaced; their memory is still preserved in the name of a street, Rue des Saints-Pères. The Camillians, whom St Camillus de Lellis (1550–1614) had just founded at Chieti—Clerks Regular ministering to the sick—were soon well known by their form of dress, a large red cross on a black habit. In France alone twenty hospitals were run by these 'Crucifères', of whom 220 died in the service of the sick in less than thirty years. The women did not lag behind. In 1624 the Venerable Françoise de la Croix founded her Soeurs Hospitalières de la Charité Notre Dame for the care of sick women and young girls in the hospital she had established on the Place Royale—now called the Place des Vosges. She received such a flood of vocations that within a few years she was able to open a second house in Paris, in the Rue de la Roquette, followed by others in Bourg, Limoux, Patay, Saint-Étienne, etc. And scarcely had the community of the Sisters of Charity been born of the pious determination of Louise de Marillac and the ever creative generosity of Monsieur Vincent, when they discovered their vocation as nurses, and brought their firm gentleness and boundless self-sacrifice into countless homes.

All these undertakings are famous; but many others deserve

remembrance. One might say that during that blissful period one had only to strike the ground, and a spring would gush forth. At Limoges, for instance, Martial de Maledent, a convert, inspired Pierre Mercier with the fire of charity; together they discussed their plans with their friend de Saige, and the result was the founding of the *Clairettes* of the Mother of Calvary and Marcelle Germain's Sisters of Providence. At Saint-Brieuc and Ploërmel, Gillette de la Pommeraye, Laurence du Breuil and Anne de Canton—three splendid Breton names—went to Father Ange le Proust, Prior to the Canons of St Augustine at Lamballe, to tell him of their desire to do good works; and in 1659 the Augustines de Saint-Thomas de Villeneuve were founded. Again, on the initiative of Marie de Petiot and Hélène Mercier, the Sisters of St Alexis were formed (St Alexis was the saint who lived under a staircase). Some of the old Orders which appeared to be dormant were revived: the Augustinian nursing sisters at Amiens, then at Beauvais, thanks to Bishop Potier de Gesvres; at Vierzon, M. Bouray undertook a similar task, and at Amboise, Catherine de Jésus. The Hôtel Dieu in Paris had its own saintly figure, Geneviève Bouquet, who did not found an Order but introduced a new manner of life which endured long after her death. Wherever physical suffering was to be found, there stood forth men and women imbued with generosity, whose zeal often carried them to the point of heroism. It was an infectious zeal, which ordinary layfolk, even men of letters, also shared; for in 1650 the dramatist Rotrou died of the purple fever while tending the sick.

But there was also the call of extreme poverty and misery. Christ's charity answered that call too. The time was coming when a voice would be heard crying aloud from the pulpit: 'God's Church is indeed the city of the poor.' True Christians already knew as much. Monsieur Vincent determined to succour all the destitute, and for that purpose he instituted the Sisters of Charity. Faced with the problem of beggary, he did not believe that its solution was a state responsibility, to be handled by way of police action and the confinement of those unfortunate creatures in what were virtually houses of forced labour. His method was persuasion and love. It was also the method of the Sisters known as Religieuses Hospitalières du Saint-Esprit, who ran a Hospice of Charity at Dijon; this was not merely a reception centre but a real house of rehabilitation for the workless poor. Love and persuasion were also the method of the Jesuits who were dedicated to similar tasks. Father Chaurand of Avignon established 126 charitable houses in Provence; Father Dunod was sent by the administrator of Caen to fight poverty throughout Normandy; and there was, of course, the beloved Father St François Régis, who, in addition to his apostolic work, set up vast charitable organizations resembling soup kitchens

*D

which provided food for the hungry, and an organization for lace-making, which found work for street-walkers. As yet there was no organized Catholic Aid or Public Assistance or Social Security. But these combined undertakings fulfilled the same purposes; and because they were not run by the state a genuine surge of love could be felt sweeping through the whole Church.

It is hardly necessary to cite more names or refer to other undertakings; they are too many and too varied. Rotrou was not the only layman who stood out as an exemplary figure. There were true saints in the world, such as M. de Renty, of whom we shall speak again, and many of his friends in the Company of the Blessed Sacrament. M. de Bernières-Louvigny actually formulated the doctrine of Christian Almsgiving. The Gentlemen of Port-Royal were no less charitable in disposition; and Blaise Pascal, when he felt the approach of death, took in a destitute person to live with him. All Paris admired Claude Bernard, the poor priest whom Cardinal Richelieu shielded, despite his innumerable eccentricities, and at whose funeral the Minister was just one of a vast crowd. There was hardly any distress or sorrow which failed to find succour in some charitable work. Monsieur Vincent was not the only one who looked after prisoners, convicts and galley slaves. Girls who had fallen into sin roused the most sincere kindliness: it was for them that the Sisters of the Good Shepherd and the Madelonettes were founded; St François Régis and the Company of the Blessed Sacrament were also concerned with them. There existed an undertaking which looked after the marriage of girls without dowry, and one under the patronage of St Martha to safeguard the morals of servants; while the abbé de Sousi welcomed in Paris the little chimney-sweeps from Savoy. There are certainly too many to mention within the compass of a short chapter; but they form an amazing picture.

10. THE CORN SPRINGS UP: (iii) EDUCATION

Missions and charitable enterprises were two powerful means of cultivating the Christian soil and raising new harvests from it. But there was still a third—education. St Ignatius of Loyala had made the profound observation that 'the training of students is one of the best means of forming true Christians'; and the Council of Trent in its fifth session made it obligatory for bishops and priests to take the greatest care over education. The result was a remarkable expansion in teaching [1] immediately after the closure of the council, when the Jesuits, Somaschi, Theatines and Ursulines took up the work. Blessed César de Bus founded his Doctrinarians, or Priests of Christian Doctrine, and St

[1] See *The Catholic Reformation*, p. 375, on this renaissance of Christian education.

Joseph Calasanz (who died in 1648) his Piarists or Clerks Regular of the Pious Schools, which made rapid progress in Aragon, and then throughout the Spanish world. This movement, however, gradually slowed down. The wars ruined many schools; acts of generosity were dried up by the high cost of living, and the expulsion of the Jesuits dealt a heavy blow to higher education in France. But at the beginning of the seventeenth century everything changed. The Church became once more magnificently true to her vocation as teacher, and this enabled her to train the intellect, and through it the conscience.

It must be emphasized that all the outstanding personalities of the period were as much concerned with this problem of education as they were with the Mission and works of charity. 'I believe', M. Bourdoise declared to M. Olier, 'that a priest who wishes to possess the science of the saints should become a school teacher; that is the road to canonization.' He insisted that 'the most urgent need is the instruction of children'. Such also was the view of Monsieur Vincent, who dispatched his Ladies of Charity in search of competent school mistresses, and asked his beloved Mlle Le Gras to open schools for little girls, which the Sisters of Charity did wherever they went. St Peter Fourier too was haunted by the nightmare of illiteracy, until his friend Alix Le Clerc set his mind at rest by founding the Sisters of Notre Dame. As for the Company of the Blessed Sacrament, here again it supported every attempt which aimed at remoulding Christian education: it gave its backing to Alexandre Colas de Portmorand, a priest of Orleans, who established a model school at Vaugirard; it assisted M. Olier to found a school at Saint-Sulpice, and also the Minim Fathers of Chaillot, who engaged in similar work.

Achievements in the sphere of education increased and multiplied, as they had done in the case of the missions and charitable institutions. King Henri IV interested himself in the reorganization of education; and Louis XIII, Richelieu and Anne of Austria followed his example. Scarcely had the Jesuits been authorized to return to France when they established colleges everywhere: forty in seven years. The Oratorians, whose labours for the training of youth received particular recognition from Gregory XV in 1623, increased the number of their houses: twenty-three in twenty-two years. There were also the Hermits of St Augustine and their Latin Schools, the Canons of the Holy Sepulchre at La Croix, the Hieronymites at Firminy and the Dominicans in about fifteen towns. As soon as the Benedictine monks and nuns were reformed, they became teachers; Faremoutier trained many society girls. There was a revival too among the Doctrinarians of Blessed César de Bus and the Piarists of St Joseph Calasanz. The teaching of young girls was undertaken by the nuns of the Order of the Visitation, the Maurist Sisters, the Daughters of the Cross of Mme de Villeneuve, and both branches of the Sisters of the Congregation of Notre Dame—those founded by Alix Le Clerc in Lorraine (often called Dames Augustines because they were Canonesses of St Augustine), and those whom St Jeanne de Lestonnac had established in Bordeaux. Undoubtedly the most prominent were the Ursulines, founded by Angela Merici in the preceding century, who owed their definitive character to the efforts of Charles Borromeo. Mme Françoise de Bermont established a convent of Ursulines in Paris, and they became immensely popular; altogether they had 275 houses in 1677. In harmony with the spirit of their constitutions they were sound teachers and living examples of holiness, in whom their pupils 'should be able to see themselves reflected'.

All this pious emulation bore fruit. During the first sixty years of the seventeenth century one gets the impression of huge progress in education. In France alone the schools which were either established or re-established during that period, and the generous endowments made to provide free education for children of the poor, could be counted in their thousands. At Angers, for example, in 1658, the bishop instructed all parish priests to set up a school wherever one was not already in existence; but that is only one instance among many. Naturally things did not always turn out for the best, and it was often extremely difficult to find really competent teachers—a problem which was tackled a little later by Charles Démia, Father Barré, Nicolas Roland and above all by St Jean-Baptiste de la Salle. But there is no doubt that worthwhile results had already been achieved.

What was the ideal behind primary education at that time? In 1654 a remarkable book was published by Pierre Targa at Paris under the title *L'École paroissiale* (The Parish School). This work summed up the experience of a priest who had been teaching in a school for eighteen years, and gave excellent advice. The anonymous author wrote some splendid pages on the way to teach children spelling, arithmetic and catechism, as well as about the spirit which should animate the teacher if he really wished to be true to his vocation. Teachers of today, both male and female, could still learn something from it. There is, of course, nothing to suggest that all the pedagogues of that period were so perfect, but it was nevertheless a splendid thing that such an ideal should be set before them.

In the realm of secondary education the Jesuits were the most prominent teachers. The *Ratio studiorum* of 1599 had laid down the precise methods they were to apply to the 27,000 young persons under training in France, of whom 13,000 were in Paris. Their most famous establishment in the capital was the Collège de Clermont, which Louis XIV in 1682 allowed them to call Louis-le-Grand; it had no fewer than 2,000 students, of whom 400 were boarders. Their college at Rennes had even more—2,800. They laid great stress on the type of culture that we term classical: that is to say, the study of Greek and Latin, especially the latter, which students in the upper forms were expected to speak and write fluently. It was only gradually that they leaned towards new techniques, in particular towards the teaching of the sciences; and Descartes, who was one of their students, reproached them with not having adapted Aristotle to the circumstances of modern science. All who were educated at their colleges agreed in regarding them as unrivalled teachers, strict disciplinarians, sometimes extremely so—the 'Father Flogger' was no mere myth!—but they produced real men. Among those who have paid homage to the Jesuit Fathers are Corneille, Descartes, Molière, Bossuet, Fléchier, Lamoignon, Condé and Luxembourg; all these great figures of the reign of Louis XIV came from Jesuit colleges.

But the Oratory produced men to rival those of the Society of Jesus, and their names are inscribed on its roll of honour: Colbert, Tourville and Villars. The college founded at Juilly in 1638 was the congregation's model. 'At the Oratory', said Bossuet, 'one obeys without being constrained; one rules without giving orders; and respect is maintained without the help of fear.' Teaching was therefore more liberal; more 'modern' perhaps in the sense that the study of the sciences—as far as trigonometry and integral calculus—were now added to the study of the ancient humanities. Father de Condren's Latin Grammar offered students a new approach, which they welcomed: it contained explanations in French. History had the distinction of a special Chair, and the students became acquainted with such other accomplishments as drawing, music, dancing and equitation.

As for the Little Schools of Port-Royal, they were much more strict than the Jesuit colleges; students were forbidden to address each other familiarly; they were obliged to draw each other's attention to faults, and were forbidden to see or to take part in plays. There was plenty of Greek and Latin and large doses of religion; yet there was one promising innovation which was destined to place these gentlemen in the front rank of modern teachers: the French language was considered as a distinct subject, and special times were set aside for lessons. It was here that Racine received his education.

For girls there was less variety in procedure. Most of the teaching communities were run on the same lines as those of the Ursulines, whose Rule, which ran to no less than 274 pages, constitutes a most remarkable pedagogic treatise. The primary aim was to give the students a moral and spiritual upbringing, developing their conscience rather than the brain. This too was Molière's ideal: 'To train the minds of children in sound morals . . . ' There was a great deal of spiritual reading and many religious ceremonies. The Ursulines were well versed in the works of Francis de Sales and Bérulle; the Pure Love of Christ was the basis of their teaching. With them discipline was strict; and they did not spare the rod in maintaining it. They held in high esteem practical training in such things as needlework and cookery; but Greek and Latin were also taught, and even a little philosophy. Nor let it ever be said that those good Sisters were not modern: few know that it was the Ursulines who introduced the use of the fork in school refectories.

There is therefore no doubt that valuable efforts were being made everywhere and at every level. It was natural that all sorts of difficulties should be encountered, and it even happened that this pious zeal was blended with a measure of embittered rivalry. The Jesuits of course were the most envied, so much so that a certain professor of Paris University systematically opposed conferment of the degree of Master of Arts even upon their best students—a mere nothing when we read that the rector of the Jesuit college at Liège was stabbed during a riot fomented by their rivals! The old 'master writers', who for centuries had had the legal right to teach calligraphy, were enraged to see such a flood of new teachers; relations were sometimes strained even between parish schools and charity schools. There were a few bishops who showed themselves openly hostile to the establishment in their dioceses of scholastic institutions run by communities outside their jurisdiction; there were even times when the government had to intervene. These, however, were minor obstacles which in no way interrupted an impressive forward movement. In fact, progress was in one sense too rapid; for efficient teachers were lacking, and from about 1660 there began a slowing down which was not checked until the teacher problem had been solved. It was none the less true that this pedagogic revival would do much to form that profoundly Christian French society of the reign of Louis XIV, and to lay the foundations of its subsequent greatness.

11. Early Endeavours of Catholic Action: the Company of the Blessed Sacrament

Priests and religious did not stand alone in this extensive effort to restore vigour and a sense of direction to the Catholic faith. And this again brings out one of the characteristic features of the period. We are not confronted with an entirely ecclesiastical movement: there were innumerable pious lay folk of both sexes who were striving towards the same end. The apostolate, works of charity and education aroused heroism among people who were unconnected with the clergy, secular or regular. Indeed there is reason to suspect that laymen took the initiative in some of these enterprises, employing churchmen as their agents.

It is not an exaggeration to say that this action on the part of laymen suggests the first remote attempts at what we call today Catholic Action. These attempts were numerous, varied and still to a large extent uninvestigated. To write their history it would be necessary to examine the influence exercised at that time by the sodalities of Our Lady which the Jesuits encouraged in their colleges, as well as the part played by the many new confraternities of Our Lady, the Blessed Sacrament, the Sacred Heart, and the Third Orders of St Francis, St Dominic and Carmel, all of which were seething with new life. One would have to ascertain whether the confraternities of penitents, black or white, grey or blue, confined their activities to hooded processions through the streets. It would also be necessary to inquire to what extent certain convents expanded—Port-Royal at Paris among others —which seemed to have been founded for the express purpose of serving as centres for seculars anxious to lead a Christian life.

A little more is known of the 'working man's apostolate'; in fact, we know a good deal about a certain Henry Buch (1600–66), a humble shoemaker who came from Luxembourg and was called 'Henry the Good'. While he worked hard at his trade, his one concern was the well-being of the members of his guild—to wean them from the wine-shops and from vice, and to lead them back to the sacraments. He met with considerable success in Paris, where he soon gained the support of some very influential people, who helped him to become a master shoemaker. Thus were born the pious congregations of shoe-makers and tailors—Frères Cordonniers and Frères Tailleurs— which gained ground. But there were many similar undertakings, such as the Frères des Œuvres Fortes (founded by Father Bénigne Joly at Dijon), and others established by the cutler Jean Clément and Baumais, a pedlar. Here we have an extremely odd mixture of attempts by different social groups to rechristianize themselves, conducted in an atmosphere that reminds us of our own specialized movements. These efforts were very much in advance of the times.

Some of these apostolic endeavours on the part of the laity are now famous. We have seen the widespread activities of the Ladies of Charity under the leadership of Monsieur Vincent, and on a smaller scale the work carried out by groups of gentlemen. These people, both men and women, were gathered together and sent into action by a saintly priest; but there were others—drawn in some cases from the same levels of society—who united, organized and set themselves to work, moved by a profound interior urgency. The Company of the Blessed Sacrament was one of these bodies; we have already seen it at work at many a cross-road of Catholic history during the seventeenth century, and its influence was undoubtedly of the highest importance.[1]

In 1627 Henri de Levis, Duc de Ventadour, a peer of France, the king's Lieutenant-General in Languedoc and Viceroy of Canada, underwent a severe spiritual crisis. He read Teresa of Avila and meditated daily on the *Introduction to the Devout Life*. A sincere Catholic, he was grievously pained by the defects and misfortunes of the Church. A remarkable idea occurred to him: if the Catholic *élite* in France united in an association to promote the Kingdom of Christ, using the thousand and one connections which it would have at its disposal, it would exercise a profound influence, both in resowing the seed of faith and in fighting the Church's enemies. He confided his scheme to three religious: Father Philippe d'Angoumois, a Capuchin and his spiritual director; Father de Condren, second Superior of the Oratory; and Father Suffren, S.J., the king's confessor. They encouraged him, and Louis XIII, who was told about it by an officer on his staff, approved. In 1629 Henri de Levis sacrificed his 'most pure conjugal love' in response to this call, and his lovely wife, Marie-Liesse, entered the Carmel at Avignon so as to leave her husband absolutely free. The Company of the Blessed Sacrament was formed in 1630.

What was its aim? M. Adrien Bourdoise explained it in his forthright manner: 'Since so many priests stand with folded arms, it is necessary that God raise up laymen to do the work of the idle.' The Companions of the Blessed Sacrament were to be apostles. They were to revive 'the spirit of the early Christians . . . to profess to be like Christ by word and by holiness of life, doing all good works for the glory of God and the salvation of their neighbour'. The Company was therefore both a pious society and a militant association. Its members met on Thursdays, a day dedicated to the Most Blessed Sacrament. They began each session with prayers, and ended it by meditating on a reading from Scripture, from *The Imitation of Christ*, or from Lorenzo Scupoli's *Spiritual Combat*; its members were obliged to make retreats, to do penance, to visit the sick and the lepers, and to give alms. But, at the same time, the Company's purpose was action in God's cause.

The Company grew very quickly. Its early members, in 1630, bore great French names—Charles d'Andelot, François de Coligny, the Comte de Brassac, French ambassador to Rome, François de Rochechouart; and they were joined by many others, great nobles and

---

[1] The secrets of the Company of the Blessed Sacrament were so well kept that its history remained unknown until 1900, when Dom Beauchet-Filleau, a Benedictine, decided to publish manuscript No. 14,489 of the Bibliothèque Nationale, entitled *Annales de la Compagnie du Saint-Sacrement, par le comte Marie-René Le Voyer d'Argenson*. Since then many publications for and against the Company have appeared (see the bibliographical notes).

prominent members of the legal profession. In its ranks were Gaston de Renty, who directed the Company after de Levis's untimely death; Jean de Bernières-Louvigny, a saintly layman; René Le Voyer d'Argenson; the two brothers Lamoignon, Christian and Guillaume; Lefèvre d'Ormesson, son of a friend of Henri IV; the Duc de Nemours; the Duc de la Melleraye; the Comte de Noailles; and the Marquis de Salignac-Fénelon—a Who's Who of the world of charity and the apostolate. The Company counted some illustrious well-wishers among the bishops, though it was careful to avoid becoming 'clericalized', and accepted only a few priests; Alain de Solminihac, Godeau, Perochel, Zamet, Abelly, were its friends. All the leaders of the reform movement were more or less directly in close touch with the Company —Monsieur Vincent and M. Olier, for example; while the Oratory was represented by Father de Condren; Bossuet too was a member. Its work, according to one of its circulars, was 'to do as much good as possible and to remove as much evil as possible'; and that task allowed for many associates.

But here we meet a strange phenomenon: this association, whose aims were so singularly praiseworthy, was surrounded by deep secrecy. Why? To begin with, it was undoubtedly through humility; unlike Tartuffe, in whom Molière purported to describe them, these truly Christian men had no desire to parade their virtues; when they gave alms they did not wish their right hand to know what their left hand did. But there was no less certainly another reason: they believed that success in their struggle against vice and abuses would be best secured if, instead of proclaiming their activity from the roof-tops, they discreetly brought into play the many contacts that each had at his disposal. The most detailed precautions were taken to maintain secrecy. Members were not acquainted with the names of those at the top, but only with those of the officers immediately over them. The minutes of the business conducted at their meetings were kept locked in a small box, bearing the name of one member, but deposited with another, so that in the event of the depositary's death, the precious box would be handed over by the deceased's family. In order to make doubly sure that other interests might not run counter to their own, 'all religious and priests bound by vows and obedience to a general superior' were by resolution excluded from the Company. What was their attitude towards official authority? Formally the Company had no legal status, either civil or canonical; Richelieu, whose information was derived from Father Joseph, approved it; on the other hand Jean François de Gondi, Archbishop of Paris, absolutely refused to recognize it. Rome was suspicious and merely sent fair words!

That did not prevent the Company from enjoying enormous success. Adherents flocked to it—too many in fact, which was detrimental both to its quality and to its secrecy. The provinces were won over: at Marseilles it had Gaspard de Simiane; at Grenoble, M. de Foresta; at Toulouse, Jean de Garibal; at Caen, M. de Bernières. In 1659 a secret congress met at Paris; it included representatives of all the Company's branches in the provinces, each of whom submitted a report on the state of his particular region. Sections were formed for women—hardly a prudent step where secrecy was concerned. It is not known definitely what was the eventual number of members in the Company; but there must certainly have been several thousand, divided into fifty groups.

Their activities extended to every sphere. There was no sector of Catholic life in which its shadow might not be glimpsed in the background. The Company helped Monsieur Vincent with his charitable undertakings and in his efforts to reform the clergy; it also lent the weight of its authority to M. Olier, M. Bourdoise and St John Eudes. The Confraternities of Charity, which cropped up more or less everywhere in France, were discreetly sustained by its influence and financial support. The Company financed missions, and encouraged the efforts of the founders and foundresses of schools and colleges. It was the warehouse wherein was stored everything destined for the poor. The rousing of public opinion in protest against English violence in Ireland was their doing; the financing of the Jesuit missions to the Huron and Algonquin Indians, and the Lazarist missions to the Hebrides, the Orkneys and Ireland was likewise their work. The corn seed sent to bankrupt farmers came from them. They were behind everything, even to the teams of surgeons who went around everywhere performing operations without charge.

All this was magnificent and worthy of admiration. Had the Company confined itself to such tasks, it would certainly have endured; but there was the other half of their programme. It was not enough to undertake good works; evil must be suppressed, and in doing so its members used the long arm; secretly, of course, but could such secrecy be maintained for ever? Priests of doubtful morals, merchants who did a flourishing trade in charms and similar objects in the vicinity of Saint-Sulpice, the butcher who sold meat on Fridays, the market gardeners who displayed their wares in the square before Notre Dame, those unscrupulous traffickers who waited for young girls as they alighted from the stagecoaches, and offered them wonderful jobs—all these people, obviously not respectable, but numerous, soon discovered who had put the police on their heels. The unruly nobles who delighted in duels took a jaundiced view of the efforts made by the Marquis de Salignac-Fénelon, a member of the Company, to discredit this absurd practice by swearing an oath never again to draw the sword: his gesture was made to appear the act of a coward. The

Protestants—heresy was one of the Company's pet aversions—learned with indignation that whenever one of their number was a candidate for a public office or some position of responsibility, the Company, warned of the fact, took steps to have him rejected. Even the craftsmen affiliated to the trade guild—the Compagnonnage [1]—were denounced by Henry Buch, a protégé of the Company, as blasphemers, men of evil life and revolutionaries; the Compagnons du Devoir were similarly attacked by the Sorbonne. Where would these methods lead? Desmarets de Saint-Sorlin, a writer who was a member both of the Company and of the Academy—the man who started the wrangle over the 'ancients and moderns' in 1656—engaged in activities that were quite definitely a kind of police investigation. The Company was blamed for the burning at the stake of the mad visionary Simon Morin. And the Jansenists, who at first were delighted with the Company's uncompromising attitude, were soon in conflict with its members. Anyone suspect was excluded from its ranks, and in the affair of the 'Five Propositions' the Company made the most strenuous use of its authority to have the new sect condemned. All in all, these activities earned for the Company a host of enemies.

It was Jansenism that dealt the blows that were to crush the Company. In 1660 an ex-parish priest of Rouen, who had been suspended as a Jansenist, counter-attacked with a letter in which he revealed the secret of the Hermitage, the Company's branch at Caen. Mazarin seized on the incident with glee: he could not forget that the Gentlemen of the Company had often urged the queen to dismiss him. On the 13th December the Parlement of Paris forbade the existence of all associations not authorized by royal warrant. Though the Company was not referred to by name it was the object of the attack. Having therefore been warned of the step three months previously it burnt all its papers and declared itself dissolved.

It did in fact continue to exist for a long time in secret, throughout the reign of Louis XIV and the eighteenth century; and it may even be considered to have survived the Revolution, for a body known as the

---

[1] The Compagnonnage, which is not to be confused with another trade guild known as the Corporation, had its origins in the Middle Ages. At the beginning of the seventeenth century it was an association of workers whose principal aim was mutual assistance in their employment and in their search for work. Its young members were sent to different parts of the country to enable them to gain experience in their trade. It happened that the Compagnons du Devoir black-listed certain masters who were known to be hard and unjust. A few of their leaders managed to exercise some strange kind of influence, perhaps even to an alarming extent, though they could hardly be accused of immoral or anti-Christian practices. At the most, some of their ceremonies were rather clumsy imitations of the Mass, and might have been in some respects more or less sacrilegious. The Compagnonnage was condemned by the Sorbonne; it did not disappear altogether, but went underground. Some of its members may have inclined towards Freemasonry in the following century, but they were far from being the majority. On the subject of the Compagnonnage see *Présences*, preface by Raoul Dantry (Paris, 1951).

Congregation and closely resembling the Company in many respects came into being under the Restoration. Officially its members were still engaged in charitable councils, forerunners of our present-day Society of St Vincent de Paul, but their profound influence remained. Perhaps the mysterious Company was behind the flourishing organization called the Good Friends, founded in the Latin Quarter by Father Bagot for moral improvement; perhaps also it was behind the A.A.—Apostolic Associations—which the Jesuits founded some twenty years later. It may have been the Company that in 1664 encouraged Father Boudon to found the Society of God's Interests. However, everything concerning the Company remained enveloped in a haze of mystery.

Although some of the Company's methods may have been open to suspicion, and however inadmissible may have been the principle of an enterprise which, unlike Catholic Action today, remained outside the ecclesiastical authority and declined to come out into the open, one cannot condemn the achievement of these splendid men and their sincerity of purpose. They certainly produced something quite different from the Cabale des Dévots—the Sanctimonious Clique—which their enemies accused them of being. They contributed towards the progress of the cause of faith and moral reform; and the spiritual life of this great century was deeply indebted to them.

12. The Spiritual Life of the Century

It is important now to try to understand the extent of the spiritual life of the day. To what depth did this living water penetrate, which we have seen gushing forth and reaching to the highest fountains of mysticism? One word characterizes the spiritual life of this great century, a word which a scrupulous historian must use—revival. The fact is beyond question. Fifty years of effort—for it all began with the Council of Trent—the strenuous activity of so many saintly men, the prayers of so many dedicated lives—all this clearly bore fruit. The figure of the average Christian, which had begun to take shape during the preceding century,[1] asserted itself in characteristics through which we can often recognize precedents, and many of which, indeed, were to exercise an influence even upon ourselves. How many customs, devotions, pious practices and prayers have come down to us from that period of great faith!

But let us be clear on this: not everything was perfect in the Church's fold. Very far from it. The spectacle that confronted Monsieur Vincent at Châtillon-des-Dombes and Folleville in Picardy was not unique; nor had every market-town and village of France a saint to lead it back to God. If priests in so many parishes set such a poor example, it

[1] See *The Catholic Reformation*, p. 374 et seq.

could hardly be expected that their flocks would be better. Very early in the century, even after the missions had begun their tremendous task of reclamation, the Christian people in many areas remained entangled in the brushwood of several glaring vices—luxury, drunkenness, sloth—at which we need not be surprised. There were also defects that are less common nowadays—unless they have merely changed their appearance; of these the most notable was superstition. Many a bishop had to do battle with sellers of 'miraculous' charms, wonder-working talismans, even alchemistic powders that had been blessed! The number of cases of witchcraft was staggering; the most famous was that at Loudun, in 1634, in which the unhappy Urbain Grandier perished. But there were others at Aix, Lille, Louviers, Auxonne, Rouen and elsewhere. Even in the most enlightened circles people were inclined to believe too readily in miracles, extraordinary graces and visions of all kinds. The cure of Mlle Périer by touching with the Holy Thorn in 1656 (an event which profoundly moved her uncle, Blaise Pascal) was officially recognized by the Church; but there were other less authentic 'cures' which enthused the masses none the less. And if the visions of Marie Parigot of Beaune, in 1636, were genuine, or those of Mother Agnès, the Dominican nun who appeared to M. Olier, or even those of Marie des Vallées (1590–1656), a saintly but tormented soul who gave advice to John Eudes and M. de Renty,[1] how much more notorious—and revered—were those of Antoinette Bourignon![2]

Such blemishes do not affect the profound reality of the Christian revival. That reality may be recognized first of all in its most tangible results: the improvement of morals. The difference was noticeable from the beginning of the reign of Louis XIII to that of Louis XIV. The practice of violence almost disappeared; the oath taken by Salignac-Fénelon, never again to fight a duel, and the work of Monsieur Vincent had a greater effect than Richelieu's edicts, and led to the law of 1651, which condemned the absurd custom altogether. The dignity of family life and the respect in which it was once held were again restored. But were the sixth and ninth Commandments any better obeyed? It is doubtful; but at least decency and external behaviour prevailed, for the Hôtel de Rambouillet declared them to be 'in good form'. The truth is that while all was not exactly perfect in Christendom, a Catholic *élite* had been formed, far more extensive than the recognized social *élite*; its moral standards had been transformed by

---

[1] Compare Émile Dermenghem's *La Vie admirable et les révélations de Marie des Vallées* (Paris, 1926). A larger work has been in course of preparation for some years by Father du Chesnay, the archivist of the Eudists.

[2] A pseudo-mystic (1616–80) whose 'visions' were recorded in nineteen volumes by Pierre Poiret! Antoinette Bourignon did, however, have some sound views on a number of problems, notably on the influence of Descartes and the danger of his philosophy.

faith, and its influence was to be profoundly felt throughout the whole of the seventeenth century. The plays of Corneille, in which the virtues were dramatized, are an example of this transformation; the character of Pauline in *Polyeucte* fills us with admiration for the Christian spirit of that age.

It was the revival of faith, then, that transformed life. By what signs do we recognize this? First by the practice of frequenting the sacraments. Gone was the medieval custom of rarely receiving Holy Communion; the Society of Jesus had condemned it. St Francis de Sales in his *Introduction to the Devout Life* crystallized the new tradition and laid down a precept which was to dominate the whole century: the good Catholic will receive Holy Communion two or three times a month; better still every Sunday, if he has the grace to do so and his spiritual director allows it. Figures, although not numerous, show a distinct increase in the number of Communions during the first fifty years of the century. More and more it began to be taken for granted that 'the spiritual life of the Christian cannot be sustained without frequent Communion'. The practice of certain strict confessors to refrain from allowing Communion until a long time after Confession, so that the penitent might be truly repentant; the lively controversy which arose over Arnauld's book on Frequent Communion,[1] the growing practice of the solemn Communion of children, introduced by the Lazarists, the Ursulines and the priests of M. Bourdoise (and especially his disciple Simon Cerné); the beginning of the 'First Friday' Communion, which came into general use through St Margaret Mary—all these things are proofs of the profound reverence in which the Holy Eucharist was held.

Simultaneously with the development of this practice and, moreover, linked with it, there arose what might be called a sense of sin and of penance. The Middle Ages experienced it as something intense and summary; it had lost its hold during the confused period of the fourteenth and fifteenth centuries; now it reappeared and asserted itself very strongly. 'The entire life of the Christian must be a life of penance, quite apart from any particular penance one may be doing.' Those were the words of M. de Saint-Cyran; but many other excellent Christians who would never have been suspected of Jansenism thought the same. This was also a matter concerning which there was much controversy; it arose between the laxists and rigorists. There were excesses in both camps, but it was none the less a splendid thing that the vast Christian public could be stirred by these problems. It is doubtful whether such questions, were they to arise in our day, would inspire such lively passions. An anonymous *Spiritual Exercise*, published about 1650, advised Christians to say this prayer while dressing

[1] Compare Chapter VI, section 6: 'The Great Arnauld'.

in the morning: 'It is my sin, O my God, which compels me to submit
to this servitude of clothes, and to so many other of my bodily necessities. When shall I reach that state when I think only of You, and love
nothing but You?' This ejaculatory prayer in relation to the putting
on of a shirt may cause a smile; but its intention is evidence at least of
an urgent need for penance, a sentiment with which the twentieth
century does not appear to be imbued.

It is undeniable then that Christians lived at a high level of spirituality. The lessons of great spiritual thinkers are inculcated mainly by
the reading of pious works. No age has seen such a profusion of
spiritual books: the libraries of the day were a prodigious success.
There were catechisms without number. That of Canisius was trans-
lated into many languages; there was another by Simon Cerné entitled
Pédagogie des familles chrétiennes; another was written by Father
Gambart for the Ladies of Charity; others, translated from the
German, by Canon Volusius and the Capuchin Denys de Luxembourg.
Prayer books and books of meditations included Father Suffren's
The Christian Year, Firmin Raissant's *Meditations for Every Day
of the Year*, the *Christian Lent*, the *Practice of the Holy Year*, *Spiritual
Exercises*, *Little Offices*. . . . The list is too long; it is impossible to
mention them all. The Bible too was read, not only in the French
translations by Lefèvre d'Étaples and the Doctors of Louvain, but
also in those of Michel de Marolles (1649), Father Amelote and Mgr
Godeau, or in the 1657 translation by M. de Sacy and his friends of
Port-Royal. The great popularity of the Psalms demands special
mention; Father de Cadenet, of the Oratory, wrote a soul-stirring
commentary on them. We are told likewise that King Louis XIII knew
long passages of the Psalms by heart, and that he liked to repeat in
Godeau's translation: '*Qu'on te bénisse dans les cieux, où ta gloire
éblouit les yeux, où tu marches sur les étoiles!*' Lives of the saints were
numerous—saints of the early Church and saints of the barbaric age,
as well as more recent saints and other great spiritual figures. The
hagiographies of La Chétardye, the large miscellanies of Daillet and
Father Proust sold in thousands. As for books of spiritual meditations,
their success was unbelievable; apparently in the French language
alone thirty-two editions of *The Imitation of Christ* appeared between
1600 and 1660; there were 254 editions in a hundred years of Lorenzo
Scupoli's *Spiritual Combat*. The *Spiritual Exercises* of St Ignatius, and
even works which were strictly speaking mystical, such as translated
extracts from Teresa of Avila and St John of the Cross, were almost as
widely read; the *Introduction to the Devout Life*, which appeared in
1608 and which, by 1656, had been translated into seventeen languages,
was for thirty or forty years the favourite book of polite society.

All these Meditations and Elevations, then, inflamed Christian souls and led them to prayer; Bremond went so far as to suggest quizzically that this relieved them of all intellectual effort: 'In their approach to God they commandeered these sublime reflections for their own use.' A large number of books of collected prayers was published for the use of the faithful: Jean de Ferrières' *Treasure*, dating from 1583, was still very widely used. But Godeau's *Christian Prayers for People of all Classes*, published in 1646, ran it very close. It contained many such beautiful passages as the following: 'A Christian should ever abide in a state of prayer, that is to say, of sacrifice, of adoration and of continual self-oblation.' 'To pray through Christ is to place one's spirit in His; it is the giving of oneself to Him, to act according to His will and under His direction.' One should pray then all the time and on every occasion; even, as we have seen, while dressing; and M. Tronson used later to teach the same lesson to his students at Saint-Sulpice.[1] Prayer tended to become, above all, mental prayer, so much so that a few spiritual men disliked vocal prayer altogether, and 'sent it to Coventry'. But Christian people generally remained faithful to vocal prayer: they loved to say their Rosary; they developed an affection for certain prayers, such as the *Memorare*, which became once more as popular as it had been in the time of St Bernard, or the prayer beginning 'O Good and Sweetest Jesus', which was recited kneeling before a Crucifix. They also favoured Litanies, the number of which increased to such an extent that Rome became apprehensive and put a check on the fashion. The Forty Hours' Adoration, instituted by Antoine de Grenoble in 1527, became obligatory at Paris from the year 1615; and the Benedictine nuns of the Blessed Sacrament, encouraged by the queen, Anne of Austria, were not the only ones who practised Perpetual Adoration of the Blessed Sacrament, a devotion introduced much earlier by St Anthony Zaccaria; there were parishes where laymen took it in turn to keep watch hour by hour. As for the Mass, it was now attended by almost all the faithful, who followed the liturgy in Mass books, the use of which was increasing. The Mass was looked upon more and more as 'the centre of religion, the heart of devotion, the soul of piety', as St Francis de Sales had said. A definite liturgical revival had set in which was to attain its flood tide during the second half of the century.

Pious practices for the further development of the spiritual life became widespread. Not the least impressive was the practice of Retreats. These were introduced simultaneously by the Jesuits and the Franciscan Recollects of the Strict Observance. They became so popular that it was continually necessary to erect new buildings for

[1] M. Tronson even recommended seminarists to 'kiss their holy tonsure before going to bed', a pious gesture which might appear to depend upon a remarkable acrobatic feat were it not rendered quite easy by the custom of wearing wigs.

their accommodation. Before long every large town and many country villages had one or more of these establishments; particularly thriving was the house attached to Saint-Lazare at Paris, which had cost Monsieur Vincent a great deal of money. Silence was observed for a week or ten days, while the retreatants retired within themselves, meditated, prayed, listened to a director speak on spiritual things, and then made a General Confession, followed by Holy Communion. The good Catholic came away spiritually restored.

He returned once more to his everyday life, and strove to keep the flame of piety burning bright within him by frequent Communion, taking part in the Perpetual Adoration, devoting himself to works of charity and in many other ways. To guide his steps and keep his fervour alive he made use of special devotions. Cult of the saints, so dear to the Middle Ages, flourished again as in old days when they were invoked on any and every occasion. Processions in their honour increased, notably that of the Martyrs of Montmartre, to which the whole of Paris flocked. Devotion to the Mother of God was more widespread than ever before. Was she not the advocate, the mediatrix of all graces? 'O Jesus, living in Mary . . . '—Bérulle's charming words were on everyone's lips. The whole French school, from Olier to Bourgoing and John Eudes, discovered and proclaimed 'the abyss of her greatness'. Her Immaculate Conception had not yet been declared an article of faith, but Paul V in 1617, Gregory XV in 1622 and Alexander VII in 1661 referred to it as a certainty. Confraternities of Our Lady multiplied. So did pilgrimages to her shrines; the one to Our Lady of Verdelais, near Bordeaux, was very popular at that time. The 15th August was a feast kept throughout the whole Church in honour of her Assumption. Some bright rays from Mary's aureole fell upon her chaste spouse, St Joseph, whom Canada adopted as its patron. But of all these devotions the most sublime, the most stirring, and one that stimulated the piety of an ever-increasing number of the faithful, was the devotion to Christ Himself, the God-Man, the High Priest, at once celebrant and victim of the sacrifice, God present in the Holy Sacrament of the Altar. The spirituality of the French school, that 'metaphysic of the saints' of which Bremond speaks, was oriented towards Christ. It is Christ in His Passion whom Pascal invokes in his 'night of fire'; to Him he refers when he says that He sheds a drop of blood for each and every sinner. This was the beginning of a cult already proclaimed by a few obscure Carmelites in Liège, and later (1670) promoted by St John Eudes—the devotion to the Sacred Heart of Jesus, the image, both spiritual and sensible, of the Saviour's infinite mercy.[1]

[1] See Chapter V, section 3: 'Decline of Mysticism and growth of Devotion to the Sacred Heart'.

What were the concrete results of this vast spiritual ferment? It is possible to recognize them by taking some examples, and looking at the lives of certain individuals and groups of men during this period.

Let us consider one village among many, a village named Saint-Didier-sur-Rochefort, in the canton of Noirétable, Loire. It contained about two thousand inhabitants scattered over numerous hamlets, and a survey compiled between 1635 and 1640 helps us to trace its religious history.[1] At the end of the fourteenth century conditions were deplorable; when Talaru, Archbishop of Lyons, made his visitation to Saint-Didier and the five neighbouring parishes in 1378, he found either priests living with concubines or no priests at all! The second half of the fifteenth century, and especially the sixteenth, showed an improvement; but by the end of the century a new decline had set in. Yet what a change from the year 1600 onwards! The situation was completely reversed. The beginnings of progress noted by the survey were now on the increase. More and more people went to Mass, which was celebrated with great dignity, and there were even High Masses during the week. It is rather surprising to discover that there was some attendance at the offices of Matins and Lauds on many feast days, particularly those of St Anne, St Catherine and St Anthony (he of the abbey of that name in Dauphiné); and, of course, on the festivals of Our Lady. This restored parish was in the hands of a team of seven or eight priests who worked together. One impressive detail in the history of this period is the fact that in 1631 a request to the archbishop for a chapel of ease in an isolated district of the parish was initiated by laymen, the worthy peasants of Saint-Didier. Their petition rightly stated that Mass in the hamlet would be a most useful means of apostolate. Surely we have here a foreshadowing of those communal parishes which are the pride of our own day.

If there were exemplary parishes, there were exemplary individuals too. Among them was Gaston de Renty, second superior of the Company of the Blessed Sacrament. If anyone deserved to be called a saintly layman it was he. De Renty surrendered his office of State Counsellor, turned his castle at Bény-Bocage into a hostel for victims of scurvy, became a stonemason, and dedicated his entire fortune to financing the Oratory Missions and other charitable works. Naturally he took a personal share in the work, and both he and his wife devoted themselves unreservedly to the noble task. He would go and talk about God to workmen and peasants, and even to the nobles whom he instructed in the Catechism. His strong and humble soul, absorbed in

---

[1] This unpublished survey has been studied by M. l'Abbé Epinat, in charge of the Geography Course at the Facultés Catholiques at Lyons. He was kind enough to offer me a summary of his work, for which I take this opportunity of thanking him. But other documents give the same impression: e.g. the *Histoire de Montmélian* (a small market-town in Savoy) by the Abbé Bernard.

the pursuit of justice and given over entirely to Christ, found expression in his *Twelve Rules of the Interior Life*. When he died there were found next to his skin an iron girdle, a crucifix backed with nails and his famous testament of vows to God written in his blood.

Saint-Didier was but one village and De Renty but one Christian among many. There was yet another witness to the spirit of the times, a royal witness, none other than King Louis XIII, who told the Duc de Saint-Simon, father of the historian: 'God made me king only that I might set an example of obedience to Him.' From the little that Louis XIII revealed of his private life and activities we are able to infer that he was a sincere and profound Christian. Throughout his life he had a great devotion to Our Lady; at fourteen he dedicated himself to Notre Dame des Vertus during the ancient pilgrimage to Aubervilliers. On several occasions he made express appeal to her. Thus in 1627, when his armies were besieging La Rochelle, he ordered public prayers, a vast offensive of *Ave Maria*s. In 1630, when he nearly died of a dreadful disease, he sent a special messenger to implore the help of Our Lady of Loretto. In 1635, when his kingdom stood on the brink of the abyss, Corbie was recaptured on the ninth day of a novena to Our Lady. All these events made a deep impression on the king, and in December 1637 he proclaimed by letters patent his gratitude to the Mother of God. Then he made one supreme appeal to her. There was no heir to the throne, and the royal couple had already been married twenty-two years. He begged the Virgin Mother to grant his request. The king's appeal was duly recorded by Parlement, and the mediatrix answered it: Anne of Austria became pregnant and would bear him a child. On 15th August 1638, when the king was with his army at Abbeville, he dedicated his kingdom to Our Lady before a chapel recaptured from the enemy for that purpose. France was to be the fief, the possession, the land and domain of the Queen of Heaven. Protestant ambassadors might well scoff; Hugo van Groot of Sweden sent his chancellor, Axel Oxenstiern, a report which the latter found highly amusing. But such a gesture, occurring on the flood-tide of a spiritual revival in which France played so prominent a part, may well be regarded as a symbol.

13. IN CATHOLIC EUROPE

Compared with the spectacle which the spiritual life of France presents during the sixty vital years of this great century of saints, the rest of Catholic Europe creates a colourless impression, although a few figures are pre-eminent. The situation had been altogether different during the preceding period. Immediately before and after the Council of Trent, though in rather a different way, the leading lights were

St Charles Borromeo and St Philip Neri in Italy, and St Ignatius, St Teresa and St John of the Cross in Spain. France was destined somewhat later to lose her hegemony; but during that half-century the real agent of Catholic reform was the land of St Louis.

This was not because the need for reform was any less urgent elsewhere than in France. Parallel symptoms were visible everywhere, and they showed that the work was far from finished. Everywhere there were moribund parishes, such as Châtillon-en-Dombes before the advent of Monsieur Vincent. Absenteeism, immorality and ignorance corrupted large sections of the clergy; everywhere there were monks who treated their vows lightly, and there were extremely worldly nuns. It happened too that the same effects were everywhere produced by the same causes: though the decrees had been recognized by most Catholic states, they were unable to supply solutions to problems which they had sidestepped, especially those relating to the appointment of bishops and abbots, and the relations between lay rulers and the Church. The frequently disastrous influence of princes over ecclesiastical dignitaries was almost everywhere as tyrannical as in France, and perhaps even more so. In Spain, for instance, His Catholic Majesty not only made all appointments, but exercised strict control through the State Inquisition. No eminent prelate who contemplated defying the monarch could fail to remember the fate of Cardinal Carranza, whom Philip II threw into prison, despite his purple, and who emerged from his prison only to die most opportunely two weeks later. Even the most powerful Orders had to compromise with authority. Thus de Noyelle, the General of the Jesuits, apologized to Charles II for having, whilst in Rome, visited the French ambassador before presenting himself to His Catholic Majesty's representative. The weight of secular power, therefore, brought about the consequences we have seen; there were schoolboy bishops and infant abbots in countries other than France; and it was not until the reign of Philip IV and Charles II that Everard Nitard, Cardinal Minister and Jesuit, set his heart upon remedying this state of affairs in Flanders. As for countries whose sovereigns were weak, the Church was no more free on that account; in Poland the tyranny of the nobles was more burdensome, more incoherent, even than that of the kings.

The situation was not so very different in France; but a study of the period contemporary with Louis XIII and Anne of Austria reveals—as has been made abundantly clear—a prodigious efflorescence of active sanctity, the equivalent of which might be sought in vain elsewhere. No country can show a pleiad of exceptional men dedicated to God such as was produced by the land of Bérulle, Vincent de Paul, Jean-Baptiste Olier, François Régis, Pierre Fourier and John Eudes. Spain, a land of great spiritual leaders, now possessed very few. St

Alphonsus Rodriguez (1531–1616), a humble coadjutor of the Society, was the sole immediate heir of Balthazar Alvarez, the Jesuit mystic. Maria d'Agreda (1602–65), the Franciscan visionary whose *Mystic City of God* met with enormous success but was condemned by the Holy Office, is clearly not on the same plane with the sublime Carmelite of Avila. St Joseph of Copertino (1603–63) was more famous for his extraordinary gifts, bilocations and levitations than for his concise teaching. Elsewhere the English Capuchin, Benedict Canfeld, was certainly admirable, and his *Rule of Perfection* is not unworthy of comparison with the *Spiritual Combat* of Lorenzo Scupoli; but he lived and worked mainly in France, and died in 1610, the year of the Italian Theatine's death. Was there then anyone of note? Father Pointers in Flanders? Paolo Segneri in Italy? They were splendid figures, but hardly on a par with the greatest. There were of course preachers, exegetists and theologians; but of saints, if any, there were very few.

All this does not mean that the spiritual effervescence we have observed in France did not exist elsewhere. In every country souls were to be found *in via*; souls whom God clearly called, and who obeyed Him. The Christian life was lived intensely in many countries besides France: in Flanders, conspicuously the home of the Counter-Reformation (the word is strictly correct here), where universities and monasteries flourished; and in the kingdom of Poland, henceforward entirely devoted to Catholicism and piloted by the most numerous band of clergy in Europe. The practices we have seen established in France were also followed elsewhere. In Spain the custom of frequent Communion gained ground; in Belgium General Communion was customary, and vast numbers of people approached the sacraments (sometimes more than ten thousand at a time in Brussels). Everywhere pious Confraternities held numerous and spectacular processions through the streets: at Seville in Spain; at Bruges, Ghent and Furnes in Flanders; nor were these pious practices confined to the Confraternities. The ancient military Orders of Santiago, Calatrava, Malta and the Holy Sepulchre regained their vigour. The same devotions, in a greater or less degree according to the country, spread everywhere. First there was devotion to Our Lady, whose pilgrimages drew the crowds; Passau, in Austria, attracted nearly two hundred thousand pilgrims a year, the slow and sublime prayer of the Rosary ascending to Our Lady (in Portugal it was recited publicly in the streets). Lastly, King John Casimir of Poland, imitating the King of France, consecrated his kingdom to her; and Strich, the Irish martyr and mayor of Limerick, did the same for his city. There was increased devotion to the saints, a vast number of saints, even the most recently canonized. At Naples, for instance, devotion to St Francis Xavier, who had been canonized eleven years earlier, and had miraculously cured the famous preacher Father Mastrilli in 1633, was honoured with an annual novena which brought crowds to the churches. Above all there was great devotion to Christ, the God-Man; and here the influence of the French school of spirituality was felt far beyond the frontiers of France. In 1634 the Bavarian peasants of Oberammergau, who had been delivered from the plague, made a vow to perform a Passion play every ten years —a vow which they continue to observe.

The evidence of individuals is no less impressive. It would hardly be true to say that the number of those resembling Blaise Pascal was legion, but in every country there were people of exacting conscience who had met Christ along their path and had come away transformed by the Divine Presence. Again it is impossible to name them all; the list would begin with the Archduchess Isabella, Regent of the Low Countries, who died in the habit of a Franciscan Tertiary, and include Ernest of Hesse, Edward of Bavaria and Christian of Anhalt, the last of whom sacrificed his throne for his faith. The list might equally well begin with Niels Stensen, a Dane, who became a Catholic at St Peter's tomb, and end with Christina of Sweden (1626–89), a wayward and unorthodox lady who preferred conversion to the throne of the Vasas, and afterwards related the story of her strange and not altogether moral life in a book which she modestly dedicated to God the Father!

There was therefore no lack of spiritual activity. It nowhere developed into the wealth of practical fulfilment which we have seen in France; but this is not to suggest that no one outside the France of Bérulle and Monsieur Vincent longed for the expansion of the Tridentine spirit. On the contrary, almost everywhere there were dioceses ruled by bishops who were determined advocates of reform and who dedicated themselves entirely to it. In Spain there was Pascal d'Aragon at Toledo, Marcello de Moscoso at Segovia, his brother Antonio at Cadiz and Malaga, Velarde at Avila, and at Valencia Estrada Manrique, who was regarded as a saint during his lifetime. In Bohemia, poor Bohemia suffering under the burden of imperial repression, two successive archbishops of Prague, Lohelius and von Harrach, opposed terrorist methods with a spirit of charity and exemplary conduct in an attempt to restore the Catholic faith to life. In Germany the reforming bishops found it harder to assert themselves: there the abuses were deep rooted, and the warlike atmosphere resulting from the Thirty Years War did not favour the development of Christian virtues; but Father de Wartenberg at Ratisbon, G. de Thun at Salzburg, J. C. de Lichtenstein at Chiemsee, H. de Knoringen, followed by J. de Freyberg, at Augsburg, and J. P. de Schonberg, Duke of Franconia, at Mainz, did their best in frequently difficult circumstances. The role of the diocesan and regional councils appears to have been even more important in Germany than in France, and more important too in Italy, where on the morrow they began to concern themselves with morality. Reform of the religious Orders continued among the Hermits of St Augustine and the Carmelites, and also among the Dominicans under the fiery Sebastian Michaelis and the prudent Nicolas Ridolfi. As for the Benedictines, Fulda Abbey, governed by Balthasar von Dernbach, played a part similar to that of Saint-Vanne in Lorraine and in France. Orval, in Belgian Luxembourg, was the pride of the Cistercians. Recently established Orders were developing everywhere; the Capuchins, for instance, and—despite all opposition —the sons of St Ignatius of Loyola.

It is clear from this sketch that nowhere was the Tridentine ardour stifled. But there is one man whose achievement must be singled out; he is Blessed Bartholomew Holzhauser (1613–58), founder of the Bartholomites. If we are to do justice both to him and to his work— which twentieth-century Catholics rarely do—we must place them on a level with Bérulle, St John Eudes, St Vincent de Paul, M. Olier and their achievements. He was a noble and radiant figure, with a profoundly mystical soul; he was also a creator and an organizer. He came from a very poor family at Laugna, near Augsburg. His father was a shoemaker with twelve children to feed. Thanks to various charitable organizations, Bartholomew was given the opportunity to study; step by step, he reached the University of Ingolstadt, where he had a distinguished career. His vocation dates from his childhood: all his life he dreamed of becoming a priest, and he was ordained in 1639. He set to work immediately. Like Monsieur Vincent and M. Olier he was distressed by the condition of the clergy. Three friends shared his solicitude; they decided to live together and work in common towards the necessary reclamation of the priestly state. They began with themselves, preaching by example, displaying magnificent charity, unreservedly dedicated to the souls of others. *The Love of God*, which Bartholomew had recently written, was a deeply spiritual work, but a practical one: a blend of St Ignatius of Loyola and St Francis de Sales. It needed only a setting for the little team to become a new institution, and that was achieved when they were assigned the collegiate Church of Tittmoning; the Union of Secular Priests living in Community was created. They were secular priests, not religious or clerks regular; they took no vows, but simply made a promise of stability. The Constitutions, which were not published until four years after the death of the founder, indicate clearly the remarkable originality of the enterprise, which was not at all unlike a number of present-day undertakings. Bartholomew Holzhauser followed a path similar to that of Adrien Bourdoise, but broader in outlook and less whimsical. He took account of the useful lessons to be learned from the history of those many groups of canons regular, which for centuries had enabled priests to strengthen their virtue through community life. He thought of his undertaking as a means of giving his colleagues the safeguards and opportunities of a communal life, without their ceasing to be fully engaged in pastoral work. The Bartholomites were to serve as parish priests or curates but living as small teams in fraternal association. He himself was Dean of Leogenthal in the diocese of Chiemsee, then of Bingen-am-Rhein in the diocese of Mainz. The centres which he established included the communal presbytery, a seminary for the training of the young (who undertook university courses), a house of retreat, and sometimes a charitable foundation. The idea succeeded, and Bartholomew Holzhauser made himself its courier. He went from country to country, multiplying his little groups, and he met with rapid success—in Swabia, Westphalia, the Tyrol and Poland. The Bartholomites soon had a house in Rome. When their founder died prematurely his youthful institution numbered over one thousand seven hundred members, and its influence extended far and wide. When, between 1639 and 1679, Laurence Neesen founded the seminary at Malines in Belgium, he drew on the ideas of Holzhauser, as well as on those of Monsieur Vincent and M. Olier.[1]

For, in everything new and original that happened in the Church at this period, French influence was strong. Monsieur Vincent, as we have seen, established his Lazarists in Rome and in Poland. In the Low Countries the Oratory had made enormous progress. Many countries, even as far afield as Canada, demanded the methods and the men of Saint-Sulpice. Such French-speaking territories as Savoy, Lorraine and Franche-Comté were in the fullest sense spiritual colonies of France. Often it was the result of the direct action, and nearly always under the influence, of Frenchmen that the Church in Europe leaped forward anew. This was true of the Mission, which during this period was comparatively rare outside France: after 1660 it expanded widely in Italy, Germany, Spain, Portugal and Poland. In Hamburg Father Schacht, S.J., emulated Monsieur Vincent; for twenty-five years (1629–54) he preached to the masses and sustained them with his amazing charity. The influence of Monsieur Vincent was felt in Spain through Jerome Lopez, and in Portugal through Antonio Vieira. This radiating influence was to remain effective for a very long time, even when the original source of warmth had cooled.

---

[1] The Congregation of the Bartholomites died out in 1770 on the death of its last superior, who had allowed it to decline. But its influence remained for a long time, even outside Germany. About 1860 Mgr Dupanloup, the celebrated Bishop of Orleans, tried to revive the work of Holzhauser. Again, even today, the *Unio Apostolica*, founded in 1862 by Canon Lebeurrier, claims kinship with him, and is endeavouring to obtain his canonization.

14. ROME AT THE TIME OF BERNINI

There was, however, one sphere in which the spiritual preponderance of France did not make itself felt. This was the sphere of art. Here Rome was in the forefront; Rome, which, since the Council of Trent, had asserted its position more strongly than ever as the capital of Christendom; Rome, which was then increasing in size, becoming more vigorous, planning its streets and its squares and building its fountains; Rome, where the Church's victorious restoration continued to be celebrated with a ceaseless outpouring of religious manifestation. The burst of joy and creative force which had proved so powerful at the end of the preceding century remained undiminished, and lasted for another hundred years. The Eternal City was still the capital of the arts, to an even greater extent than it had been in the days of the Renaissance; it would be impossible to enumerate the painters, sculptors and architects who came from all over Italy and indeed from every Catholic country, France included, to learn what she alone could teach. This vitality contrasted with a definite eclipse in other spheres.

The popes, following the example of such men as Sixtus V and Paul V, remained watchful patrons of the arts. Urban VIII commissioned Bernini to construct the baldacchino in St Peter's, wrought in bronze from the Pantheon; Innocent X restored St John Lateran and built, among other things, the exquisite Church of S. Agnese al Circo Agonale; the austere Alexander VII spent vast sums of money in modernizing the Roman College of Sapienza, clearing the area around the Pantheon and, above all, giving to St Peter's the majestic antechamber of Bernini's colonnade. But they were far from being the only ones. All the Catholic sovereigns—Louis XIII and the last wretched Spanish Hapsburgs—were great builders of churches; at Vienna, in Styria and Upper Austria, Leopold I enthusiastically continued the architectural restoration begun by Ferdinand III. The passion for building new churches was so intense that in Paris tradespeople, workmen and students could be seen meeting together to form voluntary working parties on the site of the church of Saint-Jacques du Haut-Pas; and Father de Bérulle, the future Cardinal, and his disciples, worked with their own hands on the Oratorian chapel in the Rue Saint-Honoré.[1]

This impulse to build the house of God was truly equivalent to an impulse of faith; it was even more so than at the time of the Renaissance, when a number of artists might have been seen creating magnificent works on religious themes without in any way trying to emulate the holiness of a Fra Angelico. The masters of the seventeenth century

---

[1] Which is today the Protestant Temple of the Oratory.

were for the most part believers, often staunch believers. Guercino
assisted at Mass every day, and spent an hour in prayer before settling
down to work; Bernini received Holy Communion twice a week, and
made a retreat every year according to the method of St Ignatius of
Loyola. In France Callot also attended daily Mass, and Philippe de
Champaigne based his life on the ascetic principles of the 'Solitaires'
of Port-Royal. In Spain Murillo belonged to the confraternity founded
at Seville by Mañara (the famous Don Juan who was subsequently
converted) for the purpose of recovering the bodies of the drowned,
and assisting those condemned to death. The Tridentine spirit, the
splendid ideal of reform, was everywhere alive in art.

But it was in Rome that art asserted itself in all its glory. Such was
the meaning of that style which sprang to life in the wake of the
Council, as an extension and a contradiction of the art of the High
Renaissance, and which then reached its zenith—Baroque.[1] It was not a
decadent and disintegrating style, as has been so often alleged, but one
which had its own aesthetics, its own genius and significance—a
sensuous art, one might say, ostentatious perhaps, and with a tendency
towards effect and virtuosity, no doubt open to criticism in the matter
of taste, but not in the power of its creative impulse. Everything that
mattered then, at least in Rome and in Italy at large, lay in the realm
of Baroque.

In architecture the predominant type of church had a single nave
with cradle vault, and was flanked by small independent chapels. In
front rose a monumental façade whose relation to the interior was not
always apparent. Above soared the dome, derived, through Florence,
from antiquity; the most splendid example is St Peter's. In those days
so many domes were built in every part of the Eternal City that henceforth, in whatever part of the world the traveller might be, he could
never again see one of these structures without thinking of Rome. A
colonnade spread across the façade, of which it became the principal
feature, a source of light and shade in infinite variety, peopled by a
world of statues. The austere lines of Vignola's Church of the *Gesù*,
and of the Society's churches in general, tended to assume an overload
of decoration; here indeed there seems to be some justification for the
mistaken term 'Jesuit style', used to describe these ensembles of
heavily ornamented façades, portly domes, colonnades and crowding
sculptures. The ancient churches were modified according to the new
fashion; strange to say, it gave rise to no incongruity. Genuine masterpieces were produced by a host of architects, in the forefront of whom
were the Cavaliere Bernini and his rival Borromini. It was now that the
exquisite church of St. Suzanna presented to the Roman breezes a

[1] The origin of Baroque and the meaning of the word have been explained in *The Catholic Reformation*, p. 387 et seq.

façade so supple that it seemed to have been made of rippling drapery; that the church of St. Agnese on the Piazza Navona revealed a profusion of harmonious curves, angles and recesses; that S. Ignazio began to dominate a square arranged like a theatrical scene; that Guarini, at Turin, grouped churches in the most amazing geometrical combinations; that Longhena, in 1632, remembering the lessons of Palladio, erected on an incomparable site at the mouth of the Grand Canal the church of Santa Maria della Salute, an edifice which, no less than San Marco and the Palace of the Doges, gives Venice its character.

Baroque was universal. It occurred in sculpture, so closely linked with architecture that one could no longer say which of the two predominated in a given building. So intoxicated was it with its own virtuosity that it compelled marble to play the part of velvet, satin, and even of clouds; and masses of gold were applied to every available surface as the culmination of magnificence. So also with painting, which reigned supreme on the ceilings and interior walls, recovered its former glory in the reredos, and spread itself in gigantic tableaux. Painting followed the traditions of the Carracci and of the great Bolognese school represented by Caravaggio, as also those of Guido Reni, which lived once more in the noble and passionate Barbieri (1590–1666), surnamed Guercino (the squint-eyed), and in Domenichino (1581–1641) through the Virgilian beauty of his 'Life of St Cecilia', which adorns the church of St Luigi di Francesi.

Can this art be called Christian? Undoubtedly it can, with all deference to those who protest that they experience no religious emotion except in the half-light of Norman or Gothic vaulting, and to those who base their judgment on classical canons without perceiving how intimately true Baroque is blended with the most rigid French classicism. As Émile Mâle has amply demonstrated, it fulfils the same function as did the art that flowed from the Council of Trent, of which it is the direct descendant. It represents the devotion of the age to God made man, to the saints, to Our Lady, to the Child Jesus and to the angels. It proclaims in its own way the great dogmatic truths reaffirmed by the Church; e.g. a painting by Domenichino in the church of St Januarius at Naples shows Luther and Calvin trampled underfoot by a superbly youthful Catholic. In a word, it is an art which, uniting the basic facts along which the dialectic method of Christian experience proceeds, unveils the glory rather than the Cross.

One man, Giovanni Lorenzo Bernini (1598–1680), seems to embody in his name and work all that is extraordinary, exciting and perilous in Baroque. He was certainly the most celebrated and the most successful artist of his time, so much so that Louis XIV and Colbert thought of entrusting to him the colonnade of the Louvre. The Papacy gave him the direction of the work on St Peter's; it was he, therefore, who completed the basilica of Christendom. Bernini was sensitive, a believer with a prodigious imagination, and tremendously energetic; he designed for the Piazza Navona that delightful fountain in the shape of a half-submerged boat, as well as the vast group of 80 pillars and 284 columns which embraces the piazza of St Peter's like two magnificent arms. The fertility of his powers does him small service; but one cannot deny that such fertility is also a gift of genius, and a somewhat rare gift at that. Though in Bernini's case it degenerated now and then into facility, there was in his technique that strictness and precision which are the qualities of a master. Besides, he was a veritable Christian artist, the true heir of those geniuses who succeeded each other in the shaping of St Peter's. During a long lifetime he erected over the papal altar (1633) the bronze baldacchino now inseparable from the stately nave; infused new life into Michelangelo's gigantic piers, transforming their naked mass into four amazing reliquaries; exchanged the architect's pen for the sculptor's chisel and set up the 'Chair of St Peter' at the back of the chancel—a synthesis of stone, stucco, gold and theology which has no equal anywhere on earth; and finally (1656) endowed the basilica with that antechamber of incredible majesty, adorned with perpendicular magnificence and rigorous proportion.

One may not like Bernini; one may see in him, as in all his contemporaries and imitators, the perils of Baroque—sensualism, the taste for 'enriching' and facile virtuosity. But it is extremely unfair not to recognize Bernini as occupying pride of place in that manifestation of an age and society, which it is the function of living Christianity at every period to formulate by means of art.

Originating in Italy, Baroque did not remain confined to that country. Its growth was rapid and widespread. Every country that welcomed the spirit of the Catholic Reformation also opened its gates to an artistic form which appeared to be that of Rome and of the Church triumphant. It was characteristic of such Protestant strongholds as England, Sweden and the Low Countries that they escaped its influence entirely, or almost entirely. There was consequently an Austrian Baroque, a Czech Baroque, a Spanish Baroque and, more luxuriant still, the dazzling Baroque of Latin America. It was infinitely varied too, for versatility is another characteristic of this style; it absorbed local material, traditions and folklore with extreme facility, creating everywhere a new synthesis. From the Karlskirche at Vienna, the abbey of Einsiedeln in Switzerland, St Jacob at Innsbruck, to the churches of Mexico and Brazil, an infinite variety of works, often entrancing, always unusual, sprang up along a strangely meandering road—naves hung with tapestry of gold, chapels made to look like reliquaries (sometimes even like ballrooms, e.g. the chapel with stuccos by Serpotta at Palermo), façades in which the apparent tangle

resolves itself into a complex harmony. Everywhere there blazed forth
the power of the Church and the glory of God.

One country, however, resisted the temptation presented by
Baroque—France, the very country where the spirit of the Catholic
Reformation asserted itself in its purest and finest aspects. Not that
the Italian taste failed to penetrate; it was certainly prolific at the time
of Fontainebleau. It is evident likewise in the façade of Saint-Gervais
at Paris, built by Clément Métezeau; in the church of Saint-Paul-
Saint-Louis, the work of the Jesuit architects Dérand and Martellange;
as well as in the domes of the Sorbonne, finished by Lemercier in 1635,
and those of the Val-de-Grâce, completed by Mansart in 1645. All these
were quite clearly 'Roman'. It showed itself too in the painting of
Simon Vouet (1590–1649). Better still, pure Baroque is to be seen in
many a French religious monument; Bernini, on a visit to Paris,
erected in the chancel of Val-de-Grâce a baldacchino which was a
replica in miniature of that of St Peter's. Many retables, pulpits and
confessionals would long remain as perfect specimens of Baroque amid
the triumphs of the classical era. Yet after all, was there such a distinct
difference between two styles which were to dovetail as much as they
were to compete with each other for more than a century? Between the
colonnade of St Peter's and that of the Louvre, as well as between that
of St Andrew's on the Quirinal and Saint-Sulpice, the relationships are
more subtle than one imagines.[1]

French religious art, however, remained profoundly different from
that of Italy. Was this because it found in its own medieval tradition a
realism which prevented it from yielding to a more florid style; or
perhaps some kind of poetry intimate and full-flavoured in its tone?
Was it also because the strictly spiritual influences of the French
school, so judicious and restrained, caused it in some sense to filter
out the art imported from Italy? Spiritual leaders were undoubtedly
well aware that the Council of Trent, while restoring the true religious
spirit, had taken great care not to proscribe the splendour of worship
and artistic representation. They thought it fitting to pay homage to
God by making His temples beautiful, and by assisting artists to work
for Him. The churches of France are no less beautiful than those of
Italy or Spain. In fact, some of the mystics of the great century of
saints took a direct interest in matters pertaining to art—men such as
M. Olier, of whom Bremond says that 'not content with being the
poet of the French School, he would have liked to be its painter too'.
M. Olier's influence upon Lebrun was considerable. There is no doubt
that the great spiritual movement of the age produced the extraordinary
number of churches and chapels built at that time (over thirty in Paris

[1] A book by Victor L. Tapié, entitled *Baroque et Classicisme* (Plon), throws a wealth
of new light on the subject.

alone), and gave rise to the volume of religious inspiration among contemporary painters. But those same mystics also used their influence
in fostering a more cautious form of art, a form more obedient to the
rules of reason and less given over to delirium; a form which was
neither Jesuit, nor Oratorian, nor Jansenist, but which epitomized all
that was most sincere and most exacting in French spirituality. One
has only to enter the churches of Saint-Roch and Saint-Paul-Saint-
Louis, or the chapels of Val-de-Grâce and the Sorbonne, to experience
the living reality of that art: it addressed itself less to the senses than
does Baroque; its appeal is perhaps rather to the soul. In painting it
had its counterpart in the great works of Eustache Le Sueur (1617–55)
—in his life of St Bruno—and of the realist Georges La Tour (1593–
1657)—especially in his 'Nativities', of which the subtlety of indirect
lighting is so thrilling. It was the same with the works of the Jansenist
painter Philippe de Champaigne, who came later, and the sculptures of
Sarrazin.

Italian preponderance was no less evident in music. In the period
following the Council of Trent, Palestrina and his rival Vittoria [1] were
living in Rome; they were the initiators of that style in Church music
which gradually moved away from the old vocal polyphony towards
other forms of expression. Any attempt to deviate from the rule that
the human voice alone was suitable for prayer to God had hitherto
been energetically resisted by priests and theologians alike. Instrumental music was looked upon as theatrical, not entirely free from
sensuality and pride. By the end of the sixteenth century it was regarded
differently: it might perhaps be associated with the glorifying of God.
Henceforward its triumph was assured, especially as regards the organ,
the instrument *par excellence* of church music. By the beginning of the
seventeenth century the organ had made its appearance everywhere.
Giovanni Gabrieli and the Dutchman Sweelinck were the recognized
masters among organists; they were in universal demand. As the
number of these amazing instruments increased they were discovered
to be of every conceivable type, according to the country and the
player. All at once the decline of Gregorian chant, which had already
begun, was accelerated. In an attempt to save it, a kind of Medicean
edition was produced, but this was merely a skeleton without soul, and
despite the works of Henri du Mont a long time elapsed before it was
revived. However, church music found its bearings in another direction.
Twenty thousand people often gathered to hear Frescobaldi play his
celebrated toccatas on the organ in St Peter's. The human voice went
well with musical instruments, not only with the organ but also with
an orchestra: the recitative blended with the sacred text, slightly

[1] See *The Catholic Reformation*, p. 147.

underlined by the instrument. The oratorio, born of the imagination of St Philip Neri fifty years earlier, co-ordinated both words and music with a touch of the dramatic. The great musician of this period was Monteverdi (1567–1643), whose vast output included a number of Masses; he was a man of inexhaustible invention. Behind him came a band of disciples—Cavalli, Provenzale and his German friend Heinrich Schultz, who was rather overshadowed by the master. France in this sphere too was rather reluctant to accept Italian influence; when she adopted the organ, though her organists were among the best she kept to a more restrained style. Much less theatrical, for instance, was Gigault, who wrote exquisite Christmas carols, and trained Lulli, Bouzignac and Henri du Mont. There was also Father Bourgoing, and even King Louis XIII; the former discovered a tradition of musical plain chant with quite distinctive features. But under the personal rule of Louis XIV and the hegemony of Lulli in the realm of music everything changed, and Italian supremacy asserted itself.

15. The Turning-point: 1660

The days of this extraordinary epoch were numbered. It was not merely in music and painting that a new chapter began about the year 1660. Here is a remarkable fact: this change, which occurred in every sphere, including the economic, coincided exactly with the personal rule of Louis XIV, whose accession also marked a turning-point both politically and morally. On 8th March 1661, Mazarin being dead, the twenty-two-year-old king made known to the Council his will to be in future his own first minister, though until that date he had seemed not to bother about government. He kept his word, much to everybody's surprise. The wily cardinal, the shrewdest of his courtiers, had said: 'You do not know him. He will be rather a late starter, but he will go further than any other.' A new chapter in French and world history had opened.

It was also a new chapter in the history of the Church. Monsieur Vincent died in 1660, and Louise de Marillac the same year; Jean-Jacques Olier three years earlier, and Michel le Nobletz seven; Adrien Bourdoise was to disappear from the scene five years later. Pascal, that glittering genius, was to end his short life in 1662. All these departures were significant. Of the really great personalities who had led the Church in its praiseworthy effort towards revival, only a few, e.g. John Eudes, now survived; still, they had delivered the substance of their message—their successors had only to continue the good work.

There were numerous indications that the climate was changing. In accordance with the Treaty of the Pyrenees, the young king had in the previous year married his cousin, the Infanta Maria-Theresa. But he neglected her, and played a dangerous game with another cousin, Henrietta of England, who had become his sister-in-law. Then he yielded to the silent passion of Louise de la Vallière; soon she, if not the children she had born him, appeared in public at his side. It was a far cry from the strict and austere piety of King Louis XIII. The court followed the royal example. Many an adulterous intrigue was hatched around the elegant prince. The dissolute, who became emboldened, were not alone in proclaiming that life was something to be enjoyed and that any other notion was laughable—referring to Gassendi and Saint-Évremond as their authorities. In a society where bad examples came from above too many were prepared, as Father Mersenne said, to identify 'their evil inclinations with human nature'. France, however, had no monopoly over licentiousness. The history of the court of the Stuart king, Charles II, is no more edifying; nor are the love-affairs of Charles Emmanuel II of Savoy, or the thirty-two illegitimate children of Philip IV, His Most Catholic Majesty of Spain. From top to bottom society experienced a decided moral landslide, and it continued for years.

The Church was likewise affected. It was at about this time that Abelly, Monsieur Vincent's biographer, penned the terrible words: 'The priesthood is without honour.' And after so much effort! There were many priests whose conduct, if not altogether heinous, was far from godly. Curiously enough, Innocent XI was obliged to forbid priests to become footmen or butlers; in any case his prohibition went unheeded. Once again absenteeism flourished. Speaking of the clergy whom he knew, Bossuet declared: 'The world, the world, the world . . . ! Pleasure, bad advice, bad examples! Save us, Lord; save us!' And, in order to pursuade his canons at Condom to keep residence he had to threaten them with imprisonment. The same deterioration set in once more among the religious Orders: at Chaise-Dieu, Saint-Ouen, Fécamp and Cluny the enemies of reform raised their heads; particularly at Cluny, where, in 1642, the little Prince de Conti had been appointed abbot at thirteen years of age. The fact that Monsieur Vincent had long ago been removed from the Council of Conscience was not mere coincidence. There were bishops and cardinals, appointed by royal warrants, who laid aside the *cappa* and married— Henri de Verneuil, Bishop of Metz and son of Henri IV, Maurice de Savoie-Nemours, Archbishop of Rheims, and also, outside France, Henry III de Lorraine-Guise and Archbishop Albert, ex-Cardinal of Toledo. The dissolving of the Company of the Blessed Sacrament, that austere guardian of morals, was understandable. Fewer and fewer colleges and schools were being opened; the movement was not to be resumed until very much later. Severe and painful crises tortured the souls of men; Jansenism developed rapidly, and Pascal's *Provinciales* had envenomed the controversy since 1656; Quietism was already on the threshold. But the intellectual crisis of minds was no less serious. Descartes had been dead ten years, but would the Cartesians remain faithful to what was genuinely Christian in his doctrine? Spinoza, a refugee at Amsterdam, was preparing to write his *Ethics*, in which Christ would be nothing more than one of the names of virtue. Elsewhere Atheism made progress. The quarrel of the ancients and moderns began in 1656. Soon, under the appearance of a literary dispute, the real point at issue developed into this: could reason claim to apprehend everything without the necessity for Christian revelation? The French literary School of 1660 was rich in genius; but it was more interested in the passions of the heart than in flights of the soul. It was not without significance that Molière was authorized in 1664 to present his play *Tartuffe*. Is not true piety more or less visualized in this caricature of hypocrites?

Are we to assume from all this that the new epoch was unworthy of its predecessor? It would seem a harsh judgment indeed to affirm that the age of Bossuet and Fénelon, of Massillon and Fléchier, of Bourdaloue and Rancé, of St Jean-Baptiste de la Salle and St Grignion de Montfort was a period of decadence. We can hardly speak of 'broken wings', as some have done. But what is certain is that we are no longer face to face with that spiritual upsurge and youthful daring, that extraordinary animation, which had raised aloft the Christian soul during more than half a century. The greatest Christian figures of the period which now opened were the heirs and disciples of Bérulle, Olier and Vincent de Paul; but they were not destined to infuse into the Church the new blood, so warm and bountiful, which we have seen flowing in its veins. After the crisis and relapse at the beginnng of the new king's reign, past efforts were certainly resumed and followed up with courage. But there was another side to the picture: dissension among Catholics—Jansenists against Jesuits, Gallicans against 'Romans', Bossuet against Fénelon, Mabillon against Rancé,— and soon the triumph of intolerance and the advent of free thought, occurring both together. The century of Louis XIV was beginning, and the great century was drawing to a close. In the eyes of history they do not coincide.[1]

---

[1] It must be remembered that a time-lag is not abnormal when profound social changes are taking place. It was not much before 1700 that the majority of the clergy benefited from the setting-up of seminaries; and it was not until about 1730 that these priests, who were better trained, superimposed upon the mass of French clergy the virtues which, three quarters of a century earlier, Monsieur Vincent and M. Olier were teaching their followers. There is no doubt that all that was best in Christians at the time of Louis XIV was the fruit of the lessons and examples of the saints and eminent spiritual men of that great century (see Chapter V, especially section 2).

* E

16. THE STRENGTH OF SAINTS AND THE
WEAKNESS OF MEN

One question demands an answer: why this change, this slowing down of the spiritual sap? From one point of view there is no satisfactory answer; the change resulted partly from those same mysterious designs of Providence which, having produced so many saints at the beginning of the century, was less prodigal thereafter. But there are also human reasons—all too human—which account to some extent for the slowing down and the relapse; they explain why the great furnace of spiritual life, which had burned so powerfully, cooled down and could no longer carry the fire of Christ to the entire world.

The most serious of these reasons, painful though the admission may be, was the Papacy's failure during the last forty years of the great century to live up to its role. The fact that great pontiffs had taken in hand and identified themselves with the work of reform on the morrow of Trent had enabled the spirit of revival to begin the regeneration of the Christian soul.[1] It is impossible to exaggerate the importance of St Pius V, 'the pope of the great conflicts'; [2] but Gregory XIII, the terrible Sixtus V, the pious Clement VIII, the stern Paul V, all carried on the same work, each in his own way; while the venerable Gregory XV (1621–3), during the two years of his pontificate, instituted the Sacred Congregation of Propaganda, canonized five saints (1622), and gave to the Church's new look a sanction that might have been considered final.[3]

Why was so much doomed to alter after Gregory's death? His successors were not *bad* popes—the scandals of the Renaissance were never repeated; but why did they prove unequal to the situation? Above all, why did they look upon their function in a light no longer acceptable in that age, determined to hold their own as Italian princes, influential in political schemes, and sumptuous in their administrative setting, as though their material responsibilities were more vitally important than their spiritual duties? On 12th August 1623 Maffeo Barberini was elected to the Chair of St Peter under the name of Urban VIII (1623–44), and public opinion was favourable. Even the French, indignant at first because their candidate Federico Borromeo, Archbishop of Milan, had been set aside, merely on account of Spanish opposition, accepted this well-dressed, cultured and handsome Florentine; he was fifty-five years of age, and his election terminated a

---

[1] On the popes see *The Catholic Reformation* (Index).
[2] The expression 'le pape des grands combats' is used by Cardinal Grente in the title of his book on St Pius V, republished in Paris in 1956.
[3] See *The Catholic Reformation*, pp. 308, 393.

sequence of senile popes.[1] And yet, despite appearances, Urban VIII
was far from being as good as his predecessors. He was a politician,
and not a very clever one at that; his intervention in the Thirty Years
War brought the Holy See within an ace of an imperial attack on
Rome, without increasing its authority. He ran into trouble with
Venice, and also with Portugal when he refused to recognize its
independence and the young dynasty of Braganza. Worse still, he did
as one of his predecessors had done in the time of Alexander VI: he
committed himself to a sordid war in support of his family's quarrel
with the Farnesi over the duchy of Castro. He was defeated, and
Rome would have been sacked but for the intervention of the King of
France.

Was Innocent X (1644–55) any better? He had good intentions,
and his attempts to organize the papal government on a sound basis
were commendable; the fruit of his efforts was the Secretariat of
State, the basic instrument of Vatican administration. But he was weak
and easily influenced, and the methods he adopted to re-establish order
were suspect, as were his aims. Two facts are symptomatic of this
pontificate in which the gradual landslide became more marked. One,
of considerable importance when viewed against the broad background
of history, is the Holy See's declaration that the articles of the Peace
of Westphalia were null and void.[2] The other is the story that when
Innocent X died his body was left for three days in a gardener's tool
shed, no one troubling to bury him.

With the advent of Alexander VII (1655–67) it looked as though the
Papacy was about to recover. He was known to be a virtuous man, of
outstanding honesty and energy; he proved his courage well enough
when the plague of 1656 claimed fifteen thousand victims in Rome. As
Cardinal Chigi he had failed to win victory for the papal cause in the
Westphalian negotiations; but that was not his fault. He bore the
engaging motto: 'Molto fare, poco dire' ('Do much and say little').
This Sienese scholar was a canonist and a theologian. He was credited
with a worthy entourage. His ideas were sensible: he suggested, for
example, uniting the states of Europe to withstand the Turkish
advance. But his authority very quickly crumbled. Was that his own
fault, or was it due to circumstances? France under Mazarin raised
difficulties for him in connection with Cardinal de Retz, and even
worse problems under Louis XIV. Weary of seeing the Christian
world slipping through his fingers the ageing Pope buried himself in
chagrined solitude, consoling himself in his disappointment by writing
Latin verse. His last joys were the canonization of St Francis de Sales

---

[1] Having survived all the cardinals he had created, Urban VIII had a medal struck to
commemorate the fact—which was certainly unique!
[2] See page 149.

and the condemnation of those who disparaged the Immaculate Conception. In a different epoch such a man would have done better.

The curse of these three pontificates was nepotism; it bordered on the scandalous—one might have been back in the days of Sixtus IV or of the Borgias. Indeed the practice whereby succeeding popes found employment for their families had continued, with rare exceptions, for several centuries; but it had declined since the Council of Trent. Normally the Pontiff placed one of his nephews in some governmental post and another in the Sacred College—it being tacitly agreed that neither would succeed him. The three popes just referred to broke with this arrangement. Under Urban VIII there was a positive invasion of insolent and greedy Barberini. The gibe of the scholars was, 'Quod non fecerunt Barbari, fecerunt Barberini',[1] and the people of Rome used to sing:

'Han fatto piu danno,
Urbano e nepoti,
Che Vandalli e Gothi,
A Roma mia bella,
O Papa Gabella.'[2]

It was to defend the so-called rights of his dear nephews that the Pope hurled his soldiers upon Castro, against which he formed a coalition. Innocent tried hard to force the rapacious Barberini to make restitution; but were the Panfili any better? This honest man's sister-in-law, Olympia Maidalchini, gained an increasing influence over him. She was a capable business woman, and it was thanks to her that her son, Camillo, was made cardinal; then, when he cast off the purple and married, it was the lady's nephew who succeeded him—a youngster of seventeen. The documents relating to his birth were faked! And even Alexander VII—a virtuous man—though he had good men at the beginning of his pontificate, gradually yielded to nepotism and gathered around him a little group of Chigi. These were fortunately resisted by the great Roman congregations and by Cardinal Rospigliosi, a future Pope.

All this was distressing, and would have been still more so had not these three questionable pontificates been followed by others of a totally different character, had not the courageous reaction initiated by Rospigliosi, who became Clement IX, been continued by his successor, Clement X, and, above all, had there not arisen soon afterwards the strong and saintly figure of Innocent XI.[3] It must be emphasized, however, that these weaknesses, to which history bears witness, do

---

[1] 'What the Barbarians did not do, the Barberini have done.'
[2] 'Urban and his nephews have done more harm to my beautiful Rome than did the Vandals and the Goths, O tax-collecting Pope.'
[3] See Chapter V, section 14.

not appear to have injured the prestige of the Papacy in relation to Catholic opinion as a whole. Ever since the successors of St Peter had managed to bring the long needed Council to a successful conclusion, and had taken in hand the work of reform, the faithful had held the Holy See in great veneration. There was abundant evidence of this attachment: more than 700,000 pilgrims flocked to Rome for the Holy Year of 1650; and on every occasion, for months on end, they acclaimed Innocent X. Besides, we once again behold the temporal glory of these popes of this time manifested in the stones of Rome; and not only in those of which the churches were built. It was Urban VIII who fortified the Castle of Sant' Angelo and Civitàvecchia; it was he who adorned the Piazza Navona with the graceful *baraccia*, the fountain representing a half-sunken barque; he too it was that raised Castel-gandolfo on its charming hill to serve as a summer residence. Innocent X followed his example; during his reign the Piazza Navona was decorated with two more richly decorated fountains. And the climax of this splendour was reached in two examples of town-planning undertaken by Alexander VII—the Porta del Popolo at the foot of the Pincio which commands magnificent views, and the two arms of Bernini's colonnade enclosing the Piazza of St Peter's—the courtyard of Christianity, the antechamber of a sovereign. . . .

Is such ostentation offensive? One thinks of Monsieur Vincent, of the poor whom he fed at his table, of François Régis dining on an apple, of the destitution of the poor and the holiness of saints. But such was the climate of the age and the new character of the Church since the Council of Trent, which looked to glory and victory as symbols of the authority and majesty which the pontiffs had rediscovered. Besides, it would be unjust not to appreciate the efforts of these popes to maintain the reform and to assist those who fostered it. Urban VIII, who furthered the work of propaganda, raised the Breviary, the Ritual and the Martyrology; he did his best to aid reforming bishops, took an interest in the progress of the Oratory and placed Saint-Sulpice under his immediate control. Innocent X supported popular preachers, followed closely the work of John Eudes and Bartholomew Holzhauser, and gave his backing to young institutions. One of Alexander VII's claims to glory is the fact that he summoned the Lazarists to Rome and made it obligatory for all future priests to make a retreat under the Fathers of the Mission. All that is not without significance, but it is fragmentary. These three popes were certainly right-thinking men, and did what they could to carry on the essential work; but we do not get the impression that they tried to grapple with the difficulties, or that they assumed full responsibility for the reform. St Gregory VII or St Pius V, in similar circumstances, would have acted very differently.

And that is why so many problems remained unsettled at the turn of 1660; it was not because they were hidden but because the popes, who alone might have had sufficient authority to impose solutions, were unwilling to do so. Nothing, or too little, was done to put an end to the system of holding benefices *in commendam*, or to terminate the often disastrous influence of lay authority over ecclesiastical appointments. How, indeed, could anything be done, when pontifical elections were the stake of political negotiations, the result of opposing interests, with the Roman court itself setting an example of scandalous nepotism? Another serious problem had not even been touched upon: antagonism between the secular and regular clergy, the almost continual misunderstanding between all types of religious Orders and the bishops. The avalanche of lawsuits between these various branches of the clergy is quite baffling; and the pontifical administration, instead of trying to put an end to the disputes, too often played one against the other, even the regular clergy against the bishops—a dangerous game, which was to have a bearing upon the development of great doctrinal crises, especially Jansenism and Gallicanism. Hence anarchy in both cases, which was singularly harmful to the Church. It explains the partial failure of the reform, or at any rate the length of time it took for the new ideas to gain complete victory.

But this partial failure brought in its train other harmful consequences at many levels. Mention has just been made of the doctrinal crisis arising from Jansenism. It would not be right to say that the popes of this period did not attempt to forestall it. Urban VIII condemned the *Augustinus* of Jansenius; Innocent X made a pronouncement on the Five Propositions; Alexander VII confirmed the condemnation by his predecessors and placed the *Provinciales* [1] on the Index. But were these coercive measures sufficient? Should not the popes have confronted these errors with something more than condemnations, and put forward a clear statement of true Catholic doctrine? That was not done, and the Jansenist affair was to be for many years a kind of cancer gnawing at the mystical body.

There was another and similar lack of resolution. What was done to counteract the intellectual crisis [2] which had manifestly begun and which would continue to develop rapidly? There was the condemnation of Galileo under Urban VIII, but that did not achieve very much. None of these three popes issued a great encyclical to show that the Church was alive to contemporary circumstances and was endeavouring to find solutions to the questions that were torturing mankind. It was not only at the religious level that the Papacy seemed to have lost what Father Mourret calls the direction of the world. Difficulties, and

---

[1] The whole of Chapter VI deals with Jansenism.
[2] See *The Church in the Eighteenth Century*, Chapter I.

in fact the most serious difficulties, soon arose in the political field. For while episode followed episode in the sublime conflict waged by the saints and great spiritual leaders, the world was being speedily transformed. The problem of balance between Catholics and Protestants, which no one had managed to settle by gentle firmness taking advantage of that utter confusion which the 'reformed' camp manifested at the beginning of the century,[1] was resolved by force at Münster and Osnabrück, where a balance was established from which the Catholic Church had nothing to gain. Might not a pope such as Paul V have hurled into the fray another Catholic League? Would not stronger popes have done everything possible to prevent a conflict between a French cardinal and the Catholics of the Empire? Nationalism was forging ahead in Europe, and the Church had nothing to gain from that either.

In Europe too, at the same time, absolutism was advancing. It was becoming established everywhere, not only in France, where a young and very ambitious king was about to systematize the principles which Richelieu had bequeathed to him. The masters of Europe were just as dictatorial in Spain, in England, and in many a little Italian principality. This twofold evolution of the world towards nationalism and absolutism completed the destruction of Christendom—the hardening of Catholic groups into self-centred groups inimical to each other and with whom the Church too frequently had to compromise, the renunciation of every principle of Christian policy, as when the Most Christian King Louis XIV formed an alliance with the Grand Turk.

The saints might illuminate their age, but they could not by themselves lead it back into the full light of day. The weakness and smallness of men had also to be reckoned with.

---

[1] See *The Church in the Eighteenth Century*, Chapter III.

CHAPTER III

EUROPE DIGS NEW FOUNDATIONS

1. A Period of Change

THE first half of the seventeenth century which, as we have seen, constituted a splendid period of spiritual exaltation, presented quite a different picture in the temporal sphere. A striking contrast exists between the purity, charity and radiant light of the saints, and the atrocities, violence and blood-stained gloom presented by the dreadful spectacle of politics. On the one hand there was Monsieur Vincent, his friends and his imitators; on the other were hordes of mercenaries burning, killing, plundering, reducing entire provinces to the condition of a desert. The Great Century was also a period of misery and suffering, because it was a period of profound change.

It goes without saying that the Church experienced the backlash of events. It may be true in one sense that the only history which counts in the eyes of the Church is that of the interior life—the history of souls, for ever new and ceaselessly relived; but she cannot remain indifferent to the history of those peoples which constitute the Church or of those man-made institutions known as states, with which she has to maintain relations. It was in France, torn first with military defeats followed by the Fronde, and in Germany, a panting prey to the *reiters* and *lansquenets*, that St Vincent de Paul, St John Eudes, M. Olier, Bartholomew Holzhauser and others had to carry out their task. But we may wonder whether political events might not challenge the very function of the Church, its rights and principles, its opportunity to be present and active in the world which was developing.

The political crisis about to rend Europe once more was to a large extent the continuation and the consequence of those of the preceding period. What was the position of the Christian West at the close of the sixteenth century, or in the first fifteen or twenty years of the seventeenth, when it was just beginning to assert itself? A balance seems to have been established between two opposing blocks on the basis of a geographical partition. On the far side of a line which corresponded roughly with the lay-out of the Roman *limes* was the Protestant zone; on its near side was the Catholic zone. In actual fact it was not as simple as that. The Catholic countries of Westphalia and Poland jutted into the Lutheran zone like wedges, and in the Catholic zone Calvinism had become firmly established at many points. Over the most disputed regions the problem was solved by a more precise division. It was solved for Germany by the Peace of Augsburg; Spain was forced to agree to the same solution in the Low Countries, and the Swiss cantons accepted a similar solution. But did this partitioning provide an assurance of peace?

Peace was based solely upon universal weariness. In other words, time and man's capacity to forget were working against it. Neither of the two camps was prepared to regard as final the relinquishment of territory once possessed or but recently desired. The Lutheran princes, for whom adherence to the *credo* of Wittenberg had been so profitable, dreamed of splendid ecclesiastical domains which might be secularized. Calvinism aimed at universalism. On the Catholic side things had advanced beyond the stage of shilly-shally and withdrawal, and a counter-offensive was being launched in every sphere. With St Peter Canisius and the Douai Jesuits the offensive was apostolic; with Bellarmine and Baronius, polemic. There also existed a political counter-offensive, in which strictly political forces were engaged. The role of Ferdinand of Austria, Maximilian of Bavaria, the archbishops of Cologne and Andrew Bathory II in Poland exercised considerable influence in bringing the states back to the Catholic faith.[1] Was this activity, which alone deserved the traditional name of counter-Reformation, to be relinquished? The conflict was bound to explode at the first opportunity. Would it start in the Low Countries where Olivarès, the dictatorial minister of Philip IV of Spain, refused to accept the partition which gave independence to the Northern Provinces? Or in Bohemia where Protestant ambitions clashed with the tide of the Counter-Reformation more violently than anywhere else? By 1620 war had broken out on both these fronts.

This was not just another religious war, similar to those which had already steeped so many European countries in blood as a result of the Protestant revolution. Under cover of the new religious conflict profound changes were to take place. The face of Europe was about to assume those features which, on the whole, it would retain for about two hundred years. The ratio of strength between European states was being speedily modified. The preceding period had undoubtedly been marked by the eclipse of France, to which the religious wars had to some extent contributed. But when Henri IV put an end to that tragedy the kingdom made a notable recovery. The population grew to nearly fifteen million over an area scarcely four-fifths the present size of France. Sully clearly demonstrated France's opportunities, and she led Europe in prosperity. Once France had found a man strong enough to put an end to internal disorders and restore prestige to the crown, she would no longer be satisfied with any position in Europe but the first, which she regarded as her due.

[1] See *Catholic Reformation*, p. 331 et seq.

Since England experienced an almost total eclipse during the whole of this period, busy as she was painfully resolving her internal problems, France had but one rival to face. The Hapsburgs alone determined to thwart France; they still aspired to that universal monarchy of which Charles V had dreamed. Although not so strong, now that two sovereigns shared their domains, they were no less ambitious and formidable. In Madrid Philip IV (1621–65) proudly mourned the Armada, in the certainty that he would rule an 'Empire twenty times the size of that once ruled by Rome'. In Vienna his cousin Ferdinand II longed to revive the ancient Holy Roman and Germanic Empire. However, weaknesses lay concealed beneath these haughty appearances. If Ferdinand had listened carefully he might have heard his vast edifice splitting asunder; nor could he shut his eyes to the fact that, though much prestige still remained to the imperial crown he wore in Germany, it carried very little real authority. Even Spain had overtopped the zenith of its glory and had begun to decline. Spain's golden century was behind her. Through the influx of precious metals into the country and resulting inflation, her people had forgotten the meaning of work. The expulsion of many of the Moors had sapped her economy, and her population was diminishing. In 1550 there were nine million inhabitants, but only six million in 1650. 'When Spain stirs the earth trembles.' The time was approaching when this proud proverb would no longer be true.

The religious and political grounds for conflict were therefore inextricably merged, and the old duel which for over a century had set the Hapsburgs against the royal house of France, a duel in which both sides strove for supremacy, was about to be resumed. Since both adversaries were Catholics what was to be the attitude of the Church to this encounter? Could the Holy See take sides against the Hapsburgs who posed as champions of the Catholic counter-offensive, even though it knew that their zeal in crushing heresy concealed other ambitions? Could it on the other hand condemn the Church's eldest daughter and her Most Christian King, the heir of St Louis—the one country in which the spirit behind the Tridentine reforms was bearing fruit? Once more the Holy See was forced, as it had been in the past, to play its role of supreme arbiter, and reconcile the sons of a common father. If the Holy See failed to recognize this as its task, or to fulfil that task, there was a danger that the conflict might result in an entirely secular solution, one in which political interests alone would predominate. Further, the new order established in Europe might bring about the end of the Catholic counter-offensive and the permanent eclipse of the Papacy.

Within the states themselves there existed problems no less complex, and for the Church equally disturbing. To put an end to the bloody factions kindled by the Protestant revolt two solutions were available: the exercise of authority and the use of compromise. The first was the one most generally accepted; it had been formulated in Germany under the famous principle *Cujus regio, hujus religio*, which gave religious unity the force of law modelled on the method of dealing with political differences. The Church never quite accepted this solution; firstly, because it assumed that in order to safeguard peace she might be forced to abandon territories held by Protestantism; secondly, because if she left to princes the care of establishing religious unity in their domains she would be putting temptation in their way to meddle in matters outside the jurisdiction of the political power— a temptation to which they would succumb only too easily.

As a matter of fact some rather strange theories had recently become widespread in Christian Europe. These theories insisted on the rights of secular powers to control and direct everything not only in so far as civil life was concerned, but also in matters affecting piety and Christian life. Theories such as these were formulated by Thomas Lieber, known as Erastus (1524–83). He was a Swiss-German doctor who had settled as a teacher at Heidelberg. His ideas were contained in his *Explicatio gravissima*, a work published six years after his death, and which his English disciple Wither strove to make known. Erastian ideas, which were welcomed by the Protestant princes and Queen Elizabeth, might also tempt Catholic monarchs—perhaps even the Emperor and the Most Christian King of France.

These doctrines were in harmony with the times and therefore constituted a threat to the Church. Nearly all governments, great and small, were moving in the direction of absolutism. To control the forces of disruption which smote the century, to bind together national endeavour in the struggle for life, the people turned to one man or one family who would incorporate the greatness and ambition of the nation. But it is the destiny of an absolutist state to absorb the entire creative powers of its people, to allow nothing to escape its control, and to exercise its vigilant supervision over religion itself, as well as over the economy and the intellect. The Erastian surrender of religion to politics which the famous dictum *Cujus regio* seemed to imply was one which leads to the modern evolution of governmental forms. Therein lay a grave danger to the Church and to Christendom itself.

The alternative solution to the Catholic-Protestant problem was no better. It was a compromise solution, one which had gained acceptance in France with the Edict of Nantes, in Poland with the Convention of Warsaw, and which the temperamental Rudolf II had allowed Bohemia to impose on him when he signed the Royal Charter (*Majestätsbrief*). But this solution, the basis of a *modus vivendi* between the religious groups, was not popular. In Bohemia it was shattered nine years after the notorious charter was ratified. In Poland all the bishops except one declared against the convention. In France resistance to the edict was frequent and tenacious. The Catholics could not easily resign themselves to seeing the Protestants as a state within the state, strutting defiantly in their fortified towns. The Church was unfavourable in principle to any form of compromise, and this attitude assisted her real enemies. To put an end to the policy of compromise was to strengthen absolutism. When the King of France revoked the Edict of Nantes he was congratulated by the Holy See; but he was also responsible for Gallicanism, which was more or less schismatic.

In every field, then, the Church seemed to be threatened in its authority and its rights. Perhaps the coming crisis and world evolution would lead to a kind of general secularization of policy. But that was one aspect among others of a more general crisis, a gradual process leading modern man to a profound modification of his conception of the world, of life and of himself. A crisis of the spirit and of the conscience smouldered beneath the whole series of political events which effected so profound a change in the appearance of the world. Galileo, Bacon, Descartes, Spinoza, the birth of experimental science and the establishment of a new method of reasoning [1] blazed the trail of a story on another plane, in which the collapse of the Hapsburgs and the birth of absolutism point to other fundamental ideas. Modern Europe was in the making; was it to continue to be the Europe of Christians?

2. THE THIRTY YEARS WAR: A WAR OF RELIGION BECOMES POLITICAL

There is no more striking example of the confusion of religious and political interests, and of the disappearance of the former to the advantage of the latter, than in the Thirty Years War. This phrase is, in any case, inaccurate. Some historians, easily captivated by somewhat over-simplified methods of exposition, have used it to denote a whole series of events in which the crisis in Europe during the first half of the century is examined from the diplomatic and military point of view. But these events (which, moreover, did not end in 1646, since the conflict continued in several places long after that) cannot easily be narrowed down to the traditional conception of war. Strictly speaking, if internal and external politics were merged, it meant that the whole order of Europe was being challenged. An extremely complex drama was being enacted in which great powers were struggling to establish their supremacy, while nations were fighting for their freedom and their rights, and hostile Churches faced each other in an effort to reconquer souls and property.

[1] See *The Church in the Eighteenth Century*, Chapter I.

The traditional diagram, to which French historians on the whole adhere, may be sketched out as follows. The war began in Bohemia in 1618 by the revolt of the Czechs against the Emperor Ferdinand II, the causes of which were both religious and political. In 1620, at the battle of the White Mountain, near Prague, the imperial armies crushed the rebels, who were reduced to merciless subjection. Therefore, from the very beginning, the affair was an Austrian internal crisis; but would it remain so? Keen observers foresaw that it could lead to a general war of state and religion. France, though tempted to intervene in favour of the Czechs in order to weaken the Hapsburgs, held back because her own position was precarious. But her hesitation did not prevent the war from spreading.

The storm broke in Germany, where Frederick, the Elector Palatine, a Protestant, was declared to have forfeited all his wealth and titles for having accepted the crown of Bohemia offered him by the Czechs; and he was replaced in the electoral council of the Empire by the Duke of Bavaria, a Catholic. At the same time another conflagration was kindled: the Dutch, taking advantage of the state of affairs in 1621, again took up arms against Spain on the expiry of the Twelve Years Truce. The Protestant princes, now a minority in the council and threatened by the emperor's success, looked around for allies. King Christian IV of Denmark came forward, enticed no doubt by the prospect of winning the bishoprics of the Weser (1625).

Henceforward the war was a European war. Behind the scenes France encouraged the Danish king, who suffered defeat and signed a hurried peace at Lübeck. The emperor reinforced his positions in Germany and intensified his policy of catholicizing by force. France became uneasy. When the Hapsburgs of Vienna and Madrid became allies, the possibility that they might return to their policy of encirclement, which was the policy of Charles V, remained a threat. Richelieu, who from now on held the reins of French politics, decided to act, in moderation at first and more or less secretly. By preventing the Hapsburgs from occupying Val Tellina he hindered them from securing communication between their Austrian and Italian territories by way of Splügen and Stelvio. He was anything but helpful to the emperor when the latter wished to have his son elected king of the Romans, that is to say, legal heir to the imperial crown. Christian IV's lack of success showed Richelieu that his efforts were inadequate and his diplomacy succeeded in finding a new adversary to hurl against the emperor in the person of Gustavus-Adolphus, King of Sweden. The promise of suitable subsidies persuaded him to enter the field in 1631. He was a strategist of genius. His well-trained troops roamed across Germany sweeping the imperial armies before them, and reached the Rhine. But this Caesar was becoming a nuisance! If Richelieu had no

wish to see an entirely imperial Germany, he certainly did not desire a
totally Protestant one. A cannon-ball, so well aimed that one might
suppose it was done deliberately, killed the Swedish leader at the battle
of Lutzen in 1632 as he charged at the head of his cavalry.

Richelieu then intervened. He had meanwhile crushed all his
enemies in France itself; he could now substitute open warfare for his
non-committal tactics. On the grounds that the balance of power in
Europe was in danger, he gathered around him a host of allies, including the German Protestant princes, and in 1635 he attacked. At first
he met with disaster. He was invaded in the north and the east; Corbie
fell; the enemy patrols actually reached Pontoise (1636). But such was
France's resilience that she reacted with crushing effect. Arras was
snatched from the enemy; Roussillon was occupied; an army friendly
to the French was hurled into Alsace, and the Hapsburg coalition began
to totter. Peace was in the air, but it required a little more time and the
memorable victories of Turenne in Alsace and the Palatinate before
the emperor agreed to sign the peace. The negotiations which opened
at Münster and Osnabrück in 1644 dragged painfully on for four years.
In 1648 the treaties of Westphalia settled the religious problems as well
as German and European political problems.[1]

To what extent was the Church, or religious interests generally,
affected by all these political, diplomatic and military issues? We
cannot identify those interests with Christian principles, because the
latter were monstrously violated. Probably no war since the invasion
of the Huns had been fought with such ferocity. The celebrated series
of plates by Callot, called *The Miseries of War*, constitute a truthful
record of those horrors. Mercenary armies for whom war bred war
were let loose on the provinces. They razed, pillaged, burned, tortured
and murdered for years on end, without distinguishing too closely
between friendly and hostile territory. The men who led them, such
as the lean and gaunt Tilly with his scarlet plume, and the haughty
Wallenstein with his irascible countenance, *condottieri* whose only
trade was war, were no better than their rank and file where a battle
was concerned. Almost the whole of Germany, many parts of France,
the Low Countries, Lorraine and Franche-Comté were to emerge
breathless from the struggle and ruined for a quarter of a century. And
this violence was perpetrated in the name of the Gospel, for the triumph
of this or that *credo*!

There is no doubt whatever that the Thirty Years War did begin as
a religious war, as a new phase in the conflict between Catholics and

---

[1] The war with Spain went on until 1660 despite Condé's victory at Lens in 1648. But
that was mainly because France was paralysed by the Fronde disorders. Peace was
achieved through Turenne's victory at the Dunes (1658), and was followed by the signing
of the Treaty of the Pyrenees.

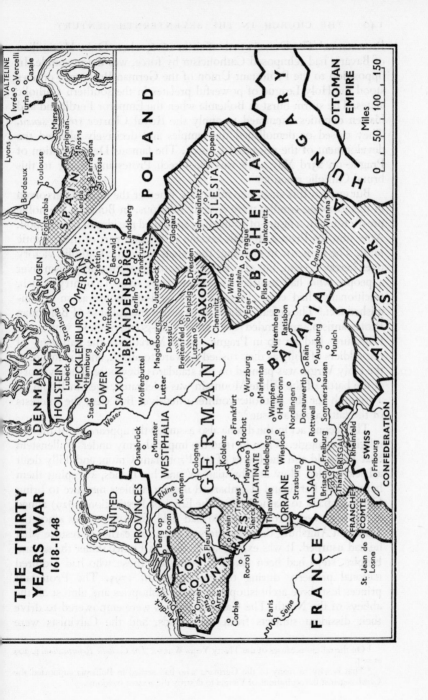

THE THIRTY YEARS WAR
1618-1648

Miles
0   50   100   150

OTTOMAN EMPIRE

HUNGARY

POLAND

BOHEMIA
Oppeln
Schweidnitz
Glogau
SILESIA
Prague ○ Jankowitz
White △ Eger
Mountain ○ Pilsen
Dresden
Leipzig ○
Breitenfeld
Lutzen ○ Chemnitz
○ Jüterbock

SAXONY
Frankfurt
Berlin ○
Dessau
Magdeburg ○
Wolfenbüttel
Lutter ○

BRANDENBURG
Berwald
Landsberg
Stettin ○
Wittstock

POMERANIA
Hamburg
Stralsund
Lubeck

MECKLENBURG
RÜGEN

DENMARK
HOLSTEIN
Stade

LOWER SAXONY
Elbe
Weser

AUSTRIA
Vienna ○
Danube
Ratisbon
Nuremberg ○

BAVARIA
Munich ○
Augsburg ○
Rain ○
Donauwerth ○
Sommershausen
Nordlingen ○
Wurzburg ○
Marlental
Wimpfen ○
Hellbronn ○

GERMANY
Frankfurt ○
Höchst
Mayence
Wieslech
Heidelberg ○
Coblenz
Cologne ○
Kempen
Berg op Zoom
Osnabrück ○
Munster ○

WESTPHALIA
Rhine

UNITED PROVINCES

PALATINATE
Treves
Sierck
Thianville
Strasburg

LORRAINE
Avein
Fleurus
Rocroi

ALSACE
Brisach
Freiburg ○
Rottweil
Thann
BRISGAU
Rheinfeld

SWISS CONFEDERATION
Fribourg ○

FRANCHE COMTE
St. Jean de Losne

LOW COUNTRIES
Dunkirk
St. Omer
Arras ○
Corbie
Mardick

FRANCE
Paris
Seine

Lyons ○
Bordeaux ○
Toulouse ○
Perpignan ○
Marseilles ○

VALTELINE
Ivrée ○ Vercelli
Turin ○ Casale
Ros'ts
Tarragona ○
Lerida ○
Tortosa ○
Fontarabia ○

SPAIN

Protestants.[1] The Donaüworth affair in 1606, where Duke Maximilian of Bavaria had reimposed Catholicism by force, was the preamble. In opposition to the Protestant Union of the German Protestant princes stood the Holy League of powerful prelates in the southern Catholic states. The storm burst in Bohemia when the Emperor Ferdinand and his ten deputies attempted to apply the Royal Charter *stricto sensu*. They closed or demolished the temples and decisively blocked the development of the reformed Church. The famous Defenestration of Prague on 23rd May 1618 was the Czech Protestants' reply to this brutal Catholic reaction.

But even at this stage one might ask whether the interests involved in this growing conflict were entirely religious. In Bohemia the noble pre-Reformation figure of John Huss embodied the idea of nationhood. After him the Protestant faith became an integral part of the patriotic ideal. The emperor in crushing the rebels made the Catholic victory over heresy certain, but also the victory of Hapsburg despotism over a people who had aspired to become free; over a country which, tracitionally, had come to regard its semi-autonomy as an accomplished fact.[2] The defeat of the Czechs sealed the collapse of Bohemian Protestantism, and ended the rather easy-going régime which the Hapsburgs had set up in Prague. 'Santa Maria' was the battle-cry of the soldiers of Tilly as they rushed forward to attack, and the image of the Holy Virgin was painted on the standards they bore. Their victory at the battle of the White Mountain was celebrated, even in Rome, as a triumph for the Catholic counter-offensive. But were the interests of the faith alone at issue?

The second act in the drama also assumed the appearance of the old religious struggle. When in 1626 the imperial army under Wallenstein beat Mansfeld and the forces of the Protestant Union, and Tilly dealt a back-handed blow at Christian IV and his Danes, sweeping them before him, Ferdinand II embarked upon a ruthless measure to bring Germany back to Catholicism. The Edict of Restitution (1629) aimed at forcing every Protestant who had held Catholic estates since the Treaty of Augsburg three-quarters of a century earlier to restore what he had usurped. It was exactly as though, in France under the second Empire, steps had been taken to dispossess those who had acquired national property during the revolution of 1795. The Protestant princes lost three archbishoprics, fifteen bishoprics and almost all the abbeys of the North. The Catholic princes were empowered to drive their dissident subjects from their lands, and the Calvinists were

---

[1] On the religious causes of the Thirty Years War see *The Catholic Reformation*, p. 209 et seq.

[2] That is why so many of the Germans who had settled in Bohemia supported the Czechs against the aspirations of Vienna to destroy the ancient freedoms.

banished *en bloc*. This was, therefore, a counter-reformation measure;
it was political counter-reformation if not spiritual, for the beneficiaries
of this recovery of property were not all entirely free from suspicion of
greed—among them the Archduke Leopold William, son of the
emperor, who, already Bishop of Strasburg and Passau, secured the
grant of three extra dioceses. This operation was not carried out in the
interests of the Catholic faith alone; its purpose was rather to support
an imperial venture in the direction of absolutism and centralization
throughout Germany, linked as an afterthought with a desire to return
to the secular struggle whose goal was the encirclement and suppression
of France. At the very moment when his Viennese cousin was carrying
out this ruthless catholicization Philip IV of Spain was intervening in
Italy to drive a Frenchman from the Duchy of Mantua, to overpower
Venice and control Savoy, while keeping a close eye on the Duchy of
Castro. In the spring of 1632 the Jesuit Pasmany, Archbishop of Gran,
champion of the anti-Protestant policy of violence in Bohemia and
Hungary, was in Rome tightening the alliance between the two
Hapsburgs—*ad majorem Dei gloriam*, but also to crush France. The
outcome was the raid by Gustavus Adolphus, a Protestant king financed
by a French cardinal, followed by the entry into the war of the Most
Christian King against the Catholic King and the Holy Roman Empire.

Thus the Thirty Years War soon lost its original character as a
religious conflict, and became wholly a political struggle. It has often
been said that the war marked a decisive turning-point in the development of armaments and the conduct of military operations. But it was
also the last of the religious wars and the first of the great conflicts of
modern times. Some of its episodes represented clear-cut religious
interests. Such was the resolute struggle waged by the German
Protestant princes grouped around Bernard of Saxe-Weimar, and that
of the Dutch under Maurice of Nassau against the terrible infantry of
Olivarès. But religion was not the only issue; it was not even the real
driving force behind the dispute. The German princes desired above
all to preserve their freedoms, their tiny anarchical sovereignties; and
Richelieu helped them on the assumption that a Germany dissected and
shared out among hundreds of petty monarchs was less dangerous to
France than an Empire united under the crown of the Hapsburgs.
As for the Low Countries, the real ringleaders in the contest were the
strict Gomarist pastors who recognized the devil in everything which,
near or far, reminded them of Catholicism; or perhaps the business
men who saw in the eclipse of Spain an opportunity to create for themselves a maritime empire, and their friends the Corsairs of Friesland
and Zealand who managed to round up five hundred Spanish ships.
Henceforward the religious war remained but a pretext; temporal
interests took precedence over the spiritual.

3. THE POLICIES OF CARDINAL RICHELIEU

A new light is now thrown upon two problems—the attitude adopted by France, the France of the Most Christian King, and the part played by the popes throughout the drama which rent Europe.

The policy followed by France, and in particular by Richelieu, France's first minister of state, has always aroused heated discussion. It seems perhaps difficult to understand how a Cardinal of Holy Church could become an ally of Protestant powers, thereby checking, and finally halting, the progress of Catholicism in Germany and the offensive of the Counter-Reformation. And why did Richelieu go so far as to establish relations with the Turks? Even while that policy was being pursued the king himself was asked such questions in no uncertain terms by Marie dei Médici, by the Papal Nuncio and by Marillac, Keeper of the Seals. They were put to the general public in such pamphlets as the *Avertissement d'un théologien*, published in 1625, the *Espion français* and the *Mysteria politica*. Many good Catholics, who were also patriotic Frenchmen, thought that the honourable policy for France was to ally herself with the Empire, with Bavaria, Spain and Poland, in order to crush heresy and re-establish Catholic unity in Europe. The Government of Cardinal Ministers, *Gallia purpurata* as it was then called, thought otherwise. But why?

To affirm as some have done that Richelieu, despite his purple, laughed at Catholicity, is pure slander. It is too easy to say, as a Venetian ambassador is often quoted as saying, that Richelieu was more of a statesman than a churchman; and it is a perversion of the truth. When young Armand du Plessis de Richelieu received the cardinal's hat, Pope Gregory XV, who was anything but stupid and had a very lofty conception of Church interests, sent him a congratulatory letter praising his brilliant qualities and signifying that he would crush heresy, and 'tread upon serpents and reptiles'. There is nothing to prove that Richelieu was not determined throughout his life to deserve those praises, and really serve the cause of the Church in the midst of events which were so complex that it was not always easy to discern just where that cause lay. In any case, it is certain, as his correspondence proves, that in politics he always aimed at putting into effect 'what the principles of theology prescribed as permissible';[1] that he resigned himself to making war only when forced into it by circumstances; and, moreover, that he never showed the slightest sympathy with Protestant theology, even when he sought the alliance of Protestants. It is beyond doubt that he regarded France as 'the very heart of all Christian States'.

[1] *Correspondence de Richelieu* (d'Avenel, v. 282).

Nothing in this suggests that there was a touch of Machiavellism in Richelieu's methods—at least not in the trite and disparaging sense of the term. 'Fascinated by Machiavelli,' says Cardinal Grente, 'he showed that he intended to reinstate him.' What he did admire in the Florentine was his healthy realism, his keen sense of what was possible and his relentless lucidity. There is no evidence that Richelieu accepted the lessons in cynicism that may also be learned from Machiavelli. Richelieu detested market-place diplomacy; he believed that secrecy is the soul of success. He even invented the term *affaire secrétissime*, but never did he play a game of double-dealing, and never was he known to break his word. To those politicians who taught that treaties were made to be broken from the moment they became inconvenient Richelieu replied: 'The Christian faith is opposed to such maxims.' His policy does not appear to have been less Christian in its methods than in its intentions.

Neither would it be true to say that he continued to uphold the Protestant cause because of his hatred of the Hapsburgs. Throughout the entire series of events his policy revealed a strategy infinitely more complex than that attributed to him under the traditional conception of things. At the beginning of the war, far from striving to help the Czechs and subsequently the Protestant Union, he approved France's abstention from the controversy. Later, when he became minister, he envisaged an extremely flexible policy in which countries Catholic like Bavaria, Calvinist like Brandenburg and Lutheran like Sweden would unite to resist imperial ascendancy. In the Val Tellina affair in 1626 he offered no opposition to a compromise which stood for a defence of Catholicism. It was only in 1630 that, disapproving the incautious efforts of his beloved Father Joseph, who still believed it possible to come to some arrangement with the emperor, his attitude hardened. But by that time the Hapsburg danger had become considerable. Aided and advised by Wallenstein, the emperor aimed at a united Germany under his rule. Catholicization by force, begun by the Edict of Restitution, was clearly seen by Richelieu to be just what it was: a means of domination. The alliance made between Vienna and Madrid was growing more compact, and the two Hapsburgs could threaten France on every frontier. The Cardinal Minister was conscious of his duty to the State: he had to defend the interests, the territorial integrity, perhaps even the liberty and life of the country entrusted to him. Hence his alliance with the Protestants, the subtle and efficient labour of Father Joseph to thwart imperial diplomacy, the effort to rally 'jusque sous les poles', as Voiture said, the opponents of the House of Austria. Hence also the subsidies to Gustavus Adolphus and, later on, the taking over by France of the Lutheran and Calvinist army of Bernard of Saxe-Weimar. This was not in the least a betrayal of the

Catholic cause. At a time when he appeared to be most preoccupied with these tactics Richelieu did not abandon his allegiance to the things which appertained to his priestly state. He rejected the offer made by Gustavus Adolphus to take similar action with regard to Franche-Comté and Alsace, an operation which would undoubtedly have moved France's frontiers to the Rhine and the Jura Mountains. Richelieu knew that he would have had to pay for it by throwing in his lot completely with the Protestant cause. He also strove to protect the neutrality of the Catholic League, and he maintained a French garrison at Trier in order to prevent the Swedes from attacking the archbishop elector. Even at the height of Gustavus Adolphus's success he offered to mediate between the King of Sweden and the emperor.

As for the results of his work, continued and finalized by his disciple Mazarin—though certainly with less breadth of vision—it would be unjust to regard them as prejudicial to the Catholic cause, and nothing more. If it is true that the Treaties of Westphalia brought about a definite return to the *status quo ante* hardly favourable to the Roman Church, it is equally true that they were warranted by the danger of imperial aims which France had to resist. But it was French diplomacy which secured for the Catholics of Holland, Brandenburg and Hanover the little tolerance they enjoyed, and which they certainly would not have done without her intervention. Considering Richelieu's policy as a whole, both internal and external, we may ask whether there did not exist behind all his realistic diplomacy the very noble and profoundly Catholic idea that a *rapprochement* with the Protestants might lead to their return to the bosom of the Church.[1]

On the whole, this policy which was advantageous to France was quite as good as that of the Hapsburgs from the Catholic point of view. Judging from the way in which titles and benefices were given back to the Church following the Edict of Restitution, we are entitled to maintain that the principles of ecclesiastical reform were better respected in the land of Bérulle, Olier and Monsieur Vincent. Moreover, an impartial estimate of Richelieu's policy obliges us to ask whether another policy were possible. Indeed, another had been put forward. It has been called the policy of the Devout, and was proposed by that other great cardinal, Bérulle, among others. The idea behind it was the defence of the Catholic cause everywhere and by every

---

[1] See section 11: 'Richelieu and the Protestants'. The only aspect of Richelieu's policy which might be seriously questioned is the priority given to Lutheran Sweden over Catholic Poland. It might not have been possible to prevent the Vasa king, Sigismund III, from entering into an Austrian alliance—which in any case proved to be detrimental to him. But Poland was already undermined by disintegrating forces which led shortly afterwards to her ruin. Perhaps Richelieu with his penetrating vision was able to gauge the true weakness of this possible ally; and, since he needed a weapon with which to threaten the enemy to the north and east, he preferred the army of Sweden.

possible means; in other words, by the formation of a *bloc* of all
Catholic powers against Protestant countries and peoples. That policy
was put into operation in England in the time of Queen Henrietta, the
wife of Charles I. It was also the policy of the ambassador Fargis in
Madrid, that of Marie dei Médici when she took refuge in the Spanish
Low Countries, and more or less that of Anne of Austria and a mixed
bag of sincere believers and trouble-makers. For a while it was even
the policy which Father Joseph endeavoured to put into effect. In the
eyes of its adherents Richelieu was the cardinal of heretics.

But was it a practical policy? It would have placed France in a
position of inferiority in relation to the Hapsburgs, which the country
would have refused to accept at the height of its expansion; nor could
France yet aspire with any hope of success to the hegemony of a
Catholic Europe. It would have been quixotic to expect from such a
policy anything but fresh dissension. Besides, it savoured of treachery
and conspiracy, whether one desired it or not. Spanish soldiers had
quite recently been garrisoned in Paris in the name of the Catholic
faith. The danger of Hapsburg intervention in France was not remote,
as the wars of the Fronde would prove. The advocates of a Spanish
alliance happened to be the very people who resisted the cardinal's
attempts to put the country in order, and if their opposition had
succeeded the result would certainly have been a return to anarchy, of
which France had grown tired. The king's brother Gaston, Ornano,
Chalais, the two Vendômes and the two queens were all members of the
Devout; had their opinions prevailed the country would have reverted
to the state that obtained during the ministries of Concini and de
Luynes. 'The more France suffers,' wrote Olivarès, 'the more peaceful
will Christendom become.' The Catholics of France were not likely to
lend their support to hopes of that sort. When Chalais's head fell
beneath the axe Richelieu put an end to a policy which, while pur-
porting to subscribe to noble Catholic aspirations, concealed others
which were pernicious. These unhealthy disputes had nothing whatever
to do with the faith, nor even with the interests of the Church. The
clear-headed Father Joseph appreciated this; he fell in with the views
of his friend, giving him all possible assistance in his policy of a
Protestant alliance.

Though it is true that Richelieu in no way deserves to be maltreated
by Catholic historians, it is evident that the Church could not have
emerged greater and stronger from this succession of tragic and chaotic
events. The defence of Catholicism and the Counter-Reformation
were bound to be pushed more and more into the background. When,
through exhaustion and general weariness, the conflict eventually came
to an end, scarcely any further thought was given to the Christian ideal
during the long-drawn-out peace negotiations.

4. THE POLICY OF THE HOLY SEE

Perhaps the foregoing explains the policy which the Holy See followed throughout these events, a policy which aimed at stability and a middle course, absolutely acceptable in principle though possibly questionable in the manner in which it was handled. The Church has been sharply criticized for that policy. French Catholic historians [1] have not forgiven her for failing to give Richelieu unwavering support; nor have German Catholic historians been less severe. Both sides have based their argument on the fact that her policy was not really successful, and that the outcome of the war was unfavourable to the Church. Yet we cannot be really sure, *hic et nunc*, that any other policy was possible and more advantageous. What is certain, however, is that the Papacy, which previously held such a strong position, wielding as it did the powerful diplomatic weapon of the nunciatures, [2] did not play the part of umpire as she might have been expected to do. The reason for this may lie partly in human weakness, nepotism and a succession of pontificates that were either second rate or too short. But it is also reasonable to think that this policy, which after all refused to side with either camp, was guided by a clear view of the facts and of the interests at stake—that it was in fact a continuation of the policy of Sixtus.

This strategy of the happy medium, if not of impartiality, was not the original policy of the Holy See. The conflict began as a struggle between the Catholic throne of Austria and the Protestant rebels, and the Papacy could have no doubt at all of where its sympathies lay. Paul V, a Borghese, was not without spirit. At the risk of a European war he had recently brought to heel the Most Serene Republic of Venice, [3] and had intervened energetically in England against the anti-Catholic measures of James I. [4] As a friend of the Hapsburgs (he had been Nuncio in Spain) he persuaded Maximilian of Bavaria to organize the Catholic League; and when news reached him that the battle of the White Mountain had ended in victory he arranged for a solemn procession of thanksgiving at Rome, during which, incidentally, he suffered an apoplectic fit. His Nuncio Caraffa and the Jesuits sent by him laboured for the reconversion of Bohemia, nor does it seem that the Pope once raised his voice to condemn their excesses.

Under Paul V's successor this policy of counter-reform was, if not abandoned, at least moderated and conducted on different lines.

---

[1] Dufourcq, for instance.
[2] See *The Catholic Reformation*, p. 330.
[3] Ibid, p. 326.
[4] Ibid., p. 212.

Gregory XV was a sound and prudent pontiff. He founded the Congregation of Propaganda and canonized five saints in 1622; but was he aware of the danger to Christian Europe that might result from excessive bolstering of Hapsburg power? On the one hand he pressed for conferment of the Palatine electorate upon Duke Maximilian of Bavaria, a liegeman of Catholicism in Germany, so as to ensure a Catholic majority in the Imperial College. On the other hand he openly sought to maintain good relations with France, asking her to use her influence in the East for the protection of missionaries. In order to please the king he raised the episcopal See of Paris to the status of a metropolitan see (1622), and bestowed the cardinal's hat on Richelieu, the young protégé of Marie dei Médici. There is no doubt that in the Val Tellina affair he endeavoured to serve as umpire. In 1621, when the Catholics of the country rose against their Protestant masters, the League of Grisons, a veritable Rhaetian Saint Bartholomew's Day ensued, and Austria grasped the opportunity to secure a foothold in the valley. The Pope intervened. He was eager to assist the Catholic population of the highlands, but also to allay the anxiety of France. France indeed had reason to fear the sight of a Hapsburg at Vienna giving help to his cousin of Spain, who was installed in Italy; for such an eventuality might precipitate a conflict. The diplomacy of Gregory XV was wonderfully flexible. It aimed at negotiating a compromise which might well have established the independence of Val Tellina and left everybody satisfied. But the Pope died when the powers were on the point of agreeing.

It was the lot of his successor Urban VIII to be Pope during the most violent years of the crisis, when it became evident that Catholicism and Protestantism were no longer the sole reason for the conflict, but that two groups of powers were defending their own interests. It has often been said that Urban was so entangled in his nephews' problems, so busy trying to put right wretched troubles like that of the Duchy of Castro,[1] that he had no time to become seriously interested in the European drama. That is a harsh judgment. What seems more likely is that while he and the whole Roman Curia watched the progress of a war which was a distressing reminder of the struggles of the preceding century, they were haunted by the memory of the year 1527, when German ruffians under the Constable of Bourbon sacked Rome. To remain altogether neutral seemed to them the best solution. Urban VIII fortified the castle of Sant' Angelo and Civitàvecchia, and established an arms factory, but he did not make it clear against whom his cannon was to be used.

To judge his policy fairly proper consideration must be given to the very delicate situation confronting the Papacy. Directly or indirectly

[1] See p. 127.

Spain dominated Italy. She controlled both Milan and Naples. Her agents financed and regimented the petty princes of the peninsula. And the only counter-measure at the disposal of France lay in her ability to threaten Avignon, which was papal territory. In these circumstances it is hardly fair to blame the Pope for having felt constrained towards a Hapsburg policy. In actual fact he did not resign himself to it. It may be true that to avoid offending Madrid he refused to recognize the House of Braganza's leadership of the restored kingdom of Portugal. It may also be true that here and there a cardinal openly subscribed to the Spanish cause. Yet he himself maintained an attitude of reserve. In any case, he had seen in the Duchy of Mantua what Spanish intransigence was capable of perpetrating, and he had experienced it himself in the kingdom of Naples. When in 1629 the emperor signed the famous Edict of Restitution, he was so uncertain of the Pope's attitude that he did not submit the draft for his approval, declaring—and this was sheer Erastianism—that however competent the sovereign pontiff might be to deal with matters of dogma, he should not get mixed up in ecclesiastical affairs. And when, after France had come into the war, Richelieu's opponents asked Urban VIII to condemn the 'cardinal of heretics' and put the country under an interdict, he refused. This must certainly be considered a courageous gesture on his part, if we recall the wild scene that took place in the Consistory, when the Spanish cardinals, backed by Cardinal Ubaldini, called on the Pope to take sides, and Cardinal Colonna had to summon the guards to restore order. However, that did not prevent Urban VIII from doing his best to oppose, and then to break, Richelieu's alliance with the Protestant princes. He tried, moreover, to prevent the Most Christian King from making an alliance with the Turks.

It cannot be doubted that this policy of equilibrium was a Christian policy, but was it humanly possible of achievement? It did not, in fact, succeed, and Urban VIII soon became suspect in both camps. Wallenstein spoke seriously of leading an expedition against Rome. In Val Tellina the solution put forward by Gregory XV was not a success, and the Val passed under the control of the Swiss Cantons—that is, more or less under Protestant influence. Good relations with France deteriorated. Richelieu's appointment of Cardinal La Valette as army commander, against which Urban VIII had rightly protested, served as a pretext for an exchange of sharp words. And Venice appeared to be on the point of rising up once more against Rome. If the Pope's role as adjudicator were to lead to ultimate success it undoubtedly needed a man of greater calibre than this Barberini, and of a moral prestige less heavily involved in mundane commitments.

None the less Urban VIII must be given credit for having, even in the worst moments of the *débâcle*, striven for peace with praiseworthy obstinacy. Papal diplomacy sought unremittingly to draw the two Catholic countries of France and Bavaria together, and the nuncios continually maintained secret negotiations between Madrid and Brussels and Madrid and Paris simultaneously. Innocent X, who succeeded the Barberini pope, bravely continued the same efforts, though he too was in an extremely difficult position, powerless to prevent the Spanish forces at Naples from marching through the Papal States to rejoin the rest of the army in Milan; yet he supported Mazarin in his slow and delicate approach to peace. But peace which the pontiffs desired and for which they strove was not to be concluded in the way they had hoped.

5. The Treaties of Westphalia

After discussions lasting nearly four years the treaties which were to put an end to the conflict were signed in Westphalia on 24th October 1648, at Münster in so far as concerned the issues between the Empire and France, and at Osnabrück to settle those between Sweden and the Hapsburgs. These treaties were inconclusive even before they were signed. A few months earlier Philip IV of Spain had offered to make a separate peace with the Low Countries, which had rebelled, and to give them complete independence. He was even prepared to hand over Antwerp on condition that they abandoned the French. He eventually carried on the war for another twelve years until the Peace of the Pyrenees. The treaties therefore affected only Germany and the Empire. By them France and Sweden were amply rewarded for having defended the 'Germanic freedoms'.[1] As for these Germanic freedoms, there could be no doubt that they had been well defended, for the sovereignty of three hundred and forty-three states was recognized. As far as France was concerned this ratification of the carving up of Germany was a more important result than her territorial acquisitions.

The religious clauses of the treaty were intimately associated with the political disintegration of states. In one sense they determined it; for the course of events set in motion by the revolution of Martin Luther reached its most extreme consequences. Freedom of conscience and worship was proclaimed—it was even extended to include the Calvinists—but the freedom existed for the princes, not for their subjects. The principle *Cujus regio, hujus religio* asserted itself once

---

[1] France won the recognition of her sovereign rights over the Three Bishoprics of Metz, Toul and Verdun, which she had held without legal title since 1552. Above all she acquired, if not the whole of Alsace, at least the grounds for total annexation in the future through certain obscure clauses in the treaty (Mülhausen, Strasburg and several states directly dependent on the Empire were specifically excluded).

F

more. It was even aggravated in its effects, for Article V of the treaty
declared that 'together with the right of territory and sovereignty the
governments would enjoy that of reforming the Church'. It was
Erastianism carried to its inevitable conclusion. Every petty king,
every princeling became a pope in his dominions, and this was an
outright contradiction of the decisions taken by the Council of Trent
at its XXIVth Session. There existed one reservation to this rule of
state religion: it was specified that the private or public exercise of one
of the three forms of worship could not be suppressed where it had
existed on 1st January 1624. And war-weariness was so general that the
clause was in fact usually honoured.[1]

The treaties also provided for a return to the *status quo ante* as
far as property was concerned. Ferdinand II very soon became
aware that the Edict of Restitution was a mistake, and decided not to
put it into operation. The treaties determined that all ecclesiastical
property would belong to the religious body which owned it in 1624.
In practice the Catholics were the losers: they had to give up two
archbishoprics, thirteen bishoprics and numerous abbeys. The Protestants saw their influence grow in the Diet, and Brandenburg soon
carried great weight in the imperial elections and in German policy as
a whole. The Protestant cause unquestionably gained much from the
treaties; but less than might have been expected, for it lacked virile
leadership and was not at that time the great evangelical and reformed
Church of which some Protestants had dreamed. But paradoxically the
great *political* victory of Protestantism coincided with the total failure
of Protestantism to organize itself into a single Church.[2] Cromwell, the
strong man of the Reformation, had only just vanquished his king
(1649), and yet was far from having achieved that coalition of Protestant forces which William of Orange was to build.[3] But it is no
less certain that therein lay a definite danger for Catholicism. Had
Richelieu still been alive, would he have allowed his vast effort to
reach such a conclusion? In exchange for the permanent weakening of
the Empire would he have been willing to pay a price too heavy for
his Catholic heart to bear? However that might be, Mazarin had no
such scruples, and his diplomacy during the negotiations was inexorably realistic. In other words, it took account of no principles which
were not entirely advantageous to France.

It is understandable that Rome should have looked askance at such
an end to negotiations which she had tried so earnestly to direct. The
Nuncio Chigi and the Jesuit Wangnereck (who used the pen-name

---

[1] In the diocese of Strasburg, however, there were violent incidents from 1660
onwards.
[2] See *The Church in the Eighteenth Century*, Chapter III.
[3] See *The Church in the Eighteenth Century*, Chapter III.

Ernestus de Eusebiis in impassioned pamphlets against the policy of surrender) both endeavoured to resist the trend towards opportunism. It was all in vain. Duke Maximilian of Trauttmansdorf, who exercised great influence over the Emperor Ferdinand II, reminded him that since he had Protestant as well as Catholic subjects he had a particular interest in the proposed arrangement. The objections raised by the Chigi were therefore ineffectual. All that the Pope could do was to lodge a solemn protest against decisions which he was powerless to prevent. His representative refused to be present at the solemn sessions during which the treaties were signed. The papal Bull *Zelus domus meae* declared these documents 'perpetually null, worthless, invalid, iniquitous, condemned, frivolous and without authority'.[1] But apart from the King of Spain and the Dukes of Mantua and Lorraine no prince of any importance echoed his protest. The Pope himself did not dare to publish his Bull, written in November 1648, until June 1650, after the departure from Rome of the Swedish and Brandenburger troops whose presence was so irksome.

6. THE BURIAL OF CHRISTENDOM

The Papacy now realized that the time had come to abandon the field of high international politics. In this, however, it was not alone. The Treaties of Westphalia finally sealed the relinquishment by statesmen of a noble and ancient concept, a concept which had dominated the Middle Ages: that there existed among the baptized people of Europe a bond stronger than all their motives for wrangling—a spiritual bond, the concept of Christendom.

Since the fourteenth century, and especially during the fifteenth, this concept had been steadily disintegrating.[2] The Protestant revolution dealt it a mortal blow, for men and nations who shared the same Gospel opposed one another with implacable fury. The Thirty Years War proved beyond a shadow of doubt that the last states to defend the ideal of a united Christian Europe were invoking that principle while in fact they aimed at maintaining or imposing their own supremacy. It was at Münster and Osnabrück that Christendom was buried.

But the tragedy was that nothing could replace it; and twentieth-century Europe is still bleeding in consequence. Henceforward no higher ideal, no higher authority existed to assert itself over states. Europe was to be little more than a collection of countries, great and

---

[1] On the occasion of the third centenary of the Treaties of Westphalia, Pope Pius XII, in a letter to the Bishop of Münster, repeated this condemnation but in milder terms.

[2] See *The Protestant Reformation*, Chapter I, and *The Catholic Reformation*, p. 246.

small, maintained in balance—and an unstable balance—by the
antagonism of might. There was nothing left to withstand the assault
of self-interest and passion. Some have rejoiced at the change which
laid the foundations of modern Europe. Among them is the French
socialist Proudhon who, in his book *La Guerre et la Paix*, after
railing against 'the alliance between the sword and the tiara', characteristically reminiscent of the Middle Ages, exclaims: 'What is the greatest
act of the European community since that famous alliance? The
Treaty of Westphalia which, by the opposition of forces and under the
protection of the god of war, laid the foundations of universal balance.'
When we consider the results achieved by this policy during three
centuries, we find it difficult to share his enthusiasm.[1] Rather are we
inclined to repeat sadly the words of Pius XII with regard to these
very agreements of 1648: 'Treaties which are not built upon moral
law collapse.'

However, the idea of a superior principle dominating politics did
not entirely disappear from the minds of men. If Europe was
destined to become the jungle we know, where only the strong would
make the laws, there would not cease to flow a stream which tended to
lead elsewhere than towards the rule of might. So long as governments
and statesmen sought to maintain an uneasy peace backed by alliances
and counter-alliances, jurists and theologians would strive to reach
beyond this empiricism, to codify the moral rules governing relations
between peoples, and even to rediscover the bases of a unity and link
Europeans in a consciousness of a common allegiance. It was a kind of
homesickness for Christendom. The defenders of the old ideal had for
heirs the promoters of international law, the protagonists of a united
Europe. This aspect, with all its endeavours, schemes, theories and
dreams of a more civilized policy, is perhaps among those least studied
by classical historians; but it is the most moving in the whole period
during which the modern world was built.[2]

Even as far back as the beginning of the fifteenth century Pierre
Dubois, and a little later Podiebrad, King of Bohemia, put forward
some splendid Utopian ideas for the setting up of a community of
nations, even a brotherhood of the human race, to take the place of
Christendom which lay in ruins.[3] At the beginning of the seventeenth
many others appeared. Wise and eminent men laid down the principles
of this solidarity. The great Spanish Jesuit Suarez (1548–1617)

---

[1] It is true that the Christian ideal did not prevent long struggles from taking place
during the Middle Ages, such as the one between the Plantagenets and the Capetians. But
the policy of balance of power did not prove any more effectual, and modern wars became
more general and more devastating.

[2] Reference must here be made to the excellent book on this subject by Bernard
Voyenne which is mentioned in the bibliographical notes.

[3] See *The Catholic Reformation*, p. 214.

declared that 'every existing state, in itself a perfect community composed of its own members, is also part of a universal community'. The indefatigable herald of this splendid idea was Hugo van Groot, known as Grotius (1583-1645). He was the glory of Holland, an eminent jurist and father of international law. He took refuge in France when the fall of Jan van Oldenbarneveldt obliged him to flee his country. Through Richelieu and Louis XIII he was granted a pension, and the King of Sweden made him his ambassador in Paris. He was indeed one of the most important and most interesting figures of his day. He too regarded it as 'necessary to establish between Christian powers a kind of corporate body, with assemblies at which disputes would be settled once and for all'. He went so far as to sketch out a plan of a League of Nations. Emeric Lacroix, known as Emeric Crucé, was more ambitious: he developed the plan, and published in 1623 a detailed work entitled *Discours des occasions et des moyens d'établir la paix générale*. In his 'United Nations Organization', the capital of which would be Venice, he included Ethiopia, Persia, China and Japan. And Sully in his old age perfected his celebrated *Grand Dessein* which he attributed *a posteriori* to his master Henri IV—a 'most Christian republic' founded upon the federation of fifteen 'dominations', the whole governed by an elected Council. Sully was a practical man and foresaw the need for a police force—a hundred thousand infantry and twenty-five thousand horse—to subdue the unruly. The idea was so popular that Richelieu gave Desmarets de Saint-Sorlin the outline of a tragedy entitled *Europe*, in which the goddess Europa puts an end to the quarrels of the wayward children of her family. Were all these just idle dreams? We might call them dreams, but they suggest a state of mind, a nostalgia that we of the twentieth century can appreciate. Vanishing Christendom left a void, and the world had not yet become resigned to recognizing that force could overwhelm it.

All these schemes and plans ran against the same difficulty, whether their authors appreciated the fact or not. How could this unity, which all declared to be so necessary, be brought about? By virtue of what principles and interests could Europeans be induced to come to an understanding? Some thought to recapture the old idea of the crusades, since it was, after all, in the crusades that Christian Europe had asserted its unity. Pierre Dubois had already used the idea, and so had Podiebrad; Sully took it into account in his *Grand Dessein*. It was also one of the main ideas—one might say almost an obsession—of Father Joseph; he went about everywhere proclaiming that war against the Turk was the only way to ensure true peace among Christian peoples, a subject with which he dealt in some thousands of Latin hexameters in his *Turciade*. The same view was entertained by Duke Charles of

Nevers-Gonzaga who in 1627 became head of the House of Palaeo-
logue and, in that capacity, deeply interested in the reconquest of
Byzantium for Christianity.

But the crusade was as anachronistic and outmoded as Christendom
itself, though the battle of Lepanto, in which the Catholic West saw
in its victory the proof of its rediscovered greatness, was still quite
near in time. Europe was so preoccupied with its tragedies that it scarcely
thought of Lepanto any more. It is true that the Order of Christian
Militia had been formed in Vienna for the purpose of resuming the
crusade; but who pursued that purpose? At most a few of its knights,
and some Poles and Wallachians, who struck some feeble blows against
the Turks in 1620 and 1621. The Ottoman Empire, undermined as it
was by internal disorders, no longer seemed a threat. It was not until
1656 that the Albanian Köprili, Grand Vizir of Mohammed V, reformed
the empire at the point of the sword and once more hurled the armies
of the Crescent against Europe. During the Thirty Years War the Turk
was merely regarded as a possible ally in the game of diplomacy. And
Father Joseph, who had often told Louis XIII, 'to me the only
Christian king is one who takes the Cross', ended by negotiating an
alliance with the Sultan against the Hapsburgs. As for the King of
France himself, he declared to his confessor, Father Caussin: 'I
should like to see the Turks in Madrid so that the Spaniards would be
forced to make peace with me; and then I should join Spain to make
war on the Turks'—all of which suggests a strange confusion of mind
as between the crusade and the principle of balance of power. Neither
the Turkish peril nor the crusade would ever again seal the unity of
European nations.

So nothing happened. The idea of unity had no future—quite the
contrary. For nations were beginning to become more and more aware
of what distinguished them one from another. The sentiment of
nationhood was spreading wider and wider. It was gaining ground in
many parts of Europe in movements towards independence. It was
growing steadily in unhappy Bohemia, for instance, which had paid
dearly for its longing for freedom, in Ireland, no less unhappy even in
Sicily, and in Naples where the Spanish yoke was severely shaken, in
Catalonia where the republic presided over by Claris had existed for
nineteen years (1640–59), and equally in the Low Countries which, in
1648, saw their victory ratified, and in the young kingdom of Portugal
which had been free since 1640.

But that same national movement which swept so many people
along and which, in so far as it aimed at liberty, was legitimate, was
also soon to lead to excesses. Nationalism had arrived; it developed
and asserted itself. It was no longer simply a question of the right of
nations to be free: each nation aspired to shut itself up in the pride of

being itself, different and separate from every other; and this pride corresponded only too closely with very definite aspirations. History was becoming 'that dangerous product of the chemistry of the intellect', which Paul Valéry would condemn. Nationalism was about to reinforce Spanish pride, and in England and Holland to become an integral part of the will for economic expansion.

The French did not lag behind. Growing conscious of the dangers resulting from their territorial boundaries, they invented the doctrine of natural frontiers, which would fix the confines of France at all those points which comprised Gaul. Already the *Savoy Letter* of 1600 had proclaimed that the Capetian kingdom should reach as far as the watershed of the Alps. Sully won back Lorraine, Franche-Comté, Savoy and the Low Countries, and in France the people sang:

> 'Quand Paris boira le Rhin,
> Toute la Gaule aura sa fin.'

Even in Germany, with its three hundred sovereigns, intellectuals extolled Germania Magna. The *Introductio in universam geographiam* by Phillip Clavier, which had twenty-six editions in twenty years, annexed to Germany Alsace, Lorraine, the Flemish Low Countries, Bohemia and Scandinavia. This forerunner of Wilhelm II and Hitler was not the only one of his kind: a number of teachers were extolling the purity, the grandeur of the German soul, contrasting it with Latin depravity; and soon Grimmelshaussen was to forge his way to fame peddling ideas like these in his *Simplicissimus*. If the French had read too much Caesar and Strabo, the Teutons were too fond of Arminius.

Europe, then, was preparing to become modern. It was not to be wondered at that some people remained nostalgic about Christendom.

7. The Halting of the Catholic Counter-offensive

What then was the position of Europe from the point of view of religion in the middle of the seventeenth century? Peace between the Churches had been re-established for the time being. Officially it had been resolved never to fight again in the name of hostile creeds. But it was impossible to estimate what progress had been made in the direction of a real pacification of minds. The perpetuation of Germany as an amalgam of small states of divers religions, and the development of Erastian ideas among all and sundry, contributed rather to intensifying intolerance. Almost everywhere an authoritarian religious policy predominated. The only point gained was that, in the name of the principle of balance of power, peace had been established on diplomatic and territorial bases which would hardly allow either of the two camps to progress any further.

From the Catholic point of view that meant the halting of the counter-offensive set in motion immediately after the Council of Trent, and which in Austria, Poland and even in some parts of Germany had met with happy results. The ideal of a counter-reformation was henceforward rejected, since it was compromised by states which, while pretending to work for it, actually made use of it. Was this to be the end of the great upsurge which had swept forward the Tridentine Church? Baronius and Bellarmine had scarcely a disciple; and we remember that [1] even on the strictly spiritual level a very decisive slowing-down was noticeable once the half-century was passed. The great sorrow it caused Innocent X is understandable.

Although this was particularly noticeable in Germany, schemes, manœuvres and intrigues multiplied *ad infinitum* immediately after the treaties. It was an enormously complex game played by the emissaries of the Holy See and the Empire, Jesuits and Capuchins, Lutherans and Calvinists, on a chessboard of three hundred and forty-three pawns. The results were barren, for no one really gained ground. The principle of *Cujus regio*, confirmed by the treaties, won the day—except that the Hohenzollerns of Brandenburg rejected it on principle. Everywhere else the Erastian-minded strove to apply it rigorously, even among Protestants. Thus a Calvinist landgrave in Hesse drove the Lutherans from his university, and in Anhalt-Zerbst the Calvinists were expelled. When the Moravian Brethren, fleeing persecution in Bohemia, arrived in Saxony they were admitted on condition that they embraced the official religion—Lutheranism. The Waldenses, who had tried in vain to make their feeble voices heard in Münster and Osnabrück, got nothing at all, and were everywhere treated without consideration. In Protestant countries tolerance towards the Catholics was most unreliable. In Saxony, for instance, they were permitted to practice their religion in private only; in Brandenburg, where the Catholics constituted a mere one per cent of the population, the government could afford the luxury of being broadminded. It goes without saying that the position was exactly the same in places where Catholics predominated. Rulers like Ernest de Hesse-Rheinfels, who made an honest effort to bring about a *rapprochement* between separated brethren,[2] were rare indeed. The fact that some of the princes were converted (and there were conversions on both sides, but especially from Protestantism to Catholicism) had little effect upon the general position. Germany remained, and was to remain until the nineteenth century, dressed in motley—to quote an Italian chronicler of the time: different religions prevailed according to the mood or the convictions of princes. The Reformation made no progress, but neither did Catholicism win back the country.

---

[1] See Chapter II, p. 123 et seq.   [2] See p. 168.

The same situation prevailed in Switzerland, where the policy of division had already been in force a long time. Peace, and perhaps even a real understanding, was an accomplished fact between the Catholic cantons linked together in the Borromean Confederacy, which was renewed in 1655. The militant spirit of the highland cantons, especially those of Saint-Gall and Lucerne, threatened it continually but unsuccessfully. The first Villmergen War in 1656 turned to the advantage of the Catholics against Bern and Zürich; but it was a paltry and short-lived advantage, and the balance was restored once more.

The Catholic offensive was also halted in territories where Catholic successes might have been expected. In the Low Countries, where an extremely interesting effort had been made, the situation remained confused. The Dutch revolted against Catholic Spain in the name of religious freedom; they were none the less allies of Catholic France and, on that account, compelled to show some regard for those loyal to Rome. The latter took advantage of the fact. Excluded from all types of employment, deprived of all official means of propaganda, the Catholics succeeded, however, in making some progress. Philip Rovenius, the Vicar Apostolic, guided their little band unswervingly, and in the space of about forty years their numbers grew from three to four hundred thousand. Such conversions as that of the great poet Joost Van den Vondel excited wide interest; in the year 1641 alone there were six hundred conversions. The Dutch section of the Cologne seminary had to refuse admissions; the Klopjes, a kind of lay sisterhood, spread everywhere. The movement was ruthlessly suppressed in 1648 when the United Provinces signed their peace with Spain and rejected their alliance with France. The office of Vicar Apostolic was suppressed in 1651, and anti-Catholic measures were tightened. Catholics were strictly forbidden to possess churches. They had to return to the practice of hearing Mass secretly in houses with numerous exits, or which were easily barricaded, where people fervently adored 'the dear Lord in the garret'. Tolerance, of which they were so proud in the Batavian regions, applied only to the various branches of Protestantism, the followers of Gomar and Arminius, the Anabaptists and others. Though all these decided to put up with each other from then onwards, the votaries of Rome had no rights whatsoever.

In England the Catholic drive took on a semi-official form. At the beginning of the century, on the death of Elizabeth, the issue between Catholicism and the Anglican religion had not yet been decided. James I (1603–25), son of Mary Stuart, declared in his first speech from the throne: 'I acknowledge the Roman Church to be our Mother Church, although defiled with some infirmities and corruptions.' The dictatorial policy of this monarch, the weight he gave to the established Church, the violent effect of the Gunpowder Plot on public

*F

opinion in 1605 [1] and the stern reaction of Paul V to the anti-Catholic measures taken at that time appeared to decide the dispute against Rome. An undercurrent still existed, however, which tended towards a great swing-back.

In 1625, after the failure of the first proposal of marriage with a Spanish princess, the new king, Charles I, married Henrietta of France, sister of Louis XIII, and the Catholics hoped for a reconciliation between Rome and the English Crown. Bérulle lent the whole weight of his authority to the plan, but it was not handled tactfully. The pious cardinal accompanied the princess to London with twelve Oratorians. He made a pilgrimage with her to Tyburn, near the spot where the remains of the English martyrs of Elizabeth's persecution reposed together with those of the authors of the Gunpowder Plot. Henrietta refused to receive the crown from the hands of the 'heretical' Archbishop of Canterbury. The Papist religion was restored in the royal palace with a pomp that bordered on ostentation. At the same time all sorts of bargaining went on: preparations were made to install a Vicar Apostolic in London, and a nuncio arrived secretly. Cardinal Barberini and the Benedictine Dom Leander studied the possibility of allowing the English Communion under both species and the validity of Anglican Orders, and even recognizing the marriage of priests. For two years it was possible to cherish the dream of union.

But the plan fell through. First, because Charles I, more dictatorial even than his predecessors, preferred a 'High Church' under his absolute control to a return to Catholicism which would have deprived him of that control. The man who acted as his agent in the whole business, William Laud, Archbishop of Canterbury, certainly Romanized Anglicanism by modelling his rites and practices upon Catholic ceremonial and customs, but it is not clear whether he wished to bring about a real reunion. Uneasy over the discontent shown by his reformed subjects, and anxious to pursue a vast foreign policy which would embarrass France by giving support to La Rochelle against Richelieu, Charles I dismissed the Catholic priests and the French women and domestic staff attending the queen. The queen wept and clung to the window bars to watch them leave. The king snatched her away so brutally that he made her hands bleed. The attempt to catholicize England seemed at an end.

Then, suddenly, strictly political events occurred which disposed entirely of the possibility. The Civil War, the victory of the Puritans, the beheading of the king in 1649 and the dictatorship of Cromwell marked the total collapse of the dream of reunion. The Protector officially professed tolerance, but, as in Holland, this tolerance applied only to the various forms of Protestantism. 'But if by liberty of

[1] See *The Catholic Reformation*, p. 212.

conscience', Cromwell exclaimed, 'you mean a liberty to exercise the Mass, I judge it best to use plain dealing, and to let you know, where the Parliament of England have power, that will not be allowed of.' England was destined to remain a stronghold of Protestantism.[1]

8. IRELAND AND POLAND: CATHOLIC MISGIVINGS

Thus the stability resulting from the Treaties of Westphalia appeared, on the whole, unfavourable to Catholicism. Halted in Holland, held in check in England, forced to accept its losses in Germany as final, Catholicism seemed compelled to recognize that it had ceased to advance, at any rate in the territorial and political spheres. But there were other and worse signs. One Catholic stronghold was collapsing, another was dangerously threatened, and these were disquieting thoughts.

Ireland was now reduced to bondage as a result of the repression inflicted on her by Elizabeth, who intended to cure the country's desire for independence. She was deprived of her most elementary freedoms, administered by ruthless English officials and subjected to the growing pressure of the official religion.[2] But the land of St Patrick clung to the Catholic creed with savage fervour and remained firm. Her faith, a sign of her liberty and right to exist, was dearer than life to Ireland, and she was resolved to do anything to preserve it intact. Since 1603 a few sporadic movements of unrest, more or less encouraged by Spain, had resulted merely in provoking reprisals.

But in October 1641, when Charles I faced great trouble in England, the Catholic Confederation, led by Phelim O'Neal, Maguire and More, launched a rebellion in the four corners of the island, and popular fury, so long pent up, expressed itself in dreadful atrocities. Protestant settlers were massacred and their farms looted. Charles I, incapable of re-establishing order, granted the Irish freedom of worship (1646), while his secret envoy, the Duke of Glamorgan, asked them for their support in the struggle which the king was maintaining against the Puritans. By joining the conflict they were sure to draw on themselves the fury of Cromwell, if he won. Nor could they be certain that Charles I, if he triumphed, would keep his word: the Nuncio Rinuccini suspected him of playing a double game. Furthermore, the situation in the island was confused. The Council of Kilkenny, which controlled the Catholic Confederation, was torn between two considerations: there were those who, like Owen O'Neill, demanded outright the complete restoration to the Church of her rights and property; while more moderate politicians, like Bellings and Preston, were ready to

[1] Regarding events in England, see *The Church in the Eighteenth Century*, Index.
[2] See *The Catholic Reformation*, p. 203-4.

come to an understanding with the king and his viceroy, the Marquis of Ormond. Siding with the former, the nuncio dismissed the council, set up another and even excommunicated Preston. This bickering merely assisted Cromwell who, as soon as the king's fate had been sealed, set about bringing order back to Ireland—an English and Puritan order.

And it was ferocious. In a campaign of a few months (1649) the Roundheads brought the country to heel. At Drogheda, as Cromwell said explicitly in his report, almost all the defenders were put to the sword. Scarcely thirty managed to survive, and they were deported to Barbados. At Wexford and New Ross similar horrors were perpetrated. The Lord Protector remarked that the sorrow occasioned by these events would, with God's help, save much bloodshed. The remnants of the army, gathered in the marshy regions of the Upper Shannon, around the ancient monastic centre of Clonmacnoise, continued the hopeless struggle. Under an Act passed by the English Parliament in 1652, the property of the Irish Catholics was confiscated and given to veteran soldiers of the Puritan forces. Those who had not taken part in the insurrection were permitted to settle in the west, in the infertile region of Connaught. Some preferred to escape to the mountains, where they led a vagabond existence. As for the vanquished, they were forced to remain as tenant farmers on their own lands, which passed into the hands of the English. Catholic Ireland was apparently pulverized. In fact, sustained by hope, she maintained an obstinate and heroic struggle for centuries. The Irish question remained like a wound in the side of England.

Was Poland, that other great Catholic bastion in the north, destined to undergo a similar fate? In the middle of the century the question might well have been asked, for the signs were disturbing. Yet the return of that noble country to the Catholic faith, accomplished with enthusiasm and resolution, was one of the major episodes of the Counter-Reformation.[1] At the dawn of the seventeenth century Sigismund III (1587–1632), a pupil of the distinguished Jesuit Warszewicki, had completed the transformation of his country into a citadel of the Roman faith in the heart of Lutheran and Orthodox territories. Poland became ever more closely identified with Catholicism. The Convention of Warsaw, set up in 1573 to lay the foundations of a compromise between the rival religions, soon became a dead letter. The Protestant communities had, in fact, lost the right of public worship long before they were officially deprived of it in 1632. The reformed writers were reduced to silence, while Catholic pamphlets multiplied rapidly. Starowolski and Kobierzycki demonstrated in their works that Poland, herself an elder daughter of the Church, was

[1] See *The Catholic Reformation*, p. 336–7.

indebted to the Church for her greatness and her opportunities. A genuine effort towards reform was undertaken by the bishops, assisted by the Jesuits and Monsieur Vincent's sons and daughters from France.

Nevertheless, this Catholic edifice, apparently so solid, was cracked and threatened internally by an absurd political system whose main purpose was to secure the freedoms and privileges of the nobles. The throne was elective; a sovereign had to sign the *Pacta Conventa* imposed on him by twenty or so of the wealthiest and most powerful families known as magnates. The crowning absurdity was reached in 1652, with the passing of the *Liberum Veto*, which recognized the right of a single deputy to oppose any decision made by the Diet. Such a practice was all the more lamentable because the Republic of Poland, a vast and complex state stretching from the Baltic to the Black Sea, from the Oder to the Dnieper, and including within itself several foreign races, was henceforward surrounded by grasping enemies. Sweden aspired to turn the Baltic into a Swedish lake; Prussia under the Great Elector Frederick William (1640–88) had yet to accomplish its high destiny; Russia was persecuting the Ukrainian Cossacks; and Turkey was putting pressure upon the Crimean Tartars.

The history of Poland during the first half of the seventeenth century was therefore a succession of crises. Pledged to a European war on the side of the Empire, King Sigismund III was defeated. He lost his Swedish throne and barely succeeded in retaining the throne of Poland (1629–32). Then followed a period of confused policy which first drew the country nearer to France and then to the Hapsburgs, with very little gain or prospect thereof. This was followed by a dynastic crisis resulting from the fact that both Vladislas IV (1632–49) and John Casimir (1649–68) died without heirs. This in turn was followed by a religious crisis. Protestantism raised its head, and a conference convened by Vladislas IV at Thorn in 1643 in an attempt to establish a *modus vivendi* came to nothing. Worse still, dissension arose even within the bosom of Catholicism: the Jesuits, maligned by the famous *Monita Secreta* of the turncoat Zanorowski,[1] were violently attacked. Several of their colleges and houses were plundered, and they were ultimately driven from Poland. A mercenary struggle went on between the magnates and the higher ranks of the clergy for the possession of the Jesuits' property, which led to violence: at Wilno the Vojevode and the bishop fought to the death.

It is hardly surprising that under such conditions Poland's adversaries regarded her as their prey. In 1649 the subject peoples—Tartars, Cossacks and Ruthenians—rebelled, supported by the Russians, Swedes, Prussians and even by some of the Polish nobility. By 1655

[1] See *The Catholic Reformation*, p. 50, footnote.

Poland stood on the very brink of ruin. Warsaw was twice captured by the Swedes; its sanctuaries at Jasna Gora and Czestochowa were saved only by the heroism of their monks, and the Jesuit St Andrew Bobola was put to death on 16th May 1657 under dreadful torture.[1] In 1657 Poland was forced by the Treaty of Wehlau to renounce her sovereignty over Prussia, and in 1660, by the Treaty of Oliva, she lost Livonia. These were premonitory signs of the tragedy which, in the eighteenth century, was to bring down the greatest Catholic nation of the north.

9. THE GROUPING OF CATHOLIC AND PROTESTANT FORCES

The slackening of the Catholic counter-offensive did not imply abandonment of the spirit that had inspired it; quite the contrary. Christian Europe at the mid century was torn by discord, but the ancient strongholds of Catholicism were just as firm, inflexible and unshakable in their determination to maintain their Roman faith as were the bastions of the Reformation to maintain the reformed religion.

The territories of the Hapsburgs and the areas under their powerful influence were the bulwarks of inflexible Catholicism. There the spirit of the Counter-Reformation carried its principles to triumph—but at what a price!

Vienna and the hereditary Austrian states in the heart of Europe constituted the foremost of these bulwarks—Vienna with its innumerable churches, its three Catholic universities, its streets swarming with an incredible number of monks of every Order. Up to the end of the century, and even beyond, the old ideal of fighting heresy with every possible weapon was maintained, inspired by the fiery eloquence of the Venetian Capuchin Marco d'Aviano and the Augustinian Abraham à Santa Chiara, who also laboured in both Bohemia and Hungary.

Brutal methods were adopted in Bohemia. Immediately after the battle of the White Mountain, repression, accompanied by a policy of frenzied catholicization, fastened upon the rebel Czech country. The sermon preached by the Capuchin friar Sabinus before Ferdinand II, based on the biblical text, 'Thou shalt chastise them with a rod of iron', was not preached in vain. The emperor, incited by Dom Onate, the Spanish ambassador, by Cardinal Dietrichstein, and by such ferocious politicians as Plateis and Slavata, was only too eager to listen to him. Heads fell on the great square in Prague—twenty-seven in one mass execution, including that of an old man of eighty-six. Czech

---

[1] St Andrew Bobola was canonized as a martyr in 1957 on the occasion of the third centenary of his death. Pius XII referred to him in an encyclical as an example of heroism in the face of unbounded violence.

Protestants condemned to flogging or imprisonment had no alternative but to flee, and more than thirty thousand of them wandered through the mountain passes of Riesengebirge and Böhmer Wald in pitiful groups, while all their estates were confiscated and given over to the Catholics. Catholicism was declared the official religion, and was made obligatory under the Constitution of 1627. The Jesuits, confessors to the new rulers, obtained control of the Czech Church; it was set up as a Fourth Estate, but henceforward held first place among the assemblies of the nation. The activities of the Jesuits, however, were not always reprehensible: the work of their preachers, among whom were Colens and Chanovsky, was truly apostolic, and the revival of devotion to St Nepomucene, a fourteenth-century martyr, did much to restore the faith. So few advantages at the cost of so much violence! For thirty years the land of the Czechs groaned and gasped. *Bohemia's Tears of Blood*, published by Holyk while in exile, painted an unhappy picture. The pathetic pleading of two successive archbishops of Prague, Lohelius and von Harrach, of the heroic Capuchin Valeriano Magni, a Milanese dedicated to the cause of reconciliation with the Protestants,[1] of Cardinal Bilenberk and even of the Jesuit Balbyn were of no avail. They pleaded that heretics should be treated as brothers, on the grounds that they could not be won over to the true faith except by kindness and holy example. Under an imperial edict of 1st February 1650 any non-Catholic discovered in Bohemia after 15th March of that year was liable to death or life imprisonment. A Counter-Reformation conducted in such a manner can hardly claim our admiration.

Vienna wished to adopt the same approach in that poor remnant of Hungary that still remained to the Empire while the Turks occupied the other two-thirds of the country. Assisted by Austrian officials, the Jesuit Cardinal Pazmany, Archbishop of Gran and one of the leaders of the political and military Counter-Reformation, established a reign of terror under which Protestants were condemned to the galleys in the hope of converting them. In Hungary's case however the reaction encountered the opposition of the magnates of the country, most of whom, including the Gabors and Raköczys, were reformed. In 1645 the magnates even managed to defeat an imperial army. In the peace that followed, the principle of religious freedom was recognized, but it was a peace which Vienna regretted from the bottom of her heart, and was soon to challenge.

The other stronghold of the Counter-Reformation was Spain, wholly loyal to the ideals of Philip II. Under Philip III ('the Pious') and Philip IV, who, after a life of indulgence developed a spiritual regard for Maria de Agreda, Madrid resembled Vienna, but was much

[1] See page 166.

more violent. Hardly a Protestant was left in the Peninsula; all had been liquidated by the Inquisition. The supervision of the Holy Office continued vigilant, and its resources remained powerful. For want of Christian heretics the authorities set about the few remaining Moriscos, semi-converts from Islam who, though under strict control since the Alpujarras revolt and the edict of Philip II, still managed to practise their Mohammedan faith in secret and to plot with the Sultan of Morocco. They were hunted mercilessly as far as the province of Algarve in the extreme south of Portugal, where a small band of survivors hung on. A few Jews, another band of nonconformists, were also taken to task. The same methods obtained in the territories under Spanish control. In the Catholic Low Countries (present-day Belgium) Protestantism was in full retreat; it became almost extinct except in small centres like Roulers, Tourhout, Ypres and Bruges. The aim was to prevent the influence of the northern Low Countries, which were heretical, from contaminating the Catholic areas. The Holy Office watched the position closely, keeping a tight control over the universities, condemning every doctrinal deviation and taking action soon afterwards against Jansenism, which it described as a rehash of Protestantism. Even in Italy where, however, the Protestant threat was almost negligible, the same measures were adopted. In Naples and in the two Sicilies a thoroughgoing Inquisitorial terror descended upon the Protestants. In the whole of the peninsula the only remaining heretical groups of any importance were the Waldenses, who had taken refuge in the upper valleys of the Alps since the persecution which assailed them during the sixteenth century.[1] The Duke of Savoy, at that time owing allegiance to Spain, let loose against them in 1655 a frightful campaign which lasted thirty years and ended by wiping out their communities. Here again the spirit of the Counter-Reformation was maintained.

A truly Christian soul can find nothing admirable in this persecution, but the position was exactly the same in the Protestant camp; we have seen it in Holland and England. Over against the Catholic bastions Protestant walls rose up no less steep and sturdy. Foremost among them was, of course, Calvinist Geneva. Surrounded by Papists, aloof from the Swiss cantons in which Catholics and Protestants still fought each other occasionally, the dour city stood proof against all Catholic penetration. Without doubt a few priests were bold enough from time to time to bring Communion to the Catholics in this sacrosanct city, and when one of them happened to be caught he was thrown into prison accompanied by the innkeeper who had been rash enough to give him accommodation. In 1621 the Consistory decreed the death penalty against any Calvinist who returned to 'Catholic idols'. Their

[1] See *The Protestant Reformation*, pp. 487, 488.

pastors were forbidden to take part in funerals and to pray over graves. The religious dictatorship along the Lake of Geneva was not much less austere than in the days of the pale-faced Calvin. A young Frenchman named Rémond, a native of Annonay, who had publicly made fun of 'Messieurs les Pasteurs' and questioned the truth of the Scriptures, was condemned to death only to be reprieved at the moment of mounting the scaffold. The Consistory strongly opposed reformed theologians who did not share its rigid belief in Predestination. Among these were the Dutchman Arminius and the Frenchman Amyrault as well as John Drury in England. If there had to be but one impregnable stronghold of pure Calvinist doctrine, that stronghold was going to be Geneva!

Unless perhaps it might be Scotland, made as John Knox had shaped it, for he was a disciple of Calvin and perhaps even more ruthless than his master.[1] There the Presbyterian Church and its *Book of Discipline* reigned supreme. Everything that recalled 'the livery of the Beast' horrified it. When Laud, who was Anglican archbishop and the king's minister in London, tried in 1637 to introduce liturgy and the official prayers, a regular tumult broke out in Edinburgh Cathedral, and an old woman flung a stool at the dean's head. The Scottish Church, victorious in its war against Cromwell,[2] regarded itself as entrusted by God with the duty of keeping the reformed religion pure, unblemished and uncompromising.

The Scandinavian countries could, however, aspire to contest that honour with Scotland and even with Geneva. In Denmark very severe laws were promulgated against the Catholics in 1613, 1624 and 1643, and Christian V reiterated them after his *coup d'état* of 1660. In Sweden the formation of a strong and independent monarchy by Gustavus Vasa was intimately linked with the adoption of Lutheranism, and during the reign of Sigismund the Holy See and the Jesuits tried without success to have the question of the national religion reviewed. Gustavus Adolphus was the flaming sword of the Lutheran religion, to which he was passionately attached. But there was a possibility that his daughter Christina (1626–89) might sever that link. At twenty-two she became disgusted with Lutheranism and, through her conversations with Descartes and Chanut, the French ambassador, she discovered Catholicism. She made contact with some Jesuits who disembarked secretly disguised as noblemen, and in 1652 decided to recant. But Protestant pressure in the country was so great, as she well knew, that she dared not face the consequences. She therefore abdicated and fled to Rome dressed as a man. Arrived in the Eternal City she publicly recanted, and thereafter led a long and adventurous life which was not

[1] See *The Catholic Reformation*, p. 194.
[2] See *The Church in the Eighteenth Century*, Chapter III.

always quite worthy of a Catholic. Both her cousin Charles Gustavus, who followed her upon the throne, and Charles XI, who succeeded him, strengthened the anti-Catholic measures. Anyone converted was banished and his property confiscated, and no priest was allowed to enter the country.

There were Catholic groups on one side and Protestant groups on the other; intolerance reigned everywhere. If Europe had shifted its bases in the political field, it still remained closely attached to the errors and fanaticism of the past in the religious field.

10. 'That They may be One'

Thus the great scandal of Christians divided from one another was to endure in the new, the 'modern' Europe, and there was nothing to indicate that it might one day end. 'That they may be one as We are one'—Christ's prayer found no echo; religious unity, the living reflection of the unity of the Trinity, was broken no less than political unity.

Yet there were souls who refused to surrender to this scandal, just as there were great minds which refused to submit to the dismemberment of Europe; and they often belonged to the same people. Comparatively little is known of the efforts of dedicated men to bring about the reunion of the Churches (even though the rift seemed final), and to restore that unique Mystical Body. Such men existed in both camps.

Among the Catholics there were princes such as Adam de Schwartzenberg, a friend of the Protestant Elector of Brandenburg, the sovereigns of Poland, especially Vladislas IV, high prelates like the Polish Bishop Lubienski and the two successive Archbishops of Prague, Valeriano Magni (1586-1661) (the Milanese Capuchin, who, as we have seen, did such splendid work in Bohemia after the battle of the White Mountain) and the Benedictine Dom Leander, who pursued inquiries in Rome in an attempt to bring the Anglicans back to the fold. All these men were convinced of the necessity of bringing together men of goodwill to discuss and study disputed questions in a spirit of real charity. And we shall see that the Protestant policy of Richelieu, very far from relegating him to the clique of fanatics, brings out his deep attachment to these very aims. Those who were close to Richelieu —Father Joseph, the Jesuits Audebert and Dulaurens, the Capuchin Father Hyacinthe and Véron, parish priest of Charenton—were certainly aware of these great schemes, and gave them varying degrees of support.

Among the Protestants we again meet the famous Dutch jurist Hugo van Groot, known as Grotius, the originator of international law, who elaborated a plan for the union of European states. 'Throughout my life', he wrote to a friend, 'I have burned with the desire to reconcile the Christian world.' And indeed, as he saw things, the two aims were identical; for only the Gospel and its teachings could form the moral bases of a 'United States of Europe'. How could Christianity be strong if its children continued to tear each other to pieces? As a Protestant with Arminian leanings, that is to say, opposed to an excessively strict doctrine of Predestination,[1] Grotius detested all forms of sectarianism, and dealt most sternly with the Genevan kind. 'Wherever the followers of Calvin become established,' he wrote, 'they cause trouble.' He reproached the Catholic Church with moral destitution, abuse of scholastic theories, excessive devotion to the Virgin Mary and to the saints (the vow taken by Louis XIII made him laugh heartily); but he had the courage to write that the distressing division of Protestantism into sects would never end until all the Churches of the Reformation became united to the See of Rome— 'That See', he said, 'without which there can be no hope of any common government within the Church.'

George Calixte (1586–1656) was less rigid in thought and less logical, but he was not less high-minded than Grotius. A Lutheran professor at the University of Helmstedt, Calixte started with the idea of trying to put an end to disunity between the reformed Churches, and eventually looked to the reunion of all Christian confessions, including the Catholic and Orthodox Churches. He suggested that they should limit their tenets to fundamental articles of faith, such as has been recognized in the early centuries. Apart from these articles, each Church would retain the right to teach what it liked. This idea of a basic Christianity, this naïve syncretism, was obviously chimerical; but there is no doubt about the magnanimity and loftiness of purpose of the thinker who elaborated it.[2]

It must be admitted that all these grandiose proposals achieved very little. Calixte was violently attacked by the reformed theologians; they accused him and his friend Conrad Hornejus of being traitors who had sold themselves to the cause of Rome, and they pointed out no less than twenty-eight heretical propositions in the works of Calixte. Grotius met with a similar fate. While he was ambassador in Paris the Lutherans in Uppsala had him spied upon by agents in their pay, in order to denounce him to the government in Stockholm. They succeeded so well that the great jurist asked to be recalled to the court of Sweden. As for Valeriano Magni, he was the object of the Jesuits' furious wrath; reports concerning him poured into the Holy Office, and he

---

[1] See *The Catholic Reformation*, pp. 224 and 225.
[2] Another splendid figure was Jan Amos Comenius (1592–1670), a member of the Bohemian Brethren, who took refuge in Poland and then in Holland. The attitude of this true apostle of Christianity was very similar to that of Grotius and Calixte.

was eventually thrown into prison. Had Richelieu lived long enough he might perhaps have made an issue of reunion during the Westphalian negotiations; but he died before the end of the war. The negotiations undertaken by Grotius during the Osnabrück conferences were cut short, and the great Dutchman was shipwrecked and drowned shortly afterwards. Mazarin could not be expected to pursue so lofty and far-reaching a policy. The wrath of the Gomarist pastors of Dordrecht and the Genevan theologians, as well as that of the Catholic Neuhaus and Vitus Ebermann, exploded against this dream of union. The question of union was not referred to at all in any of the numerous articles signed at Westphalia.

These splendid schemes, however, were not abandoned. The disciples of Grotius, notably the convert poet Vondel, carried on his ideas. George Calixte continued his apostolate until his death, defying the horde of enemies who pursued him relentlessly. Concrete efforts were made in the form of discussions at Rheinfels in 1651 on the invitation of the Landgrave Ernest of Hesse-Rheinfels (Valeriano Magni was present), at Frankfurt and Ratisbon at the instigation of the Jesuit James Massen, and then at Thorn in Poland at the request of Vladislas IV. They produced no results; at the most they were symptomatic of an attitude of mind different from the general intolerance which prevailed, however unsteady that attitude might be. Such dreams, too, raised echoes in the soul of a young French priest named Jacques-Bénigne Bossuet and in that of Leibniz, a young German philosopher. In due course these men would return to the theme. Before long that great-hearted Franciscan Spinola [1] was to come upon the scene; but in the middle of the century the possibility of a reunion of the Churches, or even of any real appeasement of minds, was so slender as to be regarded as non-existent.

11. RICHELIEU AND THE PROTESTANTS

What was the position in France in the mid seventeenth century, when intolerance was apparently victorious everywhere in Europe? Was she to be found in the Catholic coalitions bent upon counter-reformation? It was among them that she found her worst enemies. But France was certainly not in the Protestant camp. It had been evident since the days of Henri IV that the land of St Louis would remain irrevocably loyal to the Roman faith. The French Government's foreign policy during the Thirty Years War was to remain aloof from vital religious issues; indeed it might be said to have reflected an awareness of her material interests and nothing more. But

[1] See p. 298.

her internal policy in relation to religious matters was in keeping with
her foreign policy: she did not follow the path of Austria or Spain in
an attempt to impose unity of belief on all her subjects. On the contrary, she gave to the world a unique example of a state prepared to
respect liberty of conscience. This policy, inherited from the wisdom
of Henri IV, was also that of a man who on this point more than on
any other showed clearly the depths of his convictions—Richelieu.

Had the edict signed by the wise Henri at Nantes in 1598 really laid
the foundations of religious peace? To almost every Frenchman it
appeared as a political truce and a military armistice imposed as a result
of general exhaustion rather than as a charter of equality in religious
belief. 'It crucifies me . . .,' exclaimed Pope Clement VIII when he read
the text of the edict. 'Freedom of conscience is the worst thing in the
world.' The Protestants Calvin and Theodore Beza had long ago
attested similar words. In many parts of the country the Catholics
strove to circumvent the effectiveness of the edict; but the Protestants,
in districts where they felt strong, took as much advantage as they
could of the rights which had been accorded them, and did not hesitate
to make fun of priests and of the Mass. On both sides to avoid com-
pliance with the provisions of the edict was regarded as serving God
and truth.

It seemed therefore quite possible that the conflict might be resumed
and that it would start on purely political grounds. Henri IV gave
the Huguenot minority a number of guarantees precisely in order to
prevent his work being ruined by a new wave of intolerance. For
instance, to ensure impartiality in the administration of justice he set
up in Paris, Grenoble, Castres and Nérac tribunals known as *Chambres
mi-parties*, made up of councillors from both faiths. This was an
excellent measure; but not so the one under which the Calvinists were
given a hundred and fifty strong places where they had the right to
maintain garrisons. That was simply a case of allowing the Protestants,
as Richelieu wrote, 'to share the state with the king'. A veritable
'state within the state' was erected with La Rochelle as its capital. It
had its army, navy and ambassadors (two deputies at the court). It
also had a foreign policy of its own, diplomatic relations with England,
the Low Countries and the Protestant princes in Germany. 'To put it
bluntly,' exclaimed Chancellor Pasquier, 'this state within the state is
a monstrosity! It is not a matter of religion but of allegiance.'

There was therefore no doubt whatever about the danger. All the
more so because the most violent sections of the Protestant group led
by Henri de Rohan, taking advantage of the uncertainty and confusion,
got the upper hand over the 'moderates' led by the elderly Duplessis-
Mornay. They demanded that the government should make itself
responsible for the upkeep of their fortified towns and the pay of their

troops, while the Protestant Church organized itself into a regular political party, dividing the territory into sixteen 'provinces' and eight 'circles' with a central government to control the whole. 'Felony!' exclaimed Pasquier again, and there was some justification for the word.

However weak a government might be it could not allow the state to be split in this way. After the death of Concini, Louis XIII hoped he was at last in control of his realm, but he noticed a reaction setting in. Béarn, where the Protestants were slow to restore Church property to the Catholic clergy, was occupied by the royalist forces in 1619. In the following year the Huguenot Assembly at La Rochelle countered with a stroke which was clearly revolutionary: they organized the eight circles as military governments. The Duc de Bouillon as leader of the first circle automatically became commander of all the Protestant forces, though Rohan and his brother Soubise actually exercised command. Again the king took action, and poured his armies into the region around Charente and against Montauban. They were incompetently led by Luynes, the king's favourite, who had been made constable, and the operation became a fiasco: for instance, a mine which was intended to shatter the walls of the town blew up part of the king's camp! A few defeats suffered by the Protestants at Poitou and near Royan were sufficient to persuade them, at the peace signed in 1622 at Montpellier, to agree to dismantle their strongholds, with the exception of Montauban and La Rochelle, and to consent to the reaffirmation of the terms of the Edict of Nantes. But this did not after all solve the problem of the 'state within the state'.

That was the political problem which Richelieu tackled when he came to power in 1624. It was indeed a political issue, for it would be very far from the truth to imagine that he whom they called 'the cardinal of La Rochelle' was a hammer of heretics and a champion of intolerance. He left this role to the 'devout', who could hardly be considered his allies. He did not like the Protestants. He condemned their theology in his *Principaux points de la foi de l'église catholique*; in 1615, as the spokesman for the clergy at the assembly of the States-General, he denounced their transgressions. But though he resolved from the very start to ruin the Huguenot party, and in this sphere as in every other to enhance the king's name, he never yielded to the temptation to impose by force his faith and obedience to his own Church. He declared that it was his end and purpose to bring this political faction to heel; but he added: 'As for the rest, that is a matter which must be left to Providence; we must not use any other pressure than that which springs from a good life and good example.' Those were indeed Christian words, and fairly rare at that period.

The Huguenot party did not disarm. Although several of their leaders, among whom La Force and Lesdiguières, allowed themselves to be won over by pensions, a marshal's baton or the Constable's sword, the common people remained fiercely opposed to any lasting settlement with the Catholics, and increasingly hoped to establish a 'united provinces' of French Protestantism in the west on the lines adopted by their Dutch friends. The existence of Fort-Louis, the fortress which had been built especially to keep watch on the entrance to La Rochelle, annoyed them intensely, and the more hot-headed among them spoke openly of storming it. 'Either the fort must take the town or the town the fort,' they said. Could a determined minister tolerate such an attitude?

The first encounter took place during 1625–6. Seeing that Richelieu was occupied with the complicated affair of Val Tellina, and knowing that his position at court was not quite secure, the most headstrong of the Protestant leaders demanded the disarming of Fort-Louis and, when their demands were rejected, they rebelled. Soubise occupied the Île de Ré, attacked a royal fleet at the mouth of the Blavet, and then established himself on the Île d'Oléron. Meanwhile the whole Huguenot region from the Atlantic to Nîmes revolted in answer to Rohan's call. It was a foolish attempt which savoured unpleasantly of treason, and of which even England and the Low Countries disapproved, though it had the secret support of Spain. Alliances became strangely reversed and the political aspect of the conflict was evident. The cardinal was too preoccupied with the international situation to prolong a struggle in which he felt uncertain of complete victory. When the royal fleet, assisted by English and Dutch ships, recaptured Ré and Oléron he offered the rebels a *status quo* peace, contenting himself with a demand for the installation of a royal commissioner at La Rochelle. But he did not forget the treason.

He made very thorough preparations for decisive action. Public opinion was on his side; far-seeing people like the President of Bordeaux saw in an attempt on La Rochelle 'the first and last stirring of rebellion', and the 'devout' hoped it would prove an opportunity for wholesale proselytism. The Pope thought likewise. Military leaders, to quote the words of the Venetian ambassador, 'aspired to enhance their own importance by means of war'. A minority of the nobles, being subtler politicians, doubted the wisdom of handing the cardinal a victory that would make him absolute master of France: 'You will see', laughed the gay Bassompierre, 'we shall be fools enough to take La Rochelle.' Richelieu's able assistant throughout the enterprise was Father Joseph, in whom the old soldier was not altogether concealed beneath his Capuchin habit. He successfully played the unusual role of Chief of Staff, providing for all eventualities, planning the attacks, the investment of the enemy and even the provisioning of troops, all of which he did with a skill that has been described as

Napoleonic. And all the while a flood of pamphlets from his impassioned pen told France and the world why it was necessary to bring the *cabale des Rochelais* to its senses.

The siege of La Rochelle began in the early autumn of 1627 and lasted a year. Its episodes are well known; they constitute one of those vivid chapters of history which can never be effaced from the memory —the lean cardinal, in breeches and boots, wearing his pale grey breastplate, inspecting his troops with a morose and pensive air, while the plume in his large hat floated on the ocean breeze. The king, whose 'presence was worth a hundred thousand men', rode loyally beside him.

Richelieu had considerable forces at his disposal: twenty-five thousand foot-soldiers, new cannon bearing the realistic motto *ultima ratio regum*, and the fleet he had built up in three years. He was faced by an aggressive population shut in behind their walls: thirty thousand souls, every one of whom was determined to defend with his life principles more precious than life itself, and a garrison of veteran soldiers with many years' experience of warfare. Guitton, the mayor, threatened to plunge a dagger into the heart of anyone who spoke of surrender. Behind the town ran a twelve-kilometre trench; facing the sea the approach was blocked by an embankment fifteen hundred metres long and eight wide at the top, which had been built in six months. The English, now on the Protestant side, twice sent their fleet under Buckingham in a fruitless attempt to force the blockade. A ghastly famine struck the town; corpses lay about the streets, so emaciated by hunger that they would not decay. On 28th October the town was compelled to surrender. Amidst general rejoicing and a jubilant peal of bells the victorious cardinal, accompanied by his advance guards, entered the town in triumph. He was dreadfully pale and trembling with fever. Father Joseph, calm as ever, hastened to one of the temples, had it consecrated at once as a cathedral and there celebrated the first Mass. Thus was written a decisive chapter in the religious history of France.

The fact that Rohan still continued to hold the Cévennes was of little importance, for a few months later he too was forced to submit. The military stage was over. It was now quite clear that the French monarchy would no longer tolerate a faction prepared to challenge its authority, a state within the state. But though the capture of La Rochelle closed the story of the Protestant party as far as its religious aspect was concerned, it opened up new horizons, and it was here that Richelieu's policy was to prove infinitely more flexible than fanatics might have imagined.

One of the first instructions the cardinal gave on entering the captured town was that there should be no looting or any form of reprisals. He also ordered that the population be provided with food as a matter of urgency. His interview with Guitton was almost friendly. He asked him what he thought of the French and English sovereigns, to which the defeated hero replied: 'I think it is better to have as king the man who captured La Rochelle than one who was unable to defend it.'

This was a wise view, as the peace signed at Alais—the *Paix de Grâce*—on 28th June 1629 abundantly proved. The Protestants lost their privileges, their fortified towns and all the resources which might have enabled them to set up again as a faction; but it was made quite clear that they had not been attacked on account of their religion, and that as subjects the cardinal made no distinction between them and the Catholics. All the strictly religious clauses of the Edict of Nantes were accordingly confirmed.

We cannot say that Richelieu's handling of this affair was merely an act of great wisdom, one of those gestures of appeasement in which magnanimity and skill mingle in the overriding interests of the nation. It certainly looks as though the cardinal's policy was associated in his mind with other and more profound aims. He evidently wished to lead the conquered Protestants back to the Roman faith, but he had no desire to use force or even pressure. True there were some who did use force or pressure, but they did so on their own initiative. There was much more to be gained by encouraging missions in the Protestant zones and showing favour to those who were converted. In fact, this moderate and persuasive policy seems to have borne fruit. Statistics show that the number of pastors dropped between 1627 and 1637 from 10 to 17 per cent according to locality, and that the number of their adherents continued to diminish after the *Grâce d'Alais* until 1661. Even a small town the size of Leyrac the figures were reduced from three hundred to sixty.

But undoubtedly we must probe further. There is much to suggest that the cardinal minister, impressed by the idea of the union of the Churches, regarded his Protestant policy as a means of attaining that end. We know that while Grotius was resident in Paris the cardinal had long and friendly talks with the Dutchman, who was now the King of Sweden's ambassador and an enthusiastic propagandist in the cause of reunion. On his suggestion the Jesuit Audebert proposed to the reformed clergy the idea of a conference at which pastors and priests would elucidate their points of disagreement. When the ex-Jesuit François Véron, parish priest of Charenton, recommended a rather simplified form of Catholicism freed from excessive scholasticism, which—as he thought—the reformed clergy might be prepared to accept, the authorities allowed him to expound his theories from the pulpit of Saint-Germain until he was condemned by Rome.

The steps taken indicated a clear intention towards appeasement if not a *rapprochement*. On three occasions—in 1633, 1635 and 1636—the King's Council forbade Catholics to refer to Protestants in public as heretics. In 1637 the Secretary of State, La Vrillière, was informed of a ruling by the Bishop of Montpellier condemning mixed marriages, and expressed his dispproval. Still more surprising, in 1631 the Protestants obtained official subsidies for the holding of their synods and even sixty thousand *livres* for their schools. All these signs were characteristic of a policy which went much further than merely bringing to heel a rebellious faction, a policy which throws light upon that adopted by Richelieu in Germany, and which was not based entirely on the demands of French interests.

It is remarkable to observe that a handful at least of right-minded people followed his example. A closer approach between Catholics and Protestants was noticeable. Amyrault, a pastor of Saumur, dined with the Bishop of Chartres; this incensed the Genevan pastors, who expressed their disapproval loudly and vehemently. Petit, a pastor of Nîmes, was on friendly terms with the Archbishop of Toulouse, while the parish priest of Puylaurens invited his congregation to pray for the Protestant pastor of the town who was sick. Bishop Godeau was a friend of the Protestant Courant, and Rivet, a member of the reformed Central Committee, was on friendly terms with Father Mersenne. Richelieu's France thus appeared to be the only great country in which escape from the slavery of intolerance was envisaged and consideration given to the possibility of a *rapprochement* between the members of the different Churches. This fact, upon which official history lays scarcely any stress, adds enormously to the cardinal's stature.

But could such a policy, which was so far ahead of its time, endure? Its legal and administrative elements were retained by Mazarin, who readily admitted that during the period of the Fronde 'subjects adhering to the so-called reformed faith gave clear proof of affection and loyalty'. This however was not universally true, for there is ample evidence to show that several Protestant groups took advantage of the opportunity to rearm afforded by the Fronde. Moreover the Protestant Central Committee, for some obscure reason, maintained secret relations with Cromwell; but Mazarin stood in such need of religious peace that he was ready to close his eyes to the fact, and he was fairly clever at the diplomatic game of compliments. In any case he did maintain peace between the Churches. In 1649 news of the execution of Charles I of England, uncle of young Louis XIV, provoked a wave of indignation throughout France, and there was a tendency towards anti-Protestant reprisals, which Mazarin promptly checked. On the other hand, he showed no interest whatever in the other half of Richelieu's programme, his penetrating views on *rapprochement* and perhaps union—though Henri de Gondren, Archbishop of Sens, tried to make him appreciate and adopt them. Mazarin was a realist with no taste for this method of approach.

Besides, public opinion had not yet been won over to such ideas. Although pastors were able to move freely in Paris and conduct their services (which Catholic priests in London could not do) they were often insulted in the streets. Conversely, wherever the Protestants were numerous they annoyed the Catholics and provoked them by their remarks and sacrilegious acts. Almost everywhere Protestants were excluded from official appointments, and sometimes from trade, by pressure and the abuse of authority. We have seen that one of the objectives of the Company of the Blessed Sacrament was the elimination of heresy; it used its powerful resources to that end, successfully opposing the appointment of Protestants to the highest posts. In Languedoc the Comte de Rieux even attempted to forbid public practice of the reformed religion and relented only when faced with armed intervention. In 1650 the Assembly of French Clergy recommended the king to 'render the Reformation inactive and bring about its gradual downfall by diminishing and depriving it of its privileges'. In 1655 the Assembly condemned liberty of conscience even more categorically and called for the closing of the 'Synagogues of Satan', in other words, the temples. The principles of the Edict of Nantes and the *Grâce d'Alais* depended in the long run upon the goodwill of the government. Richelieu and Mazarin knew that it was in their interests to reach an understanding in matters of religion. But what would happen if the government became convinced that a diversity of faiths threatened its authority, and if a rabid wave of fanaticism were to silence the counsels of wisdom? Richelieu's policy had no chance of predominating in the Europe of 1660; the policy of 'one king, one law, one faith' was soon to compel recognition in Paris as everywhere else.

12. Towards Absolutism in Europe

We must here note yet another feature characteristic of the world which emerged from the long crisis. Absolutism, which had long been developing in most European countries, continued to make progress and assert itself everywhere—in Spain, where the old autocracy of Philip II was maintained; in England, where the vanquished Stuarts bequeathed it to their conqueror Cromwell; in the new Hohenzollern State, where the Grand Elector established it on military foundations; and in the United Provinces, where William of Orange was soon to instil it even into democratic institutions. France under Louis XIII and Richelieu offered a striking example of the growth of absolutism.

Once all resistance had been smashed, whether it came from the nobles or the Protestants, a monarchical order and discipline were imposed upon the whole nation, an administrative machine constantly being perfected and strengthened so that it was impossible for anyone to evade the will of authority. Louis XIV had only to tread the same path in order to give a finishing touch to the system.

Absolutism profited largely from existing circumstances. Internal disorders in France, for instance, or in England, caused it to be accepted as the only means of restoring order, and even of preserving national unity. As nations became conscious of their individual characters they felt ready to accept a régime which appeared to offer them opportunities and national greatness. The religious crisis itself operated in favour of absolutism. Wherever the principle of *Cujus regio, hujus religio* triumphed it became an integral part of royal authoritarianism, justifying it in theory and providing it with ways and means. But wherever the other solution was tried it had the same result. France's experience (and that of Poland too, which seems farcical) was that a policy of tolerance had to be imposed by a strong government. Everything therefore tended to move in the same direction. The era of strongly organized states under the firm control of absolute governments had now begun. It would continue until peoples decided to substitute their own authority for that of monarchs and to recognize no rights but those of a sovereign entity, the nation.

The march of absolutism, in a fair way to becoming one of the bases of the new Europe, itself set the Church some serious problems, first in the matter of principles. Almost everywhere absolutism was founded on the theory of the divine right of kings. Already an old theory, it had made positive progress for a century. In France particularly the preachers of the League had dared to parade the rights of a Catholic nation before the 'tyrant' Henri III and the heretical Béarnais Henri IV. But the advocates of order triumphed, and with them what Renan called the 'religion of Rheims'.

According to Bellarmine and Suarez political power is granted by God to the society first, and is then transmitted to kings by that society. From this theory the Church of France steadily inclined towards a different one, taking the view that a monarch, by the very fact of his having inherited a crown, is the direct representative of God on earth—'anointed by God', the trustee of a supernatural mission. This doctrine had a very large following at the beginning of the seventeenth century. Guy Coquille, André Duchesne and Jérome Bignon were its most able exponents. 'A king is the living image of God by whom he is chosen,' said one; and another added: 'A monarch holds his kingdom from God alone.' An Archbishop of Vienne told Henri IV that his crown was 'the living image on earth of the eternal government which is in heaven'. Referring to the extent of the power of kings consecrated by God, Savaron, a zealous apologist, did not hesitate to declare that a king 'exercises the functions of God'. He was not the only person to hold this opinion, any more than France was the only country to do so. When King James I of England formulated his theory of the monarchy in his *Basilicon Doron*, he wrote:

'God gives not Kings the style of Gods in vain,
For on his throne his sceptre do they sway.'

—words which served his own cause well! In France the policy of Louis XIII and Richelieu, while rescuing the country from anarchy at home and preserving it from serious threats from without, ended by implanting this doctrine in men's minds. The two ideas of law and order and the divine right of kings were henceforth intimately associated. In 1632 Le Bret, a counsellor of state, wrote in his treatise on civil rights: 'Kings are appointed by God. Royalty is a supreme power conferred on one person only. Sovereignty is no more divisible than is a point of geometry.'

There was grave risk that such principles would diminish the authority of the Church. At the assembly of the States-General in 1614 the Third Estate presented a draft of a fundamental law which, while declaring that the king holds his crown from God alone, specified that his subjects cannot be exempt on any ground or pretext whatsoever from the allegiance and obedience due to him; and that all who maintained a contrary opinion should, if they were French, be regarded as rebels and, if they were foreigners, as sworn enemies. The statement was precise: any intervention, be it ecclesiastical or pontifical, between king and people was rejected. The words seemed so revolutionary that when the clergy protested Louis XIII intervened to have them deleted; but the idea they had inspired remained.

As evidence of this nothing is more significant than the war waged for many years against the Jesuits, who were determined ultramontanists, opposed to any extreme concept of divine right which threatened the authority of the Church and the Pope. Every possible opportunity had been taken to attack them since the day in 1594 when Châtel, one of their students, made an attempt on the life of Henri IV, and the pressure increased after the king's assassination in 1610. Had not the Jesuit Mariana written that it is sometimes lawful to kill a tyrant? But the charge of regicide was merely a pretext. Libels and pamphlets bearing the signatures of famous people, e.g. Antoine Arnauld [1] and Étienne Pasquier, the public prosecutor in the department of the Advocate-General, clearly indicated what was behind the attacks on the Society. Extracts from Bellarmine's writings were denounced in

[1] A forbear of the famous Jansenist family.

the pamphlets as seditious; for instance, the statement that the Sovereign Pontiff can and must instruct kings to refrain from abusing their authority.

The uproar reached its peak in 1626 when Sébastien Charmoisy, a Parisian bookseller in the Rue Saint-Jacques, put up for sale some copies of a learned theological work from Italy, written by Father Santarelli, an Italian Jesuit. The effect of this austere work was shattering. It stated, for instance, that the Pope may, even in the temporal sphere, guide princes towards their spiritual end. If they reject the guidance the Pope may punish them, not only by excommunication, but also by inflicting temporal penalties such as depriving them of their kingdom and releasing subjects from their oath of allegiance. The Parlement stormed; the Sorbonne thundered. The Superior-General and three Fathers approved the work, and the whole Society was indicted. Called upon to repudiate it, the French Jesuits evaded the issue. Richelieu, who was hostile to Santarelli's theories but much too clever to allow the Parlement and the Sorbonne to score a victory over the Society, intervened and the affair fizzled out. But the violent reaction stirred up by Santarelli's ideas (which were in fact a mere revival of others put forward in the time of Innocent III) indicated an attitude of mind. As between the authority of the king by divine right and that of the head of the Church opinion seemed decidedly in favour of the former.

Hence, both in theory and practice, monarchical absolutism clashed with the Church's basic concepts. To be properly geared, as it were, absolutism is obliged to become totalitarian—to use the term which has become fashionable in our day though it embodies a time-honoured fact. Absolutism necessarily leads to wholesale obtrusion upon everything that concerns the life of the subject, and therefore to intervention in precisely those domains in which the safeguarding of freedom is most vital. 'This State is monarchical,' replied Louis XIII to a member of the Parlement; 'everything touching it depends upon the will of the king.' And Richelieu added: 'Order in a state demands a definite uniformity of control.' These two statements contained the germs of endless controversy. Were official appointments within the Church's hierarchy, the functioning of its departments and the disposal of Church property also to depend on the will of the king? And did the term 'uniformity of control' include the power to direct souls? The way was open to political interference in matters of religion. The doctrines of Erastus had become more real than ever; and Grotius, who adopted them, had recently revived and developed them further.

Wherever absolutism triumphed problems arose over its relations with the Church. To confirm this one has only to consider the example of two countries: one king included the word 'Catholic' in his title

and the other the words 'Most Christian'. In both these countries the
pressure of caesaropapism was intensified. In Spain the fact had been
evident since Philip II, for whom the Inquisition was to a great extent
an instrument of government. Caesaropapism was still more evident
under his successors. Philip IV's minister, the Count of Olivarès,
advocated a centralist absolutism identical with that of Richelieu, in
which 'all the realms which constitute Spain will be subject to the
conventions and law of Castille'. He interfered shamelessly in the
affairs of the Church; he controlled episcopal appointments and
ecclesiastical property, maintained an increasing hold on the Inquisition, and even went so far as to intervene in elections, arranging for
his own minions to be chosen Generals of the great Orders—Franciscan, Dominican and Jesuit. And with what offhanded insolence his
Catholic Majesty treated the Papacy! Philip II sent his infantry to
Rome; his successor, as we have seen, lectured the Holy Father in full
Consistory, urging him to take action against France,[1] and moved his
forces across the Papal States without asking permission.[2] But one fact
has always been evident since the time of Constantine and Byzantium:
the identification of personal interests with those of the Church is the
invariable and fatal consequence of absolutism, no matter how Christian
or Catholic it may claim to be.

In France the march towards absolutism was accompanied by the
development of Gallicanism, a doctrine which before long set the
Church some alarming problems. The word 'doctrine' is perhaps too
precise. Gallicanism embodied a mass of traditions, practices and ideas
of long standing, and developed in a complicated manner. Very definite
interests, such as national pride and independence, converged in
Gallicanism, combined with a veiled form of anti-clericalism, possibly
even secularism. They included, apart from a few Protestant theories,
many historical memories that went back to the time of Philippe le
Bel, the period of the Great Schism and the debates which preceded
the Concordat of 1516. Viewed as a whole, Gallicanism represents a
wave of opposition to the prerogatives of the Holy See in relation to
the Church in France and the State of France.

There were therefore two forms of Gallicanism, one political and
the other ecclesiastical, both of which, however, embraced a common
distrust of the Roman Court and a jealous attachment to the traditions
of the national Church. The political aspect was represented at the end
of the sixteenth century by the jurist Pierre Pithou (1539–96), a converted Huguenot, whose treatise *Les libertés de l'église gallicane*
created a sensation. He defended the French king's right, among other
privileges, to debar the bishops of his realm from free communication
with the Pope, to forbid appeals to Rome and the assembling of

[1] See p. 148.   [2] See p. 141.

councils in France, to oppose the publication within the realm of papal documents and canons issued by councils—even oecumenical councils. Pithou did not attempt to dispute the spiritual rights of the Pope, but he denied the Pope most of the means of making them effective. He maintained that this did not give France any unfair advantages, but merely native franchises and common rights which our ancestors have most steadfastly upheld.

Ecclesiastical Gallicanism went further still. Edmond Richer (1559–1633) was its leading spirit. He was a member of the senate at the Sorbonne; in 1611 he published a treatise in Latin on ecclesiastical and political authority. As far as he was concerned Christ did not give the power of the keys to Peter alone, but also to the college of the twelve apostles, so that the power to direct and make infallible laws rested in the full assembly of the Church—the general council. In other words it meant a return to the conciliar theory of the early fifteenth century; and it was on principles such as these that Richer based the claims of a national Church (especially the Gallican) to retain its customs, administrative procedure and privileges.

It is evident therefore that Gallicanism was advancing in the direction of absolutism. The monarchy, on the principle of divine right, turned it to good account; furthermore its theorists, Guy Coquille among them, proved to be convinced Gallicans. Whenever papal authority was in question, as in the Santarelli affair, Gallican theories and absolutist policies were found to be in agreement. But the two forms of Gallicanism—the one asserting the rights of the State and the other questioning the very spiritual authority of the Pope—did not yet merge. Richer was condemned by du Perron, Archbishop of Sens, and by his suffragan bishops, and deprived of office. The clergy as a whole were not yet won over to royal absolutism, but it was none the less fairly Gallican in outlook.

Richelieu had to face this trend. Naturally he saw at once that Gallicanism lent weight to his absolutist purpose; but not at any price would he quarrel with Rome. So once again he played his hand with restraint and flexibility. He himself persuaded Richer to submit to authority and withdraw his book. At the same time he checked the zeal of extreme Gallicans in the Santarelli affair. He was none the less completely won over to the political aspect of Gallicanism, and it was under Richelieu's patronage that Pierre Dupuy (1582–1651) published his *Preuves des libertés de l'église gallicane* and his *Commentaire de Pierre Pithou*. Then, when the Assembly of the Clergy condemned Dupuy in 1639, Richelieu instructed Pierre de Marca (1594–1662) to reopen the question and prepare a semi-official report on the relations between the Apostolic See and the Church in France. That document was the *De Concordia sacerdotii et imperii*. But Marca went too far. While formally recognizing the Pope's spiritual rights, and even using the term 'papal infallibility', he stated that 'an ecclesiastical law does not become final and binding until it has received the consent of the nation which has to apply it'. In other words, no papal decision would be admissible in France unless accepted by France—in practice, by its government. Marca also engaged in strong criticism of progressive centralization as operated within the Church, the acquisition by Rome of benefices and the role of the Pope in ecclesiastical appointments. Theories such as these opened the door to the many disputes which arose between the government and the Holy See.[1] In Richelieu's time incidents were avoided thanks to his ability as cardinal minister. There was but one serious case of friction; it concerned the appointment of Cardinal La Valette as commander, which was quite rightly criticized by Urban VIII.[2] Under Mazarin two disputes occurred; one concerned Cardinal de Retz, the minister's obdurate opponent, who fled to Rome; the other, of deeper significance, arose out of the manner in which the Bishop of Arras was appointed under the terms of the 1516 Concordat to a district which was not really French territory, though occupied by France.[3] Such conflicts were premonitory signs of much more serious disputes which were to mark the autocratic rule of Louis XIV. What would happen if absolutism, eager to lay hands upon the Church, sought to undermine the very spiritual authority of the Pope; in other words, if the two forms of Gallicanism, backed by force, were merged into one? Clearly such a situation would create the risk of schism, a problem which was soon to arise.

Thus from whatever angle we view the world at the beginning of the seventeenth century, the picture is one calculated to fill the Church with anxiety. Europe, no longer under the influence of the Pope, or even of the Christian ideal, was rent asunder. Religious fanaticism within states showed no sign of diminishing, and even Catholic states seemed committed to paths which threatened to lead to grave crises, perhaps to secession. In addition, other crises were developing in the minds and consciences of men, the symptoms of which were easily discernible through the evolution of ideas and the violence of the Jansenist controversy. All this contrasts strangely with the spectacle of the spiritual revival we have witnessed, all those saintly souls who strove whole-heartedly to strengthen the foundations of the Church and restore her to her former allegiance.

Therein lay the problem. Would the Church, restored and regenerated, be sufficiently strong to impose her discipline, a truly Christian

---

[1] Marca's book was placed on the Index. He himself after a serious illness submitted and became Bishop, and subsequently Archbishop, of Paris.

[2] See p. 148.

[3] Marca, now Bishop de Marca, was entrusted with the task of settling this controversy.

discipline, on a world that appeared to be moving away from her? Or would she remain content to spread a gloss of Christianity over ambitions, interests, passions even, which bore no relation to her principles? The struggle between holiness and the world is unending. That struggle was about to unfold in an atmosphere of splendour during an illustrious reign which began on 8th March 1661 and lasted more than fifty years.

CHAPTER IV

LOUIS XIV: 'MOST CHRISTIAN KING'

1. THE SUN KING

A FRENCH historian may be forgiven if he allows a little sentiment to appear in his approach to the study of Louis XIV—the man and his reign. For never, in the thousand years that wove the thread of her history, had France been as strong, as glamorous, as radiant as she became during that long reign when, under the rule of the thirtieth Capetian, she attained the pinnacle of her fortunes.

The image of this monarch is so colourful that the mind, somewhat dazzled by the splendour, is inclined to admiration rather than to an impartial judgment. Louis XIV was Versailles: Versailles with its palace, its parks, its glassy lakes and its masterpieces—an unparalleled *ensemble* which the world would copy but never equal. Louis XIV evokes military glory obedient to French arms, strongholds captured by Vauban, the crushing campaigns of Condé and Turenne, captured enemy flags hanging in the cathedral of Notre Dame, and Europe anxious to recognize and accept a new order based on French standards. Louis XIV represents order of another kind and a model which French genius created and proclaimed, and which Europe accepted without hesitation—the language of Molière and Racine spoken henceforth by kings and ambassadors; a French conception of creative form compelling recognition by western civilization and blossoming into an unprecedented magnificence. France's debt to this man and to his reign is so vast that it would be unjust and even absurd to deny it. He gave her fifty years of firm rule, an effective structure embodying many ideas that have survived to the present day, a language, a literature, an art, and above all a feeling of greatness born of a noble sense of urgency. The expression which Perrault used to characterize this period, 'the century of Louis XIV',[1] was undoubtedly the expression of a courtier, intended to flatter his master by comparing him with the Emperor Augustus; but it stated a reality which history has acknowledged.

Since Christianity is unquestionably associated with that glory and achievement, to what extent may a Christian historian share this admiration? The part played by Christianity is especially evident through the official documents which assign to the Catholic religion a fundamental position within the State—through the customs and

---

[1] Also used later by Voltaire.

practices accepted by the mighty king himself and the majority of the French people, through the liturgical ceremonies which year after year, from the crowning and anointing of the sovereign at Rheims to his funeral at Saint-Denis, give character and rhythm to his own life and that of the nation. The century of Louis XIV, in so far as it concerns the things of the spirit, was not merely the century of Molière and Racine, La Bruyère and La Fontaine, Mansart and Le Vau; it was also the century of Bossuet, the fearless apologist, of Fénelon, whose heart was enamoured of God; of Bourdaloue, Fléchier, Mascaron, Massillon and a group of preachers who have never perhaps been matched in any age. It was the century of St Margaret Mary Alacoque, St Louis-Marie Grignion de Montfort and St Jean-Baptiste de la Salle.

But more essentially the Christian religion was linked with everything that stood for solidity and grandeur in France during that period. It bound together members of society; it was the code of morals, the key to institutions, and it embodied the meaning of life itself—'the whole of man', as Bossuet remarked. To fail to recognize the part played by Christianity is—as Nisard said of Voltaire, historian of Louis XIV—'not to reach the heart'. On the other hand, to study the reign from the Christian standpoint is to probe the spiritual depths of the epoch, for there only its genius lies revealed. The triumph of order and authority over the forces of crisis and disintegration, to which the classical era ultimately tended in every domain, was achieved through the reawakening of a spiritual allegiance having its roots in time immemorial; that allegiance had been restored to life by the admirable upsurge of the preceding period, and the whole nation was prepared for the contest. If the century of Louis XIV honoured the man even more than it honoured France, it was because its foundations were those of the Cross.

When we consider, however, the events of this glorious epoch, too many of them appear to be out of tune with a Christian conception of life and the world. This glittering reign contains many dark patches, and the detractors of Louis XIV, among them Michelet and Lavisse, have not had to seek far for a bill of indictment. The facts are there to hand; there is no need to search for them. They are apparent in the policy adopted towards the Protestants and the Jansenists, but especially in the ghastly methods used to secure victory by force of arms. Other examples, still more surprising, are to be found in the relations between the Catholic King of France and the Sovereign Pontiff, whom a Catholic must acknowledge as the Vicar of Christ. And how is a Christian to assess that apparent indifference to the misfortunes and sufferings of the lowly, hardly compatible with the tradition established by a former Louis—Louis XII, the 'Father of his people'?

We are evidently faced with a kind of indwelling contradiction.

This appears even more manifest when we consider together the two forms of title in general use during the reign. Since the time of Louis XIII it had been the custom to distinguish the king of France by the additional title 'Most Christian King'. Paul II first used the title in 1469 in a letter to Louis XI. When Louis XIV reached the apogee of his glory his flatterers persuaded him that he was comparable with the sun itself, and they urged him to have a medal struck to confirm this humbug. To what extent can the 'Roi Soleil'—the Sun King—also be called a Most Christian King? Are not the two titles incongruous? There is, in any case, no doubt whatever that the Sun King would find it very difficult to be 'most Christian' in the manner of St Louis.

The events of the reign did, in fact, demonstrate the antithesis between the two titles. It would be unjust, and contrary to historical fact, to disregard the solid Christian basis on which the reign of Louis XIV rested; but it would also be unjust to gloss over the serious faults of which the king and his régime were guilty towards religion, its precepts and its rights. It seems that a real paradox existed between Christian principles, which neither the king nor his servants treated lightly, and the contingencies—necessities perhaps, but certainly inevitabilities—that appertain to government. Monarchical absolutism, indispensable during that period and demanded by peoples themselves as a means of controlling crises and preventing a return to chaos, was attaining its zenith, its acme of perfection. Was it reconcilable with the Gospel, the religion of humility and poverty and its ideal of justice and love? All the great religious discussions of the reign were to converge upon that question.

But the man mostly concerned with that question was he upon whom everything depended and from whom everything proceeded; he embodied the régime so perfectly as to be inseparable from it, bearing both the burden of responsibility and the glory of his reign. In many ways he was as much the prisoner of the system as he was its master. Where does pride begin and end in a king who declares, as Louis did, that love of glory held the highest place in his sentiments, and convinced himself by that very fact that he served a cause that reached infinitely beyond its scope? A leader who knows well that firm discipline is indispensable to the security of the country entrusted to him must find it difficult to decide where charity begins and ends, especially when an occasional act of injustice is the price to be paid for the maintenance of order. Every event that occurred, including those that affected religion, touched the depths of the man in Louis XIV; they influenced his attitude towards faith, towards God and the Church. Raised up by the régime itself to such an eminence that he was scarcely permitted to remain a man, would Louis XIV discover within himself sufficient moral strength, born of humility and submission to the divine will, to resist the temptations resulting from his lofty position? Could he possibly strike a balance between the demands of the high office he assumed and his obligations as a poor sinner?

When describing the 'century' of Louis XIV historians repeatedly use such words as reason, order, light, unity, discipline and balance; but in every case the words appear to skim the surface of reality. They are especially inadequate and inaccurate when used to deal with the religious aspect. The truth is to be sought among the crises that rent the long reign, and not so much in the atmosphere of solemnity that surrounded the Masses celebrated at Versailles and the eloquent funeral orations; it will be found in the conflict existing between the rigid demands of a doctrine requiring detachment, purity and humility of heart and the infinite charity of a saint, and the poor human nature of the man who had to apply it.

2. God's Viceroy

On the day following Cardinal Mazarin's death Harlay de Champvallon, at that time president of the Assembly of the Clergy and Archbishop of Rouen (later of Paris), said to Louis XIV: 'Your Majesty instructed me to approach M. le Cardinal in all matters of business; but the cardinal is dead. To whom does your Majesty wish me to address myself in future?'

'To me,' replied the king. 'I shall dismiss you shortly.'

This was the first occasion on which the king expressed his determination 'to be his own first minister in future,' a decision which he repeated to the Chancellor Séguier, to Fouquet, his superintendent of finance, to Le Tellier and Hugues de Lionne, all of whom showed great surprise.

The king's *Mémoires* suggest that his decision was by no means made on the spur of the moment. For years he had been signing the documents presented to him by Mazarin without reading them, but he had pondered things over in his mind more than he appeared to be doing. 'I continually tested myself secretly, without confiding in anyone,' he wrote, 'meditating upon every occurrence.' The old cardinal was not mistaken when he said that his pupil 'will be a late starter, but he will go further than anyone'.

What were the profound motives that decided this burly lad of twenty-two, hitherto more interested in horses and pretty girls than documents and affairs of State, to assume the burden of responsibilities that went with power? What psychological evolution brought about this change of attitude; what sentiments, what men, what reading influenced him? None of the king's biographers has asked himself that question; yet it is perhaps the key to the whole reign. Was it merely pride, a thirst for power or distrust of men, that determined the most dictatorial of kings to refuse to share the direction of affairs with anyone? Few appear to be aware that a copy of Godeau's *Catéchisme royal* (Godeau was Bishop of Grasse), which appeared in 1659, was given to the king immediately on publication. He acquired from this work a theory of royal power that was particularly prone to excite in a young mind a passion for absolutism, though the work was based upon a genuinely Christian theology. At the very commencement of a reign that lasted more than half a century, and during which the king never swerved for a moment from his decision to be 'his own first minister', he most certainly recognized the Christian obligations of this 'trade of king'. In assuming personal authority he considered that he was obeying a command from heaven.

On reaching his legal majority eight years earlier—fourteen years of age in the case of kings—he was crowned in the brilliantly lit cathedral at Rheims, its arches and pillars adorned with magnificent tapestries. Everything in that wonderful ceremony compelled his mind to seize upon the religious and sacramental significance of his office. The ancient liturgy, its rites, music and symbolism, had undergone little change since the time of King Pepin the Short; everything reminded him again and again that as king-priest, the anointed of God, successor to the Scriptural kings, Saul, David and Solomon, he occupied a positive position in the world under God's will and ratified by the Church. The tunicle, the dalmatic and the cape which he donned in turn reminded him of the three Orders of the priesthood. During the singing of the litanies he lay prostrate on the ground, just as a priest does at his ordination and a bishop at his consecration. The holy oil rubbed on his forehead, breast and shoulders was the same as that used in the administration of the sacraments. More hallowed still were the words of the antiphon: 'Almighty and eternal God, it was Your Will that the kings of France might receive the holy anointing with the balm sent by heaven for that purpose to the saintly Bishop Remigius.' Even more impressive was the Church's acknowledgment of the king's supernatural powers, for it confirmed the rite of 'touching for scrofula' (king's evil) and recognized that he possessed the miraculous gift of healing sores by his touch. Indeed, the pomp of the ceremony, the firing of guns, the ringing of bells, the cheering of the people, those priceless adornments, his crown and sceptre, the hand of Justice, the great purple mantle decked with golden fleurs-de-lys were all tangible tokens of an authority that proceeded direct from God, having nothing to do with earthly values. To add emphasis to the young king's conviction, jurists had perfected throughout the centuries the doctrine of kingship by divine right,[1] and this had been

[1] See p. 176.

further developed during the reign of his father and grandfather. The doctrine had now reached a state of perfection. 'Kings are made by God,' wrote Councillor Le Bret; Coquille, Duchesne, Bignon and Savaron went even further. Soon Bossuet, the most powerful Christian voice of the age, produced his *Politique tirée des propres paroles de l'Écriture sainte*, in which he made a definite break with the tradition of Ballarmine and Suarez. He developed and defined the idea when he wrote: 'A king's throne is not the throne of a man, but the throne of God Himself . . . . Royal power is sacred: God raises up kings as His ministers and reigns through them over nations. . . . Obedience to princes is therefore an obligation of religion and conscience. . . . One should not consider how princely authority was established; it is sufficient that it exists and governs. . . . An inherent holiness exists in the character of a king, and no crime can efface it.'

Such were the theories that Louis XIV read and heard repeated in all manner of ways, not only by jurists (e.g. Domat in his *Droit public*) but by bishops in their theological writings. He must also have read, again from the pen of the Bishop of Meaux, these words, which transcended everything that had gone before: 'According to the Scriptures princes are gods, and they participate to some extent in the independence of God.'

How could the king fail to absorb such doctrine? Ideas such as these occur time and again in his own writings (the *Mémoires* and *Testament*) under different forms. 'Here below kings fulfil a function that is wholly divine. It is the will of God that whoever is born a subject shall obey without discrimination.' And again, more precisely: 'Because a king takes the place of God he participates in His knowledge.'[1] The doctrine of kingship by divine right was therefore put into practice in a systematic and awe-inspiring manner throughout the entire reign. The king's golden rule of life was based upon what he had read in Bishop Godeau's *Catéchisme royal*: 'May your Majesty remember at all times that he is a Viceroy of God.'

A conviction such as this, rooted in the conscience of a prince, was not without its advantages. Undoubtedly it contributed towards determining the atmosphere of the reign, an atmosphere of incomparable majesty maintained for half a century—an air of solemnity, perhaps artificial and tiresome, but which none the less provided a dignity scarcely known during other Capetian reigns (the succeeding one, for instance). It produced a continual and instinctive gravitation towards an ideal of grandeur. Indeed, the king's person appears to have been stamped with these qualities. All observers are unanimous in

---

[1] Jacques Pirenne has compared these words with those used by the ancient Egyptians. The pharaohs of the fifth dynasty (the twenty-fifth century before our era) were declared to possess all knowledge 'from their mother's womb'.

agreeing that such an air of majesty emanated from Louis XIV that it impressed everyone who came into his presence. 'Everything about him', said Mme de Motteville, 'inspired respect and fear, and those upon whom he looked intently could not escape this feeling.' And Saint-Simon adds: 'No man ever inspired such awe; one had to begin by getting accustomed to seeing the king if one were not to stop short suddenly when speaking to him.' Needless to say, this conviction that he was the trustee of God's power and majesty had its dangers; but the fact that he entertained a great respect for his trust was a point in his favour.

In some respects the consequences of the king's conviction that he was God's Viceroy were favourable. By taking his role seriously, not merely on account of the rights it conferred upon him but also because of the obligations it imposed, he was drawn to assume the duties of his state in an extremely steadfast and conscientious manner. The gravity of the doctrine of divine right lay in the fact that it imposed on its recipient demands worthy of the power it granted him. Never did Louis XIV seek to escape them. His *Mémoires* and his *Testament* deal admirably with his conception of his mission and the manner in which he desired to discharge it. He regarded the 'trade of king' as 'great, noble and delightful'; but he wished to feel 'worthy to acquit himself well of everything he undertook'. This illustrious man was, therefore, the most hard-working of kings. 'That is how a king reigns,' he said. 'That is why he reigns.' He had no desire for power without work. 'To wish for the one without the other implies ingratitude and presumption towards God, and injustice and tyranny towards men.' Throughout his entire life Louis XIV devoted many hours a day to public affairs, either alone or with his secretaries of State. He continued to preside over the council until the eve of his death, and conformed to a discipline whose purpose, whatever one might say, went beyond furnishing an opportunity to exalt his kingship through court etiquette.

The actions of a king here below, in his capacity of God's Viceroy, must be providential in the sense that they reflect God's work. The king must ensure the reign of 'justice, the precious trust that God has placed in the hands of kings, and through which they participate in His wisdom and power'. The king must 'show towards peoples subject to him the same marks of paternal goodness that we receive daily from God', and have 'no greater desire than to safeguard the weak against the oppression of the strong, and relieve the destitute. He must also guarantee to maintain Christian order which is the foundation of society, defend those virtues which Christianity demands of men and, in short, protect the faith, its dogma and the Church'. Such were the duties of a king, and Louis XIV was fully conscious of them. There is

* G

no evidence that he sought to escape them. 'He is charged with a great burden' said Bossuet; and he knew.

Such a conception was genuinely Christian. 'How can we possibly imagine', writes Pierre Gaxotte, 'an absolute monarchy separated from the commandments of God?' It is precisely to the extent to which Louis XIV strove to remain loyal to such principles that he deserved the title 'Most Christian' bestowed on him by diplomatic custom. But just how much did he really strive? The doctrine had to be applied by a man made of flesh and passions like every other, ceaselessly beset by temptations and no more immune from sin than anyone else. Can a Viceroy of God permit himself certain weaknesses without creating scandal? What is more to the point, this earth-bound representative of heaven runs the risk of forgetting occasionally that his most trifling act is responsible to a higher Justice; he is liable to confuse the delegated authority vested in him with an entirely temporal authoritarianism. Between monarchy by divine right and an absolutist system of State control collusion would be almost inevitable, and that was the tendency of the age. Between the conviction that one represents God on earth and the illusion of being something more than a man there exists an incline down which it is very easy to slide. Did Louis XIV manage to avoid confusing the issue?

3. THE HEART OF A KING

It is a fact beyond dispute that Louis XIV was a believer. He spent the whole of his youth in an intensely spiritual atmosphere, under the influence of a Spanish mother of great piety and the memory of a devout father. He had been constantly told that his birth was an answer to prayer, that he was indeed Louis the 'God-given'.

In 1650 he solemnly renewed the dedication of his realm to Our Lady made by Louis XIII, and instructed 'all institutions to admonish each and every one to have a special devotion to the Holy Virgin'. One of the first acts of his personal rule was to take part in the Stations of the jubilee solemnized in 1661. He walked in the processions to show, as he said, 'that it was through God and His grace rather than by his own efforts that he hoped to accomplish his aims'.

Throughout the reign the practice of religion played an important part in the schedule and time-table that governed court etiquette. Morning and evening prayers formed part of the ceremony of the *lever* and *coucher*—when the sovereign rose from or retired to bed. The king assisted at Mass every day, respectfully kneeling from the *Sanctus* until the priest's Communion. At nightfall he never failed to take part in the evening service. He attended in person a number of processions—at Corpus Christi, for instance, and those arranged three times a year by the Order of the Holy Ghost (on 1st January, 2nd February and the feast of Pentecost). He also followed in the procession of 10th February to commemorate the dedication of France to Our Lady. In Advent he listened to the Sunday sermons, and sometimes on Wednesdays and Fridays; during Lent he attended them all, and scrupulously obeyed the Church's laws relating to fasting and abstinence. He publicly warned the court that he expected everyone else to do likewise. He attended the offices of Holy Week regularly, even during the years when his personal difficulties with the sixth and ninth Commandments prevented him from making his Easter duties. On Maundy Thursday he washed and kissed the feet of thirteen poor children in the presence of the Chaplain-General; afterwards he served them a meal, and the princes of the blood, headed by the Dauphin, acted as waiters and cup-bearers.

All this clearly constituted a splendid and steadfast homage to the Christian religion. It is difficult to say to what extent these ceremonies were an expression of the king's faith. From what we know of his practices we cannot regard him as extremely devout. He received Holy Communion five times a year at the most: 'At the parish church on Holy Saturday,' Saint-Simon tells us, 'and in his private chapel on other days, such as the eve of Pentecost, the feast of the Assumption, the eve of All Saints and Christmas Eve.' We know of no recorded instance of his having felt impelled to approach the altar out of a personal desire or to satisfy an interior need. During Divine Service he was reluctant to use a prayer book; even Mme de Maintenon was often unable to persuade him to do so. When he had one he scarcely opened it and contented himself with saying the Rosary, which seems to have been his favourite devotion. All his life he kept the beads he had inherited from his father, and which had previously belonged to Henri II and Henri IV. It was, in any case, a peculiar Rosary: the beads were tiny skulls in ivory. There seems to be no record either of any spontaneous desire to read spiritual books, a practice which his father and his cousin, Philip IV of Spain, always followed. His father had been a fervent admirer of Lorenzo Scupoli, and Philip of Maria d'Agreda. Mme de Maintenon often complained to the king that he paid little attention to the books she read to him. There is no mention anywhere of his having made retreats, as did St Louis, who was accustomed to withdraw frequently to some monastery. All the evidence suggests that the spiritual tide of the century of saints did not sweep the great king's soul towards mystical heights.

It has often been said, and perhaps unjustly, that the religious practices of Louis XIV were simply a matter of form, a way of showing his sincere respect for the religion of his forbears. The king might have read in a letter addressed to him by Fénelon,[1] if indeed it ever came to his notice, this unsparing criticism of his faith: 'You do not love God; you only fear Him with the fear of a slave. Your religion consists of nothing but superstitions and petty superficial practices. You resemble the Jews whom God accused of honouring him with their lips and not with their hearts. You are scrupulous in trifles and obstinate in things that are dreadfully wrong.' It is difficult to know to what extent the Archbishop of Cambrai was right; to judge properly one would have to probe the depths of a heart that was never inclined to be prodigal with its secrets, but strove rather to conceal its innermost thoughts.

We do know, however, from certain characteristic traits and from what the king has said, that he possessed a faith that was anything but formal. When he was eighteen he confided to an intimate friend that he could not understand how anyone in a state of mortal sin could sleep at night with an easy conscience. 'On great feast days', said Mme de Caylus, 'he experienced twinges of conscience because he could not pray, or prayed badly.' And the Abbé de Choisy aptly commented: 'More than once, despite official whispers, the king preferred to abstain from the sacraments than approach them unworthily.' This was a source of scandal to the common people, but of edification to the wise and enlightened. In 1704, on the brink of old age and consequently very much wiser, he admitted to Massillon after one of those dramatic sermons in which the celebrated preacher was so proficient: 'Whenever I listen to you, Father, I am displeased with myself.' Those are not the words of a man whose religion is a matter of mere routine, decorum or policy.[2]

There were no spiritual complications attached to the faith of the Roi Soleil. The reassuring simplicity of his beliefs sheltered him from the insidious subtleties of Jansenism and Quietism, and certainly held him aloof from disturbing ideas such as those of Pascal, from anxious searchings and shattering revelations. Yet he was not a man whose conscience was easily satisfied, contenting himself with a few superstitious practices and assuming that he was thereby saved; it was not as simple as that. Through the outward show of splendour we get a glimpse of a man like ourselves, face to face with his soul, and like us, wrestling with the Angel.

For this king who loved court etiquette was well acquainted with

---

[1] The letter was written to the Duc de Chevreuse, but intended for the king. It is included in Fénelon's *Oeuvres complètes* (tome vii, pp. 321–5). No one can say whether the king read the letter or not; but it seems that some passages regarding the necessity for signing a peace must have had some influence on him. Traces of this influence may also be found in the conversations that the king had with Maréchal de Villars.

[2] Saint-Simon relates that he was deeply impressed by the eagerness with which the king inquired, on being informed that Louis XIII was dead, whether his father had received the Last Sacraments.

those human passions that play havoc with the soul and endanger eternal life. He yielded to some and vanquished others, as all men do. His life appears to have been a conflict of the will. In his youth he was subject to fits of violent anger; he eventually succeeded in curbing them so that he always remained supremely master of himself. He never allowed anyone to notice that he was in pain, either morally or physically; he did not even allow himself to be ill, and above all to appear so. In the face of death he displayed a praiseworthy strength of mind.

In other matters he was undoubtedly less exemplary. Historians, in an attempt to prove that he was, as one has said, 'unacquainted with the refinements of Christian morals', have strongly emphasized his waywardness where love was concerned; and certainly the picture is hardly edifying. He wrote in his *Mémoires*: 'If it is true that the heart, unable to reject its natural weakness, experiences despite itself these common emotions, reason at least should conceal them.' It must be admitted that Louis did not succeed very well in putting this precept into practice. His display of mistresses and legitimized children was offensive; but was the conduct of his Catholic Majesty, Philip IV of Spain, any better? The Most Christian King's resounding, and some-times simultaneous, love affairs present a rather disagreeable picture resembling that of a sultan with his harem—the tender Mlle de la Vallière, the disturbing and attractive Mme de Montespan and other beautiful but less famous women, such as Mlle de la Motte Argencourt, Mlle de Marivault, Mme de Ludre and Mlle de Fontanges. Does this picture suggest that, as a slave of violent passions, he did not suffer in consequence? On several occasions, as the feast of Easter drew near, he was seen to make an effort to return to the right path in order to receive Holy Communion. There were one or two moving incidents. On Maundy Thursday, 1675, a courageous priest refused Mme de Montespan absolution, and the king, far from punishing the bold man, admitted that the fact perturbed him and ordered his mistress to leave the court. This she did—though it was only for a short time. What is also remarkable, and indeed to the king's credit, is that he allowed Bossuet, Bourdaloue, Massillon, Dom Cosme and other preachers to lecture him from the pulpit. The precision and violence of their censure were astonishing. We have only to read the devastating attack Bour-daloue made in his sermon on impurity, uttered in the very teeth of the culprit! No twentieth-century dictator would endure such a castigation. Louis XIV was a great sinner, a public sinner, and he was fully aware of the fact; the sense of sin can be profoundly beneficial to the soul.

Furthermore, we must remember that about half way through his reign the king put an end to these violent love affairs once and for all.

This may have been due to the decisive influence of Mme de Maintenon and her devout circle, for we must not underestimate the qualities of this good and clever convert, grand-daughter of Agrippa d'Aubigné and widow of the paralysed poet Scarron. She became governess to the king's illegitimate children by Mme de Montespan, gradually won her master's favour, and ended by secretly marrying him. She was no common sycophant, playing on the king's scruples in order to secure him for herself. 'Lord God,' she wrote, as though making a confession, 'all my life I wish to adore whatever Your Providence ordains for me; I submit to it without reserve. Let me be of service to the king in the salvation of his soul. . . . Let me be saved with him!' These words were written with sincerity; and equally sincere were the king's spiritual impulses, his disgust with his past and his weariness of repeated sin. The alleged conspiracy between Mme de Maintenon and Fénelon to worry and beset the king does not entirely explain his attitude. Even when respect and a strong tinge of boredom were the only feelings he retained for his wife, Louis XIV still did not return to his former excesses. He was forty-six when he married Scarron's widow, and he led an absolutely upright life during the last thirty years of his reign. The approach of old age is not sufficient to explain this victory over himself.

One aspect, however, of Louis XIV's character must appear distressing to a Christian: we might call it pride, egoism or hardheartedness, for all three are usually found together. He was naturally proud, but the defect was intensified by the education he had received. As a mere child he had been the object of a form of flattery which might have turned anyone's head. His mother prostrated herself before him, declaring that the 'respect in which she held him was greater even than her love'. His first lessons in handwriting consisted in copying the words: 'Homage is due to kings; they do whatever pleases them.' The doctrine of divine right could only emphasize this tendency towards pride, and there is much to suggest that what he had been told about his 'miraculous' birth might easily have driven home the conviction that he was entrusted with a superhuman mission.

The danger of excessive pride was therefore inevitable, and no doubt Fénelon was right when he said: 'You love only your glory and your comfort. You view everything in terms of self as if you were the god of earth, and everything had been created to be sacrificed to you.' Bossuet expressed himself more prudently, but he evidently thought the same when he spoke of the dangers of unlimited power, and referred to Nabuchodonosor and Balthasar. Saint-Simon went further, referring to the king in stinging terms as 'loving and valuing only himself and having no purpose outside himself'.

Indeed, the amazing thing is not that the great king should have been proud in view of the upbringing he had received and the worship with which he was surrounded,[1] but that a prince so flattered did not yield to hysteria. It has very often been said that 'only the fear of hell prevented him from demanding adoration', but this is pure malice. He was too clever to lose sight of the precariousness of things human and the fear of judgment. Bossuet called this 'the remedy God Himself has prescribed to kings against the temptations emanating from power'. Mme de Sévigné relates that some members of the Order of Minims dedicated a thesis to the king in which they likened him to God, as though God were but the copy of the king. Bossuet had no difficulty in convincing him that such praise was indelicate, and Louis XIV, of course, rejected it.

It is none the less true that on many occasions he was severe and indifferent to the point of inhumanity. Despite many acts of spontaneous kindness, especially towards the young, there were too many occasions when he proved to be sadly lacking in the most elementary kindness. That might not be regarded as serious if his harshness were merely a principle of government. Olivier d'Ormesson quoted the king as having said: 'I know I am not loved, but I am not bothered about it, for I wish to reign by fear.' He could hardly be condemned on these words alone, for one may argue long as to whether the use of gentleness or force is of more value in the management of men. Even his reputed cruelty, that quiet cruelty towards the women he loved, may easily be excused on the sensible principle, which he stated in his *Testament*, never to allow love to interfere with politics. But it is very distressing to think that this hardness, pride and egoism seemed to enclose his heart in steel, rendering him insensible to great suffering, heedless of flagrant wrongs and somewhat lax where justice was concerned. We are painfully surprised to see a young king bring pressure to bear on the judges in the trial of Fouquet, his superintendent of finance, in hope of securing his execution; and to read of the brutal and irrevocable disgrace of Olivier d'Ormesson because his conclusions in his report on the affair were not in the king's favour. Even more painful is the fact that in his old age the king went so far as to imprison Vauban for his moving appeal on behalf of social justice. And what are we to think of a military leader whose armies laid waste the Palatinate, of a king who organized the *Dragonnades* in Languedoc? France's 'Great King' lacked the very qualities which would have made him a really Christian king; the quality that was also wanting in that other great Catholic king, Philip II of Spain—the fragrant spiritual bloom of mercy—the charity of Christ.

---

[1] Bearing in mind the persistent and fulsome praise showered on Louis XIV there is some excuse for his pride. The Abbé Dangeau, brother of the memorialist, even produced a *Dictionnaire des bienfaits du roi*.

4. THE KING AND THE CHURCH

The oaths taken by Louis XIV during his coronation ceremony were many and elaborate. He swore 'to protect the Church in his kingdom, as it is the duty of every king to do', 'to safeguard peace at all times' within the Church, and to prevent the Church from falling victim to disorder and evil. Such was the basis of that alliance between the Crown and the Church, which had been the foundation of French monarchy since the time of Clovis. One of the oaths taken by the king was even more precise: to preserve 'the canonical privileges, rights and jurisdiction of the Church'; and those who officiated at the ceremony replied in a prayer which resembled a warning: 'As the clergy stand nearer to the holy altar than the rest of the faithful so must you endeavour to ensure that the clergy are treated with the greatest respect and maintained in suitable places, that God's mediator on behalf of men may make you mediator between the clergy and the people.' The recognized position of the clergy as the first Order of the realm was thus clearly defined.

It goes without saying that Louis XIV did maintain that ancient alliance between the Altar and the Crown. He maintained it as a believer, wishing to remain loyal to the vows made at Rheims. But it was also good policy; he appreciated that it provided his throne with its most solid foundations. There are, however, many ways of interpreting that alliance. In principle it meant a collaboration between two authorities working together in the best interests of the people, but each having its own sphere of activity, the one spiritual and the other temporal. In actual fact this collaboration, founded on equality of authority, almost ceased to exist as time went on. Sometimes the Church sought to bring the lay power into subjection; at other times, and especially after the great theocratic ventures had run their course, kings strove to control the Church. As far as appearances went that was the underlying, if not expressed, purpose of Louis XIV. The question was bound to arise sooner or later whether the Church, honoured, flattered, its hierarchy surrounded with marks of esteem, could avoid becoming a part of a system, a cog in the machinery of government under a régime that tended more and more towards centralization and dictatorship.

The exclusion of ministers of the Church from positions of authority was a hard and fast principle of the régime of Louis XIV, and one to which there was no exception. Doubtless the king remembered the power of Richelieu and Mazarin. Saint-Simon relates that when someone expressed surprise to Louis XIV that he did not place on the

Council a certain cardinal whose services he commended, the king replied: 'I have made a rule, to which I adhere, never to have a minister of the Church on my Council, especially a cardinal.' And in his *Testament* he stated explicitly and with a touch of humour his reasons for this ostracism: ' . . . because ecclesiastics are a little too inclined to take advantage of their profession, and sometimes make use of it to minimize their rightful duties. . . .'

But if the king did not wish the clergy to interfere in his affairs he did not by any means think that he should abstain from interfering with the business of the Church. Quite the contrary: the collusion of the spiritual and the temporal, and unfortunate consequence of the 1516 Concordat which did so much harm to the Church and against which the Council of Trent failed to take a strong stand, became a factor of government during the whole reign of the *grand monarque*. Louis XIV used to the full his right, recognized in the Concordat, of nominating candidates for bishoprics and abbeys. That the Pope reserved to himself the right of canonical investiture was a minor consideration to the king. In actual fact it was he and he alone who appointed the higher clergy.

It must be appreciated that in the king's eyes this was a task of some importance: 'The most hazardous part of his duties,' as Bossuet said. And Louis had every intention of performing it worthily. He even wished, as he assures us, 'to observe in the sacred army' the same rules that he applied to the promotion of his military officers, and admit 'to the bishoprics and other high positions only those who have served the Church in missions or in carrying out the functions of parish priests or curates'. The Council of Conscience was available to assist him in his choice. The king himself presided over the Council and, especially from about 1682 to 1684, was very concerned with what took place at its meetings. His confessor (Father La Chaise [1] at first, and above all Father Le Tellier) occupied a prominent place in the Council as representative of the French clergy, dealing with religious affairs and disposing of titles and benefices. But Mme de Maintenon, after her marriage to the king, managed things over the heads of the

---

[1] A well-known cemetery named after Father La Chaise or de la Chaise (1624–1709) now stands to the north east of Paris on ground which at that time belonged to the Jesuits. Father La Chaise exercised a considerable influence over the king. He was not, as Rébelieu stated in his *Lavisse* (viii. 1), 'Secretary of State for religious affairs, sole representative of the Church of France to the king, chief treasurer and paymaster of the royal bounty', but he did advise the king as to the disposal of benefices. Every Friday after Mass Louis XIV spent many hours with him either working or discussing matters affecting his soul. La Chaise courageously endeavoured to avoid nominations which might have given scandal, despite the flood of applications he received. An article by Father Guitton entitled 'Le père de la Chaise et la feuille des bénéfices' appeared in the *Revue d'histoire de l'Église de France* (1956, p. 29 et seq.), and dealt with La Chaise and the promotion-hunters.

Jesuits, and eventually became a kind of minister for ecclesiastical affairs.

The king's good intentions and the influence of those who assisted him did not lead to really satisfactory results. The very system of control which Louis XIV exercised, his gradual isolation in the restricted environment of Versailles where active control became more and more centralized, inevitably resulted in the majority of bishops and other Church dignitaries becoming minions of the court, the government and the administration. Le Tellier, Archbishop of Rheims, Jean-Baptiste Colbert, Bishop of Montauban, and André Colbert, Bishop of Auxerre, were the sons, brothers or cousins of ministers. The former chaplain to the Queen Mother was appointed to Saint-Malo and the king's chaplain to Auch. Mme de Maintenon had her beloved confidant the Abbé Godet des Marais (who was none the less a very pious priest) installed at Chartres. Still more surprising, many bishops were taken into the king's household, e.g. Valot and Daquin, Bishops of Nevers and Fréjus respectively; Sanguin, Bishop of Senlis, whose father was a *major-domo* at Versailles—all 'cads in purple', to use the words of Saint-Simon. The most ridiculed prelate of them all was Ancelin, Bishop of Tulle, whose mother had been one of the king's nurses.

Abbots and abbesses were appointed in the same arbitrary manner. The competition was lively, for these posts yielded a good income. The *in commendam* system, denounced by all reformers during the preceding period, was practised more than ever. Abbesses transferred from one Order to another to acquire a wealthier convent; bishops would offer some abbey in their diocese to a highly placed minister. Both Mme de Montespan and Mlle de Fontanges obtained from the king splendid convents for their sisters. We have the famous story, told by Saint-Simon, of the little Comte de Toulouse, a natural son of Louis XIV, asking for a bishopric for his valet Picard to compensate him for the fact that the valet's brother Vexin had been given some profitable abbeys. To crown all, the king took it into his head to seek a dispensation from the Holy See in order that one of his legitimized sons might enter the Church.

It was surprising that this state of affairs did not infect and corrupt the episcopate under Louis XIV. Although it was not generally up to the standard of its counterpart in the time of Louis XIII and Richelieu it was, in fact, not bad; it even included some splendid personalities who had either survived the previous epoch or had simply remained loyal to the duties of their state.[1] But members of the higher clergy, the worldly minded bishops and commendatory abbots, were absolutely devoted to the king, zealous in his service and dazzled by his splendour.

[1] See Chapter V on the qualities of certain bishops.

That was a serious matter. Even Bossuet and other bishops who possessed the most brilliant qualities as churchmen allowed themselves to be captivated by Versailles, the court and the fact that they came under the king's notice. 'Whatever will you do at Rheims?' a lady of fashion asked Le Tellier when he was returning to his diocese. 'You will be bored to death there!' Racine satirized the 'petite assemblée' of fifty-two prelates who followed the court around. For ambitious priests who wanted to make headway Versailles became the object of their pilgrimage *ad limina*. Bishops and important Church dignitaries were certainly no longer employed in official lay positions to the same extent as in the past, but one or two were diplomats and administrators. An archbishop, for instance, occupied the post of King's Lieutenant and Governor, and Henri de Sourdis was at the head of the Admiralty. But by all appearances they were as much a part of government machinery as they were a means of enhancing the king's glory. When Colbert met with resistance in his attempt to bring production under his control there were bishops in several localities who shouldered the responsibility of making the working class conform. The subordination of the episcopate was such that, when the Bishop of Agen openly criticized Colbert's policy the powerful minister rebuked him before the whole court, and threatened to have him taken back to his diocese under guard. Needless to say the bishop made no reply, terrified lest the punishment might be carried out.

One of the most unhappy consequences of this subjection of the higher clergy was that it became practically cut off from Rome. 'To write directly to the Pope, to his ministers or to anyone representing him in this court,' said Saint-Simon, 'or to receive any letter whatever without the king or his Secretary of State knowing the reason for it and permitting it, was an unpardonable crime against the State. The practice was punished and therefore ceased entirely.' Thus, at a single stroke, attachment to the Holy See, if not loyalty to Rome, disappeared. 'Osmosis exists between the universal Church and a particular Church; they are distinct but not separate. They open out into one other, the interests of the one being bound up with the interests of the other. When their relationships become strained it does harm to the very life of both.' [1] The Gallican crisis showed in a painful manner the conse-quences of this factual and spiritual separation. And there is no doubt that the evident slowing down of the spiritual upsurge noticeable at the beginning of the reign of Louis XIV must be seen in relation to this separation.[2] The laws made by the Council of Trent were not officially accepted in France during the reign of Louis XIV any more than they had been under his predecessors; they were not even taken

---

[1] From Father Broutin's *La Réforme pastorale de France au XVIIe siècle*, ii. 52.
[2] See Chapter II, p. 123.

into account in the assemblies of the Clergy, where henceforward only Gallican freedoms were considered.[1]

We must not overlook the fact that, although the king's subjection of the clergy to his will was part of a broad policy, he could not have failed to consider other very material advantages. His idea of ownership was strictly totalitarian. 'Everything within our realm, of whatever nature, belongs to us. . . . Kingship implies the right to dispose absolutely of all property possessed by churchmen and laity.' In the view of Louis XIV everything that had been said about the object of Church property and the intention of the founders was merely a groundless scruple. 'The principle will not, in fact, be invoked unless it be to thwart any tendency on the part of the clergy to elude their public duties.' In his *Testament* Louis even attempted to demonstrate under five heads that as ecclesiastics are not burdened with heavy expenses they should pay more taxes than the other orders of society. But what justification had the government to encroach upon Church property by so disposing of benefices that the proceeds found their way into the ever-empty Treasury? The affair of the *Régale* (the king's right to receive revenues of vacant bishoprics) was the occasion, if not the cause, of the serious controversy that arose between the Most Christian King and the Holy See. Even though the royal treasury might not have gained a great deal from the *Régale*, the fact that the trouble seems to have originated as a question of pounds, shillings and pence is typical of the *modus operandi*.[2]

Thus, in every sense, collusion between Church and State was flagrant. This fact is recognized even by historians who are not inclined to condemn the mistaken ideas of caesaropapism. 'Was there ever a close union of Church and State?' asks Cardinal Baudrillart. 'The Church of France was closely bound to the king and almost merged into the State,' says Pierre Gaxotte. And Gabriel Hanotaux is even more categorical: 'Religion was nothing other than the State.' A Catholic mindful of the lessons of history cannot wax enthusiastic over this type of identification. How can a national Church remain loyal to the principles of which she is the guardian if she is to be subject to the State whose interests are mainly temporal? Since the time of Constantine and Byzantium the Church has learned to distrust sovereigns who are 'bishops from without'. There was some ground

---

[1] We can see that Gallicanism was a cast of mind common among the French clergy of that day, and quite distinct from the question of doctrine. There were, moreover, degrees in this tendency towards moral particularism and ecclesiastical chauvinism. They could be recognized in the cassock worn by the bishops: the deeper the blue the more closely was the wearer inclined towards Gallican ideas. Saint-Simon speaks of the 'blue patch' of bishops; and Rigaud's celebrated portrait of Bossuet (in the Louvre) shows the bishop dressed in a violet cassock with a very definite tinge of blue.

[2] Despite appearances the origins of the *Régale* affair were spiritual rather than financial. See p. 218.

for Fénelon's burst of indignation: 'Abuse of our rights and usurpa-
tions no longer originate in Rome. The king rather than the Pope is
the master of the Gallican Church, and the king's power over the
Church has passed into the hands of laymen who lord it over the
bishops!' Had that been all, the situation might not have been so bad;
but once the king had become master of the national Church, he might
seek to intervene in more restricted fields. At a very critical phase of
the Jansenist *débâcle* the Attorney-General d'Aguesseau threatened
that the king might establish a new article of faith when he thought it
desirable, and enforce it upon his bishops. There was much wisdom
in the prayer uttered by Bossuet: 'May God prevent our Most
Christian Kings from aspiring to sovereignty over things sacred.'

In short, this confusion between Church and State determined the
religious policy of Louis XIV throughout his reign. His intervention
in things sacred moved steadily towards absolutism and caesaropapism, striving to achieve that totalitarian unity which was his evident
purpose in every other field, whether it concerned economy, intellectual
life or the fine arts. The result was a series of crises and catastrophes
ending in downright failure.

5. DEFENDER OF THE FAITH AND OF MORALS

The religious policy of Louis XIV did not, in fact, assume at once
the emphasis and ruthlessness that characterized it during the crises
arising out of Protestantism, Jansenism, Quietism and even Gallicanism,
until after the period from 1680 to 1685. In many ways these years
marked a turning-point in the reign. By 1682, when the king was
finally installed at Versailles, he had reached the height of his glory.
The medal comparing him with the sun had just been struck, and Paris
had recently bestowed on its master the title of Louis the Great. In
1684 the Peace of Regensburg marked the apogee of the French Sun
over Europe. By that time the king was a widower and in his forty-
fifth year; he had abandoned his youthful indulgence, married Mme
de Maintenon and was on the way to a sincere conversion. Henceforward his religious policy and interior development were closely
related, and to some extent intermingled. Having become devout without being any less dictatorial, Louis XIV would intervene in religious
matters in the role of defender of the faith and of morals and protector
of the Church, a Church whose powers were in his view strictly sub-
ordinate to his own.

He had never in the past failed to insist on respect for the Catholic
faith and the Commandments, even when his personal conduct ill
qualified him to play the role of Father of the Church. It seems hardly
probable that Louis XIV applied to himself those words in Molière's

Tartuffe, which Cléante hurls at devout people of every type: 'Why do you take upon yourself what is Heaven's responsibility?' One of the first acts of his personal rule was to republish an edict under which blasphemy was punishable by death. In 1661 Parlement ordered the arrest of two men under that edict: the first a blasphemer who was condemned to the galleys; the other a skittle-player who could not cure himself of the tiresome habit of taking the name of God in vain when his ball missed the skittles, and was duly hanged. When three years later, in 1664, the nuns of Port-Royal refused to submit to the authority of their archbishop, they were actually disbanded by the police. Such was the solicitude of Mlle de La Vallière's lover in defence of the faith.

As time passed he went still further. About the middle of the reign several decrees were issued to safeguard the holiness of the Sabbath and all feasts preceded by a vigil fast. They amounted to seventy-eight days in the year and, if we are to believe La Fontaine's mischievous cobbler, they caused some inconvenience to artisans and craftsmen. A royal ordinance reminded generals that their troops were obliged to fast during Lent; when military leaders objected that it was difficult to comply with such orders during a campaign they were told that their Quartermaster-General's department should apply to the bishops to obtain the necessary dispensation.

When Louis XIV himself returned to a more rigid practice of religion he used his authority to ensure that his *entourage* followed his example. Dangeau's *Journal*, dated Easter Monday, 3rd April 1684, contains the following entry: 'On rising, the king spoke severely about courtiers who failed to make their Easter duties. He said he had a high opinion of those who made them well and urged everyone to think seriously about it, adding that he would be grateful to them if they did so.' This certainly suggested a great improvement on the sentiment expressed by Cléante in *Tartuffe*! Whether pressure of this kind resulted in any spiritual improvement in the court is perhaps doubtful. A joke played by the Marquis de Brissac on some of the 'devout' ladies of the court caused a great deal of amusement at Versailles. One evening the Marquis said loudly that the king would not be present at prayers. On hearing this some of the lovely ladies hastily blew out their candles and hurried from the chapel, but were very upset to learn later that the august worshipper had attended after all. The irony of La Bruyère in his famous *Caractères* is very much to the point: 'Nowadays piety consists in . . . knowing your way about the chapel, being acquainted with the position of seats which allow you to be seen or not seen. A devout person would just as soon become an atheist if the king were one.'

Louis XIV was evidently not content to 'defend' the faith at

Versailles merely by urging his courtiers to approach the confessional. When difficulties arose over doctrine he again intervened with the same enthusiasm. He appeared more anxious than the Pope himself to revive animosity in the Jansenist dispute.[1] The nuns at Port-Royal were forbidden to accept novices, and four or five obscure Jansenists were thrown into the Bastille. Later, when the affair took a turn for the worse, the king intervened personally, and urged the Spanish authorities to have Father Quesnel arrested. In conjunction with Mme de Montespan and Father La Chaise he examined the documents relating to the suspect, asked the Pope to condemn unequivocally a number of harmful clauses, decided on the demolition of Port-Royal-des-Champs, and 'at his express command' had the Bull *Unigenitus* accepted by his stubborn Parlement. By the time Louis XIV died, over two thousand people had been imprisoned on account of Jansenism.

He dealt similarly with Quietism. In his handling of the *Maximes des Saints* and the *Nouveau Testament en français* he acquitted himself like a theologian; and, when the authorities in Rome were divided and hesitant in their examination of Fénelon's theories, the king submitted a memorandum of his own opposing the supporters of the Swan of Cambrai, as Fénelon was called. Another example was the arrest of Father Lacombe by the king's police. Imprisoned for a while in the Bastille and on the Île de Ré, he afterwards spent nine years in the château at Lourdes and fourteen at Vincennes, and was eventually declared insane and sent to Charenton,[2] where he died.

Saint-Simon, referring to the king's behaviour, caustically observes that as Louis grew older he imagined he was doing penance when he did it on the backs of other people. The irony is perhaps not altogether fair. It is just as reasonable to believe that as Louis XIV returned to a stricter observance of the faith he became more conscious of the duties to which he was bound by his coronation vows, and that he sincerely wished to assume the role of 'God's sergeant'—a role which his ancestor St Louis regarded as the primary duty of kings. If such were the case, Louis XIV would naturally have discharged that duty in a manner recognized and understood at that period. Moreover, under a régime of thorough-going absolutism such as he intended to establish those who deviated in the matter of religion were regarded as rebels, destroying that national unity of which the Catholic religion

[1] Chapter VI deals with the history of Jansenism and Quietism.

[2] As 'defender of the faith' Louis XIV must also be credited with having re-established Catholicism in Alsace, whence it had been wellnigh eliminated by Protestantism. The annexation of Alsace was advantageous to the Catholics. On 21st October 1681, three months after the surrender of Strasbourg, Mass was celebrated in the cathedral the first time for a hundred and twenty-two years. Two days later Bishop Fürstenberg, a German well disposed towards France, received Louis XIV at the portal. The Jesuits of the province of Champagne immediately set to work. It was they who suggested the colonizing of Alsace by Catholics.

constituted the bond. Doctrinal deviation, let alone heresy, was utterly incompatible with the principle 'one king, one law, one faith.' The greatest religious drama of the reign was to prove this abundantly.

6. THE REVOCATION OF THE EDICT OF NANTES

When Louis XIV assumed personal control the problem of Protestantism was already a complex one.[1] The 'religionnaires', as the Calvinists were usually called, numbered over a million adherents; they had 136 pastors and 650 temples. Their members included sailors (among whom Duquesne) along the coasts of Normandy, Aunis and Poitou, manufacturers and merchants at Montauban, Nîmes, Montpellier and Grenoble, and peasants in the Cévennes and the mountains of Dauphiné. On the whole they were peace-loving people, only too anxious to be left alone. Deserted by their leaders, who had merely taken advantage of disorder to seek fortune and adventure, they were favourably reported upon to the king by Mazarin in 1652. Perhaps that was an astute stroke of diplomacy on the cardinal's part. 'The pasture may be rank,' he said, 'but at least the little flock does not wander away.' Colbert, whose influence was growing, appreciated the hardworking qualities of the Protestant population. That illustrious soldier and champion of the throne, Turenne, had not yet been converted. There was nothing to suggest that peace would not continue.

But the fanatics, whether Catholics or Protestants, did not lay down their arms. Wherever the 'reformed' were most numerous they continued to harass the 'popish' population in every possible way; and, if the authorities shut their eyes to their activities, they strove to expand, shamelessly violating the provisions of the Edict of Nantes. In the district of Gex alone twenty-three new temples were opened in fifty years. The Catholics on their part regarded the pacificatory edicts imposed by Henri IV as a truce that might be revoked at any time. Even though the Protestants no longer existed as a political party, there still remained the deeply rooted memory of the state within the state and the dangers the country had recently faced as a result of Protestant power. 'England and the northern Protestant countries', said the discerning Jacques Bainville, 'had set an example by suppressing what remained of Catholicism, and excluding Catholics from employment.' If the king of France decided on action similar to that which had taken place in England public opinion was certain to approve.

There is no doubt whatever as to why Louis XIV adopted a policy so radically different from that of Richelieu and Mazarin. Religion was

[1] See Chapter III, p. 175.

the main reason; but a religion too narrow in conception and indeed hardly Christian. It was, however, the religion of the vast majority of the people. On the day of his coronation the king had sworn to exterminate from his realm and all places under his jurisdiction any whom the Church declared to be heretics. He therefore deemed this to be a duty to which he was bound by conscience. Bossuet reminded him of it in his *Politique tirée de l'Écriture sainte*: 'The king should use his power to destroy false religions within his State.' Louis XIV was certainly sincere when he wrote: 'I do not doubt that it is God's will that I endeavour to lead back to His ways all my subjects.'

Needless to say, this psychological motive was reinforced by the political incentives we have noted. There is no doubt whatever that the whole country was convinced that diversity of religion within the State was incompatible with perfect law and order. 'If uniformity of external worship and interior faith are not maintained among the king's subjects', said Fléchier, 'they will always be as different races at war within the bosom of the Church and the country; they will be two bodies instead of one.' This inflexible Catholic totalitarianism was echoed by certain Protestant voices. Élie Benoist, for instance, declared that 'diversity of religion disfigures the State'; and Turenne: 'The independence of pastors is incompatible with order.' The unifying character of absolutism as expressed in such sentiments was desired by the whole country, and it tended towards the elimination of differences in religion.[1]

From the very beginning of the king's personal rule his coldness towards Protestants bordered upon hostility. When the representatives of corporate bodies presented their customary congratulations at court he declined to receive the Protestant ministers, and Pastor Vignoles, sent by their chamber at Castres, was expelled from Paris. The Assembly of the Clergy had complained of a number of infringements by the Calvinists, and the king ordered a court of inquiry to be set up in every province under the joint presidency of a Catholic and a Protestant. In every case a lukewarm Protestant was chosen. Sixty-four temples were demolished in Poitou; in the Gex district only two remained. Another edict (1662) went still further. By applying *stricto sensu* Article 28 of the Edict of Nantes, which permitted Protestants to have schools without stipulating the number of teachers allowed or taking account of educational requirements, it was decided that there would be one teacher to each school. At Marennes, for example, one

[1] In 1657 the delegates of the reformed Churches met in Paris, and passed a somewhat surprising resolution assigning a theological basis to royal absolutism: 'Our opinions in relation to politics and religion are identical. We believe that a subject may never merit a reward from his sovereign, even though he render him the most outstanding service. Any favour granted by the sovereign should be regarded as an act of grace on his part; a subject who expected a reward would be guilty of insolence.'

teacher was allowed for six hundred Protestant children! In June 1662 a number of Huguenots who failed to remove their hats when a procession was passing were sent to the galleys. One might have expected a little more tolerance at a time when the court was applauding Molière's *École des Femmes, Tartuffe* and *Don Juan.*

There were good Catholics who strove by other methods to lead the straying Calvinists back to Catholic unity. Nicole and Arnauld, who published three works refuting Calvinist errors, were among the Jansenists who had recently become reconciled under the Clementine Peace, and endeavoured to convince the Protestants. Bishops, among whom was Hardouin de Péréfixe de Beaumont, at that time Bishop of Rodez and later Archbishop of Paris, espoused the cause in their pastoral letters. There was, among others, the Jesuit Raimbourg, assisted by secular priests and laymen who worked together in the Compagnie du Salutaire Entretien. The young Bossuet outshone them all with a handbook, admirable for the precision and depth of its doctrine: his *Exposition de la doctrine catholique* which was approved by Innocent XI and followed soon afterwards by the *Histoire des variations des églises protestantes.* The Protestant reply is to be found in the writings of Jean Claude (1619–87), Aubertin, Jurieu (1639– 1713) and Basnage. In 1678 Mlle de Duras organized a debate which brought Claude and Bossuet face to face in a verbal duel, and the Catholics declared that their champion had crushed his opponent.

These controversies were to some extent fruitful. They resulted in a few sensational conversions that were largely due to the arguments of Bossuet, Montausier and Dangeau. Mlle de Duras herself was converted; but the most outstanding event was the conversion of Turenne, who in 1668 returned to the faith of his fathers with the dignity and sincerity of a soldier. It is probably true to say that his conversion had a more beneficial effect than any other of that day. Some embraced Catholicism to win the king's favour, but the motives of others were even more worldly. Pellisson, a former clerk to Fouquet and himself a convert, invented a kind of 'conversions account', maintained from the revenues of extremely rich abbeys to which the king had not appointed an abbot. It also derived its income from a third of the *régale* under a statute of 1676. A commoner who recanted would receive six *livres,* a trooper thirty and a sergeant forty. Compensation to a member of the nobility might take the form of a yearly pension up to three thousand *livres.* Whatever the motives of the people concerned, the conversion of nobles such as the Duc de la Trémouille and the Duc de la Force had some effect; though the latter's conversion remains uncertain.[1] They led the king to believe

---

[1] Another Duc de la Force, a descendant of the above, has written a book entitled *Louis XIV et sa cour* (Paris, 1956). See p. 58 of that book.

that the return of all Protestants to Catholicism was a possibility, and thus contributed towards an intensification of his efforts in that direction.

Pressure came from every quarter. Whenever the Assembly of the Clergy met, its members reiterated their complaints against the transgressions of the Protestants. Following a military victory in 1675 the coadjutor to the Bishop of Arles exclaimed to the king: 'Are you not indebted to God for this glorious victory? It now remains that you show your gratitude by using your power to exterminate heresy completely.' What was there to prevent Louis XIV from becoming another Theodosius or a new Charlemagne? 'All Catholics regard freedom of conscience as a dangerous precipice,' the Assembly emphasized; 'a trap set to ensnare simple minds, a door leading to libertinage. Take it from them, Sire; remove this deadly freedom!'

Undoubtedly Mme de Maintenon whispered similar ideas into the king's ear, and with increasing insistence as his power developed. Did not this grand-daughter of Agrippa d'Aubigné say in 1679: 'If God spares the king there will not be a Huguenot left in twenty years'? Louvois, whose prestige was growing, spared no effort to achieve the same ends; not only on account of his hatred of Colbert, who offered protection to Protestant and Catholic manufacturers and workpeople alike, but because he had no wish to allow his enemy Mme de Maintenon the satisfaction of success. The sanctimonious set at court were in favour of strong measures. And we cannot exclude the possibility that some courtiers, jealous of the commercial and industrial prosperity of the Huguenots, may have used their influence to pursue aims that were anything but apostolic. At the very moment when the persecution was being intensified Mme de Maintenon wrote to her brother: 'Now is the time to buy Protestant estates; they are going for a song.' We can hardly avoid a feeling of discomfort at this undisguised expression of sentiments.

'In order gradually to reduce the number of Huguenots in my realm,' wrote Louis XIV in his *Mémoires*, 'I decided to refrain from imposing further restrictions and to ensure that they enjoyed the privileges allowed by my predecessors. I determined to grant them no more, but rather to maintain existing privileges within the narrowest limits that justice and propriety permitted. I would allow no personal favours whatever, so that they might be compelled to ask themselves whether it would not be in their best interests to become Catholics.' This was precisely what had been suggested by Councillor Bernard of the Presidial at Béziers in his *Explication de l'Édit de Nantes* (1666) and by the Jesuit Meynier in his *Édit de Nantes éxécuté selon les intentions de Henri le Grand* (1670).

The Protestants were thus subject to all kinds of vexatious measures —and in the name of the Edict! Whatever had not been formally authorized was forbidden. For example, there was nothing in the Edict to the effect that Protestants could bury their dead by day; they were therefore compelled to bury them at night. It was not stated that they could invite their friends to weddings; attendance was therefore limited to twenty persons. There was no formal statement in the Edict giving them the right to be judges, notaries, bailiffs, royal secretaries, lawyers, doctors, booksellers or printers; they were therefore driven from all the professions. Rarely has the art of textual misrepresentation been used to better advantage. Mixed marriages were prohibited, and children born of them were declared illegitimate and snatched from their parents to be brought up in the Catholic religion. Occasionally tragedy was softened by comedy, as in the case of an old man of eighty when someone called to take him to the catechism class! It was decreed that Protestant children could become Catholics on reaching the age of seven, and their parents were required to make an allowance towards their education in the Catholic faith. These measures resulted in a flood of emigrations. An edict was therefore promulgated under which captured fugitives were sent to the galleys, and sales of real estate executed by them during the previous two years were rendered void.

Such measures led to conflicting results. The weak and lukewarm yielded and recanted; people of strong convictions resisted. Disorders broke out in Dauphiné, Vivarais, Languedoc, and even on the outskirts of Bordeaux; and a number of Protestants, among them a pastor, were broken on the wheel. When Colbert died in 1683 Louvois gained considerable influence, and the situation became more serious.

Either Louvois or Marillac, governor of Poitou, invented the loathsome method of winning converts known as the *Dragonnades*. Soldiers, especially *dragoons*, from whom the *Dragonnades* derived their name, were billeted in the houses of Protestants with authority to do whatever they wished. It is not difficult to imagine the excesses of which these booted missionaries were capable. An engraving of that period shows a dragoon, a sword at his side and in his hand a musket levelled at a kneeling Protestant about to sign his recantation. They committed the most abominable crimes; there were thousands of cases of looting, torture and rape. They roasted the feet of men and children; they dragged women through the streets by their hair; they flogged old men in the presence of their children. Their atrocities were such that Catholics frequently gave shelter to Protestants who were visited by the king's dragoons. Bishop Le Camus at Grenoble, Cardinal de Coislin at Orleans, the Bishops of Gap, Lescar, Tarbes, Saint-Pons and others protested publicly and opposed the sending of troops into their dioceses. In 1685 the Assembly of the Clergy passed a resolution condemning the use of force.

It would be surprising if, as some historians have suggested, Louis XIV knew nothing about the *Dragonnades* and the tragic state of affairs that existed. It is difficult to believe that the protestations of the clergy, of several bishops, of the Maréchal de Vauban and others were never brought to his notice, especially in view of the fact that he eventually removed Marillac from office. He may have thought that these excesses were the work of a few extremists; but he was more impressed by the results obtained, the news that reached him every day of mass conversions. They were a source of great joy to him, as Mme de Maintenon said. Indeed, Protestants were being converted in large numbers: in the district of Nîmes alone sixty thousand in three days. At Montauban and Bordeaux the whole population became Catholic under a resolution passed by the municipal council. Castres, Montpellier and Uzès followed their good example. In many places the very news of the arrival of the dragoons was sufficient to awaken an intense zeal for abjuration. The more discriminating Catholics questioned the value of such conversions; and Mme de Maintenon was anxious about the spiritual condition of all those unhappy people who recanted without knowing why. But they themselves knew only too well.[1]

Louis XIV was led to believe that there were scarcely any Protestants left in France; that those who had not fled had been converted or were on the point of conversion. Almost every day Le Tellier, Louvois and Father La Chaise informed him of mass conversions, the news of which was brought by special courier. On 18th October 1685 an edict drafted by Le Tellier was presented at Fontainebleau for the king's signature, and registered by Parlement on the 22nd: it was the Revocation of the Edict of Nantes. 'Whereas the greater part of our subjects of the so-called reformed religion have embraced the Catholic faith, the enforcement of the Edict of Nantes is no longer necessary. . . . We have therefore decided to efface the memory of the disorder, confusion and evil which the development of this false religion has occasioned in our realm, and nothing can be more to the purpose than to revoke absolutely the Edict of Nantes.'[2]

[1] Not satisfied with their activities at home the king's administrators intervened in Savoy, where the twenty-year-old Duc Victor-Amédée II was experiencing a temporary attraction towards everything French. The persecution of the Waldenses which had commenced thirty years earlier (see p. 164) had abated slightly, but now broke out again with greater fury. The Waldenses of the Briançon and Pignerol districts fled from France and took refuge in the valleys of Piedmont. Savoyard troops gave chase, assisted by French soldiers from Catinat. This was not war but butchery; three thousand women and children were massacred in a meadow, and the prisons of Savoy were packed.

[2] The revocation did not apply to Alsace, which was administered under the provisions of the Treaties of Westphalia, but the province did experience some pressure from the *Dragonnades*.

All the temples were demolished. Protestant assemblies, even in private houses, were everywhere forbidden. Pastors were given two weeks in which to leave the country. Children born of Protestant parents had to be baptized by priests and brought up as Catholics. Persons who remained loyal to the new religion or attempted to emigrate were condemned to the galleys. These measures were in every respect comparable with those taken against Catholics in many Protestant countries.[1] That such methods should have been adopted by the grandson of Henri IV is lamentable, for France was thus stooping to the level of countries where intolerance had become the rule; Louis XIV was breaking completely with the policy of his wise predecessors.

We are tempted to describe the revocation of the Edict of Nantes as 'something worse than a crime—a blunder!'[2] Public opinion welcomed it none the less with deplorable enthusiasm. It fired the imagination of poets, and inspired artists and writers. Six medals were struck to commemorate the event, and seven engravings were made. The French Academy set a competition on the subject of 'Apollo victorious over the serpent Python', and the prize was won by Fontenelle. It inspired the painter Le Brun and the sculptor Coysevox. The measure won the approval of the most brilliant intellects of the day: Racine, La Bruyère, La Fontaine, and also Mme de Sévigné, who wrote: 'It is the greatest and finest thing that has ever happened.' The Abbé de Rancé called it a miracle, 'a miracle we might never have hoped to see in our time!' Such was also the opinion of Bossuet who, in his funeral oration on Michel Le Tellier, praised to the very skies 'this new Constantine, this new Theodosius, this new Marcianno, this new Charlemagne!' Though Vauban expressed his doubts on the efficacy of the measure, as did Saint-Simon later, it would have been difficult to find anyone sufficiently courageous at that time to express disapproval. Public opinion was unquestionably with the king.

Pope Innocent XI's attitude was ambiguous. He declared publicly to Christina of Sweden that 'the use of force propagates heresy; it never conquers it'. He asked James II of England to show consideration towards the Protestants who took refuge in his country, and he endeavoured to persuade Louis XIV to mitigate the severity of his measures. None the less he congratulated the King of France officially, and a year later caused the *Te Deum* to be sung to dispose of rumours concerning his attitude. It seems likely that the Duc d'Estrées, French ambassador to the Holy See, was exaggerating when, in his desire to

[1] See pp. 164 and 165.
[2] The words were first used in connection with the execution of the Duc d'Enghien; they have often been attributed to Fouché or to Talleyrand, but were in fact used by Boulay de la Meurthe.

flatter his master, he told the king of the Pope's 'joyous outburst' on hearing the news. In fact the words used in the Pope's congratulatory letter might have had several meanings: 'It is a deed', the letter said, 'that will endure for ever in the annals of the Church.' Political events, such as the Gallican dispute, which was at its height, perhaps explain the Holy Pontiff's attitude of reserve.[1]

It cannot be denied, however, that this general enthusiasm for what constituted a crime against conscience was lamentable. It may be interpreted as an expression of the intolerance of the age, the desire for national unity and the conviction, especially among the more enlightened, that many of the 'reformed' had indeed returned to the Catholic Church of their own volition. The attitude of Bossuet was above all significant. We have referred to his enthusiasm over the revocation of the Edict; but he was also among the bishops who rejected violence in their dioceses, and condemned the abuse of power. He stated publicly that it was wrong to force recent *réunis*—converts from Protestantism—to receive Communion and assist at Mass; he claimed that they should be treated with tact and instructed with gentleness. He even undertook soon afterwards to revive the work of *rapprochement* between opposing religions. The position adopted by this great Christian prompts us to be wary in our criticism of what may appear to us a dreadful and repugnant measure, but which, in the eyes of its contemporaries, seemed politically wise and justified on religious grounds.

According to the judgment of history the revocation of the Edict is seen to be a glaring error. It involved France in grave material loss. Despite royal injunctions, a great number of Protestants were reluctantly compelled to flee the country rather than recant. The estimated numbers involved vary from sixty thousand to two million, though the latter figure is obviously absurd. The number was probably between three and five hundred thousand. The distressing flight of the refugees resembles many we have known in our time. They fled by sea in stormy weather from the coasts of Aunis and Brittany; they made their way at the height of winter across the precipitous passes of the Alps and the Jura. Many fugitives died *en route*. Those who were captured by the police were sent to the convict ships; the more fortunate were struck down on the spot. Most of these emigrants were sailors, soldiers and teachers; good craftsmen and excellent people, energetic and hardworking. The wealth in men and money lost in France in this way was enormous, for many of the refugees succeeded in taking out of the country considerable sums in gold. Many countries willingly offered

[1] An illustration of the Pope's attitude is suggested by the fact that he raised Le Camus, Bishop of Grenoble, to the dignity of cardinal when he fell into disgrace for having opposed the violent persecution of the Huguenots (8th September 1686).

asylum to the French Protestants. The Grand Elector populated Berlin and Brandenburg with them. The Dutch welcomed all the intellectuals and the savants, among them Pierre Bayle, Jurieu and Claude, who taught in Holland. Sweden, the English colonies of America, Ireland and South Africa also accepted them. These emigrants took with them French technical skill hitherto unknown to the countries in which they settled. Thus Ulster developed the linen trade for which Belfast has become famous; Germany developed the culture of the artichoke; the Cape began to grown the vine and the olive tree. Denis Papin, who found refuge in Marburg, invented a boat with wheels that were turned by a steam engine (1707). Wherever French Protestants settled they occupied all the important posts; their departure weakened their own country and strengthened France's opponents. So great was France's error that Christina of Sweden aptly compared her with 'a sick man who cuts off his arms and legs'. Perhaps the greatest tragedy of the emigration was that French Protestants served against France in hostile armies. At the battle of the Boyne the Huguenot Armand de Caumont, Marquis de Montpouillan, was in command against his Catholic cousin de Lauzun. In 1914 five hundred officers of French origin and bearing French names fought in the Prussian Army.[1]

Meanwhile in France itself the Protestant problem was a long way from being solved by the revocation of the Edict. Nobody quite knew how to dispose of the fugitives' property. Should it be sold to the advantage of the State, or sequestered? Or should it be passed on to the nearest Catholic heirs? The handling of these concrete and definite problems was the source of much confusion and many malpractices.[2]

As for the *réunis*, it soon became evident that they were 'converted' in name only. The priests of Normandy admitted that the old Huguenots were more zealous than ever in their Protestant convictions. Claude Brousson and other heroic pastors returned, and preached everywhere. The Catholic Church replied by sending its best preachers to the provinces where the converts were most numerous; Fénelon went to Saintonge and Bourdaloue to Languedoc. But the Church lacked an enlightened and dedicated clergy capable of winning hearts.

[1] An excellent survey of the present position of the Huguenots may be found in the magazine *Réforme*, 9th November 1957. Apart from the actual Protestant emigration of the period, mention must also be made of several hundreds of Waldenses who were hunted throughout France and Savoy. Most of them settled in Odenwald, Taunus and Württemberg, where villages may still be found with such names as Grand-Villars, Petit-Villars, Pérouse, Pinacle and Serres.

[2] Mlle Hélène Delattre has made a special study of the subject in her thesis at the École des Chartes presented in January 1936: *L'aide financière aux protestants convertis. Étude sur le tiers des économats et la régie des biens des religionnaires fugitifs, des origines à 1724.* See *Position des thèses de l'École des Chartes*, 1936.

The formative training of the seminaries made very little impression. Fénelon, writing from the town of Saintes, said that his teaching had moved the people's hearts, but that his new converts tearfully complained: 'As soon as you leave us we shall be at the mercy of monks who preach Latin at us, and talk of indulgences and confraternities. No one will speak to us without threats.' The truth was, no one really knew how to handle the situation. An inquiry set up by the Council in 1698 revealed a rapid rise in Protestantism. How was it to be met? One governor recommended gentleness and another coercion. Bossuet and five other bishops protested strongly against certain disgraceful practices, such as the dragging of corpses of Protestants in the mud and throwing them on refuse dumps. In 1699 the king commanded the use of moderation, and district governors were deprived of their powers in religious matters; but it was almost impossible to curb the fanaticism aroused by the revocation. In many places government agents and parish priests pursued suspects, and forced the *réunis* to make at least a show of being Catholics. Time tended to fan the passions rather than allay them. Loads of anti-Roman pamphlets arrived from Holland, England and Lausanne, and were distributed secretly. Many of them were written by Jurieu, who announced that the hour of deliverance was at hand.

A Protestant resistance movement was organized in the mountains of Dauphiné, Lozère and Languedoc. In these secret communities an extraordinary atmosphere of emotion developed: women and children prophesied, among them 'la Belle Isabeau', a wool carder from Grenoble. Uprisings broke out near Castres, at Velay and other places. In 1690 Lieutenant-General de Broglie crushed the first rebellion, but failed to halt the Protestant movement. The Assemblées du Désert met the more frequently. They gathered on the moors, usually at night, where their pastors or chosen leaders spoke to them words of faith and hope. Claude Brousson was caught and broken on the wheel at Montpellier, but nothing could dishearten those fierce 'Children of God'.

In 1702 the decisive upheaval occurred in the diocese of Mende. A priest known for his anti-Huguenot zeal managed to organize the arrest of a small convoy of fugitives; but the peasants of the district set them free, butchered the gaoler-priest and two others, and burned a number of castles. A veritable war had commenced.

Wherever Protestants were fairly numerous they rose up at the call of their preachers—Séguier, Mazel, Espérandieu, Ravanel, Couderc, Pierre Esprit, Gédéon Laporte—and revolution broke out. The Church which had gone to ground in the desert marched off towards conquest, like the chosen people about to enter the Promised Land. Everywhere their prophets predicted crushing victories. Those

H

who were taken by the police marched to their execution with cries of joy. 'My soul is a garden of pools and shady trees,' replied the preacher Séguier when the judge condemned him to be burned alive. They produced splendid leaders: Gédéon Laporte, a blacksmith built like a Hercules, Jean Cavalier, a twenty-year-old baker's boy who proved to be a strategist of genius in guerilla warfare, and Roland, his able lieutenant, a youngster of seventeen. Operations were undertaken against presbyteries, churches and convents. In order to recognize each other at night the partisans wore white shirts over their clothes. Soon the whole of France and Europe were talking of the exploits of the *Camisards*—the 'white shirts'.

While France was being attacked on all sides by foreign enemies and had insufficient forces to cover her frontiers, trained armies commanded by Broglie and Montrevel were indulging in savage suppression of rebellion. The letters of Fléchier, Bishop of Nîmes, present a frightful picture of the degree of violence resulting from the civil war between Frenchmen.[1] The best generals available, Villars and Berwick, had to be sent to suppress the rebellion. For three successive years (1702–5) the fighting and destruction continued, and nearly five hundred villages were destroyed. Villars tricked Cavalier into leaving his camp by granting him a commission as a colonel, and giving him a vague promise that he would be free to practise his religion. Roland was killed in battle. Little by little the fever subsided, and the opposing sides discussed an amnesty. But the Protestant Church was not vanquished; it emerged from the conflict strengthened and tempered by its trials. It gravitated back to the countryside and the people where its real roots were to be found.

A few days before Louis XIV died he signed a new edict that reintroduced the old repressive measures. At about the same time Antoine Court, a preacher from Languedoc, assembled the first synod in a disused quarry near Nîmes, marking the reconstruction of

---

[1] 'You are right to pity me in the unhappy situation which has obtained for nearly two years now . . . the practice of our religion has almost ceased in three or four dioceses. More than four thousand Catholics, including eighty priests, have been butchered in the neighbourhood, and nearly two hundred churches burned. . . .

'. . . As for ourselves, we have neither rest nor recreation; in this town we are bereft of all consolation. When the Catholics are stronger the others are afraid they will be massacred; but when the fanatics are numerous in the district, the Catholics in their turn are afraid. I have to console and reassure them all in turn. We are shut off here and dare not move fifty paces beyond the town without risk of being killed. From my windows I have seen all the houses in the country round about burned down with impunity. Hardly a day passes without my learning in the morning of some fresh misfortune that has happened during the night. My room is often filled with people who have been ruined, poor women whose husbands have just been killed, fugitive priests who tell me of the unhappy plight of their parishioners. It is horrible. I comfort some and calm others, trying to help and succour them all as their father and shepherd. A large band of these rebels has recently been routed, and people think that it is all over. But they are mistaken; their minds are so distraught that they can think of nothing but their losses.'

French Protestantism. As always where religion is concerned, the policy of force had served no useful purpose.[1]

7. THE MOST CHRISTIAN KING VERSUS ROME

When Louis XIV struck at the Jansenists and the Protestants he did so on behalf of the Catholic faith, in the interests of Church unity, which he was unable to distinguish from national unity. We find it hard to believe that during the very period when he was imprisoning the supporters of Port-Royal and his dragoons were carrying out their 'missions' against the Protestants, the Most Christian King was engaged in a violent conflict with the Apostolic See, playing a dangerous game with schism and even running the risk of excommunication. But that is exactly what was involved in the Gallican dispute, the episodes of which had such a shattering effect on the minds of contemporaries.

Unpleasant incidents began to occur at the very commencement of the reign. The king was then in the full pride of his youth, determined to use every opportunity to manifest his pomp and power. His teacher Mazarin had accustomed him to adopt a free and easy manner towards the Holy See; he threatened to 'examine closely the conduct of the election' of Innocent X; and he abused Alexander VII for having given asylum to his foe the Cardinal de Retz. Hugues de Lionne, who had previously failed in his efforts to get the irrepressible cardinal interned, endeavoured to worsen relations between Paris and Rome, whereupon the king sent to Rome the Duc de Créqui, 'a high-ranking soldier with extensive powers and great arrogance, but lacking in tact'. The purpose of his mission was to wipe out by a display of sumptuousness the impression of failure bequeathed by the Retz affair. The duke followed his instructions to the letter. His manner was abrupt; in matters of protocol he was haughty and overbearing. His entire *entourage* resembled a miniature court, and every member copied his manner. Things reached such a pitch that in August 1662 the Corsican Guard, too often provoked by the ambassador's footmen, took advantage of a quarrel to avenge themselves. They besieged the Farnese Palace, and a bullet whistled past the nose of the ambassador's wife, killing one of his pages. Louis XIV treated the affair with an arrogance that amazed Europe. He sent an insolent letter to the Pope, had the Papal Nuncio escorted to the frontier, recalled his ambassador

[1] It is necessary to add that the repressive measures referred to had also a disastrous effect on France's foreign relations by clinching the alliance of all Protestant countries against her (see *The Church in the Eighteenth Century*, Chapter III). The effect was just as disastrous from another point of view: Michelet regards the revocation of the Edict of Nantes and the resulting episodes as a kind of incubation period of the Revolution, and Albert Sorel remarks that 'the jurists of the Terror had only to dig into the miscellany of decrees against the Protestants to find weapons for their own use'.

from Rome and sent troops to occupy Avignon. An army of fifteen thousand men threatened the Papal States. It was really a storm in a teacup, but the young king intended to make it clear that he would suffer no opposition to his will. Unfortunately some of the French bishops supported him. Alexander VII had to give in: he agreed to send a cardinal to France to present his apologies, to disband the Corsican Guard and, for good measure, to erect a monument in Rome to commemorate not only the offence but the atonement.[1]

Disputes of this nature had nothing to do with doctrine; other incidents, however, were much more significant though less resounding. As absolutism gathered momentum it could hardly be expected to tolerate any authority in France but that of the king, whether it came from the Pope or anyone else. Pierre de Marca died in 1662, but his learned treatise *De Concordia sacerdotii et imperii* [2] continued to furnish abundant polemic material to the enemies, avowed or otherwise, of papal authority. The State counsellor Le Vayer de Boutigny popularized this method in a small manual which ran to many editions. He compared the State with a ship controlled by a captain and a pilot, the captain exercising full authority as to the ship's progress, its safety and the discipline of the crew, and the pilot being in charge of navigation; but de Boutigny reasoned that the king was the captain, and the Pope merely the pilot. It went without saying that the captain had the right to supervise the pilot, and even to reprimand him if he flagged!

Thus developed a trend of thought which, as we have seen,[3] began during the time of Pithou and Richer and which we today call Gallicanism, though its contemporaries were unacquainted with the term. Such expressions as Gallican Church, Gallican precepts and Gallican freedoms were for ever on the lips and in the writings of people of the Great Reign, in a jungle of bitter debates and arguments. Not that Gallicanism ever attempted, as Anglicanism did, to establish itself seriously as a national Church, taking schism for granted; nor did it constitute a homogeneous body of doctrine, still less a sect. Gallicanism was a complex blend of theories, traditions, interests, susceptibilities and disappointments, all of which embodied the common but definite purpose of limiting the power of the Pope and his interference in matters affecting France. That fact alone was quite sufficient to win the sympathy of Louis XIV, and dispose him to personify the fusion between the parliamentary and the ecclesiastical aspects of Gallicanism.

Furthermore, to understand the Gallican dispute and to appreciate

---

[1] For a true appreciation of the psychological atmosphere and the reactions of public opinion, the reader is recommended to consult Father Mortimort's 'Comment les Français du XVIIe siècle voyaient le Pape', which appeared in Bulletin No. 25, *XVIIe siècle* (Paris, 1955).

[2] See p. 180.

[3] See the end of Chapter III, p. 179 et seq.

the daring required to oppose the authority of Rome—an idea quite inconceivable today—it must be remembered that the dogma of Papal Infallibility had not yet been defined by the Vatican Council; it was not, in fact, defined until two hundred years later. Despite proposals put forward by the Jesuits, the Council of Trent had not stated the doctrine categorically. That the Pope possessed supreme authority was clearly understood; but so did the Oecumenical Council, which had stated the solid truths on which the Church had been reconstituted. At that time it was not absolutely clear which of the two authorities took precedence over the other, and it was permissible to hold either opinion —*in dubiis libertas*. On the evidence of the jurist Domat, a well-known Gallican, 'the Regulars had spread the doctrine of papal infallibility to such an extent that the common people, not well versed in such matters, regarded it as Catholic doctrine and the contrary opinion as heresy'. Enlightened people, however, were not inclined to adopt that view.

Within the first few weeks of the king's personal rule an incident occurred which clearly suggested his attitude in the matter. The Jesuit father Coret of the Collège de Clermont supported a thesis claiming that the Pope, having received the gift of infallibility from Christ, was indeed infallible. The battle was on. The Jansenists, only too pleased to get the Jesuits into trouble, let loose their wrath. Arnauld launched two vigorous pamphlets in defence of Gallican freedoms; and the king, although a determined enemy of Jansenism, flew into a rage over the Jesuits' thesis. Thanks to the pleading of his confessor Father Annat and the suppliant letters of Pierre de Marca, the king resisted the impulse to seize the thesis and imprison its rash author.

Two years later another incident occurred, again arising out of a thesis. A young Breton student, Gabriel Drouet de Villeneuve, was preparing to present his thesis at the Sorbonne when it was rumoured that the paper contained 'Roman' theories that were unacceptable to the free Gallican Church. There was, in fact, very little in it: a mere statement to the effect that the privileges of certain churches had been granted by the Popes, and that Councils, however useful 'were not indispensable'. Another uproar; and again Arnauld and his friends intervened. At that time the affair of the Corsican Guard in Rome was at its height. Louis XIV was furious. 'Humiliate Rome by every possible means!' he thundered. Parlement therefore censured the unfortunate student, forbade him to present his thesis, and the Sorbonne, after making a show of protest against this intrusion into its affairs, abode by the decision.

There is no doubt that incidents such as these were deliberately stirred up. Every opportunity was seized upon to foment and increase tension. When a Cistercian named Laurent Desplantes happened to

write that 'the Pope has authority over all Christians and full jurisdiction over the whole Church', Parlement was indignant that anyone
should thus strike a blow at its authority. And when the Sorbonne was
again called to account it replied by stating its tenets specifically in a
Déclaration en six articles (4th May 1663). The paper was extremely
cautious in tone, but maintained none the less that papal infallibility
was not officially taught in the learned *penetralia* of theology; upon
which the king warmly congratulated the Sorbonne.

These incidents among many others reveal a state of mind. Gallican
influence developed in proportion to the growth of royal power. All
sorts of people were Gallicans: politicians set on absolutism and
national prestige; bishops so closely associated with the régime that
they were prepared to follow ministers 'blindly like flunkeys', as
Bossuet said; prelates of irreproachable character (among whom
Bossuet himself), utterly devoted to the Church, its unity and its
hierarchy, though perhaps a little too opportunist; and parliamentarians who had inherited the theories of Pithou and were anxious to
retain their privileges. A large number of Jansenists, whose hostility
to the Pope arose out of their hatred of the Jesuits, were also Gallicans.
'Scratch a Gallican, and beneath you will find a Jansenist,' was a
popular saying. Naturally enough the king's *entourage* and most of the
courtiers were Gallicans; they were only too eager to flatter his pride
by provoking his wrath against the one rival who dared to challenge
his authority. The quarrel between the Most Christian King and the
Holy See continued, with an occasional truce, for many years. Every
possible pretext was used to prolong the conflict—a controversial
thesis at the Sorbonne, the publication in France of a book by a
Spanish Jesuit, an edict by Colbert to reduce the number of religious
and so provide more labour for agriculture, the annulment of the
marriage of Marie de Savoie, a ridiculous story about the administration of Extreme Unction to a nuncio in circumstances which the
French clergy regarded as irregular. Finally, in 1673, came the affair
of the *régale*—the king's prerogative of enjoying the revenues of
vacant sees—which brought the conflict to a head.

In its early stages the cause of the trouble appeared to be merely
financial; but the root of the problem lay in the king's claim to control
and direct the Church in France as though he were the Pope. It must
be remembered that Louis XIV believed that Church property was
entirely at the disposal of the king. Although in principle ecclesiastics
were exempt from tax, it had become an established custom to vote a
Don Gratuit—a free gift—every five years, and the money went into
the treasury. In 1661 the *Don* amounted to two million *livres*, and in
1675 four and a half million. In addition to this, from about the time
of the Merovingians the king had possessed the *droit de régale*, under

which he was entitled to receive the revenues of all bishoprics and some abbeys from the moment a See became vacant until the new incumbent was installed (*régale temporelle*); he even had the right to make appointments to ecclesiastical livings in a diocese where conferment depended upon the Ordinary (*régale spirituelle*).[1] The question that still remained undecided was whether the king's right extended to the southern dioceses where it did not exist at the time those areas returned to French rule. The bishops, supported by the Pope, opposed the king's claim, and they invoked the authority of a council held at Lyons in 1274. The ministers and the Paris Parlement supported the king, and they traced their case back to Philippe le Bel.

The question was reopened in 1608 and was debated for more than sixty years. Early in 1673 it was settled out of hand by an edict which decreed that every diocese in France without exception was subject to the *régale*. The extent of the king's control over the clergy then became evident. Of 130 bishops 128 accepted, while 59 were affected by the measure. The only two to protest were Pavillon, Bishop of Alet, and Caulet, Bishop of Pamiers, highly respected and upright men who were in no way influenced by personal interests. Caulet appealed to the Assembly of the Clergy at its meeting in 1675, but the Assembly cautiously declined to get mixed up in the business. Rome could not let the matter pass without a protest. When Pavillon died the Bishop of Pamiers continued to fight alone, determined to prevent the king from appointing anyone unworthy of the office to his See after his death. Although he was accused of Jansenist sympathies, the Holy See gave him its full support. Twice the Archbishop of Toulouse condemned him, and each time the Pope quashed the decision. When he was condemned a third time and deprived of his See he appealed to Rome. Thus began an intensely violent crisis which continued for fourteen years after the death (in 1680) of Caulet.[2]

---

[1] The *régale temporelle* was not valuable to the king from a financial point of view. Since 1676 two-thirds of the revenue were used for pension purposes and the balance was allocated to the 'New Converts'. Some of the buildings fell into a bad state of repair while the appointments remained vacant, and a special financial grant known as *économes-sequestres* was made for restoration. The *régale spirituelle* (which came into existence in the twelfth century) was extremely valuable to the king, for it enabled him to accommodate his minions (cf. C. Laplette, 'L'administration des évêchés vacants et la règle des économats', *Revue d'Histoire de l'Église de France*, 1937, p. 161 et seq.)

[2] One of its episodes was known as the 'schism of Pamiers'. On the death of Caulet his spiritual son Jean Cerle was appointed Vicar Capitular, against which the king reacted energetically. Four companies of cavalry were sent to Pamiers and billeted on the king's opponents—a repetition of the *Dragonnades* methods. Jean Cerle had to flee; he led a wandering life, but exercised his episcopal authority *by right and in fact*. On 16th April 1681 he was condemned to death *in absentia*, and he retaliated by excommunicating the *régaliste* canons. Public opinion was on his side, and the Pope supported him, though feebly. Under a brief dated 1st January 1681 the diocesan administration set up as an expedient by Montpezat, the Metropolitan of Toulouse, was condemned as illegal and a trespass. Hence the schism. There were two opposing groups of clergy: those who were

The atmosphere in which the crisis developed was much more depressing, and the circumstances very much more complex than is generally supposed. Superficially the question at issue was whether the King of France was entitled to assume control over the Church's property and spiritual prerogatives. But quite apart from the legal aspect Rome was also concerned with Gallican theories as a whole and the fact that Louis XIV was inclined to favour them. Furthermore, his foreign policy was a cause of scandal. The anti-French clique did not lack arguments which might arouse the Holy Pontiff's anger: the king's desire for supremacy, his wars against other Catholic powers, his alliance with the infidel Turk and his annexations of territory without formal declaration of war. What strikes one as remarkable, however, throughout the episodes of the dispute is the extraordinary docility of the Pope, his reluctance to deal severely with the king, and the magnanimity with which he endured grievous wrongs. Innocent XI had been Pope since 1676.[1] He was a wise and prudent man, of stable character rather than of vast intellect. His was a truly priestly soul, overflowing with the virtues of justice and charity—a saintly figure whom the Church would canonize. Far from despairing of the 'eldest daughter of the Church', who was acting like a stubborn child, he allowed her a great deal of latitude. He seized every opportunity to declare his desire to maintain 'a very close relationship' with the Most Christian King, and refrained from using pressure against him until it became impossible to avoid doing so any longer. Louis XIV on his part treated him with great respect, even at the height of the conflict when the official mood was at its worst. His personal relations with the Pope remained good, and he declared that 'it behoved him to kiss his hand'. The king's attitude was not entirely based upon his need of support in his policy towards the Protestants and the Jansenists. At that period he was returning to a more earnest practice of religion, and under the influence of Mme de Maintenon and Bossuet he could

---

loyal to Cerle and those who favoured the measures taken by the king and the Archbishop of Toulouse. In 1681 fourteen priests of the diocese who had gone over to the *régaliste* principle solemnly retracted their error. The seriousness of the schism is emphasized by the fact that the Holy See gave to priests loyal to Cerle power to validate marriages which had been performed by the *régaliste* priests. Carle died in hiding on 16th August 1691. He was a splendid figure who remained courageously loyal to the See of Peter, though unknown to the public generally. Despite the fact that he was hunted by the king's agents he had a high regard for the principle of royal authority; the language he used in his pastoral letters when referring to the king was very similar to that used by the bishops at Versailles. On the downfall of James II he was the only bishop in France to prescribe prayers and expiatory fasts. Monsignor Vidal has given an excellent account of this schism, which very few historians apart from Lavisse mention. See the résumé of 'Le schisme de la régale au diocèse de Pamiers' (Paris, 1938), published in the *Revue d'Histoire de l'Église de France* (1939), p. 505.

[1] On Innocent XI, see Chapter V. The relations between Innocent XI and Louis XIV have been exhaustively studied by J. Orcibal in *Louis XIV et Innocent XI* (Paris, 1949).

never have accepted the idea of schism; it would have been inconceivable to him to act like Henry VIII.

In 1687 Innocent XI wrote to Louis XIV on three occasions to put him on his guard against 'those whose only desire was to curry favour by their flattery' and to draw his attention to the effective spiritual weapons at his disposal. Months went by and the king did not reply. The most astonishing rumours were current: it was said that the king was about to be excommunicated, and that a French army of 200,000 men was preparing to march on Rome. In 1680 the French Assembly of the Clergy signed a declaration of complete and unreserved loyalty to the king 'from whom nothing could possibly separate them'.

The temperature was rising. The situation was aggravated still further by an incident connected with the convent at Charonne. Under the 1516 Concordat the king had the right to submit to the Pope nominations for the office of abbess, but he had no power to appoint. When the Augustinian nuns of Charonne were suspected of slight Jansenist tendencies the Government appointed a mother superior from the convent of the Order at Cîteaux, without referring the matter to Rome. The nuns refused to accept her, barricaded themselves in their convent and elected another superior. The police finally closed the convent and disbanded the nuns—a use of force against which the Pope protested indignantly.

To gain support in his resistance to the Pope, Louis XIV then appealed to the clergy. The atmosphere was tense. 'The Pope has pushed us too far,' exclaimed Harlay. 'He will regret it.' The obsequious and worldly Archbishop of Paris who led the opposition to Rome held a meeting of a few members of the Assembly at his palace, and it was decided to convoke a General Assembly of the clergy of France, composed of two bishops and two priests from each province. Harlay acted as their spokesman. Opposing him was Bossuet, the new Bishop of Meaux, a much more colourful figure whose influence would soon be felt in France. The Assembly's discussions consisted mainly of a tussle between these two men: one was a zealous supporter of the king's authority, a finished courtier and a Gallican extremist; the other, infinitely more prudent and restrained, just as devoted to his king, but a respectful son of the Church, dominated by a desire for unity and an open supporter of papal authority. Bossuet began with an able speech in which he endeavoured to reconcile both points of view; he held that the Holy See alone was the pivot of the Church, to which the faithful are united through their bishops and the king, who are the trustees of divine power on earth. For a while it seemed that a solution might be found to the problem of the *régale*, but the Gallican extremists increased their pressure. Spurred on by Colbert, who was fanatically hostile to Rome, Louis XIV asked the Assembly to determine the

* II

official doctrine of the Gallican Church and to define the spheres of authority as between Church and State.

This gave rise to lively discussions. Choiseul-Praslin, Bishop of Tournai, made a long statement on Rome's transgressions and short-comings; the Assembly argued heatedly for or against papal infalli-bility, and the problem of the *régale* was completely forgotten. Some members of the Assembly even mentioned schism, and Bossuet, torn between his loyalty to king and Pope, again endeavoured to keep the Assembly within the bounds of moderation; he drew up his *Déclara-tion en quatre articles* (1682), which the seventy-two members of the Assembly unanimously approved. The first article confirmed that the temporal power was absolutely independent of the Church; the second, that the authority of the Council was higher than that of the Pope (reference to this had been made at the Council of Constance); the third stated that the Gallican Church enjoyed special privileges because of its tradition of 'rules, customs and constitutions'; the last article rejected papal infallibility outright. It acknowledged that the Holy Pontiff was 'the highest authority in matters of faith', but held that 'his decision is not irrevocable until it is confirmed by the judg-ment of the Church'.

As soon as the *Déclaration des quatre articles* had been passed by the Assembly it was registered by Parlement and promulgated as law.[1] Naturally enough Innocent XI condemned it outright, 'with a shudder of disgust'. Even in France one or two theologians made a feeble attempt to oppose the declaration, and the Sorbonne, furious at not having been consulted, did likewise; but the king had no difficulty in disposing of all opposition.[2] It was not such an easy matter to get the better of the Pope. Not that Innocent XI used any of the weapons at his disposal; he neither excommunicated the king nor placed the country under an interdict; but he firmly refused to confer canonical investiture on the bishops nominated by the king. He remained deaf to all appeals, and allowed the vacant sees to grow in number until they reached thirty-five. It seemed as though the Catholic Church in France might eventually be deprived of legitimate leaders.

Louis XIV alternated between resignation and wrath. At first he complained that the Pope had become 'hard-hearted'. He instructed his ambassador, Cardinal d'Estrées, to say that the Declaration of the Four Articles was 'merely a formality'. This provoked a smile in

---

[1] The Four Articles remained law for a long time. The *Codes de la législation française*, by Napoléon Bacqua, may still be found in use in many French courts of justice. They were the fore-runners of the famous *Codes d'audience Dalloz*. This work contains a chapter dealing with ecclesiastical matters, beginning with the 1682 *Déclaration*. The Bacqua *Codes* were republished in 1843.

[2] In any case, Louis XIV dismissed the Assembly. He probably regarded it as even more royalist than the king!

Rome. Then the king changed his attitude; troubled maybe by doubt and remorse he played the bully when a rather trivial incident brought the dispute to a head. Embassies in Rome had enjoyed certain privileges which gave them immunity from police supervision. The privilege was abused to such an extent that it gradually included the whole neighbourhood in which the embassy was situated; in consequence the police had become almost powerless in half the city. Innocent XI wished to discontinue the custom. All the ambassadors agreed to surrender the franchise, in so far as it affected the neighbourhood of their embassies, but Louis XIV haughtily refused. When the Duc d'Estrées died the Pope warned the King of France that he would not receive his new ambassador unless he agreed beforehand to surrender the franchise. Louis XIV replied by sending the Marquis de Lavardin with an escort of six hundred armed men. Innocent XI excommunicated the French ambassador, but that did not prevent priests, and even bishops, from giving him the sacraments at the church of Saint-Louis-des-Français. A well organized campaign rallied French public opinion to the king's side. French forces occupied Avignon at once, and the nuncio was placed under house arrest. There was even some talk of appealing to a council. The patience of Innocent XI was exhausted, and he assumed the offensive by excommunicating the king on 16th November 1687. However, as a supreme gesture of trust and affection, he refrained from publishing the fact, and the king was informed privately.[1]

In truth, Louis XIV had grown weary of this squabble which, as a Christian, he found distressing. Mme de Maintenon, who had been decorated with the Golden Rose, the highest papal distinction, was striving for a reconciliation. The Jansenist troubles were going from bad to worse, and they could not be resolved without the aid of Rome. The death of Innocent XI in August 1689 simplified matters, for the king pretended that the dispute was a personal one between himself and the late Pope, and the new one, Alexander VIII, met him half way. The Pope allowed it to be known at Versailles that he was disposed to 'settle the affair of the *régale* to the satisfaction of the king and the Holy See'; whereupon Louis XIV withdrew his troops from the Comtat Venaissin. But Rome did not intend to yield in the matter of principles; the Bull *Inter multiplices*, drawn up by Innocent XI, was published in 1681, declaring that the conclusions of the 1682 Assembly were 'all invalid and without authority'. Moreover, from his deathbed the Pope addressed a letter to the king in which he appealed to his conscience.

[1] The secret excommunication of Louis XIV was overlooked by historians for many years. Father Dubruel discovered the fact while preparing his work on the *Régale* dispute. It was first made known in an issue of *Études*, dated 5th December 1913 (cf. Dubruel, *En plein conflit: la Nonciature de France sous Louis XIV*, Paris, 1927).

It was quite easy for Innocent XII to take advantage of the king's conciliatory attitude, which was accentuated by the fact that France was at war with the League of Augsburg. An understanding was reached in 1693: in exchange for a retraction in due and proper form the Pope approved the canonical investiture of all the bishops nominated since 1682, and extended the right of *régale* to the whole of France. Louis XIV gave instructions that the Four Articles were no longer to be regarded as legally binding, a retraction which the Parlements in most cities declined to register. In any case, the Gallican quarrel ended with the undoubted victory of the spiritual power over the temporal.

Not that Gallicanism really disappeared. It became very closely associated with Jansenism, and remained a source of trouble to the Church in France long after the death of the Great King—almost until the outbreak of the French Revolution. When Louis XIV signed the *Édit des cinquante articles* in 1695, prescribing, 'in pursuance of the rights of the Holy See', the organization of the Church of France, the authority of the crown over the clergy, the system of ecclesiastical jurisdiction, and even the fees of parish priests and other clergy, he may have been attempting to pay off old scores. But by that time the quarrel was over, and Rome let the matter pass. The document had a strong Gallican flavour, but its provisions remained the basis of Church policy in France until 1789.

8. 'I HAVE BEEN TOO FOND OF WAR'

The pride of Louis XIV was at the root of every distressing event that marked the relations between him and the Holy See; a pride so dominating that for many years it silenced the voice of conscience and maintained in the king an attitude of mind that should be foreign to a Catholic.

Moreover, we cannot fail to recognize this pride in the continual bloody wars that stained the great reign; and in the objects and methods of the king's foreign policy which undoubtedly contributed much to his personal glory, but brought discredit upon France.

On several occasions Louis XIV had very good reasons for entering into war. His father's aims had not been achieved, and France did not by any means possess all the territory which she might have legitimately claimed on the principle of language and population. Her frontiers to the east and to the north were badly protected; the ambitions of the Hapsburgs had not diminished; across the Channel England was developing rapidly, and resented the presence of a great power under her very nose. In many European capitals, and even in Rome, anti-French feeling was so strong at that time that a king who was solicitous of his country's interests had to be careful. Louis's assaults against Europe were therefore far from being entirely unjustified.

But there is also no doubt whatever that in numerous cases Louis XIV flung himself into the fray a little too lightly, without even attempting to negotiate in the hope of securing results by peaceful means. 'I have been too fond of war,' he admitted on his deathbed. When he was a child his teachers used to talk to him of conquests and victories; and, surprisingly enough, Bishop Godeau's *Catéchisme royal* had set before him the examples of the greatest butchers in history— Tamerlane and Genghis Khan. We can hardly be surprised therefore that Louis XIV should write: 'The attributes of a conqueror are deemed the most noble and most lofty.'

Did he knowingly aspire to world supremacy? Did he dream of establishing a French monarchy over the whole of Europe? We cannot find in his *Mémoires* any trace of such aims, or even a policy of 'natural frontiers'; but he conveyed the impression that he cherished these ambitions, and it is possible that his fawning courtiers put into words what he pondered in his heart. He certainly did not prevent Aubery (though later he imprisoned him for two months) from publishing a Latin treatise on 'the king's rightful claims to the Empire' (1667), in which he referred to France's claim to 'the patrimony and ancient heritage of her kings', that is, all the territory which had been 'in the possession of Charlemagne as king of France'. Jacques de Cassan's book, *La Recherche des droits du roi*, was republished in 1670. This precursor of geopolitics affirmed the rights of the French Crown to Navarre, Naples, Sicily, Majorca, Milan, Genoa, Flanders, the Low Countries, Ravenna and Avignon. The document aroused feelings in the king similar to those awakened by previous theses: insolence in his relations with other monarchs, an offensive boasting of his successes, a desperate desire to humiliate opponents and (more important) a contempt of right and an often repeated conviction that one need not abide by treaties—that force should decide everything. In a way this was the broadly realistic policy established by the Treaties of West-phalia. But in view of the principle of balance of power in Europe such a policy could end only in catastrophic failure and the weakening of France. Much worse, it led the country to discard its noblest traditions. The Spanish writer and ambassador Francesco de Lisola published a satirical work entitled *The Shield of State and Justice*, in which he criticized the aggressions and transgressions of the king. 'The fate of Europe is at stake,' he wrote, 'and sentence must be passed as to its freedom or enslavement.' Even if we allow for the extravagance of language natural in controversy, it is depressing to see such words applied to an heir of St Louis.

This aggressive policy of Louis XIV was not the only one possible at that time; others had, in fact, been suggested. The one put forward by Claude Fleury in his *Lettre sur la justice* was bold enough to proclaim that 'the same spirit of justice should exist between states as between individuals', that 'most conquests are unjust', and that a policy devoid of ethics can end only in tyranny. The one proposed by Fénelon was perhaps too idealistic. It claimed that all Christian princes should restore their unjust conquests, and compensate peoples for whatever losses they had sustained. The same theory was developed by Saavedra Fajardo. It was unquestionably Utopian, but it embodied a genuinely Christian ideal of which Innocent XI had quite rightly reminded Louis XIV. The diplomacy of the Holy See was neither very skilful nor very far-seeing; it failed to discover in time the Protestant peril in the person of William of Orange, and made no attempt to reconcile the great Catholic powers; but it had at least the merit, especially under Innocent XI, of having courageously pointed out to the mighty King of France that even in the field of politics he had obligations as a Christian, and that the day must come when he would appear to answer for his actions before a tribunal that did not depend upon the power of the sword.

One matter on which the Holy See had occasion to reproach Louis XIV was his Eastern policy: his hesitation and ultimate refusal to join the crusade against the Turks which the Papacy longed to see organized. Not that the idea appeared anachronistic and absurd to the King of France, for the cycle of events since the beginning of his reign remained a continual reminder of the dreadful reality. In 1663 the Grand Vizier Köprili, who had reorganized the Ottoman Empire, flung against the West an army of 120,000 men, composed of janissaries, Tartars, and Cossacks. Their hordes swept across Moravia and Silesia laying waste the country; more than eighty thousand Christians were sold in the slave markets of Constantinople. In every town in Germany the *Türkenglocken*—the bells of the Turks—were rung at noon every day. With this danger threatening the West, Louis XIV was torn between his duty as a Christian and the alliance which had bound France to the Sublime Porte since 1536. He decided eventually in favour of the Christians, and sent six thousand men, the flower of the French nobility, to help his brother-in-law, Leopold I. The Turks called these young heroes 'The Maids', on account of the customary wigs they wore. Their arrival decided the victory of St Gothard on the island of Rab (1664). Despite this intervention Louis XIV carefully avoided destroying his connection with his Turkish ally.

Although the Ottoman threat had been temporarily removed, it had not been entirely disposed of. Twenty years later the Grand Vizier Kara-Mustafa proved just as aggressive as his predecessor Köprili, and openly began preparations for a new offensive against the

Empire. It was then that Innocent XI, ignoring the existing quarrel with Louis XIV on the subject of the *régale*, tried to interest his conscience in a vast scheme to effect peace and unity among all Christian peoples and to stem the assault of the infidel. For a moment he nearly succeeded, but discord again developed among the Christians. The annexation of Strasburg by Louis XIV caused the Pope the greatest sorrow. In 1683 a new Turkish offensive by 250,000 men threatened Vienna. A special messenger was sent by the Holy See to beg the King of France to think of the safety of Christendom. The Nuncio himself approached the king. 'War against the Turk is God's will,' he said, 'and He will severely punish all who oppose or distract from it.' The Most Christian King remained deaf to these appeals. No Frenchmen fought at the battle of Kahlenberg (12th September 1683), when the heroic Polish expeditionary force under John III Sobieski cut down the Turks; neither did they take part in the sixteen years war (1683–1699) during which the armies of the West drove the Crescent from Hungary. The Nuncio wrote to Louis XIV in 1687: 'If Your Majesty, having rid your own country of heresy, were to be favourably disposed towards the barbarian and the infidel, the whole of Christendom would stand amazed. You cannot do this without serious injury to your glory and, which is more important, without grave detriment to your conscience, of which you will one day have to give the most strict account to God.' Yet the Franco-Turkish alliance became even stronger.

One hesitates to pass judgment on a policy which appeared so remote from the traditional Christian ideal. Might it not be justified on the principle of European balance of power, the desire to retain an ally capable of attacking the Empire from the rear? Events seem to suggest that the diplomacy of Louis XIV was the right one; the eventual Turkish defeat, which French support could not prevent, resulted in an enormous increase in Hapsburg power, followed by the ruthless subjection of Hungary to the throne of Vienna, the mass executions at Eperies and the defeat of Francis II Raköczy, a friend of Louis XIV. Prince Eugene created a veritable empire from the mountains of Bohemia to Serbia, a formidable power which might have threatened France. Who can say whether all these events might not have happened even if the *grand roi* had placed himself at the head of the Holy League, as the Pope wished him to do, led the crusade against the Turks, and built a peaceful Christian Europe around the French throne? These are prospects with which the imagination may play; but other schemes lay concealed behind the foreign policy of Louis XIV.

We may indeed ask ourselves what were the objects of the continual wars waged for thirty years of his long reign of fifty-four years; or whether, in fact, this foreign policy based on force really did embody a coherent plan. Was the purpose dynastic, as in the War of Devolution (1667–8) and the disastrous War of the Spanish Succession (1701–1714), which sealed the ruin of France and put an end to her supremacy? Was it a question of commercial interests, as in the war against Holland (1672–8), or the need to stem the ambition of the Hapsburgs, as seems to have been the case in the War of the League of Augsburg (1688–97)? But in this painful and fruitless struggle France confronted not only the Protestant coalition (led by William of Orange), roused to indignation by the revocation of the Edict of Nantes, but even the Catholics of the Empire. One might well wonder whether France's acquisition of Franche-Comté and a part of Flanders was adequate compensation for the dreadful sacrifices in men and materials that were the evident consequences of all this bloodshed. And from a Christian point of view there was absolutely no justification for them.

Above all, how can we explain away the methods employed to execute that policy? At the very commencement of the reign France occupied the southern Low Countries on the controvertible principle of Devolution; this was a clear demonstration of Louis's lack of respect for international law. Then came the plan of 'reunion', whose purpose was to reintegrate with France all territories which had at any period (even from the time of King Dagobert!) belonged to regions recently acquired by France. Europe regarded this demand as an intolerable provocation. Montbéliard, the Saar, Deux-Ponts and most of Luxembourg were successively occupied. The annexation of Strasburg (28th September 1681), which was an open city, was universally condemned as an act of unpardonable aggression, though the action might have been excused on the grounds that the city had allowed armies hostile to France to pass through it on three occasions. The Pope was horrified, and the incident may have caused the failure of the scheme outlined at that time by Spinola to reunite the Protestants to the Catholic Church.[1] The whole of Europe shuddered with anguish at the prospect of a universal French dictatorship. France's old friends abandoned her. Towards the end of the reign she stood alone, haughtily alone, facing a dangerous threat of opposition. 'Alone against all,' cried Louvois proudly. But the consequences had yet to come.

The methods adopted by Louis XIV during the course of his wars were quite often discreditable. Perhaps the Dutch pamphleteers exaggerated (as may be expected in this kind of propaganda) when they denounced 'the unheard-of cruelties which the French have perpetrated'; but what we know of the occupation of Franche-Comté and Alsace by the troops under Condé and Turenne respectively can hardly excite our admiration. The event which, however, more than any other has left an indelible stain upon the 'great century' was

[1] See Chapter V, section 12: 'An Unfulfilled Hope'.

the dreadful invasion and devastation of the Palatinate, carried out by the order of Louvois at the beginning of the War of the League of Augsburg. Its object was to create a barren region extending along the whole frontier, and the leaders Duras and Tessé executed the task with dreadful zeal. Vineyards and orchards were utterly destroyed; towns and villages were razed to the ground or burned; rare and beautiful castles—among them the Château of the Electors, one of the wonders of Europe—were demolished; Mannheim, Spire, Oppenheim, Frankenthal, Bingen, Landenburg and Heidelberg were set ablaze. The unhappy populations fled through the snow, and those who survived hunger and cold described the kind of war waged by the King of France. It was little wonder that Europe in those days regarded Louis XIV as a madman.

When Innocent XI learned of these events he wrote a touching letter to his Nuncio concerning the brutality of the French troops in Flanders and the despicable burning of the town of Tongres, urging him to inform the king 'how badly His Majesty is served by those who perpetrate sacrilegious and inhuman crimes in his name, drawing down upon his arms the hatred of Christian peoples; how the extermination of so many innocent people offends the honour of God, who has granted the king such prosperity and so many victories, and could, by a flick of the finger, reverse the situation and punish the authors of such dreadful massacres'. In vain the supreme voice of the Church reminded Louis XIV of 'the moment of death from which the sovereigns of the world, however great and victorious, are not exempt'. In reply to this moving appeal a curt note from Father La Chaise stated that such incidents were inevitable in war, but that the King of France would see that the churches destroyed were rebuilt. Reminded of the charity of Christ and clemency towards innocent populations, Louis XIV, no doubt in good faith, thought to allay the Pope's sorrow by promising to rebuild walls!

9. 'RELIEVE THE DISTRESS OF THE PEOPLE'

When the old king was giving his last words of advice to his great-grandson, the future Louis XV, having referred to the liking he had always had for war, he added: 'Try to relieve the distress of the people—a thing which I unfortunately have not been able to do.' An expression of belated regret, but also of sad truth. This final aspect of the reign remains to be discussed. It casts a shadow over the picture, for the splendour of Versailles, its luxury and its magnificent festivities, cannot obliterate the misery and suffering discernible in the background. It is a spectacle no Christian can contemplate without emotion.

The circumstances of the common people of France seem to have been wretched during the period. La Bruyère was perhaps exaggerating the condition of the peasantry when he wrote in his *Caractères*: '. . . wild animals can be seen, male and female, roaming about the countryside, dirty and ghastly. . . . They appear to be able to talk, and when they rise to their feet they are seen to have human faces. . . . At night they disappear into dens where they live on black bread, roots and water. . . .'

We like to think that this language is hyperbolical, and that today we would use the word 'vegetables' instead of 'roots'. There is, however, abundant evidence to confirm the truth of this melancholy picture. In 1675 the district governor of Berry reported that in his province 'the peasants are more wretched than slaves in Turkey'. The same year the Duc de Lesdiguières drew attention to the fact that in Dauphiné 'the greater part of the population had lived entirely on acorns and roots, and were reduced to eating grass and the bark of trees'. And Mme de Sévigné wrote in 1680: 'Everywhere I see people who have no bread.' A royal commission sent into Maine and the old province of Orleans described a very similar situation. 'The common people', Vauban wrote in his diary, 'eat meat scarcely three times a year. Three-quarters of them are dressed in rags, winter and summer, and they wear clogs over their bare feet.' This state of things, which gradually worsened towards the end of the reign, when trade and industry had been ruined by wars and excessive taxation, provoked dreadful peasant risings which were even more dreadfully suppressed. The revolt of twenty-five thousand peasants in Brittany has become famous for the cruelties which the province endured when the uprising was crushed. The ten thousand soldiers let loose over the country committed countless crimes. 'They do nothing but kill and rob,' wrote Mme de Sévigné. 'A few days ago they put a little child on a skewer.'

Would it be right to say that Louis XIV was personally responsible for such a situation? To a great extent he was probably not even aware of it. Versailles was a long way from the provinces, and neither his ministers nor the courtiers would have been anxious to keep him in the picture. Were the governors' letters laid before him, and the evidence of such courageous men as Vauban, Fénelon and the Bishops of Montauban and Mende? Louis XIV has been described as a kindly prince, happy to have an occasional chat with a peasant. It is possible that if he had known the truth he might have wished to do something about it; but he was a slave of the very system he had created and which did not permit him, absolute though he was, to know and act except through an intermediary.

Furthermore, as we survey the details of this long reign we are impressed by a decline in what was perhaps one of the most attractive moral phenomena of the preceding epoch—what we might call the spirit of St Vincent de Paul. People had certainly become less anxious to fight against destitution and the abuse of law. Of course, the great charitable works established at the beginning of the century still survived: hospitals were opened; confraternities of charity, successors of the Company of the Blessed Sacrament, still strove to do good. The king himself was well aware of these institutions and frequently encouraged them by his gifts; but there is no doubt whatever that he did not regard such activities as a major interest, as Louis XIII and Anne of Austria had done. In short, he did not experience the anguish of Christ's charity. When Fénelon, in his *Plan de gouvernement*, pointed out that the king should examine his conscience according to the heart of God, begging him to 'relieve those who are at the last stage of exhaustion', to give bread to the unemployed, to 'have every convict set free at the end of his term of punishment as fixed by the courts', he could not expect the right kind of response from a sovereign like Louis XIV. That sense of social sin which is one of the highest achievements of twentieth-century Christianity did not exist in the seventeenth, except in a few rare and privileged souls.

In contrast, however, with these permanent departures from charity there were some men who spoke a truly Christian language. Bossuet's resounding words, uttered in 1659 in his celebrated sermon on the eminent dignity of the poor within the Church, will echo through the world for ever: 'The poor you so despise were set by God as his treasurers and collectors. . . . The Church was built for the poor alone . . . the rich, as such, are suffered merely as a favour. . . .' Later, when the position deteriorated, especially where children were concerned, other voices rang out denouncing errors, corrupt practices and injustice. The words of Boisguillebert, who wrote *Le détail de la France*, were all the more convincing because he was an economist. That illustrious soldier Vauban put forward a complete scheme of reorganization, administrative, financial and social, in his *Dîme royale*; many really moving paragraphs came from his pen. Fénelon too made his voice heard in the *Examen de conscience* and *Remonstrances*, and even in the novel *Télémaque*.

Louis XIV paid no heed to these voices; neither did he appear to take Bossuet's appeal seriously: 'Look at these accusers: they are the poor who will bear witness to your unrelenting callousness.' In any case, police action was his answer to those who pleaded for a more humane régime. Pontchartrain and d'Argenson treated such works as *Dîme royale* and *Télémaque* as though they were obscene books or licentious newspapers, or suspected of Quietiest heresy as was the *Maximes des saints*. A few days before old Maréchal Vauban died, the King's Council seized his book and gave instructions that he was to be prosecuted for having published it; Boisguillebert was similarly dealt with. Fénelon was dismissed the court on suspicion of Quietism. He was not in disgrace, but the circumstances of his dismissal were such that he could not leave his diocese of Cambrai.

We can imagine the hopelessness and indignation experienced by this sincere priest in the face of such obstinacy in what he considered to be injustice and sin. When France stood alone against Europe in 1710, and seemed at the point of collapse, he addressed a daring letter to the Duc de Chevreuse, but intended for the king.[1] He condemned absolutely the king's religious policy, his attitude to war and social evils. 'You may reply that God will sustain France,' he wrote; 'but I ask you what promise you have had. Do you deserve miracles at a time when not even the threat of utter and imminent disaster can reform you, when you persist in remaining hard, haughty, ostentatious, incommunicable, unfeeling and always willing to delude yourself? Will humiliation without humility appease God? Though overwhelmed by your faults you refuse to acknowledge them, and you would certainly begin again if you could survive a year or two. Can you satisfy God with a devotion that consists in decorating a church, saying the Rosary, listening to a piece of music, being easily scandalized, or pursuing some Jansenist? It is not sufficient to bring to an end a foreign war; you should provide bread for your starving people at home. . . . You should remember the true state of your country, and keep within bounds that despotism which is the cause of all our ills.' A terrible indictment; we may wonder how a man dared to write such a letter, and, if Louis XIV knew of it, how he could have endured it without throwing its author into the Bastille.

On the surface these accusations were merited, and the holy anger of the Archbishop of Cambrai appeared justified. But we are apt to wonder whether the judgment of God who probes the depths of the heart was so severe. Bossuet's language was more moderate. He saw clearly the fundamental opposition between Christianity and unlimited absolutism when he exclaimed: 'It is not proper to man to have no superior. The very idea is bewildering, for man's condition does not lend itself to such independence.'

Perhaps the Most Christian King did occasionally forget that he had Someone over him to whom he would one day have to render an account. He failed, in any case, to penetrate the meaning of that eternal lesson of the Gospel which, during his reign, the Sacred Heart repeated to the humble nun, Margaret Mary—'God is Love.' [2]

[1] See p. 192, note 4.
[2] On the devotion to the Sacred Heart, see Chapter V, section 3: 'Decline of Mysticism and Growth of Devotion to the Sacred Heart'.

10. 'GOD ALONE IS GREAT'

Despite everything the king did not forget that, like all men, he was in the hands of God. When the hour came to settle his final account he proved to be the Christian he had always longed to be, even during the wayward years when sensuality and pride seemed to be in control.

The last years of his reign were a long succession of trials, a painful apprenticeship of utter renunciation. Within the bosom of the king's family death struck with such frequency that everyone began to imagine it had an ally among men. The Dauphin died in 1711; his son the Duc de Bourgogne, Fénelon's pupil, died six months later, preceded by his wife and followed within a month by his eldest son, the Duc de Bretagne. The heir to the throne, the little Duc d'Anjou, was still a baby scarcely out of the cradle.

The general situation was no brighter. Over and over again the war that had been raging since 1701 appeared almost lost: the disasters at Ramillies, Turin and Oudenarde appeared to toll the knell of France once glorious. An extraordinary revival of national spirit produced a counter-thrust at Malplaquet, followed by a victory at Denain. But although the peace signed at Utrecht and Rastadt settled the Spanish dynastic problems it was not advantageous to France, who received nothing in return for her immense sacrifices. The war had left her in a deplorable condition: bled white, drained of money and men, her economy bankrupt, her population had fallen from nineteen to seventeen million inhabitants, and desolation and savagery reigned everywhere.

Confronted with such a painful situation the old king showed his customary strength of mind. He accepted his trials with the dignity which the consideration of his glory demanded, but also with the resignation of a believer—even with a surprising and admirable humility: 'Few people have experienced the misfortunes that have befallen me,' he said to the Maréchal de Villars. 'God punishes me, but I have well deserved it.' When he made this admission was he thinking of his former mistresses, of the Protestants who had been the victims of his *Dragonnades*, of the unhappy people of the Palatinate fleeing in the snow, or of the prophetic words of Innocent XI who warned him that God would punish his revolt against the Vicar of Christ? But though repentant he had no intention of covering his head with ashes. He insisted that nothing in his routine should be changed; the requirements of court etiquette were to be strictly adhered to; there was to be no visible sign of the sorrow which everyone, he above all, bore in their hearts. This dignity was also a Christian virtue.

He faced death with the same admirable courage. Towards the end of August 1715 he was stricken with senile gangrene in the legs, and was cared for—if one may use the expression—by his aged and rather incompetent doctor Fagon. He soon became aware that his end was near, and demanded to be told the truth about his condition. When he knew that he could not live beyond the beginning of September he organized his last days with touching determination. Three days before his death he presided over the Council for the last time, dictated some details relating to his will and settled a few court matters. On the eve of his death he commanded that his great-grandson, the future Louis XV, be brought to him, and he gave the child his last words of advice. He said playfully to those whom he caught trying to hide their tears: 'Did you then think me immortal?'

This was indeed the attitude of a Christian who had rediscovered himself. All his life he had aspired to dominate events, but now he abandoned himself to God with moving simplicity. Just before the end, an elixir administered to him by an empiricist seemed to give him back his strength, and someone told him he would soon be well. He replied: 'Life or death—whatever God wills.' Assisted by Mme de Maintenon, who knew his faults so well, he made his confession to Father Le Tellier. He said that he felt he was at peace with God and had every confidence in His mercy, 'but would ever regret having offended Him'. On several occasions he asked forgiveness of those present for any scandal he had given them and wrongs that he had done them. During the night of 31st August, in a strong and apparently calm voice, he joined the priests in the prayers for the dying. His last words were the recital of the *Nunc in hora mortis* and the well-known verses of the psalm, 'O Lord, come to my assistance: O Lord, make haste to help me'. The long and painful struggle was over; the struggle of a man in whom the demands of religion had battled with human frailty and the force of circumstances. Louis the 'God-given' was then indeed 'Most Christian'.

A few days later, in the Sainte-Chapelle decked for the royal funeral, a Christian voice pointed to the moral of that amazing and adventurous reign. Massillon, pronouncing the funeral oration of the king who had made Europe tremble, took for his text these words (from the Book of Ecclesiastes): [1] 'I am become great, and have gone beyond all in wisdom that were before me in Jerusalem: . . . I have perceived that in all that there was only labour and vexation of spirit.' At first Massillon remained silent, his eyes cast down. Then he gazed a moment over the congregation, and pointing to the coat of arms— L. L. G., 'Louis Le Grand'—he began with these unforgettable words: 'God alone is great.'

[1] Eccles. i. 16 (Douay version).

CHAPTER V

CHRISTIANS OF THE CLASSICAL PERIOD

1. CLASSICAL CHRISTIANITY

CLASSICISM is traditionally linked with the reign of Louis XIV, or rather with his century. It has left its mark in many beautiful works of art and countless literary masterpieces. The plays of Corneille, Molière and Racine, the precepts of Boileau, the funeral orations of Bossuet, the sermons of Bourdaloue and, above all, Versailles itself, the very centre of beauty in its supreme severity—all spring to mind when we speak of the *classical age*. At the same time it evokes an attitude of mind which is reflected in an adherence to rigid rules, constant control of intellect over imagination and passion, a desire to attain an ideal of perfection and stability through order and discipline. The concept was a moral, aesthetic and political one, and not confined to France, though that country led Western nations in their assimilation of its principles. The concept is embodied in the theory of absolute monarchy, the splendour of court etiquette personified in the great King Louis XIV.

As with all traditional concepts we cannot accept classicism without certain reservations. Though it is quite correct to regard the seventeenth century, especially the second half, as the classical age, it is true only in a superficial sense, however splendid that superstratum may be. The more we study the Great Century the more we appreciate that beneath the surface of magnificence a crisis was developing 'which touched the whole man in the whole range of his activities, economic, social, political, religious, scientific, artistic; in his entire being, to the very depths of his will and his emotions. . . . The State, the public, the upper classes and the individual strove ceaselessly to re-establish order and unity within themselves and within their own spheres'.[1] From a political standpoint the monarchical structure that had been built up at the beginning of the century in the face of obstacles had stood wonderfully firm for fifty years, maintained by the genius of a great king, though towards the end of the reign it began to show real signs of decay. Thus the whole classical system is shown to be the result of a struggle to maintain an equilibrium painfully achieved and under a continual threat of destruction.

From the point of view of religion the position was the same. What

---

[1] Roland Mousnier: *Les XVIᵉ et XVIIᵉ siècles* (*Histoire générale des civilisations*), Paris, 1954, p. 276 et seq.

has been described as *Christian Classicism* was indeed a reality: it had its own definite characteristics. Linked with the established order, it sustained absolutism and was its trustee, sharing with it the splendour of the régime. Sainte-Beuve aptly summed up the relationship when he said that 'the Throne and the Pulpit stood back to back'. Classical Christianity is displayed in the pomp and magnificence of its ceremonial on the occasion of princely weddings and funerals. It was strikingly represented by its lordly, but sterling, bishops with their imposing *entourages*, their large retinues of servants and their six-horse carriages. It is recognizable in its masterpieces: the splendid works of Bossuet, such as the *Politique tirée de l'Écriture sainte* and the *Discours sur l'histoire universelle*, the beautiful chapels of Val de Grâce and the splendour of the Invalides. That was an austere and stately form of Christianity. It aspired, though often unsuccessfully, to control morals. It was more submissive than spontaneous, and founded on fear rather than on love; but its faith was exact, solid and unshakable. One would no more have dreamed of questioning it than one would have questioned the authority of the king. Such was the faith of Jacques-Bénigne Bossuet.

These outward appearances are not exactly misleading, but do they reveal the whole truth? In the sense in which classical Catholicism reveals a kind of conformity with rules it is not truly representative of the profoundly religious life of a vast number of people. No pause occurred in the upsurge of spiritual ardour noticeable at the beginning of the century. The followers of such men as Bérulle, St Vincent de Paul and Olier still toiled on, and the leaven of reform was still working. Although there were Christians who, broadly speaking, resigned themselves to the established order and a conception of the world which, after so many years of torment and chaos, they had come to appreciate, there were still a great many who remained quite untouched by 'classicism'. Just as there were bishops who refused to live a life of ostentation, so did many a simple soul lead an unfettered spiritual life under the gaze of God, even within the recognized framework of classical Catholicism.

The facts prove that in the religious field itself order, discipline and stability—splendid 'classical' qualities—were not achieved without continued effort, and sometimes only after a spectacular struggle. Within the Church the classical age was an age of violent crises brought about by Jansenism, Quietism and Gallicanism, and of an altogether more insidious crisis which tormented minds and consciences. Side by side with official orthodoxy profound spiritual aspirations asserted themselves, and it would be difficult to fit them into the framework of the system. The century of classicism was not merely an era of royal pomp and ceremonial in which the apparent function of the Church was to buttress and bestow its blessing upon absolutism. It was also an era of contention in the name of sanctifying grace and pure love, and the very violence of the conflict demonstrated that despite hidden cracks the vital structure of spiritual liberty survived.

We may even wonder whether 'classical Christianity' did not conceal an inner contradiction which might have caused the system to fall to pieces. Was not Christianity superimposed upon the classical ideal, to which it was diametrically opposed? Pierre Gaxotte was right when he said: 'The seventeenth century was the human century *par excellence*, the century of man's glory.' Was not the pompous cult of royalty simply a man-made religion? God occupied a very unimporant position in the immensity of Versailles; even in the chapel, if the king's eyes turned to the altar the courtiers turned their eyes to the king. The purpose behind all that magnificent literature—the works of Corneille, Racine, Molière, La Bruyère and La Rochefoucauld—was man, and man only. During the preceding period the 'devout humanists' and the masters of the French School surrendered man utterly to God, although they held him in high esteem. This is also true of the succeeding period so far as formal expression is concerned, but much less so in fact; and to a certain extent this attitude explains the definite slowing down of the spiritual upsurge and creative power of the period. It also explains the development of libertinism or disbelief which predominated in the eighteenth century. Classical Christianity was therefore destined to succumb to its own inconsistency.

But it did not yield without a struggle. Religion continued to remain firmly rooted in institutions and in men's souls. Disintegrating ideas cannot seriously and suddenly attack the admirable order that binds faith and the political and social sinews into an entity. Saints, doctors and great preachers would fight with all their strength to prevent the dissolution of legitimate hierarchies—the real causes of which no one, except perhaps Fénelon, really understood, although the signs were easily recognizable. Christians of the classical age have written the passionate and grandiose story of that struggle waged on the world's stage and in the depths of souls. Our impression of the Church during that half-century is something more than an exhibition of solemnity and stilted majesty; it offers us a picture of pathetic tenacity.

2. AN ERA OF FAITH

The outstanding fact of Western society in the Great Century was its sense of religion, deeply rooted in the life of the community, controlling and dominating its principles; decidedly a fortunate counterpart to the unwarrantable interference of officialdom in religious matters, an occurrence of which the reign of Louis XIV was a remark-able example, though all the sovereigns of his day vied with each other in the same direction. 'In the Catholic world the close union of and the mutual relationship between the two powers established by God, their intimate association in the common field of public life,' to use the words of Pius XII,[1] strove to keep alive the spirit of Christianity with which institutions were imbued. The least a viceroy of God can do is to defend God's rights among His people. That the Church was the trustee of the deposit of faith and the guarantor of stability and harmony in the life of the community was a fact recognized by every-one. Domat, the king's counsellor in the presidial Chamber of Cler-mont, in Auvergne, based his *Traité de droit public* (1697) on the axiom that 'Religion is the foundation on which social order is built'.

The efficacy of religion was everywhere manifest: in the family circle, within the framework of society, and especially in marriage, which is the basis of society. Henri Bremond was right when he observed that Christian marriage, which experienced a grave crisis at the time of the Renaissance and the Reformation, recovered its dignity during the seventeenth century when there developed 'a mysticism in marriage which was as far removed from animal coarseness as it was from the artificial modesty of the pseudo-spirituals'. St Francis de Sales's bold and emancipating passage on the sanctity of matrimony went a long way towards restoring its dignity. Bossuet wrote to Sister Cornuau, whose spiritual notions were rather muddled: 'I have often told you, my child, that the married state is holy. Those virgins who despise it are not wise virgins.' Le Maître de Sacy praised the goodness and the wisdom of God, who raised the physical union of man and woman to the dignity of a sacrament. Admittedly these are common-place and time-worn notions today, but in the seventeenth century they had the force and freshness of a rediscovered truth.

The family therefore retained a definitely spiritual character because it was founded upon a sacrament. 'Any man who fears God will be a good husband, a good father, a good son, a good brother, a good master, a good servant . . .' wrote Fortin in his *Conseils fidèles d'un père à ses enfants*. There existed at that period a widespread custom of recording family events, great or small, in books popularly known as *livres de raison*. The opening pages of the books usually contained a few basic principles of faith and some really beautiful prayers. The father of the family, as the responsible head of a small social cell, exercised an authority over the family comparable with that of a monarch over his realm; and, like the king's authority, it was essentially spiritual. With our modern ideas of equality we can scarcely imagine today the extent of the father's jurisdiction and the respect accorded to

[1] Speech to the World Congress of the Lay Apostolate, 14th October 1951.

him. The scope of his testamentary rights was much wider than it is today, so that a father's authority endured even after death—a fact which, as Leibniz so profoundly observes, 'would be meaningless without belief in an immortal soul'.

The fact of religion also entered into a man's work, which is another aspect of social life. As in the Middle Ages, the Christian calendar of feasts prescribed the days on which men refrained from work, and there were too many of them if we are to believe the cobbler in La Fontaine's fable. Linked with the system of trade guilds, which were specifically economic in character and are still just as strong today, there were confraternities of arts and crafts. These associations afforded mutual assistance where necessary and were based on religious principles, though quite distinct from the pious confraternities, whose purposes were spiritual. The election of the executives of a guild was conducted in the presence of the priest in charge of the church to which it was affiliated, and the men elected promised 'to do their duty well'. The rules of these trade guilds included penalites for those who infringed them: the penalty almost always consisted of some act of devotion, the giving of alms or payment of a fine, and the proceeds went into a collecting-box to honour some patron saint.

The parish was yet another sphere in which religion united men. It experienced a definite recovery under the influence of the reforming ideas of the early part of the century. We remember how Monsieur Vincent changed Châtillon des Dombes from a centre of disorder, selfishness and corruption into a living parish. Until 1667 the parish priest alone was responsible for the maintenance of registers of births, marriages and deaths,[1] and he read government statutes from the pulpit. A spirited atmosphere therefore existed in parish life, and under a good priest it could be a really Christian atmosphere. The bell-tower was the voice of the village; its measured peals set the rhythm of daily life. The bell called the people to prayer, sounded the alarm and celebrated important events within the community. The registers of that period provide evidence of countless examples of devotion to parish work by Catholics of all classes.

There is therefore no doubt whatever that, just as in the Middle Ages, the religion of that period was conjoined with a living faith, directing customs and laying down rules to impose on everyone respect for the Commandments of God and of the Church. Because men lived within the framework of Christianity it was naturally very difficult for

---

[1] Under a Statute of Villers-Cotteret (1539) the parish priest registered baptisms and burials and, after the Statute of Blois (1579), marriages. He was therefore responsible for the complete record of a person's civil status until the time of the Revolution, with the single exception that from 1667 (under the Code Louis) he had to maintain the parish registers in duplicate: the original was sent to the bailiff's office and the copy retained at the presbytery.

them not to lead Christian lives. Bossuet was thinking along the same lines when he wrote in his *Conférence avec Monsieur Claude*: 'I admit that individuals may be ignorant of some articles of faith . . . but they profess them in general when they declare their belief in the universal Church.'

And indeed belief in God was general. To people of the Great Century faith was natural. 'Free-thinkers' existed, but they were still rare; they could be found only in those small groups of intellectuals and men-about-town of whom Saint-Évremond (who was compelled to seek refuge in London in 1661) was a typical example. Their number grew towards the end of the reign of Louis XIV, and not only in France; none the less they were not very numerous. Father Mersenne estimated that about the year 1660 there were fifty thousand atheists in Paris, a figure we can no more accept as reliable than we can the lament of Mme de Maintenon that 'there are no longer any Christians in the provinces', or the Princess Palatine's statement that 'the faith is extinct'. The wise Father Garasse said that he knew of only five atheists in Paris, three of whom were Italians.

It is important to understand that a Christian is one who lives within the structure of a Christian society, and not one who merely conforms. We have only to pick at random any personality of the classical epoch, and we find a soul deeply penetrated with Christian sentiments. Neither is it necessary to select a champion of the Catholic cause, of whom there were many. A woman of the world such as Mme de Sévigné (who, as appears from her famous letters, enjoyed her fair share of lawful pleasures), read spiritual books and religious history, delighted in discussing problems of faith with her friends Nicole and Abadie, and recognized the hand of Providence in every occurrence. She thought, spoke, acted and reacted quite spontaneously and naturally as a Christian. In this she was not alone. The scoffing La Fontaine prayed like a child; so did Colbert, Turenne and many others. Even many less respectable personalities showed signs of possessing a deep faith: Mme de Montespan weighed her bread during Lent to avoid breaking her fast. The rugged Cardinal de Retz experienced moments of repentance, and acted like a true Christian when he made amends to all those whom he had treated badly.

Moreover, this great but worldly minded century was also the century of outstanding conversions, including that of Retz. Mme de Montespan dabbled in witchcraft before coming back to the Church, after which, as Saint-Simon tells us, she distributed her enormous wealth in alms, worked for the poor, wore nails in her belt, garters and bracelets, and, the mischievous memorialist adds, as a supreme act of penance she imposed silence upon her tongue! At Port-Royal there were at least a score of conversions, among whom Antoine Le Maistre,

Hamon, Pascal and Racine. In such places as Mont-Valérien, near Paris, Mont-Voiron, in Faucigny, and the forest of Orleans, members of the nobility, the middle classes and former worldly minded priests lived a completely eremitical life. It would be impossible to compile a list of all the converts, even French ones. Rancé, the Duchesse de Longueville, the noble house of the Contis, the shadowy figure of Mlle de la Vallière—all these are well-known personages. Eustache de Beaufort, Antoine de Chanteau, Gaston de Fieubet, chancellor to Queen Marie-Thérèse, Louis de Bailleul, a president of the High Court, the Chevalier de Reynel, one of Turenne's lieutenants, and many others besides left everything to spend their lives in a cloister. Though the breach between God and the world may sometimes be flagrant, it is very often mended in this way.

There are others to whom the word 'conversion' may hardly be appropriate, but whose death was utterly and magnificently Christian. We have already described the exemplary death of Louis XIV himself. The last hours of Michel Le Tellier, the great Condé, the Comte de Bussy, Montausier and many others were no less splendid. Two weeks before La Fontaine died he wrote to a friend: 'Dying is nothing, my friend, but do you realize that I must appear before God?' When Colbert was almost at his last gasp he received a letter from the king, and upon his wife asking him if he wished to reply to it he answered calmly: 'There is plenty of time for that; I am thinking of my answer to the King of Kings.' The vicar of the church of Saint-Eustache told Colbert that the parishioners were praying for his recovery. Colbert interrupted him: 'No, Father, not that. Let them beg of God to have mercy upon me.' A society which thus practised 'the art of dying' must be a profoundly Christian society. How wrong was Vauvenargues when he said: 'Nothing can be more misleading than to judge a man's life by the way he dies.' The contrary is true: the Christian life is best judged at the moment of death.

Thus the facts contradict the gloomy assertions of Father Mersenne and the two great ladies of the 'Devout' circle. If we examine further we shall see evidence of the existence of faith. The frequent reception of the Sacraments, resumed during the preceding period, became more or less general. After a very careful investigation G. Le Bras [1] concluded that the practice of frequent Communion was universal at the beginning of the eighteenth century, and he was inclined to think that it never had been more general than during the period between 1660 and the Revolution. There is evidence [2] that in the diocese of Séez, for

---

[1] G. Le Bras: *Introduction à l'histoire de la pratique religieuse*, Paris, 1942 (especially i. 95 and ii. 24).
[2] The position is examined by Father Flament in the *Revue d'histoire de l'Église de France* for July–December 1955, p. 235.

instance, the number of those who received Holy Communion frequently was considerable. And elsewhere nearly everybody made their Easter duties. In Spain many confessors counselled daily Communion. Salazar had to protest against 'inordinate frequentation of the Sacraments'. In France the Jansenist Arnauld, whose treatise on *Frequent Communion* made such a stir, was not alone in demanding that no one should approach the Sacraments without serious preparation. The arguments raised by the subject indicate the intense interest it aroused.[1] It is true that the excessive strictness of the followers of Port-Royal would eventually end in keeping scrupulous souls from Holy Communion; but abstention would certainly not result from indifference.

The enormous amount of spiritual literature produced was another sign of intense devotion. Evidence of this is to be found even today in the attics of country houses and on the shelves of second-hand bookshops along the Seine embankments. One out of every three or four of those little calf-bound books are books of piety published during the Great Century: Lenten sermons by Bourdaloue and Massillon; methods of mental prayer by Father Pomey, Father Nepveu and Father Nicolas; Letourneux's *Année Chrétienne* and his *Histoire de la vie de Jésus-Christ* (1673), Little Offices, *Élévations*—spiritual works of every description. And their success with the public was extraordinary. The *Exercice spirituel* which three anonymous authors dedicated to the wife of Chancellor Séguier in 1664 went into innumerable editions; a hundred thousand copies were printed of the *Heures catholiques* (1685), by Harlay de Champvallon—for the publication of which God will forgive him much. *Lives of the Saints* on the model of those compiled by Bishop Vialart de Herse were to be found everywhere, and the *Bible* by Le Maître de Sacy was in every good library. How can we doubt the faith of a public which so nourished the soul?

Included among this spiritual literature was the Catechism, a compact and very useful manual of Christian instruction which became widely used. It began to spread throughout the Church immediately after the Council of Trent. At that time an attempt was made to adapt for use by the general public the larger Catechism compiled by the Fathers. Canisius launched his Catechism throughout all the German-speaking countries. The great reformers attached enormous importance to the catechetical method of teaching in book form, intended for the general Catholic public rather than for the use of parish priests. One after another the bishops caused Catechisms to be produced for the adults and children of their dioceses, notably Rheims, Luçon, Bordeaux, Toulouse, Rodez, Vabres, Châlons and Agen. By way of

[1] The following figures from a statistical survey made at the Jesuit college in Molsheim, Alsace, are significant: in 1650 there were 7,000 Communions a year; in 1670, 21,640, and in 1706, 23,000.

experiment an inter-diocesan Catechism was introduced for the three Sees of Luçon, La Rochelle and Angers, but unfortunately it had Jansenist tendencies. Generally speaking these little books were a success; the questions put became more and more precise and the answers were short and arresting. The catechesis on feast days began to acquire liturgical significance. The best of these works was the one by Bossuet, which d'Astros used as a model when he composed his 'Imperial Catechism' in 1806.

Many earnest people strove to maintain the popularity of these pious works and to foster the faith which they taught. Pilgrimages were almost as successful then as they had been in the Middle Ages. Houses for Retreats continued to increase; they developed under the twofold influence of the Jesuits and the Recollects,[1] and continued under the Lazarist Fathers. Much of the initial success of Port-Royal was due to the retreatants who congregated there. We know for certain that the mission and retreat given at Vannes in 1695 was attended by 2,436 men and 2,519 women. Saintly people desirous of assisting each other in the attainment of spiritual perfection, succouring the unfortunate, or uprooting vice, joined the 'Associations Apostoliques' (some of whose members had belonged to the Company of the Blessed Sacrament)[2] or the Congregations of Our Lady. These societies were directed by the Jesuits and the Lazarists. Ordinary layfolk gave proof of remarkable piety: in many a church in Paris and Rome men and women watched every night before the Blessed Sacrament which was always exposed for adoration. Many of them, too, wore some scapular, or even a hair shirt. During the day-time the faithful were to be seen spending long hours at prayer in the churches, bowing down five or six times in succession and then going to kiss devoutly the feet of the crucified Christ. Faith was more demonstrative then than it is today. When a number of people came together they would begin to recite the litanies, despite the opposition of a section of the hierarchy who feared that these praises might be recited parrot-fashion. New litanies were always being composed; among them the Litany of the Holy Angels, the litanies of Providence so much admired by Jean-Jacques Rousseau, and others taken from the Holy Scriptures.

The number of devotions multiplied. The traditional cult of the Blessed Sacrament never ceased to grow. In some ways it was comparable with royal ceremonial; the beautiful monstrance glittering with gold and precious stones was perfectly in keeping with the ostentation of official ceremonies in the 'salutations to the Blessed Sacrament', a practice which was spreading. The Benedictine nuns of the Blessed Sacrament, approved by the Pope in 1661, passed their lives in adoration before the Sacred Host with remarkable fervour. There is even a

---

[1] See Chapter II, p. 108. [2] See Chapter II, p. 98.

record of a 'clock of the Blessed Sacrament' having been invented by a Carmelite friar; it automatically summoned the people to prayer at certain hours in order that they might atone for offences committed against the Sacrament of the Altar. The Oratory recommended devotion to the Child Jesus as perfectly representing that childlike spirit to which the Kingdom of Heaven has been promised. Devotion to the Sacred Heart, the importance of which will be seen shortly, arose from several quarters. Devotion to Our Lady continued to grow. In 1683 Innocent XI instituted the feast of the Holy Name of Mary; and in 1716 the feast of Our Lady of the Rosary was extended to the whole Church. In Germany a few pious women in attendance upon the Empress Eleanora of Neuburg, third wife of the Emperor Leopold, began to dedicate to Mary the month of May, the loveliest of the year, and at Naples a number of ladies in the parish of Santa Chiara pressed the clergy to establish the practice. It soon spread to the whole Church. Some writers are of opinion that there is a danger of affectation in certain forms of Marian cult. Among these were Father Crasset, and especially Father Windenfeld, whose good intentions carried him so far that his writings were placed on the Index; but there is no doubt that devotion to Mary is a great help to piety, and assists countless souls to remain pure and humble. St Louis-Marie Grignion de Montfort was fully alive to the fact, and became the staunch champion of devotion to Mary.

Christians of the classical period could not doubt that the Blessed Virgin had a special interest in their era, for they knew that high in the Alpine valley of Laus, where numerous miracles occurred, the Mother of God had deigned to appear to a humble shepherdess, Benoîte Rencurel, and had repeated her visits over a period of fifty-four years, from 1664 to 1718.

3. Decline of Mysticism and Growth of Devotion to the Sacred Heart

A profound and lively faith was apparent therefore throughout the seventeenth century. We cannot, however, help noticing the change that took place as the great century of spiritual revival merged into the century of Louis XIV. After what we have seen it would be an exaggeration to talk of spiritual decline or decay; but there were several definite signs of an approaching weakening in intensity.

The spiritual tide still flowed vigorously, but it was less lively than hitherto: it ceased to race. The problem affected France more than any other country because she had remained the spiritual guide of the entire West until about 1660. Up to that time a number of mystics who were also extraordinary men of action had been hard at work, but in the succeeding period there were scarcely any. They had their followers, but these lacked creative qualities. The spiritual men of those years profited from the lessons of their predecessors. Bossuet and Fénelon were writers of genius, but they were not saints.

The personal rule of Louis XIV had begun in a very different atmosphere from that of his father, and by that time such great spiritual leaders of the preceding period [1] as Bérulle, Vincent de Paul and Olier were either dead or about to disappear from the scene. That wonderful Ursuline nun Marie de l'Incarnation had gone to die in far-off Canada; Father Surin was fighting his last fight against the Devil in the haze of madness; for Maria d'Agreda the day of the great awakening was drawing near. Of all that glorious cohort John Eudes alone remained, having laid the theological foundations of the devotion to the Sacred Heart.

There was no lack of spiritual men, even mystics of some consequence, but they were disciples rather than masters. Along the path traced by Father Chardon came Father Piny, the apostle of pure love, and Father Massoulié, an ascetic rather than a mystic. After Louis Lallemand, whose *Doctrine spirituelle* was published by his followers in 1695, came Fathers Nouet and Crasset of the Society of Jesus, men of no mean spiritual qualities. It was Father Crasset who guided the humble and sensitive soul of Mme Helyot in the way of holiness. That saintly woman would buy the wares of flower-girls so that she might have the opportunity to speak to them of God; and her radiant holiness changed her commonplace husband into a mystic who wrote some extremely beautiful meditations. Later came Father de Caussade (1675–1751). His admirable *Instructions spirituelles* defended mysticism when it was most bitterly attacked, and upheld the principle of 'Surrender to Divine Providence'. Among the Carmelites was René de Saint-Albert, who taught the prayer of simplicity; he had two serious competitors in Portugal—Joseph of the Holy Ghost and Anthony of the Holy Ghost, and in Spain another Joseph of the Holy Ghost, who was General of his Order. Father Philippe de la Trinité was a theorist rather than a mystic but all were inspired by the writings of St John of the Cross. Perhaps the most outstanding fact was the reappearance in Italy of a spiritual school, whereas scarcely anyone of note emerged during the preceding period other than St Joseph of Copertino. Among those who occupied a leading place in the band of spiritual writers were the stigmatic Franciscan nun St Veronica Giuliani of Turin, Blessed Sebastiano Valfre, Blessed Gregorio Barbarigo, who deserves to be called the Charles Borromeo of Padua,

---

[1] See Chapter II, p. 123.

I

Cardinal Giovanni Bona, and above all St Leonard of Port Maurice, O.F.M., whose activities belong more especially to the following epoch.[1] In short, the only figures comparable with such leaders as Bérulle, St Vincent de Paul, J. J. Olier and St John Eudes, from the point of view of experience and influence on their age, are Louis-Marie Grignion de Montfort (1673–1716) and St Margaret Mary Alocoque (1647–90), a sister of the Visitation. The former did magnificent work as a missionary, was a mystic of a high order and had a great devotion to Our Lady. St Margaret Mary led a wonderful life of prayer in her convent at Paray-le-Monial, and gave the world the devotion to the Sacred Heart of Jesus.

More disturbing than the decrease in the number of great spiritual men and women was a kind of backward pull on spiritual life, occasioned by a violent conflict between two hostile concepts.

From the earliest Christian ages various methods have been devised to help souls in their ascent to God. Some have insisted upon asceticism, on the necessity for man to learn in the agony of his soul to understand his own profound wretchedness, and to subdue his flesh and his mind. Others, relying on the truth that 'God is Love', believe that if love is sufficiently strong in a man's heart it will eradicate his sinfulness and enable the soul to soar towards God. Genuinely spiritual-minded writers know that both ways are inseparable; the 'purgative way' precedes the 'mystic way', and no one can hope to reach the heights until he has conquered himself. This view was natural to such saints as Francis de Sales, Vincent de Paul, Teresa of Avila and John of the Cross. But from about 1660 antagonism between the two tendencies became more marked, possibly because Cartesian rationalism had accustomed men's minds to distrust the irrational or because the austere morals of the Jansenists emphasized the abyss between human and divine virtues. It was certainly due in part to the excesses of the Quietists, disciples of the mysticism of pure love—the allegedly 'quick way' to God.[2] An anti-mystic reaction was unleashed. Maria d'Agreda's *Mystic City of God* was condemned by the Holy Office in 1681, reinstated by Innocent XI, then condemned by the Sorbonne. The attacks became more violent against the 'easy methods of prayer' as advocated by Father Pomey, Father Nepveu and others, against the Viennese writer Avancini's *Life of Christ*, and other suspect authors. It required three lively treatises by the Augustinian Father Nicole, a prominent member of Port-Royal, to hammer those whom he described as visionaries. Bossuet and the Jesuit Bourdaloue joined the fight and in turn opposed the 'short way'. The true mystics were thus compromised by the Quietists and were engulfed in their defeat, with the

---

[1] See *The Church in the Eighteenth Century*, Chapter V.
[2] See Chapter VI, p. 369 et seq.

result that their popularity waned and they eventually suffered a verit-able eclipse that lasted until our own era. The fact that between 1687 and 1799 Rome condemned no less than eighty spiritual works demonstrates the extent of the hostility.

On the other hand the ascetic tradition ran the risk of deviating as a result of Jansenism. It was not perhaps the doctrine of the Bishop of Ypres that mattered in this domain so much as the interpretation that the Abbé of Saint-Cyran [1] characteristically drew from it. Under the influence of the 'ascetics' Christian experience became austere, severe almost to the point of being unnatural. The sense of sin, which, as we have seen,[2] was so profound at the beginning of the century, may very well be stimulated to the point of exaggeration. Jansenism coloured the faith of countless souls even in those circles in which it failed to score success. There is an undoubted grandeur in the stern demands of Christianity. Of course it was a splendid thing that so many souls in classical times should have been able to say in their distress, as did Mme de Sévigné: 'What is my position in relation to God? What have I to give Him? What can I hope for? Am I worthy of heaven, or have I deserved hell?' But was it right to deny the soul that great upsurge of love that might whisk it away from its uncleanness and cast it at the feet of God? This rigid tendency threatened to harden the Christian experience and render it inaccessible to even a modest awareness, and for that reason the so-called 'casuistical' Jesuits fought against it. It also runs the risk, as will be seen in the long dramatic struggle against Jansenism, of restraining the faithful from approaching the Sacraments, on the ground that they are unworthy: a dangerous incline that provides an excuse for all sorts of weaknesses. And what was left to prevent the spiritual life from collapsing when the tragedy of Jansenism had more or less discredited the ascetic approach?

We have a striking example of this profound crisis of the Christian soul in the manner in which devotion to the Sacred Heart, the most providential acquisition of the classical century, asserted itself; it was the greatest mystical fact of the era. The devotion has become so well established today that we are apt to overlook completely that for a long time it stood as a sign of contradiction within the Church. The origins of the cult go far back. St Augustine had already said that the heart of Jesus, pierced by the soldier's lance, shed its blood for the remission of men's sins. In the Middle Ages St Bernard, Guillaume de Saint-Thierry, Richard de Saint-Victor, and later St Mechtilde, St Gertrude, St Anthony of Padua, and later still Tauler and Suso, had spoken of the heart of Jesus as a refuge and a shelter offered to the poor heart of man. The more ascetic saints—Lutgard, Angela of Foligno,

[1] See Chapter VI, especially p. 340 et seq.
[2] See Chapter II, p. 106.

Catherine of Sienna—stressed the need to study the heart of Jesus in order to live better, rather than the personal relationship of the Christian to Christ, as one heart to another. During the sixteenth century devotion to the Sacred Heart flowed like a subterranean stream through almost the whole of Catholic thought. It came to view in the lives of Blessed Louis de Blois, St Ignatius of Loyola, St Peter Canisius, St Francis Borgia, the Venerable Louis of Granada, St Teresa and many others. St Francis de Sales spoke of it to his Sisters of the Visitation in terms which suggested the devotion that would soon come to birth. Already the cult existed among the Carmelites in Liège, in the convent of Unterlinden in Colmar and in the Chartreuse at Cologne, where John Justus Lanspergius was its zealous advocate.

St John Eudes, who founded an Order,[1] established seminaries, and was a tireless missioner and reformer of the clergy, was also the great apostle of the Sacred Heart in the seventeenth century. As a result of long meditation, a deepening of his faith and the grace of interior light he came to see in the flesh of the Heart of God made man the symbol of the uncreated love of the Almighty for His creature. In the Divine Heart he discovered the great mysteries of Christianity: Creation, the Redemption. Through an understanding of this Heart he approached the Real Presence in the Holy Eucharist. It compelled men to desire to make reparation for the indignities and sufferings which sin has inflicted upon it. Filled with this grandiose idea, which indeed profoundly sums up the whole Christian theology, St John Eudes composed his beautiful Office of the Sacred Heart in 1670. Two years later he established the Feast of the Sacred Heart in the houses of his Society. Thirty years previously he had already instituted a feast of the Heart of Mary.

This devotion was theological in character; it could never have emerged from any organization of limited scope, or from any 'Third Order' of the Sacred Heart, had not Margaret Mary Alocoque, the humble nun of Paray-le-Monial, been favoured with extraordinary graces. Christ appeared to her, spoke with her, commanded her—an 'abyss of unworthiness and ignorance'—to 'spread the flames of His burning charity'. The Heart of Christ, 'encircled by a Crown of Thorns and surmounted by a Cross', would be exposed for the veneration of Christians 'as the supreme effort of His love on behalf of the ransomed world'. These revelations were repeated three times between 1673 and 1675.

Devotion to the Sacred Heart was suddenly to assume extraordinary proportions. Millions of Catholics would repeat throughout the centuries the tremendous words of Christ to Margaret Mary: 'Behold this Heart Which has so loved men.' But it did not happen immediately.

[1] See Chapter II, p. 73.

The epoch proved to be stubbornly opposed to revelations of this kind. At first her superiors treated St Margaret Mary as though she were mad. Father de la Colombière was replaced; as Superior of the Jesuit house at Paray he had directed her soul, and declared his belief in the truth of the revelations. Father Croiset, a teacher at Lyons who took over the nun's instruction, was also transferred elsewhere; and such was the universal distrust of mystics and everything connected with the theory of 'pure love' that his book was placed on the Index. An attempt made in 1697 to induce Rome to recognize the feast of the Sacred Heart failed. Margaret Mary died in 1690; she had never ceased to repeat that God had charged her with a mission, and that the 'adorable Heart' would reign over the world. But she did not live to see the triumph of that devotion to which she had dedicated her life. She only just managed to see the devotion adopted in a few convents of the Visitation, and a few confraternities of the Sacred Heart approved and enriched with indulgences. Wherever rigorists were to be found they put obstacles in the way of this mystical devotion. We are surprised to find that even Bossuet, whose voice might have trumpeted the good news abroad, did not press this intensely theological and profoundly moving devotion upon his age. Such a lack of appreciation clearly points to the anguish of the Christian conscience. Yet the ascetic and the mystic meet in two prayers which sum up the whole devotion to the Sacred Heart of Christ: 'O God, who joinest together in one will the hearts of Thy faithful, grant that nations may love Thy commandments'; and 'Jesus, meek and humble of Heart, make our hearts like unto Thine.' [1]

4. Faith and the World: the Theatre

Society may be undivided in its belief in Christianity, but the extent to which that belief reacts on morals remains an eternal problem; so prone is man's sinful nature never to live fully in accordance with the

[1] Opposition to the devotion to the Sacred Heart continued well beyond the seventeenth century. In 1720, at the time of the great plague in Marseilles, the Bishop of Belzunce consecrated his diocese to the Sacred Heart and introduced the feast. Despite his earnest and repeated entreaties Rome, suspicious of anything resembling inordinate mysticism, refused to approve the devotion. It was not until 1765 that Clement XIII approved it at the request of the Polish bishops. Maria Leczinska, a Pole who became Queen of France, was then able to spread the devotion throughout the country. But even then it was permitted, not prescribed. Moreover, when an attempt was made to establish the devotion in Paris, incidents were provoked by Jansenists who, at their 'synod' held at Pistoie in 1786, described the devotion as idolatrous. It was not until 1856 that Pius IX extended the Feast of the Sacred Heart to the Universal Church. The process of beatification of Margaret Mary was opened in 1714, interrupted, and then reopened in 1819. She was not beatified until 1864, and not canonized until 1920. It remained to our epoch to interpret the true meaning of this devotion. This Pius XII expressed in glowing terms in his Encyclical *Haurietis Aquas* on the occasion of the centenary of the feast in 1956.

demands of faith and conscience that no era has yet been able to solve the problem. Racine's famous lines, inspired by St Paul and St Augustine, remain true in any century:

> '*Mon Dieu, quelle guerre cruelle,*
> *Je trouve deux hommes en moi,*
> *Je ne fais pas le bien que j'aime,*
> *Et je fais le mal que je hais.*'

('What a cruel war, my God, is waged between the two men within me; I do not the good that I love, but the evil that I hate.')

In considering that profoundly Christian society we must not be surprised to encounter some very dark background shadows in the picture. The progress made during the preceding period was undoubtedly maintained, and the savage cruelty of the upper classes no longer existed. Though the practice of duelling had not altogether disappeared it was at least less common; and moral behaviour had improved. But there still remained much to be done. The scandal consequent upon the conduct of Louis XIV and other European sovereigns did not tend to encourage virtue. Passions were violent and instincts wild. The criminal use of poisons was evidence enough.

Among the mass of the people ordinary faults were widespread. If we are to accept the verdict of many bishops of the period we must believe that debauchery and drunkenness were common among Christian people. Every occasion provided an opportunity for merry-making: Sundays, fairs, even pilgrimages and the feasts of patron saints. The events at Séez, described by Daquin, were exactly similar to those which Cardinal Le Camus mentions as having taken place in Grenoble, and to those at Autun which caused such pain to Roquette. In Bavaria a pastoral letter criticized the conduct of some who took part in a pilgrimage to the shrine of Our Lady at Altötting. In Italy the brawls and free fights which broke out at every opportunity caused great indignation. Superstition was rampant; there was no country in which people did not believe in witches and sorcerers. 'To get a true picture of the ridiculous superstitions prevailing and foolish practices of every description resulting from ignorance and simplicity', writes a contemporary, 'one has to know something of our country people and above all the peasants in our most outlying provinces.' Superstition permeated the whole of Christendom, and many bishops had to take steps to check the stupid worship of relics and images. Bayle, author of the famous *Dictionnaire*, was obviously exaggerating when he wrote that 'the devil indeed put his shoulder to the wheel to turn religion, which is the finest thing in the world, into a mixture of foolishness, eccentricity, nonsense and appalling crimes'. But perhaps he was not altogether wrong.

Such dark shadows, however, were not, the worst of the evils. They have always existed, and those who see irregularities in everything, as a few pious bishops were apt to do, might have had an almost professional tendency to exaggerate them. St Augustine says that the work of the Holy Ghost in the Church is accomplished slowly, almost unconsciously, but without interruption. It must be allowed time in which to become effective. Here we must draw attention to a tendency characteristic of the age, but one which in a sense was more disturbing than the drunken squabbles and sexual indulgence of the peasants.

We might describe this tendency as a growing distinction—at least in certain circles—between religion and life. The real conflict, denounced by so many preachers from the pulpit, lay between 'the world' and faith. Such was indeed the essence of the struggle between Christianity, which strove to remain one in its teaching and universal in its scope, and those who in different ways aspired to limit its activities to a restricted field. It consisted in allowing preachers and spiritual directors to intervene in some spheres of life (even though their advice was rarely followed) and excluding a great part of man's life from ecclesiastical jurisdiction.

This was diametrically opposed to the teaching of St Francis de Sales, whose whole purpose was to combine Christian faith and life into a single entity, even in its lesser aspects and activities, and thus enable the soul to weave the thread of small virtues in the factory or the kitchen, in the court or in the shop. That conception of Christianity was now threatened: one might be a Christian without having to live entirely as a Christian. The people had before them the example of the Great King himself, a convinced believer whose behaviour was questionable from many points of view. There was a definite tendency even among the best people to confine religion to the seclusion of the inner man, a propensity fostered by the spiritual atmosphere of the early part of the century, and resulting in a kind of deep-seated cleavage. It is thus possible for a very lively faith to go hand in hand with an attitude of mind that is substantially non-Christian. Many chronicles of the period bear witness to the danger of formalism. 'All people know of religion is based on confraternities, indulgences and congregations,' wrote Cardinal Le Camus in a letter in which he condemned 'the love of pleasure and luxury among all classes'. There existed a type of casuistry which allowed men to think they could save their souls by making some sort of compromise with human frailty. At court excellent Christians, e.g. Mme de Sévigné, were proud to be seen frequenting the *salon* of Ninon de Lenclos, who was notorious for his intrigues and his atheism. Among the middle class, who were becoming increasingly important, there existed an economic and business morality that deviated more and more from the Christian moral code. The Jansenists failed completely in their attempt to secure the condemnation of loans against interest. A type of social morality with which medieval Christianity was imbued began to part company with religion, and the time had not yet come when great popes would raise their voices against this state of affairs. Class selfishness was growing; it would become manifest in the eighteenth century, which was to fall a victim to the evil. Society was hardening, becoming more segmented and less inclined to charity. Massillon was right when he wrote: 'Without exactly losing our faith we allow it to weaken within us, and make no use of it.' Such was the advent of the modern world with its dechristianized *élites* and its great evils—'Money has appropriated the Kingship of God'.

We shall see that the cleavage between faith and life was perceptible in literature and art. To be a Cornelian hero it was not essential to be a Christian; with the exception of Polyeucte the characters of Corneille's plays, so jealous of honour, so prone to vengeance, possess none of the evangelical virtues. Neither is Christianity to be found in the passion of Racine's heroes and heroines. The author of *Phèdre* resorted to some extremely skilful arguments to persuade his old masters of Port-Royal that his tragedy really illustrated their own moral theories! Too many classical writers convey the impression that they have raised a barrier between their faith and their art, so that the former may not intrude upon the latter. La Fontaine is an example: the 'moral' in most of his fables runs counter to the precepts of the Gospel. Among others, La Rochefoucauld and Mme de La Fayette tacitly advance the theory that reason is sufficient to make a lady; Christian morality is not rejected outright, but its repudiation is implied by omission.

Nothing emphasizes this separation more than the famous dispute that arose over the theatre and was debated so passionately, especially in France. The Fathers of the Church condemned the theatre during the era of the decadent Roman Empire, when the stage served to parade scurrility. By the Middle Ages the theatre had so successfully made its peace with the Church that it took its subjects from religious themes, and was able to stage its plays in the porches of cathedrals. But the 'mystery plays' gradually deteriorated. They declined from the comic to clownery; they parodied the creed and made fun of the hierarchy. Some restrictive action was necessary, and the Paris Parlement forbade them in 1548. Official censure embraced the whole theatre despite really serious attempts by several responsible people, including Richelieu, to narrow it down. In other Catholic countries, such as Spain, there was no censure whatever. The tradition of the Spanish mystery play was maintained by Calderòn de la Barca (1600–1681) with his *Auto di Nascimiento* and *Farsa del Sacramento,* rich in symbolism in which his dramatic genius was placed at the service of the Catholic faith. 'Devout comedies' combined sermons with biblical plots or with themes taken from the lives of the saints, and they met with enormous success.

In France, where the craze for the theatre was unbelievable, the position was extremely odd. The halls were packed, the actors were earning money, leading actors and actresses became celebrities, and tragedies and comedies were given at court. At the same time the official attitude of Christianity was such that all plays and players were absolutely condemned. The combined influence of the Company of the Blessed Sacrament and Port-Royal undoubtedly explains the rigid attitude adopted. In 1666 Nicole described 'poets of the theatre' as poisoners of the public, and likewise condemned writers of novels. A similar attitude was evinced by the Protestant synods. The production of Molière's plays *Tartuffe, École des Femmes* and *Don Juan* let loose a storm of protest. In 1693 the Theatine Father Caffaro published a letter in which he discussed the question whether plays should be allowed or absolutely forbidden. Bossuet replied with his *Maximes et réflexions sur la comédie,* and the least one can say is that his language was not temperate. Bossuet regarded all plays as depraved: Molière was soundly trounced. The *Rituel parisien* excommunicated actors by name,[1] and, as we know, Molière's remains were refused the right of Christian burial. The parish priest of Saint-Barthélemy, referring to Molière, said publicly: 'He is a devil in man's clothing, and should be burned.' The King of France, however, discountenanced these outbursts; he was godfather to one of Molière's sons, and publicly encouraged plays. Meanwhile Rome, where comedy flourished, declined to join in this hostility. The result was that all the Italian comedians in Paris professed to be the Pope's subjects in order to escape excommunication!

This vigorous condemnation achieved no result after all; perhaps because it was too severe, in which case the responsibility for the rupture between religion and life lies with the authorities rather than with the Christian people. 'What a strange situation,' exclaimed La Bruyère, 'when a crowd of Christians of both sexes gather together in

---

[1] Excommunication was not a mere matter of form. 'In order to receive the Last Sacraments actors had to read a statement renouncing their profession. Some had not the courage to do so. The case of Mlle Champmeslé is touching. She refused to repudiate her past, and declared that it was noble to remain true to one's art to the last. "If I get well I wish to return to the theatre." It was only a few hours before her death, and probably because there was no hope of recovery, that she yielded.'—A. M. Carré's *L'Église s'est-elle réconciliée avec le théâtre?* (Paris, 1956).

* I

a hall to applaud a crowd of actors under sentence of excommunication!' Chalucet, Archbishop of Toulouse, acted more logically when in 1702 he excommunicated the audience. Fortunately the Nuncio, who enjoyed the theatre, was then resident in Paris.

5. THE VOICE OF THE PULPIT

Society did not, however, lack advice and warnings during the Great Century. In fact, one of the most striking features of the epoch is the important part played by preaching. If it were not impertinent one might say that the success of the pulpit competed with that of the stage. As great an audience listened to those who 'made man tremble under the judgments of God' as there were spectators who laughed at the pranks of Scapin and the cryptic profanity of Don Juan. The writers of great sermons were as famous as the comedians and the tenors; some of their names are legendary. The miracle of their eloquence was discussed in the streets and in the news-sheets. At the end of a sermon by Massillon on the Last Judgment the whole congregation rose as though he, the supreme judge, were about to place the elect on his right and the damned on his left. It is impossible to exaggerate the importance of pulpit oratory during the classical period. If it reflects the spiritual maladies which still remained to be cured it was without doubt one of the chief instruments, perhaps *the* chief, in the transformation of morals.

The phenomenon was general, for all the great Catholic countries had illustrious preachers at that time. In Italy the Jesuit Paolo Segneri (1624–94) joined the conflicts against Quietism and Probabilism. His limpid and tasteful eloquence nearly always avoided the comical buffoonery then fashionable. The Capuchin Giovanni Francesco d'Arezzo, who later became Cardinal Casini, lashed his audiences so vigorously that we are inclined to wonder whether his words can have been really effective. In Portugal Father Antonio Vieira (1608–97), another Jesuit, was for a long time a great missionary in Brazil; he returned to his own country, where he stirred vast crowds. In Spain Father Tirso Gonzalez, who became General of the Society of Jesus, and Don Jaime y Cordoba, nicknamed 'Father of the Poor', both reacted against the bombastic and pompous style of eloquence; while the Augustinian de Carayon went so far as to say during the funeral oration of a queen that 'the very moon has gone into mourning so that human beings may don their black'! The fashion in Germany contrasted with the French classical taste; sermons were sentimental, little concerned about logic and enriched with legend and symbolism. A very successful exponent of this *genre* was the Augustinian Ulrich Megerle

(1642–1709), who in religion bore the name Abraham of Saint Clare; he was the official preacher at the court of Vienna, and his collected sermons on 'Judas, the Master Rogue' are still read today. More popular orators were Rauscher, Pursel and Knelling, who added a pleasant touch of humour to the sentimental.

But it was in France that pulpit oratory reached its zenith. Preachers had the advantage of an almost universal language that had reached an unprecedented state of perfection to which they themselves had contributed; and their audiences were growing more and more appreciative of lucidity and finesse in sacred eloquence, which had attained a level never before known. The king himself set a high value on the art, and encouraged it as much as possible by showing marks of favour to the most eloquent among the preachers. He recognized that they held a special place among the great men who contributed to the glory of his reign.

Pulpit oratory had been completely transformed in a short time. The first half of the century was a period of development during which the burlesque type of sermon gradually disappeared. The famous 'Little Father André', who died in 1657, used to compare the four evangelists with the four kings in a pack of cards. On one occasion, seeing a few members of the congregation so near the altar that they touched it, he said the biblical prophecy that calves would be seen on the altar was about to be fulfilled!

St Vincent de Paul taught his Lazarist priests that true eloquence should be direct; that it should strike the heart and the mind and avoid 'monumental periods' and booming effects. Fathers Le Jeune and Senault, both Oratorians and later masters at Port-Royal, Saint-Cyran and Singlin, instilled into preachers a sense of gravity and dignity which had so often been disregarded in the past. The Jesuit Lingendes and Bishop Godeau followed precisely the same idea. It is surprising to find that Cardinal de Retz did likewise; his Lent and Advent sermons from 1640 to 1648 brought all Paris to the church of Notre Dame.

By about 1660 pulpit oratory in France was at the height of its success, though it was not entirely free from serious and obvious defects such as affectation, bad taste and a superficial gloss of erudition. Even the best preachers did not escape these faults. Bossuet, for example, referring to the fall of great empires, which he regarded as proof of the intervention of Providence, mentioned those of 'Bacchus and Hercules, renowned conquerors of the Indies and the East'. He compared the Blood of Christ with the blood that Catiline forced his fellow conspirators to drink. On another occasion, when recalling to mind the tortures suffered by St Gorgonius, he spoke of the 'foul effluvia emanating from the fat from his roasting body'. But apart from all such extravagances there were great qualities in those sermons produced in such profusion. The richness of their style and the soundness of their doctrine were amazing. Great skill went into the composition, the general arrangement, the setting out of facts, the realism of the imagery and, among the greatest preachers, the melodious arrangement of words. Bossuet was renowned for the harmony and rhythm of his periods, Bourdaloue for his impact and Fénelon for the music of his words. And what courage these men had! They denounced the folly of splendour, sensual pleasures, pride and hardness of heart; they handled invective and innuendo with a precision that would never be tolerated in our day, despite our professed broadmindedness. Massillon preached against the thoughtless cruelty of men in high places, who imagined they were in the world entirely for their own benefit. There is Bourdaloue's famous sermon on impurity, preached before the young Louis XIV, the lover of Mlle de la Vallière and Mme de Montespan. These two sermons were not far removed from the great biblical reproaches of the Jewish prophets to the guilty kings of Israel. When the nobles complained to Louis XIV of the acrimony of Mascaron, he replied: 'He did his duty; now we should do ours.' It is to the credit of the king, his court and society generally that they actually listened to those great voices reminding them from the pulpit of their duties towards God.

Not all the preachers of the classical age won a lasting reputation. Many who drew the crowds are quite forgotten today; some are mentioned, but not on account of their eloquence. Soanen made a great impression at court before becoming Bishop of Sénez and subsequently involved in the Jansenist affair. Another, the Abbé Charles Boileau (unrelated to 'the lawgiver of Parnassus') was so much appreciated by Louis XIV that the king had him elected to the Academy. But who now remembers the Capuchin Father Séraphin, whose improvised sermons, before Massillon's time, electrified the court? Or Father Nicolas of Dijon, another Capuchin, who had the rare gift of making apt quotations from the Scriptures and the Fathers of the Church? There was the Abbé Anselme, who was the fashionable orator at Versailles about the year 1686; Cassagnes and Cotin, whose eloquence took them to the French Academy; and Dom Cosme, who preached as many Lenten sermons at the court as Bossuet did, but whose name was none the less omitted from Cardinal Grente's exhaustive *Dictionnaire des Lettres*. Some there were who did not deserve such unaccountable indifference; the Oratorian Fromentières, for instance, who preached the funeral oration of Anne of Austria and the sermon on the occasion of the taking of the veil by Mlle de la Vallière; and Father de la Rue, a Jesuit who became an important figure at court from 1687, where he preached the Advent and Lenten sermons for four years running, and pronounced the panegyric upon Bossuet at Meaux. Father Gaillard, another Jesuit, was the last preacher whose sermons the king enjoyed in his old age. The number of preachers of the classical century is inexhaustible. When Father Houdry, himself a prolific preacher, produced a collection of the masterpieces of sacred oratory, the work ran to twenty-three volumes, and even then he had to omit three-quarters of the material.

Of these great men six emerge as having withstood the test of time with varying degrees of success. It is interesting to note, however, that although their contemporaries recognized the greatness of them all, they did not classify them in the order we follow. When the Abbé de Clérambault spoke in praise of Bossuet before the Academy, he said that Bossuet had 'allowed his rivals to attain the highest level of eloquence'. It was not until the advent of Nisard and the nineteenth-century critics that the Bishop of Meaux was given his rightful place in literature.[1] The keenest minds, among them La Bruyère, were struck by the 'power and magnetism' of Fénelon's oratory though he was not immediately successful in drawing the crowds.

Whom then did the classical century deem to be the principal representatives of pulpit oratory? One was Fléchier (1632–1710), whose funeral oration for Turenne we so much admire, together with his elegant and polished style and his 'noble church music', those little ornaments which he claimed would create 'a taste for virtue'. But he is so often solemn and pompous that we are inclined to endorse all the criticisms hurled at academic sermons. Another was Mascaron (1634–1703); the court doted upon him, and Mme de Sévigné praised him to the skies. Though his oratory does not leave us untouched we find him uneven, and he is apt to mistake metaphors for ideas. Later, towards the end of the reign, we have Massillon (1663–1742). He it was who preached the funeral oration of Louis XIV, with its famous dramatic exordium, and who continued into the first half of the eighteenth century the great tradition of classical sermons. Voltaire and the Encyclopédistes would set him in the forefront of pulpit orators. Though Massillon's similes, hyperboles, paraphrases and antitheses appear to depend upon an extremely questionable form of rhetoric, he was certainly not lacking in psychological precision, in critical acumen, and even in lyricism and warmth.

[1] In ten years (1659–69) Bossuet preached four 'Stations' at the court, that is, no more than Dom Cosme and a third of those preached by Massillon. His funeral oration for Henrietta of England was given in a little chapel at Chaillot, while François Favre preached his at the church of Saint-Denis, and Father Senault the most important one at Notre Dame. Mme de Sévigné wrote that she found the sermon preached by Bossuet for the Profession of Louise de la Vallière 'less divine' than that preached by Fromentières at the clothing of the king's former favourite.

6. THE SEVERITY OF BOURDALOUE

Bourdaloue was the typical preacher, 'the attorney-general of moral law', as Bishop Calvet remarked. It seemed that his sole vocation, the one purpose of his life, was to remind his contemporaries of the Commandments of God and the demands they make on man. He never relaxed in his determination to point out to man the narrow way, clearly determined by reason and experience, that leads to heaven through the light of faith. For thirty-five years, tirelessly and unflinchingly, he shouldered this responsibility; and indeed without regard for people's feelings. 'He strikes out unmercifully,' wrote Mme de Sévigné, 'uttering truths right and left. . . . It is every man for himself! But he goes straight ahead.' Indeed nothing could stop him. He denounced the court as 'the seat of pride, the centre of corruption, the school of godlessness', a treacherous sea 'where the noblest virtues are shipwrecked'. He spoke with accents worthy of Amos and Osee. When the poisoning scandal burst he did not hesitate to refer to it, pointing at Mme de Montespan, who was still the king's mistress. Those whom he assailed showed their disgust secretly, or at least discreetly. One day when he was ascending the pulpit at Saint-Sulpice, the great Condé sneered: 'Look out, gentlemen; there goes our enemy.' On another occasion, when Bourdaloue successfully launched one of his 'furious attacks against the conscience of his audience', and the congregation had evinced some measure of annoyance, Maréchal de Grammont exclaimed loudly: '*Morbleu!* He's right!'

To say that people ran to hear him speak would be an understatement; they literally fought to get in. They arrived long before the sermon was due to start, and the wealthy had their places kept for them by their lackeys. The atmosphere was rather like that of a theatre before the curtain rises, everybody chatting and calling across to one another. Suddenly the preacher arrived, elbowed his way through the crowd, ascended the steps and appeared high up in the pulpit. There he stood until there was perfect silence, motionless and with eyes closed, praying.[1] At length he opened his eyes and began to speak, softly at first, as if to clear the way. Then he gradually increased his speed, rising to that 'thundering and dreadful pitch' described by the journalist Robinet, reaching such a pitch of menace and holy violence that he frequently had to stop and sit for a moment to recover himself.

'I felt so powerfully attracted by the force and correctness of his arguments', wrote Mme de Sévigné, 'that he staggered me. I could not regain my composure until he decided to pause.' It is impossible not

---

[1] This was the pose depicted in Jouvenel's engraving; hence the legend that Bourdaloue learned his subject by heart and spoke with his eyes closed.

to think of Bourdaloue when we try to imagine the great esteem in which preachers were held in classical times. He was born in 1632, at Bourges, where his father was a counsellor of the presidial court. Bourdaloue was above all else a Jesuit. Nothing else was of importance. As a student, novice and teacher he received the long and sturdy training that St Ignatius had planned for his sons. He represented the Society at its best, in such a way that his every word and gesture refuted the criticisms of Pascal's *Provinciales*. In him there was nothing secretive, nothing underhand, no element of guile; still less did he tend towards the lax or easy-going. He spent most of his time in the lone-liness of a cell devoid of ornament except for a portrait of the king given him by Louis, which his superiors allowed him to retain. Beneath a shy exterior he concealed a profoundly intimate spiritual life, as far removed from the disturbing fantasies of the Quietists as it was from exaggerated Jansenist austerity. He did not confine himself to the preparation and delivering of sermons. 'His sublime eloquence', as Lamoignon said, 'sprang above all from his thorough knowledge of the world'. A confessor and spiritual director, he exercised a con-siderable influence apart from his preaching, because his life, as Mlle de la Vallière so wisely said, was 'penetrated with the truths he preached'. When he felt the approach of death he expressed a wish to retire into some secluded house of the Society; but on being told by his superiors that he was irreplaceable, he yielded and remained at court. He died, still active, in 1704.

Bourdaloue's art—if art it may be called—was based above all on logic, fact and absolutely methodical argument. Others might take wing and soar to such heights of eloquence that they lost contact with the earth; he based his pathos on pure reason. Bourdaloue usually divided his sermon into three or four parts, each being subdivided into sections. This arrangement tended to deprive it of dramatic swing and forceful impact, but it gave the discourse an admirable orderliness that appealed to his contemporaries—despite Fénelon, who scoffed at the method. Moreover, Bourdaloue was a moralist rather than a theologian; too often he neglected to support his arguments with dogmatic facts, but he had a profound knowledge of souls. He was another La Rochefoucauld, lacking the bitterness of the author of the *Maximes*, but possessing his sense of truth. His ability to analyse the human heart, to lay bare its secrets and its frailties great and small, has rarely been equalled. So precise was he in his descriptions that shrewd minds thought they could name the sinners, male or female, whom his pictures conjured up. He might have been really great had he possessed the breadth of view and the abundant intellectual qualities of Bossuet, the sensitiveness and the unflagging curiosity of Fénelon, without mentioning their other gifts of genius. Bourdaloue was a preacher, the greatest of his time, but he was nothing more. Bossuet called him 'our master'. As far as technique went he was the master of French preaching, and for that reason has survived to the present day. But order and method can be learned; genius cannot.

7. BOSSUET

When we think of Bossuet, the great Bishop of Meaux, whose name stands for all that was Catholic in the classical age, we imagine him first as a preacher, a religious orator. His activities were indeed devoted to these necessary tasks: expounding Christian doctrine, exhorting his fellow men to a better way of life, exalting the truths of religion on great occasions in order to redeem through them the nation's soul.

So too he appears in the full-length statue of him that stands beneath the dome of the French Academy. Such was the pose in which his contemporaries often saw him—grave and reserved, looking straight ahead, his hand extended to emphasise his exordium or his reproach, so obviously engrossed in his sacred task that it would be difficult to imagine him in any role but that of the mouthpiece of God. When we utter his name and remember what he left to posterity we cannot but think first of his oratorical writings. He delivered eleven funeral orations, of which the most famous were those of Henrietta of England and Condé, with their gripping exordia flowing majestically into the body of the subject, like folds of the funereal tapestry that adorned the church; remarkable too were such descriptive passages as the death of the queen and the battle of Rocroi. His innumerable sermons, almost all written up from short notes, still have the power to move us, even though they lack the glamour of his eloquence and the warmth of his presence. Among these were his sermons on the unity of the Church, the 'eminent dignity of the poor', and death.

With Bossuet pulpit oratory attained its zenith. Though solidly buttressed by dogma and by his voluminous reading, his words never lost that spontaneity and easy flow which are the hallmarks of great oratory. He developed his thoughts relentlessly and coherently, but without any of the deliberate rigidity that limited the powers of Bourdaloue. Bossuet thus succeeded in contriving a blend of opposite qualities: strength allied with flexibility, conciseness with richness of vocabulary, logic with persuasive warmth. His mood varied; in turn he could be solemn, realistic, lyrical, logical, poetic, didactic and occasionally familiar. His psychological analysis probed to the very depths of the being; his historical references gripped the attention by the force of their relevancy. What consummate art lay in the series of periods, the balanced development of his argument and that 'domelike sentence' of which Valéry speaks, rising by stages, each one awakening more deep-toned reverberations, then descending in flowing accents until it reaches the deliberately sought words that bring it to a close in perfect harmony—a powerfully abrupt closure or the whispering echo of a lingering lament.

Bossuet was all that, but he was much more besides. Belonging to those few 'who have most superbly made use of the power of speech', he could not confine himself within the limitations of oratory. He was also a writer who possessed the qualities of sensitiveness, imagination, rhythm and precision; he was the greatest historian of his day, a moralist who rivalled La Rochefoucauld and La Bruyère, and a spiritual director comparable with St Francis de Sales. As a polemist he was the equal of Pascal, and so brilliant that his contemporaries admired him above all as a controversialist. In a way he was also a politician; but at the same time his *Lettres sur l'Amour de Dieu* and his *Méthode pour faire oraison de simplicité* show that he was a remarkable spiritual writer. More than anything else he was a doctor, a direct descendant of the Fathers of the Church, among whom he would certainly have been numbered had he lived in their time, for he was a capacious religious thinker, the most solid of his century. He achieved all these things with regal facility; his manifold flexible qualities enabled him to engage in every kind of activity at once, any single one of which would have been sufficient to absorb one mind and fill a lifetime. Behind everything he was and did lay an intensely rich experience of humanity; in consequence he was the guiding light of his era, its witness and its most typical representative. If his intellectual stature is to be measured by the extent of ground he covered, that is to say by the range of his interests rather than by the results he achieved, we may rightly describe Bossuet as a genius. One might hardly have expected genius to spring from a family of provincial magistrates whose ancestors had been vine-growers and cloth merchants; but such indeed were the Bossuets—honest, headstrong, of good reputation and above average intelligence. Jacques Bénigne, the seventh child, revealed great gifts from an early age. He was born on 27th September 1627; his godfather read his horoscope and discovered that a great career awaited him. The child soon confirmed that prophecy. At the Jesuit college in Dijon he proved a serious student, a stickler for Latin and of a piety which his teachers admired. He clearly deserved to bear the family motto 'Good Wood Bossuet' inscribed around a twisted vine-plant. He received the tonsure at nine years of age, though not on account of his piety; it qualified him to receive the revenues of a canonry at Metz and involved no religious obligations. His resourceful father, who had settled in that city, managed to secure the dignity for him when he was fifteen years of age. His intellectual qualities were so evident that his parents sent him to the Collège de Navarre at Paris, the teachers' training college of the day, where he made a great impression and became the favourite pupil of Nicolas Cornet, who occupied the chair of theology. At twenty-five Jacques Bénigne became a doctor of the Sorbonne. On the day of his ordination, the same day upon which he presented his thesis, the great Condé himself was present, and he caused general astonishment by a sermon delivered extempore, as though for fun, during a social evening at the Hôtel de Rambouillet.

But his new state was no mere game; to him the priesthood was something more than a career. By the time he was fourteen he had read the Scriptures through, and declared he received from them 'a sense of joy and enlightenment'. Later, under the austere Cornet, he acquired a taste for theology, which he never lost. The turning point was reached at the age of twenty-one. He was making a retreat in preparation for the subdiaconate when he experienced a spiritual crisis very much like Pascal's 'night of fire'. He came to appreciate the instability of human affairs, and in a sublime piece of writing set down his anguish and his resolutions. That date was a milestone in his life; it showed clearly that the greatest conflict of his life was the one that took place within himself. His reading of the works of Bérulle, and above all his meeting with St Vincent de Paul, added the finishing touches. From that eager, ardent lad, as Bossuet described himself, Vincent formed a man of the Church, a man of God. Bossuet was acquainted with the atmosphere of Saint-Lazare, having taken part in the Tuesday Conferences [1] at which he later preached; he therefore understood the meaning of a lived religion and a true priestly vocation. His mind was made up. When the young doctor learned that his master Cornet was about to offer him the chair of theology he declined this 'open sesame' to an exceptionally brilliant career. As a zealous priest he assumed the responsibilities of his canonry at Metz, of which he already held the title and revenues.

That was the kind of man he would remain throughout his life. The cast of his character was clearly outlined in his youth, and though it matured it never really changed. The artists Mignard, Nanteuil, and later Largillière and Rigaud, have portrayed him at different ages; but the several paintings reveal very little change. They all show a healthy balance, self-control, a robust pride, a kindly disposition with a touch of condescension and a great deal of confidence in life and in himself. The thick lips and the broad nostrils suggest perhaps fulsome appetites, and that his apparent serenity was not acquired without a great struggle. But this Burgundian was a healthy fellow, a tireless worker; after a day of priestly duties he could spend half the night wrapped in a bearskin rug, writing letters, sermons and treatises. And he had a healthy mind: logical, precise, with an instinctive dislike of the vague, the doubtful and the morbid; more brilliant than intelligent, but not unduly precocious. He was sensitive, however, and capable of exquisite tact, to which his penitents bore witness; so fundamentally good that his occasional simplicity allowed him to be taken in by the wiles of the wicked—of whom his nephew was one. He was generous at all times except when carried away by the excitement of battle; then, as in his clash with Fénelon, he would lose his sense of proportion and even of charity. He had few other faults apart from his passion for a fight, an inordinate liking for court life, its pomp, its honours and the desire to wield power and influence.[1] Had he been more humble, more meek and more detached from the world, he might have been a saint. He was but a man, yet a man whose greatest merit was to desire to put into God's hands all he did, said and hoped. He was a man of faith.

Faith was the central fact of his character and of his life. He staked his all upon eternity. His faith was simple and direct, rejecting doubt and ambiguity whenever essentials were at issue. Yet it was a lucid faith, sure of its foundations, aspiring to dominate every facet of life and possessing a natural horror of sin. Such a faith was absolutely and wholly Catholic; in other words it was not born of personal cogitation and the arguments of conscience, but of profound adherence to authority and tradition, and of the felicitous sensation of 'feeling with the Church'. Nothing could be further from Bossuet than the heretical mind. He described a heretic as 'one who has an opinion', and it would have been impossible for him to hold any opinion that was not within the framework of revealed truth and dogma. He has often been unjustly described as a Jansenist because he condemned those who 'make the gate of heaven too wide', just as he condemned those 'whose hardness makes piety dry and odious'; but he tended to be Augustinian and was certainly more inclined to a religion of fear than to a religion of tenderness. That did not, however, prevent those quasi-mystical elevations (apparent in his *Méditations sur l'Évangile* and his *Élévations sur les mystères*) that led him to 'consume his heart in the infinite depths of love' and enliven his devotion to Christ, Our Lady and the saints. In short, he was the most solid, the most well balanced of the Christian thinkers of his day.

[1] He also had a liking for material wealth, money and good living. He owned real estate in Paris, and charged his tenants a high rent. But the famous story, spread by Voltaire, that he was secretly married to Mlle de Mauléon has been absolutely refuted, especially by Amable Floquet in his *Études sur la vie de Bossuet*, and by Canon Urbain. The truth is that out of sympathy for the lady Bossuet stood surety for her in connection with a loan she raised when buying some shares. The contract was seen by one Jean-Baptiste Denis, a priest who had been driven from Meaux for misconduct, and he confused it—perhaps deliberately—with a marriage contract. (See the details of this affair by A. Augustin-Thierry in *Ecclesia*, Paris, December 1952.)

Such a man seemed so clearly predestined to wage war on God's behalf that it appeared quite natural for him to have chosen the career he followed. He spent seven years at Metz as archdeacon of the Chapter, and was an enthusiastic propagandist among Protestants and Jews, but he continued to cultivate his mind in the privacy of recollection. Then he was called upon to preach in Paris, where six 'Stations' (four of them at court) and as many funeral orations enhanced his renown, and he soon became an outstanding success. In 1670 he was made Bishop of Condom, though he never resided there; and in the same year he staggered the court with his magnificent funeral oration on Henrietta of England. A few months later Louis XIV chose him from a list of a hundred candidates to be tutor to the Dauphin. It was a difficult task which lasted twelve years, and he performed it with more zeal than pleasure, more credit than personal satisfaction. In 1681, as first chaplain to the Dauphin's wife, he was given the bishopric of Meaux; it was an unassuming see, but near Versailles. Henceforward until his death he devoted himself to his episcopal duties with the earnestness he applied to everything he undertook. He supervised the administration of his diocese, controlled the seminary, presided over meetings of the trustees, prepared a draft catechism and busied himself with the poor. Meanwhile he remained the great official orator, always at the service of the court on ceremonial occasions or when some responsible person was needed to solve a difficulty or settle a dispute. He was the guide, philosopher and friend of the Church of France and, in a way, of the Great King.

It is difficult to say whether Louis really liked him; but he certainly respected him. As Sainte-Beuve so aptly put it: 'They understood each other.' Bossuet's character and even the quality of his faith led him to identify himself naturally with the accepted order of things, which seemed to justify his own way of life; and he strove not merely to adhere to that concept of the world which pertained to the principle of monarchy by divine right, but even defended and consolidated it. His *Politique tirée de l'Écriture sainte* was written with this purpose in view; so was his *Discours sur l'histoire universelle*, in which, by showing God's work through human acts and events, he vindicated a system in which everything was stable, well ordered and based upon obedience and faith. He knew the dangers and limitations of the system, and when royal absolutism ran the risk of compromising through pride the established order of God, Bossuet intervened with the object of preventing a rift and fostering harmony between the two authorities whose responsibility it was under heaven to rule the world. He acted thus in the Gallican crisis.[1] It was through this attitude rather than through his language and style that he showed himself to be the

[1] See Chapter IV, p. 222.

classicist *par excellence*—if it is really true that classicism is the result
of a conflict with, or perhaps a victory over, the forces of destruction
and disintegration.

Thus the life of Bossuet was a contest; especially after he had
shaken off the shackles of his official duties as tutor to the Dauphin and
felt free to do battle with anything that threatened the Catholic order,
to which he was passionately devoted. He did not lack adversaries;
indeed, they were innumerable and powerful. First there was 'the
world', that looseness of morals which extended even to those circles
where one would expect an example of virtue and loyalty. He knew
the danger better than anyone, and against the world he 'followed his
profession conscientiously,' as Lanson said, 'without brutishness or
flattery, without complacency or insolence'. The world had its
accomplices: casuists, probabilists, laxists and all those impudent
theorists who imagined and taught that it was easy to lead a Christian
life. There were also the free-thinkers, whose ideas absolutely horrified
him. Their influence appeared to be spreading; Fontenelle had just
been elected to the Academy. The absurd intellectual pride of incredulity, the irony of the sceptics, the animal-like indifference—all those
factors seemed to him as 'seditious' as they were shameful. Again,
there were heretics who strove to shatter that unity of the Church
which he extolled in his writings. Finally there were the Protestants,
whom he did not hate but regarded as brothers. For them he had
written in his youth his *Exposition de la doctrine catholique*, a small but
brilliant book which had stirred many consciences; it was against the
Protestants too that he later wrote his *Histoire des variations des
églises protestantes* in order to convince them of their errors.

Up to about 1690 it seemed to Bossuet that he had won all his
battles, and that his enemies acknowledged defeat; the king had been
won over, the errors of Probabilism had been condemned, and the
Huguenots were clearly nonplussed by his *Histoire des variations*.
Later, however, the beautiful harmony which seemed to reign as a
result of his endeavours appeared to disintegrate. New perils rose up
before him. Suddenly he perceived a danger in the philosophy of
Descartes, whom he had approved as a sound thinker and to whose
philosophy he had introduced the Dauphin. Now he saw the conclusions which unscrupulous men might draw from it. He exclaimed
prophetically: 'I see a great combat preparing within the Church.
More than one heresy will spring from the misunderstood principles
of Cartesian philosophy.' He was also disturbed by Malebranche, the
Oratorian metaphysician, whom he suspected of wishing to reduce
ethics to a mere question of order, eliminating the supernatural and the
spirit of penance, and glorifying a form of liberty which made nonsense
of authority and tradition. He considered that, even if the aims of

Malebranche himself were honest, his disciples were plunging headlong into heresy. And Richard Simon, another Oratorian even more suspect, ventured to apply the critical method to the Bible, thus 'substituting grammar for theology'. On one occasion Bossuet managed to persuade Chancellor Michel Le Tellier to forbid the publication of one of Simon's works, but the adversary repeated his offence and the attack had to be renewed.[1]

Continual strife and his uneasiness at seeing God's order gradually threatened made Bossuet obstinate, almost unfeeling, and his clear-sightedness began to diminish. He failed to perceive that once the vocabulary of Richard Simon's theories was explained, those theories could serve as weapons of Christian apologetic against atheistic criticism. When, under the influence of a book by Father Caffaro, he raged and fumed against the theatre, insulted Molière and included the plays of Corneille and Molière in his condemnation of the Byzantine spectacles, he was unable to recognize that his excessive severity was crippling his own constant endeavour to permeate life with the spirit of Christianity; he was almost forcing Christians to secede. When he published his letter to the Pope on the subject of Chinese idolatries and superstitions, he was unaware that the attitude he adopted against 'Chinese rites' and the possibility of establishing a Chinese Church was diametrically opposed to the attitude of St Paul, who, in order to convert the Gentiles, became 'a Greek among Greeks'.[2] Finally, when he lent the whole weight of his authority to crush not only Father Lacombe and Mme Guyon, but even Fénelon, his own disciple, friend and colleague,[3] and when he took up cudgels against the mystics and all the Maria d'Agredas of this world, he failed to see that in condemning mysticism outright he was depriving Christian experience of the precious stones in its crown, and reducing it to a kind of emaciated moralism and dogmatism. It was this lack of understanding, as well as his taste for austerity in religion, that caused him to be too lenient, if not too complacent, towards Jansenism, which was really more dangerous than Quietism. This was noticeable in the Quesnel affair.[4] Undoubtedly these were errors of judgment; they reveal the limitations of his genius and intellect, but they also suggest that his normal approach to problems was that of one who struggles to hold his ground rather than to extend his conquests, and that he was a prophet of the past rather than a creator of the future.[5]

[1] Descartes, Malebranche and Richard Simon are dealt with in *The Church in the Eighteenth Century*, Chapter I.
[2] See *The Church in the Eighteenth Century*, Chapter II.
[3] See Chapter VI, p. 388.
[4] See Chapter VI, p. 398 et seq.
[5] Joseph de Maistre's criticism is none the less excessively severe: 'He flattered the powerful, while the wretchedness of the people never drew a protest from him.'

He died eleven years before his king, on 11th April 1704, and thus did not witness the sudden decay that marked the end of the reign. He died, not like a saint, but like an upright man in an age when men knew how to die. Almost his last words were addressed to his secretary, who spoke to him of his glory: 'Enough of this talk. Let us ask pardon of God.' Yet he achieved a renown that has increased with time; for time has eliminated accidentals from his work and emphasized only the essentials. His glory is perhaps somewhat cold and pompous—'one of the religions of France', as Sainte-Beuve said; a glory that failed to recognize the humanity concealed beneath the solemn exterior, and in which much injustice is blended with admiration. The noble title given him by Fénelon [1]—the Eagle of Meaux—describes him perfectly in his steadfastness and courage, in the manner in which he soars to the heights, or in which he strikes down an adversary. In short, what we admire in Bossuet is not so much the outstanding figure of that great court, or even his mastery of the French language, but the man who fought so hard to promote loyalty to Christian principles, the champion of Christ's cause.

8. The Anguish of Fénelon

It might appear unnatural to rank Fénelon among the great preachers of the seventeenth century, as though we were approaching him through one of the lesser aspects of his rich personality. Although he did preach a great deal, at the *Nouvelles catholiques* at Saint-Cyr, during missions for the conversion of Protestants and especially in his own diocese, he could not be included among the leaders of religious oratory of his day. In fact, we have only six of his sermons, firstly because he was in the habit of improvising, and secondly because most of his notes were destroyed in a fire at his palace at Cambrai. His contemporaries, however, admired him as a pulpit orator. 'One feels the power and ascendancy of this rare mind,' wrote La Bruyère, 'whether he preaches spontaneously or whether his sermon has been well prepared.' Reading his *Dialogues* on the subject of eloquence generally and pulpit oratory in particular, we are able to appraise the soundness and relevance of his views upon this difficult medium. He makes great fun of those preachers 'who speak Latin in French', who are for ever dividing, subdividing and paragraphing (so much for Bourdaloue!), and those who, to avoid appearing second rate, try to be lofty (so much for Fléchier, and perhaps also for Bossuet!). He recommends simplicity, no shoddy brilliance or affectation which is afraid to appeal to the

---

[1] 'I picture you', he wrote to Bossuet, 'in your skull-cap, holding M. du Pin as an eagle holds a frail sparrow-hawk in its talons.'

emotions; let the sermon even be passionate, but let it preserve grace, gentleness and harmony, seeking to convince rather than to terrify. His own sermons followed precisely these principles; the flow of the sentence and the persuasive force of the sentiments are in perfect accord, and a touch of lyricism gives life to the argument and softens down the erudition. Such a style of eloquence was rare in his time; it was the forerunner of the form popular today, and it earned for Fénelon the famous title Swan of Cambrai.

Fénelon's dominant position among the preachers of the Great Century was not, however, entirely due to his brilliant gifts. If it is true that the role of those who speak in God's name is to convey His judgment to men and to remind them of their baptismal vows, Fénelon above all others stands out as the living conscience of his era. Bourdaloue, Mascaron, Massillon, and Bossuet in a lesser degree, courageously denounced social evils and the positive failure of society to follow the precepts and spirit of the Gospel; but no one asked himself the question whether from the point of view of Christ's teaching the system of classical Christianity did not contain deficiencies and errors. Fénelon alone, at least among the higher clergy, dared to pass a Christian judgment upon the established order; and though he did not condemn it outright, he proposed measures which might have made it more Christian. He was affected by the profound crisis of his epoch, probably to a greater extent than Bossuet, because he was more prone to anguish of the spirit; he appreciated the necessity to overcome the disintegrating forces which threatened the structure of Christianity. But instead of fighting simply to defend and resist he struggled to build anew and to create. He looked as passionately to the future as his rival did to the past, and he asked himself what he should do to keep faith alive in a new kind of world. To achieve his purpose he looked to a young, daring and conquering form of Christianity such as he had acclaimed in that splendidly impetuous sermon on the Calling of the Gentiles—the religion of the Revolution of the Cross, which addresses itself to the heart.

There is something fascinating about Fénelon as a man. In Bossuet we admire his genius, his power, the unrivalled balance in his life and thought. Fénelon is nearer to ourselves. He is more prone to human frailty, is more apprehensive, more anxious and more delicate. At twenty-one years of age the young Bossuet solved his spiritual crisis by binding himself so completely to the demands of Christianity that he never again appeared to experience any painful spiritual conflict. Fénelon, on the other hand, spent his whole life searching for interior peace. He suffered in consequence of his contradictions. Psychologically he lacked balance: he vacillated between self-assurance and disgust of self, optimism and despair. This lordly archiepiscopal duke, owning a wealthy and beautiful diocese, was none the less unhappy within himself. If he appeared agreeable, kindly and charitable in the eyes of men, he knew that before God he was full of pride, hardness and selfishness, 'an abyss of subtle defects', and this knowledge over-whelmed him. He admitted moreover that he did not understand himself: 'I cannot explain my inner self. It escapes me, and appears to be for ever changing. I have no idea what I am.' It was a tragedy, and shows how vain and inadequate were the epithets 'tender, charming, refined, changeable, romantic' with which too many contemporaries have labelled him. It is sufficient, in any case, to study his portraits, especially those that show the pained and reticent expression of his old age, to appreciate that he was something more than the charmer who, as Saint-Simon said, 'was as careful to win over servants as he was their masters', a handsome man of such noble bearing 'that one had to make an effort to avoid looking at him'. He possessed gifts quite different from the 'finesse, grace, decorum and above all nobility' with which the curt memorialist credited him. His sensitiveness caused him suffering, his ardour provoked anguish of mind and his generosity made him imprudent. He was one of those rare and lofty souls who remain untouched by the temptation to act shabbily or to do any-thing for personal gain.

With these fascinating qualities went true genius, a profound and brilliant intellect that immediately and instinctively transformed every-thing it touched. Even in matters that did not necessarily concern an archbishop or even a preacher the attitude he adopted was always the right one, and yet original. For example, the ideas contained in his well-known treatise on the education of girls were so obviously sensible that we might be tempted to regard them as truisms were we to over-look the fact that they now form the basis of our modern teaching practice. He dealt similarly with the French language in his celebrated *Lettre à l'Académie*; he was far ahead of his time when he claimed that historical works should be critical, impartially written and supported by evidence. Unlike Bossuet, who condemned the theatre, he did not altogether disapprove of it; he discriminated between the good and the bad, and the future confirmed the justice of his attitude.

He excelled in almost every field. As a moralist he equalled Bour-daloue; in vision and the niceties of analysis he excelled Bossuet. As evidence of this we have his letters on indolence, on pride and the vanities of the world—all masterpieces of style, fluency and precision. He was an artist and a poet with a lively imagination, but above all he was impressed by the world's beauty—a rare quality in his day, especially among preachers—and very conscious of man's place within that world of beauty. He was much more of a philosopher and metaphysician than Bossuet: in his *Traité de l'existence de Dieu* he set forth brilliantly the traditional arguments and, as a good dialectician, criticized Malebranche forcefully though a little unjustly. A parish priest at Saint-Sulpice accused him of 'lacking theology', and others have repeated the charge; and the fact that his *Maximes des Saints* was condemned (in rather strange circumstances) [1] has caused some writers to pass a hasty judgment. They overlook the twenty or so works produced prior to the Quietist crisis, and which were never suspect. Those writings 'constitute a mass of mystic theology without precedent'; [2] and his *Dialogues sur le système de Jansenius* is perhaps the most lucid account ever produced of Jansenist doctrine, and contains its most convincing refutation. These works of Fénelon may not cover such a vast field as those of Bossuet, but in many respects they equal Bossuet's in quality. Fénelon lacked the capacity to give his thought that rigid, unbroken front which his rival achieved naturally; neither did he succeed in attaining internal unity and intellectual synthesis.

Under such conditions and with his temperament, his deficiencies and his reverses, how could his life be anything but exceptional, beautiful and sad, brilliant and, in a way, a failure? Cardinal Grente, one of his most impartial admirers, has pictured Fénelon 'attaining high honours at a single bound, where he shone and exerted an influence . . . then, at the summit of his hopes, his hand outstretched to seize the object of his ambitions, embarking upon a venture . . . encountering the Church's condemnation and the king's disfavour . . . meeting with disappointment . . . and finding consolation in magnificent self-sacrifice'. The human destiny of François de Salignac de la Mothe Fénelon was such that he rocketed to great heights, at great speed, and then crashed cruelly back to earth; but what complexity, what emotional and intellectual adventures, and what interior violence within the space of that unusual life!

Fénelon was born on 6th August 1651 at the Château de Fénelon. The earnest zeal with which the thirteen-year-old lad from Périgord attacked his classical studies at the college in Cahors, the zeal that developed and moulded the young seminarist at Saint-Sulpice under the direction of the ascetic M. Tronson, also bound the adult to the duties of chaplain to the *Nouvelles catholiques*, to the Protestant converts and potential converts and to the missions undertaken at the king's command in Aunis and Saintonge after the revocation of the Edict of Nantes. He never did anything by halves. Appointed tutor to the Dauphin's three sons he did not confine himself, as Bossuet had done in the case of their father, merely to giving them a correct education; he strove to make them (and especially the eldest, the difficult

---

[1] See Chapter VI, p. 392.
[2] François Varillon, whose book is quoted in the bibliographical notes.

Duc de Bourgogne) princes after the heart of God. Better still, he dreamed of making France, through the eldest, who would one day be king, a realm worthy of St Louis. It was the same urge that influenced his relations—imprudent though they were—with the Quietists; and he thought he recognized in the dubious Mme Guyon the messenger of the truth for which his soul thirsted. With the grace of a great nobleman he still remained absolutely loyal to her in her sorrow, even after his eyes had been opened. Then came the test. When he saw that the king was determined to destroy him [1] he most certainly knew that it was not solely on account of his religious theories; perhaps the great despot could not endure that Fénelon should see him with the eyes of a priest, and resented the archbishop's attempt to educate the heir to the throne in principles that refuted the errors of the régime. But Fénelon did nothing to soften the king's anger; he did not descend to flattery and grovelling. His heart was torn, but he reacted vigorously. Exiled to his diocese, he devoted himself with the same enthusiasm to his episcopal duties, dedicating himself to the best of his ability to the tasks God had entrusted to him. He proved himself capable of sublime charity in dealing with the miseries resulting from the War of the Spanish Succession, though something in his complex and inconsistent nature continued to draw him towards Versailles, to which he hoped to be recalled and restored. When the death of his pupil the Duc de Bourgogne destroyed his last illusions he buried himself in solitude, endless work and sadness. At the approach of death he at once abandoned grief and anguish, and his soul rose up sublime to face God's Providence. In his agony, on 7th January 1715, he murmured: 'I love Him more than I fear Him.'

Faith was the one stable factor, the very pivot of this eventful destiny and complex personality. Fénelon's faith was admirable; he was just as typical as Bossuet of the religion of an age when God was not 'dead'. His whole being teemed with faith: 'His very arguments were instinct with the spirit of adoration.' Faguet remarks that nothing could be more absurd than to see in Fénelon 'a sensitive and humanitarian philosopher, an apostle of tolerance, a friend of the people and a fore-runner of intellectual emancipation'. The proof of his faith can be seen in the austerity of his episcopal life, his unquenchable charity, the continual reference to the will of God which marks his thought and his uninterrupted devotion to God's cause. He certainly did not fight for that cause in the manner of Bossuet, but their goals were identical. His faith had not the monolithic character of his rival's; though it was not assailed by doubt it experienced the effects of his complex temperament. We must not imagine that these two men did not agree on the essential loyalty to tradition and submission to the Church, merely

[1] See Chapter VI, p. 389.

because they opposed each other on one point. They both professed adherence to fundamentals and to the exacting demands of Christian morality. 'Acts of magnanimity and all natural tenderness are simply a more refined, more alluring, more flattering, more pleasant, more diabolical form of self-interest. We must die unreservedly to all friendship.' Those were not Bossuet's words; neither were they written by Saint-Cyran or the great Arnauld. Fénelon addressed them to Mme de Maintenon, who was then his penitent. In so far as Quietism might be deemed synonymous with a sort of easy-going attitude, Fénelon was certainly no Quietist, despite serious errors in his use of words and a certain rashness of approach. But he saw his religion—whose demands he accepted—in the light of his own personal temperament; that is to say, with passion, gentleness and tenderness, with that utter confidence in God so well expressed in his last words. He was a true mystic; his was a soul for whom Christianity was not discipline, order and a system of precepts and institutions, but primarily adhesion, love, the offering of one's whole being to supreme love, an abandonment to the promises of the Redeemer, even to the harrowing consciousness of our own spiritual destitution. When so many saints and outstanding figures throughout the whole history of the Church have experienced this spiritual approach no one can reject the message of that great seventeenth-century trustee of the doctrine of 'Pure Love'.

Ultimately that is what gives Fénelon's genius its originality. Because this semi-invalid and zealot was able in his best moments to see everything from God's point of view, he discovered things which he was almost the only one to perceive. He towers over his era like a wild swan in flight. To so many problems that soon brought anguish to men's souls he put forward Christian solutions destined to prevent catastrophe. Fénelon the 'politician', a picture that delighted the eighteenth century, cannot be understood without Fénelon the mystic. When he wrote his *Télémaque*, a poetic tale in which he subtly sat in judgment on the world of his day; when he addressed his famous letter to the Duc de Chevreuse; [1] when, even more rashly, he composed the *Tables de Chaulnes*, he was denouncing the evils of the régime itself, the very evils that right-minded Christians condemned and which would eventually compass his own destruction. Louis XIV might well treat him as a 'visionary wit'; history has not proved Louis right. Fénelon was ahead of his time, a fact which after all explains his failure. His lucid genius enabled him not only to see the monstrosity of violence, the social injustice of his age, and the folly in the pomp of the Great Reign's ostentation, but also to discern what was unacceptable to a Christian in unlimited absolutism. From certain points of view he may have erred; to some extent he may have laid himself open to

[1] See Chapter IV, p. 192, note 1.

criticism by those who recognized in him a harbinger of the intellectual crisis which would shatter the traditional order of things.[1] None the less his is the most moving voice of that age.

9. THE REFORM IN JEOPARDY: RANCÉ

It is sufficient to mention such names as Bossuet, Fénelon, Bourdaloue and Massillon to show that the great tide that had its source in the Council of Trent a hundred years earlier was of a lasting nature despite the preponderant factor of classicism. In whatever field the Tridentine spirit had asserted itself that trend was to be found, less ebullient perhaps since it had undergone change, but more efficacious. The Church of France continued to furnish examples of the reforming and missionary spirit, but it was also still present in Italy, Spain, Poland and Austria.

Following the Council of Trent the most eminent agents of reform were the bishops, such as St Charles Borromeo, his disciples and imitators. They were more numerous immediately before and after 1600, giving example of the highest virtues, with St Francis de Sales at their head.[2] The 'Borromeans' too were still active: in Italy there was Blessed Gregorio Barbarigo whom we have mentioned as one of the great spiritual leaders of his time. From 1664 to 1697 he laboured in Padua and Bergamo. He was a remarkable bishop, anxious about the training of priests, continually visiting his flock, preaching, holding conferences and writing a great deal. In France several of the best bishops of the Great Century were still hard at work at the beginning of the personal rule of Louis XIV; e.g. Étienne de Vilazel at Saint-Brieuc, Pavillon at Alet and Vialart de Herse at Châlons-sur-Marne. The example given by Blessed Alain de Solminihac was continued by other splendid figures. Among them was Louis de Lascaris d'Urfè, Bishop of Limoges from 1676 to 1695, who wore himself out in pastoral visits, hearing confessions, presiding over synods and Church conferences; in short, he was a veritable hero of penance and charity. There was the austere Cardinal Le Camus, Bishop of Grenoble from 1671 to 1707, who turned what has been called 'France's sink of iniquity' into a well-ordered and healthy diocese. Le Camus has been referred to as the 'Rancé of the episcopate'.

Lascaris and Le Camus were nominated by Louis XIV, a fact which shows that the episcopate was not altogether bad during his reign. We have seen [3] that the king was careful in making such appointments.

[1] Intellectual posterity has been prejudicial to him, as frequently happens in the case of great thinkers. Rousseau's great admiration for Fénelon, of whom he said, 'If he were to return here below I should become his slave', has rendered him suspect.

[2] See Chapter II, p. 63.

[3] See Chapter IV, p. 198.

Not that all of them were as perfect; politics, blood ties, court influences and other less honourable reasons too often led to the appointment of bishops who should never have been in charge of a diocese. Courtier-bishops, who were more concerned with the intrigues of Versailles and the 'Journal of Benefices' [1] than with the needs of their dioceses, were still plentiful. Worse still, some of the bishops were also members of the nobility. They added the revenues of various abbeys to those of their diocese and kept a stately retinue; some had about thirty servants in livery, and they built those beautiful episcopal palaces that have survived to the present day. They were not necessarily bad men. François de Canisy, and Antoine de Charpin de Genétines who succeeded Louis de Lascaris d'Urfè in Limoges, were typical of the bishops who were members of the nobility but were also good administrators and even reformers. Naturally there were politicians among them of doubtful morals, such as Harlay de Champvallon, and some absurdly conceited, e.g. Clermont-Tonnerre and others. Some of them were excellent: Bossuet of Meaux, Fénelon of Cambrai, Massillon who was so popular in Clermont, Fléchier of Lavaur and subsequently of Nîmes, Mascaron of Tulle and later of Agen; all these were beyond criticism. We even have examples of outstanding episcopal virtues: Claude Joly, Bishop of Agen, Louis d'Estaing, Bishop of Clermont-Ferrand, Gabriel de Roquette, Bishop of Autun. At Besançon Antoine-Pierre de Grammont worked valiantly for the restoration of a tumble-down diocese; Jean d'Aranthon d'Alex did better still in Annecy. Tournai, which was then French territory, had the stern Choiseul, while Gap from 1706 onwards had Berger de Malissoles, the 'Saint of the Alps', who visited every parish once a year and five times refused to leave his impoverished diocese for a more wealthy one. We cannot overstress the important part played by those sterling bishops, who were wisely allowed to remain a long time in the same Sees and thus maintained the solid structure of the Church. This was true not only of France but of all the great Catholic countries. A body of excellent

---

[1] The 'Journal of Benefices' was the object of lively rivalry on account of the financial rewards involved. The incumbents of 'dirty' bishoprics were envious of those who were well endowed. We have the evidence of François Hébert, priest of the 'royal parish' at Versailles from 1686 to 1704. No one in France had a better opportunity to observe intrigues, and he wrote of them in his *Mémoires*: 'It is astonishing to see bishops indulging in the kind of luxury one would condemn in a woman. Their retinue and their furniture were affected by the depravity of the age. . . . It was this habit of luxury which prompted some of them to secure transfer to sees that offered a greater income than the one they began with; and these changes were continually taking place because everyone desired a better table, a larger number of servants, more of life's amenities. . . . A number of bishops rarely resided within their dioceses because, in their eagerness to become richer, they would do anything to achieve their aim. Not only were they subservient to the king, but they would woo courtiers whom they knew to be in favour, and worse still they paid attention to ladies whose morals they should have reproved had they been inclined to do their duty.'

bishops laboured in Spain; among them Severo Tomas in Gerona, Pascual d'Aragona in Toledo, Estrado de Marroqui in Palencia, and Jaime Cordone, who introduced the devotion to the Sacred Heart into his diocese and whom his flock called 'Father of the Poor'.

Slowly the clergy improved, thanks to the perseverance of many bishops. But corrupt practices still existed, and we have only to glance at the record of some of the seniors to form a fairly dismal picture of the state of the lower clergy. Claude Joly of Agen had to order his priests under pain of excommunication to wear the tonsure and sou-tane, to reside in their parishes, to hear confessions and say Mass correctly, to teach the Catechism and refrain from visiting taverns. These facts speak volumes for the obstinate persistence of such evil practices. Many other bishops were obliged to issue similar instruc-tions, among them Roquette of Autun and Le Camus of Grenoble. The same kind of thing was happening in Gratz, Barcelona and Florence, while the Patriarch of Venice was compelled to issue a directive governing the participation of clerics in the carnival celebra-tions. But the situation was nothing new, and the subject requires no special emphasis.

Despite these obvious defects the mass of the clergy remained a vital force during the Great Century. On the whole it preserved its prestige and authority. The number of priests was still large and there was no shortage of vocations. All rural parishes had a priest in charge and a vicar; in the towns the parish priest had two or three assistants and a whole body of approved auxiliaries, unbeneficed priests and chaplains in charge of confraternities. Not every priest in this motley collection was a happy choice, but the efforts made since Trent—reinforced by Bérulle, St Vincent de Paul, Olier and others—to train priests and make them true to the 'sacerdotal ideal', had unquestionably born fruit. In some respects the classical mind seemed most perfectly reflected in the priests. There emerged, as Bishop Calvet said, 'a priestly type, grave, temperate, of exemplary behaviour and good sense, wedded to order and uniformity', a type which Jansenism would eventually confine within the rigidity of its doctrine and practice, and even of dress. No doubt such men were rightly blamed for their lack of originality and for not leaving enough room in religion for 'the folly of the Cross'; but the really important fact is that those priests, many of whom were heroically virtuous, reacted against the bad old ways of spiritual laxity.

By degrees the movement to establish seminaries either on the Tridentine or French model gained ground. When Bishop de Choiseul was entrusted with the diocese of Tournai, after the territory became French, his first care was to found a seminary. Cardinal de Fürstenberg did likewise in Strasburg when France took over the province. Cardinal

Le Camus made it one of his first duties to find sound directors for his seminary; and Bishop de Roquette eagerly set about building one. Many were the bishops who called on the Lazarists and especially the Sulpicians to assist in the training of their young students for the priest-hood.[1] Numerous seminaries began to operate in Italy—at San Miniato near Florence, in Andria, Pistoia, Lareno, San Severo, Catania and Naples. Cavalieri, Vicar-General to Cardinal Orsini and a zealous Dominican, introduced the French type of seminary into Spoleto, Cesena and Benevento, where future clerics remained longer and did not mix with lay students. In German territory seminaries were opened at Würtzburg and Ratisbon; the same was done at Brixen, Breslau, Vienna, Olmutz, Prague, and in Switzerland at Freiburg. Original foundations should also be mentioned, for even where official seminaries existed private ones were also established. Among these was the Trente-Mois, which owed its existence to the generosity of the holy priest Claude Bernard. Others were the Presbytery Schools of Pierre Crestoy (1622–1703), parish priest (from 1678) of Barenton in Normandy. They were real country seminaries. The most remark-able of such institutions was that of Claude Poullard des Places (1679–1709), whose aim was to attract to the priesthood young men from the poorest classes. His Séminaire du Saint-Esprit (1702) provided the Church of France with a body of vicars for the poorer districts; they were called 'Bouics' from the name of his first successor. These seminaries also provided men of devotion and courage for the most difficult missionary work in pagan lands.[2]

The facts were there to demonstrate the eventual results of these patient efforts, especially in the opposition put up by the general mass of the clergy during the eighteenth century to the forces of unbelief, and the courage shown by the French clergy during the Revolution. Moreover, notable figures stand out from the vast number of good and saintly priests whose names are forgotten. Before Claude Joly became Bishop and Count of Agen he was an excellent parish priest at Saint-Nicolas-des-Champs in Paris; and courageous too, for he dared to tell the Duchesse de Noailles to supervise the conduct of the ladies of honour at court when they came under the eye of young Louis XIV. At Saint-Sulpice, Baudrand de Lacombe, M. Olier's biographer, and

---

[1] It must be emphasized, however, that it was not yet obligatory in all dioceses for students to pass through a seminary. Where it was the rule, the period of training varied from four to eighteen months. The seminarists paid for their board and lodging, but those who were too poor were allowed to do their own cooking, and they could go into the town to buy provisions. The quality of the buildings varied a great deal. In some cases they were set up in disused inns. Ordinary laymen were generally permitted to join the classes with the seminarists, and in any case to attend divine service with them. One of the rules of the seminary at Coutances provided for a student to take over the duty of 'driving away dogs and keeping beggars quiet' during Mass.

[2] See *The Church in the Eighteenth Century*, Chapter II.

La Chétardye, who refused the bishopric of Poitiers in order to remain a parish priest, were other fine examples. Every great Catholic country had its own exemplary priests. Regarding them as a whole we might be justified in taking an optimistic view, but they were badly paid and often despised by the higher clergy, with the result that there developed a social consciousness and a tendency towards dogmatism and insistence on their demands. When therefore the Jansenist crisis occurred the movement assumed considerable importance—a veritable 'Catholic Presbyterianism' which drew its arguments from Richer. The movement found a champion in the facetious Abbé Jacques Boileau (who said he wrote in Latin so that the bishops might not understand!). By 1700 it was powerful enough to send to the astonished Bishop of Chartres a well-considered document inviting him to recognize in priests the same spiritual powers possessed by the bishops—a sign of grave and dramatic antagonism ahead.

The position was also favourable in the religious Orders and congregations, but much depended upon circumstances. Generally speaking institutions dating back to the sixteenth century or the early part of the seventeenth remained efficient forces in the service of the Tridentine ideal. The Jesuits were still a powerful influence; they were made the subject of official inquiries, calumniated and even persecuted in some areas; in others they were praised to the skies, and continued all powerful. They constituted the *élite* of the priesthood in every Catholic state, acting as confessors to princes and spiritual directors to countless souls. In 1701 they became publicists and journalists by founding the famous *Mémoires de Trévoux*. All the Generals one after another were excellent men: the German Nickel, the Genoese Oliva, the Spaniard Tirso Gonzalez and the Milanese Tamburini. Despite a little friction resulting from Probabilism, the Society of Jesus, eighteen thousand strong, remained a bulwark of the Church—as Voltaire would find out. The Capuchins were not so far up in the scale, and were therefore less open to suspicion. Their growth was extraordinary: by about 1700 they numbered thirty thousand members, had eighteen hundred houses, and were to be seen everywhere. It was they who maintained the great Franciscan tradition at its liveliest.

Recent institutions were less numerous, but they retained the bloom of youth. Bérulle and his Oratory were much talked about, mainly on account of Mascaron, Massillon and Malebranche, and the Jansenist affair in which the Oratory was somewhat compromised; all of which proves that it exercised a considerable spiritual influence. The progress of the Lazarists continued: 'Bestowed upon all, dear to all', runs an inscription on the tomb of one of them in Warsaw. The wise Matthieu Beuvelet, who strove to improve the organization of M. Bourdoise's

K

congregation, was superior at Saint-Nicolas-du-Chardonnet. As for Saint-Sulpice, its renown as a source of seminary teachers was assured. Numerous dioceses asked for Sulpicians; in Canada they were the 'Lords of Montreal', and they gave the country that sound body of priests which it has had ever since. The glory of the Congregation at that time was Louis Tronson (1622–1700)—'Monsieur Tronson'. He was the third Superior-General and truly representative of its spirit; a corpulent but ascetic man who resigned an attractive post as chaplain to the king, and later refused a bishopric, to dedicate his life to the training of priests. His book *Examens Particuliers* (1690) was the offspring of a fervent soul and long experience as seminary director. The book has remained a classic; some of its precepts may cause a smile, but the high quality of the writing, its delicacy of analysis and its common sense make it an undisputed masterpiece in the training of priests.[1]

Less satisfactory were conditions among the priests and nuns of the old religious Orders. No doubt Bossuet was thinking of them when he wrote to the abbot of La Trappe: 'The Church's affairs are in a very bad state . . .' The *in commendam* principle governing the revenues of unoccupied benefices was still in force, and not even the best people— among them Bossuet, who derived benefit from the custom—found fault with it. We have seen the disastrous effects resulting from the system, which hampered the efforts for reform made during the preceding period. The behaviour of some communities was conspicuously scandalous; the Benedictine nuns at Metz dispensed entirely with communal fasting and took turns, one at a time, to carry out the fast for all the rest. During carnival time they dressed up their porters and gardeners in their own habits. The sons of St Bernard got rid of the *Histoire générale de la réforme de Cîteaux* from their libraries, because the work laid bare their vices. The Franciscans and Dominicans were hardly better. However, it is unnecessary to stress these known facts.

Furthermore, in one way and another relations between the Regulars and the hierarchy were bad: often because of a clash of interests. 'There would be greater spiritual independence', said Fénelon, 'if there were no material interests at stake.' But the discord was also due to the fact that so many religious of all Orders had lost their sense of discipline. Strife broke out at every opportunity: in France, in Italy, and even in Poland, where an incident involving the abbey of Andrezejow caused a riot, and in the Low Countries, where a group of Benedictines were in open conflict with all the bishops of the country.

Notwithstanding this picture of decadence there were some encouraging exceptions. In every sphere of religious life attempts at reform

[1] Jean Gautier has furnished an excellent portrait of M. Tronson in *Ces Messieurs de Saint-Sulpice.*

met with a measure of success; nowhere, however, was the fundamental issue faced squarely: that is to say, whether the organization of the regular clergy really corresponded with 'the needs of an age when the social structure was so varied and centralized State control predominated'.[1] In France that question would be put bluntly in 1765 by the public authority.[2] The French Benedictine congregation of Saint-Maur, made famous by Mabillon, was beyond reproach, and a revival was under way at Reichenbach and at Michelfeld in Bavaria. Not all Benedictine nuns by any means resembled those at Metz, who gave so much trouble to the Archdeacon Bossuet. At Faremoutiers, for instance, one of the two oldest convents in France, a splendid spiritual revival developed under the direction of two successive abbesses whose lives were models of holiness. The Carthusians were scarcely affected by the decline. Their Superior-General Dom Innocent Le Masson published an excellent guide to mental prayer in 1695, and he managed the Order with a firm hand. Father Samaniego, General of the Friars Minor, strove bravely to lead the Franciscans back to discipline and observance of the Rule. Among the Dominicans the man who so magnificently embodied the ideal of the reform was Father Antonin Cloche, a lean Gascon from Saint-Sever, who was elected Master-General in 1686. He spent no more than five hours a night in sleep and ate once a day; he travelled continuously, preaching, reviving missions among the people and doing his best to prevent the purchase of titles or their bestowal upon favourites. 'The face of the Order has changed', he frequently complained; 'its beauty is declining, souls are perishing, and I am afraid God will call us to account for it.' He was one of those who did not resign themselves to the unhappy situation.

Among the numerous reformers of the Great Century Jean Le Bouthellier de Rancé has an undeniable claim to recognition. His was a strange destiny, as romantic as anyone could wish. His name will always be associated with La Trappe, one of the most original spiritual families in the history of the Church; a family which suggests to the uninitiated the most exacting form of Christian experience and one somewhat contrary to nature.[3]

On 28th April 1657 Jean Le Bouthellier called at the city residence of the Montbazons, with whom he was on familiar terms. It was early in the morning, for he had been worried about the health of the *duchesse* for several days. On the steps he met M. de Soubise, who exclaimed: 'It is finished; the play has ended.' Le Bouthellier collapsed with grief on the stone steps, making no attempt to hide his feelings.

[1] E. Préclin.
[2] See *The Church in the Eighteenth Century*, Chapter IV.
[3] The French word *trappe* also means 'trap' and 'trap-door', and is therefore liable to create the idea of a trap into which a man may fall and disappear for ever.

He was a handsome young man of thirty-one, of brilliant intellect and such wide culture that at fifteen years of age he had published a translation of Anacreon. He was of a violent, impulsive disposition and inclined to extremes in everything. Bremond called him 'the thundering abbot'. He had already had a dazzling career in the Church; partly through his father's influence and partly through the kindness of Richelieu, his godfather, ecclesiastical benefices had been piling up for him ever since he was eleven. He was a canon of Notre Dame at Paris, chaplain to the King, abbot of Saint-Symphorien-Lès-Beauvais, of La Trappe, of Notre-Dame du Val, of Saint-Clementin in Poitou, and prior of Boulogne—an amazing achievement, but such was the custom of the age.

When he rose from the steps he went to pray beside the dead body of the woman whom he loved tenderly as a friend rather than as one of his penitents. He spent the whole of the following summer in one of his castles examining his conscience and writing down his thoughts. Had God sent him upon earth to be a worldly priest intent on cultivating useful connections, surrounded by lackeys, enjoying the pleasures of the hunt and his magnificent carriages? He went through a heartrending spiritual crisis. God seemed to speak to him and reproach him so severely that the deep repentance he felt never afterwards left him. He determined to be as lavish in his penances as he had been in worldly enjoyments. The priests of the Oratory, Pavillon and the austere Bishop of Alet, all set him on the right path, and he determined to follow it to the end.

He suddenly relinquished all his livings: of his titles he retained only that of abbot of La Trappe. The Cistercian abbey of La Trappe was in the diocese of Séez, in Normandy. Like most monasteries of White Monks, it had badly deteriorated. The walls were cracked, the ground overrun with brambles; of the two hundred monks who had once dwelt there only six remained, and they lived like poachers, or rather like thieves. Rancé, the commendatory abbot, set to work; he decided to reform that wretched community and restore life to La Trappe. If it were God's will a salutary influence would spread from this restored community to the others, perhaps even to the whole Order of St Bernard.

He had to face strain and stress, and even danger, for the six ruffianly monks were capable of using dagger and poison. But 'the thundering abbot' held his own. He succeeded in replacing the reprobates by Cistercians of the strict observance, who followed his way of life. Moreover, throughout the Order everyone became seriously disturbed by the prevalence of unseemly ways. Eustache de Beaufort reformed Sept-Fons, near Moulins, with Rancé as its leader. But attempts by the abbot of La Trappe to impose a more strict observance upon every monastery were unsuccessful; the 'mitigated' opposed him, and even won over the authorities at Rome. Rancé was not distressed; he would be satisfied if La Trappe became the only community in which God would be served by a life of penance, and his example must prove contagious. After all, everything seemed to show that he was right: vocations were numerous, and often quite surprising—a former sea-faring man, an unfrocked priest, the ex-provost marshal of Touraine and so on.

It was the spirit of penance that drew them all to La Trappe—the same spirit that took others to Port-Royal. Rancé progressed passion-ately along the path of renunciation, as it was in his nature to do. He did without fish, eggs, butter and wine; he gave up sleeping on his straw mattress. The monks were no longer allowed to leave the monastery; they maintained perpetual silence; their lives were governed by the singing of the Office day and night and the carrying out of heavy manual work. To what limits would the spirit of penance lead this great and terrible abbot? The ordeal of singing the Psalms standing barefooted on the icy flagstones for ten or twelve hours at a time seemed natural to him. But it undoubtedly proved too much, and he had to slacken a little in face of protests and an increase in the number of sick. La Trappe became, however, the very home of penance, a model of renunciation carried to the limits of human endurance. Innocent XI approved the reformed Rule in 1678, and La Trappe became foremost of all the monasteries of St Bernard in striving to renounce their former laxity and adhere to strict observance. So it has remained to the present day.

It has often been said of Rancé, in his own time and since, that his behaviour was immoderate. It is true that some of the hardships practised in various Trappist monasteries were beyond the limits envisaged by the kindly St Bernard. It is equally certain that Rancé's scorn for the parading of intellectual pursuits, an attitude that brought about his violent quarrel with Mabillon [1] and Le Masson, was very different from the attitude of him who had declared that it was 'not becoming for the spouse of Christ to be illiterate'. But it is remarkable that in a century so obviously worldly and frivolous so many souls turned to La Trappe as to a haven of salvation; that so many penitents from court and city should have approached the abbot for guidance in the leading of better lives. One may argue about Rancé, but there is not the slightest doubt that when he died in 1700 one of the great spiritual lights of his time was extinguished.[2]

[1] See *The Church in the Eighteenth Century*, Chapter I.

[2] In connection with the movement towards reform we must mention a Benedictine community set up by Peter Mekhitar, an Armenian who came over to Catholicism from the Greek Orthodox Church. He was driven from Greece by the Turks, and he and his brethren settled in Venice. The monastery of Saint Lazarus near Venice still houses the 'Mekitarists'. The community also has a branch in Vienna and another in Trieste.

10. CHARITY: THE MISSION: ST GRIGNION DE MONTFORT

The spirit of revival in evidence during the first half of the century was just as decisively concerned with charity and the apostolate as it was with reform. But what was its position during the classical age? Here again we should not speak of an eclipse, but rather of a slowing down of creative effort. St Vincent de Paul was no longer on the scene, but his lessons continued to bear fruit.

The spirit of charity was not wanting during the Great Century. Preachers extolled the virtue in stirring accents. The mystery of the poor (their 'eminent dignity', to use Bossuet's phrase) and the duty of the rich to give alms were frequent subjects of sermons. 'When God made the rich', said Fléchier, 'His purpose was to make them charitable. He chose them to be the instruments of His goodness, the channels along which flow His exterior graces within the Church. He imposes upon them a command and a necessity, not merely a counsel.' And Bourdaloue exclaimed: 'Why are you rich unless it be for the sake of the poor?' It was not a case of finding a subject for eloquent oratory. Many of those who listened to these admonitions put into practice the precepts they learned, and the example came from those in high places. When members of the nobility died they bequeathed their property to the poor; organizations, such as the Apostolic Association to which we have referred, recruited its members from among the wealthy classes, and continued the charitable work of the Company of the Blessed Sacrament. For half a century laymen had become more and more aware of their responsibilities in relation to charity, and works undertaken by saintly people tended to become organized and formed part of definite charitable enterprises. Governments co-operated with the Church towards the same end. More and more hospitals and hostels were established. To the General Hospital in Paris were added the Val-de-Grâce and Les Invalides. Throughout the French provinces twenty-seven hospitals were opened between 1661 and 1715, in addition to those built during the preceding period. In the territories conquered by the Great King the bishops usually opened a hospital as soon as they took over the administration of their dioceses; e.g. Bishop Choiseul at Tournai. Italy and Austria did likewise. Three hospitals were built at Turin, two at Milan, two at Venice and four at Vienna.

All the religious Orders dedicated to charity prospered; this was partly due to the decline of the mystics, for the contemplative Orders lost recruits to the advantage of active institutions. The splendid community of the Sisters of Charity began to develop at this period.[1] The Brothers of St John of God—*Fate bene fratelli*[2]—were also

---

[1] See Chapter I, p. 33 et seq.   [2] See Chapter II, p. 92.

expanding rapidly; in France, Italy, Spain and even in Spanish America their houses multiplied. Their hospital in Rome, built on an island in the Tiber, was continually enlarged. The various Charité hospitals in Paris and in the French provinces experienced the same growth. The Brothers even established small hospitals in country districts run by a brother who was a doctor. The Camillians undertook similar work. All the female Orders and communities devoted to charity were developing rapidly. New ones were founded with specific vocations: refuges for fallen women were opened at Besançon, and institutions for Protestant converts and the *Nouvelles catholiques*, to which the Sisters of Christian Union were dedicated. Founded by Vachet and his sister Mlle de Crézé, they opened eighteen houses in ten years. Prisoners, convicts, condemned criminals for whom the heart of Monsieur Vincent had bled—none was forgotten. Few people know that in Italy the great scholar Muratori devoted all the hours he could spare from his library work to those poor outcasts. Mercedarians, Trinitarians and, of course, Lazarists were ever mindful of the fate of those unfortunate people, and the first two institutions established in Spain strove heroically to ransom those who suffered in the Berber prisons. The former Hospitallers of St John of Jerusalem, henceforward known as the Knights of Malta, experienced a revival and returned to their traditional role.

The charity of Christ was not dead. There was certainly too much dissipation of effort and too little organization, resulting in reduced efficiency; but the effort was none the less splendid.

The Mission, which was one of the flowers that blossomed during the Great Century,[1] continued to thrive, though less vigorously than in the time of Monsieur Vincent. Of the old team St John Eudes still remained, and continued to wear himself out during the first twenty years of the personal rule of Louis XIV. The indefatigable Father Maunoir worked on in Brittany until 1683. A way had been found to kindle the spiritual flame in souls; the best bishops were adopting it systematically and establishing numerous diocesan missions. Antoine Pierre de Grammont, Archbishop of Besançon, entrusted the Josephites with a mission to Lyons that lasted two months. He organized in all about a hundred, which were undertaken by Capuchins, Jesuits, Oratorians, Benedictines and a group of secular priests 'whose work in the Lord's vineyard', he said, 'was very fruitful'. At Limoges, Louis de Lascaris d'Urfé sent for Father Honoré, a Capuchin from Cannes, who had preached no fewer than three hundred missions and was therefore an expert. Every important Order and community took part in this great work: the Lazarists with Father Planat, apostle of Auvergne, and Father Bonal, a pioneer from Rouergue; the Capuchins with Father Séraphin of Paris; the Jesuits with Father de Lingendes and

---

[1] See Chapter II, p. 86.

Father de la Colombière, a champion of devotion to the Sacred Heart. René Lévêque added to their number his Compagnie des Piétistes de Saint-Clément.

It is a remarkable fact that the idea of the mission spread from France to the great Catholic countries. In Italy its unflagging leader was the Jesuit Father Paolo Segneri, the most famous preacher of his day. There was not a province in the country where he did not preach missions between 1665 and 1692. After his death his cousin and friend Father Segneri the younger and father Pinamonti continued his work. In southern Italy, which suffered great distress, Father Cristofarini laboured in the Abruzzi, and the ascetic Father Ansalone battled for forty years against the vices of Naples. Father Francisco de Geronimo, another Jesuit, also preached in Naples. To assist him he established two lay communities known respectively as the 'Two Hundred' and the 'Seventy-two', the latter working in secret. All these great Italian missioners were extraordinary men: they used the discipline in public, preached in the streets, in the squares and before the theatres; they engaged in violent debate with their opponents and called a spade a spade, railing against sin in holy anger. They were true men of action. It is said that during Father de Geronimo's missions he made between one hundred and five hundred converts yearly.

The mission also progressed in Spain, but it was less vigorous and less spectacular. Father Tirso Gonzalez was a remarkable missioner before being elected General of the Society of Jesus. So was the famous Portuguese preacher Antonio Vieira; he preached a 'Station' at the court and journeyed to the West Indies. The missions multiplied in Germany. The Jesuit Father Schacht laboured in Hamburg, Jemingen in the south, Ampferle in Breisgau, Scheffler in Silesia; the Capuchins Prokop von Templin and Martin von Cochem were the apostles of the Rhineland. Bishop Fürstenberg of Paderborn left nearly 100,000 thalers on his death to finance missionary work. It would be impossible to overestimate the importance of this great kneading of the dough of Christianity. It was thanks to the missions that the canton of Valais was restored, and that the greater part of the Helvetic canton of Thurgau returned to Catholicism. Protestantism was repelled in Hungary through the missionary activities of Father Stankoviez and Bishop Erdoddy.

Towards the end of the seventeenth century and in the early part of the eighteenth Louis Marie Grignion de Montfort was the embodiment of the missionary spirit as well as of the spirit of charity and penance. He was a man of vast energy and a great saint. He stood aloof from his time, a sort of misfit in the religious life around him, utterly outside the austere and rather uniform pattern of the existing priestly ideal. We might say he was an eccentric; but there have been many such in

the Church who have none the less played an important role. St Philip
Neri was one; St Francis of Assisi another. Let us say that our saint
was 'mad about God'. Everything we know of him through reliable
witnesses suggests that he was a strange figure, a ragged and penniless
priest who begged his bread and proclaimed his poverty as others
display their wealth. He was a wonder-worker who healed the sick by
laying his hands upon them. He had experience of spectacular and
mysterious occurrences: good and bad angels fought for possession of
the sinful soul of a dying man, and not without coming to blows. To
demonstrate the meaning of charity he would kiss the purulent sores
of the sick, as Catherine of Siena had done. Most certainly all holiness
is not necessarily expressed in actions of that kind, but they are a
manifestation of holiness. Indeed, it was not a bad thing to remind
Christians of the Great Century that the ethics of the Beatitudes are
not identical with those of human wisdom, and that no scandal ever
shocked more than the scandal of the Cross.

Louis Marie Grignion was of Breton stock, Montfort being a village
of the old diocese of Saint-Malo. His father was a briefless barrister
who had great difficulty in bringing up his eighteen children. When the
future saint, whose piety had astonished his masters in the Jesuit school
at Rennes, decided to go to Paris to study for the priesthood, he had
nothing approaching the 300 *livres* necessary at that time to enter a
seminary, and had to depend upon the generosity of some good friends.
Thanks to them he was admitted to the annexe of Saint-Sulpice, where
M. de la Baroudière accepted the sons of poor families. He was then
twenty years of age, having been born in 1673, and was already well
known for the strangeness of his behaviour, the violence of his penances
and his thirst for humiliation. This young John the Baptist's continual
talk of the Holy Ghost and the end of the world caused a smile at
Saint-Sulpice; he was more severe than a Jansenist and had more
devotion to Our Lady than a Jesuit. Some strange tales were current
about him. Once when he accompanied one of his superiors who had
business with a bank, he was found on his knees in the main office
among the employees and servants, praying without paying the
slightest attention to those around him.

Louis Marie was ordained priest in 1700, and was invited to Nantes
by the aged René Lévêque, whose Compagnie des Piétistes de Saint-
Clément emulated the Lazarists in preaching missions in country
districts. He went about preaching everywhere, and met with success;
but his manner did not please the traditionalists. Ten months later
Bishop Girard, who surmised what good a priest of his type might
achieve in the denser parts of Poitiers, invited him to that city. Louis
Marie Grignion roused the people so effectually that the bishop
entrusted him with the chaplaincy of the hospital. It was a badly run

* K

hospital, lacking in generosity and the spirit of dedication; it therefore provided the saint with his first opportunity to exert his influence. He found the sick neglected, and the nurses, who were lay folk, were wanting in discipline. The new chaplain took this chaotic little world in hand. A wonderful and pious idea occurred to him: he decided to associate the sick with the running of the establishment, especially from the spiritual point of view. He elaborated his plan, and formed his willing helpers into a congregation. He gathered his 'daughters' together in a large ward, in the centre of which he stood a cross—he called it the Hall of Wisdom—and he made them recite the Office as nuns do. News of what he was doing spread around the city. The daughter of Trichet, a public attorney of the presidial court, offered to help him; she left the world and donned an ashen-grey woollen habit, taking the name of Marie-Louise de Jésus. The squalid hospital became a model of cleanliness and the Daughters of Wisdom were founded. The saint achieved all this in five years. The community was very small, but today it numbers more than five thousand members.

These achievements were merely a beginning, enabling him to lay the foundations of his work. The hospital at Poitiers no longer needed him, but the peasants, whose faith was threatened, were waiting. Louis Marie Grignion was grieved, as Monsieur Vincent had been, to find that the spirit of the Gospel no longer lived among the country people. Armed with his rosary and a great crucifix, which he held above his head as though for protection, he set out to give his missions. He preached, erected Stations of the Cross and rebuilt churches. Soon he was in demand almost everywhere in Brittany and Normandy, and even beyond. From Saint-Malo he went to Saintes, from Saint-Brieuc to Coutances and La Rochelle. Enormous crowds gathered when he spoke, and he brought tears to their eyes when he talked to them of their misfortunes and Christ crucified. Many were the cities, market-towns and villages through which this tall, thin man passed in his ragged soutane. Many were the crowds that succumbed to the magic of this unattractive orator with gaunt face, large mouth and stubby nose; but his eyes shone, and his voice penetrated to the depths of their conscience. He was also a great walker, trekked everywhere, and made pilgrimages to many shrines including those of Notre-Dame des Ardilliers and Chartres.

His charity became a byword. It is said that while a seminarist at Saint-Sulpice he used to call on the servants of nobles and teach them the catechism. When he was working at his hospital in Poitiers everyone in the city had seen him sauntering along the streets and roaming around the markets leading a donkey carrying baskets for the food he begged. One day, when he came across two swordsmen about to fight a duel, he threw himself between them, grasping the murderous blades in both hands. On another occasion he found some dandies importuning young laundresses; removing the discipline which he always carried attached to his belt, he made such good use of it on their backs that they ran away. His idea of charity obviously did not exclude the use of violence! All sorts of stories were current about him. He even found his way into houses that were so unsparing in their hospitality that it would have been regarded as most unseemly for a priest to be seen there; yet he compelled the guests to leave by talking to them of the salvation of their souls.

His method of saving souls was one of which the authorities did not always approve without some hesitation; at least not until a long time afterwards, when he was canonized. One after another the bishops, even those who had welcomed him to their dioceses, concluded that he went too far. 'If wisdom consists in undertaking nothing new for God and in not getting oneself talked about, the apostles made a great mistake when they left Jerusalem; in any case, St Paul should not have travelled so much, nor should St Peter have set up the Cross on the Capitol.' That is indeed the language of Christian truth; but this difference of opinion gave rise to a great deal of discord from which Louis Marie Grignion drew supernatural lessons: 'More than ever am I impoverished, crucified, humiliated; men and devils wage a sweet and agreeable war against me. Let them calumniate me, mock me, tear my reputation to pieces and cast me into prison, for these are precious gifts; to me they are dainty dishes. Oh, when shall I be crucified and dead to the world?' Most certainly he had no rule of life but the 'folly' of the Cross.

Such was the nature of his strong and original spirituality. As a student of Olier and Tronson, a voracious reader of Boudon, and 'Bérullian' in outlook, Louis Marie Grignion added new material to what he had received from his predecessors, and that material was drawn from his personal experience. He declared that one must 'empty oneself of self' and 'adhere to God', as his teachers had said. He demanded of those who listened to him that they 'cleave to God' and practise a 'holy slavery'. This great ascetic was a mystic who instinctively reconciled both tendencies. He was a belated defender of the principle of 'pure love'. Furthermore, Jansenists and their supporters held him in great contempt. But this paradoxical saint, who attempted to manage the world, wished to emphasize one important fact above all others: God's wisdom in what to men is foolishness, the sublime absurdity that is the sole legitimate end of the Christian. His remarkable book entitled *Amour de la Sagesse éternelle* reiterates this principle, 'the placing of all wisdom in the wounds of Christ', the preaching of Christ humiliated, despised and crucified, and nothing else. His entirely Pauline and Augustinian doctrine compensated for the occasional too human element in the Christocentrism of the seventeenth century. His teaching, however, did not cease to address itself to men's hearts; for Louis Marie Grignion not only pointed to the end, he offered the means to attain it: recourse to Mary, the sweet Mother, the mediatrix of grace; and such was the purpose of his moving *Traité de la vraie dévotion à la Sainte Vierge*.

However, this wholly dedicated life exhausted him. His work had prospered despite every difficulty. He went to Rome—on foot, of course—where his efforts won approval, and he was given the title of 'Apostolic Missioner', a term made famous in the past by Jacques de Vitry. So many people came forward to help him that he was able to found a community of priests destined for the mission fields, of which he had dreamed since his early years as a priest. In 1712 he founded the Company of Mary or Missionaries of Mary, who carried on and expanded his apostolate of the countryside. Around them he gathered a group of fellow workers, originally laymen, under the name of Brothers of the Holy Ghost.[1] He allotted them the task of educating the children of the poor, for he was as much concerned with the problem of training the young as with the apostolate. Shortly before his death he sent Sister Marie-Louise de Jésus to open a school at La Rochelle for the daughters of working-class families. But he had worn himself out at an early age by his ascetic life and his superhuman efforts. In 1716, at the age of forty-three, he went peacefully to God.

The Great King had died shortly before, and with the Regency began an era in which Christianity rapidly disintegrated. St Louis Marie Grignion de Montfort foresaw more than anyone else the march of events leading to that circumstance. He was the prophet of those latter days, the Jeremias of the dying seventeenth century, and with all his strength he shouted his warnings in moving words: 'Remember, Lord. Now is the time to fulfil Your promise. Your divine law has been transgressed, Your Gospel slighted, Your religion rejected; torrents of iniquity flood the earth and there is abomination even in the holy places. Will You remain silent for ever? I appeal to You through Your Mother. Remember her compassion and do not cast me aside. Rise up, Lord, in Your mercy.'

Such was the last witness whom the Great Century had to offer of its faith, its torments and its hopes. The important point is that this barefooted priest, so foolish in the sight of men, but so holy before God, had little or nothing in common with the traditional conception of the 'classical Christian'.

---

[1] In 1835 they were reorganized as a separate congregation by Father Deshayes, who called them Brothers of St Gabriel.

11. CHRISTIAN EDUCATION: FROM CHARLES DÉMIA TO ST JEAN-BAPTISTE DE LA SALLE

St Louis Marie Grignion was not alone in his anxiety for the education of children: he shared his concern with a number of contemporaries. One, of course, was Monsieur Vincent, whose saintly followers, led by Marguerite Naseau, became teachers;[1] equally concerned were M. Bourdoise, Pierre Fourier,[2] the Jesuits, the Oratorians, the Ursulines and many others. The education of the young remained one of the major cares of society in the seventeenth century. That concern, indeed, was among the brighter aspects of the period, although the attempts made to increase the number of schools and to make education available to all classes of society are some of its least appreciated features. Our democratic régimes pride themselves on having made education widespread, but before them the old Catholic régime, especially in France, carried on a work that in many respects the former have merely inherited.

About 1660, educational undertakings experienced something in the nature of a pause following upon a fruitful period; but they soon regained momentum, and public authorities became interested. The king insisted on many occasions that every parish should have its school. In 1700 an edict instructed judges and attorneys to ensure that parish priests checked the regular attendance of children at school. In this field as in that of charitable enterprise the State looked to the Church to organize education and provide the means of carrying it out. Moreover, in accordance with the spirit of the times the two spheres merged; 'the exercise of charity and the education of youth' are two terms which are very often found together in the annals of the seventeenth century. The provincial assemblies gave the name 'Office of Public Welfare' to the department which combined matters relating to relief, education and agriculture. The Church, loyal to a duty it has never shirked, entered fully into the effort to provide against the inadequacy of the educational system and to adapt it to the needs of the time. Education, according to Fléchier, 'appertains neither to charity nor to human institutions, but is a divine command and a matter of justice'. But the teaching had to be Catholic, for it was inseparable from a Christian education—a fact expressly stated in an ordinance of 1698. This is the answer to the legend that the ancient régime of the Church was the myrmidon of ignorance.

By 1661 some remarkable results had been achieved in various branches of education. In so far as higher education was concerned, the universities, after a period of crisis, were reorganized during the fifteenth and sixteenth centuries. The Sorbonne retained its high reputation; it was a veritable oracle of Christendom, and its doctors, universally famous, were a closed circle to which it was impossible to gain admittance without strict tests, including the presentation of a thesis which lasted a whole day. But the students' colleges, even the celebrated Collège de Navarre, were dominated by routine, and were out of touch with the educational discoveries of the day. The type of education which might be called secondary approached the higher standard of the universities in so far as the upper forms were concerned, and it tended more and more to remain in the hands of the religious Orders which inclined to this method at the beginning of the century.[1] The education of the children of the nobility and the upper middle class was mostly in the hands of the Jesuits. Their colleges multiplied, not only in France where they numbered about a hundred in 1700, but also in Germany, in Bohemia and Austria (101), in Italy (135), in Spain (105) and in present-day Belgium (26). They have often been taken to task for the uniformity and lack of originality in their teaching, as well as for needless insistence on discipline which left too strong an impression on the child. But they produced first-class men, admirably trained in self-control and capable of undertaking methodical work. The colleges run by the Oratory [2] were more modern in their teaching methods and were the only serious rivals of the Jesuits after the Jansenist crisis had almost eliminated the 'Little Schools' of Port-Royal. They too were among the *élite* of educationists, especially in their college at Juilly. As for the education of young society girls, the most prominent teachers were the Ursuline nuns, the daughters of St Angela Merici.[3] In France alone they had three hundred and twenty houses. They were closely followed by the Visitandines, the Sisters of the Holy Child Jesus,[4] the Dames de Saint-Maur and many others; and Port-Royal ran schools under the rule drafted by Jacqueline Pascal.

This was a very satisfactory state of affairs. Elementary education for girls had been given a strong impetus during the preceding epoch, and many Orders and congregations were dedicated to that work. The Sisters of Charity were most prominent, but the Ursulines, the Visitandines and the Notre-Dame Sisters ran schools for the daughters of the poor side by side with those for the children of the wealthy. An extremely large number of local congregations and institutes were established and developed: the Sisters of Providence; the Sisters of Ernemont, founded in Rouen in 1698 by a friend of Renty and Bernières;[5] Grignion de Montfort's Sisters of Wisdom, a number of

---

[1] See Chapter II, p. 96.   [2] See Chapter II, p. 97.   [3] See Chapter II, p. 97.
[4] To be distinguished from the modern Society of the Holy Child Jesus.—Tr.
[5] The Sisters of Ernemont were initiated by the Company of the Blessed Sacrament and the efforts of St John Eudes; the Baron d'Ernemont was acquainted with them both. The sisters also fell under the influence of Saint-Sulpice, for one of their early superiors was the Sulpician M. Blain; they were typical of the numerous congregations of nuns who

whom were dedicated to teaching; the Sisters of the Holy Family at Besançon; the Filles de l'Enfance, who were forced to disband on account of their Jansenist tendencies; the Sisters of the Christian Doctrine in Nancy; and the Sisters of the Adoration of the Blessed Sacrament in the Avignon district. The fecundity of educational establishments during that period is staggering; they were perhaps a little chaotic, but there is no doubt about the amount of good work done. The fact that generally speaking more women than men today practise their faith in all the Catholic countries of Europe is in a large measure due to the work of the good teaching sisters.

The position in relation to elementary education was not quite the same where boys were concerned. Not that they were neglected; we have seen [1] that 'parish schools' and 'charity schools' were widespread during the first half of the century. We have also seen how public authorities insisted on the need to open schools and the importance of regular attendance; and the bishops, or at least the best among them, moved in the same direction. At Autun, Gabriel de Roquette drew up a complete plan for primary education, and his successor Colbert, son of the great minister, went so far as to compel parish priests to bring in from the fields children who failed to attend school. Pavillon, Bishop of Alet, allotted 7,000 *livres* from his annual budget of 20,000 for the education of the poor. Broadly speaking it is correct to say that in France (though much less so in Spain and Italy, and still less within the Empire) the majority of parishes had a primary school which normally depended upon the parish priest. But the problem of teachers still remained unsolved; they were in dreadfully short supply. No religious congregation was entirely devoted to teaching, so that the situation was very different from that affecting girls. The Brethren of the Common Life, the Piarists and the Doctrinarians leaned towards secondary education; the efforts of the Lazarists and M. Bourdoise's priests were limited in scope. In consequence a definite retrogression was noticeable about 1660. When Jean-Baptiste de la Salle arrived in the neighbourhood of Saint-Sulpice only one 'charity' school had survived of the thirty that functioned in the time of M. Olier, and with very inadequate teaching staff. Such a deficiency, which could have been made up solely by institutions devoted to teaching poor children, was indefensible.

---

at that period gave their lives to teaching and hospital work, and embodied the Catholic spirit of the day. But they were unique in two respects: they were the first religious congregation of women to be formed by Colbert (1690), then Archbishop of Rouen, into a congregation taking simple vows, unlike the Daughters of Charity, whom St Vincent de Paul made into a Society; in addition, under the spiritual influence of St John Eudes they were the first to be called 'Sisters of the Sacred Heart'. On the eve of the Revolution they had more than a hundred schools and nearly a hundred hospitals. (Cf. Canon Levé's *Qu'est-ce qu'une religieuse d'Ernemont?* Rouen, 1932.)

[1] See Chapter II, p. 96.

In 1666 the magistrates of Lyons received a long report under the heading *Remontrances* 'dealing with the need for and usefulness of Christian schools for the teaching of poor children'. The author was Charles Démia (1637–89), a young priest of Lyons. He was a former student of Saint-Sulpice, a familiar figure belonging to the group of priests at Saint-Nicolas-du-Chardonnet, where the words of M. Bourdoise were still quoted: 'If St Paul were to return to the world he would become a school-teacher.' Démia's memorandum was doubtless read by one or other of the magistrates, but he received no official backing. He therefore decided to begin alone. The children he wished to reach were the poor, the homeless, those whose parents could ill afford the expense of education, or who could not gain admission to the few 'charity' schools that existed. It was for them he created his 'Little Schools', admission to which was quite free. The first was opened at Lyons in 1667, and others soon followed, for groups of pious laymen took an interest in the enterprise. At Lyons sixteen schools were opened in twenty-two years, and ten more in the neighbourhood. Démia established the Seminary of St Charles to train the teachers he needed. Families began to ask this splendid priest to do something for their daughters also, and he founded the Sisters of St Charles. Such work required proper organization and money. This was taken in hand by the Bureau des Écoles, composed of priests and laymen; its officers handled the running of the schools in regard to hygiene and curriculum. The undertaking was so successful that the archbishop entrusted Charles Démia with control of all schools in his diocese. Démia's work survived in the district around Lyons until the Revolution. It was not only as a man of enterprise, a creator and an organizer that this astonishing man made his mark; everything which today goes by the name of 'modern progress' in our schools already existed in his achievements, including aptitude tests and career guidance. The extremely secular Ferdinand Buisson in his *Dictionnaire de Pédagogie* paid homage to him as the author of 'the first attempt at methodical organization' in primary education. If the Assembly of the Clergy, before whom he first laid his scheme in 1685, had followed it up, France would have been the first nation to have a Minister of Education, and he would have been a Christian.

Charles Démia was not alone in his vocation. We have seen what was accomplished by St Grignion de Montfort and his disciples. Father Barré, a Minim, a saintly and contemplative man associated with the foundation of the Sisters of the Holy Child Jesus and the Dames de Saint-Maur, tried to establish at Rouen, and later at Paris, a community to be known as the Brothers of the Holy Child Jesus, with the object of giving free education to poor children. In fact he made little progress, but his *Statuts et Règlements* laid the foundation of future achievements. One of his followers, Canon Nicolas Roland, an extraordinary character who at fifteen years of age performed in a play at the coronation of Louis XIV and later sailed in a pirate ship, took up Father Barré's idea and initiated at Rheims a scheme for the education of girls. He intended to establish a college for teachers, but did not live long enough to complete his work. Another disciple of Father Barré was Adrien Nyel, a humble teacher of burning enthusiasm and simplicity of soul. He attempted to set up schools all over France, and he might have achieved a great deal had he been a better organizer. All these efforts were not futile; they prepared the way for one who was a teacher of genius, a methodical organizer and a true saint who reaped the fruit of all that went before: St Jean-Baptiste de la Salle.

In the spring of the year 1688 the parish of Saint-Sulpice in Paris was in a state of great excitement. From the Rue Dauphine to the Invalides, from the Seine to Notre-Dame des Champs, everyone was talking of the new ideas that were being introduced at the old school in the Rue Princesse, where the poor children of the district had been taught since the time of M. Olier. Some people thought the new master's strange methods absurd; others thought them excellent. He was a priest from Rheims, assisted by two laymen both oddly dressed. His first decision was to exclude Latin from the curriculum, and he abolished compulsory manual work; the whole class received instruction together, not individually. The dunces thought the discipline too severe; the parents thought it too lax. And the parish priest wondered whether he had done right to call on the services of this M. de la Salle.

The charity school in the Rue Princesse was in very poor shape when the new team took over. It was the last surviving school of the thirty functioning in M. Olier's time, and numbered two hundred pupils whom poor M. Compagnon, assisted by a fifteen-year-old boy and a voluntary worker who was a hosier by trade, found great difficulty in controlling. M. de la Salle and his two companions did not easily win obedience from these 'wild young animals', as they called them. But apparently their methods were not bad, for order gradually returned to the school in the Rue Princesse. The number of pupils quickly grew, and they worked. The censure of the pessimists and everlasting critics came to nothing. The inquiry undertaken by M. Forbin-Janson on behalf of the authorities did not bear out the accusations brought by scandalmongers. Better still, the new parish priest M. Baudrand pressed M. de la Salle to open a new school in the Rue du Bac, and three hundred pupils were accepted. Thus the work prospered.

Who was this M. de la Salle whose methods were so effective? He was a priest of thirty-seven years of age (born in 1651) whose family

came from Champagne. They had grown rich in business and rediscovered their ancient nobility in exercising the responsibilities of the
magistracy. Intended for the Church, Jean-Baptiste was made a canon
at the age of sixteen and thus provided with a sound living. He studied
zealously under M. Tronson at the seminary of Saint-Sulpice. At
twenty-seven he was ordained, returned to Rheims and settled down
to the life of a well-to-do canon with an income of 40,000 *livres*,
acquired quite legitimately. But fate—or rather Providence—unexpectedly brought him into contact with Nicolas Roland, his colleague in
the cathedral chapter; later he met Adrien Nyel, who was obsessed
with the idea of teaching as a method of reaching souls, and had
answered the call of some pious women in the town who wished to
open charity schools. Everything happened naturally and inexorably
for Jean-Baptiste de la Salle. He was caught as it were in a net, but it
was the net of God's will. How could he possibly have escaped the
obligation he was under to Nicolas Roland who, on his deathbed, left
the care of his orphanage to Jean-Baptiste? He was equally susceptible
to the warmth of Adrien Nyel, who appealed to his charity. To please
Adrien he bought a house to accommodate the teachers of the schools
for the poor; and he began to take an interest in these good people who
had meant little to him and whom he had rather looked down upon
from his prosperous middle-class position.

At length he plunged into the work, preaching a retreat to his boarders
and providing them with a Rule of Life. Without really intending to
do so he found he had created a training college for primary school-
teachers. The teaching profession thus came to him suddenly and
unexpectedly. When Adrien Nyel one day went to establish a school at
Guise, Canon de la Salle took his place in the classroom. His family
thought he was mad, and when he installed the teachers in the family
home they were convinced that he was; so much so that his own
brothers left home in disgust. Things got even worse when, on the
advice of Father Barré, whom he went to consult in Paris, he obeyed
to the letter Christ's command to the rich young man. He resigned his
canonry and distributed all his wealth to the poor, providing for the
destitute during a dreadful famine. Immediately he became poor among
the poor, as were the teachers around him and with whom he now felt
on close and brotherly terms. His little group was established. It was
not yet an institute, much less the congregation to be known as the
Brothers of the Christian Schools; but in the sight of God and man it
was already in existence on 28th May 1684. About a dozen school-
teachers made a vow to dedicate their lives to teaching the children of
the common people, to live as lay religious in poverty and self-
sacrifice, with Jean-Baptiste de la Salle as their leader and soul of their
little group. A great work was unobtrusively born into the Church.

Jean-Baptiste de la Salle was indeed an extraordinary man. This well-to-do canon of gentle and refined disposition, modest and unassuming in his way, became a stern ascetic, using the discipline, wearing a hair shirt and a painful belt against his skin, sleeping on a plank and fasting more often than the law enjoined. But he was also a mystic, as is clear from his splendid book *Méditations pour le temps de la retraite*. He was a true son of the French school, of Saint-Sulpice and of Bérulle; his one aim in life was, to use the words of his predecessors, to 'adhere to God' and to promote His Kingdom. The efficacy of his spiritual life may be compared in some respects with that of Monsieur Vincent's. The influence he exerted, the sweet force that attached men to him, despite his extreme humility, sprang from his interior life. He would, of course, have been the last to regard his work as unique, vastly ahead of his time and stamped with the seal of genius; but it was so none the less.

He devoted his whole life to this unforeseen vocation to teach. He was to be nothing but a pedagogue, but in the noblest and fullest sense of that word. He had the primary and indispensable quality of a teacher, an understanding of children; he knew them and loved them. Moreover, he did not hesitate to lend a hand himself, taking the classes, going from desk to desk pointing out mistakes, and assisting those who were slow. His experience was unrivalled, and his splendid book, *Conduite des écoles*, shows him to have been a brilliant theorist. He regarded the ability to adapt oneself to a child as the foremost quality of a teacher, to be direct and realistic in order to reach the child's understanding. For that reason he did away with the teaching of Latin in beginners' classes, an old and rather silly practice.[1] To create a spirit of competition among students he made them work in teams, correcting each other's work. Before his time the teacher endeavoured with varying degrees of success to give individual instruction to each child in turn. In future the class was taught as a whole, the students following the lessons in a book, each being questioned in turn. This is now the essential principle of modern teaching practice in primary schools, where spelling and arithmetic hold first place.

But many other ideas developed around this central principle. Teachers had to be trained to practise the new method of teaching. His modest institute aimed at providing this type of training; he founded training establishments to which every diocese sent prospective teachers and which eventually became the basis of our teachers' training colleges. And, thought Jean-Baptiste, why should there not be special courses for adults and young people already working? These he organized, and they were the forerunners of our present-day

---

[1] This was also the opinion of Comenius in Moravia, but he did not succeed in getting it approved.

continuation courses, clubs and study circles. The arrangement of special training facilities for difficult and backward pupils—a quite recent undertaking—was also the idea of Jean-Baptiste de la Salle. This great teacher appreciated that Latin was not indispensable to many middle-class children on completion of their primary education; they required instead a knowledge of the sciences and technical subjects. For them he founded the first of what are now our modern technical institutes. So manifest in his achievements are his genius for education and his talent for educational technique that even the most secular-minded of our modern French theorists, such as Ferdinand Buisson and Victor Duruy, pay homage to him and regard him as the precursor of modern educational practice.

Such was the man who staggered Paris by his innovations, after trying them out at Rheims and a few small towns. The success achieved in the neighbourhood of Saint-Sulpice gave new strength to the little band. In 1691 he took a large house in Vaugirard, and in October of the following year a training centre was opened with ten young trainees. The time had come for Jean-Baptiste de la Salle to establish his work on more solid foundations, and on 6th June 1694 he and six of his most dependable colleagues made a vow to the Blessed Trinity 'to form a society for the purpose of maintaining free schools together and with others'. The Institute of the Brothers of the Christian Schools was founded. They were not to be priests, nor even clerics. To enable them to remain loyal to their vocation as teachers they would undertake no ministry. They would pursue only the ideal of the Christian teacher, subordinating every purpose to the formation of children—a sufficiently vast and noble ideal in itself. Their attire, adopted at Rheims where it caused great amusement among those who were ill-disposed towards them, was a cassock of rough serge, a white collar turned down, a three-cornered hat and a large cloak with loose sleeves similar to the one then worn by working people. As news of their success spread, this garb would be seen more and more frequently in French towns. Mme de Maintenon's confessor, Godet des Marais, invited the Brothers to teach at Chartres, and the Duc de Béthune established them in Calais at his own expense. Soon they were at Troyes and Avignon, in Normandy and Burgundy. Wherever bishops or governors desired to open schools they called on the Brothers: Mende, Alès, Grenoble, Valence, Moulins, Boulogne-sur-Mer and even at Versailles. Wherever Protestantism still remained strong the authorities relied upon the teaching of the Brothers to instil faith into the minds of the children.

Such success was not attained without provoking violent opposition; the life of Jean-Baptiste de la Salle was indeed a perpetual cross, as is the privilege of all great pioneers. Desperately he fought all who stood in his way and whose rule-of-thumb methods he upset. The 'master writers' and schoolmasters who earned their living by teaching the children of those who could pay were furious at the development of an institute whose members offered education without payment. There were even incidents in which the schools were ransacked and the Brothers maltreated. A few bishops, either prompted by these people or perhaps to avoid trouble, refused to accept the Brothers even when they themselves had sent for them. Strange and sometimes sordid intrigues were instigated against the great pioneer; legal proceedings were instituted in which justice was thwarted to the end that he might lose his case. He also had to defend himself and safeguard his work against those who endeavoured to take it over and use it for purposes different from his own: the Jansenists, especially in the south of France, showed excessive interest in the schools and the Brothers, and when their founder reacted against their schemes their wrath exploded, and they set out to destroy his work. In the face of countless and never-ending trials Jean-Baptiste de la Salle's weapon was a sublime confidence in God and humble submission to His will. The internal crises which shook his Institute caused him the greatest pain; they were perhaps the normal teething troubles of a new enterprise, but they were to him the source of intense suffering. There came a day when he had doubts about himself, his vocation and the usefulness of the work he had undertaken. St Teresa had also experienced similar moments of black despair.

But his soul was too magnanimous and too strong to yield to discouragement. The great majority of the Brothers remained loyal to him, even when, almost outlawed, he was forced to leave Paris; even when a tactless bishop endeavoured to have him replaced as Superior of the Institute; even, above all, when an attempt was made to break up the Institute and distribute its fragments among the dioceses. There exists a letter of matchless beauty signed by the directors of all his houses, begging their old superior, indeed commanding him 'in the name of the society to which he had promised obedience', to return and place himself at their head and save the work he had undertaken. He obeyed and came back; that was in 1714. The reign of the Great King was nearing its end; but St Jean-Baptiste de la Salle had given his Institute, tormented though it was by so many formidable forces, the means of preserving Christianity in the souls of the children of the common people, even after the outbreak of the Revolution.

When he died on 7th April 1719 the Brothers of the Christian Schools numbered 274 members. By 1900, the year of their heroic and illustrious founder's canonization, they numbered 20,000, with over 350,000 pupils in their schools.

12. AN UNFULFILLED HOPE

Despite such figures as Jean-Baptiste de la Salle, Louis Marie Grignion de Montfort and Margaret Mary Alacoque, not forgetting Rancé and the glorious pulpit-orators, there remained aspects of the classical age which did not encourage optimism. From some points of view the outlook was distressing. At the end of the sixteenth century the Church had hoped that simultaneously with the work of order and renovation the work of reconquest might proceed, for she was not content to abandon for all time to the Protestants the territories in which they had settled. Unfortunately the 'Counter-Reformation' did not continue during the reign of Louis XIV. There were two methods envisaged by Catholics to reconquer lost souls, and they attempted to put both into effect together: conversion and the use of force. Both methods, demonstrated respectively in St Peter Canisius and the Battle of the White Mountain, seemed condemned to failure.

During the first half of the seventeenth century high-minded men considered that a reconciliation between Catholics and Protestants was possible.[1] These men were to be found in both camps, and serious efforts had been made towards reconciliation without worth-while results. The Lutheran Calixte, the master of Helmstedt, was criticized both by his co-religionists and by Catholics, and the great Capuchin Valerio Magni was eventually thrown into prison. The idea of reunion of the Churches was not however abandoned: it was taken up again during the last thirty years of the century and actively pursued. The situation appeared favourable, for the early fanaticism of the Reformation had seemingly diminished and various princely families of the Empire had returned to Catholicism. The various shades of Protestantism were more or less in the throes of a crisis and incapable of organizing a Church;[2] they were uneasy about the progress of Socinianism[3] and worried about the growing power of the princes.

It was considered that a skilful policy of maintaining contact and a disposition to make concessions might furnish good results, and this was attempted in 1665 by Cristobal de Rojas y Spinola, a zealous Franciscan, more subtle, skilful and conciliatory perhaps than he was prudent and thoughtful. He was, nevertheless, a true apostle of reunion. As Bishop of Tina in Dalmatia, later of Wiener-Neustadt and confessor to the empress, he persuaded Rome that only he could bring about a *rapprochement*. Innocent XI, who was grieved by the Turkish threat and the great rift between Christians, put whole-hearted trust in him, and the Emperor Leopold firmly supported him. Armed with

---

[1] See Chapter III, p. 166.
[2] See *The Church in the Eighteenth Century*, Chapter III.
[3] See *The Catholic Reformation*, p. 224.

this twofold mandate, Spinola visited the various states of Germany, called on the princes and made numerous contacts with theologians of the reformed Church. The Papal Legate Bevilacqua was sent especially to follow up his efforts, and the ardent Spaniard imagined that victory was in his hands. He felt convinced of the early conversion of the Elector of Saxony and the Elector Palatine; in Hanover, in any case, John Frederick, won over to Rome, was assisting the Capuchins and Jesuits to convert the masses, and abjurations were so numerous that Rome appointed a Vicar Apostolic. A wave of optimism spread despite the pessimistic reports of the Nuncio at Vienna. It was at this juncture that the Dane Niels Stensen (or Stenon) became a convert, was ordained priest and eventually consecrated bishop. Molanus, the Lutheran abbot of Lokkum, appeared to be on the point of recanting. When Spinola went to Rome in 1678 to give an account of his mission his infectious enthusiasm influenced well-intentioned people, including the Pope, into believing that they were on the eve of a great victory.

In actual fact, when it came to the preparation of a plan for reunion, matters appeared less straightforward. In 1683, after many discussions, Spinola and his questioners agreed upon the following points: Rome would concede the marriage of priests, Communion under both species for the laity, and approve a German liturgy; in consideration of which the Lutherans would recognize the Pope. Other points of doctrine would be submitted to a new council; meanwhile the Tridentine decisions would be held in abeyance. By all appearances Spinola went too far, and the Holy Office, despite Innocent XI, who continued to rely upon the generous Franciscan, was right to protest. Further, two questions remained unanswered: one concerned Catholic property which had been secularized, and the other concerned the role which the princes had assumed within the Churches. It soon became clear that the latter was the stumbling-block. In Hanover, John Frederick's successor proved hostile to every approach. Everywhere else, in Sweden, Denmark and Brandenburg, the situation hardened. It was the same in Catholic countries: in France, where the Edict of Nantes was about to be revoked; in Bohemia, where the saintly Cardinal von Harrach, a great pioneer of missionary work, was being more and more hampered in his activities; in Hungary, where the Primate of Gran continued to effect conversions by the use of force, exile and the galleys. Repudiated by Rome, thwarted in Germany by vested interests, Spinola continued in vain, though tirelessly, his travels in search of reconciliation. When he died in 1695 he had achieved nothing definite.

While Spinola was active in the practical sphere, theoretical discussions began between the Catholics and the Lutherans. The Lutheran representative was Gottfried Wilhelm von Leibniz (1646–1716), an encyclopedic genius, learned in literature and science, theology and history, philosophy and law; a remarkably engaging personality, thoughtful, shrewd and generous. His splendid qualifications were the result not only of vast erudition, but also of his travels in Europe, where he had made the acquaintance of such men as Malebranche, the great Arnauld, Newton and Huyghens. Leibniz was a member of the Aulic Council at the court of Hanover, that is to say one of the most active centres of irenicism. He had an intense desire for unity; he revived the grandiose ideas of Sully and Grotius, and dreamed of rebuilding the unity of Europe through the creation of a Christian republic. To him Christianity was one and the Church was one; one in her belief in a few great fundamental truths that guaranteed salvation; one in the love that united all her members. Leibniz was by no means hostile to the Catholic and Roman Church. He admired her discipline and her religious Orders, whom he called 'a saintly, a heavenly host'. He even understood the customs, liturgy, ceremonial and music of the Church. He reproached her, however, for being loaded with too many corrupt practices, for being intolerant—in his eyes excommunication was as reprehensible as schism itself—and with clinging to useless dogma. Moreover, Leibniz did not regard Protestant churches as being universal either; they were individual churches, just as intolerant and just as intractable in their dogmatism. In short, the author of *Traité de la Souveraineté*, *Essais de Théodicée* and *La Monadologie* demanded the adherence of all Christians to an invisible Church built on charity and faith, while adherence to a visible Church might be maintained by diversity within unity.

About 1680 intellectual circles of Christian Europe were giving Leibniz's ideas serious attention. The Holy See was slightly misled by the terms he used in referring to the religious Orders, the Blessed Virgin, the saints, and even papal authority itself; it saw him as a messenger of reconciliation, so much so that it offered him a post as librarian at the Vatican! He maintained relations with the Archbishop of Mainz, the Papal Legate Bevilacqua, Father Malebranche, and even the Nuncio in Vienna. But his relationship with Bossuet was the closest of all. From his early youth Bossuet had always enjoyed discussions with Protestants. He embarked upon them loyally and seriously, certainly with the firm intention of winning Protestants over to the Catholic Church, but he was equally determined not to yield on basic principles. When Bossuet published his *Explication de la doctrine chrétienne* Leibniz assured him that he had an extremely high opinion of his work; similarly Bossuet's later book, *Histoire des variations*, claimed the attention of the German philosopher. In 1692 there began a correspondence between the two which, with a short interruption, lasted until 1702. Both these brilliant men passionately defended their respective points of view, utilizing all their resources of knowledge and logic.

But it soon became as clear as day that their two concepts were irreconcilable. To begin with, how could a Catholic, a member of the Roman Church, accept Leibniz's theories as to the very meaning of 'Church'? Leibniz, logically pursuing his arguments, rejected the oecumenical character of the Council of Trent, while Bossuet rightly claimed that the Tridentine decisions constituted the very bases of the restored Church because they were the genuine voice of Tradition. An even more profound difference between the two minds lay in their conception of faith, where there was no possible chance of agreement; here Leibniz claimed liberty of thought, while Bossuet stood for full adherence to the truth of the Church. When Leibniz broke off the correspondence in 1702 under the pretext that 'he found the peremptory tone of his correspondent discouraging', it was in fact because, as the Duke of Hanover's representative on the Aulic Council, he could not continue to discuss a reunion which must deprive him of his rights, since the duke expected to become King of England on the death of Queen Anne. The relationship had at least proved that no compromise was possible between two absolutely incompatible doctrines. It meant the end of the conciliatory discussions. A few intrepid souls continued indeed to labour the subject, but they were modest attempts with no far-reaching consequences. On the threshold of the eighteenth century it became clear that Catholic propaganda was no longer gaining any ground from the various branches of Protestantism.

Hopes that Catholicism might recover some territory in the East, in the areas of schismatic 'Orthodox' Christianity, were also dashed. More serious still, the Uniate Church was threatened. Reunion had been the means of leading back the Christians of Lithuania and the Ukraine [1] to the Catholic fold in 1596, enabling them to reform and reorganize their Church, which was then declining. The hostility of the Orthodox, culminating in the murder of St Josaphat Kuntsewycz in 1623, continued, and the conflict broke out again between the Metropolitan Orthodox and the Uniate bishops. The reunion was honoured under the authority of the energetic Metropolitan Peter Mokyla, but the Cossack Wars continually weakened it. In 1705 Peter the Great himself caused Uniate priests to be put to the torture; others were exiled to Siberia. Worse still, Catholics of the Latin rite treated their Uniate brethren badly on account of their particular form of liturgy, the marriage of their priests and the fact that they used leavened bread for the Holy Eucharist. The nobles and the Catholic bishops excluded the Ruthenian bishops from the Polish senate. The situation had become so tense by 1714 that the Metropolitan Kiszka, assisted by the Nuncio at Warsaw, undertook to call a synod at Lemberg in an

[1] See *The Catholic Reformation*, p. 337.

attempt to 'Latinize' the Uniate Church, but there was little hope of saving it.

The situation was nowhere very satisfactory among the Orthodox. The Patriarchate of Constantinople (which was under Turkish rule) continued to argue peevishly over the validity of the Latin form of baptism and transubstantiation as understood by Rome. In Serbia, Catholics were so badly treated that about forty thousand of them crossed over to Hungary, and the Orthodox clergy attempted to use force against those who remained. In Rumania some Catholic nobles managed with the aid of a few bishops to reconstitute a church, but it remained under threat from both the Turkish authorities and the adherents of Orthodoxy. It did not become established until about 1730. The only serious attempt made by Catholicism to penetrate the Orthodox zone was that undertaken in Russia by the Croat Krijanich and a few Jesuit missions. The pan-slavism of Peter the Great offered them little hope of success. It seems that everywhere we look we see the work of peaceful reconquest and expansion being brutally arrested; and this at the very moment when the quarrel of Chinese Rites was undermining the work of missionaries in Asia.[1]

13. A WASTED PAST: THE POLITICAL COUNTER-REFORMATION

The halting of the century-old dream of *political* Counter-Reformation—the attempt to reinstate Catholicism by force—was just as brutal. This attempt was, as we have seen, halted at the beginning of the century,[2] but the spirit that inspired it still survived, though of a very different quality from what it had been. In consequence, its efforts resulted only in failure.

Was it only to serve the interests of Catholicism that Louis XIV used coercion in his dealings with the Protestants,[3] ultimately revoking the Edict of Nantes? Was it not rather with the intention of pressing his principle of unification to its logical conclusion? At all events, it is plain that his severity, which drove so much excellent material from the country and caused the bloody revolt of the 'White Shirts', did not succeed, for it had to be replaced by more tolerant methods.

A comparable policy within the Empire had even worse consequences. In the hope of achieving in Hungary what it had done in Austria, and making general use of the coercive measures adopted by Cardinal Pazmany,[4] the Imperial Government destroyed the *modus vivendi* so painfully established with the Magyar Protestants. Profiting

---

[1] See *The Church in the Eighteenth Century*, Chapter II.
[2] See Chapter III, p. 155. [3] See Chapter IV, p. 204. [4] See Chapter III, p. 163.

by the impetus derived from victory over the Turks [1] the Government quartered German troops in the land of St Stephen, and rebellion ensued. Following the proclamation of Croatia-Zrinyi, in answer to the call of the son of Raköczy, and more especially of Imre Tökölli, fighting began around the Danube similar to that carried on by the 'White Shirts' in France. It was savagely suppressed; the rebel bands were easily overcome by the Austrian regular army. Most of the leaders were captured, and others took refuge with the Turks. Their pastors were condemned as heretics and traitors, their temples were closed, and the Grand Master of the Teutonic Order became governor of Pressburg. The reaction was so violent and so obviously intended to smother Hungarian nationalism as much as Protestantism that the rebellion broke out anew with even greater fury. This time Catholics and Protestants united, which resulted in a bitter struggle with cruel fighting on both sides. The Hungarians stood alone against the enormous power of the Empire, and history has recorded the courage and tenacity of their resistance. The struggle was carried on by Imre Tökölli, assisted behind the scenes by France, and even supported by a revolt of the Czech peasants. Finally, appreciating the hopelessness of his position, he appealed to Turkey as a last resort; and the Sultan replied by launching a gigantic army against Vienna. Such was the consequence of the so-called Counter-Reformation conducted in the worst possible manner. When the Turks were driven out, Buda and the Danubian fortresses recaptured and Hungary completely subdued and systematically Germanized, the unifying authoritarianism of the Hapsburgs triumphed, but not Catholicism.

In England an attempt to reinstate Catholicism was crushed even more decisively, for the outcome resulted not only in political defeat but also in the final eradication of Catholic traditions. For a time, however, it seemed that the country might return to its former loyalties. For as yet there was no real concord within the ranks of Protestantism itself; [2] a struggle went on more or less openly between Anglicanism and each of the other reformed sects with the object of imposing their respective creeds upon the country. But the one point on which all these hostile brethren were agreed was that Popery must be eliminated; not on any account were the 'Jesuits' to regain a foothold. Cromwell's Commonwealth led, in fact, to a Puritan dictatorship under which Catholics were denied every right. The restoration of the monarchy under Charles II (1660–85) in no way changed the situation, despite his own leanings towards Catholicism and pressure from his mother and sister, the two Henriettas. His Declaration of Indulgence, under

[1] At St Gothard; see p. 309.
[2] Concerning events in Protestant England and the consequent crises see *The Church in the Eighteenth Century*, Chapter III.

which priests were authorized to celebrate Mass in private houses, provoked such a furore in Parliament and had such a bad effect on public opinion that he was forced to hurry through Parliament his Test Act (1673), under which all persons holding office were required to take an oath of supremacy, recognizing His Majesty as supreme head of the Church. The king's brother, the Duke of York, a convert to Catholicism, renounced all his appointments, including the post of High Admiral of the splendid fleet he had created, in order to avoid taking an oath which he regarded as blasphemous. But even those measures proved insufficient. Hatred of Catholicism was shared by every shade of Protestantism. The Popish Plot, fabricated by the ageing Anglican minister Titus Oates, was believed without question: the Jesuits were supposed to be organizing a new Gunpowder Plot, Catholics to be awaiting the landing of French forces and Ireland to be implicated. Six Jesuits and nine other priests were hanged; two thousand Catholics were either thrown into prison or compelled to flee the country. The question of depriving the Duke of York of his right of succession was under consideration.

In the midst of this tempestuous atmosphere the Duke of York became king as James II (1685-8). The English people had such unpleasant memories of Cromwell's Commonwealth that their loyalty to James overcame their religious bigotry, and he was accepted without demur. James was courageous, upright and virtuous, but stubborn and narrow-minded. No sooner had he become king than he thought it his duty to restore Catholicism by law. He openly attended Catholic services, received Holy Communion and surrounded himself with Catholic advisers; and with such inordinate haste that Innocent XI advised prudence. Monmouth, an illegitimate son of Charles II, landed in Puritan Scotland, and the country rose up in response to the call of Argyle, son of a Protestant executed after the restoration of Charles. Monmouth was defeated at Sedgemoor, and Lord Chief Justice Jeffreys was sent to punish the insurgents at the 'Bloody Assize'. James II set up a court of ecclesiastical commission and prepared the way for a return to Catholicism. In 1687 he annulled the Test Act; Father Petre, S.J., was given a seat on the Council; the Archbishop of Canterbury and seven Anglican bishops were committed to the Tower. It was at this time that Dryden, a convert to Catholicism, wrote his strange poem, 'The Hind and the Panther', glorifying the Roman Church. The king considered he did a wise thing when he issued his Declaration of Indulgence, the aim of which was to link Non-conformists, Baptists, Presbyterians and even Quakers with the Catholics against the Anglicans. Staunch Protestants were suspicious of such company, and public opinion was roused when all Anglicans were gradually excluded from important official appointments. Parliament refused to approve the Declaration in favour of the king's 'innocent Catholic subjects'; a jury acquitted the seven bishops of seditious libel, and the stage was set for revolution. Protestant England had tolerated her unpopular king for three years in the hope that he would soon be succeeded by his elder daughter Mary, a Protestant, who had married the Protestant William of Orange. Their fury burst when a Catholic heir, James Edward, was born in the palace. James II prepared to retreat before the growing storm.[1] William landed his Huguenot army at Torbay. His standards carried the legend *Pro religione protestante*. With the flight of James II Catholicism had lost the day.

Henceforward the small band of English Catholics, numbering about a thirtieth of the population, diminished in importance. They were treated as inferior citizens and barred from posts of responsibility; they alone among the 'non-conformists' were refused religious freedom. The Declaration of Rights (1689) allowed freedom of worship to all others who recognized the schema of Christian faith as laid down in the Thirty-Nine Articles; the only bodies excluded were the Catholics, the Unitarians and the Jews. Harsh measures were taken against all Papists, and the 'crime of the Mass' was again punishable. It is doubtful whether William and Mary (1689–1702) themselves approved of this fanaticism, but they were compelled to yield to public opinion. Anne Stuart (1702–14)—'Good Queen Anne'—second daughter of James II and wife of Prince George of Denmark, treated the lower Anglican clergy kindly, but continued to apply to Catholics the full rigour of the penal laws. The Act of Settlement passed by Parliament in 1701 excluded all Catholics from succession to the throne, and Anne, who would gladly have bequeathed her crown to her half-brother James Edward (James III), was obliged to sign the Act. She was succeeded in 1714 by her cousin of the House of Hanover, who became George I, a moderate but thorough-going Protestant. No further hope remained to the Catholic cause in the land of St Edward and St Thomas à Becket.

The Counter-Reformation in England was therefore not only a conspicuous failure, but it brought about a very strong Protestant reaction. A similar reaction was experienced elsewhere, e.g. in Scandinavia. In Denmark, after Christian V's *coup d'état* of 1660, all previous anti-Catholic enactments were collected together as a code of laws and enforced (1683). Priests entering the country were liable to execution;

---

[1] The extent to which public feeling had been roused is suggested by a curious incident which took place on 22nd December 1688. On learning that the king had left the palace Londoners became panic-stricken. It was rumoured that the Irish were attacking London. There was a beating of drums, a great bustle of muskets and pikes; the streets were illuminated and barricades were set up. A state of uncertainty reigned, but nothing happened after all. Someone shouted, 'No popery!' and the crowd flung itself upon all Catholic embassies. The incident became known as the 'Irish Night'.

anyone converted to popery ran the risk of banishment and confiscation of property. When the French ambassador claimed the right to build a Catholic chapel he had to undertake not to allow any Danish Papist to enter it. Furthermore, the vitality of the Catholic faith in Denmark definitely languished, despite the notable conversion of the savant Niels Stensen, who was appointed Vicar Apostolic but was forced to live in exile; despite also the secret missions financed by the Bishop of Fürstenberg and organized by the Jesuits at Münster. By 1715 the Catholics of Denmark numbered no more than one in five thousand.

The position was no better in Sweden. The conversion of Queen Christina [1] had created a sensation, but none had followed her example. Her cousin and successor, Charles XI, strengthened the anti-Catholic laws, and from 1686 onwards they were precisely the same as those of Denmark. Converts were banished and their property confiscated, and priests could enter the country only secretly. So great was the distrust of anything akin to popery that Ussadius, a venerable champion of Lutheranism, was condemned to thirty years' imprisonment for having dared to teach that works were useful towards salvation. Only in the last twenty-five years of the eighteenth century, under the philosopher King Gustavus III, was it possible for Oster, the Vicar Apostolic, to reinvigorate the unhappy Catholic Church in Sweden. [2]

In Germany the position was not much better, though legal measures seem to have been less severe in certain areas. Many German states, such as the episcopal electorates and Bavaria, remained absolutely loyal to Catholicism, as did the ecclesiastical principalities of Fulda, Münster, Ratisbon and Würtzburg. In Hesse and the Palatine a *modus vivendi* was established between Catholics and Protestants; while in Saxony, Frederick Augustus, converted to Catholicism and elected King of Poland, came to an arrangement under which Catholics were given the right of private worship. Everywhere else, however, notably in Prussia, Protestant reaction was violent, either openly or beneath the surface. The Grand Elector Frederick William proved tolerant, but from 1688 his successor Frederick III was relentless, encouraged as he was by those French refugees who had settled in Prussia after the revocation of the Edict of Nantes. In any case, Frederick entertained rather extravagant ideas: he desired religious unity in his states, but his readiness to reach an agreement with Rome was dependent upon the Pope's agreeing to crown him king. When his plans were frustrated he withdrew from Catholics the right to practise their religion, and reinforced the old decrees, which resulted in persecution and the expulsion of the Jesuits. The Catholic population of all the Prussian states scarcely exceeded 3 per cent, and was definitely on the decrease.

In some parts of Europe the situation was even worse, and Catholics

[1] See Chapter III, p. 165.   [2] See *The Church in the Eighteenth Century*, Chapter IV.

were severely persecuted—in the Low Countries especially, though here Catholicism put up a vigorous defence. Since 1648 [1] Catholics had been continually frustrated, and they were suspected of being pro-French. The falsity of this accusation was proved by their staunch loyalty in the struggle against Louis XIV; nevertheless they were treated as enemies of the State and forced to lead a more or less underground existence. Officials were forbidden to visit them; their votive chapels and crosses set up on the highways were demolished, and they were unable to protest. Many priests and religious were exiled, but the Church, though virtually outlawed, struggled on in grim determination. Mindful of the lessons of Rovenius, they bribed Protestant officials into allowing them to practise their faith; they educated their young, and trained their priests in Germany. About 1671 there were ten thousand Catholics in Amsterdam and eighteen 'houses of prayer'; by 1715 there were approximately three hundred thousand Catholics in the whole of Holland. The deplorable affair of the Jansenist schism in Utrecht [1] severely hampered the forward movement of Dutch Catholicism, but only for a while.

Nowhere in the whole of the West was Protestant savagery more in evidence and Catholic resistance more heroic than in Ireland. The religious and political aspects of the conflict combined to render it implacable. Since the days when Cromwell's Roundheads subjected Catholic Ireland to English discipline by means of barbarous repression, that country, though reduced almost to helplessness, had continued to strike fear into her executioners. To the Irish people loyalty to the Catholic faith and to her national consciousness were inseparable. She defended both freedoms with her blood. It was not surprising therefore that the Irish interfered in England's politics, were hostile to her Anglican kings and allied themselves with her Catholic pretenders. But this confusion of interests could result only in more harsh repression. When under Charles II tempers were roused in consequence of the consternation provoked by the 'Popish Plot' fabricated by Titus Oates, the Irish were the first to be accused of having fostered the conspiracy. Oliver Plunket, Archbishop of Armagh and Primate of Ireland, was sent to the gallows at Tyburn in order to satisfy public opinion. Peace returned to the Emerald Isle during the very short reign of James II; the Irish Catholics recovered under the viceregency of Talbot Tyrconnel—'Mad Dick'—and were allowed a measure of autonomy. But the revolution of 1688 plunged them into misfortune. They rose against the Protestant monarchs William and Mary, and assisted James II to land at Kinsale with five thousand men whom Louis XIV had placed at his disposal. James was defeated at the battle

[1] See Chapter III, p. 157.   [2] See Chapter VI, p. 420.

of the Boyne (1690) and returned to France. The Irish fought their last desperate battles, and were forced to yield at Limerick (1690). The subsequent treaty promised them freedom to practise their religion, but William and Mary, under pressure from the Protestants, were unable to keep their word. Persecution was quickly resumed. Catholics were excluded from Parliament; they were forbidden to have priests, to carry arms or to open schools. They were literally blockaded in their island, and any man who sent his son to be educated on the Continent was forced to pay a fine of £100. They were treated as inferiors and obliged, on pain of a £60 fine, to assist at Protestant services. Many were driven from their estates, which were taken over by their enemies (a total of one million acres were thus confiscated), and they were the victims of any extortions that the English cared to impose upon them. Terror reigned throughout the country; as cruel as, if not worse than, that experienced by the French Protestants after the revocation of the Edict of Nantes. But their resistance did not weaken. Patrick Donnelly, assisted by seventy-seven priests, twenty-two religious and nine nuns, journeyed from place to place throughout the country. Mass was celebrated at secret meeting places upon an altar-stone, the *corrig-an-aifrion*. Donnelly was eventually captured, and most of the bishops had to flee to France and Portugal. Many, however, with the aid of French bishops, opened seminaries on the Continent for training young priests who would continue the struggle. The eclipse of the Catholic Church in the land of St Patrick was merely apparent: Ireland was not conquered; she was not even discouraged.

Poland, another bulwark of Catholicism at the other end of Europe, appeared on the point of collapse. For a long time the country had been a source of grave anxiety to the Church,[1] but she remained as magnificently loyal at the end of the seventeenth century as she had formerly been. The dramatic events of 1655, when the monks of Czestochowa repulsed the Swedes, seem to have had the effect of sublimating their faith. Nowhere was the Church surrounded with more love and veneration; nowhere were the feasts of Christmas and Easter celebrated with greater devotion, or the prayers said to Our Lady more fervent. And nowhere were the clergy more powerful. They owned 800,000 serfs, and one archbishop was the proprietor of sixteen towns. All the Orders, including such new French congregations as the Lazarists and the Sisters of the Visitation, were active, and mission work was in full swing. Yet the position of Poland was extremely dangerous, squeezed as she was between schismatic Russia and Protestant Prussia and Sweden, and unable to communicate with the Catholic West except through Bohemia. At home she was in even greater peril from the elective monarchical system, from the ambitions

---

[1] See Chapter III, p. 160.

and incurable anarchy of the nobles, and from the underlying disagreement between the different regions and classes of the population. This state of affairs whetted the appetites of her neighbours, two of whom —Prussia and Russia—were rapidly expanding. King John Sobieski (1674–96) halted the march of decadence; on his death a Frenchman, Louis de Conti, victor of Steinkirk, was elected king, but England and Brandenburg-Prussia opposed his nomination. The Elector of Saxony therefore became king and reigned at Warsaw as Augustus II. The War of the League of Augsburg, the Great Northern War and the War of the Spanish Succession isolated Poland and deprived her of the support of France. Bordered by Russia, Sweden and Saxony, lacking a strong army to safeguard the integrity of her frontiers, torn more and more by the forces of anarchy, the unhappy country could only await the edicts of Peter the Great, communicated to her through the Russian ambassador. The tragedy of partition already loomed on the horizon.

It was indeed a far cry from the time when the Catholic world, led by the newly born Tridentine Church, seemed on the point of overcoming her adversaries; the days of the White Mountain and the political 'Counter-Reformation' seemed very far away. The spirit of reform, however, the same spirit that had made possible the victory at Lepanto, still survived, and it found expression in the sphere in which it had met with its greatest success. Christendom, if we may still use the word, was threatened not only by internal dissension; another and a very old peril had just raised its head in the East—the Turkish threat. An offensive had been preparing since 1656, when the Albanian Köprili, Grand Vizir of Mohammed V, took control of the Ottoman Empire. In 1663 it was unleashed against the Danubian territories. Hungary, the bastion of the Cross, was the victim of brutal anti-Protestant measures devised by the emperors, and many Hungarians had thrown in their lot with the Turks. Faced with this danger, the Papacy assumed its ancient role and called for a crusade. In 1664, responding to an appeal by Alexander VII, an international army under the command of the Italian Montecucculi halted a Turco-Tartar army 200,000 strong in the neighbourhood of the St Gothard monastery on the Raab, where a contingent sent by Louis XIV and including the flower of the French nobility fought with great distinction. But the threat of the Crescent was not thereby repelled, because the Emperor Leopold was in too great a hurry to sign peace through fear of his Hungarian subjects, and also because Hungary had been ravaged by war for many years. The Turks then launched a new attack, this time against Crete, a dependency of Venice. Despite Clement IX's earnest appeals and the help sent by Louis XIV, Candia was compelled to capitulate (1669). A second Turkish assault upon the Danube was

L

made in support of the Hungarian rebel Tökölli, who had asked for their help. A complete rout followed. Two hundred and fifty thousand soldiers of ten nations flung themselves upon Vienna and its fifty thousand inhabitants, and the dawn of the year 1683 seemed to herald the end.

But once again the Pope acted. Innocent XI begged all Christian states to abandon their internecine quarrels and unite against the advance of Islam; Louis XIV alone of the great Catholic princes of the West remained deaf to his entreaties. In Vienna labourers, middle-class citizens and students, inspired by the eloquence of a Capuchin, Marco d'Aviano, fought side by side at the barricades under the command of Roger von Stahremberg. Meanwhile the counter-offensive was under way. As the sixty thousand imperial troops commanded by Charles de Lorraine were of poor quality, the Pope sent financial assistance together with an army of twenty-five thousand crack troops led by John Sobieski, King of Poland; it was their heroic charge against the slopes of Kahlenberg that saved Vienna. The Turkish retreat began. The fact that the Polish forces had saved the day humiliated the emperor; he showed his resentment towards Sobieski and declined even to thank him for his support. The emperor reorganized his army, putting excellent generals in command, and once again took the offensive. One after another the fortified towns of Hungary were captured, and in 1686 the fortress of Buda, 'the shield of Islam', which had been held by the infidel for a hundred and forty-five years, was reoccupied. A Holy Christian League organized by Rome, and joined by the czar despite his contempt for it, carried the war into the Ottoman Empire. It invaded Zante, Cephalonia and Leucade, and captured Corinth. When the League bombarded Athens, the Parthenon, used by the Turks to store gunpowder, was blown up and suffered irreparable damage (1697). Prince Eugene and the Venetian Morosini won great glory. The Sultan was forced to sign the peace of Carlovitz, under which he abandoned Transylvania and the whole Hungarian plain. All that remained to him was Temesvar, from which he was later driven by Christian forces at the request of Clement XI. The peace of Passarovitz (1718) confirmed the overthrow of Turkish power in the Balkans. This was the first step in a long series of events that was to continue into the twentieth century, and eventually brought about the downfall of the Sublime Porte. It is doubtful, however, whether we may regard this achievement as a Christian victory, a crusade. Christian principles played very little part in the emperor's Hungarian policy or in the Venetian campaign of pillage which destroyed so many monuments of ancient art. The spirit of Lepanto was no more. The defence of religious interests was no longer at issue; there were other interests to defend.

14. THE TROUBLES OF THE PAPACY

What was the position of the Papacy during this momentous period in which the Church, while apparently enjoying a glorious present, had cause to be uneasy about the uncertainties of the future? We have seen with what an admirable sense of duty she conducted the struggle against the Turks. The victory of St Gothard could never have been achieved without Alexander VII; the victory of 1683 would not have been so outstanding without the enormous amount of money collected by Innocent XI to finance Sobieski's expedition; and behind the military achievements of Prince Eugene in 1715 and the Christian counter-attack in Morea lay the diplomatic skill of the wise and energetic Clement XI. But did all this mean that the Papacy had regained its authority, that it was in a position to resume its former role as leader of the Christian world?

It is certainly true that the Church was no longer governed by unworthy popes. The seven pontiffs of the classical age may have been very different from each other (Alexander VIII and Innocent XII were far from agreement on all points); but all were worthy of esteem and two of admiration. None could certainly be compared with Julius II or a Borgia.

The strong and courageous Alexander VII died in 1667 after a troubled pontificate,[1] sad at heart because of the humiliations inflicted upon him by Louis XIV,[2] and immersed towards the end of his life in a gloomy piety. He left behind him the memory of indomitable energy, a good life and an upright character. Clement IX (1667–9), who occupied the Chair of St Peter for less than three years, was a shrewd and wise Tuscan, hard on himself and kind to others; *aliis, non sibi clemens* was his motto. He strove with remarkable determination to fulfil his duties, and was the very embodiment of charity, a spirit of conciliation [3] and courage—as on the occasion when a decision had to be made to snatch Crete from the clutches of the Turks. The aged Cardinal Altieri was next elected Pope after the interregnum of five months. The election was marred by disputes arising from the fact that the new Pope was eighty-four years old, and his reign seemed certain to be ineffectual. He wept bitterly before agreeing to accept the heavy responsibility, but after his coronation as Clement X (1670–6) he proved to be anything but incompetent. He worked extremely hard on behalf of the Missions, resisted Louis XIV in the affair of the *régale*, and helped Poland with subsidies to maintain the struggle against the

---

[1] See Chapter II, p. 148.
[2] See Chapter IV, p. 215.
[3] It was in connection with his efforts that the expression *Pax Clementina* came into use; he arranged a temporary settlement of the Jansenist affair (see Chapter VI, p. 363).

Turks. Deep down in that soul inspired by the spirit of reform dwelt a degree of holiness badly needed by the age.

With Innocent XI (1676–89) sanctity returned to the Chair of St Peter, such as had not been seen since Pius V a century earlier. The Christian people had acclaimed him as a saint long before his beatification by the Church in 1956. His name was Benedict Odescalchi; his family came from the shores of Lake Como in the north of Italy. He was a noble figure with all the solid qualities characteristic of men from that part of the country: tenacity, courage in the performance of duty, frugality and a love of discipline. According to his portraits he was slim and rather delicate looking, with a long nose and face, elongated still further by a goatee beard; there is a look of thoughtfulness on his face, anxiety even. His biographers relate that he experienced such emotion when he said Mass (which he considered himself too unworthy to do every day) that he often shed tears at the altar. He was a model of piety, austerity and simplicity of life—the perfect example of an utterly dedicated priest who has renounced all things. But his personal austerity was accompanied by infinite tactfulness towards others. As Papal Legate at Ferrara, and later Bishop of Novara, he was already well known for his unbounded generosity, his visits to the sick, the criminals and the destitute. Innocent X who, despite his weakness, was a good judge of men, gave him the cardinal's hat and entrusted him with tasks at the Vatican that were subsequently included in the duties of the Secretariat of State—an appointment that struck fear into the hearts of many of the Roman nobility, the ladies of fashion, and even the superiors of religious congregations.

Everyone had good reason to beware, for Innocent XI attacked abuses of every description from the moment he was elected Pope. He abolished sinecures, and none of his nephews received advancement. The regular clergy were strictly controlled and led back to the discipline of their Rule, especially the Dominicans and Cistercians. Before appointing a bishop the Holy Pontiff made a very thorough personal investigation into the candidate's spiritual qualities and the extent of his learning. Parish priests were called upon to preach, to be 'simple and pious', to teach the Catechism, reside within their parishes and conduct themselves properly. The behaviour of Roman ladies of fashion was censured; many of them objected to the Holy Father's regulations concerning dress as their husbands did to his decrees on the subject of gambling. Some have accused Innocent XI of Jansenism, because of the severity with which he defended morals. Though he attacked the Quietism of Molinos [1] and gave his whole-hearted support to Father Tirso Gonzalez, the great adversary of all Laxists and Probabilists, he showed no sympathy whatever with the doctrines of

1 See Chapter VI, p. 373.

Jansenius; it was moreover during his pontificate that Port-Royal disintegrated. Benedict Odescalchi was no great theologian, but he was a defender of the faith.

He was an equally forceful defender of the rights of the Church and the Catholic world. It is touching and even paradoxical that a man physically frail and whose life was so deeply spiritual could fight so fiercely. He was the one Pope who stood firm against the might of Louis XIV, even to the point of excommunicating the French ambassador Lavardin; rather than yield, he preferred to see his Avignon estates seized by French troops.[1] By sheer energy and diplomacy he succeeded in forming the coalition against the Turks, and was therefore the real victor of Kahlenberg. All these courageous achievements were in harmony with the charity that he evinced to the end of his life. When he was compelled for political reasons to refrain from condemning the revocation of the Edict of Nantes, he approached James II of England on behalf of the unhappy Huguenot refugees. Even at the height of conflict with the Turks he found time to interest himself in a field hospital which he had sent with Sobieski's forces and which may be considered the forerunner of Catholic Red Cross work. When Innocent XI died on 12th August 1689 the whole of Rome flocked to watch the funeral *cortège* as it proceeded from the Quirinal to the Vatican. With difficulty the hearse pushed its way through the eager crowd striving to touch the coffin with a piece of material or some other object to be kept as a relic. No Pope of that period had such a deep and lasting influence upon events.

The brief reign of Alexander VIII (1689–91) was very different. Not that this shrewd Venetian was unimportant; he was proficient in canon law, very well acquainted with ecclesiastical administration, and had acted as adviser to seven Roman congregations. His foreign policy too was praiseworthy, for he worked to restore peace with France. But while Rome rejoiced at the revival of those ostentatious and licentious festivals which Innocent had forbidden, she was angered by the new Pope's weakness for all his relations. The nepotism of the Ottoboni was soon as proverbial as had been that of the Barberini; but it did not last for long.

When Cardinal Pignatelli became Innocent XII (1691–1700) it was not without good reason that he took the name of his saintly predecessor. Beneath a gracious exterior he retained the severity of an inquisitor, which office he had previously held. His harsh measures against nepotism created a deep impression, and he made it clear to priests, bishops and even to cardinals that they must preach by example. He attacked Quietists and Jansenists alike; but he also knew how to care for the poor and the orphans of Rome with the tenderness

[1] See Chapter IV, p. 223.

of a father. His death in the middle of the Jubilee Year came as a surprise, and saddened the Catholic world.

He was followed by the first Pope of the eighteenth century, Clement XI (1700–21), who proved a worthy successor. He was an eminent jurist and a former governor of the papal cities of Urbino and Rieti; he had such an impressive personality that he was unanimously elected by the Conclave despite the fact that, though a cardinal for ten years, he had been ordained and had said his first Mass only two days before the Conclave. Immersed in countless political problems, he maintained against the emperor and the Duke of Savoy the same firm attitude he had adopted towards Louis XIV. It came quite naturally to that kindly and erudite Umbrian, the friend of art and literature, to defend the Church against Christian princes as against the Turks: he was likewise the champion of morals, of the spirit of reform and of the true faith. The Bull *Unigenitus* was his work.

This impressive series of popes has earned much unfair criticism from French historians, who have resented the Holy See's opposition to the policies of Louis XIV. It is therefore imperative to emphasize their qualities, for they were imbued with the true Christian spirit. In those days not every aspect of Roman life was commendable, whether we consider the papal *entourage*, the religious Orders or even the Sacred College. The secret dispatches of the nuncios and the Secretariat of State suggest that there was some truth in the bantering satire of Saint-Simon. Fabio Chigi, Pope Alexander VII, made no secret of his opinion of his namesake, Cardinal Sigismund Chigi, whose gay parties and quail-shooting set tongues wagging. Neither had Ginetti, Mellini or Bassadonna much regard for their purple. So many rumours circulated concerning Cardinal Carpegna that Innocent XI instructed another cardinal, the virtuous Casanetta, to hold an inquiry. These imperfections, so close to the Apostolic See, saddened and disturbed the saintly Pope, and Cardinal d'Estrées records that he heard him deplore them. When a cardinal died the Pope deliberately refrained from appointing a successor until twenty-four vacancies remained in the Sacred College; he thus reduced the number of cardinals to fifty in the hope that he might improve their quality. When Cardinal Maidalchini had himself ordained priest the Pope forbade him to celebrate Mass! But the existence of a few black sheep should not lead us to exaggerate the evil; many of the clergy were excellent and worthy of the greatest praise. Blessed Gregory Barbarigo was a model of zeal, charity, piety and learning. Cardinal Bonvisi, Nuncio in Vienna, the Spanish Cardinal Saenz d'Aguire and the Austrian Cardinal Leopold von Kollonitz were no less virtuous. After Innocent XI an intense effort was made, especially by Innocent XII and Clement XI, to refine the Sacred College and combat every abuse.

The struggle against nepotism, which had been a veritable scourge of the Holy See during the preceding epoch, is typical of the efforts made in this direction. If we exclude Alexander VIII, not one of the pontiffs we have just mentioned permitted himself to yield to this very natural but disastrous tendency. Urged by Bonvisi, Kollonitz, Saenz and Albani (who became Clement XI), Innocent XII decided to strike an effective blow against these long-established abuses, and in 1692 published his Bull *Romanum decet Pontificem*, under which the Canons forbidding bishops to enrich their near relations with ecclesiastical property were applied also to the Holy See. 'Popes may appoint one nephew only as cardinal. Under no pretext whatever may they give money, property or responsible posts to their relatives. If any of their relatives are without means, Popes may assist them as they would help any poor people. If a relative of the Pope becomes cardinal as a result of personal merit, his emoluments shall not exceed 12,000 Roman crowns.' At the same time this energetic Pope abolished all appointments, whether civil, military or ecclesiastical, that were traditionally granted as sinecures to the relatives or agnates of the reigning Pope.

These and similar gestures had a far-reaching effect. It is interesting to note that in the great doctrinal disputes of the period (Jansenism and Quietism) Rome always had the last word in the long run. Even Louis XIV had willy-nilly to reach an understanding with the Pope in order to settle the question of Port-Royal. In the Church of the classical age everything pertaining to the permanence of the spirit of reform depended upon the popes and had their support. This was just as true of Rancé and his Trappists as it was of Father Cloche and his Dominicans. We shall see [1] evidence of the personal intervention of the popes, often a deciding factor, in overseas missionary work. It is also interesting to note the number of saints canonized and beatified by those pontiffs, especially by Clement X and Alexander VIII. Among those canonized were men who reflected the priestly ideal, such as Francis Borgia, Laurence Giustiniani and Pius V; such reformers as Cajetan of Tiene; such great missionary figures as Louis Bertrand, Francis Solanus, Rose of Lima; souls utterly dedicated to God, such as John of the Cross, Peter of Alcàntara, Mary Magdalen dei Pazzi. There existed an undoubted relation between the choice and the purpose.

It stands to reason that this determined effort to give back to the Papacy its position of authority increased its prestige. Even when, politically speaking, things were going badly for the Pope, Louis XIV was careful to show him great personal respect. The respectful manner in which public figures spoke of or to the popes during that period was not in the least comparable with their former treatment, e.g. at the

[1] See *The Church in the Eighteenth Century*, Chapter II.

beginning of the sixteenth century. The deference with which the sacred office of Pope was surrounded was plain for all to see; there existed a real distinction between the man and his position. Everyone knew that papal elections were the occasions of all kinds of political schemes, and that pressure was brought to bear on behalf of various interests. It was often said of a cardinal that he was 'of the crown', meaning that in the Sacred College he was less a man of the Church than the representative of some monarch. In this connection Mme de Sévigné wrote: 'You have only to read history to appreciate that a religion which owes its origin and its survival to a permanent miracle cannot be regarded as a figment of man's imagination. Believe me, despite all that goes on in Conclave, it is always the Holy Ghost who chooses the Pope.' The crowds who flocked to Rome from the four corners of the earth during the great Jubilee Year of 1700 did not, of course, concern themselves with such questions; at other periods in history, less propitious as far as the Holy See was concerned, such manifestations always drew the crowds, for the glory of Rome and of the Vicar of Christ has always been resplendent. It is none the less important that thinking Catholics should be aware of the facts.

The idea of Papal Infallibility began to make positive progress during the seventeenth century, although the age appeared to have surrendered to victorious caesaropapism. It is true that the old conciliar theories were still occasionally advanced, even by Bossuet; but no one took them seriously any longer. Papal Infallibility had not yet been defined as a dogma, and still had numerous enemies, but the fact seemed to be gradually forcing itself upon men's minds. A great impression was created by St Robert Bellarmine's comment in his splendid treatise on the Roman Pontiff, referring to Christ's words in the Gospel of St Luke: 'But I have prayed for thee that thy faith fail not: and thou being once converted, confirm thy brethren' (Luke xxii. 32). In fact, no one questioned the sovereign right of the Vicar of Christ to make laws. On that point even Jansenius entertained no doubt. During the period 1703–5, when the French bishops endeavoured to oppose a procedure that tended to reserve to the Holy See alone full and exclusive jurisdiction in doctrinal matters, Clement XI retorted bluntly: 'Who made you judges? The bishops hold their prerogatives from the Roman Pontiff alone. The Pope has no use for their opinions; he calls upon them to obey.' Public opinion approved language of this kind. The doctrine of Infallibility was demonstrated more and more ably by the works of Viva, Billuart, Kilber and Orsi in the *Biblioteca Pontificia Maxima*, and later on in the treatises of Petitdidier and Fénelon; but its elements were still not precisely defined. Fénelon saw Infallibility as the privilege of the Roman Church, Billuart as the personal prerogative of the Sovereign Pontiff;

but, in any case, the idea was on the way to becoming common doctrine.

However, this lovely picture contained dark shadows. Here, as in every other field, the Great Century, especially the classical period, was remarkable less as an era of perfect stability than as a time of grave crisis during which dogged and courageous attempts were made to maintain the ever-threatened order of things. The Papacy was very well aware that formidable forces were ranged against it: absolutism, Erastianism and Gallicanism.[1] All three endeavoured to impose the notion of complete independence of the monarchs in relation to the spiritual power, and even to justify the ascendancy of the State over the religious sphere of influence. It is to the glory of Innocent XI that he boldly threw the whole weight of papal authority against the Great King's caesaropapism which had been so cautiously handled by his predecessors. It was the Holy See that finally won the battle against Gallicanism, although Louis XIV took cunning revenge by publishing his Fifty Articles. The same problem arose in all other Catholic countries. The Pope protested to the emperor concerning the handling of Peter's Pence. In Spain there was ceaseless argument about levies and taxation; indeed the dispute became so acrimonious under Philip V that diplomatic relations between Madrid and Rome were broken off. Similar problems arose in Bavaria and Poland. But it was not simply a question of money. As in France, where the affair of the *régale* precipitated the Gallican conflict, the underlying issues were everywhere much more serious than a mere matter of finance.

In the sphere of international politics the Papacy was not only attacked by hostile forces; she was nearly defeated. She never recovered her position as arbiter of the Christian world. The fact that the Pope's representatives were excluded from the negotiations at Osnabrück and Münster, where the treaties of Westphalia were agreed upon with complete contempt for the interests of the Church, confirmed the political eclipse of the Papacy; in other words, all hope of securing the triumph of a Christian political morality was killed. Not that the Popes did not seek to resume their ancient role. Alexander VII and Clement IX endeavoured to unite Catholic states against the Turks; Clement X worked for peace between Genoa and Savoy, and offered to mediate between Paris and Vienna; Innocent XI devoted himself body and soul to the reconciliation of nations; and Clement XI embarked upon similar negotiations. On the whole all these efforts proved unsuccessful; the secularization of international policy continued. In vain, for example, did Innocent XI take it upon himself to guide the conscience of Louis XIV, to remind him, often in moving terms, of his duties as a

---

[1] See Chapter III, section 12: 'Towards Absolutism in Europe'.

* L

Christian.[1] Henceforward decisions were reached on all important political matters without consulting the Holy See or taking any account of the higher interests of Christendom. On the threshold of the eighteenth century states even disposed of the Pope's fiefs, under the treaties of Utrecht and Rastadt, without the least consideration for his sovereign rights. The political eclipse of the Holy See reached a climax with the criminal partition of Poland while the popes looked on helplessly.

A similar eclipse took place in the field of ideas. The novel trends invading minds and consciences [2] no longer took account of papal views—a fact which emphasizes yet another weakness on the part of Rome towards the end of the seventeenth century. Did they appreciate the gravity of the crisis and the importance of the issues at stake? Did they lack the ability or intelligence to anticipate the future? Their usual approach to subversive doctrines was to counter by condemning them. But was it sufficient to place on the Index the *Provinciales*, the *Discours de la méthode* (subject to amendment), Fontenelle's *Histoires des oracles*, Bayle's *Dictionnaire*, and even the biblical works of Richard Simon? Twentieth-century Popes, including Pius XI and Pius XII, have realized that mere condemnation of modern errors is not sufficient in the war against them; the world and its problems need to be 'rethought' from genuinely Catholic viewpoints. This the popes of the seventeenth century scarcely understood, and their silence was disturbing.

The popes of the classical age, infinitely more praiseworthy than their immediate predecessors, do appear to have made a valiant attempt to lessen the effects of the contemporary crisis, but we cannot refrain from thinking that they might have achieved more in the circumstances. The eighteenth century could not deny the temporary eclipse of papal power.

15. CHRISTIAN ART DURING THE GREAT REIGN

Was it coincidental that the classical age corresponded with a lowering of vitality in religious art? [3] From 1670 to 1680 the fact was obvious. Borromini died in 1667, Bernini in 1680; and during the year 1682–3 Louis XIV became established in Versailles. The climate had changed. Clement X erected the two fountains in the piazza of St Peter's and planned the Ponte Sant' Angelo. Clement XI encouraged tapestry and mosaic, thus enabling Rome to compete with the schools of Venice and Ravenna. Generally speaking, however, the popes were occupied with cares of a different nature, and were no longer deeply

[1] See Chapter IV, p. 229.
[2] See *The Church in the Eighteenth Century*, Chapter I.
[3] See Chapter II, p. 118 et seq.

interested in art. Even in France, at that time resplendent as the home of all the arts, very few works can be considered distinctively Christian. Churches already in course of construction were completed, among them Saint-Sulpice, whose architect, Le Vau, who died in 1670, had been able to finish only the choir, the transept and a small portion of the nave. But very little new work was commenced. The masterpieces of religious architecture during the Great Reign were the dome of the Invalides and the Chapel of Versailles, both of which tended to the glory of the king as much as to the glory of God. The vast work undertaken at Saint-Denis under the direction of Robert de Cotte towards the end of the reign was destined to receive the body of the all-powerful monarch himself.

These facts do not by any means imply that the artists of this period were less imbued with faith than their forbears. The solid sense of Christianity that we have seen so firmly rooted in the souls of other men during the Great Century was just as much alive and exacting among painters and sculptors. Le Brun, Puget and Girardon each devoted part of his fortune to the building of a chapel in his favourite church; the first at Nicolas-du-Chardonnet, the second at Saint-Madeleine de Marseille; the third at Saint-Landry in Paris. Jacques Courtois, nicknamed 'the Raphael of Battles', was among the famous converts of the day, and he became a Jesuit. Even Coysevox and Watteau, who left to posterity the pagan grace of 'Vénus à la coquille', 'Aphrodite accroupie' and 'Embarquements pour Cythère', were none the less sincere Christians who seemed in no way to suffer from the distinction between their profession and their spiritual life. 'Rigaud's last painting,' observes Langevin, 'when he was rich in years and blessed by fortune, is one of the only two religious pictures we have from his brush; I refer to his "Presentation in the Temple", which re-echoes so clearly the artist's *nunc dimittis*.'

The fact that Christian art did not occupy the eminent place it had held formerly did not point to a diminution of faith, but rather to a change of attitude on the part of society towards art. Society was invited less frequently to praise God, because it was expected to exalt man, especially through the apotheosis of kings. The amount of money devoted to the building of churches during the reign of Louis XIV cannot be compared with the sum spent on Versailles. The vast hall of the Great King's palace, in which he received the homage of his loyal subjects, was perhaps the true sanctuary rather than the chapel. This trend is not noticeable in France alone; in Prussia, Portugal, Austria and Poland princes followed the example of Versailles. It has been estimated that thirty thousand sumptuous town and country houses were built throughout Europe between 1660 and 1715. Secularization was therefore evident in art as in all other fields. Towards the

end of the reign it developed into a process of sensualization confirming
that final breach with faith, as we shall see when dealing with the
eighteenth century. It may be said therefore that immediately on the
death of Louis XIV the sails were set, as in Watteau's picture, in the
direction of Cythera.

But Christian art did not cease to exist. When the vast assets of
states and the capital of wealthy patrons, so essential to the development of architecture, were diverted from the building of churches,[1]
religious art turned towards painting and sculpture to adorn existing
churches or to decorate private chapels. Pierre Puget (1622–97), the
genius who carved 'Milo of Croton', also sculptured the wonderful
'Stoning of St Stephen' at Aix and the moving 'Magdalen's Communion'. Girardon (1628–1715), on the recommendation of Le Brun,
dedicated to the memory of Richelieu the sensitive mausoleum in the
chapel of the Sorbonne. Coysevox (1640–1720) compared very favourably with him as the sculptor of Mazarin's tomb, but excelled him in
his 'Descent from the Cross' in the chancel of Notre Dame at Paris.
Nicolas Courtois (1656–1719) commemorated in marble the vow made
by Louis XIII. Finally Sebastien Slodtz (1655–1726) was responsible
for the statue of Faith, a little-known masterpiece in the chapel of the
palace at Versailles.

During that period painting was more fashionable than sculpture.
The taste spread both from Flanders and from Italy, and churches
everywhere teemed with paintings. They covered walls, overcrowded
chapels, and attained enormous dimensions. Vicarages, cathedral
chapters, confraternities, the residences of nobles and wealthy citizens
—all wanted paintings. At the church of Saint-Germain l'Auxerrois
the pictures were changed throughout the year according to the feasts!
The guild of goldsmiths and silversmiths at Paris ordered every year
a gift for Our Lady, and it usually took the form of a huge painting.
This *genre* produced its own specialists; among them were Philippe de
Chennevières, who painted a large number of such pictures, and
Sacquespée, who was seven times prize-winner of the 'Palinods de Puy
de l'Immaculée Conception.' But the masters who won fame in profane
art had Christian pictures also to their credit: Le Brun (1619–90), his
'Triumph of the Virgin', 'Martyrdom of St Stephen' and 'Elevation
of the Cross'; Mignard (1610–95), a friend of Molière, his graceful
'Virgin with Grape', which hangs in the Louvre, and among many
other works, his amazing 'Baptism of Christ' in the church of Saint-
Jean. There were also the two Coypels (father and son), de la Fosse

---

[1] This does not include abbeys; a good number of abbots, whether commendatory or
regular, put in hand repairs or rebuilding in the classical style of architecture, which
resulted in edifices of great dignity. A splendid example is the Premonstratensian abbey
of Mondaye, in Normandy, which has often been imitated.

and Jouvenet (a student of Rubens and the Carracci), all less famous but far from inconsiderable. We have already referred to Rigaud, but we might also mention Largillière's 'Offering of St Genevieve'. It must not be forgotten that all these artists took their religious paintings seriously. Lomazzo's book, *The Temple of Painting*, read at that time in a French translation, warned painters that before beginning to portray a Christian subject they should ascertain from theologians 'how to represent God, the angels, the soul, the devil, the saints and heaven; their appearance, colours according to their functions, and, generally speaking, any pious stories attached to them'. And no one failed to follow the injunction. Le Brun based his work on these principles when he attempted to express the theology of his master M. Olier.

Though fewer churches were built in the classical age, the period remained fertile in religious art, thanks to painting and sculpture; not only, of course, in France, but in every great Catholic country. To place all this work under one heading and label it 'classical art' is hardly satisfactory. It seems to flow from two great sources. Baroque on the one hand had its hour of glory during the preceding period, and continued along its course. It produced no more masters of Bernini's eminence, but a multitude of talented votaries. From the Tyrol to Sicily, from Portugal to Bohemia, and even as far as Latin America, hundreds of churches and chapels were still being built and decorated in that style. Swept along by its strange genius, Baroque became more and more luxuriant, more complicated and over-elaborate, perhaps even wanton and artificial. Rocaille and Rococo began to make their appearance, and the form retained very little Christian inspiration.

The other trend was altogether different. A reaction set in against the excesses of Baroque, and an attempt was made to subject art to rules and standards, to logic and a more ordered taste. No more church façades resembling drapery lashed by the wind; no more naves overladen with ornamentation. From the models of antiquity artists selected the austerity of their colonnades and their harsh equilibrium. Henceforward the taste was for façades of orderly appearance, whose beauty emanated from the strictly mathematical harmony of their parts; naves that were spacious, cold and naked, whose glory proceeded from the quality of the material, depending no longer upon the lavishness of their decoration. Such a conception of art corresponded to a very formal religious expression linked with an all-powerful monarchical system: the religion of such a man as Bossuet.

This opposition between two trends of Baroque was purely theoretical; it had no foundation in fact. A great deal of Baroque survived even in the great classical art of the age of Louis XIV; it was apparent in the component members of architectural types. Were the colonnade and the dome borrowed from antiquity or from Baroque? Was not the influence of the 'Jesuit churches' and Bernini's colonnade considerable? But decoration owes more to Baroque than one usually cares to admit. This applied to altar-pieces, which, as we have seen, were so ornate and so often exhibited the influence of the Carracci and Rubens. Baroque also were those characteristically 'classical' sculptures, in which marble was shaped in a manner to suggest the pliability of cloth. Baroque was the reredos, which in so many churches rose up behind an equally Baroque and lavishly decorated altar. The arrangement of sumptuous funerals was similarly affected. When illustrious personages were to be buried the nave was hung with voluminous black draperies ornamented with braid and silver tears, accompanied by symbolical figures, torches and ornamental chandeliers. In some way the sense of the grandiose, the ostentatious and the majestic visible in classical art was not inconsistent with Baroque tradition, but was rather a direct continuation of it.

Briefly, we might almost say that Christian art in the Great Century was 'classical' as to its exterior structure, but retained much that was Baroque in its interior arrangement. It is astonishing that this blend did not result in lack of harmony; but the artists of those days, thanks to good taste and an innate sense of proportion, apparently knew how to harmonize elements that were naturally opposed. But did not the spiritual life of that time inherit the lessons of the Council of Trent and the French School? Is it not possible to feel the tension between opposing tendencies? Not only did Baroque and the Classic coexist, but the faith of Rancé and Bourdaloue coexisted with that of Bossuet and Fénelon, because the religion of that day was vigorous.

The two aspects of classical religious art may be considered in what are perhaps the only two French monuments dating from the reign of Louis XIV which achieved fulness of expression: Saint-Louis des Invalides and the chapel of Versailles. The value of the first lies in its purity of architectural line, the perfect balance in the colonnades of the façade, the majestic thrust of the dome set so firmly upon its drum. It is the Christian masterpiece of Mansart (1598–1666), wherein he displayed the 'classical' in the most formal sense of the term. In style Mansart stands out as the heir of antiquity; indeed this architect, who must have read Descartes, brought antiquity back to life. The beauty of the chapel of Versailles lies in its interior decoration, so rich in detail, so graceful and of such remarkable freedom of touch; austere restraint is certainly not its overriding quality. Both these works are typical of France under Louis XIV, and are in keeping with the religion of the Most Christian King and his age.[1]

---

[1] See V. L. Tapié's excellent book, *Baroque et classicisme*, mentioned in the bibliographical notes.

Music was equally wedded to the glory of the Great King.[1] One cannot imagine the festivities of Versailles without the accompaniment of orchestras scattered about the gardens, and human voices mingling with the *arpeggio* of the fountains. The reign of Louis XIV was the period when opera, which had recently known such rapid development in Italy, took France by storm; it was the age when the instrumental concert that came to the fore about 1660 became rooted in the life of the nation. But there was clearly nothing specifically Christian about that.

Religious music was not, however, omitted from society's infatuation with musical expression. Every great master of the day included sacred music in his compositions. Even Jean-Baptiste Lulli (1632–87), a free-thinker from Florence (and probably an atheist), wrote a *De Profundis*, a *Miserere* and a number of motets, apart from his successful operas. Among other composers of motets and similar works of Christian inspiration were J.-B. Moreau, the author of the two choral works *Esther* and *Athalie*, Clérambault, Couperin le Grand (1668–1733) and Rameau (1683–1733), most of whose compositions were adjuncts of secular entertainment during the Regency and the reign of Louis XV. Moreover, the king himself was interested in music. The standard of performance at the chapel of Versailles, in which Du Mont and Lalande won fame, was extremely high. The organs at Versailles, the Invalides and in the more important provincial cathedrals were first-class instruments. Sung Masses with organ and orchestra achieved beauty that still has power to move us; those of Du Mont and Couperin le Grand have a worthy companion in Lalande's *Office of Tenebrae*. Motets were likewise enormously popular. Lully wrote twenty-three, which, though they lack feeling, reveal an occasional upsurge of fervour and magnificence. On the death of Lalande, Louis XV commanded that his forty motets be published in collected form. Apart from the formal type of music, in which Lully (and after him Lalande) was a sort of dictator, there were some ingenious Psalms by André Campra. Marc-Antoine Charpentier (1634–1704) drew on sacred history for subjects from which his strange genius produced such masterpieces as *The Prodigal Son* and *St Peter's Denial*.[2]

In Italy too profane music began to develop rapidly. Every little court had its theatrical company for the purpose of presenting opera. Venice outshone them all; but there also religious music benefited from the vogue. Operatic orchestras played at High Mass; the Sistine Chapel was celebrated on that account as well as for its *castrati*. The fashionable oratorio and motet continued to flourish side by side with

[1] See Chapter II, p. 122.
[2] It must not be forgotten that great missioners—among them St Grignion de Montfort—composed canticles that are not lacking in quality.

Masses, of which Alessandro Scarlatti wrote no fewer than twenty. The oratorio was the favourite form of Carissimi, and of the venturesome Stradella, whose style was elegant, lucid and precise. Immensely successful was the cantata, in which solo and choral vocals alternated; popular too was the recitative, invented by Alessandro Grandi in 1620, shortly before his untimely death.

The same forms were adopted in Germany. Hitherto the German-speaking world had been relatively unproductive in other spheres of art; but now, under some mysterious influence, Germany revealed herself as the land of music, and above all of religious music. She came into her own in the biblical atmosphere of Protestantism, and ultimately produced such illustrious men as Bach and the exuberant George Frederick Handel.

16. THE DAWN OF A NEW CENTURY

The period known as the classical age could not last for ever; and, as in the case of all great eras, it closed at a time when society appeared to have attained a state of fulness and stability. It is not man's destiny to achieve a permanent synthesis of passions and principles, interests and ideals. The century of Pericles was doomed to pass; so was that of Augustus, and the century of Louis XIV was no more eternal. In every field classicism reveals a courageous and determined attempt to impose order upon the forces of destruction which cruelly tormented the age. For a short time the attempt succeeded; an unhoped-for harmony was achieved. The political régime became an integral part of spiritual aspirations, and the social element endeavoured to identify itself with the religious ideal. But that stability, splendid though it was, was condemned to impermanence, for it depended upon circumstances and the presiding genius of a few men. Time would challenge its constancy.

Thus the end of the reign of Louis XIV marked a turning-point. After the melancholy events and the pressure of the preceding ten years a reaction was inevitable. It occurred during the Regency and the reign of Louis XV, and was as much a moral and intellectual reaction as it was political. Indeed, premonitory signs might have been detected almost throughout the reign, certainly from 1680 onwards, when the principle of kingship by divine right began to be questioned at the very height of its triumph, and when the coalition of European states threatened the ascendancy of Louis XIV. At the time of the despot's death thirty-five years later the threats had become more alarming, and the menace of disintegration loomed on all sides.

By a strange coincidence, just as a change of political climate occurred in the entire West at the very moment when Louis XIV assumed personal control of affairs, so did his death seem to be irresistibly significant; for the seventeenth century died with him. In every sphere and from every point of view the eighteenth century was clearly destined to be different. What had happened to the theory of divine right in England, where on two occasions—when the crown was given to William of Orange and then to George I—the 'right' was exercised by a perfectly human will? And what was it worth to the House of Brandenburg and the House of Savoy, who owed their leadership of Germany and Italy respectively solely to their own courage and ingenuity? A transformation had taken place in social life; those classes that were deemed to be at the bottom of the ladder began to question the right of the hierarchical system which placed them there. The economic evolution of the West tended to challenge the old order of things; capitalism was born, money increased in importance at the expense of land, and the role of bankers was magnified.

But there were other more disquieting signs. At that period, as always when great changes are imminent, the true causes of the crisis lay in man himself. He questioned his very conception of life and of himself. Very early in the seventeenth century indications of this 'crisis of the European conscience' were evident. The crisis, which according to Paul Hazard began around 1675, was really an indissoluble blend of crises relative to the intellect and the moral conscience. Furthermore, a spirit of libertinism manifested itself early—a growing cleavage between faith and life, the first satanic attack in the revolt against God. Many leading figures noted these evident signs—even Bossuet, who was seldom endowed with the gift of prophecy. They were the source of the great onslaught soon to be made against the concepts under which the world had hitherto been governed, and against the human powers that controlled it.

That onslaught would be directed likewise against divine authority, for the Church was deeply involved in the impending crisis. She was intimately linked with the principles of statecraft and the organization of society during the classical age; she sustained and buttressed the entire system. If the régime were threatened how could the Church possibly avoid involvement? We appreciate that this relationship was essentially provisional; the Church, the spouse of Christ, the trustee of an eternal message, was bound to the régime only in that sense. In no other sense was she tied to any particular form of civilization. She was capable of dovetailing into any transitory system that history might produce without changing her destiny, which transcends time. There was a Church in pagan times and in medieval times; there was even the Church of the Renaissance and of Humanism. The Church of the Classical Age might in her turn drift towards the abyss; but 'the Church' as such must always survive.

To enable that to happen it was essential that the sap within her remain vigorous enough to engender future growth, that those in authority become quickly aware of gathering clouds, and do not confuse the transitory with the eternal in relation to the promise. They must be capable of distinguishing between a moribund world and one about to be born. That twofold function was magnificently fulfilled by the Church from the fifth to the tenth century, when she created the civilization of cathedral and crusade out of the bloody chaos of a barbarous Europe. We shall see her faced once more with the need to exorcize it again in modern times.

Several questions therefore present themselves. How did the Church react to the crisis of mind and conscience, and was she aware of what was at stake? Would she manage to give the correct answers to the questions men were asking themselves in the name of intellectual progress? Had she anything to offer beyond overruling authoritative statements by way of reply to a change of intellectual outlook that cast doubt upon her tenets? These questions constitute one of the serious problems facing the Church on the threshold of the century of Voltaire and the Revolution.[1]

Another question that was already being posed in a different form around 1660 was whether the Church had the energy and vitality required to renew herself while restoring the world. No doubt splendid work had already been done by saints and men of faith and talent to impregnate the marrow of society with the spirit of Christianity. It could not be said that the Church had failed to accomplish the mission imposed upon her from the beginning to raise up the baptized but sinful masses. Yet the fact remains that there was still a great deal to be done; that pure lustrous and radiant Christianity of which the greatest Christians have dreamed, a religion sufficiently robust to counter the difficulties of new times without harm, was still far from being a reality. By the end of the century there were many signs of an impending landslide: fewer missions, fewer books of instruction, and a return to many abuses. Furthermore, the Church herself experienced internal crises which shook her severely, one of which had not been disposed of by the beginning of the eighteenth century. These crises so reduced her power and prestige that she was unfortunately unable to face the storms of tomorrow with her forces intact.

[1] See *The Church in the Eighteenth Century*, Chapter I.

CHAPTER VI

THE DOCTRINAL CRISES OF
JANSENISM AND QUIETISM

1. A Theological Alliance

AT THE end of summer, 1621, two friends, both priests, met at the college of Sainte-Pulchérie in Louvain. Both had formerly been pupils at the city's university, one of the glories of the Church for nearly two centuries and an important cultural centre made famous by Erasmus, Latomus, Busleyden and Justus Lipsius. The university was also the centre of disputes and brawls, frequently occasioned by theological discussions.

It was a long time since the two friends had left college. One of them had returned to the Flemish city to become president of the college, in other words superior of the seminary. The other had come from Paris, where he resided. The younger was a Dutchman born in 1585, in the village of Accoi near Leerdam. He was lean and gaunt, all bone and muscle; the type of Dutchman whom the Spaniards had found unconquerable in Holland's struggle for independence. He was tall, with a long, slightly aquiline nose and a high brow; his chin jutted out, and his pointed, goatee beard made it seem even longer. His biretta gave him the appearance of a fighting man rather than a man of prayer. His eye was keen, and through the apparently unbroken calm of his features might be glimpsed an occasional flash of subdued storm. Those who knew him well were aware that his imperturbable air concealed intense emotion and a spirited character.

The Dutchman's parents were very poor, but he turned to Holy Orders, following in the footsteps of an uncle on his father's side who had succeeded in becoming Bishop of Ghent and a delegate at the Council of Trent. He had a brilliant career at the university, obtaining a first in literature and philosophy and a mastership in theology. He began by seeking admission to the Society of Jesus, but was rejected for some obscure reason, probably because he was ill-suited by disposition to a life of absolute obedience. Having returned to Louvain after a long absence in France he enjoyed a considerable reputation on account of his learning, piety, eloquence and strong principles. His name was Cornelius Jansen but, in the manner of the Humanists, he used the Latin name Cornelius Jansenius.

The Frenchman, whom Jansenius welcomed with open arms before

the fine marble statue of Our Lady which adorned the entrance to his
seminary, was a very different man. This restless little Basque was
prematurely bald, deeply lined and of stocky appearance; he had an
ardent and pained expression which was both disturbing and fascinating. His name was Jean-Ambroise Duvergier de Hauranne, and at
that time was forty years of age. Born in Paris in 1581 of a well-to-do
family, he received the tonsure at the age of ten, and was educated by
the Jesuits under the care of Bishop Bertrand d'Eschaux whom Henri
IV held in high esteem. A rosy future faced the young man. At twenty-
five he was given the well-endowed parish of Ixtassou, and in the
following year a canonry. It seemed therefore that he was destined to
lead the easy-going life of a rather worldly minded cleric, of whom
there were so many at that time. But that was not to be. He had within
him a hunger and thirst which the pleasures of the age could not
satisfy; neither could the intellectual attainments which had come to
him so easily in Paris and Louvain. His soul pined for God, reaching
out to an inaccessible holiness. Indeed, he was a strange and extraordinarily complex man whose character was made up of obvious
contradictions. Quarrelsome, bitingly and passionately critical of
everything, he adopted the discourteous and domineering air of a
prophet; yet he was capable of gaiety and tact, and displayed a winning
simplicity and an almost Franciscan charity. Undoubtedly this engaging
personality, this unfinished genius, could have been a saint. A few
months before the Frenchman's journey to Louvain the Bishop of
Poitiers, who admired him, presented him with a wealthy abbey which
rendered him secure from all material cares; in accordance with the
custom of the times he assumed the title of his living—Abbot of
Saint-Cyran.

It is very likely that these two men became acquainted at Louvain,
in the library or during one of the study-courses. They certainly met
again between 1604 and 1606 in Paris, as former students of the same
faculty; a little lost perhaps in the big city and rather unwelcome at the
Sorbonne where the theological tenets of the Louvain Jesuits were not
highly esteemed. They must have passed the long evenings debating
many a great problem during the interminable discussions which were
the joy of student life. The Dutchman Jansenius was well acquainted
with the problems of Protestant reform; and they no doubt touched
upon the different spheres of ecclesiastical and lay authority as expounded by the Gallican professor Edmond Richer [1] whose courses
they were following. As former students of the Jesuits they both
shared an intense and bitter antipathy towards their old masters, which
possibly explains the harsh judgments passed upon them by the Jesuits.
Temporarily separated, the two friends were later able to renew their

[1] See Chapter III, p. 180.

frequent discussions when Jansenius stayed five years in the Basque country, first as director of the college of Bayonne and later at Camp-de-Prats, the family estate of the Haurannes, where Jean-Ambroise's mother, 'the lady of Hauranne', treated him as a son. The two young men had reached a point in their relationship when feelings were subordinated to their common search after vital truths, neither really knowing what part each played individually in their work. Later they parted once more, one going to Louvain and the other to Poitiers and then to Paris. But distance was no barrier, for they maintained a communion of souls and minds by means of a continuous flow of letters written in the rather affected style of the time.

In September 1616 Cornelius sent Jean a particularly important letter; he told him of an intellectual revelation he had had, the truth of which he considered to be of such grave significance that he felt compelled to inform his friend at once. With passionate insistence he returned to the subject in letter after letter. Eventually the abbot of Saint-Cyran shared his friend's mental anguish: he became convinced that Jansenius was right. Surely it was absurd to occupy themselves with Greek and Latin authors, the Fathers of the Church, and even probing the Scriptures as they had both been doing up to then, while neither of them had found the reply to the fundamental question that tormented every Christian—'Shall I attain salvation, and how must I attain it?'

After a meeting with Father de Condren, the celebrated Oratorian, Saint-Cyran had become 'converted', in the Pascalian sense of the term, and he was ready to devote his whole mind to this single problem. Was it possible that his friend had indeed found the solution? Without delay he set out for Louvain.

The problems of divine grace and free will were among those that had racked men's consciences for twenty centuries, especially in the West, where personal salvation had always been regarded as the supreme problem. In the East, the East of Arius and Nestorius and metaphysical discussion, controversy had always raged around the dogma of the Blessed Trinity and the two natures of Christ. It was on such problems as the former, those stumbling-blocks that straddled the paths of faith, that Martin Luther had come to grief. Free will, man's helplessness, efficacious grace and sufficient grace—over these terms theologians were still in conflict even though the Council of Trent had formulated precise Catholic definitions. Thirty years earlier, in Louvain itself, Michel de Bay, nicknamed Baius, master and subsequently chancellor of the university (he died in 1589), endeavoured to reconcile Protestant concepts with the teaching of the Church. He was, however, condemned by St Pius V in 1567 and by Gregory XIII in 1579, and he submitted. But his ideas survived him, and his friend

Janson, professor of Holy Scripture at Louvain, maintained them, though cautiously through fear of the Holy Office, and they continued to be held. Others circulated similar ideas; among them the Irish Franciscan Conrius, whose courses, definitely Augustinian in character, created a sensation among the students. It became clear that the controversy relating to grace was not at an end when the Jesuits and the Dominicans confronted each other over Father Luis de Molina's book [1] *Concordia*, which dealt with the problem of reconciling grace and free will. The strict Thomists led by Bañez strenuously opposed it on the grounds that, apart from other defects, it led to a too facile moral outlook. A special Congregatio de Auxiliis was instituted by Clement VIII in 1597 to settle the controversy—which it declared itself unable to do. As bitterness increased Paul V forbade all theologians to refer to the matter publicly. But how was it possible to prevent Christians from discussing in secret, and to enthuse over and devote their life to questions which concerned issues most vital to man?

Jansenius, therefore, wrote to his friend that the only subject worthy of their complete attention and their whole existence was that of grace; in other words, salvation. And he added that he thought he had discovered the unique solution to its most complex problems, a solution that would reconcile all opposing theories, and provide the answer for which all men of faith were waiting.

But how, and where? Jansenius declared that the essentials of his discovery came from his reading of St Augustine. He was sure that within the voluminous and inexhaustible writings of the Bishop of Hippo everything was to be found—every question and every answer. Was he not called the 'Doctor of Grace'? He it was who had mapped out the right path through a maze of errors; he had defended God's rights against Pelagius and the rights of man against the Manichees. St Augustine! He was far and away superior to all those babblers who entangled themselves in Molinism and the arguments of the Schoolmen. Jansenius was quite definite: all truth dwelt in the inspired works of the African bishop.

Such was the subject of the ardent discussions of the two friends during the ten or twelve years that Jean Duvergier resided at the college of Sainte-Pulchérie. Undoubtedly Jansenius sketched out for Saint-Cyran the main points of the doctrine he had evolved and of which, as he considered, St Augustine would furnish the proofs. They discussed them together, while the naturally critical acumen of the little Basque raised objections to which the Dutchman was forced to reply.

---

[1] He was a Spanish-Jesuit who died in 1600, and must not be confused with another Spanish priest, Molinos, whose theses gave rise to the Quietist crisis. Molina's system is known by the name Molinism; but Molinosism is used with reference to the theories of Molinos.

Together also they grew excited over the grandeur and beauty of their discovery. What great service they would render the Church if they formulated in precise terms, with incontrovertible arguments, the doctrine they glimpsed!

Thus their great scheme was developed. Jansenius would devote himself to probing St Augustine in order to extract the substance of the work. He would read through the books on grace ten times, fifty times or more if necessary. He would write a commentary worthy of that genius; a work so profound, so perfect that it would meet with the approval of all enlightened minds. Thus their doctrine, their solution, would penetrate deeply into innumerable souls, passing into the very marrow of Catholicism. Saint-Cyran would assist him by research, criticism, testing the force of Jansenist arguments on this and that person, and generally paving the way for the spread of their doctrine. They had to be careful however; precautions were necessary to prevent their undertaking from encountering the same fate as that of Baius. But they intended to keep the secret until the moment when the bomb would burst. Accordingly they perfected a code—admittedly a little childish—to prevent their design from becoming known if their correspondence should be read. The code name for their great project was 'Pilmot'; Jansenius called himself 'Boèce' or 'Sulpice', and his friend 'Celias' or 'Solion'. The Society of Jesus was dubbed with the rather disagreeable name of 'Gorphoroste', and its members were 'Les Fins'. St Augustine himself was given the pseudonyms 'Seraphi', 'Aelius' and 'Leoninus'. Other personages referred to occasionally were given esoteric names; e.g. Richelieu was 'Purpuratus', Bérulle 'Rougeart', and the King of Spain 'Carpocre'. As for the Protestants, for some unknown reason they were called 'Cucumer'.

Having thus perfected their great scheme and the details of their code, the two friends separated after agreeing not only to write to each other but also to meet periodically in order to acquaint each other with the work's progress. Jansenius remained in Belgium, at first in Louvain, where he was given the chair of Holy Scripture, and then at Ypres, of which he became bishop in 1635. He rarely left the country, except for a mission to Spain and a few brief visits to meet Saint-Cyran. In 1627, having no doubt sufficiently read and re-read St Augustine, he began to draft his celebrated commentary *Augustinus*. He had just finished it in 1638 when death overtook him. He died in dispositions of great piety, submitting his book to the decisions of the Church and entrusting it to his chaplain Lamaeus with instructions to publish it after his death.

Saint-Cyran left the theoretical aspect of the undertaking to his friend and devoted himself to the practical side. He settled in Paris, where he endeavoured to win influence. He was acquainted with Richelieu, who publicly referred to him as 'the most learned man in the world'. He struck up a friendship with Father de Condren, Cardinal de Bérulle, the energetic Adrien Bourdoise and even with St Vincent de Paul. As a spiritual director he guided the souls of a large number of men and women, most of whom belonged to the fashionable world. The doctrine in which he instructed them was solid, exacting and imbued with the spirit of reform, such as was taught by the leading spiritual men of that earnest epoch. Bishoprics were offered to him on several occasions, but he refused them: he was satisfied to remain the living conscience of his day and to exercise his influence discreetly. The attitude he adopted in public was a skilful one; he wrote a crushing pamphlet condemning the somewhat farcical apologetics of the Jesuit Father Garasse, thus bringing the laugh to his side. The works he published under the name 'Petrus Aurelius' (Petrus after the apostle, and Aurelius after Augustine!) secured him the goodwill of the Gallican bishops. The plan was therefore well on the way to realization; and it seemed likely that the young community of the Oratory, won over to the influence of Saint-Cyran, would serve as the vehicle for the new ideas. Indeed, Jansenius, as Bishop of Ypres, had already helped the Oratory to found houses in Belgium. Thus, little by little, and even before it was known, 'Pilmot' emerged from the confines of intellectual conception and tended to become a religious movement capable of attracting souls. And the abbot of Saint-Cyran had already discovered the most appropriate centre from which to raise up the movement and disseminate its doctrine: the abbey of Port-Royal.

2. PORT-ROYAL AND THE ARNAULD FAMILY

Port-Royal, an abbey of the Bernardines, situated in the valley of the Chevreuse, about six leagues (between sixteen and seventeen miles) from Paris, was founded in 1204 by the wife of a soldier of the Fourth Crusade to obtain from heaven the safe return of her husband. It stood in the hollow of the narrow valley, and the hills cut off the horizon on all sides: a melancholy region, in which a state of meditation and prayer seemed to come naturally to the soul. For a long time the abbey had sheltered pious women, living in seclusion, unknown, but following steadfastly the rule of Cîteaux. Since the end of the Middle Ages its discipline had become relaxed as in so many other convents of every Order. The nuns' way of life was not actually scandalous, but they had certainly become worldly. They were not enclosed; anyone who wished could enter the convent, and the religious could go out whenever they so desired. As a recreation these rather foolish virgins organized masquerades; their servants did likewise under the direction of the chaplain. The latter, a Cistercian, could not even translate the *Pater Noster*, and the convent's library contained but one spiritual book—a Breviary. In forty years the nuns had not heard more than seven or eight sermons.

On the threshold of this abode so ill-disposed to receive grace there suddenly appeared one day a new face—a child of eight. Her father, very much in favour with King Henri and naturally anxious to see his six daughters established, had secured Jacqueline's appointment as coadjutrix of Port-Royal, while her younger sister, aged five, was appointed to Saint-Cyr. Such were the lamentable customs of the times.

When the abbess died three years later (1602) Jacqueline, who had become Mother Angélique, succeeded her. On one and the same day she made her First Communion and was solemnly blessed as abbess. It seemed that very little could be expected from this eleven-year-old mother superior. She found the convent very boring, and was so terrified at the thought of having to pass her life there that she fell sick. But there was no way of escaping her fate; the abbatial Bull under which she was appointed had been duly sealed, and by a piece of trickery, for the authorities in Rome had been informed that she was eighteen years of age. And her dreadful father, taking advantage of her weakness, persuaded her to sign a document renewing her solemn vows. 'Bursting with spite', she obeyed him.

But God, of course, makes use of everything, even of the most unlikely instruments. Though this abbess had no vocation she had within her the seed of sanctity; and here, where she expected perpetual boredom, grace lay in wait for her. At the age of seventeen she already gave evidence of those qualities which she exhibited throughout her life: depth of soul, a tendency to impulsiveness, a virile strength of purpose even in the midst of intense suffering; but she lacked perhaps that true simplicity of heart which might have placed her among those pious women who approach near to God. During Lent in 1608 a certain Franciscan Father Basile, a wandering monk of doubtful morals,[1] preached such a moving sermon at Port-Royal that the young abbess was deeply stirred. While she listened to him speaking of the self-abasement of Christ, she gradually came to perceive in an agony of grief the wretchedness of the worldly life of her convent, and she decided to change it.

She began to effect reform by reforming herself. She dressed in a habit of coarse wool, bathed the loathsome sores of a sick novice, returned to the practice of rising at night for prayers and the use of the discipline morning and evening. She grouped around her a nucleus of sisters as determined as herself to change their mode of life. The movement gained ground. Assisted by a visiting Franciscan, the young abbess persuaded her sisters to return to strict poverty. They all laid

[1] He gave up the priesthood and became a pastor, but later returned to the bosom of the Church.

at her feet their small personal treasures, their fine linen, their jewellery and caskets, and decided unanimously to re-impose strict enclosure. The 25th of September 1609 was a dramatic and splendid day—the 'Day of the Grating'—which remained famous in the annals of Port-Royal. Mother Angélique refused her own father admission to the convent, and closed heart and ears against his indignant protests; she even remained inflexible to her mother's entreaties and went away victorious, though almost at the end of her tether.

This young woman of steel belonged to an old Auvergnat family of parliamentarians and lawyers named Arnauld, who, though tainted with an hereditary strain of pettifoggery, were not without merit and talent. Jacqueline's grandfather, a Huguenot, had rejected Calvinism after the Massacre of St Bartholomew. Five years later he was raised to the peerage. Her father Antoine, who became successively Commissioner of Audit and Public Attorney, was finally called to the bar, and became famous for his lawsuits against the Society of Jesus, which was at that time in conflict with the university. Her mother, Catherine Marion, was the daughter of an Advocate General in the Parlement de Paris. Thus the family belonged to the upper legal class, and were elbowing their way towards the peerage. Antoine Arnauld had twenty children, of whom ten survived him. Mother Angélique was the third; the eldest, Robert Arnauld d'Andilly, was the father of the Marquis de Pomponne, minister of the Great King Louis XIV; the sixth, Henri, became Bishop of Angers. His other five daughters, including the widows, took the veil at Port Royal; and the youngest son, Antoine, born in 1612, became the 'Great Arnauld'.

When the Arnauld family recovered its equanimity, they looked a little more kindly upon the courageous act of the young abbess. Her father, no doubt recognizing his own qualities in this display of character, changed his attitude. He accepted the situation and lent his influence in support of the reform undertaken by Mother Angélique. Rumour reached Paris of the splendid happenings at Port-Royal. The Great Century had just begun, and all that was best and loftiest in the Church was ready to grow enthusiastic over such a creditable enterprise. Instead of an illiterate Bernardine or a visiting Franciscan, Port-Royal could now have first-rate men, even saints, as its spiritual directors, among whom were Father Archangel of Pembroke, a celebrated Franciscan and a real mystic, and Sébastien Zamet, the admirable Bishop of Langres. Other welcome visitors were the Fathers of the Oratory, even Bérulle himself and more frequently Condren. St Francis de Sales also, while staying in Paris, desired to visit the good nuns in the valley of the Chevreuse. Mother Angélique made a general confession to him, and after his return to Annecy he continued to correspond with her on spiritual matters.

THE ARNAULD FAMILY
ABRIDGED GENEALOGICAL TREE

Antoine Arnauld = Mlle Marion
(barrister)   (later Sister Catherine
    de Sainte-Félicité)

- Robert Arnauld d'Andilly (father of fifteen children; later became a 'solitary')
  - Arnauld de Luzancy (solitary)
  - Arnauld de Pomponne (minister under Louis XIV)
- Catherine = I. Le Maistre (later Sister Catherine de Saint-Jean)
  - Antoine Le Maistre (solitary)
  - Simon Le Maistre de Séricourt (solitary)
  - Le Maistre de Sacy (Director of Port-Royal; translator of the Bible)
- Jacqueline (Mother Angélique, abbess of Port-Royal)
  - (Mother Angélique de Saint-Jean, abbess)
- Jeanne (Mother Agnès, abbess)
- Henri (Bishop of Angers)
- Antoine (surnamed the 'Great Arnauld')

Flattering reports concerning Port-Royal eventually reached the ears of Louis XIII, who instructed the intrepid abbess to go and reform the royal convent of Maubuisson, near Pontoise, which another Mother Angélique, sister of Gabrielle d'Estrées and her brilliant rival in intrigue, had allowed to fall into a lamentable state. In the face of violent opposition, even armed opposition on the part of the deposed abbess, Jacqueline Arnauld more or less succeeded in her difficult task, an achievement which put the finishing touch to her reputation.

It is almost impossible to imagine the fame that surrounded this twenty-year-old girl. When she returned from Maubuisson, accompanied by thirty nuns who had refused to leave her, Port-Royal became an important intellectual centre that drew a vast number of souls yearning for a life of renunciation and absolute mortification. Yet one of the most touching features in the character of Mother Angélique was her constant longing to retire still further from the world and bury herself in a life of total renunciation. She asked St Francis de Sales to receive her into his community as least among his Visitandines, but he refused her request.

There is one black spot in this wonderful story. The valley in which the monastery was situated was very unhealthy. Many of the religious died from fever; and while Mother Angélique gladly accepted this as the will of God it disturbed her. She therefore took a decision which circumstances seemed to demand: they must leave the valley. At Saint-Jacques, on the very outskirts of Paris, her mother bought her the 'Hôtel Clagny', which she pulled down and replaced by a spacious convent. It became the Port-Royal of which a Parisian boulevard still bears the name and of which the building has been used as a maternity hospital since 1814. Suddenly the centre of activity was transferred to the very gates of the capital, and the influence of the reformed community increased still further. Port-Royal became fashionable; all the 'devout' people of the city, the nobility, judges, priests and religious of all Orders, gathered there to pray.

What is more, the strict and powerful gentlemen of the Company of the Blessed Sacrament, that celebrated lay body whose activities could be traced behind every reforming effort of the day, took notice of those nuns whose ideals were identical with their own. They even thought of selecting some of them to establish a new contemplative Order— the Institute of the Blessed Sacrament—more or less directly attached to themselves, the members of which would dedicate themselves to continual prayer in order to bring down God's blessing upon France. The idea won the enthusiasm of Mother Angélique, who agreed to leave her convent and go to the Rue Coquillière to manage the new foundation; but all her sisters, 'because of their great devotion to the Blessed Sacrament', asked to join the new Order. They decided that henceforward their convent would be called 'Port-Royal of the Blessed Sacrament', and that they would bear on their white scapular a large red cross. In any case, Mother Angélique did not long remain in the Rue Coquillière because the worldly success of the convent displeased her, and she returned to her beloved community in the *faubourg*.

And so about 1630 Port-Royal had every appearance of being the very model of reformed monasteries, ideally conducted according to the spirit of the Council of Trent. In the eyes of countless Catholics the habit of the Order, which so many young girls longed to wear, seemed to be the symbol of Christianity restored to its full splendour. There was obviously no question so far of doctrinal deviation, still less of heresy and rebellion; and if anyone had dared to tell Mother Angélique and her daughters that one day they would be condemned by the Church they would have died of grief. Yet the danger was already on their doorstep.

3. PORT-ROYAL AND THE ABBOT OF SAINT-CYRAN

Some time in 1620 Jean Duvergier de Hauranne met Robert Arnauld d'Antilly at the house of a friend, and they discovered that they had a lot in common. Jacqueline's elder brother closely resembled her: eager, forceful, inclined to solitude and prayer, and obsessed by life's great problems. He did not, in any case, find peace of mind until he left the world in 1646 and retired to Port-Royal. A strangely intense friendship developed between the two men, and Robert Arnauld often spoke to his sisters of the brilliant spiritual qualities of his friend. At that period the influence of the abbot was growing perceptibly. His reputation for mortification gave him a halo of glory. The words he uttered were on everyone's lips: 'God has made it known to me that His Church ceased to exist five or six hundred years ago'—a statement which allowed it to be understood that he would remake it. All his penitents sang his praises. Why should the nuns of Port-Royal, themselves aspiring to sanctity, hesitate to place their souls in the hands of this new Augustine?

And that is precisely what happened as a result of a fortuitous circumstance. Mother Agnès, the younger sister of Mother Angélique, had long since left Saint-Cyr for Port-Royal, where she wrote a short work containing sixteen meditations in honour of the sixteen centuries since the foundation of the Holy Eucharist. Her work, entitled *The Secret Chaplet*, was a pious treatise, obviously over-sublimated and weak in theology, though not much fault could be found with it as to substance. Sébastien Zamet and Father de Condren approved it; in consequence of which M. de Bellegarde, Archbishop of Sens, envious

of the influence of his colleague the Bishop of Langres in the Institute
of the Blessed Sacrament, referred the work to the Sorbonne, which
found therein 'several instances of nonsense, irrelevance, error,
blasphemy and impiety'. The Jesuit Father Binet took the same view.
It seemed that a great fuss was being made over such a little book,
but behind the criticism of Mother Agnès the real purpose was probably to attack Father de Condren and the Oratory. This was a fairly
common procedure among theologians.

There suddenly appeared in Paris a little pamphlet entitled *Apologie
pour servir de défense au Chapelet*, and it soon became known that
Saint-Cyran was the author. The famous abbot stated that, having
examined the sixteen meditations with the greatest care, he could find
no fault with them; on the contrary, he admired their doctrine. He
went further: he won the support of his friends in Belgium, and had
the work approved by Jansenius and Froidmont, eminent masters of
Louvain University. Finally Saint-Cyran wrote a crushing reply to the
criticisms of Father Binet. The gratitude of the Arnauld family was
overwhelming, as well as that of the Institute of the Blessed Sacrament,
the whole of Port-Royal and, of course, Sébastien Zamet.

Zamet was so grateful that he entrusted Saint-Cyran with the
spiritual direction of his nuns, on the grounds that he himself lived so
far from Paris that he could not give the task his uninterrupted attention. Thus arose a delicate situation fraught with possibilities. On
either side of the grille in the parlour of Port-Royal, Angélique and
Saint-Cyran, the two great protagonists in the drama, faced each other
—'the flint', as Sainte-Beuve put it, 'which would eventually throw off
the spark'. From the very beginning complete harmony existed
between the abbot and Mother Angélique. In a short time he became
the spiritual director of all the nuns at Port-Royal, and he suggested to
them that the method followed by M. Zamet was much too easy-going
and should be changed. These holy women were seized with a veritable
craze for mortification. The 'supereminent ideal of the primitive
Church' became the sole topic of conversation at Port-Royal. The
Bishop of Langres bitterly resented seeing himself utterly superseded.
The community's official preacher for Lent 1635 was Saint-Cyran,
who had now become the master of Port-Royal.

Master not only of the monastery that bore the name, but also of the
circle of people that henceforward thronged around those sacred
walls. The radiance of Jean Duvergier continued to extend. A youngster
of twenty, precocious and burning with the love of God, became the
abbot's disciple as soon as he made his acquaintance, and under his
instruction launched into the study of St Augustine, assisted by little
books of commentaries that arrived from Louvain and later from
Ypres. That young man was Antoine Arnauld, the Benjamin of the

Arnauld family. Serious-minded men of 'great intellect, learning and virtue', men of good standing in the world, voluntarily grouped themselves together on the advice of the reformer; they took no religious vows, but agreed to lead a life of silence, work and prayer. Among them were Catherine Arnauld's son Antoine Le Maistre,[1] a celebrated barrister who suddenly renounced the world and built himself a little hermitage in the garden of Port-Royal; his brother, Le Maistre de Séricourt, an outstanding military officer; de Bascle, a member of the nobility; and M. Vitart, a member of the upper middle class whose sister had married a gentleman named Racine. There were also two clerics: Claude Lancelot, a student of Bourdoise and sub-deacon in the community of Saint-Nicolas-du-Chardonnet, and Antoine Singlin, who, having become a priest on the advice of St Vincent de Paul, abandoned the Lazarists to join the ranks of the Solitaires of Port-Royal. In order to assist the further development of his group by drawing to himself the young, Saint-Cyran put into effect a plan to set up *Petites Écoles*— 'Little Schools'—based upon a new educational system and intended primarily to form character. The execution of this project was entrusted to Lancelot, and pupils began to come in.

The plan outlined by the two friends at Louvain fourteen years earlier appeared therefore to be a success. They had both worked hard, each in his particular field. It was now time to instil the great theories of the Bishop of Ypres into the minds most capable of receiving and disseminating them. Saint-Cyran, disturbed by certain rumours that had come to his ears, left Paris and retired for a while to his abbey at Poitiers. Although Jansenius died about that time it seemed certain that their ideas would triumph.

4. THE THREE STAGES OF JANSENISM

Augustinus was published at Louvain in 1640, in flagrant violation of papal instructions forbidding any public statements concerning grace. While the work was being secretly printed the Jesuits succeeded in obtaining a number of pages and requested the Internuncio to warn Rome, so that publication might be forbidden. Despite this, the enormous volume came off the press duly authorized and dedicated to the Cardinal-Infante, governor of Belgium. It seemed to appear everywhere at once. In September 1640 copies were sold at Frankfurt fair. In Holland the Calvinists were enraptured with it—an anagram of the name Cornelius Jansenius produced *Calvini sensus in ore*. So many people read the book in France that it had to be reprinted at Paris in the following year, and at Rouen shortly afterwards. One cannot but be astonished at the success of such a book; it was written in Latin,

---

[1] Or Le Maître. Both spellings are to be found in documents of the period.

was extremely bulky and made such heavy reading that the very sight of it would discourage Christians of our time. Publicly, Saint-Cyran was enthusiastic about the work, though he had personal misgivings as to the wisdom of certain expressions. He did, however, declare with the air of a prophet that it was 'the book of devotion of this last age', 'a book that would endure as long as the Church', and 'it is the kind of book that can never be destroyed, despite King and Pope'.

What then was the doctrine expounded by *Augustinus*? In order to obtain a true picture of that doctrine, it should be studied in relation to theories which had already been subjects of controversy within the Church; for the aim of Jansenius was to formulate a solution that would reconcile opposing tenets and put an end to disputes. The basis of the Catholic faith is that man, having lost his original state of innocence through sin, cannot be saved without God's help, without grace. But this divine support is related to man's freedom, and man must strive to save himself. It is extremely difficult to reconcile these two means of salvation. To allow too much to grace might destroy man's liberty; to exaggerate the role of liberty might result in denying grace its proper function and power. Hence the doctrinal deviations in one direction or the other that arose during the course of centuries.

Already during the fifth century the Breton monk Pelagius had stated that man was entirely free by the exercise of his will to do right or not to do right; to save his soul or to lose it—free to say yes or no to God.[1] In other words, original sin had not prostrated man irrevocably. According to Pelagius divine grace is nature itself, and man possesses it because he has reason and can choose his destiny. In such a scheme of things man depends entirely on himself. 'By free will man is emancipated from God'; so said the Pelagian Bishop Julian of Eclanum. It follows, therefore, that Redemption has no meaning, and Christ ceases to be necessary. St Augustine devoted four large works to the refutation of this heresy concerning free will.

The great doctrinarians of the Protestant Reformation,[2] Luther and Calvin, held the opposite view: they rejected free will, and denied man any positive action in the work of his salvation. They considered that salvation depended solely on grace and the will of God, decided from all eternity by the infinite but inscrutable wisdom of God. Predestined man could do practically nothing of himself in order to be saved or to avoid damnation.

The teaching of the Catholic Church over the centuries is to be found between these two extreme systems; it refuses to make everything dependent upon free will, but it does not leave everything to

[1] See *The Church in the Dark Ages*, page 31.
[2] Two chapters of *The Protestant Reformation* are devoted to the study of Luther and Calvin.

grace. Such problems were considered as early as 853 by the Council of Quierzy-sur-Oise, which made this profound statement: 'To those who are saved salvation is a gift of God; but those who perish are lost through their own fault.' Here grace and liberty are reconciled; it is an agreement in principle, which leaves a vast field for discussion. This had become very clear from recent controversies in which the Molinist Jesuits laid greater emphasis on free will, with the object of building up a moral effort on man's part; while the Dominican Thomists stressed the importance of grace in order to extol faith. Because the Congregatio de Auxiliis established for the purpose of settling the dispute had declined to make a decision, both theories could be taught from the pulpit in Catholic churches. Who then would put an end to this quarrel? Jansenius declared that he would; he, and he alone, was the authoritative interpreter of St Augustine!

According to Jansenius no one before him had discovered in the work of Augustine the synthesis of the demands of both grace and free will. Original sin created an abyss between man's first state and the fallen state that followed. Man was entirely free in his state of innocence, and his will tended naturally towards what was right. In his fallen state he was no longer free but a slave of sin, for ever dragged along by earthly delights; all that he did led him to the abyss of corruption. But, argued Jansenius, God in His goodness offered humanity a chance to snatch itself from the abyss. Through Christ's merits He gave man efficacious grace, which ennobled the human will. Those who possessed it were indeed free, delivered from the slavery of sin, and the grace in their souls coincided with man's interior demand for the good. But nothing could be done for those who did not possess it; they were without hope. Even the just could not obey the divine commands without grace—St Peter, for instance, denied Christ before Pilate's judgment-seat. Grace, however, Jansenius declared, was not given to all humanity. Many are called, but few are chosen. Only a few exceptional souls were capable of exercising free will in regard to salvation. As for the rest, God did not condemn them, but, because grace has not been given to them, they remained *in massa damnata* as a result of original sin. The Jansenist synthesis, at least as far as the word was concerned, recognized free will in man, but limited it to those few who received grace—a doctrine which parted company with Protestantism in its first assertion, but drew close to it in its second. It rejected the Catholic doctrine which teaches with St Paul that God 'will have all men to be saved' (1 Tim. ii. 4), and gives everyone sufficient grace to enable him to carry on the struggle for salvation. Perhaps it would be an exaggeration to describe Jansenism as a 'rehash of Calvinism', as has so often been done. It would be more accurate to describe it as a kind of semi-Protestantism.

M

Such was the substance of Jansenius's vast work *Augustinus*, the essentials of what we might call 'doctrinal Jansenism', speculative and metaphysical, born 'in the library of an intellectual', as Bremond so rightly said. But when the theories of the Bishop of Ypres were injected into the atmosphere of Port-Royal they assumed a totally different character, and found expression in moral directives applicable to the daily life of the Christian. Thus a 'moral Jansenism' developed and asserted itself, to which real Jansenism gradually gave way. The term 'Jansenist' in our day has come to signify almost exclusively an excessively severe moral attitude. The relationship between these two aspects of Jansenism was not binding. The Jansenist doctrine of grace no more demanded a stricter form of moral behaviour than did Luther's Protestantism (as was very evident in Germany). For if man is not granted efficacious grace, if, despite his efforts, he is to remain *in massa damnata*, why should he strive to live according to the Commandments?

But the *milieu* in which the doctrine was disseminated was already predisposed to apply the most 'Jansenist' interpretation to the bishop's ideas. The people of Port-Royal were inclined towards austerity; they entertained a gloomy and tragic outlook on Christian life. But the austerity of Port-Royal was not unique; quite the contrary. The writings of many prominent Catholics of the day, including among others St Vincent de Paul, Bérulle, Olier, and even the gentle St Francis de Sales, contained statements that the solitaries of Port-Royal would gladly have claimed as their own. Mother Angélique's reformed nuns were not alone in refusing all compromise, all worldly entanglement. Nor was the Jansenist Pascal the only one to suffer spiritual torment in wrestling with great problems. The early intentions and the first leaders of Port-Royal were beyond criticism—'Everything we admire in them', said Bremond, 'is Catholic.'

Deviation came later, and it happened through Saint-Cyran. There is no doubt whatever that doctrinal Jansenism developed into moral Jansenism in the soul of that ardent, immoderate mystic to whom Mother Angélique had entrusted the spiritual direction of her community. In fact, Saint-Cyran selected from *Augustinus* its moral and practical conclusions only. But he cogitated upon his friend's transcendent ideas in order to adapt them to a novel spirituality suggested to him by his personal experience. He had most definitely a keen and harrowing sense of man's misery as a sinner. What had undoubtedly moved him most of all in St Augustine was the idea of the 'cruel war waged between the two men within me', that exhausting conflict which man, without God, is doomed to lose. Jansenist theories confirm his tendency towards rigorism, an austere and gloomy religion. Already in his *Apologie pour le chapelet secret* he had written: 'We have within us a perpetual source of sin flowing towards everlasting death, unless God places within us the fountain of life that flows into life eternal.' These few words embody the whole Jansenist doctrine on grace. When Saint-Cyran reminded his penitents 'that the judgments of God are terrible', that all men are wretched sinners, that no one can be sure of salvation even though he strive doggedly to that end, he was repeating truths that many other preachers had proclaimed in his time and before him; but he gave the words a doctrinal background that came from Jansenius's book.

It is easy to understand how, with the best intentions, the pious daughters of Mother Angélique, and even the solitaries, were able to drift into doctrinal deviation; and that so many souls should have yielded later on, drawn by the movement's spirit of mortification, its 'most deadly talisman', as Sainte-Beuve says. It was quite easy to go astray; the Jansenists used the same language as St Charles Borromeo, St Vincent de Paul and Bourdaloue. Indeed, Bossuet saw clearly that 'this severity puffs out presumption, fosters an arrogant sorrow for sin and a spirit of ostentatious singularity'. Such faults would become more and more apparent as the various episodes in the history of Jansenism unfolded.

For Jansenism was not to remain merely a doctrine of grace bound up with a complete, coherent and rigid conception of religion and strict morality. It was a subject which had cropped up under different forms throughout the Church's history, and it soon concerned itself with matters of discipline as much as it did with doctrine and morals. A third aspect of Jansenism was soon added to the other two: we might call it 'sectarian Jansenism'. Its origins were complex. They may be traced through the arrogance of the Arnauld family, proud of its triumphs, and later on of the holiness of so many of its members. 'To acknowledge the name of our family', said Mother Agnès boldly, 'is almost like acknowledging God.' Its origins are also evident in the undeniable pride of Saint-Cyran, in his 'haughty and insolent zeal' to which Jean-Jacques Olier referred; in his immovable conviction that he and Jansenius alone could claim to represent true Christianity. They may also be traced to the polemical and quibbling tendencies of the sect—especially of the Arnaulds, who were professional lawyers—and a reluctance to accept humbly the decrees of the Church and submit to her judgment. From the very beginning Jansenism was on excellent terms with Gallican circles in the parliamentary field, which were anti-Rome on principle and anti-Jesuit by temperament; there Jansenism gained numerous adherents. It won friends among other classes of society, especially the lower clergy whose 'presbyterian priesthood' Jansenius extolled as the trustee of grace on equal terms with the hierarchy. A Jansenist 'party' was thus established—in the sense in which the word 'party' was then used. Its members became less and less concerned with Augustinian doctrines relating to grace, but increasingly interested in the triumph of their side. It is well known that great doctrinal struggles tend more and more to develop and consolidate the sectarian spirit. Thus, during the hundred and fifty years of its history Jansenism, having commenced as a doctrinal deviation on grace, merged into an exacting conception of Christian morality, then gradually became a heresy against the Church, even going as far as to ally itself unintentionally with the enemies of Christianity itself. We may feel justified in thinking that this eventuality was not foreseen by Jansenius, Saint-Cyran or Mother Angélique.

5. THE ATTITUDE OF CARDINAL RICHELIEU

When *Augustinus* was published the battle of Jansenism had already entered upon its first skirmishes, and the abbot of Saint-Cyran was in prison. Enlightened people had for some time been forming guarded opinions of the celebrated spiritual director. Father de Condren, who had known him since the beginning of his career, said of him : 'He has an inaccessible mind; he loves novelty, and has an inordinate leaning towards the eccentric.' Sébastien Zamet, Bishop of Langres, enlightened by the bitterness of his experience at seeing himself thrust from Port-Royal by his former protégé, described him as 'an insulting and violent personage, without the slightest respect for those who in any way disagree with him'. As for Monsieur Vincent, saint that he was, he bore with humility his being treated by Saint-Cyran as an ignoramus when he gently reproved the abbot for claiming to save the Church single-handed. 'Ignorant? I am even more ignorant than you think . . .' he replied with a pleasant smile. But he remained aloof from Saint-Cyran, and saw less and less of him.

Richelieu shared that mistrust, though his reasons were not entirely praiseworthy. At first the proud cardinal endeavoured to lure this new force into his own service, but Saint-Cyran refused to be drawn. He was not a man to be bought. It then came to the all-powerful minister's ears that words of criticism had been uttered concerning governments 'that desired to have none but minions in their service'. The cardinal's opinion of the reformer suddenly changed; he was no longer 'the most learned man in the world', but a 'visionary', an unbalanced, headstrong man. Before long His Eminence declared that he regarded Saint-Cyran as 'more dangerous than six armies'; an obvious exaggeration. It is very doubtful whether the master of Port-Royal did in fact plot against the cardinal, but it cannot be denied that his behaviour was that of a conspirator. He wrapped himself in mystery, instructed his correspondents to burn his letters and continually influenced people and events. Richelieu might have believed, or given a convincing impression that he believed, that Saint-Cyran was capable of the 'most evil designs' (to use Bremond's words), and that he exercised control over a sect as dangerous as the Protestants. In fact, these two men were absolutely incompatible. 'There is not a potentate in the world', declared Saint-Cyran, 'who is more naturally qualified to rule than I am.' 'Purpuratus', as Saint-Cyran and Jansenius had nicknamed Richelieu, was not the man to make allowances for people with pretentions of that nature.

Various incidents brought his anger to a head. Jansenius, whom everyone knew to be Saint-Cyran's friend, published from Louvain a pamphlet entitled *Mars Gallicus*, a bitter condemnation of Richelieu and his policy of alliance with the Protestants. And when the cardinal had the marriage of Gaston d'Orléans and Marguerite de Lorraine annulled, Saint-Cyran publicly declared that his action was a disgraceful scandal—which incidentally was quite true. Finally, when a certain Father Séguenot of the Oratory published a commentary on St Augustine's treatise *De Continentia*, the inquiry instituted to examine the work, on the grounds that it contained a number of unreliable statements, revealed that it had been directly inspired by Saint-Cyran.

On 14th May 1638, a week after the death of Jansenius, the king's police arrested Saint-Cyran, and confined him in the Château de Vincennes. The least one can say about the ensuing trial is that it was hardly a fair one. The defendant's old friends and even his confessor were questioned. Sébastien Zamet accused of heresy the man whose theology he had praised to the skies a short time previously. Saint-Cyran's letters containing spiritual advice to the sisters of Port-Royal were seized by the police and read in court. And Father Joseph, 'the Grey Eminence', worked efficiently in the background. There is no doubt whatever that the trial, conducted by the State, was canonically illegal; for only an ecclesiastical tribunal was competent to try Saint-Cyran, who was indicted solely on his religious opinions. St Vincent de Paul had the courage to state this fact clearly in his evidence; he refused to incriminate his old friend, and pressed for acquittal pure and simple. Despite everything Saint-Cyran spent five years in prison.

The ordeal was very painful to him; but not physically, for Richelieu saw that the prisoner was treated with consideration. He allowed him to receive visitors, to correspond with his friends and even to write and publish books. This enabled Saint-Cyran to remain the leader of the movement, to continue to guide numerous souls and even to effect conversions among the imperial officers who were at that time prisoners in Paris. But morally he suffered a great deal; so much so that he experienced a dramatic spiritual crisis during which he asked himself whether he was right after all, whether his opinions were justified and whether his boldness was not merely empty fool-hardiness.

His captivity, however, raised him still higher in the esteem of his followers. Port-Royal had a martyr! 'Remember', exclaimed Mother Agnès, 'that the abbot of Saint-Cyran is confined to prison only because he pointed out the true way to penance.' Neither his spiritual daughters nor his friends intended to yield to persecution. In vain did the authorities suppress the 'Institute of the Blessed Sacrament'; the house of 'Port-Royal of the Blessed Sacrament' still remained a centre of mystic fervour. Nothing was achieved by the disbandment of the solitaries. Driven from Port-Royal-des-Champs, where they had settled, they returned without any fuss, continued to recruit adherents and calmly set up their 'Little Schools'.

While all this was going on, *Augustinus* was published, and it created a tremendous sensation. In Louvain the Jesuits set about its wholesale destruction. In Paris the diocesan theologus Habert attacked it violently from the pulpit of Notre-Dame. In Rome the aged Pope Urban VIII, an advocate of the policy of appeasement, having tried at first to impose and maintain silence, was forced under pressure from the Jesuits to sign the Bull *In Eminenti* (March 1641). Publication was none the less delayed for two years. All these events were mere skirmishes; preparations were being made for more strenuous conflicts ahead.

When Richelieu died, Mazarin, who was more conciliatory, agreed in February 1643 to set Saint-Cyran free. His nuns, the solitaries and friends in every walk of life welcomed him with idolatrous demonstrations. At the convent of Port-Royal the abbess announced the news to her nuns by loosening her girdle, thus avoiding a breach of silence. As soon as he became free Saint-Cyran began to write against the Protestants, probably to gain the goodwill of the queen mother and the court. But a few weeks later he died, a tired man. His zealous followers shared his body amongst them, everyone wishing to keep some member as a relic; the less fortunate had to be satisfied with pieces of linen steeped in his blood, or a little of the dust 'that was made when his head was sawn off'. This ardent leader, this disturbing and fascinating mystic, vanished from the scene at the critical moment of the conflict, aware that he left behind a successor capable of continuing and developing his work still further. That man was Antoine Arnauld.

6. THE 'GREAT ARNAULD'

The youngest child of the famous Arnauld family was at that time just thirty years of age, but physically and intellectually he appeared much older. He had a little, wiry, energetic body that always seemed about to leap. His features were swarthy, rather ugly and with large wrinkles, and he had an unshapely nose. But his eyes glowed like embers; they looked straight into a speaker's face, reaching to the very soul. A strange power emanated from this ungainly man; it might have been irresistible had he possessed warmth of heart and some hidden tenderness. Antoine Arnauld was a brilliant dialectician and polemist who gave the impression not so much of embodying his convictions as possessing a capacity for establishing their truth and setting them out as dogmas. In that role he excelled.

From his childhood his own family had treated him as an infant prodigy. His mother guided his steps towards the priesthood, and from 1638 to 1641 he presented his four set theses before the assembled bishops and judges at the Sorbonne, who applauded his work. Moreover, 'Jansenist' tendencies were already noticeable in his outlook. He had studied St Augustine and extracts from the work of the Bishop of Ypres, but he had not yet found his way into the movement. His nephews in the Le Maistre family, the solitaries, who were older than he, were disturbed to see him so satisfied with his efforts, content to ride in his stately carriages and eagerly pursuing worldly success. But like all the Arnaulds he had a craving for things divine; and Saint-Cyran, a profound psychologist, suspected as much. Once, when Saint-Cyran was visited by the young theological student in his prison at Vincennes, he induced him to confide in him and talk about the 'perpetual state of lethargy' in which he had so far lived. He warned him against pride, and persuaded him to restore himself spiritually by solitude, prayer and fasting—advice that he offered his penitents. The last of the Arnaulds responded admirably to the master's expectations as the rest of the family had done, and entered joyfully into the exercise of mortification and austerity of life which 'Jansenism' had now become. Saint-Cyran had no equal in his ability to lead people along the one path that enabled them to give of their best. It did not take him long to ascertain the part this slim boy might play, endowed as he was with the intelligence that the conflict demanded. While still in prison Saint-Cyran wrote to his pupil on 1st February 1643: 'The time has come to speak out; it would be a crime to remain silent.' Thus he who was to become the 'Great Arnauld' entered the lists.

The field selected—no doubt by his master rather than by himself—had nothing to do with the theology of grace, but concerned morals and practice. Perhaps it was one way of distracting men's minds from the criticisms that were being hurled at *Augustinus*; and, more precisely, a means of attacking Jansenius's adversary, the Society of Jesus. It was in fact a Jesuit, Father de Sesmaisons, who permitted his penitent the Marquise de Sablé (a lady on good terms with Port-Royal) to attend a dance on the day on which she had received Holy Communion. Saint-Cyran had forbidden his penitent the Princesse de Guéméné to do that very thing. This mundane incident inflamed the theologians in both camps, for the moment was ripe for an explosion. On 25th August 1643 Antoine Arnauld published his *De la Fréquente Communion*, in which, taking the fathers, the popes and the councils as his authority, he claimed to restore the true doctrine concerning reception of the Sacraments. This doctrine, he asserted, had been vitiated and corrupted by Jesuitical laxism. The pamphlet was not without merit. Its language was lucid and precise, its arguments solid, and the work contained some very beautiful passages and sublime thoughts on the Holy Eucharist, expressed with impressive piety. Hence its success. But Arnauld maintained some curious opinions. Instead of regarding Holy Communion as a means of acquiring spiritual sustenance and increasing grace, he presented it as a sublime reward to be obtained only at the cost of strict mortification and, in any case, to be received very infrequently. In other words—and here we have the ideas of Jansenius—only those should communicate who felt the definite call of divine grace. Not to communicate became a sign of exemplary piety and profound humility. Before confessors permitted their penitents to approach the Blessed Sacrament they should impose on them long waiting periods and severe penances. It was possible to reconcile all this with the intention of the Council of Trent to restore to the Holy Eucharist its former dignity; but Arnauld's treatise clearly ran counter to the tendency of the times, which was to present the Sacred Host as the soul's sustenance. But this emphasis upon the rigorous, rendered inhuman by dint of mortification, was discouraging to poor sinners who constituted the majority of Christians.

The reaction was lively; and not only among the Jesuits. St Vincent de Paul remarked that anyone reading Arnauld's book on frequent Communion was forced to ask himself 'whether there could be any man on earth who held such a high opinion of his own virtue as to believe himself worthy to receive Holy Communion'. St Paul would have dreaded the idea of doing so. 'None the less,' added St Vincent mischievously, 'Monsieur Arnauld boasts that he says Mass every day.' It seemed obvious that such a book would turn the faithful away from Holy Communion, and encourage weakness and apathy. In fact, a few years later parish priests drew attention to an impressive drop in religious practice among their parishioners. 'If this book', to quote Monsieur Vincent again, 'has benefited a hundred people by making them more respectful towards the sacraments, it must have done harm to more than ten thousand by drawing them away altogether.' But not everyone was as far-seeing as Monsieur Vincent. Highly placed prelates such as Bishop Caulet, Bishop Pavillon and many others approved the book. In Rome the Jesuit Cardinal de Lugo hoped to put an end to the dispute by suggesting a simple censure of the body of the work while condemning the preface because of a clumsy paragraph in which St Peter and St Paul were treated as equals within the Church. Despite these pacificatory intentions the brawl developed. When the first Jesuit was put out of action, Father Pétau launched a pamphlet entitled *La Pénitence publique et la préparation à la communion*, a well-thought-out work but so badly written that the Jansenists were able to say that the good Father 'knew every language except his own'. M. Olier intervened publicly, and he was joined by the whole of Saint-Sulpice. At the other extreme every Gallican and anti-Jesuit at the Sorbonne and in the Parlement de Paris bestirred himself, even urging Arnauld to appeal against his indulgent condemnation by Rome. This he wisely decided not to do. The quarrel over *Fréquente Communion* was at its height when the controversy over *Augustinus* entered a new phase.

7. THE 'FIVE PROPOSITIONS'

The Bull *In Eminenti* hardly affected the prestige of *Augustinus*, which continued to be read and remained a subject of controversy despite the interdict. In 1644 Father Pétau launched against it two weighty treatises in Latin; though extremely erudite they were the despair of his publisher, the bookseller Charmoisy. Arnauld replied with two works under the title *Apologies pour Jansénius*, which had a very wide circulation as a result of the vast success of his *Fréquente Communion*. But a young and talented Jesuit, Father Deschamps, a more powerful fighter than the excellent Pétau, dealt a stinging blow against the late Jansenius by proving from a comparison of texts that his book revived the theories of Baius which had been condemned by the Sorbonne in 1560. Now at last the anti-Jansenist offensive began. Habert, a former lecturer in theology at Paris who had been appointed Bishop of Vabres, in Tarn, led the attack. A group of Jesuits joined in. Then Arnauld committed the greatest mistake of his career, and it was to do great harm to his side.

When Father Véron, a notable preacher, publicly referred to the Jansenists as Calvinists, they denounced him to the Sorbonne and demanded redress. Nicolas Cornet, doctor of the Faculty of Theology and an extremely just man, decided to deal with the matter personally. He read *Augustinus* carefully, and extracted from it, by a method very common in theological discussions of this kind, a certain number of 'propositions' which, it appeared to him, summarized the whole conception of Jansenius. On 1st July 1649 he submitted them to the judgment of the Sorbonne. Arnauld and his friends suddenly became uneasy, and obtained a ruling from the Parlement to forbid examination of the case. Nicolas Cornet and his fellow theologians were indignant; they passed the 'propositions' to the Assembly of the Clergy with the suggestions that they be submitted to Rome. A petition drafted by Habert was presented to all bishops. Under it the Pope was requested to give 'a plain and explicit judgment'. St Vincent de Paul was terrified by what he learned at that time concerning the Jansenist peril and the falling away in the practice of religion in the parishes; he therefore lent the whole weight of his authority to the proposal, and pleaded personally for signatures. Eighty-five bishops signed the petition. In spite of the fact that eleven Jansenist prelates drew up a counter-petition requesting Rome to refrain from passing judgment, Innocent X accepted the appeal, and appointed a commission consisting of five cardinals and thirteen consultants to settle the question once for all.

The case dragged on for two years; innumerable influences were at work in one direction or another, both sides having dispatched qualified representatives to Rome. The Jansenists subsequently took revenge when they attempted to have the judgment modified by publishing a lively account of the gossip which had surrounded the affair; but that had no effect on the ultimate decision. On 31st May 1653 the Bull *Cum occasione* was signed by Innocent X formally condemning the 'Five Propositions'. All five were declared heretical, and in addition several were described as 'blasphemous, impious and an insult to divine mercy'. In substance the first four propositions expressed the idea that efficacious grace was indispensable to salvation, but that God did not give every man sufficient grace. The fifth affirmed that Christ did not die for all men; He did not shed his blood for all.

The condemnation of Jansenius and his theories was thus precisely stated. What were Antoine Arnauld and his friends to do? Nine years earlier the condemnation of a passage from the preface to his *Fréquente Communion* had driven the hot-headed polemist to take shelter 'beneath the wings of God'; that is to say, he buried himself in a château belonging to the Princesse de Guéméné. Since then, however, the position had appreciably changed. The Jansenist movement had spread and had grown more powerful; the 'Jansenist party' was a body of some consequence. To begin with, vocations continued to increase in the convent. In 1648 it became necessary to reopen Port-Royal-des-Champs, which had become less unhealthy since the solitaries had had the low-lying ground drained. And the little band of solitaries grew; the six original residents had been joined by many learned men who had abandoned the world to come and pray, sing canticles, dig the land and write books. Robert d'Andilly, the oldest member of the Arnauld family, was among them; he cultivated beautiful pears, and sent Anne of Austria the 'blessed fruits' from his espaliers; there was his son Arnauld de Luzancy; and Pallu, a doctor who was followed by Hamon, another doctor. Among the clerics were Manguelain, Giroust and Duchemin, and even a bishop named Listolphe de Suzarre, and Pierre Nicole, the most eminent Latinist of his day. Finally there was Antoine Singlin, a former pupil of St Vincent de Paul. Singlin began by deputizing for Saint-Cyran as spiritual director of the whole of Port-Royal, and eventually took his place. He had an equally deep understanding of souls, but he was wiser and more gentle than Saint-Cyran. But the 'Great Arnauld' became the real master.

Thus the second generation now occupied Port-Royal; and being, as is usually the case, more committed than the first, they were tougher and more daring. Among the nuns was a daughter of Robert d'Andilly, Mother Angélique's niece, a young girl of twenty who, because of her brilliant gifts, had been appointed novice mistress. She had a most unusual disposition; apart from her burning enthusiasm, she was extraordinarily energetic, and her frigid air of composure concealed the most intense feeling. Her name was Mother Angélique de Saint-Jean. Among the men of that second generation was Blaise Pascal. As a preparation for the future Port-Royal had had its Little Schools since 1638, to which Lancelot, Nicole and Le Nain de Tillemont dedicated their lives. These schools were destined to compete with the Jesuit colleges and rival those of the Oratory. A new teaching technique was developed, based upon example and mutual confidence between child and teacher. For the first time in the history of education the French language became a distinct subject in the school's curriculum.[1]

The nuns also took boarders into their convent school. Sister Sainte-Euphémie who, before she took the veil, was Jacqueline, sister of Blaise Pascal, watched over them with zeal and tenderness.

The 'Jansenist Party' developed out of the publicity attaching to the dispute. Its adherents came from the legal profession and from parliamentarians, supporters of the freedoms of the Gallican Church and hostile to Rome on principle, and even from members of the nobility who hated the cardinal-minister on the rather doubtful grounds that he was the Pope's man. Jansenism was in very good odour among the supporters of the Fronde. To obtain an idea of the network of influential members of society that the party included throughout France we have only to quote the names of some of the fashionable women who, from far and near, flocked to Port-Royal: Anne de Rohan, the Princesse de Guéméné, Elizabeth de Choiseul, the Comtesse de Plessis-Guénégaud, Madame de Souvre, the Marquise de Sablé, the Duchesse de Longueville, Louise Marie de Gonzague, future Queen of Poland and friend of Monsieur Vincent, the Duchesse de Liancourt,

[1] See Chapter II, p. 97.

the Duchesse de Luynes, and even Madame de Sévigné who, as Sainte-Beuve remarked, was 'an amateur Jansenist' just as she was a 'volatile friend'.

Knowing, therefore, that he had the advantage of strong support Arnauld could not avoid the temptation to resist his condemnation. It was a difficult decision to have to make; for Mazarin was about to set up a council of letters-patent to make the Bull law, and was even then calling together the bishops then in Paris, to instruct them to accept the Bull. In fact, all the French bishops, including the Jansenists, did accept it. Even at Port-Royal hesitation predominated: Mother Angélique, despite occasional sudden and violent outbursts against Rome, was inclined to silent submission; Singlin and Nicole were similarly disposed. Had Saint-Cyran still been there, he too might have chosen that way out of the impasse, for notwithstanding his faults he was a high-minded man and not given to subterfuge. But Antoine Arnauld thought he could hedge and evade the issue.

Hence the famous distinction between 'fact and law'. Arnauld adopted the attitude that the Pope had quite rightly condemned the 'Five Propositions'. They were monstrous heresies; but the propositions were not to be found in the *Augustinus*. They were a complete forgery by people inimical to Jansenius and his doctrine, and they distorted his ideas. It was a clever line of argument, but dishonest. Not one of the sect's representatives had raised the point during the discussions in Rome. It reeked of the spirit of double-dealing, the cunning of the quack lawyer. Arnauld, however, adopted that line of argument even though he may not have invented it. Nicole may have put it into his head, but Arnauld clung to it with characteristic determination.

The brawl became more violent than ever. Were the five propositions really contained in Jansenius's work? In 1654 the Assembly of the Clergy solemnly confirmed that they were, and a brief statement from Rome said so even more expressly. But were the bishops qualified to settle a point of fact (which any intelligent person could decide for himself) as to whether this or that statement was to be found in a book? Was the Pope really infallible when he set himself up as a judge as to whether a thing was or was not? The way which led to the answer to such questions might also lead to open revolt, even to schism. Whatever the position might be, many upright people were profoundly disturbed. Before giving absolution confessors would ask their penitents if they rejected Jansenist ideas and whether they accepted the Bull. Father Picoté, a Sulpician, refused absolution to a very prominent personage, the Duc de Liancourt, because he stated that the five propositions were not to be found in *Augustinus*. Thereupon the Great Arnauld flew into a passion, and retorted with two letters which he published; one to 'this Monsieur Picoté' and the other to his superior, M. Tronson, and the whole of Saint-Sulpice. The letters created a great stir, but produced a brusque reaction from his adversaries. The Sorbonne took the matter up, examined the letters, which it declared to be 'scandalous and an insult to the Pope', and then disposed of the question of 'fact and law' in two well-defined judgments. Arnauld became extremely apprehensive. He drew up two statements which his opponents might have found it easy to accept as a withdrawal had tempers not been over-heated. His enemies intended to make him bite the dust—a fact which shows that not all the faults were on his side. The Sorbonne condemned him, and even threatened to have his name struck from the list of Doctors of Theology if he did not submit formally. All his friends at the Sorbonne could do was to make an impressive exit from the hall as a sign of protest. Even the Parlement dared not accept the appeal lodged by Arnauld.

The Jansenist position appeared to be critical. Rome, the King, Mazarin, the Jesuits, Saint-Sulpice, Saint-Lazare and nine-tenths of the bishops were against Arnauld. They constituted a formidable mass of enemies, and Arnauld felt the approach of disaster. He was obliged to go into hiding, and was able to leave his retreat only at night. For twelve years he led a wandering life, continually changing his hiding-place. Then occurred a sensational circumstance that brought up the whole question once again.

8. BLAISE PASCAL AND THE 'PROVINCIALES'

On 23rd January 1656, the very day on which the sixty Jansenist doctors walked out of the Sorbonne to avoid taking part in the condemnation of Arnauld, a pamphlet appeared that was pounced upon by all classes of society in Paris. The style was incisive and satirical; the arguments vigorous and striking. It was written in the form of a letter to the Jesuits and to an imaginary person living in the provinces, and the subject was the policy and morals of the Jesuits. Police inquiries failed to reveal how this little leaflet had been prepared, printed and distributed. Other 'Provincial Letters' appeared at irregular intervals during the succeeding months. Altogether eighteen were published up to the middle of 1657, when they were collected and published in one volume. The third letter bore the signature of Louis de Montalte; either a misleading attempt to be precise or intended to arouse a little more curiosity. The reading public thought it must be a pseudonym; Monte Alte might come from *mons altus*. Could the author be Clermont d'Auvergne?

Be that as it may, Mazarin devoured the *Provinciales*, and 'laughed heartily over them'.

To those in the know there was no mystery about the person hiding behind the pseudonym. He was a close friend of Antoine Arnauld and under the spiritual direction of M. Singlin. His father, a superintendent of taxes in Normandy, was himself a friend of the movement, and one of his sisters was a nun at Port-Royal. The writer's name was Blaise Pascal (1623–62). He was a young man of thirty-three whose influence was out of all proportion to his age. He had a lean face, an aquiline nose and long, thin lips. The interior fire that burned within him lit up his delicate features, and his restless look seemed to be continually questioning life and peering into its mysteries. Everything in him betrayed an extreme and poignant tension, the strain endured by a sick man who, in order to create and to live, had to overcome continually the pressure of trifles; he had the troubled look of a genius to whom the abyss speaks. At twelve years of age Pascal rediscovered alone all the theorems of plane geometry; at sixteen he composed a treatise on conical sections; at nineteen he invented a calculating machine, and had since given ample proof of an intellect of which the scope, power and penetration staggered those who knew him. In 1647 his *Nouvelles expériences touchant le vide* aroused the enthusiasm of scientific circles, but his eager mind was already moving in another direction. Until that time he had shown very little interest in religious problems. But a year earlier he had made the acquaintance of two doctors from Rouen— De la Bouteillerie and Deslandes—in attendance upon his father who had injured his leg. These gentlemen were enthusiastic Jansenists. Everyone in the Pascal family had read the works of Jansenius, Saint-Cyran and Arnauld, and Blaise also was much impressed by them. The result was a sort of 'first conversion', which is apparent in the famous *Prière* he composed for the use of sick people and the excellent letter he wrote to his elder sister Mme Périer on the death of their father. For the time being things went no further than that, and while his younger sister Jacqueline took the veil at Port-Royal, Blaise was leading a fairly worldly life, mixing with people of fashion, riding in his six-horse carriage and apparently quite unconcerned with questions of grace and salvation.

But God evidently lay in wait for him. Once when he was crossing the bridge at Neuilly he came very near to death. His two leading horses bolted and plunged into the Seine. He experienced a mysterious interior stress in which physical pain (of which he always had his share) played as great a part as metaphysical misgivings. He was thus slowly drawn towards that 'night of fire', 3rd November 1654, that darkness pierced with light, when his beloved Christ imposed upon him His presence, His truth and His message never again to be challenged. Henceforward his irrevocable choice was made; with all his being he believed. Obedience to the demands of Christianity meant staking everything on victory at the moment of death without risking any loss. Converted at last, he placed himself in the hands of M. Singlin, who sent him to Port-Royal-des-Champs to make a retreat.

Thus Blaise Pascal was introduced into the headquarters of Jansenism at the very moment when the crisis was at its most serious. The indomitable Arnauld, after a brief period of anxiety and weakness, decided to resume the struggle. It now became for him not so much a question of St Augustine, of grace, of God's rights, but rather of knowing who would prevail—the representatives of true Christianity or the Jesuit clique. It was imperative to return to the contents of the letter which the Sorbonne had recently condemned, but they had to be handled in a different, a cleverer and a more efficient way. Arnauld determined to try. But one may, as Henri Bremond so nicely put it, be a 'theological machine-gun' and yet be a mediocre polemist. When, therefore, Arnauld read the new draft to his assembled colleagues he was forced to recognize that their enthusiasm had waned. 'I do not think you find this piece of writing very effective,' he declared, 'and I believe you are right.' Mme Périer said of him: 'He was not the kind of man who thirsted for praise.'

Arnauld turned towards Blaise Pascal. 'You are young,' he said. 'You certainly should do something.'

A little over a week later that 'something' was done: Pascal produced his first *Provinciale*.

'Excellent!' exclaimed Antoine Arnauld. 'That will be appreciated; we must have it printed.'

Whether or not this dazzling polemist who within eighteen months brought men's minds back to the subject of Jansenism actually agreed with all its concepts has always been, and perhaps always will be, a matter of controversy.[1] All we really know of Pascal's religious convictions is gleaned from fragments, the *disjecta membra* of a great unfinished work. It is not even certain whether some of his short notes express his own opinions or those he intended to refute. The discreet Nicole has assured us that Pascal 'thought many Jansenist writings were in need of some slight adjustment'. The moral climate of Port-Royal, its lofty and exacting demands, its atmosphere of sombre austerity, together with its undeniable dignity, were qualities that were bound to appeal to a convert like Pascal who was continually rent with spiritual torment, haunted by the anguish of his misery and unworthiness, seeing himself as a mite hopelessly remote from God. But did he really accept the doctrine contained in *Augustinus*? He told Nicole that if he were one day to write about grace 'he hoped he would succeed in

[1] Before forming an opinion on this subject one might well read Maurice Blondel's excellent article, 'Le Jansénisme et l'antijansénisme de Pascal', in the April–June 1923 issue of *La Revue de Metaphysique et de Morale*.

divesting it of the fierceness that had been given to it, and make the doctrine so commendable that it would suit all types of people'. But Pascal was not a theologian; he was therefore amenable to the influence of any theological theories that he might admire; he might even over-colour their expression. At the same time, as a result of this ceaseless and dramatic dialogue that he maintained within himself, he was often led to adopt a very different attitude. Perhaps it was the Jansenist in him that led him to declare among other things that 'without grace man is merely a creature filled with natural and ineffaceable error'; that to 'people deprived of faith and grace' there remained nothing but 'uncertainty and darkness'; that 'to find God a mediator is necessary'. But from Pascal's pen flowed other sentiments that had no Jansenist flavour: 'I thought of you in my agony; I shed that drop of blood for you',[1] or, 'I love you more ardently than you have loved your stains'; such expressions as 'God perceptible to the heart', 'the heart bowed by God'. Pascal also extols 'the Pope who comes first', the 'trunk' of the tree which is the Church. Though we may not say with Blondel that 'Pascal showed himself to be extremely anti-Jansenist', we may agree with Bremond that 'beside, or perhaps beneath, this Pascal more or less intoxicated by the theology of his masters, there existed another who escaped from them and whose influence was one day to lead innumerable souls back to the bosom of the Catholic Church'.[2]

Why then did he join in the controversy and embark upon a work so far removed from such sentiments? It could not have been entirely due to the influence of those whom he followed as his true guides, or to a young man's pride in being associated with his elders in a struggle. He quite sincerely hated those whom he regarded as public dangers, corrupters of the hearts of Christians—in other words those who supported the easy-going moral attitude that he had learned to hate within himself. What was that violence if not the reaction of an exacting soul against her own inner complicity? A taste for battle did the rest, together with his temperament, less impartial than his intellect, which never yielded but was rather stirred to further activity by contradiction. He believed that he should not obey his own convictions only, but also become the mouthpiece of the group, the appointed advocate of theories with which he did not altogether agree. When Madame de Sablé asked him one day 'if he was quite sure of everything he put in his letters', he replied that 'he was satisfied to avail himself of the reports with which he was provided; it was not his responsibility

---

[1] This expresses the very opposite thought to that contained in the condemned 'fifth proposition'.
[2] From the splendid chapter entitled 'Religion de Pascal', in vol. iv of Bremond's work. See also *En prière avec Pascal* (Paris 1923).

to examine whether they were factual'. Pascal the physicist would never have argued thus in connection with his experiments on the void!

From the very first *Provinciale* it seemed that the Great Arnauld's prophecy would be realized; the work was appreciated. Its literary beauty alone would have guaranteed its success. The harmony between matter and form, its supreme facility and its absolute simplicity were remarkable—'the only modern work worthy of the ancients', as Bossuet, an excellent judge, described it. All the experts admired 'Louis de Montalte'; it was impossible for him not to continue.

At first he lived near the Luxembourg and the gate Saint-Michel (there were two entrances to the house),[1] and later, under the name of M. de Mons, he retired to an inn under the sign of King David in the Rue des Poirées, facing the Collège de Clermont—a Jesuit establishment! He spent the whole of 1656 writing his pamphlets, and wherever Jansenists were to be found in France they distributed them, happy in the knowledge that every blow went home and that their adversaries betrayed signs of the fact.

Furthermore, how could Pascal doubt that he was right when heaven itself gave him a sign? On 24th March 1656, four days after the publication of the fifth *Provinciale*, a miracle occurred within Pascal's own family. It was the Friday of the third week in Lent, the day on which the Church sings at the Introit: 'Show me a token for good, that they who hate me may see and be confounded.' A precious relic, a thorn from the Crown of Thorns, was exposed for veneration at Port-Royal de Paris, and a little girl of ten who suffered from a dreadful weeping ulcer of the eye prayed fervently before the relic that she might be cured. Her name was Marguerite Périer, the daughter of Pascal's elder sister. She was cured, and the prodigy was duly confirmed by the community, the secular power and the doctors, among them Guy Patin, who could hardly be considered credulous. It created a great sensation, the more so because other wonders followed at Port-Royal, as though the efficacy of the relic were reserved only for the Jansenists. The hero of the 'night of fire' could not have failed to see this Miracle of the Holy Thorn as a sign of encouragement.

Thus the offensive developed before a public that was no less amused than enthusiastic. For it very soon became an offensive in the grand style, conducted with the object of creating a diversion, deflecting criticism from Port-Royal so that it might fall back upon its opponents. The first three *Provinciales* sought to defend the Augustinian theses on grace, to justify Arnauld and lacerate the doctors of the Sorbonne who 'considered it easier to censure than to assess, because it is so much

---

[1] He spent eighteen months there. It can still be seen at No. 54 Rue Monsieur-le-Prince. Cf. J. Mesnard, 'Les Demeures de Pascal à Paris', in *Mémoires des serv. hist. de Paris*, t. iv.)

easier for them to find monks than reasons'. From the fourth, and especially from the fifth *Provinciale*, it was no longer a question of defence but of attack. The real heretics, the true poisoners of the public mind, were not the saintly people of Port-Royal but the Jesuits, 'who put cushions under the elbows of sinners', and made the Christian religion 'indulgent and accommodating' in order to recruit adherents, a religion in which the scandal of the Cross was abolished, and the sacrifice of Calvary no longer had any meaning! One had only to read the books written by the Jesuits—those by Father Escobar,[1] for example, whose manual of moral theology was the casuists' guide! And Pascal would quote—though not always accurately—extracts intended to cause horror or laughter. His vehement criticism was not entirely untrue, however, and the polemist's arrows, aimed at an obviously too facile moral outlook, did not fail to reach their targets. But he implicated the whole of the Society of Jesus, representing it as a monster of hypocrisy and laxity. This was a singularly odd manœuvre at the very moment when Fathers Isaac Jogues, Brebeuf, Lallemant and Garnier had shed their blood in Canada, thus giving proof of the heroism of the Jesuits. But in controversy adversaries frequently hit below the belt, Pascal no less than others. Furthermore, he was not always honest or self-consistent. In the last *Provinciale* he praised Thomism to the skies (no doubt to win over the Dominicans), though he had jeered at it in the first. On several occasions he was guilty of mental reservation, garbled quotations and false innuendoes; all the faults, in fact, with which he reproached 'Jesuitism'. The heat of battle alone cannot be offered as an excuse for his attitude and some of the methods he adopted.

Was Pascal aware that he was going too far, that he was acting discreditably and perhaps even doing injury to the Church?[2] Did he heed the advice of Mother Angélique and M. Singlin, who considered the *Provinciales* too spirited and too uncharitable? Did he perhaps experience an intellectual and moral crisis of such a nature that the arguments he attributed to his opponents found an echo in his own soul ceaselessly in torment? Replying in the seventeenth *Provinciale* to Father Annat, who had described him as the 'Secretary of Port-Royal', he declared: 'I do not belong to Port-Royal. . . . I have said nothing to support such impious propositions. . . . And even if Port-Royal

---

[1] Father Antonio Escobar y Mendoza (1589–1669) was a holy religious who, in 1630, published a *Manual of Cases of Conscience*. The tenor of the work appeared so strict that he was denounced to the Inquisition. No one was more surprised than he when he learned that a French writer was accusing him of laxism!

[2] Blondel has spoken very harshly of Pascal's role: 'He makes a laughing-stock of theology; he exposes the sacred delicacy of the religious life to the mockery of a foolish and corrupt world.' Bremond expresses his judgment concisely: 'Louis de Montalte is guilty; Pascal is innocent.'

upheld them ... I am not attached to anything on earth but the Catholic Roman and Apostolic Church alone, in which I desire to live and die in communion with the Pope.' He wrote a nineteenth and twentieth *Provinciale*, but he never published them. No doubt he regretted having gone too far.[1]

Nevertheless Pascal had given valuable service to his masters' cause. If ever the weapon of ridicule was used with deadly effect, this certainly was the case in the battle of the *Provinciales*. Mazarin's laugh echoed throughout France. Such counterstrokes on the part of the Jesuits as *Entretiens de Cléandre et d'Eudoxe*, by Father Daniel, and the *Bonne foi des Jansénistes*, by Father Annat, fell flat. The ideas of Jansenius gained ground. The brisk language of the *Provinciales* made much easier reading than the dry Latin of *Augustinus*. Of course the Holy Office placed the famous letters on the Index (6th September 1657), and three years later the king commanded them to be burned by the public executioner; but that delay itself and the severity of the measures proved that the work was still very widely read. Perhaps it was on account of the letters or the Miracle of the Holy Thorn that the persecution undertaken against Port-Royal was suspended in July 1656, that the Little Schools, closed in February, were allowed to reopen, and that the solitaries, dispersed after the condemnation of Arnauld, were permitted to return to their beloved solitude. Whatever the case might be, the climate had changed.

9. Louis XIV and Port-Royal

Basically, however, the problem remained unchanged. The preceding year it occurred to Pierre de Marca, Archbishop of Toulouse, to draw up a Formulary in which he explicitly condemned Jansenism, and called upon his priests to sign the declaration. In August 1656 the Assembly of the Clergy did likewise, modified the declaration a little and submitted it to Pope Alexander VII. The latter, when Cardinal Chigi, had been one of the commissioners charged by Innocent X to

---

[1] This attitude lends some support to the assertions of those who claim that Pascal underwent a 'third conversion', this time from Jansenism to complete Catholicism. Facts and documents have been quoted to substantiate this theory; among them the evidence of the parish priest of Sainte-Étienne-du-Mont, Father Beurrier, who was Pascal's confessor in 1661, six weeks before Pascal's death. Father Beurrier's *Mémoires* provide further evidence. But the strongest proof lies in the change that took place towards the end of Pascal's life. He devoted himself to acts of charity and to the service of the poor, and abandoned all forms of controversy. On the other hand Pascal never signed the episcopal document formally rejecting Jansenism; he simply declared himself a Catholic subject absolutely to the Church. His family did not seem to think he had retracted. Controversy over this aspect of his life appears to be endless. Such historians as A. Gazier, Father Petitot, as well as Faguet and Hallays, have argued *against* a 'third conversion', while others, among them E. Jovy, Henri Bremond, Father Yves de la Brière and T. de Wyzews, have argued *for*.

examine the 'Five Propositions'; he was thus perfectly familiar with the situation, and gave formal approval to the text of the document. The Assembly of the Clergy therefore made it obligatory for all bishops to sign the Formulary, stating: 'With heart and mouth I condemn the doctrine in the five propositions of Cornelius Jansenius contained in his book *Augustinus*.' The problem of distinguishing between 'law and fact' ceased to exist.

What were Arnauld and his friends to do now? The question at issue was no longer the holding of a simple theological opinion concerning grace and a strict or less strict moral attitude: it concerned the very authority of the Church. The Pope had now settled the problem of fact by stating that the five condemned propositions were indeed to be found in the work of Jansenius; to hold the contrary view was to question his authority. The danger of heresy, and even schism, was imminent. The more reasonable among the Jansenists, including Nicole, advised submission. Others suggested signing the Formulary with 'mental reservation'; in other words, doing precisely what the Jansenists accused the Jesuits of doing so often. They would maintain a 'respectful silence' without modifying their thoughts on the subject. The more impetuous Jansenists, who were the most numerous, demanded an out-and-out rejection. Among them were Pascal, his sister Jacqueline and the indomitable Mother Angélique de Saint-Jean. As for Arnauld, he continued to write pamphlets and to approach the right people; in the name of the Gallican freedoms he secured from the Parlement a refusal to register Alexander VII's Constitution, and in the absence of Cardinal de Retz, the Vicars-General in Paris published an ambiguous document reopening the question of the distinction between 'fact and law'. It needed a *lit de justice* to bring the Parliamentarians to heel, and strong threats to lead the Vicars General to rescind their publication. It was understandable that Mazarin became weary of all this uproar, more especially as the Jansenists had struck up a friendship with his enemy Cardinal de Retz. When the latter escaped from prison in Nantes the parish priests supporting Port-Royal had the impudence to cause the *Te Deum* to be sung. And Retz himself, from his exile in Rome, sent to the French clergy a letter (drafted by Arnauld) in which he compared himself with St Athanasius, St John Chrysostom and St Thomas of Canterbury. He extolled the theories of Port-Royal and posed as the defender of their doctrines concerning grace. It all seemed rather comical coming from this 'Cardinal Don Juan' who dispensed with both sufficient grace and efficacious grace.[1] But Jansenism, having become a sect, set itself up

---

[1] Moreover, having no very firm convictions, he made an offer to the Queen to 'exterminate the Jansenists if she were to join forces with him'; that is to say, give him Mazarin's post as first minister.

as a kind of ecclesiastical Fronde. Before Mazarin died he advised Louis XIV to distrust that 'refractory clique', and 'no longer to endure the Jansenist sect or even its name'.

Undoubtedly the young King needed no encouragement in that direction. Anything which might cast a shadow over his power, and more especially anything which tended to remind him of the Fronde, horrified the King. The gay young prince, busy trying to seduce his wife's maids of honour, was certainly not the man to perceive what was estimable, admirable even, in the spirituality of Port-Royal. He introduced Pierre de Marca and Father Annat into the 'Council of Conscience', and instructed Port-Royal to dismiss its novices and boarders, which occasioned painful scenes and a rather inordinate shedding of tears. M. Singlin had to leave to avoid arrest, and Arnauld had to decamp once more. The old foundress, Mother Angélique, died of grief, followed shortly afterwards by Jacqueline Pascal, Sister Sainte-Euphémie. By the King's command a feeble attempt was made to bring about a *rapprochement* between the Jesuits, through Father Ferrier, and the Jansenist leaders headed by Arnauld; but it came to nothing. Jansenism remained stubbornly entrenched and prepared to give battle. 'Under the pretext of avenging the outrages perpetrated against God,' said the Protestant Jurieu, 'these gentlemen appease their own particular passions'—which was certainly true.

Of the entire Jansenist clique the most determined in their resistance were the nuns of Port-Royal du Saint-Sacrament in Paris,[1] of whom Mother Angélique de Saint-Jean was the mainspring. Despite a demand by the court that they sign a declaration (a much more subdued document, in any case, than the Formulary) submitting to the decision of Innocent X, they remained obstinate, unresponsive, proud and grim. Heaven was theirs, and everything tended to prove it. Sister Sainte-Suzanne, daughter of the great painter Philippe de Champaigne, was miraculously cured of rheumatism. More important still, the new Archbishop of Paris, Pierre de Marca, having replaced Retz who had resigned, and from whom Port-Royal had everything to fear, died suddenly within three days of his having been appointed; an event which filled the holy women with uncharitable joy. De Marca was replaced by the Bishop of Rodez, Hardouin de Péréfixe, a pleasant man with a conciliatory disposition, but somewhat lacking in intellectual qualities. He was a good courtier, anxious to please the King, and he set about 'putting things in order'. To that end he published a non-sensical instruction in which he asserted that the question of law pertained to divine faith and the question of fact to human faith. He then instructed the sisters to sign a newly worded statement.

Mother Angélique de Saint-Jean was not the woman to be caught

---

[1] Henri de Montherlant's play *Port-Royal* stresses the convent's spirit of resistance.

by episcopal bombast of that kind. It seemed as though her ice-cold head had suddenly become seized with some kind of vertigo, and that it had spread to almost the whole community. Port-Royal of Paris began to play the martyr. Let the executioners come; the victims were ready! The good sisters looked upon Péréfixe as another Diocletian. In vain the archbishop pleaded with them through Lancelot to yield 'to please the King'. This clumsy phrase merely stimulated their courage. They pleaded liberty of conscience. To which the good archbishop, with all the grandeur and firmness of his vocation, replied that they confused 'delicacy of conscience with obstinacy'. And he was quite right.

The assertion by one of the most eminent theologians of the twentieth century [1] to the effect that objection on grounds of conscience is invalid against the Church points to the very root of the drama played at that time at Port-Royal. To resist in the name of conscience an order given in the name of the Church was to destroy the very foundations of the Church; and, because the Church is not merely a human society, it meant saying 'No' to God. Did Mother Angélique's pious daughters appreciate that fact? The words of Archbishop Péréfixe—profound for once—described them perfectly: 'As pure as angels and as proud as demons.'

On 9th June 1664 the archbishop visited the convent for the first time, and questioned the nuns one after another. As he got no satisfaction, their stubbornness irritated him more and more, and he went so far as to tell some of them that they were mad. The interview with Mother Angélique de Saint-Jean was especially loud, tense and disappointing.

What was to be done? The archbishop had tried every possible means of conciliation. He had even sent the young Bossuet, a highly reputable preacher, to explain their duty to the nuns. They still held out. They considered it to be God's will that they should do so; and the proof lay in the fact that when Mother Agnès opened the New Testament to seek the answer she came upon these words of St Luke: ' . . . this is your hour, and the power of darkness' (xxii. 53)! This attitude verged on illuminism; they entered into the darkness with gloomy zeal. It was a dramatic episode well suited to inspire the playwright Henri de Montherlant.

On 26th August the archbishop returned with police and armed men. Twelve nuns were selected to be removed from Port-Royal and distributed amongst other convents, and the order was carried out in deathly silence broken only by stifled sobs. We can appreciate the 'dreadful solemnity' of the archbishop, compelled to resort to such

---

[1] Father de Montcheuil, a Jesuit, chaplain to the 'Maquis' at Vercours in 1944; he was shot at Grenoble on 8th August of that year.

measures and no longer acting like the simple, good-natured man that he was. Mother Angélique de Saint-Jean was transferred to the Couvent des Annonciades; and the 'Blue Sisters' with five Visitandines settled in Port-Royal in company with the new provisional superior, Mother Eugénie de Fontaine, a spiritual daughter of St Francis de Sales. But the firm gentleness of the Bishop of Geneva left these aggressive virgins unmoved. Those who remained of the original Port-Royal nuns carried on an unbearable war of nerves against the hated Visitandines, while those who had been banished to other convents continued silently stubborn, writing 'accounts of their captivity' of which page after page revealed the pride of the dark angel. It eventually became necessary to strike harder; the refractory nuns were regrouped at Port-Royal-des-Champs, cut off from the world and completely deprived of sacramental life. Yet they remained unconquered for four years.

10. THE 'CLEMENTINE PEACE'

Not only the nuns resisted. Some of the bishops did likewise, and their resistance, though less spectacular, was more serious.[1] In the spring of 1644 Louis XIV instructed the Parlement to register a declaration under which all priests were ordered to sign the Formulary under pain of losing their benefices. Four of the bishops, who were inclined towards Jansenism—Pavillon of Alet, Caulet of Pamiers, Choart de Buzenval of Beauvais and Henri Arnauld of Angers—protested that the King had no right 'to make canons and laws within the Church'. They probably imagined that the Gallicanism of Louis XIV would restrain him from calling upon the Pope. The king, however, felt compelled to do so, and Alexander VIII replied to his request with the Bull *Regiminis apostolici*, making it obligatory for priests to sign a new Formulary expressed in more precise terms than the previous one. The outcome was rage and confusion in the Jansenist camp, some of their number pressing for submission while Arnauld and Nicole pressed for resistance. Once more the four Jansenist bishops adopted a definite attitude, instructing their flock to accept the Formulary as to law, but to maintain 'a respectful silence' as to the question of fact. The Pope condemned this strange directive and, in agreement with Louis XIV, decided to set up a commission to sit in judgment on the rebels. The affair had begun to take a very serious turn when Alexander VIII died in 1667.

At once the atmosphere changed. The new Pope, Clement IX, was

[1] 'Since the women have shown the courage of bishops,' said Jacqueline Pascal, 'the bishops must have the courage of women.'

of a conciliatory disposition; so was Bargellini, his Nuncio in Paris. The friends of Port-Royal, especially the Duchesse de Longueville, who had a long arm, bestirred themselves to get the proceedings stopped. The three principal ministers of Louis XIV, Lionne, Le Tellier and Colbert, each hoped for different reasons that some kind of a settlement might be reached. The whole Gallican clique pointed out to the King that he himself had allowed Rome to intervene in a matter that strictly concerned France alone, and that his action had not perhaps been very shrewd. Arnauld, relying upon this decoy, addressed a circular to all the bishops of France in which he accused Rome of 'demeaning episcopal dignity' and 'overthrowing the holy canons' of the French Church. It was in this rather extraordinary atmosphere that ultra-secret negotiations were entered into without the knowledge of Péréfixe and the Council of Conscience. They were to terminate in 1669 with an official statement by Clement IX, announcing a general easing of the situation and the return of the lost sheep to the fold.

A close study of the 'Clementine Peace' shows that it was founded on a host of misunderstandings; for the Jansenists continued to intensify their quibbles and reservations, while the Pope did not appear to have been kept fully informed. In France an idea became current which may be summed up as follows: 'The Holy See does not claim that the signing of the Formulary makes it obligatory to believe in the implicit or explicit presence of the five condemned propositions in the book by Jansenius, but only that they should be regarded as condemned and heretical in whatever book they might appear.' But it is not at all certain that that was the meaning Clement IX wished to attach to his declaration. The truth is that everybody, including Arnauld, was weary of so many squabbles, so much secrecy and underhand dealing. Within the framework of the interpretation given above the Jansenists, and even the nuns of Port-Royal, agreed to submit. The bells rang out again in the valley of the Chevreuse; the candles were re-lit in the chapel; the solitaries returned to their hermitages and a rousing *Te Deum* was sung.

Then began an idyllic period during which men of goodwill were persuaded that the Jansenist problem was solved. *Giansenismo estinto* —Jansenism is dead!—the Nuncio Bargellini wrote to Rome. The Council of State published a decree under which the king's subjects were forbidden to discuss the question of grace or to accuse anyone of being a Jansenist. Le Maître de Sacy was freed from the Bastille, and Arnauld de Pomponne, son of Robert Arnauld d'Andilly, was made Secretary of State in the Department of Foreign Affairs. Louis XIV received the Great Arnauld with extreme politeness; and when Arnauld expressed his regret that he should have been embroiled in so many controversies the king interrupted him: 'All that is over; we must not talk about it any more.'

Bossuet had always maintained a guarded attitude towards the Jansenists. He had condemned their revolt and made short work of the question of 'law and fact'; but he admired none the less their moral aspirations and shared their aversion from laxism. He therefore decided to make use of Arnauld's vigour in his struggle against Protestantism. There was even some talk of making the leader of Port-Royal a cardinal. To commemorate this happy hour in the history of the great reign a medal was struck depicting the hand of Justice clasping the Keys of St Peter over an altar—a symbol of the union of the spiritual and temporal powers.

Giansenismo estinto, Bargellini had said. But Jansenism was by no means dead. The period of the 'Clementine Peace', which, for better or for worse, lasted to the end of the century, was just another period of expansion for the movement; in fact, its third. During that time it reached its zenith. Once again Port-Royal became fashionable. The 'charming friends' of the convent, Mme de Longueville and Mlle de Vertus, had small houses built for themselves in the vicinity. Mme de Sévigné, Mme de Sablé, Mme de Liancourt and many other ladies visited the nuns very frequently. The roads in the valley were cluttered with the carriages of duchesses. The common people flocked there on foot from Paris as on pilgrimage. Well-to-do families contended for the honour of having their daughters educated by the famous nuns of Port-Royal. Even the dying asked to be buried near the holy house. All this, as Nicole, Mother Agnès and a few others wisely agreed, was going too far.

The solitaries returned and occupied the lodges they had built not far from the convent, and their numbers increased. The most outstanding among them were Lancelot, the gentle and industrious Le Nain de Tillemont, the scholarly Pierre Nicole and Dr Hamon. None, however, was as brilliant as the early occupants. When Singlin died in 1664 Le Maistre de Sacy (1613–84), nephew and contemporary of the Great Arnauld, became spiritual director of the group; a learned exegete, he also possessed a profound understanding of the human soul. De Sacy was succeeded by Claude de Sainte-Marthe. This third generation of Jansenists had an even greater passion for writing and publishing than their predecessors. The works of Saint-Cyran were published posthumously, and a collection of notes by Blaise Pascal, originally intended to form the basis of an apologetical work, were published in 1670 under the title *Les Pensées* and aroused widespread interest. Le Maistre de Sacy undertook the colossal task of translating the Bible (1672–96), and his version, written in exquisite French, met with tremendous success. The Little Schools were unable to open officially after the crisis of 1661, but houses affiliated to Port-Royal sprang up everywhere; the Jansenist educational system, based upon their own works, e.g. *Grammaire, Logique* and *Règles pour l'éducation des enfants*, spread into many other schools, where it functioned during the whole of the eighteenth century. The excellence of their teaching methods was vindicated by the famous pupils they produced; among them Jean Racine, nephew of the solitary M. Vitart and author of *Andromaque* and *Britannicus*. Racine had been the much-loved pupil of M. Le Maistre, and at that time was winning glory with his dramatic works. Other famous men of letters were also friends of the movement. Nicolas Boileau, like Mme de Sévigné, was something of an 'amateur Jansenist', though his brother Jacques, author of the *Traité contre l'abus des nudités des gorges*, was militant; and even the worthy La Fontaine, whose life was far removed from the austerity of the sect, agreed to back a volume of *Poésies chrétiennes* composed at Port-Royal.

It was at this time that the Jansenist spirit really penetrated into French Catholicism. Many Christians who were quite unmoved by theological arguments allowed themselves to be influenced by those men and women of Port-Royal whom Mme de Sévigné described as 'angels on earth', rivals of the hermits of the desert, saints descended from heaven. Never before had it been so easy and so defensible to confuse a movement towards general reform in the spirit of Trent with those equally austere tendencies that concealed questionable doctrine. There is no question whatever that some saintly souls did succeed in drawing from this well the pure waters of spiritual vitality; but the danger was no less positive. The Jansenist spirit insinuated itself everywhere; it would soon be traced in Orders far removed from Port-Royal, such as the Benedictines and even the Visitandines. It could be detected also in new foundations, such as the Filles de l'Enfance, founded at Toulouse by Mme de Mondonville. The image of the crucified Christ with the arms extended above the head became common among the clergy, even in the most reliable circles. Many parishes adopted it, e.g. Saint-Jacques and Saint-Maur in Paris, and others in Toulouse, Grenelle, Orleans, Alet, Angers and Rouen. It was the period when the famous black wooden Cross was to be found everywhere;[1] and today large numbers of these crucifixes with the body of Christ carved in bone or ivory, showing the arms stretched taut above the head, may still be found in antique shops. The same

---

[1] This type of Cross was not, however, of Jansenist origin. The museum at Cluny possesses one dating from the sixteenth century. The Crucifix was sculpted in bone, and the position of the arms was generally as described above; but it became very popular among the Jansenists. Pascal's Christ, however, which may be seen in Lafuma's large edition of the *Pensées*, as well as on page 174 of Albert Béguin's little book, *Pascal, par lui-même*, certainly shows the arms stretched above the head.

profound sentiments of the sect influenced painting, as is clear, for example, from the works of Philippe de Champaigne, father of the nun who was miraculously cured.

Outside France, Jansenism prospered in the Low Countries, both in the United Provinces and in the territories under the dominion of Spain. In the very regions where the movement was born its scope remained limited for a long time to theological circles. Jacob Boonen, Archbishop of Mechlin, Antoine Triest, Bishop of Ghent, and many of the doctors of Louvain University refused to accept the judgment against *Augustinus*. The success of the *Provinciales* helped to imbue the masses with Jansenist ideas. In 1671 Alphonsus de Bergh, who favoured the sect, succeeded to the archbishopric of Mechlin; he allowed the ideas of Saint-Cyran and Arnauld to be preached publicly, and his successor, William de Precipiano, tried in vain to combat them. Henceforward Belgium seemed to become a hotbed of Jansenism, and it was not long before Catholic Holland felt its influence, especially after the Great Arnauld finally sought refuge in that country. Utrecht, in fact, became a Jansenist headquarters.

All this tends to create an impression of enormous success, the triumph of Jansenism. Yet the more reasonable members of the sect knew that they had good cause for uneasiness. After all, what was the enthusiasm of the worldly minded worth? Was the spirit of the abbot of Saint-Cyran present in the carriages of the duchesses? Even the best of their adherents betrayed signs of weariness. Robert Arnauld d'Andilly was half-hearted in his wish to return to Port-Royal when peace had been restored. He seemed to be somewhat caught up in the attractions of the world. There was evidence of occasional friction within the group. Nicole began to work more and more alone. Were not the splendid years of Port-Royal, described by Sainte-Beuve as 'the lovely hours of a soft autumn, of a rich and lazy sunset', rather years of apparent glory and hidden decline? And no one knew how long the 'Clementine Peace' would last.

11. QUIETISM, THE HERESY OF DIVINE LOVE

A new controversy flared up shortly afterwards, causing a commotion among all sections of society, although it was not a subject calculated to excite the feelings of ordinary Christians. Although doctrinal deviation does occasionally result in real moral aberration, the finer points of heresy are generally perceptible only to the trained mind of the theologian. It is not a common occurrence to see two of the most famous bishops of the day engaged in such bitter controversy that one of them is brought to ruin. Quietism was a trifling matter in itself; but its historical importance was derived from the great conflict between Bossuet and Fénelon.

It has generally been assumed that this new type of deviation was essentially opposed to Jansenism; but this notion is too shallow. Some basis of Augustinianism existed in Quietism as well as in the theories of Jansenius, but in both cases they were exaggerated and distorted. The Quietist conception of man was not very much more optimistic than that of Saint-Cyran, Pascal and Arnauld. In the eyes of Catholics as a whole the emphasis was rather on the general attitude of the soul to moral practice and its conclusions. Jansenism bowed man to the ground before a dreadful God who, according to His whim, called some and rejected others. Jansenist morality clouded over and dried up the heart. Quietism reached conclusions much less pessimistic; we might say that the Quietists deviated in favour of *softness* as opposed to the *harshness* of Port-Royal.

The Quietist starting-point did not differ from the tenets held by the Jansenists and the most orthodox French school regarding the miserable state of man, this 'nothing', as Cardinal de Bérulle said, 'this most vile and useless creature', or, as Pascal put it, 'this outcast of the universe'. From such a concept the great spiritual leaders of the French school, Bérulle, St Vincent de Paul and Olier, had educed that practical and mystical doctrine that raised man towards God through his own conquest of himself and the giving of his whole being to Love. The Jansenists, in their frantic contempt of human nature (although Pascal declared man to be the 'glory' as well as the outcast of the universe), had merely emphasized the first aspect of spiritual experience, namely the ascetic. The Quietists overstressed the second aspect.

St Francis de Sales in his great wisdom counselled a form of abandonment to God which consoled man in the midst of his many miseries. 'I shall do my best', he said, 'to avoid having sores on my face; but if I have them I shall love the humiliation it causes me.' The idea of trusting in God and not 'overrunning' grace might console troubled souls, but the true doctrine, as contained in the *Devout Life* of St Francis, in the works of the great St Teresa and St John of the Cross, and even in *The Imitation of Christ*,[1] taught that God's infinite bounty bestows its gifts upon those who are wholly faithful, who progress heroically towards God's goodness, overcoming the temptations to which sinful nature is prone. Absolute abandonment, self-abasement by all means—but of our egoism, not of our spiritual faculties and the striving of the soul.

Confusion was all the easier because the doctrine of abandonment to God was linked with a tendency which has always existed in Christianity; it existed even among the ancients, in the *apatheia* of the Greeks,

---

[1] *The Imitation of Christ*, Book III, chapter xxxix.

in the scepticism of Pyrrho and in the famous words of Seneca, *Deo non pareo, sed assentior* (I do not obey God; my desires are like his)— and we know that that concept is essentially Islamic. Looked at from a Christian point of view the doctrine of 'indifference' had numerous supporters. Was St Augustine really so very far from Seneca when he declared that those only have true liberty who submit entirely to God, to His will and to His law? The Alexandrian philosophers, together with Isaac the Syrian, St John Climacus, author of *Scala Paradisi*, and St Maximus of Constantinople—'Maximus Confessor'—all repeated in different ways that the first degree of contemplation consists in utter indifference to earthly passions. During the Middle Ages, and more so in the great mystical school of Flanders and the Rhine, indifference had become synonymous with the spirit of renunciation, which, according to Eckhart, Tauler, Blessed Henry Suso and even the author of *The Imitation of Christ*, is indispensable to the soul's impulse towards God. By the sixteenth century this idea had become universally accepted. For St Ignatius of Loyola total indifference was the means by which man renounced all inordinate affections and desires; for St John of the Cross it was the point of departure of the soul's journey towards the mystic heights; for St Francis de Sales indifference alone enabled the human will, having shed self though not yet resigned to accept everything, to abandon itself utterly to God, to love 'nothing except for the love of God's will'.

During the Middle Ages this state was described as *quies mentis*, 'quiet of the mind'. The expression itself suggests the danger contained in this doctrine if it were but slightly misunderstood. It is easy to drift from legitimate 'quiet' towards a state of complacent sloth; and that facility exists not only in the psychical domain. Is it necessary for the soul, utterly abandoned to God and closely bound to Him, to continue to make any effort, to perform any act or to mortify itself? According to the Quietists it was sufficient that the soul rest in God, passive and indifferent to everything, even to the temptations that might assail it, and indeed indifferent to its own salvation. 'My desire is to desire nothing,' said Sister Marie-Rosette, a well-known Quietist; 'my will is to will nothing, to remain attached to nothing. . . . But I do not even desire to desire nothing, because I think that would also be a desire.' What a strange moral and spiritual world such a doctrine leads to! Is the soul still in a Christian climate, or has it attained some vague condition of *Nirvana*? It is very easy to 'wait until God moves us', and to 'do nothing and be led'. But how do we know the devil is not leading us?

There had always been Quietists in the Church. St Jerome had long ago denounced this tendency in the monk Evagrius. About the year one thousand the 'Hesychasts' of Byzantium remained still and silent, with their eyes fixed on the navel, in order to arrive at the contemplation of the uncreated light of God. They considered that in this state the soul is altogether incapable of sin. In the twelfth century, in the West, the followers of Amaury Bène and Ortlieb's 'Brethren of the Free Spirit' [1] were Quietists; the Brethren, on the plea of total renunciation, attained a condition of depravity that was anything but spiritual. Quietists also were the enigmatical Begards [2] among whom good and evil were to be found side by side. Even Luther in his youth, between 1515 and 1518 when he despaired of salvation, recommended total surrender to God, the suppression of all effort and every desire, the acceptance of everything, even hell; a doctrine so discouraging that he rejected it.

In the seventeenth century, especially in France, the lure of Quietism was noticeable even among the most lofty and sincere mystics, champions of the principle of Pure Love.[3] They rejected it instinctively, however, remaining within the bounds of a love of God which their prudence enabled them to understand and to which they endeavoured to remain loyally responsive. But it was always possible to misunderstand the counsels of spiritual leaders. M. Olier wrote to a nun: 'You must purify yourself to please God alone.' He advised priests to 'so abase themselves in serving God that they no longer looked for a reward'. Father de Condren counselled his penitents to leave themselves to God, abandoning all desire to live and to be. Jean-Pierre Camus, Bishop of Belley, the friend and biographer of St Francis de Sales, preached that the soul should aim at a renunciation so perfect that it would be prepared to accept damnation instead of salvation if such were God's will—which, of course, it is not possible to imagine. Such precepts, so susceptible to misinterpretation, were plentiful. They were to be found in the writings and on the lips of such men as Father Surin and Father Nouet, Jesuits both; the celebrated Capuchin Benoît de Canfeld; the pious layman Jean de Bernières-Louvigny, author of Chrétien intérieur; his friend M. Bertot, spiritual director of the Benedictine nuns at Montmartre; and M. Boudon, the great archdeacon of Evreux and author of Dieu Seul. False mysticism lay in wait for those who lent a too willing ear to sincere calls to a holy indifference and surrender to the mystical impulse. By the light of the Molinosist conflagration the Church would perceive the danger more clearly.

[1] See Cathedral and Crusade, pp. 521, 522
[2] See Cathedral and Crusade, pp. 557, 595.
[3] See Chapter II, p. 61.

12. The Enigmatical Miguel de Molinos

It was not only in the Church of France that the tendency existed to distort what Henri Bremond called the 'Charter of Love, sublime and holy', on which religious life during the Great Century had been founded. The tendency itself consisted in regarding divine love as a kind of sensual pleasure, and prayer as a 'vague celestial hashish'. Similar views were held in Italy by Achille Cagliarde, author of *Breve compendio intorno alla perfezione cristiana*, and his penitent Isabella Bellinzaga—the 'Milanese Lady'—a capable woman who in her youth had helped St Charles Borromeo in the running of a hospital. In Spain also there were two very saintly men who thought along the same lines: Gregorio Lopez, who went to Mexico and lived the contemplative life of a hermit, and the Venerable John Falconi, author of *Alphabet pour apprendre à lire dans le Christ*. 'The short way to perfection', wrote Falconi, 'is to remain in peaceful and silent rest, in pure faith in God and total surrender to His holy will'. The same, or in any case less orthodox, tendencies were to be found in less commendable spheres. In certain confraternities, called Schools of Christ, the 'prayer of quiet' embraced a blend of ideas that originated in Islam and India; and the Illuminati, such as those who were condemned in Seville in 1625, practised a spirituality fairly closely related to it. Their counterparts also existed in Italy, notably among the 'Lombardists' of Dom Giacomo Lombardi in the Italian region of the Marches and the devotees of St Pelagia, who assembled in chapels dedicated to that saint. All these movements were eventually linked together and swept along by the violence of the tide.

History is far from having solved the secret of the strange Miguel de Molinos.[1] Prudent, learned and eminent men have disagreed as to whether he was a saint or an impostor. Some regard him as a kind of Rasputin who duped the papal court just as the famous monk later fooled the court of Nicholas II. He seems to be condemned by his own admissions; yet the official judgment was surprisingly lenient in view of the crimes attributed to him. France and the world learned from the Dreyfus affair how difficult it is to see clearly in discussions of this nature in which a man becomes a symbol of contention.

Molinos was born near Saragossa in 1628 of poor parents, and studied under the Jesuits in Valencia. He received the degree of Doctor of Theology at Coimbra, and was ordained priest at the age of twenty-four. Intellectually he was brilliant; he radiated an air of authority which observers have described as 'at first disconcerting, and then

---

[1] He is not to be confused with the Jesuit Luis de Molina whose sophistry has been much discussed. See *The Catholic Reformation*, pp. 35, 345, and note on p. 330 of the present work.

supercilious'. At thirty years of age he was already the idol of religious circles in Valencia, a fashionable preacher, a confessor in demand in all the convents. His fellow townsmen sent him to Rome in 1664 as procurator in the beatification cause of Jerónimo Simón, who was dear to them; and Miguel Molinos met with the same success in the Eternal City. Whenever he said Mass those in search of the path towards mysticism gathered round him; even members of the Sacred College of Cardinals, and among them the future Pope St Innocent XI, at that time Cardinal Odescalchi. Letters reached him from all over Italy, and above his signature he wrote: 'Moved by the Holy Ghost', or 'In the light of the Most High'. He was at that time 'submerged beneath a torrent of souls, though he remained as detached and solitary as a hermit'. His triumph lasted unalloyed for ten years.

In 1675 Molinos published in Spanish, and subsequently in Italian, an account of his teaching; the work was entitled *Guía Espiritual—* 'Spiritual Guide'. Its success was enormous, not only in the two languages in which it was published but also in Latin, French and German. Less notice was given to his *Tradado de la Comunión cuotidiana*. He received the most flattering tributes, and when his opponents dared to criticize his theories it was they whom the Holy Office condemned, including even Father Paolo Segneri, at that time the most famous among the Jesuit preachers and a renowned ascetic doctor. Meanwhile Molinos himself remained aloof from all this, and declared that 'his one desire was to be annihilated for Jesus and contemned by all'.

Molinosist doctrine was unqualified Quietism. Its spirituality culminated in two fundamental themes: absolute passivity and contemplation in complete spiritual tranquillity. The soul must aim at 'mystic death', annihilation in God; allowing God to substitute Himself for the Ego and to dominate the whole being. The soul should have no desire, should make no act of love. In fact, every act is displeasing to God because it interrupts the state of passive resignation. Devotion itself is harmful if it is addressed to the visible, e.g. the humanity of the Man-Christ, the Blessed Virgin or the saints. Thus one way only was offered to the mystical soul: the 'inward way'. The 'purgative way' was no longer necessary: away with asceticism!

Had Molinos meditated on the Gospel of St John, in which Christ said: 'He that hath my commandments, and keepeth them, he it is that loveth me' (John xiv. 21)? Not that he denied sin and man's falling into sin, but he held that our very vices were acceptable to God, provided that the soul humbled itself. When these onsets occurred it was because God allowed the demon to use violence against the will of perfect souls, even to the point of making them perform shameful acts. Under the doctrine of abandonment it was harmful to resist.

What might have appeared to be serious faults were regarded by Molinos as simply miserable snares of the Spirit of Darkness. *Etiam peccata. . . .* That was carrying things far indeed.

That these theories were not condemned out of hand could only be explained by the prestige Molinos enjoyed with Innocent XI, the Cardinals Ricci, Azzolini, Cybo, the Secretary of State, Capizucchi, who was responsible for the *Imprimatur* granted to the *Guía Espiritual,* and Petrucci, author of a book containing similar ideas; not to mention many of the Roman princesses and ex-Queen Christina of Sweden. What is even harder to understand is that opinion suddenly turned against him. There might have been several reasons for this. A number of confessors drew attention to the fact that some of their penitents— especially female penitents—were giving anything but a moral interpretation to Molinosist ideas. Inigo Caracciolo, Archbishop of Naples, declared that the 'prayer of quiet' had ousted all vocal prayer as well as confession, especially in convents. The elderly Cardinal Albizzi of the Holy Office took a similar stand. Perhaps Quietism appeared to Innocent XI as the antithesis of the Jansenist error which had been condemned, and considered that it also should be stamped out in the general interest. Perhaps also the Pope's confessor, Father Maracchi, pressed for condemnation because he wished to show clearly that the Society of Jesus had no connection whatever with such doctrines, even though it had fought the myrmidons of Jansenius and the over-strict moral code of Port-Royal. Strange rumours were current in Rome, and accusations regarding the holy man's relations with his female penitents reached the Inquisition.

In 1685 he was arrested by the papal police. His household staff protested the absolute innocence of his life, and kissed his feet as he entered the carriage which took him to prison. Mabillon, who was then in Rome, noted in his diary that no one knew exactly why Molinos had been arrested: 'No one believes that it is on account of the doctrine contained in his published writings, but rather on account of his letters, or at least the unfortunate interpretation put on his ideas by his followers.' To defend the victim of the Inquisition pamphlets were posted up on the famous 'Pasquino'—the mutilated statue to which lampoons were affixed. The mood of hostility developed rapidly, and many of the mystic's disciples were also thrown into the prisons of the Holy Office. It was proved beyond a shadow of doubt that Molinosism was working havoc not only among the women who strove to attain the Nirvana of imperturbable tranquillity, but among others who sought joys of a less celestial nature. Molinos himself confessed to everything of which he was accused; he agreed with whatever his accuser wished to plead against him, whatever the demon, doing violence to his will, might have been able to make him do. His attitude

N

was clearly that of a Christian who, under blows and insults, rejoiced at being like the outraged Christ. Sixty-eight propositions were extracted from his writings and condemned by Innocent XI. He submitted at once, and solemnly agreed to renounce his errors. This he did in the church of Santa Maria Sopra Minerva, on his knees between two *sbirri*, and holding in his bound hands a candle, while the crowd on the square shouted: 'To the stake, to the stake!' He evinced a mysterious air of gaiety and imperturbability, possibly in that state of complete spiritual passivity in which 'No glad tidings bring joy, and no misfortune brings sadness'. Innocent XI flatly refused to allow him to be condemned to death, a fact which gave rise to doubt as to the truth of the moral turpitude of which Molinos had been accused, though he had admitted his guilt. He passed the last nine years of his life, until 1696, in prison, with every appearance of a life of mortification and prayer, if not of repentance.

13. Madame Guyon

From the very beginning Molinosism penetrated into France, where, as we have seen, it found conditions favourable. Although, however, the French Quietists exaggerated the state of passivity and assimilation with God, they never adopted the extraordinary theory of evil and man's lack of responsibility embarked upon by Molinos. Thus, in 1664, the blind mystic Malaval, 'the lay saint of Marseilles', as his fellow townsmen called him, published a practical manual on contemplation which achieved immense popularity; Father Segneri discovered seven 'illusions' in the work but nothing more serious. With Father Lacombe and Madame Guyon, however, the deviation developed into something much more significant.

The circumstances surrounding these two personalities were very much on a par with those pertaining to Miguel Molinos. They were the centre of such a maelstrom of heated controversy and vehement quarrels, and were attacked with such violence, that the historian hesitates to accept at their face value indictments in which equity does not always appear to have been observed; or even to recognize confessions which may have resulted from their own fanatical, but Christian, humility.

Father Lacombe was born in Thonon in 1643. He does not appear to have been endowed with that very sound sense of proportion and practical wisdom normally recognizable in natives of Savoy. According to Mgr Calvet he was 'a simple man and a zealous missioner', but also 'a pious visionary'; emotional and incapable of marshalling his ideas. He admitted: 'I make foolish blunders which I have to pay for soon afterwards . . . more often resulting from the painful reproaches I feel within me than from the punishments I bring down upon myself '. A man of such temperament was inevitably exposed to the accidents of fortune. Having joined the Barnabites, an Order founded in the preceding century by St Antony Maria Zaccaria, he became a teacher of theology in the mother house of the Order, and later Superior of the community at Thonon. In Rome he became acquainted with the theories of Molinos, and was on friendly terms with Augusto Ripa, Bishop of Vercelli and an ardent Molinosist. He explained his spiritual doctrine, very similar to that of Molinos, in two short works, one of which was written in Latin. They passed almost unnoticed, and perhaps the good father would have remained an obscure Quietist had not chance—or the demon—brought him into contact with Jeanne-Marie Bouvier de la Mothe, widow of Jacques Guyon de Chesnoy and sister of his provincial, Father Dominique Bouvier.

At Gex, facing Thonon across the Lake of Geneva, a house belonging to the organization 'Nouvelles catholiques' had been recently set up to guarantee the perseverance of Protestant converts. It was founded at the request of the Bishop of Geneva by a woman whom everyone regarded as an unusual person, and for whom Father Lacombe, the new spiritual director of the house, had boundless admiration. This little middle-class woman from Montargis certainly was extraordinary within the full meaning of the term. She was born in 1648. Even when very young she declared that she had 'visions like those of St Teresa'; she said that 'with a large needle' she had sewn on her flesh a piece of paper bearing the name of Jesus! She was physically abnormal, a prey to strange swellings of the body when her skin became pitted with purple marks. She did not seem very much more balanced psychologically. At fifteen her reading of romantic works and a natural tendency towards day-dreaming created a queer tumult in a mind ceaselessly in a whirl. This explosive mixture led her into marriage with a good-natured cousin twenty-two years her senior. On the day after the wedding she declared amidst tears that marriage was to her a hateful sacrifice and that she would rather have been a nun. Though she had four children she somehow (under a process which Freud has studied) transferred her unsatisfied passion as a great lover to the religious plane, and lived in a mystical delight which made her forget her real life; she applied to herself all the spiritual states the details of which she had read in books, and went so far as to claim that the Child Jesus had placed on her finger the invisible ring of mystical marriage.

In this unusual woman the features of mystical experience were amazingly blended, and hysteria undoubtedly exercised a stupendous influence over her. As a young girl she was pretty and coquettish, with alluring lips and the gentle eyes of a doe; but smallpox had left ugly marks upon her face and she regarded them as an extraordinary grace. She had little need of the everyday weapons required to charm and assert her personality. Her tremendous flow of words disconcerted even those who were most unamenable to persuasive eloquence. She wrote with a speed that St Jerome might have envied. In a week she produced a commentary on the most difficult of the biblical books, and wrote one on the Canticle of Canticles in twenty-four hours! When Jeanne-Marie Guyon became a widow she was at last able to devote herself to her true vocation: the winning of souls. 'Our Lord has made it clear that He has destined me to be the mother of a great people!' she said. And she added: 'Deep down I have a natural aptitude for sound judgment, and it never fails me'. In the matter of humility at least this Christian evidently stood in awe of no one.

When this preposterous woman came in contact with Father Lacombe their meeting put the finishing touches to her ardour. Entirely free from material worries, thanks to an income of fifty thousand *livres* left to her by Jacques Guyon, she could without hindrance abandon herself to an apostolic zeal continually inflamed by her interior voices. She dragged the worthy Barnabite along with her in that spiritual Odyssey into which he was already inclined by temperament to plunge. It ended in a complete fusion of souls, the mutual discovery 'of a land entirely new to them both, so divine as to be utterly inexpressible'. There followed the ebb and flow of graces interchanged; a supernatural silence in which their minds, independent of words, were united. Which of the two controlled the other? It needed but one word from the priest, the magnetic touch of his hand on the penitent's brow, to dispel a sick headache or a stubborn cough. But the Barnabite confessed that when he was away from her he felt bereft of a part of himself. Did their relationship develop into something rather less unearthly? At least Louis XIV, Mme de Maintenon, Bossuet and Cardinal de Noailles thought so, and stated it publicly. Mme Guyon herself never admitted to anything of a serious nature, apart from a few innocent kisses; but Father Lacombe later confessed to moral turpitude. That confession, however, occurred after he had become insane, when the truth of his admissions might have been regarded as open to doubt.[1] Whatever the case may be the mystico-sensuous nature of their relationship was sufficient to throw off balance two dispositions that were already on the threshold of error.

For a while Mme Guyon took the habit of the Ursulines at Thonon. There, and at Gex, Marseilles, Lyons and Dijon, she conducted an apostolate, while she carried out the duties of a simple medical attendant at hospitals in Turin with admirable charity. There were no limits to

---

[1] Henri Bremond has clearly stated: 'It is certain that Mme Guyon was never proved guilty of the slightest fault with Father Lacombe or with anyone else.'

· the zeal of the visionary. The enthusiastic and ardent Father Lacombe followed her despite the warnings of his provincial, Mme Guyon's brother, of his bishop, Jean d'Aranthon of Alex, who was very disturbed, and of Cardinal Le Camus, Bishop of Grenoble. They were surrounded by a fanatical nucleus of 'devout' of both sexes; for them only was reserved the teaching of hidden ineffable truths, while the public was given the mere outline of their doctrine. In 1683, after a dreadful crisis, both physical and spiritual, during which Mme Guyon knew not whether she was carrying the Child Jesus or tormented by the great dragon of the Apocalypse, she experienced a period of tranquillity during which she drafted her *Moyen court et très facile de faire oraison*. It was published two years later and met with enormous success. In two leaflets—the *Torrents spirituels*—circulated secretly she formulated mystical theories for the initiated. This was intensified Quietism, unrestricted Molinosism: surrender, passivity, 'recollection in God', the mystical marriage, 'unimaginable innocence' and indifference to human acts. There was nothing new in it all. The only point in which Mme Guyon and Lacombe differed from Molinos was the matter of sin. They did not refer to it as violence used by the demon, but they affirmed that 'extreme surrender' and detachment from self could lead the soul to commit faults; 'to commit a sin of which one had the greatest abhorrence' was to offer the greatest sacrifice to God! Such statements confirmed the worst suspicions.

When Father Lacombe and his 'soul-mate' arrived in Paris their doctrines found an immediate hearing. A number of society ladies went into raptures over the visionary. They were anything but mad, but were, on the contrary, souls sincerely in search of spiritual advancement. They included such ladies as the Duchesse de Charost, Colbert's three daughters, the Duchesses of Chevreuse, Beauvilliers and Mortemart, Mme de Miramion, foundress of the Sisters of the Holy Family, known as the 'Miramionnes', and Mlle de la Maisonfort, Canoness of Saint-Cyr, who happened to be Mme de Maintenon's cousin. The mystic couple created such a stir that the Archbishop of Paris became uneasy; in order to please Rome where, as a matter of fact, Molinos had just been arrested, he secured an order from the authorities to confine the Barnabite to the Bastille 'on account of his scandalous conduct',—an action which gave rise to gossip and mirth, for there was nothing edifying about the conduct of Archbishop Harlay de Champvallon. Shortly afterwards Mme Guyon was confined to the convent of the Visitandines in the Rue Saint-Antoine, a trial which she welcomed with great strength of mind, rejoicing to be 'deemed infamous'; she even talked of facing the scaffold, a fate with which she was not in the least threatened.

Meanwhile her friends were indignant; they busied themselves trying to secure her release, and Mme de Maintenon, who was then at the height of her influence, agreed to intervene. Poor Father Lacombe became more and more absorbed in God, lost in a prayer of quiet which left him insensible to trials. He went from prison to prison: from the Bastille to the Île d'Oléron, from the Fort in Lourdes to the one in Vincennes. In 1712 he died insane—or so it is claimed—in the asylum at Charenton, and his penitent left the convent of the Visitation to return in triumph to the fashionable circles. It was at the house of the Duchesse de Charost that she met a young bishop of thirty-five, whose irresistible charm and noble bearing seemed predisposed to inspire a spirit of mysticism, the surrender of the will, the annihilation of the being in divine love. His name was François de Salignac de la Mothe Fénelon. 'They found each other's mind to their taste', said Saint-Simon, 'and the sublime in each intermingled.'

14. The Semi-Quietism of Fénelon

That remark of Saint-Simon's, like many of his witty sayings, was not quite true, for the sublime did not immediately blend in the two friends. At first Fénelon was reserved. After a good three hours' conversation with the mystical lady in the carriage which took them from the Château de Beynes to Paris the principles she discussed began to touch him. When at the end of the journey Mme Guyon asked him if he accepted all she had said, he replied: 'It has gone in by the coachman's door.' In other words, he was almost won over.

Is it surprising that a man in whom burned the fire of genius should have allowed himself to be caught up in this way? There might have been many indications that the widow of Jacques Guyon was neurotic, and that 'her mind was clouded over by subconscious dreams which she accepted as divine impulses', but she undoubtedly had within her also an ardent love of God and the conquering strength of an apostle. At the time Fénelon met her she was free from the cumbering influence of Father Lacombe. For the moment she appeared to be well balanced, and no one in the pious coterie frequenting Colbert's noble daughters (with whom Fénelon was on very close terms) had any doubt about her loftiness of purpose. Fénelon's prejudice against her was therefore bound to collapse. Furthermore, he had reached that stage in his life when a youngish but maturing man, laudably uneasy about his destiny, asks himself questions about the future life; he must also, despite his enjoyment of the full flavour of success, find in it a bitter taste, and to some extent be predisposed to heed as a messenger of Providence a woman who, in a burning voice, speaks to him of abandonment, an inner call and the prayer of simplicity. After all, what did it matter to be a celebrated preacher, the favourite pupil of the great Bossuet and the Superior of Nouvelles Catholiques at twenty-eight years of age? How important was it to be one of the missioners especially appointed by Louis XIV to convert the Protestant provinces, if he experienced an anguish, more intense because it was hidden, that the firmest faith was not sufficient to conquer? What Mme Guyon told him was undoubtedly what Fénelon was waiting to hear.

From their very first meeting Mme Guyon herself experienced, as she said, 'an inexplicable urge to open her heart' to the young director. Without over-emphasizing the likeness between Fénelon and Ulysses, the hero of his book *Télémaque*—'his eyes full of fire, the look steady, the smile delicate, his movements casual, his speech soft, ingenuous and winning, and concealing behind his reserved manner a depth of charm and sparkle'—we may yet be permitted to think that Mme Guyon had a sufficiently keen understanding of human nature to guess that Fénelon was an exceptional man in whom burned a mysterious flame. From her point of view it was a veritable venture of spiritual seduction, the lover feeling her soul 'in perfect harmony' with the one she wishes to win, her soul 'adhering to his as the soul of King David adhered to Jonathan's', and having but one aim: to render this sublime harmony fruitful. There is not the slightest doubt that their relations were chaste. Bossuet did not enhance his stature when he accused them of moral turpitude and compared their relationship with that of the heretic Montanus and his concubine Priscilla. Despite the obviously uncommon appearances which this type of mystical union assumed, theirs was the harmony of two souls in pure love, never departing from the bounds of the supernatural.

What we know of their relationship—and we do know a lot from their letters—certainly causes astonishment; even if we allow for the fact that the language of the day was different from our own (and in this respect we have only to compare the correspondence between St Francis de Sales and St Jeanne de Chantal), and that words which may be ambiguous nowadays possessed at that time a delicate transparency. Though we may also agree with some writers that Fénelon had 'a certain simplicity of soul, at once naïve and profound', we cannot but feel that the filial trust he evinced towards the woman he regarded as his spiritual mother led him to express himself in a manner distressingly puerile. It is embarrassing to see such a great man childishly stringing together doggerel lines to the tune of *Taisez-vous, musette*; lines which run: 'Comme au maillot, je suis en grace . . . à peine je bégaie, je ne sais pas mon nom' (I am in favour, like the baby in the cradle. . . . I can scarcely lisp a word, and I do not yet know my name). It is even more distressing to read that he called the widow Guyon his 'Maman Téton', and that she should reply by calling him 'Bibi'. How strong must have been the spirit of purity in the tender and passionate soul of the future 'Swan of Cambrai' to ensure that all these sentiments did not develop into anything worse! 'I experience no feelings towards you', he wrote to his spiritual mother, 'and yet I am attached to no one more than I am to you. Nothing can be compared with my *cold, dry* fondness for you.' The words in italics are important.

Mme Guyon's influence over Fénelon was therefore beyond question. He thought and believed with all his strength that she had been placed by God along his path to guide him and provide him with the answer he sought. 'My confidence in you is complete', he wrote, 'because of the brilliance of the light you bring to bear on interior things and God's designs through you.' And he never repudiated that trust and admiration; even when he was compelled to part company with his friend, and ceased to write to her. When she was defeated and rejected by all he remained faithful to her with the grace of the nobleman that he was. 'Hold fast to what I have told you,' she commanded; 'it is of God!' Undoubtedly he obeyed her deep down in his heart to the end of his days.

Not that he accepted all Mme Guyon's opinions and made her errors his own. When he wrote, 'From you I receive my daily bread', he was presumably not referring to his correspondent's dogmatic assertions, but to the spiritual impulse she gave him, to the interior peace he had won back through his contact with her. Apart from that he meant to remain free. 'You mistake your illusions for divine impulses . . . ' he wrote. 'I have never doubted the honesty of your intentions, but I express no opinion as to the details of your doctrine. I believe in you without judging you, although it demands an effort not to judge you. You have often made a mistake in temporal matters. . . .' Those are not the words of a man who adheres to a doctrine and follows a guide blindly.

Fénelon refused to agree with his friend on very many fundamental points in which Quietism proper deviated seriously and deserved to be condemned as a heresy. Mme Guyon was not very sure of her ideas and her theological terms. She became entangled in the worst snares of Molinosism, accepting the theory that evil is imposed upon the innocent by the violence of the demon, and that God allows the innocent to become 'stained' in the interest of their spiritual progress. She even maintained that a soul in a state of perfect passivity should be indifferent to its own salvation; she went so far as to declare that a soul in a state of imperturbable peace 'would be content to live deprived entirely of the practice of religion'—which *ipso facto* would render the sacraments almost useless. Not for a moment did Fénelon recognize such reckless propositions. On the contrary, he strove to lead his friend to correct them, which she did to a great extent. In

Fénelon's hands Mme Guyon certainly grew to resemble less and less the Mme Guyon of Father Lacombe—which suggests a somewhat feminine type of mimesis. Thus the spiritual son also exercised an influence over his 'mother'. 'Guyonism' became 'Fénelonized', as Mgr Calvet has judiciously remarked.

Although the future Archbishop of Cambrai was not a Quietist in the heretical sense of the term, it is none the less true that from a doctrinal point of view, and especially from the standpoint of his profound aspirations—for he was never an ardent Schoolman—he was drawn very close to the basic doctrines of the 'spirit of quiet'. He was born and had developed in the atmosphere of 'pure love'. During his childhood at Cahors, where the memory of the Venerable Alain de Solminihac still lingered, he had read in Father Chastenet's book on the great bishop that he had extolled the virtue of being childlike and preached a love of God detached from all desire of heavenly reward. And in the Chartreuse, where he made his retreats, he had listened to Dom Beaucousin talking about Mme Acarie, Marie de l'Incarnation, and her mysticism of love. His uncle, Salignac Fénelon, an influential member of the Company of the Blessed Sacrament, had brought him into contact with the ideas of M. de Bernières-Louvigny. Later at Saint-Sulpice the famous director M. Tronson taught him the pedagogics of divine love, and instilled into him the habit of the presence of God, introducing him to the bountiful source that originated with M. Olier, in which the Christian ideal begins with complete forgetfulness of self. All these influences operating in the same direction, combined with the doctrine of pure love and perfect surrender to God, were bound to bear fruit in a soul which, as Fénelon himself admitted, 'bore the burden of itself' and awaited in torment an answer to its problems. What an antidote to the poison of doubt and scruple was this doctrine that counselled the rejection of all things, utter surrender to God and the whisperings of the silent voice! In the circle of his friends, the pious duchesses, Fénelon was able to sense the tendency to dryness in certain forms of asceticism of which Jansenism was the extreme example. Should the life of a Christian consist merely in fighting against sin? Did it not consist rather in living in God and in His love?

Thus Fénelon adhered not so much to Quietism as to that long tradition of spiritual *indifference* that permeated the whole history of Christianity; a sentiment intrinsically bound up with theocentric thought. He who seeks only the will of God is compelled to be indifferent to everything else. 'Holy indifference', he wrote, 'demands that we desire nothing for ourselves, but everything for God.' Did St Francis de Sales, M. Olier and Monsieur Vincent say otherwise? It was the alpha and the omega of what Bremond called 'the metaphysics

* N

of the saints'. There was no question of destroying the human will, but rather of delivering it from everything that fettered it, releasing it from *possessing* in order that it might tend towards *being*. The quintessence of this endeavour was the very experience of the mystics: complete renunciation, absorption in God. Holy indifference, the 'Fénelonian' state of passivity, meant more than vague contemplation; it meant supreme submission to the divine will. To love God was to die to oneself; it implied rejection of egoism, even of the selfish desire to be ultimately rewarded for one's trust. Briefly, was it unorthodox to 'dispossess' oneself? St Augustine said much the same in other words; and Pascal said: 'The one true virtue is to hate oneself.' The most admirable and profoundly Christian thing about 'Fénelonism' was its expectation of God, 'an ever-present God who envelops us and continually calls us; whom we often fail but who never fails us'. [1] Even when, in some of Fénelon's statements, his doctrine lends itself to misinterpretation, it remains in keeping with the fundamental ideas of Christian tradition; or, more precisely, to one of the two essentials of that tradition.

For there are two Christian conceptions of the spiritual life, and the Church has always striven to reconcile and fuse them. One views the spiritual life more especially from the theological standpoint, stressing its elements rather than the principles that ultimately draw the two conceptions together on the highest levels; it considers above all dogma, the doctrinal assertions to which faith adheres and the rules upon which life must be ordered. The psychological aspects of human problems remain somewhat outside this conception. But the other places religious experience in the psychological sphere, and requires that faith consist primarily in a perfect state of expectation, the reply to the *irrequietum cor nostrum* of which St Augustine speaks. When the soul knows definitely that it has been called, that it has been pierced by the dart of love that quivers in the hearts of the great mystics, then is everything else added to it: loyalty to dogma and obedience to the Commandments. In a word it is precisely this total merging with God which is the goal of all genuine religious experience, the consummation underlying St Paul's words, 'And I live, yet not I; but Christ liveth in me'; providing always we do not forget that this fusion is possible only at the cost of heroic mastery of self. There is not the slightest doubt that Fénelon was the perfect embodiment of the second of these conceptions; but he had to contend with Bossuet, who was the perfect embodiment of the first. When Fénelon, thinking of those souls who aspired to the plenitude of the spiritual life, offered them his doctrine, his adversary, bearing in mind the needs of less ambitious

---

[1] Jean Lacroix, in the 23rd February 1957 issue of *Le Monde*, with reference to J. M. Goré's book, *La notion d'indifférence chez Fénelon et ses sources*.

souls who required safeguards rather than wings to soar to the heights, replied that all this mysticism was very dangerous and might lead to serious doctrinal aberrations. From their own points of view both had cause to claim that religion was at stake; but both were wrong in not recognizing that true Christian experience results from the harmonious blending of these two conceptions, which are complementary. It was over this perplexing question that Fénelon came into conflict with his old friend and master Bossuet.

15. STORM AT SAINT-CYR

Meanwhile the early success of the young prelate and the visionary Mme Guyon gradually became a triumph; their most resplendent period being from 1689 to 1694. Fénelon had just been selected to be tutor to the king's grandson the Duc de Bourgogne, and he set about transforming this temperamental and quick-tempered boy (who was, however, steady and upright) into a prince pleasing to God, with the result that much was expected of him. His father, the Dauphin, was a remote nonentity living in his little court of Meudon. He knew nothing about France apart from what he read in the society columns of the *Gazette de France*. Fénelon devoted himself to training the future heir to be an exemplary king who would establish in France the reign of piety and the pure love of God. Fénelon felt within him 'a disinterested urge to engage in the conduct of important affairs of State, a task for which he considered himself to have been born'. Might he not become the Richelieu of this future Louis XV? Mme Guyon prophesied that he would be the light of the realm, the star that would lead kings towards the Child Christ. Fénelon's novel *Télémaque*, which he began to write for his pupil the Duc de Bourgogne, set out his ideas of a policy founded entirely upon moral principles. He went so far as to address to the Great King himself an explosive letter worthy of the prophets of Israel, in which he cast the king's faults into his teeth and threatened him with the thunderbolt of divine justice.[1] It was all very beautiful.

A little group gathered round the mystical couple creating something of the atmosphere of a secret society—a community of saintly souls, the Order of 'Michelins', who, like the archangel of old, would conquer 'Baraquin', the devil. It had a general, assistants, a master of novices, a secretary, even brother porters and brother gardeners; there was no task which the Order did not provide for. It was a childishly mystical scheme to which were added one or two more worldly aims; for, after all, the Duc de Bourgogne was destined one day to rule France. Mme de Maintenon, the queen without a crown, was kept well

[1] See Chapter IV, p. 192 and note 1.

informed, and she approved these pious endeavours which she hoped would bring about the complete conversion of her husband and the spiritual rebirth of society.

Yet it was through Mme de Maintenon that the troubles began. To begin with she confided utterly in Mme Guyon, 'hoping to find joy and consolation in the sweetness of her intercourse'. But all that changed. Mme de Maintenon had recently founded Saint-Cyr, where she intended to educate young society ladies who would become the *élite* of French womanhood. Fénelon lectured there, pointing out the way that lay open to the little children of God. He spoke eloquently on the pure love of God, mental prayer and the suppression of methods based on reason. It did not take Mme Guyon long to find her way into Saint-Cyr, where she spoke with equal ardour. The new institution, having no religious tradition, was literally seized by a wave of fervour and joy. About that time Racine was putting on his plays *Esther* and *Athalie* at Saint-Cyr. The king himself watched them at the door of the theatre, and Mme de Sévigné was in raptures over them. Mme Guyon had a staunch supporter at Saint-Cyr in her cousin the bewitching Mlle de la Maisonfort, even more of a Guyonist than herself, who disseminated strange doctrines among the students: there was no further need for prayers or good works; no need to practise virtue and perform acts of penance; the way of union and passive purification was sufficient. It was indeed a strange doctrine. Mme de Maintenon might have been influenced by subconscious jealousy at seeing another woman exercise so much sway over the young ladies, and she opened her heart to the Bishop of Chartres and her spiritual director Godet des Marais. The latter, perhaps also subconsciously, might not have been very happy about Fénelon's success. An inquiry was instituted among the students, and it was found that they were all more or less Quietist in outlook. When the king was informed he expressed a desire to read some of Mme Guyon's writings and those of her great friend, with the result that he found all this spirituality too fanciful for his taste. A group of theologians was secretly consulted, and all, except Tronson and Bourdaloue, had some very definite comments to make. Father Joly, Superior of the Lazarists, even went so far as to use the word heresy. Mme de Maintenon decided to submit the matter to an adjudicator, and she chose Bossuet.

This choice, which Fénelon accepted with great marks of respect, was sufficient in itself to cause the Saint-Cyr incident to miscarry. Though Bossuet was an excellent theologian and very well acquainted with patristic studies, he was not really familiar with the mystical writers of the previous two centuries, even St Teresa and St Francis de Sales; he was therefore instinctively suspicious. Thus his approach to mysticism was through the writings of an unbalanced woman concerning whom the most unpleasant rumours were current; and he was expected to express an opinion. All this was sufficient to cause him to confuse to some extent true mysticism with the false, Fénelonism with Guyonism, Quietism and moral decadence. As he read the works of Mme Guyon, and especially her autobiography, and after several interviews with her—or rather cross-examinations to which he subjected her at the Visitation convent in Meaux, where the visionary had agreed to settle—he became more and more convinced that he had to deal with a madwoman. This may have been a rather drastic conclusion, but he was not entirely wrong. In any case he looked upon her as a very dangerous woman.

Thinking herself lost Mme Guyon asked for two other judges in addition to the terrible bishop to be appointed to consider the matter. This request was granted her, and the commission of three members met at Issy in a country house belonging to the seminary of Saint-Sulpice. The members were Bossuet, M. Tronson and Noailles, who was at that time Bishop of Châlons. The inquiry lasted eight months, much to the disgust of Mme de Maintenon, who hoped for a speedy settlement. Mme Guyon defended herself with the help of enormous volumes, and endeavoured to prove that she was vindicated by the Fathers of the Church and the spiritual writers. Fénelon discreetly lent her his support. The attitude of the three judges was not altogether similar. Bossuet arrived at Issy in a carriage loaded with books, determined to prove that he was right beyond the shadow of a doubt. Tronson was more subtle; he feared that an out-and-out condemnation might harm the cause of genuine mysticism. Noailles kept in mind the court of Versailles. And the Archbishop of Paris, Harlay de Champvallon, aware of the general opinion, once more condemned poor Father Lacombe and Mme Guyon's *Moyen Court* in order to steal a march on the commission. A draft judgment was eventually prepared. It condemned a number of 'articles' extracted from the works of Mme Guyon without mentioning the author's name. Mme Guyon still had many friends, and there was no desire to discredit publicly one who had been so prominent at Saint-Cyr; besides, the noble Fénelon had powerful connections.

During the course of the discussions at Issy, Fénelon's personal position in the matter had not been questioned; he remained in the background, but stated openly that he was ready to agree in advance with the decisions of the three judges. In February 1695 he was appointed Archbishop of Cambrai, which Saint-Simon contemptuously described as 'a country diocese'. However, it brought in an income of 200,000 *livres*. This may have been a reward for Fénelon's attitude at the inquiry, or a means of removing him from the court at Versailles; it might even have been the outcome of skilful manœuvres on the part of his friends the duchesses. He immediately took advantage of his new appointment to make himself a member of the committee of judges and to add a number of clauses which toned down the verdict. Mme Guyon agreed to retract publicly and it seemed that everything would be settled satisfactorily. Bossuet consecrated the new archbishop in the chapel at Saint-Cyr, in the presence of Mme de Maintenon and the Duc de Bourgogne. The problem of Quietism appeared to have been solved; but it had only just begun.

16. BOSSUET VERSUS FÉNELON

Why was the controversy resumed? Why should these two great men who had so far not opposed each other openly engage in a duel from which neither would emerge with enhanced reputation? No one knows precisely, but the causes were certainly complex. Bremond held the rather romantic view that the Jansenists planned to discredit the Church which had condemned them; but that is pure hypothesis. It seems more likely that the motives were psychological.[1] It is quite possible that Fénelon, whose submission was sincere when he assured Bossuet that henceforward he would hold no opinion that differed from his, changed his mind in one of those spasms of conscience that were habitual with him. In certain respects he was unstable. He admitted: 'I could not say anything that might strike me as false a moment afterwards.' His friends may have reproached him with having given in and betrayed the cause of Pure Love and true mysticism. Perhaps also those who had staked everything on him, and dreamed of attaining high office through the 'Michelin' scheme, were thinking along the same lines. Mme Guyon stood as a living sign of contradiction. Bossuet kept her within arm's reach in the convent of the Visitation at Meaux, in the hope of bringing about a more complete conversion. Unable to bear it any longer she escaped and fled to Paris, where she was arrested by the police and imprisoned in Vincennes. The extremely tactless manner in which she was interrogated concerning her relationship with Fénelon ended quite rightly by ruffling the Archbishop of Cambrai. His dismissal from Saint-Cyr and his replacement by Bossuet really hurt the sensitive archbishop. Even Mlle de la Maisonfort turned anti-Quietist. Bossuet probably suspected his one-time protégé of playing a double game, but his reaction to Fénelon's courageous loyalty towards his harassed friend may have been too harsh. Did Bossuet view with displeasure the fact that Fénelon had

[1] To some extent they may also have been political, as R. Schmittlein has indicated in his book, *L'aspect politique du différend Bossuet-Fénelon* (Baden-Baden, 1954). It was in the field of Quietism that Bossuet's support of the king's authority and Fénelon's attitude of reserve in regard to absolutism clashed.

become his equal, even his superior, in ecclesiastical dignity? Certain rather tactless words used by the Bishop of Meaux in a pastoral letter weighed heavily upon the heart of the Archbishop of Cambrai.

These two men were really so different in disposition that their antagonism appeared almost natural. One cause of the trouble was the difference in their ages. Bossuet was nearly seventy, and the ardent forty-year-old Fénelon was in the prime of life. Then there was the clash of temperaments between the proud peer from the south, so easily offended, quick and unsophisticated into the bargain, and the son of middle-class Burgundian parents, with his feet firmly on the ground, little inclined to dreams, more sound than subtle. But the greatest difference between them lay in their spiritual outlook. And we have seen how closely this was in keeping with the particular genius of each. Finally the conflict between these two extraordinary men was based on their doctrinal concepts, each being convinced that he was upholding the rights of God and the Holy Spirit: the one defending the integrity of dogma and morality against dangerous innovation, and the other striving for the liberty of the interior life against religious conformism and its deadening effects. This controversy between two geniuses concerning problems of such magnitude was indeed a great controversy, even though human frailty led both antagonists to make use of weapons that did them little credit.

In July 1696 Bossuet wrote a second *Instruction pastorale sur les états d'oraison*,[1] and when it was finished he sent the manuscript to Fénelon seeking his approval. Undoubtedly his intention in doing so was to establish the fact that they were in perfect agreement on the clauses set out during the inquiry at Issy. But Fénelon was suspicious, and scented a trap. When he opened the manuscript he noticed that quotations from Mme Guyon's *Moyen Court* had been made in the work without any attempt to be lenient. He put away the work indignantly. Was he expected to be so dishonourable as to overwhelm his defeated friend? Was he being asked to repudiate what he held most dear? At the end of three weeks he returned the work without having read it, still less approving it. Then, taking pen and paper, he wrote at top speed his *Explications des Maximes des Saints sur la vie intérieure*, in which he explained his doctrine on religious experience, and in addition showed how easy it was to turn true mystics into heretics by distorting their ideas. When reading these two books today we do not see as much opposition in the views expressed as did their authors. There is great beauty in both books, especially in Bossuet's; and if Fénelon had only studied it a little more calmly he might have found

---

[1] Bremond remarked shrewdly, and perhaps with a touch of irony, that the best pages Bossuet ever wrote were precisely those in which, without knowing it, he upheld the theories of pure love (*Bossuet, maître d'oraison*).

grounds for agreement. But at the back of their minds they already felt bitter towards each other. As soon as Fénelon finished his book he sent the manuscript to his friends. The Duc de Chevreuse took it to the publisher at once without apparently obtaining Fénelon's clear approval. Everything moved so quickly that the *Maximes des Saints* was published (in 1697) a month before Bossuet's *États d'Oraison*. Bossuet's pride as an author was wounded and, not without good reason, he regarded Fénelon's behaviour as discourteous.

This brought about the final rupture. Bossuet was furious against the 'perfect hypocrite', as he described Fénelon, and threw himself at the king's feet to beg his pardon 'for not having revealed earlier the heresy of Monsieur de Cambrai'. He knew what he was doing. A strong anti-Fénelon group existed at the court of Versailles: those who were jealous of his success, those who envied his appointment as tutor to the king's grandson, those who hated the Jesuits—well disposed towards Fénelon but opposed to Quietism. There was Noailles, the new Archbishop of Paris, and Mme de Maintenon, who could not forget the trouble at Saint-Cyr. As for the king, his feelings towards Fénelon were uncertain. He admired him, but regarded him as 'a chimerical person', which, coming from the king, was a severe censure. Perhaps he was also aware of Fénelon's criticisms, albeit discreet, of his morals, his policy and his costly wars. All that was quite sufficient to destroy the 'Swan of Cambrai'.

The *Maximes des Saints* was violently attacked as soon as it was published, and frequently by people who had never read the work and who were indeed utterly incapable of understanding it. The most unkind rumours were current in the court and throughout the capital. It was claimed that the book was nothing more than an attempt by the archbishop to plead the case of Mme Guyon; what sort of a relationship must therefore exist between them? Generally speaking, the theologians who read the work were extremely hostile; even the prudent M. Tronson dealt cautiously with it. When the stern Abbé de Rancé, the reformer of La Trappe, was consulted, he replied that, 'If M. de Cambrai was right the Gospels should be burned; and one might complain that Christ had come into the world only to deceive us.' Fénelon was kept aware of all this fuss, the ill-natured gossip and the pamphlets,[1] and he knew that his enemies deliberately confused his ideas not only with Guyonism but even with Molinosism, of which he disapproved. But he committed one tactical error. He refused to participate in any discussion of his book if Bossuet were to be present;

---

[1] The echo of this campaign against Fénelon is reflected even in La Bruyère's *Dialogues*; in the seventh dialogue, for instance—the account of the 'Spiritual Nuptials'—where a young penitent is shocked, and exclaims, 'Fancy talking like that, Father, before a girl of my age!' Fléchier also refuted Quietism in verse.

and he added that he would not retract, in any case, as his conscience told him that he was right. The outcome was open war.

One would prefer to pass over the various episodes of the quarrel, not only for the sake of the honour of the Church, but on account of our admiration for these two great men. They hurled numerous pamphlets at each other, which were a mixture of theology and polemics, and their methods were sometimes unsavoury. As far as ideas went it was, said Cardinal Grente, 'a magnificent contest' lasting two years, the indignant Bossuet 'riding full tilt' against his adversary, and Fénelon 'parrying swiftly and brilliantly, remaining ever courteous, and assuming, with devastating elegance, an air of injured innocence'. [1] But their conduct towards each was shabby. Their intrigues involved the palace and the police; there were thefts of correspondence, abuse and slander, both in private and public. Everything was done to render the business 'unfortunate and lamentable', as Innocent XII described it.

Indeed the Pope was drawn into the controversy despite himself. Fénelon refused to submit to the judgment of his peers: he appealed to the Pope, saying that he recognized but one judge, the Vicar of Christ. It was a bold stroke, and as far as Rome was concerned a clever move which pleased everyone. But the appeal was a blunder in so far as it affected his relations with the king, who regarded his action as a betrayal of the rights of the Gallican Church. And all this was taking place fifteen years after the business of the 'Four Articles!' The Great King's reaction was swift, and rendered all the more forceful by the fact that extracts from Fénelon's *Télémaque* had been circulated in secret, together with a number of political comments which were later to constitute the *Tables de Chaulnes*. Louis XIV did not relish being told how to rule. The king gave an order that Fénelon should leave the court, return to Cambrai and remain there. The Duc de Bourgogne pleaded for his former tutor, but to no avail. Fénelon left Versailles 'under a deluge of affronts'. He was refused permission to be present at the marriage between his pupil and Marie-Adélaide of Savoy, and even to visit his niece who was very ill. His brother, his family and his friends were all swallowed up in his disgrace, which endured for the rest of his life; for the premature death of his pupil in 1711 removed all hope of reinstatement. Even after Fénelon's death the canons of his chapter dared not pronounce a funeral oration, and his successor in the French Academy hurried through the traditional panegyric, in which the *Télémaque* was not even mentioned. [2]

Disgraced and defeated, exposed to innumerable attacks, Fénelon put on a bold front. With a sad touch of humour he warned those of

---

[1] See the article entitled 'Fénelon', in the *Dictionnaire des Lettres, XVIIᵉ siècle*.
[2] This suggests that politics were not entirely excluded from the French Academy.

his friends who still had the courage to remain faithful to him: 'Be careful; I have the plague'. He fenced so dexterously, however, that Bossuet was nettled on many occaions. Pamphlets followed each other week after week, and their tone became more and more bitter. The dispute reached a climax with the publication in June 1698 of Bossuet's *Relation sur le Quiétisme*, a veritable lampoon equal in literary quality to the *Provinciales*; the bishop of Meaux adopted the same methods as Pascal, transferring the controversy from the field of ideas to the field of facts, accusing his opponent of dishonourable intentions and buttressing the weakness of some of his arguments by the violence of his abuse. It was a masterpiece of style and insincerity. Worse still, by making use of the original documents concerning the relations between Fénelon and Mme Guyon he went so far as to make all kinds of scurrilous insinuations, comparing them both with Montanus and Priscilla—an imputation which, however, he was later to regret. Fénelon was able to profit from the very violence of the attack, and with such subtlety that his rival exclaimed: 'That man *is* clever! The power of his intellect is frightening.' One retort especially struck home. Without exactly accusing Bossuet in precise terms, Fénelon hinted that his former master and friend had used a written confession he had made to him in confidence and out of the fullness of his heart before the Issy discussions took place. There is no doubt that, strictly speaking, this was not a sacramental confession, but it constituted a glaring indiscretion on Bossuet's part, and did him no credit.

The affray continued just as briskly in Rome, and the methods adopted were no less shameful. Both camps had their supporters and agents. On Fénelon's side stood the ambassador, Cardinal de Bouillon, nephew of the great Turenne, who detested the Noailles family; the Jesuits, who wrongly suspected the Bishop of Meaux of Jansenism. He also had the support of several cardinals who feared that his condemnation might be regarded as an attack on true mysticism. Furthermore, Fénelon's appeal had pleased the Pope and the Roman Curia, who were well acquainted with the virtuous life of the Archbishop of Cambrai. His own agent was the Abbé de Chanterac, a highly respected priest. Bossuet sent his nephew, the Abbé Bossuet, to the Eternal City. He was a dubious character, but wily and an excellent theologian. He had the backing of all who had fought Molinos, and his personal prestige was considerable. Two rather contemptible incidents give some idea of the extent to which the power of influence was utilized in the controversy. The 'Bossuetists' communicated to the Holy Office the record of the cross-examination during which the unhappy Father Lacombe, who was half mad, had confessed to a guilty relationship with Mme Guyon. The 'Cambraisians' for their part cast a slur on the Bishop of Meaux by saying that he was merely influenced by jealousy; they circulated the distressing story of the love affairs of his nephew the Abbé Bossuet, whom the flunkeys of Duke Cesarini had soundly thrashed for having tried to seduce their master's daughter. Zeal for the Pure Love of God was lost sight of in all these squabbles.

Considering all this mud-slinging one feels almost grateful to the King of France for having intervened to ask the Pope to put an end to the quarrel as soon as possible. If Innocent XII had resembled Julius II or Paul IV, or even Innocent XI, the king's interference might have induced him to act energetically, and he might have confined in the Castel Sant' Angelo the insolent Abbé Bossuet who, like a true Gallican, told the Pope what to do, and suggested that he should word his Bull to the satisfaction of the French bishops! In fact the Pope gave in and agreed to sign a condemnation, but he did so in subdued terms to the effect that Fénelon's book was prone to 'lead the faithful imperceptibly into errors already condemned by the Church . . .' and that it contained propositions which were 'rash, offensive to the ear and discreditable'. The condemnation made no mention whatsoever of heresy.

It did, however, mean repudiation and defeat for Fénelon, but he accepted it with dignity. On 25th March 1699 he received the news of his condemnation just as he was entering the pulpit. Putting aside the subject of the sermon he had prepared, he improvised a sublime discourse on obedience to the authority of the Holy See and the virtues of submission. Two weeks later he published the papal brief declaring his adherence to it 'simply, absolutely and without the shadow of reservation'. Perhaps he experienced a sort of bitter joy at feeling himself 'held in low esteem and an object of pity', and remaining, as Chanterac told him, 'steady and calm at the foot of his Cross'. For all that his attitude was worthy of admiration, and gave him a strange grandeur. The fact that in one of those sudden spasms of moodiness which were common with him he subsequently wrote to some of his friends that he had been condemned for expounding theories which he had never held, or that he may sometimes have given the impression that he adopted the attitude of 'respectful silence' with which he had so often reproached the Jansenists, made little difference to the general dignity of his behaviour. Neither should we attach importance to the fact that he rejected a vague gesture of reconciliation by Bossuet—a rejection which the embittered bishop countered with a desperate attempt to secure yet another formal condemnation. Fénelon's submission brought the affair to a close. Mme Guyon ended her days in 1717 in exile at Blois, at the home of one of her daughters. Her spiritual son's letters had become fewer and fewer. Quietism was dead.

But what were the consequences of the crisis? Considered objectively the literature that was born of the crisis might have fostered a greater knowledge of the spiritual life; it might have led to a fuller and more grandiose definition of the role of the mystic impulse, of reason and of the soul's activity. But there existed an atmosphere of emotion that impeded such a favourable outcome. To compensate for this, however, some of the effects of the crisis were beneficial though less ostentatious. By justly condemning the Quietism of Molinos, Father Lacombe and Mme Guyon, as well as the semi-Quietism of Fénelon, Rome undoubtedly warded off grave perils—the perils of an easy-going morality. But at the same time did it not have a detrimental effect on true mysticism, as Innocent XII feared it might do? And was this not so in France especially, where a certain rationalist tendency had begun to develop which sought out motives for distrusting every inner impulse and denouncing those 'possessed of God'? This tendency was one of the factors that gave rise to a narrowing-down of the Catholic mind. On the other hand, by insisting on the play of sentiment and interior experience did not the followers of Fénelon open the flood-gates to that tide of romantic egoism which in the next century found expression in the works of Jean-Jacques Rousseau? Again, the ruthless controversy between the two heads of the French Church gave encouragement to free-thinkers: the cruel language used by the Bishop of Meaux against the Archbishop of Cambrai made them shake with laughter! At that time a song was being sung in the streets of Paris, for everything that happens in France is eventually turned into song:

> Dans ces combats où deux prélats de France
> Semblent chercher la vérité,
> L'un dit qu'on détruit l'espérance,
> L'autre soutient que c'est la charité:
> C'est la foi qu'on détruit et personne n'y pense.[1]

Such is the wisdom of the people.

Was it really wise to provide malignant tongues with an opportunity to turn Pure Love into an object of jest?

Another outcome of the Quietist controversy, but on a different plane, was soon apparent: once again the Jansenist threat became grave, and at the very moment when Rome had settled the bishop's quarrel. Bossuet was perhaps so carried away by his zeal to fight false mysticism that he remained blind to the imminent revival of Jansenism. He may have regarded the *Réflexions morales* of Father Quesnel as a sort of antidote to the errors of Fénelonism. His distrust of Pure Love seems to have provoked him into defending theses which, by crushing love under the weight of fear, resulted in keeping the faithful away

---

[1] 'In the conflict in which two French bishops appear to be seeking the truth, one says that hope is being destroyed, while the other maintains that it is charity. No one seems to know that faith itself is being destroyed.'

from the sacraments, and prepared the way for irreligion. As often happens in violent controversies, it is Christ's truth, and especially Christ's charity, which emerges battered. Strictly speaking, only the Pope was victorious. The controversy was brought to an end through the appeal made to his authority; by the same token it was he who emerged triumphant from the great Jansenist contest. But from a spiritual point of view was not the whole Church the loser?

17. RESUMPTION OF THE JANSENIST CONTROVERSY: RACINE

Scarcely ten years after the pious Clement IX thought he had put an end to the Jansenist heresy it appeared to be on the point of revival. Indeed the Jansenists displayed an utter lack of prudence. The popularity of Port-Royal, the fuss that was made over the convent and Antoine Arnauld were bound to arouse the king's suspicions: Louis XIV did not like anything to become fashionable which might deprive him of the limelight. The most zealous champions of the sect went about declaring that they had never been condemned or conquered, and that they had therefore never submitted. The Jansenist bishops, led by Henri Arnauld, Bishop of Angers, continued to rebel against the *Formulaire*, so that once again, in 1676, the king had to publish a decree to bring them to heel. At that time a new factor was introduced which greatly aggravated the situation.

In 1673 the Gallican crisis [1] had just blown up as a result of the *régale* affair. The conciliatory attitude of Clement X failed to check it. When the energetic Innocent XI followed him to the Chair of St Peter in 1676, it became evident that the struggle was about to take a decisive turn. Who would triumph, the Pope or the Most Christian King? To aggravate the situation further the two bishops—Pavillon, of Alet, and Caulet, of Pamiers—who had protested against the government's claim to extend the right of *régale* to the whole country, were well-known Jansenists. Collusion between the friends of Port-Royal and the king's enemies appeared obvious. As a matter of fact, the Roman Curia had been extremely lenient towards Arnauld's supporters, and everyone was convinced that the Pope had promised Arnauld the cardinal's hat and had asked him to formulate a broad scheme of Church reform. In Jesuit circles Innocent XI was being discreetly referred to as 'the Jansenist Pope'. And did not the Probabilism affair seem to confirm these suspicions?

Arnauld and his friends had not forgiven the Jesuits, and they sought to get their own back. Pascal had shown them the Society's weak spot.

[1] See Chapter IV, p. 215 et seq.

That indefatigable polemist had gleaned inspiration from various casuistic treatises, even among Jesuit writings, and found no less than sixty-five propositions which he regarded as responsible for moral laxity. Many of them proceeded from a 'Probabilist' doctrine, a weak variety of laxism. It allowed that everything not formally rejected by the Church, or condemned by one of the Commandments, might be regarded as probable.[1] The sixty-five propositions were condemned by the Pope in 1679, and the Assembly of the Clergy at Bossuet's instigation reiterated the condemnation. The Society of Jesus was not mentioned by name, but it was the object of the attack. Innocent XI made a formal request that Father Tirso Gonzalez, a well-known anti-laxist, be appointed the Society's General. Thus public opinion came to regard the Jansenists as the real defenders of Christian morals which had been jeopardized by the detestable defects of laxism. Consequently Jansenism immediately began to forge ahead in various provinces of religious life, in Italy and Holland as well as in France. It was a practical form of Jansenism, having very little in common with Jansenius and the problems of grace, but very much concerned with moral austerity. Innocent XI had certainly not intended that; he desired simply to preserve doctrinal integrity against the laxists, as he intended later against Molinos and the Quietists. But his action ended by making Louis XIV apprehensive, for the king regarded it as an admission of an alliance between Rome and Port-Royal.

The atmosphere became oppressive. In the spring of 1679 the Duchesse de Longueville died—a loyal friend of Port-Royal and one of the very few people whom Louis XIV permitted to speak frankly to him. For the last ten years of her life she had spent six months in every year at Port-Royal-des-Champs. The good-natured Péréfixe had been succeeded in the episcopal See of Paris by Harlay de Champvallon, to whose part in the Quietist affair we have already referred. His private life was not very edifying, and he aimed at high office, an ambition he was not to fulfil. He distrusted the Society of Jesus, which had the king's ear through Father La Chaise, the king's confessor. At the same time, in lending its support to the revelations which Margaret Mary Alacoque had had four years earlier and to the new devotion to the Sacred Heart, the Society was promoting a form of piety radically opposed to the harsh Jansenist observance. The whole business made Bossuet uneasy.

It was Archbishop Harlay de Champvallon who, having learned how to please the king, initiated new coercive measures. On 17th May

---

[1] Probabilism went a long way towards moral laxity. For instance, it argued that 'when opposite parties in a lawsuit are supported by opinions that are equally probable, the judge may quite rightly accept money to persuade him to give a verdict in favour of one party rather than the other'.

1679 he visited Port-Royal; he was polite and all smiles, but implacable. He ordered all the postulants, the young boarders and the priests to leave forthwith. The convent was forbidden to accept novices, and the number of nuns was not to exceed fifty. Port-Royal was condemned to death by extinction.

At the same time Antoine Arnauld was asked to drop the spiritual reunions that he held in the suburb of Saint-Jacques. Imagining himself threatened he fled to Flanders and then to Holland, and the gentle Nicole was persuaded to do likewise. Not that the great fighter had laid down his arms: he refused to return to France despite the fact that his safety was assured (though Nicole did take advantage of the offer), and continued to produce polemic writings to the end—more and more of his 'machine-gun theology'. He remained firmer than ever in his conviction that his trials were his guarantee of right, and that he was one of God's elect.

Before leaving France for ever the Great Arnauld had one consolation: Jean Racine, the most brilliant of the students issuing from the Little Schools, returned to the fold. Arnauld and his friends had considered him for ever lost to heaven, a slave to the world and the disastrous passions which his plays portrayed. After his marriage and the comparative failure of *Phèdre* (1677) Racine began to reflect. The Abbé Jacques Boileau, brother of the 'lawgiver of Parnassus', reconciled him with Nicole and subsequently, though not without difficulty, with Arnauld himself. In a famous speech before the whole Areopagus of the Jansenist *élite* the dramatist demonstrated that his play *Phèdre* was not immoral, and at the end the great Antoine took him in his arms. From that moment Port-Royal had no better friend than Racine. When he described the persecution of the Jews by Haman, in his play *Esther*, was he not depicting the persecution of Jansenism? In any case Mordechai made a good portrait of Arnauld, and Esther's maidens bore an extraordinary resemblance to the nuns of the valley of the Chevreuse. He went further: courageously taking the part of the persecuted, he took upon himself the task of writing a history of Port-Royal; and in his will he asked to be buried among the 'Solitaries' in the cemetery of Port-Royal-des-Champs, at the feet of M. Hamon.

18. THE AGONY OF PORT-ROYAL

In 1698 Jean Racine died. Arnauld had died four years earlier, but just as he had taken the torch from the hands of Saint-Cyran, he left behind him another to take it up: Pasquier Quesnel (1634–1719), an Oratorian. It will be remembered that when Jansenius and his friend developed their first plans they dreamed of making the spiritual sons of Bérulle the shock troops of their great offensive. But that did not happen; the Oratory never became Jansenist *en bloc*, though its members regarded the Port-Royalist movement with less animosity than hitherto. Some manifested an attitude of benevolent neutrality because they recognized the undeniable qualities of Port-Royal, and feared that a sweeping condemnation of its principles of austerity might simply foster a tendency towards a soft spirituality. Pasquier Quesnel was among those who held this view. While Director of the Paris Oratory he did not intervene in the Jansenist quarrels. He was a pious priest who was certainly not on a par intellectually with Arnauld and Saint-Cyran, as suggested by his dull look and ovine cast of features; but morally he was among the most upright. In 1671 he published a small book entitled *Réflexions morales sur le Nouveau Testament* which competent judges deemed to be an excellent spiritual treatise, severe in tone but containing nothing suspect. To the moderns it has a Pascalian flavour, and many of the ideas expressed read very much like Pascal's *Pensées*.

Father Quesnel became the victim of a circumstance fairly frequent in his day but which we of this age find surprising: some of his personal notes were published without his permission, and they proved to be very much more Jansenist in tone than his former work. It was useless for him to disclaim publication; he was still held to some extent responsible. When, therefore, his friend Father Abel de Sainte-Marthe, General of the Oratory, was forced to resign his office in 1681 on account of his friendship with Arnauld, Father Quesnel was involved in his downfall. Various incidents aggravated the dispute between him and his congregation; he left and settled in Brussels near the Jansenist leader.

In the meantime the *Réflexions morales* met with success, and went into several editions. In the manner of La Bruyère, Quesnel went on adding to his work with each new edition; so much so that it eventually appeared to be a book altogether different from the original edition, and infinitely more Jansenist in tone. Moreover, a number of very pious people had approved the first edition, notably Félix Vialart de Herse, Bishop of Châlons-sur-Marne, who had even recommended it to his clergy. Both Father La Chaise and the Bishop of Meaux had praised it, and it was known that the Pope himself had read it. But did the succeeding editions warrant such commendation? And were the episcopal prefaces which Father Quesnel retained at the head of succeeding editions still valid? The alert opponents of Jansenism could not risk letting such trickery pass unheeded. They began a campaign against Quesnel, who was accused of being Arnauld's lieutenant, and in 1694 the *Réflexions morales* was denounced to the Sorbonne and the Holy Office simultaneously.

It was about this time that Louis-Antoine de Noailles, bishop and later cardinal, appeared on the scene of this unending drama of Jansenism. One hesitates to judge this pious and kindly prelate too harshly; his morals were perfect, his life austere and his intentions absolutely beyond reproach; none the less the part he played was an unfortunate one. It is sufficient to study his portrait painted by Largillière to recognize that this man, with his expressionless face, ungainly red nose and kindly smile, had nothing of that quality of shrewdness and authority required for the position he held. He succeeded Vialart de Herse to the See of Châlons and, as we have seen, played a prominent though ambiguous role in the Quietist affair, acting as judge with Tronson and Bossuet of Mme Guyon's writings. When Harlay de Champvallon died in 1695 several preachers refused to pronounce his funeral oration—'prevented equally', as one of them said, 'by the manner of his life and his death'. Mme de Maintenon then had Noailles nominated to the See of Paris that he might break with the past, but also because Noailles was a friend of Bossuet's and his selection would definitely bar the way to Fénelon, whom she pursued with her resentment. 'He was a man of limited understanding and a confused mind, and he was weak and soft-hearted. He said white to one and black to another. It was useless to seek his opinion, for he had none.' Such was the description of him given by the 'Swan of Cambrai'; it was hardly flattering, but not untrue.

One of the first things Noailles did was to devote a pastoral letter to Father Quesnel's book, redoubling the praises bestowed upon it by his predecessor. 'This book is as good as a whole library,' he told his priests. The Jansenists hailed the appointment of Noailles to the See of Paris as a great victory, whereas their opponents suspected him at once. An incident that occurred shortly afterwards amused the gallery. The Jansenists had republished an old book propounding their ideas; it was entitled *Exposition de la foi touchant la Grace*, by Barcos, a nephew of Saint-Cyran. The Jesuits asked the archbishop to censure it, and this embarrassed Noailles. To approve Quesnel and condemn Barcos appeared to involve a contradiction, even to 'a man of limited understanding'. He called on Bossuet to help him, and the bishop got him out of the difficulty by drafting for him a statement repudiating Barcos but extolling St Augustine! Shortly afterwards a small leaflet appeared under the title *Problème ecclésiastique*, and it caused much amusement. Its anonymous authors (two Benedictines of Saint-Maur) pretended to ask innocently if the Noailles who had disapproved of Barcos was the same bishop who had so warmly recommended the *Réflexions morales*.

Bossuet then attempted to put things right. It occurred to him to prepare a new edition of Father Quesnel's book, after pruning it of everything that might be deemed suspect. He did even better: he wrote a *Justification des Réflexions morales*, expressed in the warmest terms. 'We oppose the *Réflexions*', he wrote, 'purely in a spirit of contention'; but, went on Bossuet, 'we cannot find anything in it but good advice and instruction'. He went so far as to add: 'Is it not manifest calumny to upbraid the author of the *Réflexions* for having spoken as so many saints have done? If his language is suspect . . . we shall have to be continually on our guard against the words of the Gospel, lest some quibbler comes along and accuses us of being Jansenists.' On this last point at least Bossuet was quite right; a frenzied anti-Jansenist attitude could do a great deal of harm. But there is no doubt at all that in his desire to plead a cause the great bishop did more or less delude himself in the matter of the *Réflexions*, and failed to discern the other danger—the imminent revival of Jansenism. He did not publish his treatise,[1] but informed Quesnel of its contents. At that time Quesnel was living in Belgian Flanders and, considering himself safe from attack, absolutely refused to make the corrections suggested by Bossuet. He published yet another edition of his book emphasizing his attitude.

Fénelon was the one man who did not permit himself to be misled by Quesnel's ideas. The Quietist conflict during which he had been made to bite the dust had just come to an end. Fénelon has very often been accused of wishing to get his own back on Bossuet and Noailles, whose embroilment in the new controversy was causing them embarrassment. We cannot entirely discountenance the theory, for Fénelon was a man of complex character, and he might well have entertained the notion side by side with the more praiseworthy desire to re-establish his good name with the Pope and the king. But undoubtedly his conscience and a sense of duty impelled him to resist Jansenism. His diocese of Cambrai swarmed with Jansenists. Their gloomy doctrine could only horrify him, for he had never ceased to proclaim that 'we must not approach God with the respectful fear of a slave, but with the surrender and trusting tenderness of a son'. He conducted a considerable correspondence from his retirement in Cambrai, and his letters warned his friends of the dangers of Jansenism and the increasing harm the heresy was doing to souls. As a result of his efforts Godet des Marais, Bishop of Chartres, who was among those who first attacked Quietism, also became concerned. At the Assembly of the Clergy in 1700 it was the influence of Fénelon and Godet des Marais which predominated, not that of Bossuet and Noailles. On that occasion the Assembly condemned a posthumous work by Arnauld in which the old fighter had endeavoured to prove

---

[1] It did not appear until 1710, six years after Bossuet's death; it preceded a new edition, more Jansenist than ever, of the *Réflexions morales*. In consequence Quesnel was accused of yet another breach of faith.

that Jansenism was a mere phantom invented by his opponents. He claimed that laxism, to which the observance of Port-Royal was the antidote, was indeed the real heresy.

These battles between theologians and bishops did not lend a great deal of excitement to the discussion, yet it suddenly became violent. The Jansenist leaders, aware of the temperament of Noailles, endeavoured to persuade him to take a definite stand on their behalf. They presented him and his mentor the Bishop of Meaux with a particular 'case of conscience'. Father Gay, superior of the seminary at Clermont-Ferrand, refused absolution to a Father Fréhel, parish priest of Notre-Dame du Port, because he himself had given absolution to the Abbé Périer, Pascal's nephew, a hardened Jansenist who had always adhered to the principle of 'respectful silence' on the question of 'law and fact'. Had Father Gay the right to refuse absolution? Forty doctors of the Sorbonne declared that he had. A pamphlet dealing with the case was being read all over France, and Bossuet was furious at being unable to hush up this new quarrel. He sent a strongly worded protest to Noailles. Clement XI condemned both the pamphlet and the forty doctors of the Sorbonne. In four pastoral letters Fénelon returned to the condemnation of all 'so-called Augustinians'. Bossuet himself, unhappy at the way matters were going, made known to the king the danger 'evident in innumerable writings emanating from the Low Countries'. A kind of Holy League was developing against the 'phantom' of Jansenism, which still seemed very much alive.

Louis XIV had become weary of all this commotion. The older he grew the more he detested non-conformists; especially the Jansenists. He said that he regarded them as republicans and, according to Saint-Simon, he deemed them to be just as heretical as the Protestants.[1] He asked for details of recent incidents, and decided that the person really responsible for the whole trouble was Father Quesnel. It was quite an easy matter for him to obtain from his grandson, Philippe V, the new King of Spain, a promise to have the former Oratorian arrested in Brussels. The Spanish police were so accommodating that they sent to Versailles all the documents they had seized. The 'Quesnel Papers' were decoded, broken down, commented upon, and read to the king by his confessor every evening over a period of ten years in the presence of Mme de Maintenon. Since the introduction of *Pilmot* the Jansenists had always retained a mania for assumed names and disguised expressions. Consequently there was no doubt whatever in

---

[1] His hatred of the sect reached such a pitch that it bordered on the ridiculous. An army general whom the king took to task for having appointed to his general staff a Jansenist notary, replied that the officer in question was a complete atheist. 'Is that so?' replied the king. 'Can you vouch for it? If it is true there is no harm done, and you can keep him.' The Duc d'Orléans almost died with laughter when relating this story to Saint-Simon!

the old king's mind that Jansenism was anything but a phantom; it was an intrigue and a public danger.

He then asked Clement XI to publish another Bull condemning the sect and especially the 'Case of Conscience'. Clement XI agreed, but not without some hesitation, for he suspected a flavour of Gallicanism. The Bull *Vineam Domini* was published in 1703, registered by the Paris Parlement and approved by the Assembly of the Clergy—which alone made the Gallicans regard it as valid; it was even accepted by Cardinal de Noailles in an involved pastoral letter. Fénelon was unpretentious in his triumph. Briefly the Bull declared that it was not sufficient to sign the *Formulaire* without believing that Jansenism was a heresy— 'as though it were permissible to deceive the Church by an oath, and to say what she says without thinking what she thinks'. Henceforward there was no possible means of evasion, no way of playing with the idea of 'law and fact'; there was no longer even any chance of hiding behind 'Gallican freedoms' since the king had no desire to quarrel with Rome.

It was easy for their opponents to drive the Jansenists to the wall: at least those who were unskilled at the game of mental reservations, implications and misrepresentations. Among these were the nuns of Port-Royal-des-Champs. The valley very quickly ceased to be fashionable. The nuns had grown old; they were less numerous than formerly for they no longer took novices. They remained firm, however, in their austere piety, very much attached to their memories of a great past, and on the whole very much out of touch with recent squabbles. Who was the enemy of Noailles who thought of using them to strike at the archbishop? The nuns of Port-Royal-des-Champs [1] were invited to sign a formal acceptance of the Bull. It was a clever stroke because everyone expected a refusal. If then the archbishop agreed to take the stern measures demanded of him he would become an object of loathing to the Jansenists; but if he refused to be co-operative he would be acknowledging that he was a Jansenist. And Bossuet was no longer alive to disentangle him! This backhanded stratagem occasioned one of the most famous and dramatic episodes in the whole ghastly business.

The nuns suspected a trap but agreed to sign, adding simply the words: 'Without prejudice to the Clementine Peace.' The Pope would have been content to accept this conditional submission; but the king's new confessor, the Jesuit Father Le Tellier, pointed out to him that these stubborn old ladies were defying his authority. Louis XIV then went a step further; he asked for a bull of suppression. For a long time no decision was reached; partly because the religious, as worthy heirs of Arnauld, appealed again and again; but also because the Pope was

[1] Port-Royal de Paris had become little more than a convent for ladies of fashion.

reluctant to be too severe. Noailles groaned; he reproached the nuns with ingratitude for refusing to listen to him and not striking out their restrictive clause. As of old Port-Royal-des-Champs became the symbol of Jansenist resistance to every form of authority. The 25th September 1709 marked exactly one hundred years since the 'Day of the Grating'—when the young Mother Angélique closed the door of her monastery against her father.

On Tuesday, 29th October, d'Argenson, the chief of police, entered the convent with the constable of the watch and his patrol. The community was made to assemble in the chapter room and d'Argenson, courteous, frigid and formidable, read out the royal decree. To carry out the provisions of the Bull the nuns, numbering twenty-two, were to be dispersed. Twenty-two carriages had been brought for that purpose. Each nun entered a carriage and, accompanied by an old woman, set off for the convent allocated to her—Autun, Rouen, Nantes, Amiens and so on, all over France. Each was also accompanied by a military escort on horseback, as though they were dangerous criminals. The convent remained empty, and left to be looted by the soldiers charged to guard it.

'Such a way of exercising authority', said the Duc de Chevreuse, 'can arouse only pity for these poor women and indignation against their persecutors.' And that was precisely what the Pope had feared. Supporters of Jansenism all over France, many of whom were people of sincere faith and truly Christian hearts, longed to make a pilgrimage to the beloved valley and its deserted convent. Disconsolate women came to weep and pray in the deserted cloisters.

These demonstrations exasperated Louis XIV, and he decided to put an end to them: he gave orders that Port-Royal was to be demolished. In January 1710, during a dreadful winter of national famine, distress and defeats on the battlefield, gangs of workmen proceeded to raze to the ground the convent, the houses and even the church; only Les Granges des Solitaires was spared. But the cemetery remained, and again pilgrims flocked to it. An order was given to destroy that also. Influential families were authorized to remove the remains of their own dead. Saint-Etienne-du-Mont, in Paris, where Pascal's body lay, received the remains of Racine, Saint-Médard those of Nicole, and Saint-Jacques-du-Haut-Pas those of Saint-Cyran. As for the others, the poor and the unknown, and all who had wished to lie near the nuns and the 'Solitaries', they were disinterred and cast into paupers' graves. Saint-Simon and later Sainte-Beuve, whose pens were perhaps more vindictive than veridical, have described the dreadful scene—the drunken grave-diggers at work in the cemetery, while the dogs fought over the remains that had not yet decayed.

It was not only a shocking decision but a ghastly blunder. To make martyrs of twenty-two stubborn, elderly nuns was anything but clever. 'For the stones thereof have pleased thy servants: and they have pity on the earth thereof.' Henceforward the Psalmist's words would be whispered in prayer by countless souls moved by so much injustice. One day when the unhappy Noailles was bewailing the straits into which Jansenism continued to plunge him, a witty woman replied: 'What can you expect, my Lord? God is just, and the stones of Port-Royal are falling on your head.'

19. The Bull 'Unigenitus'

It was an easy matter to disperse a few nuns, to raze a convent to the ground and throw bodies into a common grave; much easier than to eradicate Jansenism from people's souls. Glaring signs of its vitality existed everywhere. Jansenist convents still survived. At the convent of Gif in the Île de France, the young nuns headed by Françoise de Ségur tried to persuade the abbess to take up the standard of Port-Royal; in Toulouse the Daughters of the Holy Childhood were so openly Jansenist that they had to be suppressed. The behaviour of the Sisters of Saint Martha, recently founded by the widow of the sculptor Théodon, was more moderate; they worked as peasants, and sustained the spirit of the sect in their humble life of prayer without aspiring to any connection with the great Cistercian Order. Bishops did not conceal their Jansenist outlook, and there were innumerable sympathizers in the lower ranks of the clergy. The three parishes which had welcomed the remains of the famous men whose bodies had been disinterred remained the bastions of resistance in Paris. Jansenist schools continued to function in the capital and in several provincial towns, and eventually the link-up between Gallicanism and Jansenism became complete; for those who had regarded the king's reconciliation with Rome in 1693 [1] as a betrayal of Gallican freedoms made common cause with those overtaken by the agreement between Pope and king. They counted many supporters in legal circles and among the foremost politicians; even among high Church dignitaries who considered that the authority wielded by the Holy See was excessive and its demands exorbitant.

It was Father Quesnel who fired the powder magazine. The *Réflexions morales* were condemned by the Holy See in 1708 after fourteen years of discussion. Instead of abiding by the decision the one-time Oratorian replied with a cleverly written pamphlet entitled *Entretiens sur le décret de Rome*. The Gallicans who were members of the King's Council, Chancellor Pontchartrain, Torcy, Foreign Affairs

Secretary, and d'Aguesseau, Procurator General, opposed France's acceptance of the papal brief on the grounds that the carrying out of the sentence was, as stated in the document, entrusted to the Inquisition. Emboldened by this Quesnel republished his *Réflexions*, very much enlarged and rendered all the more discreditable by the fact that the work was prefaced by Bossuet's famous *Justification*, which had obviously not been written for this enlarged version. The 'Eagle of Meaux' had died in 1704, and could have no say in the matter!

The result was a violent outburst against the Jansenists and their supporters. Fénelon forewarned his friends, and Father Le Tellier brought the whole weight of his influence to bear. A certain student of the Archbishop of Cambrai named Chalmet persuaded Champflour, Bishop of La Rochelle, and Valderies de Lescure, Bishop of Luçon, to sign a directive that had been prepared for them, under which they associated themselves with the papal condemnation and described those who had approved the pernicious work as 'abettors of heresy'. But to make quite sure that there should be no doubt as to the identity of the person alluded to, young seminarists from Saint-Sulpice were sent to post up the pamphlet on the very walls of the archbishop's palace! At the same time Fénelon denounced Percin de Montgaillard, the elderly Bishop of Saint-Pons and a well-known Jansenist, in a pastoral letter. Rome congratulated the authors of the directive and condemned the unhappy Percin.

Cardinal de Noailles grasped the purport of this salvo perfectly well. Tired and old, less capable than ever of governing the largest diocese in France, his reaction to the attack was extraordinarily clumsy. He was, as Fénelon somewhat ironically remarked, 'exceedingly scrupulous where honour was concerned, and very particular about his reputation'. He became cross and obstinate. 'He made the great mistake', wrote Saint-Simon, 'of imitating the dog that bites the stone instead of the hand that threw it.' The first thing he did was to dismiss from Saint-Sulpice the nephews of the authors of the directive; this resulted in complaints to the king and to Rome, backed by several bishops and Mme de Maintenon. Next, recognizing that he had made a tactical error, he openly attacked the Society of Jesus, which he accused of being the instigator of the whole affair; he deprived its priests of the authority to preach within his diocese and to hear confessions, and publicly deprecated their complacent attitude towards 'the superstitions and idolatries of China'.[1] He even went so far as to write a letter to Mme de Maintenon, asking her to persuade the king to dismiss Father Le Tellier.

The reaction was swift. Father Le Tellier, Cardinal de Rohan

[1] The distressing Rites controversy was at that time being hotly debated. See *The Church in the Eighteenth Century*, Chapter II.

(who had succeeded Bossuet to the See of Meaux) and Cardinal de
Bissy, taking the advice of Fénelon, who was supported by his staunch
friends Chevreuse and Beauvilliers, suggested to the king that the Pope
be asked to pronounce a formal condemnation of Quesnel's book, on
the king's promise to compel all the bishops to abide by the decision.
It was just as bitter a defeat for the Gallicans as for the Jansenists.
Clement XI knew that he was doing them a great honour by issuing a
Bull against the *Réflexions morales*, but he was careful not to throw
away such an opportunity which the king offered him to exercise his
authority. A committee was set up to examine the work once more;
the extraordinary thing was that only one of its members was well
acquainted with French. Several months had elapsed before the Pope,
pressed by the king, promulgated, on 8th September 1713, the Bull
Unigenitus, which began: 'When the Only Begotten Son of God, who
became man . . . ' The Bull made history. The condemnation of
Quesnel's work and, in a wider sense, Jansenism itself, was categorical.
Quesnel was described as 'a ravening wolf, a false prophet, a teacher
of lies, a knave, a hypocrite and a poisoner of souls'. It contained nine
lines of similar adjectives describing the ex-Oratorian, and there were
some who thought he did not deserve either the distinction or the
humiliation. From a doctrinal point of view the Bull merely confirmed
and emphasized previous condemnations. Among the hundred and
one propositions condemned Rome did, however, slip in a few which
were not Jansenist but Gallican; and they were taken word for word
from Richer.

It now remained to fulfil the second part of the programme: to
enforce acceptance of the papal ordinance throughout every diocese
in France. Would the bishops agree? Fénelon immediately made himself the 'guardian angel' of the Bull. He wrote a memorandum on the
way in which it should be dealt with, and the Assembly of the Clergy
gave its verdict accordingly. Subsequently a hundred and seventeen
bishops accepted the Bull 'purely and simply'. About fifteen, however,
qualified their acceptance. Eight openly rejected it, declaring that they
intended to appeal to the Pope for further details. The Bull *Unigenitus*
thus divided the French clergy into two camps, those who opposed it
being backed absolutely by the whole Gallican party. Threatened with
a command under the king's seal the Parlement decided to register the
Bull, and the Sorbonne was induced to submit when it saw seven or
eight doctors shut out. Events appeared to be moving towards a
schism. Cardinal de Noailles's own brother, who succeeded him at
Châlons, wrote: 'If the Pope is in error in straying from the traditions
of his See, it is he who is parting company with the Church.'

As for Noailles, at first the blow took him by surprise and left him
dumbfounded. For a moment he spoke of accepting the Bull, and

suggested that the Pope be asked to *forbid* Quesnel's book, not to *condemn* it! Subsequently he endeavoured to draw closer to Versailles. The people of Paris called him 'Our back-sliding Eminence', and they sang:

> '*Et Noailles jusqu'au bout*
> *Sera semblable au pendule*
> *Qui vient, revient et recule . . .*' [1]

Suddenly the pendulum stood still. In a magniloquent, but not entirely lucid, pastoral letter he forbade his priests under pain of suspension to recognize the Bull because, he said, the papal decision was irregular as to procedure and offensive to French bishops. At the same time, however, he condemned Quesnel's book.

The king was furious and intervened. Would there be no end to this Jansenist hydra, these conspirators and republicans? Books containing noxious ideas, such as the widely read *Hexaples*, which claimed to demonstrate the complete orthodoxy of Quesnel's theories, continued to appear. The king's attention was drawn to the unrest among the lower ranks of the clergy. D'Aguesseau openly declared that the Bull, having been registered under pressure, certainly did not possess the force of law in France. The old king, more jealous than ever of his authority, brought the weight of his fury down upon the Cardinal Archbishop of Paris. He was denied access to the Assembly of the Clergy, forbidden to go to Rome to plead his case, and was treated 'almost like a heretic'. There was even talk of 'decardinalizing' him! Amelot, the councillor of state in Rome, lent his support to the idea, and it was suggested to the Pope that a national council be assembled to depose the archbishop. To this Clement XI replied with a touch of defiance that he did not mind if he and his Bull were 'thrown as fodder to the bears'.

Father Le Tellier then advised Louis XIV to get Parlement to register a straightforward declaration that they adhered to the Bull and that it should be signed by all the bishops. Whereupon the king summoned the president, the procurator and the advocates general; but he was unable to overcome their resistance. The rumour went around Paris that when d'Aguesseau was leaving for Versailles his wife said to him: 'Go. Forget your wife and children when in the presence of the king. Throw away everything—but not your honour.' It was considered that a *lit de justice* should be convened to compel the 'Parlementaires' to agree, but the aged king was sick and lacking in strength. Meanwhile, however, the police arrested about two thousand Jansenists and their associates, and interrogated about ten thousand more. Fénelon remained calm, relishing his revenge. Before he died he dealt some well-directed blows against the hostile sect with

[1] 'To the end Noailles will resemble a pendulum swinging to and fro.'

his *Instructions en forme de dialogues*. The crisis appeared to have reached its climax. The pope yielded, and agreed to assemble a council; but thoughtful men wondered what good he hoped to achieve. Then, on 1st September 1715, the Great King died.

20. HOPES AND DISAPPOINTMENTS OF THE JANSENIST PARTY

The reign of the little Louis XV began with the Regency. It also saw the rise of 'that eighteenth-century type of Jansenism' of which Sainte-Beuve said: 'Not all the gold in the world nor all the promises of heaven could move it.' Indeed, it was a type of Jansenism that became more and more pernicious, drifting further and further away from the ideals of the early Port-Royalists. It took the shape of a 'party' pure and simple, not in the seventeenth-century meaning of the word, but in the political sense of the present day. The famous words of Péguy— 'Everything has its origin in the mystical and ends in the political' —were never more pertinent than in the present instance.

The 'Jansenist Party' would therefore assert itself under the direction and management of high ecclesiastical Gallicans, gentlemen of the Robe and politicians hostile to Rome who, as we have seen, were supporters of the sect. As was natural, the mass of militant Jansenists hardly counted; they were honest people who could no more understand Gallican theories than they could the arguments relative to grace. However, a sort of 'Catholic Presbyterianism' was seen to develop and make its influence felt, deriving its inspiration both from Richer and Jansenius's concepts of the priesthood; and demanding that the lower ranks of the clergy be granted privileges equivalent to those exercised by the wealthy incumbents. This was the first sign of that antagonism which became so painfully evident during the Revolution. More disturbing still was the fact that certain elements, who made an absolute mockery of grace of any kind, whether 'efficacious' or 'sufficient', also joined the 'Party'. Such were the free-thinkers, sceptics, men inimical to religion. Their numbers grew, for they saw in the diverse episodes of the long Jansenist dispute an easy method of attacking the Throne and the Altar. This species of support given to the descendants of Saint-Cyran, Pascal and Arnauld by such unworthy allies was just retribution for their sectarian outlook and rejection of authority. Cardinal de Forbin-Janson had said of Cardinal de Noailles: 'One day he will be the leader of a party without intending or knowing it.' And that is precisely what happened.

When the body of the Great King had been laid in the church of Saint-Denis to the almost unanimous relief of the whole of France, weary of that long reign of seventy-two years, the Jansenists made merry. It did not seem, however, that the austere ideal of Port-Royal was destined to turn to account the succeeding period, which Voltaire described as 'the pleasant period of the Regency, when Folly jingled its bells and skipped light-footed throughout France, and people did anything and everything except penance'. But it was only necessary for Jansenism to stand as an opposition party against the ideas of the late reign for it to gain the sympathy of the new groups, and especially of the Regent, Philippe d'Orléans. The fact that this vice-monger showed goodwill towards the spiritual descendants of Mother Angélique should have been sufficient to open their eyes. But the party was too overjoyed at seeing their new master overhaul all the orders issued under the late king's seal, set free the imprisoned Jansenists and withdraw the Journal of Benefices from Father Le Tellier, whom the Regent sent to La Flèche. Bishops forbade the Jesuits to preach and hear confessions in their dioceses, and Cardinal de Noailles was made president of the Council of Conscience. The courtiers, previously so devout, loudly applauded these measures—Tartuffe was being transformed into an unscrupulous Turcaret, but claimed kinship with Quesnel!

Resistance to the Bull immediately stiffened. It was not popular with Catholics generally, for they were unable to understand why propositions that had every appearance of being orthodox had been condemned. The Sorbonne announced that it had accepted the Bull purely under duress, and the faculties of Rheims and Nantes followed suit. Twenty-five bishops took advantage of the new political situation to announce that they 'had accepted the Bull only conditionally'. Once again Cardinal de Noailles shifted his position; he stated that on the whole the papal text appeared to be acceptable subject to a few modifications. His clergy begged him to keep quiet, and a deputation from the Sorbonne asked him not to yield. By the end of 1716 the Parlements of six cities including Paris had revoked their former acceptance.

Before long all this fuss began to annoy the Regent. He had more serious troubles on his hands; the most important was his attempt, with the aid of the brilliant Scotsman John Law, to avoid financial bankruptcy. He had also to guard against the intrigues of the wily Spanish minister Alberoni. His one desire was to be left in peace and free from all politico-religious troubles. These were legitimate aims, in which he was assisted by his personal secretary and former tutor Guillaume Dubois (1657–1723), who was popularly known as 'The Abbé' although he was not a priest. Furthermore, Dubois was not the contemptible, intriguing, hypocritical monster portrayed by the famous Saint-Simon, whose ducal pride was hurt at seeing 'this commoner . . . from the dregs of the people rise to power', and succeeding 'by sheer force of Greek and Latin'. This 'thin, weasel-faced little man with the intellectual air' was above all clear-sighted and ambitious; his purpose was to become first minister and cardinal, and he required a springboard from which to attain his ambition.

It was the affair of the 'Jansenist Appeals' that offered him his opportunity. Four bishops—Soanen of Sénez, Colbert of Montpellier, de la Broux of Mirepoix and de Langle of Boulogne—appealed to the Council against the Bull. Their appeal was supported by the Sorbonne and twelve other bishops, of whom Noailles was one. As a matter of fact these 'appellants', as they were called, represented a very small proportion of the Church in France; not more than sixteen bishops out of thirty-three, and three thousand priests out of a hundred thousand. Languet de Gergy, Bishop of Soissons, the most spirited defender of the Bull, was quite right when he declared in his ardent epistles that they were but a weak minority. They constituted, however, a turbulent minority, backed by the entire Jansenist party. The Regent charged Cardinal de Rohan to negotiate with the agitators; but nothing came of it.[1] The Jansenists' resistance provoked Clement XI beyond measure. He wished to 'decardinalize' Noailles, an action which the Regent opposed through sheer Gallican pride. The 'appellants' were condemned by a Holy Office decree and subsequently by the Bull *Pastoralis Officii*; they were even excommunicated. In the meantime Noailles, carried away by his determination to resist, appealed against the new Bull as he had done against the *Unigenitus*. Schism was openly discussed; a Gallican Church would be established independent of Rome, and the Archbishop of Paris would be its head. The situation was pregnant with possibilities.

At that moment Dubois acted, and with supreme skill. He let it be known in Rome that he was in a position to bring the two hostile factions together. On his advice the Regent intimidated the diehards by having Jansenist writings publicly burned and insisting that the Sorbonne expunge from its records an offensive resolution regarding papal infallibility. He persuaded Noailles to preside with Cardinals de Rohan and de Bissy over a committee of bishops to prepare a vaguely worded form of acceptance of the Bull satisfactory to everyone; and the king signed an edict to the effect that no one should publish any attack on the Bull—all of which soothed the feelings of its over-enthusiastic defender, M. Languet. Thus in 1720 a settlement was reached known as the *Accommodement*. After much hesitation Noailles

---

[1] An amusing scene took place at the church of Saint-Léger, in Soissons, when the Vicar-General came to read Bishop Languet de Gergy's pastoral letter condemning the 'appellants', and it gives some idea of the intense feeling prevalent at the time. The parish priest, who was a Jansenist, first ordered the congregation to leave, and then instructed the cantors to drown the Vicar-General's voice with a loud singing of the Canticles. Finally he ordered the church bells to be rung!

agreed to sign it. As for Dubois, he reaped the reward of his zeal: he was given the revenue of the See of Cambrai, and received Holy Orders a week later; Cardinal de Rohan consecrated him bishop, and a year later the Pope made him cardinal. In the meantime he had become Secretary of State for Foreign Affairs, was nominated to the King's Council, and eventually became first minister. The shrewd Dubois had succeeded.[1]

21. 'NO MIRACLES, BY THE KING'S COMMAND'

In actual fact the *Accommodement* served no useful purpose. A rumour was current that Cardinal de Noailles had prepared two versions of his directive: the first, expressed in compliant terms, was sent to the Pope; the second one contained mental reservations, and was dispatched secretly to his most reliable supporters. As a result the whole party felt strengthened in its resistance. Yet 1720 marked the final turning-point in the history of Jansenism. Quesnel died at Amsterdam on 2nd December 1719 after having stated in his will, which contained some fine sentiments, that he had 'never intended to say, write or think anything contrary to the beliefs and teachings of the Holy Catholic Church'. With him ended the third season, as it were, in the Jansenist story—a troubled and declining autumn. Saint-Cyran had heralded in the mild spring, which was followed by the sizzling summer of the Great Arnauld; what now remained was a dreary winter, laden with darkness and heavy storms. Jansenism was entering upon its agony, becoming more and more political, a prey to internal squabbles and secessions, buffeted even by a wave of madness.

During the entire pontificate of Innocent XIII (1721–4) chaotic negotiations were undertaken, but without result. The new Pope, Benedict XIII, a Dominican of the Thomist school, was determined to have done with the matter. A council held in Rome declared the Bull *Unigenitus* to be an article of faith. Noailles's attempts to formulate a compromise doctrine in four articles were repudiated. Colbert, Bishop of Montpellier, invoked the Clementine Peace in order to bolster up the Jansenist position, and the government, with the agreement of Rome, appropriated his benefice. The Soanen affair created an even greater disturbance. Soanen was bishop of the unimportant diocese of Sénez in Haute-Provence. He was a pious priest, but fiery and obstinate. In 1726 he published a pastoral letter in which he retracted his submission to the *Accommodement*, praised the 'appellant' bishops as 'the

---

[1] See also Carreyre's *Le Jansénisme durant la Régence* (Louvain, 1932), where the facts are given in detail. The work also contains an account of the part played by Bishop Languet de Gergy.

sole defenders of truth', and without beating about the bush pressed for open revolt and schism. The Government instructed Archbishop de Tencin, of Embrun, to assemble a provincial council to try the refractory bishop. De Tencin was not a happy choice, for he was far from worthy of the task. Furthermore, the interference of the civil authorities could only irritate the bishops, who by no means approved of Soanen. Thirty-one bishops supported him, and he himself appealed again and again, basing his case on legal quibbles. Finally the little Bishop of Sénez was suspended by the Council. He took refuge in the monastery of Chaise-Dieu, where he died in 1740 at ninety-three years of age, without having made the vaguest gesture of submission. The Jansenists described the council as 'a band of brigands', and fifty Parisian advocates signed a legal document declaring its decision null and void.

There followed a violent outburst of Jansenism in Paris and in various other parts of France, and Soanen was treated as a martyr. Anybody who at all criticized authority was susceptible to the influence of Quesnel, whether they were parish priests, magistrates, intellectuals, middle class or lower class. Cardinal de Noailles assumed the leadership of this Jansenist revival. But suddenly he changed his mind again; feeling the approach of death and influenced by his niece, the Marquise de Gramont, and Fleury, the shrewd first minister, he decided to submit and become reconciled with Rome. This he did in precise terms in July 1728. He withdrew all the directives he had issued, condemned Quesnel and the *Réflexions morales*, and affirmed his acceptance of the Bull. Shortly afterwards he died, and the people of Paris sang an ironical epitaph:

> '*Ci-gît, Louis Cahin-Caha*
> *Qui dévotement 'appela'*
> *De oui, de non s'entortilla*
> *Perdit la tête et s'en alla.*'[1]

Only the poor mourned him, for throughout his life he had relieved their misery; so much so that he sold his silver to provide them with bread. He may have had a small mind, but he had a large heart.

It naturally followed that immediately after his death letters of his were published in which he repudiated his submission. But they carried no weight; episcopal Jansenism died more or less with him. His successor, Mgr de Vintimille, accepted the Bull without reservation. Most of the theologians in Paris did likewise, and only three refractory bishops remained. The king then decreed (in 1730) that all ecclesiastics who did not sign a straightforward acceptance would be deprived of

---

[1] 'Here lies Louis the Muddler who piously made his "appeal". In a maze of Yeses and Noes he lost his head and departed.'

their livings, which could be appropriated by law. The threat was quite sufficient to cool the ardour of the bulk of the party.

Not that Jansenism was by any means crushed. Its resistance hardened in three domains: amongst the lower clergy, where 'Presbyterian' ideas developed side by side with the growing antagonism of the higher clergy; among parish priests and vicars with their *portion congrue*, who to some extent supported Jansenism on the assumption that by opposing the bishops as ecclesiastics of dubious morals and minions of the temporal power they were defending true Christianity, the Church's freedom and their own rights. Thirdly, resistance was strong in parliamentary circles, which seized every opportunity to stand up to authority. When parliamentarians attacked the Bull in defence of the rights of the Gallican Church, their activities acquired a political significance; in 1730 the Paris Parlement went so far as to publish a memorandum to the effect that 'the ecclesiastical power acquired the exercise of its jurisdiction through the secular power', and also that 'the authority of the Crown is not above that of Parlements, for the latter are the Senate and the Supreme Tribunal of the nation'—and that was a revolutionary declaration. Obviously such statements immensely gratified the 'progressive intellectuals' who were sceptical and anti-religion in outlook, and were already being described as 'the philosophers'. Ever since 1727 a weekly news-sheet called *Nouvelles ecclésiastiques* had been secretly produced by two brothers from Vendée who were priests—Etemare and François de la Roche. It was printed in the deep forest of Puisaye, in the country around Vitry-le-François, and distributed in the back streets of Paris. It vigorously denounced the scandals, great and small, of the clergy; railed against the Jesuits and lampooned the obsequious bishops of the court and the cardinal ministers.[1] All this was, of course, very far removed from the ideals of the 'Solitaries' of Port-Royal. In any case those of the party who desired to remain loyal to the traditional spirit had other misfortunes to put up with. First there was the alleged 'Letter to Monsieur Nicole', followed by a treatise by a certain Petitpied on the subject of 'fear and trust'. The movement's spiritual leaders fought desperately among themselves, and there was no Arnauld to patch up their quarrels. The situation became ever more confused.

And then some very surprising things happened. For three or four years the Jansenists had been saying that God had revealed Himself, and had come to their help as He had done in the past with the Miracle of the Holy Thorn. Indeed there was an abundance of miracles. In the parish of Sainte-Marguerite a paralytic was cured by a parish priest, a

---

[1] *Les Nouvelles ecclésiastiques* continued to appear in France until 1794, and was for a long time published at the abbey of Hautefontaine, near Vitry-le-François. It survived until 1803 in Holland.

well-known 'appellant'; in the diocese of Rheims two other unaccountable cures took place at the tomb of a 'Quesnelian' canon. But
all that was nothing compared with the miracles that occurred in the
cemetery of Saint-Médard at the tomb of a pious young deacon named
François de Paris. He was the son of a magistrate and, out of humility,
became a weaver. On his deathbed he cursed the Bull and all who had
accepted it. He accounted for no less than eight miracles in a year: a
case of dropsy, a woman suffering from cancer, three paralytics, two
cases of blindness and an eighth not clearly defined! The extraordinary
nature of these cures was officially recognized in due course.

But once the story began to spread the cemetery of Saint-Médard was
besieged by a swarm of sick, blind, the bandy-legged, the deaf and
dumb and, which was more distressing, people who were mad or half
mad. They all declared that as soon as they stepped inside the cemetery
they were seized by an irresistible power which shook them, threw
them to the ground and dragged them to the tomb, upon which they
rolled; and all this took place amidst cries and shouting. 'One could
hear groaning, shouting, whistling, prophesying and caterwauling,' a
chronicler relates. 'But above all they dance; they dance until they are
breathless.' Men were to be seen swallowing pebbles, or slashing their
flesh with glass; women 'twisting and throwing themselves about' in
a frenzy, and adopting attitudes that could hardly be described as
decent. The 'convulsionaries of Saint-Médard' were the talk of Paris.

A report of these 'strange goings-on' came to the ears of the king
and his former tutor, the Cardinal de Fleury (1653–1743), whom he
had just made his first minister—and a very autocratic minister he was.
This baby-faced man of sixty-three with the calm, blue eyes was
discreet and peaceable. His greatest wish was that his ministry might
be uneventful. He reacted immediately to the Saint-Médard affair by
ordering the police to close the cemetery. Paris composed a couplet
which became very popular:

> *De par le Roi, défense à Dieu*
> *de faire miracle en ce lieu.*[1]

But the 'convulsionaries' continued their activities. They assembled
in private houses, in the countryside, in cellars and attics. 'Sisters'
began to prophesy; others went off to heal the blind by using a paste
made of spittle and dust. There were 'Figuristes' who proclaimed the
revival of the Church by means of their antics and through the conversion of the Jews. There were also the 'Secouristes' who gave first
aid to the sick, especially to the neurotic, whom they treated by beating
them soundly with a stick. There were even 'Augustinists' who confused Molinos with Quesnel, and authorized illicit relations between

---

[1] 'By royal decree God must not work any miracles on this spot.'

men and women on the grounds that by yielding to divine impulse they could commit no sin.

All these foolish pranks discredited Jansenism, which the 'convulsionaries' claimed to profess. It is true that the early 'miracles' were received with enthusiasm, even by such bishops as Soanen and Colbert; and the Jansenist Abbé d'Asfeld went so far as to compare them with the miracles of Christ! But the madness and hysteria that were seen at Saint-Médard created consternation. Certain doctors belonging to the sect endeavoured to explain the convulsions, but the majority wisely repudiated them; this resulted in bickering. Fleury took advantage of the occasion to exercise a little authority; the insolent memorandum issued by the Paris Parlement was annulled by the King's Council, and, when the advocates replied by walking out, Fleury had ten of them arrested, a move which induced the remainder to adopt a more reasonable attitude.

22. JANSENISM OUTSIDE FRANCE

Opportunitities for the expansion and permanent development of Jansenism did not exist outside France to the extent which had enabled various forms of Protestantism to become firmly rooted beyond the countries of their origin. The austerity of Jansenism did, of course, reach out beyond France; in some countries it even exercised a profound influence, but it evinced nothing like the conquering force of Lutheranism and Calvinism. Nowhere in Europe did the struggle to impose Jansenist ideas assume the vigour it had displayed in the country of Saint-Cyran and Arnauld; not even in Belgium where Saint-Cyran had lived.

Yet the movement did at first seem to have taken deep root in Belgium during the Port-Royal days, when Alphonse de Bergh, Archbishop of Mechlin, authorized the preaching of the new ideas. Though his successor, William de Precipiano, gave all his support to the Jesuits—so much so that Innocent XII had to urge moderation — large bands of theologians hostile to the Society and to Molinosism rallied around Ruth d'Ans, and conducted a campaign that was more or less Jansenist in scope. The Collège du Faucon, which exercised a great influence on the University of Louvain, openly set up as a Jansenist centre. But when Philippe V, grandson of Louis XIV, succeeded Charles V, a violent reaction set in. Philippe was not satisfied with arresting Quesnel; he exiled Ruth d'Ans and his friends, and so they remained until the Spanish régime, overwhelmed by the combined armies of Protestant England and Holland, eventually collapsed. Canon Van Espen of Louvain then took over the leadership of the movement, and published a series of pamphlets violently Erastian and

*o

anti-Roman. Ruth d'Ans returned, and many of the bishops rejected the Bull *Unigenitus*; but it was a mere flash in the pan, for they received very little support from the bulk of the clergy. When the Austrian administrators arrived they hastened to publish the Bull, and the regent, Marie-Elizabeth, together with Philippe d'Alsace (1716–50), Archbishop of Mechlin, began a systematic war against Jansenism, so that it disappeared leaving scarcely any trace. Van Espen went to Holland and remained there until his death.

Jansenism therefore made its greatest stride forward in the Low Countries to the north, secure from Spanish and Austrian interference. There it was that the Great Arnauld had sought refuge, and that Quesnel had fled to escape the episcopal prisons of Mechlin. Several of the vicars apostolic charged by Rome to supervise the small band of Catholics, including the heroic Rovenius,[1] living amidst a Calvinist majority, had shown great sympathy with the theories of Port-Royal. One of these, a certain Peter Kodde, went even further: having refused to sign the *Formulaire* in 1699 he was declared suspended by Rome, but continued to govern his church. Thus the way to schism was opened, and it had been reached by the time the Bull *Unigenitus* was published. A group of 'appellants', acting independently, revived the Cathedral Chapter of Utrecht without informing Rome, and, in 1732, elected Cornelius Steenhoven archbishop. Varlet, a French priest from the foreign missions, having recently been consecrated Coadjutor Bishop of Ispaham, agreed to consecrate the new archbishop; he had been assured that the French bishops, among them Soanen, approved their action. This was schism indeed. A Jansenist Church was thus established in Utrecht, flouting condemnation by Rome, but in very good odour with the Calvinist authorities, who had cause to be elated over this dissension among Catholics. Varlet retired to Holland, and on the death of Steenhoven he was available to consecrate his successor. In a very short time the suffragan dioceses of Haarlem and Deventer were linked to the See of Utrecht.

Yet this schismatic church meant very little. Its position was ambiguous, for while it professed to be anti-Jansenist and condemned the five propositions, it rejected *Unigenitus*. It proclaimed emphatically that it had not separated from Rome, but that Rome had become separated from the true Church! Despite the contribution made by French emigrants the schismatic church had at the most fifteen thousand adherents. Furthermore, they were far from agreeing among themselves. The arrival in Utrecht of the 'convulsionary' Pierre Le Clerc and the violence of his teaching contributed to create confusion in their ranks. One of his books dealt with the theme that Rome had become worse than pagan. In 1763 the Synod of Utrecht split the sect

[1] See Chapter III, p. 157.

in twain, and one section gradually returned to the bosom of the Roman Church. At the beginning of the French Revolution the schism of Utrecht numbered scarcely eight or nine thousand adherents, thirty of whom were priests. It has managed to survive until the present day, but its importance has dwindled.

Elsewhere Jansenist penetration was moderate because it lacked support. The minds of men no longer enthused over the metaphysics of grace or the morality of Port-Royal; they were concerned rather with the virulent anti-papism with which Jansenism seemed to have become identified. In the Austrian states Maria-Theresa, followed by Joseph II, endeavoured to keep the Church under control,[1] and gave their support to all anti-Roman elements; the empress's confessor and doctors were members of the Church of Utrecht. But really sincere Jansenists were very rare; the Austrian temperament did not readily lend itself to excessive austerity. In Germany, where the works of Nicole and Quesnel were translated, together with Racine's *Histoire de Port-Royal*, interest did not extend beyond the limits of curiosity, combined with a little ridiculing of Rome. In Portugal a small Jansenist nucleus gathered around the Oratorian Father Pereira, and provided the famous minister Pombal with arguments in his struggle against the Jesuits and the Holy See. In Savoy and Piedmont, where 'convulsionaries' and a few followers of Quesnel had taken refuge, Jansenism merely took the form of a type of anti-papism; the same thing occurred in Venice, where Jansenist canonists urged His Most Serene Highness to demand, from the popes, privileges modelled upon those which were the pride of the Gallican Church.

In all this dissension politics rather than the spiritual life of the soul were the issue. There were exceptions, however: in Hungary, for example, where the pious Francis II Rakóczy led a life comparable with that of the 'Solitaries'; and in Italy, where the sect gained many adherents because the stern morality of Port-Royal, freed from condemned doctrinal errors, savoured of the spirituality of the great reformers of the early part of the century. They included Mgr Bottari, the librarian at the Vatican, the famous scholar Muratori, who was rector of the seminary at Pistoia, and even the secretary of the Congregation of Propaganda. But as far as all these well-intentioned 'Romans' were concerned there was definitely no question of encouraging a sectarian movement, although their leniency unconsciously brought about a similar result. The Abbé Grégoire wrote that 'Italy was perhaps the one country in which Port-Royal contained the greatest number of genuine admirers'. Port-Royal itself most certainly; but not the political movement that Jansenism had become.

---

[1] See *The Church in the Eighteenth Century*, Chapter IV.

23. THE END OF THE STRUGGLE: THE 'BILLETS DE CONFESSION'

France was to witness the passage of a few more incidents before the Jansenist controversy ceased to be of any further interest. They occurred in an atmosphere very different from that with which men like Saint-Cyran, Arnauld and Quesnel had to contend.

It was literally a pre-revolutionary atmosphere. The questions at issue concerned the distribution of the sacraments, the recognition and condemnation of devotions. Something very different altogether was at stake. Henceforward convinced Jansenists, the 'appellant' type, became fewer and fewer; hardly any of them really believed that the Bull *Unigenitus* threatened the doctrine and morals of Catholicism, or that the Bull represented an attempt by Rome to 'domesticate' the Church in France. But there emerged an increasing number of wily and intriguing persons, bent on taking advantage for purposes anything but spiritual of the extraordinary passion the public continued to show in such questions.

Faced with the ever-increasing failure of authority and a rapidly deteriorating financial and social situation, the Parlements of the main cities, without any mandate whatsoever (for their members were not elected as in England, but functioned rather as courts of justice), took it upon themselves to stand up to king and government. In doing so they gratified public opinion because they appeared to be safeguarding national privileges. The La Chalotais affair illustrated the limit to which the overbearing insolence of the magistrates could lead them in the pursuit of their ambitions.[1] Jansenism's full collusion with parliamentary circles was transparent: a glaring instance of this lay in the refusal of the Paris Parlement in 1738 to register the Bull of canonization of St Vincent de Paul on the grounds that the document dealt severely with Jansenism! By associating itself with every incident created by the sect, and from the contents of its 1730 memorandum, the magistracy made abundantly clear that it aimed at nothing less than complete control of Church and State and the imposition of its will on the régime itself.

But the parish priests who rebelled against their bishops, and declared that 'the humblest priest possessed full power and jurisdiction', that he held direct from Christ his spiritual authority, that the bishops had no right either to empower priests to hear confessions

---

[1] La Chalotais was the parliamentary representative of Rennes. He quarrelled with the Duc d'Aiguillon, second in command to the governor of Brittany, over some new taxes which the government wished to impose. The incident was the starting-point of an attempt, which unfortunately failed, by the chancellor de Maupéou to reform justice and abolish the sale of public appointments.

or to withhold that licence—all these priests were indeed real revolutionaries, whether they recognized the fact or not. These 'Presbyterian' ideas were developed by a parish priest named Nicolas Travers, who managed to exercise a great deal of influence despite the fact that he spent his life either in prison or in hiding. All these activities constituted a definite attempt to aid the 'appellant' priests and secure for the Jansenists authority to administer the sacraments. But this wave of independence went to many people's heads: these so-called 'presbyterians' bore such hatred towards the Bull *Unigenitus* and the episcopate which had accepted its provisions that they were prepared to envisage a Church independent of Rome, no longer hierarchic but democratic, Gallican and equalitarian. This dream did materialize later on, and became known as the Civil Constitution of the Clergy.

No event brings to light more clearly the collusion between these various forces than the circumstances surrounding the 'Billets de Confession'. In itself it was a trivial matter affecting ecclesiastical discipline, but wantonly exaggerated and over-coloured by the Parlements, with the object of asserting their rights and embarrassing the Government. In 1746 Christophe de Beaumont became Archbishop of Paris. He was a pious, charitable and upright man, but lacked tact and skill in the handling of difficult situations. He was known to be aggressively anti-Jansenist; on several occasions he had belauded the Bull, and from the moment of his consecration as archbishop he became the butt of the Jansenist party. Everything he said and did was sytematically distorted, and slanderous rumours were spread abroad regarding his relations with a nun whom he had placed in charge of the Paris hospital Hôtel Dieu. Even his charity was criticized.

The archbishop discovered that Paris was full of priests who were not empowered to administer the sacraments though they continued to hear confessions and give absolutions which were invalid, and sometimes even sacrilegious. He therefore directed his parish priests to require from the dying who wished to receive Extreme Unction a Billet de Confession, signed by a priest approved by the diocese, in default of which burial in sacred ground would be refused. This administrative measure was a severe blow to the Jansenists, for no priest was 'approved' who had not declared his acceptance of the provisions of *Unigenitus*. It was, therefore, not long before incidents occurred. Father Bouettin, parish priest of Saint-Étienne-du-Mont, began by refusing the last sacraments to Father Coffin, former rector of the university, and then to an aged priest named Lemerre, both of whom had refused to produce the precious Billet de Confession. Every Quesnelian priest in France rose up against Archbishop Beaumont. The Paris Parlement, to whom families appealed, three times instructed Bouettin to administer the sacraments—in other words, to disobey his archbishop. As he persisted in his refusal his living was seized. The king annulled the verdict, but Parlement replied by issuing a viciously worded decree forbidding parish priests to demand Billets de Confession or to attack Jansenism from the pulpit under pain of being prosecuted as disturbers of the peace! A few months later they proceeded even further, and labelled the Archbishop an 'abettor of schism'.

Extremely annoyed by these quarrels, Louis XV forbade by letters patent that anyone should be prosecuted for refusing to administer the sacraments; whereupon Parlement sent the king such an insolently worded protest that he dispatched his musketeers to the magistracy with an order under his private seal exiling its members to the provinces. A few months later, assuming that the storm had blown over, he allowed them to return, and published a *Déclaration* (1754) in which he imposed silence on both camps. At the same time he advised Beaumont to be a little more moderate.[1] But it was useless. When an elderly Jansenist woman refused to produce a Billet de Confession the archbishop instructed her parish priest to remain firm; this resulted in further proceedings and another verdict. This time, however, the archbishop was exiled for infringing the 'law of silence' imposed by the king's *Déclaration*, and his pastoral letter was burned by the public executioner.

The controversy became increasingly violent. Encouraged by their victory the magistracy and their supporters let loose their wrath. A pamplet by Voltaire on the subject of the 'precious Billets which the dead took with them to hell' was disseminated throughout France. In the towns of various provinces, in Amiens and Troyes, for instance, pastoral letters were forbidden, and if published were burned by the Parlements; in some cases the revenue of the bishops was seized by officers of the law. Neither the court nor the Government did anything to put matters right. One bishop was very near the truth when he said: 'We have been abandoned to the rough treatment of Parlements'. At the same time in the lower ranks of the clergy refractory priests formed teams to move by night, taking the sacraments to those at the point of death who were known to be hostile to the principle of the Billets.

Indeed many bishops thought Christophe de Beaumont was carrying matters too far, and that it was quite unnecessary to be more Roman than Rome herself; the Bull contained no reference to Billets de

---

[1] The following extract from a letter written by Mme de Pompadour to Archbishop Christophe Beaumont is interesting in that it lacks neither wisdom nor Christian sentiments: 'I should wish that some prelates, instead of regarding themselves as kings of the Church and writing pastoral letters which Parlement merely burns and the nation scorns, might be disposed to give us an example of moderation and a love of peace. What I mean is that your Billet de Confession may be an excellent thing in itself, but charity is worth much more.'

Confession, why then should the archbishop demand them? While the Assembly of the Clergy vigorously and unanimously opposed lay interference in religious matters, they were divided on the fundamental question, and asked the Pope to decide the issue. Benedict XIV replied with the brief *Ex omnibus* (1756), which decided in favour of the moderates. Only those who were notoriously insubordinate, and had expressly stated their opposition to *Unigenitus*, were to be refused the sacraments. The matter of the Billets de Confession was not even mentioned.

Thus ended an episode which derived its importance solely from the fact that, much to the amusement of the gallery, it had brought into relief the conflict between the Church and the Parlements. There were other less boisterous disputes, during which the intractable Mgr de Beaumont went into exile no less than three times. Other sources of trouble between the archbishop and the unfriendly Parliamentarians were his censure of a community of Jansenist nuns and his publication of a pastoral letter without stating the name of the printer and quoting the authority for publication. More unpleasant, though in a sense rather amusing, was the incident which occurred in 1765, when the ageing archbishop proposed to the Assembly of the Clergy that the feast ot the Sacred Heart, already recognized in many dioceses, be extended to the whole of France. There followed an outburst of protests against the 'visions' of Margaret Mary Alacoque (whom her enemies referred to as *Marie à la coque*!) and against those who had a devotion to the Sacred Heart. A number of melodramatic demonstrations took place. For instance, on the day on which the archbishop went to his cathedral to celebrate the new feast he found that all the vestments required for the service had disappeared. No doubt some Jansenist sacristan had made away with them.

But interest in the whole business was on the wane. The number of Jansenist leaders was diminished following the publication of royal decrees, and the party's importance grew ever less. It existed in one or two dioceses, where a few 'appellants' took advantage of an occasional indulgent attitude towards them which was more or less deliberate; and in Paris, where the really zealous militant Jansenists lived in hiding. The climate of the age was growing ever less favourable to religious controversy on a grand scale. Jansenist morality had long ceased to have anything in common with the easy-going morals of the period. Lack of restraint in matters of sex and an unbridled taste for speculative thought could scarcely be expected to accord with Jansenism's stern precepts. Rousseau, despite Mgr de Beaumont, who had condemned his *Émile*, wrote of the benevolence of nature, life and human activities; all of which absolutely ran counter to Jansenist theories of grace and the miserable state of man. In the midst of general indifference [1] Jansenism was beginning to sink into the sands of time. But before disappearing altogether it witnessed its supreme victory when its parliamentary supporters imposed judicial interdiction on the Society of Jesus, whose crime had been its constant and fearless opposition to Jansenism. In 1773 Pope Clement XIV was weak enough to yield to those governments which demanded the Society's dissolution.[2]

During the worst moments of the trouble over the Billets de Confession Voltaire wrote to his friend d'Argental: 'Jesuits and Jansenists continue to tear each other to shreds; we must fire on them while they are biting each other.' And a little later he wrote to Helvetius: 'Would it not be fair and reasonable to suggest that by strangling the last Jesuit with the intestines of the last Jansenist the whole matter would have been brought to a satisfactory conclusion?' These flashes of wit, accompanied no doubt by a Voltairian burst of laughter, point clearly to the moral in the story, and show the harm done to the cause of Christ in the long run by this interminable Jansenist quarrel.

24. THE AFTERMATH OF JANSENISM

By the eve of the French Revolution Jansenism had had its day, both as a great spiritual movement and as a political party. What remained of it after the crisis was insignificant. In Holland the small schismatic church of Utrecht has remained until our time,[3] but growing ever smaller; although its vehement hostility to the principle of Papal Infallibility led it in 1872 to absorb some old Catholic elements equally hostile to the newly defined dogma. Its present tendency towards allowing the marriage of priests draws it closer to Protestantism pure and simple. In other countries there remained nothing but tiny cells of Jansenism secretly linked together and feeding a common relief fund called 'La Boîte à Perrette',[4] into which the living gathered the legacies of the dead. Even to-day, lost amidst the countless sects and small churches that abound in Paris there exists a 'Jansenist' Church, canonically dependent upon the Bishop of Utrecht; its centre is near Saint-Jacques-du-Haut-Pas, formerly one of the three strongholds of

---

[1] It should also be mentioned that Jansenism had to contend with the indomitable spiritual influence of elements that still remained Christian, and were diametrically opposed to Jansenist tendencies. Especially important was the influence of St Alphonsus of Liguori (see *The Church in the Eighteenth Century*, Chapter V).

[2] See *The Church in the Eighteenth Century*, Chapter IV.

[3] See Erich Kunhelt Leddin's article in the December 1954 issue of *La Table Ronde*, entitled 'Les foyers jansénistes contemporains en Hollande'.

[4] We might call it in English 'the money-box'. Perrette was the name of Nicole's servant—the Jansenists always had a taste for cryptic nicknames,

Jansenism in the capital. Religious Orders directly descended from Port-Royal have survived to the present day; the Sisters of St Martha, although condemned by Mgr Affre, continued to a limited extent. It was not until 1918 that the white head-dress of those pious women, who by then had had the wisdom to submit to their bishop, ceased to be seen in the village of Magny, near Chartreuse, where they had conducted a welfare centre.[1] The 'Frères Tabourin' was founded in 1709 by Charles Tabourin to carry on the teaching work of Port-Royal. After a short period of modest success, especially in the Saint-Antoine district of Paris, their schools—more or less contemporary with those of St Jean-Baptiste de la Salle and his spiritual sons—foundered in 1887 through financial difficulties.

All that meant very little. Much more important were the scars left by Jansenism upon the Christian conscience, the halo that still envelops the great figures of Jansenism and the continued interest that exists in the vast issues they raised. A shoal of books has been written on Port-Royal; scholars continue to confront each other supported by copious documents, almost as in the days of the *Formulaire* and the Bull *Unigenitus*. A veritable cult has grown up around the illustrious memory of the nuns and the Solitaries, the flame of which is kept alive by the 'Friends of Port-Royal'.[2] The success in 1838 of Sainte-Beuve's six volumes and the recent play by Montherlant are equally significant of that attitude of mind which continues to present problems. The French have a weak spot for those who stand out against established authority; they are easily moved to pity the persecuted and the vanquished, and they have a sneaking dislike for excessive solemnity and an admiration for those really worthy of admiration, strong characters, men deserving of a better cause. A blend of all these sentiments lies at the root of that lingering veneration of Jansenism, or more precisely of Port-Royal; for its eighteenth-century successors are very much less famous and less admired—as though one could praise the source and scorn the river that flows from it!

Jansenism undoubtedly introduced new elements into Christian experience, incessantly varied down through the centuries, giving a new resonance to the eternal message. Literature and art themselves testify to this. It may not be quite true that Pascal and Racine owe

[1] When they were condemned, about the year 1840, another institution—the 'Sœurs de Sainte-Marie'—sprang from them. It was a perfectly orthodox organization, subject to the Church, engaged in teaching and nursing the sick. To-day it is a flourishing community which has spread beyond France, even as far as Mexico. (For further information relating to Orders descended from Jansenism, see M. Th. Le Moign-Klippfel's 'Les derniers Jansénistes', in the September 1955 issue of *Ecclesia*; S. M. d'Erceville's book, *De Port-Royal à Rome* (Paris, 1956) and, of course, Gazier's *Histoire générale du mouvement janséniste*, mentioned in the bibliographical notes.)

[2] For a long time Henry Jaudon, Counsellor of the Supreme Court of Appeal, has been their president.

everything to Port-Royal, as certain materialist historians [1] try to prove by parading these two writers as the product of the social-religious cellule of the valley of the Chevreuse; but their genius would never have developed in the way that it did had they not been nourished on the ideas of Saint-Cyran and the 'Gentlemen of Port-Royal'. And there is no doubt whatever that the pathetic contrast of grief and supernatural light portrayed in the features created by the brush of Philippe de Champaigne is just as much the fruit of the mournful doctrine of the *Augustinus* as of the stern morality which he practised as a Jansenist.

It would be unjust to ignore the role played by Jansenism in the rebuilding of Catholicism, especially in France and Italy. The raising of moral standards during the seventeenth century, the stricter—even ascetic—tendency in the practice of religion, owes something, as we have seen, to the influence of those men and women of Port-Royal who offered such splendid examples. But only to a certain extent; for after all the Port-Royalist movement was not entirely divorced from all those institutions which stirred the Christian conscience during the great century—the Oratory, Saint-Lazare, Saint-Sulpice. Their methods were different, but they laboured towards the same end without drifting into rebellion. It may be justly claimed that Jansenism, through its books and its schools, succeeded in penetrating the masses with a certain spiritual gravity, a respect for holy things which may be discerned in Catholicism today. The practice of standing during the reading of the Gospel, though it existed in the Middle Ages, was not always adhered to in the early part of the seventeenth century; but the Jansenists enforced it in their parishes. Similarly they revived the custom of rising during the saying of the *Credo*. An effort made by the Jansenists to induce the faithful to participate more actively in the liturgy has left its mark; the most noticeable instance is the reading of the Gospel in the vernacular.[2]

Though such positive contributions [3] were considerable they could not compensate for the losses and the injury which Jansenism inflicted on Catholicism and the Church. In the strictly spiritual sphere its responsibility appears overwhelming. It is quite certain that the work of such saints as Jean-Baptiste de la Salle and Louis-Marie Grignion de

---

[1] Cf. Lucien Goldmann's *Le Dieu caché* (Paris, 1955), and, concerning that work, A. Blanchet's article 'Pascal est-il le précurseur de Karl Marx?' (*Etudes*, March 1957).

[2] 'Under the influence of Port-Royal a new tendency developed during the second half of the seventeenth century: the faithful were urged not to be content with extracts or paraphrased versions of the Scriptures, but to become acquainted with the sacred text itself.' (From the article entitled 'Écriture', by Father du Chesnay, in the *Dictionnaire de Spiritualité*).

[3] We must also include the contributions made to Christian scholarship and learning in general. Le Nain de Tillemont was a master in this branch of instruction, and historical criticism owes a great debt to the Jansenist Launoy.

Montfort was frequently thwarted by sectarians whose conception of holiness was based on their own standards and, in their opinion, it did not exist outside their own ranks. More serious still, it was the Jansenists and their followers, led by Nicole, who began, and continued with dreadful zeal, the action taken against the mystics; we cannot attribute to the Quietist trouble alone those proceedings which eventually stifled the mighty impulse sweeping so many souls towards God at the beginning of the seventeenth century. Even the solid doctrine of St Teresa and St John of the Cross did not emerge altogether unscathed from their attacks. Mystical union appeared to many Catholics as a state so rare as to be inaccessible; it was not, in any case, considered either meritorious or tending towards spiritual perfection. Beneath the anti-mysticism of Nicole and his friends lurked a religion of commandments and precepts and the threat of formalism.

Such a tendency was all the more disturbing because, at the same time, Jansenism was conducing to a decline in the practice of religion; that is to say, it was robbing souls of the support of the sacraments. By virtue of the scruples that arose, as we have seen, from an absolutely false notion of what the sacraments really are, confessors, in the manner of Saint-Cyran, turned the faithful from confession and Communion. Innumerable documents testify to this attitude of mind and its consequences. At the beginning of the eighteenth century a priest of the diocese of Auxerre was recorded as being proud of the fact that he made some of his parishioners wait up to ten years before giving them absolution and Holy Communion. In Dauphiné a parish priest proudly told his bishop: 'I am sure that there has not been a single sacrilegious Communion in my parish during the last year, because no one has been to Communion.' It was only at the end of the eighteenth century that, under the influence of St Alphonsus of Liguori, another path was distinctly mapped out, as far removed from laxism as it was from austerity; a path to which Pius X in 1905 would direct the whole Church. But, in the meantime, how many souls must have lost their way to the confessional and to the Sacred Banquet!

Just as serious were the consequences of Jansenism's approach to discipline. Their refusal to submit unhesitatingly to authority, their cavilling, their arguments and, in short, their revolt, dealt the Church some heavy blows. If we can also establish that Jansenius's theories constituted a definite heresy in relation to grace, then it cannot be denied that the behaviour of the sect resulted in a heresy against the Church itself, as it questioned the very authority of the Sovereign Pontiff and his legitimate claims. In addition the 'Presbyterianism' which Jansenism encouraged in the eighteenth century undermined the authority of the bishops and the very structure of religious society; the 'subordination of the lower ranks of the clergy', to use the words of the regent in 1717, was at stake, and with it the entire structure of the Church. The Civil Constitution of the Clergy would show where this democratization would lead. And there is scarcely any need to add that the frenzied attacks conducted since Pascal's time against the Society of Jesus by every Jansenist capable of wielding a stinging pen finally discredited for a while an institution which might have had its faults, but nevertheless remained one of the strongest supports of the Church. The Jansenists threw down the pillars of the Temple.

But that was not all. In very many other ways the Jansenist crisis did great harm to the cause of Christianity. It will be remembered that, when the Port-Royalist movement began, it appeared as the vanguard of the saintly company set on their way by the Council of Trent; many excellent Catholics made no distinction whatever between St Francis de Sales, Bérulle, Condren and Saint-Cyran. All were equally animated by the spirit of reform. When Jansenism became a doctrinal deviation, and then a revolt against the Church, and when the Church was forced to condemn it, an atmosphere of uncertainty hovered over the Tridentine reform and all that proceeded from it. A long time elapsed—even to our own day—before Catholics really appreciated the work of the Council and ceased to mistake the counterfeit for the true message of holiness.

Furthermore, the obvious consequence of these repeated dissensions among themselves in which Catholics engaged so readily occasioned a loss of prestige affecting Catholicism generally. In the Quietist controversy contemporary Catholics were well aware of the worsening effect and the dangers underlying such conflicts. 'The free-thinkers owe their success to them', wrote Bossuet. 'They seized the opportunity to turn piety into hypocrisy and to deride everything pertaining to the Church.' As for the 'convulsions' and other antics that took place in the Saint-Médard cemetery, there is scarcely any need to mention that they shocked sincere men, who were puzzled by this kind of Christianity.

To say that Jansenism was the harbinger of incredulity may be a harsh accusation, but it is in a large measure true. If the Church in the eighteenth century was, as Sainte-Beuve has said, 'so powerless, so defenceless, that it was straightway riddled by the arrows of Montesquieu's *Lettres persanes*', not all the blame can be laid upon Port-Royal and its heirs, but they must bear a great deal of the responsibility; and not merely on account of their censures and their insubordination. The excessive austerity which they wished to impose alienated from Christianity the average man, the general run of Christians who felt ill at ease under a religious system in which, as Father Bonal said, 'Nothing was virtuous unless it was heroic, nothing Christian unless miraculous and nothing tolerable unless inimitable'. Yet it was the most illustrious of the Port-Royalists who has told us that by trying to be angels we run the risk of becoming animals. By dint of repeating that man's state of sin is so frightful that nothing moves him but his passions, we are liable to force him to conclude that it is much simpler to deliver himself up to his instinct for pleasure. By continually 'denying school and Church a say in theological matters, and leaving decisions on doctrine to the laymen', are we not serving the cause of rationalism? Surely by stressing the transcendence of God, rendering Him more and more inaccessible, we are in danger of discouraging man from ever attaining Him; or, as a writer with Marxist tendencies [1] has observed, man lays himself open to replacing, as happens today, the transcendence of a superhuman God by that of mankind, 'both of which are at once outside the individual and within him'. If the enemies of Port-Royal, by exaggerating the role of nature and reason, encouraged Rousseau and the philosophers, it is beyond question that Jansenism immensely contributed to the crisis of minds and consciences which proceeded side by side with the shattering episodes of that interminable controversy. 'Through the open crack', to quote Sainte-Beuve once more, 'Saint-Évremond, La Fontaine and Bayle entered' —and many others besides.

'Pascal paved the way for Voltaire', wrote Lanson, and the reflection is not as paradoxical as it sounds. But it was certainly not the purpose of those profound believers of Port-Royal, or of Pascal, the hero of the 'night of fire'.

[1] Goldman, loc. cit. Father Blanchet, reviewing *Le Maistre de Sacy et son temps*, the extremely erudite work of Geneviève Delassault, in the April 1958 issue of *Études*, remarks that in these days many people who are not by any means Christian pose as the champions of an uncompromisingly strict Jansenism.

ATE	HISTORY OF THE CHURCH	POLITICAL AND SOCIAL HISTORY	ARTS, LITERATURE AND SCIENCE
602	Jacqueline Arnauld becomes Abbess of Port-Royal		
603			Foundation at Rome of the Accademia dei Lincei.
604		France renews the 'Capitulations' with the Turks.	
605	Leo XI (April). Paul V (1605–1621).		
608			*Introduction to the Devout Life.* Death of Annibal Carrachi.
609	'Journée du Guichet' at Port-Royal.		
610	Foundation of the Visitation.	Assassination of Henri IV. Louis XIII (1610–43).	St Francis de Sales's *Treatise on the Love of God.*
611	Bérulle founds the French Oratory.		
612		Death of Rudolf II. Mathias, Emperor of Germany (1612–19).	
613		Acadia ravaged by English corsairs.	Aubigné's *Tragiques.*
614	Beginning of persecution in Japan.		Franz Hals (1584–1666).
616			First condemnation of the ideas of Galileo.
617	Decree of Louis XIII against irreligion.		Napier invents logarithms.
618		Defenestration of Prague; beginning of the Thirty Years War.	Kepler formulates his laws.
619		Ferdinand II emperor (1619–1637).	
620		Battle of the White Mountain. The *Mayflower* in America.	Bacon's *Novum Organum.*
621	Gregory XV (1621–3). The Benedictions of Saint-Maur. Jansen and Saint-Cyran elaborate their great project.	Renewal of the Dutch war against Spain. Death of Philip III of Spain. Philip IV (1621–65).	
622	Bishopric of Paris becomes a metropolitan see. Congregation of Propaganda created. The martyrs of Nagasaki.		Callot, engraver (1592–1625).
623	Urban VIII (1623–44). Success of Fr de Nobili in India.		
624		Richelieu (1624–42).	Nicolas Poussin (1594–1665).
625	Foundation by St Vincent de Paul of the Priests of the Mission (Lazarists). Père Joseph, the Grey Eminence, appointed Prefect of Missions in the Levant.	Henrietta, sister of Louis XIII, marries Charles I of England. Death of James I of England. Charles I (1625–49).	Death of Breughel de Velours.

DATE	HISTORY OF THE CHURCH	POLITICAL AND SOCIAL HISTORY	ARTS, LITERATURE AND SCIENCE
1626		The Santarelli affair.	
1627	Foundation of the Collegio Urbano. Fr Pacifique de Provins in Persia.	Siege of La Rochelle (1627–1628).	
1628			Death of Malherbe. Harvey demonstrates the circulation of the blood. Bernini (1598–1680).
1629	Foundation of the Daughters of Charity (confirmed 1634).	Edict of Restitution in Germany. Quebec taken by English corsairs.	Van Dyck (1599–1641). Velasquez (1599–1660).
1630	Foundation of the Company of the Blessed Sacrament.	Foundation of Massachusetts (New England).	Claude Gelée, 'Lorraine' (1600–82).
1631	Adrien Bourdoise founds the community of Saint-Nicolas-du-Chardonnet.		Work of Gassendi on the planets.
1632		Gustavus Adolphus killed at Lützen. Renewal of French settlement at Quebec.	Philippe de Champaigne (1602–74). Roberval invents the balance and also the cinematic.
1633			Second condemnation of Galileo.
1634		Foundation of Maryland.	
1635	Saint-Cyran spiritual director of Port-Royal.		
1636	Missions of Michel le Nobletz then of Fr Maunoir in Brittany.		The French Academy. Corneille's Le Cid.
1637	Bartholomew Holzhauser founds the 'Bartholomites'.	Ferdinand II emperor (1637–1657).	
1638	The vow of Louis XIII. Arrest of Saint-Cyran.		
1639	Marie de l'Incarnation founds the first girls' school in Canada. Creation of Holy Synods in the Orthodox Church.		
1640	Death of St Peter Fourier and of St Francis Régis.	Portugal, under the Braganzas, recovers independence. Frederick William of Prussia, the Grand Elector (1640–1688).	Jansenius's Augustinus. Mignard (1610–95).
1641	Death of St Jeanne de Chantal.	Revolt in Ireland.	Descartes's Discourse on Method. Horace. Cinna.
1642	St Vincent de Paul founds the seminary of Saint-Lazare. M. Olier founds Saint-Sulpice.	Death of Richelieu. Rocroi.	Death of Galileo.
1643	St John Eudes founds the Eudists.	Mazarin (1643–61).	Antoine Arnauld's La Fréquente Communion. Polyeucte.
1644	Innocent X (1644–55).		
1645	Beginning of the quarrel of Chinese Rites.		Death of Hugo van Groot, called Grotius (1583–1645)
1646	George Fox and the Quakers.		Le Sueur (1617–55): 'Life of St Bruno'.
1647			Murillo (1617–82.)

DATE	HISTORY OF THE CHURCH	POLITICAL AND SOCIAL HISTORY	ARTS, LITERATURE AND SCIENCE
1648	François Picquet in Syria.	Treaties of Westphalia (end of the Thirty Years War). The Fronde (1648–53).	Torricelli and Pascal weigh the atmosphere.
1649	The Jansenist 'Five Propositions'.	Execution of Charles I of England. Cromwell (1649–58). English repression in Ireland.	Lebrun (1619–90).
1650	Spread of Jesuit 'Reductions' in Paraguay (1610–1773).		Death of Descartes.
1651	Suppression of vicariate apostolic in the Netherlands.		
1652	Nikone, Patriarch of Russia.	In Sweden, Queen Christina abdicates after being converted to Catholicism. In France, end of the two Frondes.	
1653	Bull *Cum occasione* condemning the 'Five Propositions'.		Lenôtre (1613–1700).
1654			Hobbes's *Leviathan.*
1655	Alexander VII (1655–67). Massacre of Vaudois in the Alps.	Poland invaded.	
1656	Decree on the Chinese Rites.	In the Turkish empire, the Grand Vizier Koepreli.	The *Provinciales.* Beginning of the quarrel of Ancients and Moderns.
1657	Death of J.-J. Olier. The Sulpicians at Montreal.	Peace of the Pyrenees. Leopold I emperor (1657–1705).	The Bible of Lemaistre de Sacy. The *Provinciales.*
1658	Appointment of vicars-apostolic in the Far East and at Quebec (Montigny-Laval).	Death of Cromwell.	Claude Perrault, architect (1628–1703). Girandon, sculptor (1628–1715).
1659	Foundation of the Society of Foreign Missions of Paris. The *Instructions* of Propaganda.	Treaty of the Pyrenees.	Molière's *Précieuses ridicules.*
1660	Death of St Vincent de Paul and of St Louise de Marillac. Dissolution of the Company of the Blessed Sacrament.	Charles II of England.	
1661		Personal rule of Louis XIV. From 1661 to 1683 Colbert minister.	
1662	Incident of the Garde Corsi. In England the Act of Uniformity.		Death of Pascal. Molière's *École de femmes.* In London, foundation of the Royal Society.
1663			*Discourse on Method* placed on the Index. Lully (1633–1687).
1664	Reform of La Trappe by Rancé.	In China the Emperor Kang Hsi (*d.* 1722).	Molière's *Tartuffe.* Beginning of extensions at Versailles.
1665	Work of the German Pietists (Spener).		Rochefoucauld's *Maximes. Le Journal des Savants.*
1666	In Russia beginning of the Raskol. At Lyons, Charles Démia founds the Priests of St Charles.	The Great Fire of London.	*Satires* of Boileau. *Le Misanthrope.*

DATE	HISTORY OF THE CHURCH	POLITICAL AND SOCIAL HISTORY	ARTS, LITERATURE AND SCIENCE
1667	Clement IX (1667–9).	War of Devolution (1667–8).	Racine's *Andromaque*.
1668			*Fables* of La Fontaine.
1669	The Clementine Peace puts an end provisionally to the Jansenist quarrel.		Bossuet's funeral oration on Henrietta of England.
1670	Clement X (1670–6).		Pascal's *Pensées*. Maria of Agreda's *Mystic City of God*. Spinoza's *Treatise*.
1671			Quesnel's *Réflexions morale*. Bossuet's *Exposition de foi catholique*.
1672		Dutch War (1672–8).	*Les Femmes savantes*. Newton (1643–1727).
1673	The *régale* affair. Voyages of Fr Marquette. Apparitions to Margaret Mary Alacoque.	Louis XIV clashes with the Holy See.	
1675			Molinos's *Spiritual Guide*. Malebranche's *Recherche de vérité*.
1676	St Innocent XI (1676–89).	New York receives its name.	Mansart works at Versailles. Roemer calculates the speed of light. Mariotte formulates his laws of gases.
1677			Death of Spinoza. Racine's *Phèdre*.
1678			Richard Simon's *Histoire du Vieux Testament*.
1679	St Jean-Baptiste de la Salle opens his first school.		The Observatory of Paris.
1680			Invention of the anchor escapement in clocks.
1681	Bossuet Bishop of Meaux.	Annexation of Strasburg by Louis XIV. William Penn in Pennsylvania.	Bossuet's *Discours sur l'histoire universelle*.
1682	Gallican declaration of the French episcopate.	Louis XIV takes up residence at Versailles. In Russia, Peter the Great (1682–1725).	Infinitesimal analysis revolutionizes science. Newton discovers universal gravitation.
1683		Defeat of the Turks before Vienna.	
1684		Charles XII, King of Sweden (1684–1718).	Leibniz's *Meditations on Knowledge*.
1685	Revocation of the Edict of Nantes. At Rome, arrest of Molinos.	James II of England (1685–8).	
1687	Affairs of the 'franchises' at Rome. Condemnation of Molinos.		Fénelon's *Traité de l'Existence de Dieu*. Lalande, musician (1657–95).
1688	Revolt of the Camisards.	Revolution in England: William of Orange becomes William III (1688–1702). In Prussia Frederick I first king. War of the League of Augsburg (1688–97).	Bossuet's *Histoire des Variations*.
1689	Alexander VIII (1689–91).	The Palatinate ravaged by troops of Louis XIV.	*Esther*. Scarlatti (1659–1725).

DATE	HISTORY OF THE CHURCH	POLITICAL AND SOCIAL HISTORY	ARTS, LITERATURE AND SCIENCE
90		In Ireland, Treaty of Limerick.	Denis Papin's steam-engine. *Athalie.*
91	Innocent XII (1691–1700). Dispute between Mabillon and Rancé. Correspondence of Bossuet and Leibniz (1691–1702).		
91	Bull *Romanum decit* against nepotism.		
93	End of the Gallican dispute. Decree of Mgr Maigrot against the Chinese Rites.		
94			Death of Antoine Arnauld; birth of Voltaire. Leibniz's *New System.*
95	Fénelon Archbishop of Cambrai.		Locke's *Reasonable Christianity.* Palace of Versailles completed.
96			Toland's *Le Christ sans mystère.*
97	Conflict between Bossuet and Fénelon on the subject of Quietism.		Pierre Bayle's *Dictionnaire.*
98			Couperin (1668–1733).
99	Submission of Fénelon.	Hungary reconquered from the Turks.	Death of Racine. *Télémaque.*
00	Clement XI (1700–21). In Russia, Peter the Great suppresses the Patriarchate.		

SELECT BIBLIOGRAPHY

The following are the principal works to which the author refers in his extensive bibliographical notes.

CHAPTER I. A BUILDER OF THE MODERN CHURCH: ST VINCENT DE PAUL

L. ABELLY: *La Vie du vénérable serviteur de Dieu, Vincent de Paul* (the earliest biography of the saint), 1664; republished 1891.

A. LOTH: *S. Vincent de Paul et sa mission sociale*, 1880.

U. MAYNARD: *S. Vincent de Paul*, 4 vols., 1880–6.

R. DE CHANTELAUZE: *S. Vincent de Paul chez les Gondi*, 1882.

H. LAVEDAN: *S. Vincent de Paul, Aumônier des Galères*, 1928.

L. CELIER: *Les Filles de la Charité*, 1929.

P. COSTE: *Monsieur Vincent le grand saint du Grand Siècle*, 1932.

J. ROBIGNET: *Saint-Lazare*, 1939.

M. D'ESCOLA: *Misère et Charité au Grand Siècle*, 1942.

M. D. POINSENET: *Louise de Marillac*, 1958.

CHAPTER II. AN AGE OF SPIRITUAL GRANDEUR

E. MÉRIC: *Le clergé sous l'Ancien Régime*, 1890.

DOM BEAUCHIT-FILLEAU (ed.): *Annales de la Compagnie du Saint-Sacrement*, 1900.

PERE BOULAY: *S. Jean Eudes*, 1905–8.

P. DENIS: *Le Cardinal de Richelieu et la réforme des monastéres bénédictins*, 1912.

MONIER: *Vie de M. Olier*, 1914.

MGR. PRUNEL: *La Renaissance catholique en France au XVII siècle*, 1921.

H. BREMOND: *Histoire littéraire du sentiment religieux en France*, 11 vols., 1924–33.

J. HARANG: *Bourdoise*, 1935.

J. GAUTHIER: *L'Esprit de l'École française de spiritualité*, 1936.

MGR (afterwards CARDINAL) GRENTE: *L'Eminence Grise*, 1941.

G. LE BRAS: 'La Vitalité religieuse de l'Église de France', in *Revue d'Histoire de l'Église*, 1945.

S. M. BOUCHEREAUX: *La Réforme des Carmes en France*, 1950.

A. CHAGNY: *L'Ordre hospitalier de Saint-Jean de Dieu en France*, 1951.

J. DAGENS: *Bérulle et les origines de la restauration catholique*, 1952.

M. D. POINSENET: *La France religieuse au XVII siècle*, 1954.

P. RENAUDIN: *Un maître de la Mystique française Benoît de Canfeld*, 1956.

P. BROUTIN: *La Réforme pastorale en France au XVII siècle*, 2 vols., 1956.

J. GAUTHIER: *Les Messieurs de Saint-Sulpice*, 1957.

CHAPTER III. EUROPE DIGS NEW FOUNDATIONS

G. HANOTAUX: *Histoire du Cardinal de Richelieu*, 6 vols., 1896.

V. MARTIN: *Le Gallicanisme et la Réforme catholique*, 1919.

A. LEMAN: *Urbain VIII et la rivalité de la France et de la Maison d'Autriche*, 1922.

B. VOYENNE: *Petite Histoire de l'Idée européenne*, 2nd edition, 1924.

W. S. KNIGHT: *Grotius*, 1925.

V. MARTIN: *Gallicanisme politique et le clergé de France*, 1929.

L. BATTIFOL: *Richelieu et le roi Louis XIII*, 1934

J. CASTELNAU: *Christine de Suède*, 1944.

CHAPTER IV. LOUIS XIV: 'MOST CHRISTIAN KING'

E. MICHAUD: *Louis XIV et Innocent XI*, 1883.

CH. GÉRIN: *Louis XIV et le Saint Siège*, 1893–4.

G. LACOUR-GAYET: *L'Éducation politique de Louis XIV*, 1898.

A. DUCASNE: *La guerre des Camisards*, 1946.

P. GAXOTTE: *La France de Louis XIV*, 1946.

T. ORCIBAL: *Louis XIV contre Innocent XI*, 1949; *Louis XIV et les protestants*, 1951.

F. GOUSSEAU: '*Religion fondement de l'ordre social au Grand Siècle*,' in *Verbe*, May–July, 1954.

DUC DE LA FORCE: *Louis XIV et sa cour*, 1956.

CHAPTER V. CHRISTIANS OF THE CLASSICAL PERIOD

J. BARUZI: *Leibniz et l'organisation religieuse de la terre*, 1907.

MGR. GAUTHEY: *Marguerite Marie Alacoque*, 1915.

CROUSAZ-CRETET: *Paris sous Louis XIV*, 2 vols., 1921.

H. BREMOND: *L'Abbé Tempête* (Rancé), 1929.

G. TRUC: *Bossuet et le classicisme religieux*, 1934.

M. DENIS: *Art chrétien*, 1939.

GILLET: *L'éloquence sacrée*, 1943.

L. LE CRUM: *S. Louis-Marie Grignion de Montfort*, 1946.

A. M. CARRÉ: *L'Église va-t-elle se reconcilier avec le théâtre?*, 1956.

P. VARILLON: *Fénelon et le pur amour*, 1957.

V.-L. TAPIÉ: *Baroque et classicisme*, 1957.

CHAPTER VI. THE DOCTRINAL CRISES OF JANSENISM AND QUIETISM

L. SÉCHÉ: *Les derniers jansénistes*, 1891.
CH. VINCENT: *Malaval*, 1893.
J. PASQUIER: *Qu'est-ce que le Quiétisme?*, 1910.
H. BREMOND: *Apologie pour Fénelon*, 1910.
P. DUDON: *Le Quiétisme espagnol: Michel de Molinos*, 1921.
SAINTE-BEUVE: *Port-Royal*, 8th edition, 1923.
A. GAZIER: *L'Histoire générale du mouvement janséniste*, 1924.
J. LAPORTE: *La Doctrine de Port-Royal*, 1925.
G. HARDY: *Le Cardinal de Fleury et le mouvement janséniste*, 1926.
J. CHAIX-RUY: *Pascal et Port-Royal*, 1930.
L. CARREYRE: *Le Jansénisme pendant la Régence*, 1929–32.
J. ORCIBAL: *Origines du Jansénisme*, 1947.
J. F. THOMAS: *La Querelle de l'Unigenitus*, 1949.
L. COGNET: *La Réforme de Port-Royal*, 1950.

ENGLISH SUPPLEMENT

H. S. LEAR: *Priestly Life in France in the Seventeenth Century*, 1873.
L. VON PASTOR and others: *History of the Popes*, 20 vols., 1929–50.
H. BELLOC: *Richelieu*, 1930.
A. LUDDY: *The Real De Rancé*, 1931.
N. ABERCROMBIE: *The Origins of Jansenism*, 1936.
C. BARTZ: *Louis XIV* (trans.), 1937.
SIR C. A. PETRIE: *Louis XIV*, 1938.
T. MAYNARD: *Apostle of Charity: St Vincent de Paul*, 1940.
A. HUXLEY: *Grey Eminence*, 1941.
VOLTAIRE: *The Age of Louis XIV*, 1751 (trans. M. P. Pollack, Everyman's Library).
CARDINAL DE RETZ: *Memoirs*, 1717 (trans. P. Davall, Everyman's Library).

INDEX OF PRINCIPAL NAMES

INDEX OF PRINCIPAL NAMES

(Main references are show in heavy numerals)

439